MARKET SHARE REPORTER

ISSN 1052-9578

MARKET SHARE REPORTER

AN ANNUAL COMPILATION
OF REPORTED MARKET SHARE
DATA ON COMPANIES,
PRODUCTS, AND SERVICES

2000

ROBERT S. LAZICH, Editor

Detroit
San Francisco
London
Boston
Woodbridge, CT

Robert S. Lazich, *Editor*

Editorial Code & Data Inc. Staff

Susan Turner, *Contributing Editor*
Joyce Piwowarski, *Programmer/Analyst*

Gale Group Staff

Terrance W. Peck, *Coordinating Editor*

Mary Beth Trimper, *Composition Manager*
Wendy Blurton, *Senior Buyer*

Gary Leach, *Graphic Artist*
Cindy Baldwin, *Production Design Manager*

27500 Drake Rd.
Farmington Hills, MI 48331-3535

ISBN 0-7876-2449-7
ISSN 1052-9578

Printed in the United States of America

TABLE OF CONTENTS

Indexes

TABLE OF TOPICS

The *Table of Topics* lists all topics used in *Market Share Reporter* in alphabetical order. One or more page references follow each topic; the page references identify the starting point where the topic is shown. The same topic name may be used under different SICs; therefore, in some cases, more than one page reference is provided.

INTRODUCTION

Market Share Reporter (MSR) is a compilation of market share reports from periodical literature. The eighth edition covers the period 1996 through 1999; while dates overlap slightly with the ninth edition, the tenth edition of *MSR* has completely new and updated entries. As shown by reviews of previous editions plus correspondence and telephone contact with many users, this is a unique resource for competitive analysis, diversification planning, marketing research, and other forms of economic and policy analysis. Features of the 2000 edition include—

- More than 2,000 entries, all new or updated.
- SIC classification, with entries arranged under 511 SIC codes.
- Corporate, brand, product, service and commodity market shares.
- Coverage of private and public sector activities.
- North American coverage.
- Comprehensive indexes, including products, companies, brands, places, sources, and SICs.
- Table of Topics showing topical subdivisions of chapters with page references.
- Graphics.
- Annotated source listing—provides publishers' information for journals cited in this edition of *MSR*.

MSR is a one-of-a-kind resource for ready reference, marketing research, economic analysis, planning, and a host of other disciplines.

Categories of Market Shares

Entries in *Market Share Reporter* fall into four broad categories. Items were included if they showed the relative strengths of participants in a market or provided subdivisions of economic activity in some manner that could assist the analyst.

- ***Corporate market shares*** show the names of companies that participate in an industry, produce a product, or provide a service. Each company's market share is shown as a percent of total industry or product sales for a defined period, usually a year. In some cases, the company's share represents the share of the sales of the companies shown (group total)—because shares of the total market were not cited in the source or were not relevant. In some corporate share tables, brand information appears behind company names in parentheses. In these cases, the tables can be located using either the company or the brand index.

- ***Institutional shares*** are like corporate shares but show the shares of other kinds of organizations. The most common institutional entries in *MSR* display the shares of states, provinces, or regions in an activity. The shares of not-for-profit organizations in some economic or service functions fall under this heading.

- ***Brand market shares*** are similar to corporate shares with the difference that brand names are shown. Brand names include equivalent categories such as the names of television programs, magazines, publishers' imprints, etc. In some cases, the names of corporations appear in parentheses behind the brand name; in these cases, tables can be located using either the brand or the company index.

- ***Product, commodity, service, and facility*** shares feature a broad category (e.g. household appliances) and show how the category is subdivided into components (e.g. refrigerators, ranges, washing machines, dryers, and dishwashers). Entries under this category cover products (autos, lawnmowers, polyethylene, etc.), commodities (cattle, grains, crops), services (telephone, child care), and facilities (port berths, hotel suites, etc.). Subdivisions may be products, categories of services (long-distance telephone, residential phone service, 800-service), types of commodities (varieties of grain), size categories (e.g., horsepower ranges), modes (rail, air, barge), types of facilities (categories of hospitals, ports, and the like), or other subdivisions.

- ***Other shares.*** *MSR* includes a number of entries that show subdivisions, breakdowns, and shares that do not fit neatly into the above categorizations but properly belong in such a book because they shed light on public policy, foreign trade, and other subjects of general interest. These items include, for instance, subdivisions of governmental expenditures, environmental issues, and the like.

Coverage

The tenth edition of *Market Share Reporter* covers essentially the same range of industries as previous editions. However, all tables are *new* or represent *updated* information (more recent or revised data). Also, coverage in detail is different in certain industries, meaning that more or fewer SICs are covered or product details *within* SICs may be different. For these reasons, it is recommended that previous editions of *MSR* be retained rather than replaced.

Changes in Coverage. Beginning with the fifth edition, *MSR*'s geographic area of coverage became North America—Canada, the United States, and Mexico. As in all past editions, the vast majority of entries are for the United States. In the first four editions of *MSR*, international data were included at greater or lesser intensity depending on availability of space. This necessitated, among other things, frequent exclusion of data organized by states or regions of the United States—which are popular with users.

In order to provide better service to users, a companion publication, called *World Market Share Reporter* (*WMSR*), is available. *WMSR* features global market share information as well as country-specific market share and/or market size information outside North America. At the same time, *MSR* features more geographical market shares in the North American area.

MSR reports on *published* market shares rather than attempting exhaustive coverage of the market shares, say, of all major corporations and of all products and services. Despite this limitation, *MSR* holds share information on nearly 4,000 companies, more than 1,250 brands, and more than 1,980 product, commodity, service, and facility categories. Several entries are usually available for each industry group in the SIC classification; omitted groups are those that do not play a conventional role in the market, e.g., Private Households (SIC 88).

Variation in coverage from previous editions is due in part to publication cycles of sources and a different mix of brokerage house reports for the period covered (due to shifting interests within the investment community).

As pointed out in previous editions, *MSR* tends to reflect the current concerns of the business press. In addition to being a source of market share data, it mirrors journalistic preoccupations, issues in the business community, and events abroad. Important and controversial industries and activities get most of the ink. Heavy coverage is provided in those areas that are—

- large, important, basic (autos, chemicals)
- on the leading edge of technological change (computers, electronics, software)
- very competitive (toiletries, beer, soft drinks)
- in the news because of product recalls, new product introductions, mergers and acquisitions, lawsuits, and for other reasons
- relate to popular issues (environment, crime), or have excellent coverage in their respective trade press.

In many cases, several entries are provided on a subject each citing the same companies. No attempt was made to eliminate such seeming duplication if the publishing and/or original sources were different and the market shares were not identical. Those who work with such data know that market share reports are often little more than the ''best guesses'' of knowledgeable observers rather than precise measurements. To the planner or analyst, variant reports about an industry's market shares are useful for interpreting the data.

Publications appearing in the March 1998 to June 1999 period were used in preparing *MSR*. As a rule, material on market share data for 1999 were used by preference; in response to reader requests, we have included historical data when available. In some instances, information for earlier years was included if the category was unique or if the earlier year was necessary for context. In a few other cases, projections for 2000 and later years were also included.

''Unusual'' Market Shares

Some reviewers of the first edition questioned—sometimes tongue-in-cheek, sometimes seriously—the inclusion of tables on such topics as computer crime, endangered species of fish, children's allowances, governmental budgets, and weapons system stockpiles. Indeed, some of these categories do not fit the sober meaning of ''market share.'' A few tables on such subjects are present every edition—because they provide market information, albeit indirectly, or because they are the ''market share equivalents'' in an industrial classification which is in the public sector or dominated by the public sector's purchasing power.

Organization of Chapters

Market Share Reporter is organized into chapters by 2-digit SIC categories (industry groups). The exception is the first chapter, entitled *General Interest and Broad Topics*; this chapter holds all entries that bridge two or more 2-digit SIC industry codes (e.g. retailing in general, beverage containers, advanced materials, etc.) and cannot, therefore, be classified using the SIC system without distortion. Please note, however, that a topic in this chapter will often have one or more additional entries later—where the table could be assigned to a detailed industry. Thus, in addition to tables on packaging in the first chapter, numerous tables appear later on glass containers, metal cans, etc.

Within each chapter, entries are shown by 4-digit SIC (industry level). Within blocks of 4-digit SIC entries, entries are sorted alphabetically by topic, then alphabetically by title.

SIC and Topic Assignments

MSR's SIC classifications are based on the coding as defined in the *Standard Industrial Classification Manual* for 1987, issued by the Bureau of the Census, Department of Commerce. This 1987 classification system introduced significant revisions to the 1972 classification (as slightly modified in 1977); the 1972 system is still in widespread use (even by the Federal government); care should be used in comparing data classified in the new and in the old way.

The closest appropriate 4-digit SIC was assigned to each table. In many cases, a 3-digit SIC had to be used because the substance of the table was broader than the nearest 4-digit SIC category. Such SICs always end with a zero. In yet other cases, the closest classification possible was at the 2-digit level; these SICs terminate with double-zero. If the content of the table did not fit the 2-digit level, it was assigned to the first chapter of *MSR* and classified by topic only.

Topic assignments are based on terminology for commodities, products, industries, and services in the SIC Manual; however, in many cases phrasing has been simplified, shortened, or updated; in general, journalistically succinct rather than bureaucratically exhaustive phraseology was used throughout.

Organization of Entries

Entries are organized in a uniform manner. A sample entry is provided below. Explanations for each part of an entry, shown in boxes, are provided on the facing page.

1 *Entry Number.* A numeral between star symbols. Used for locating an entry from the index.

2 *Topic.* Second line, small type. Gives the broad or general product or service category of the entry. The topic for Salad Dressing Market - 1998 is Salad Dressings.

3 *SIC Code.* Second line, small type, follows the topic. General entries in the first chapter

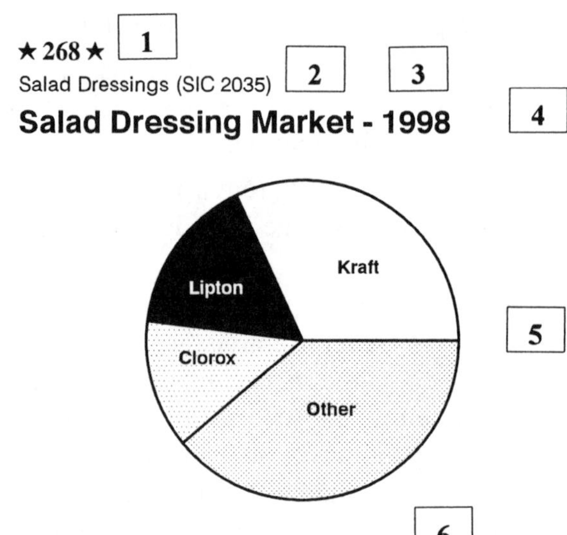

Shares are shown based on $1.34 billion in sales for the year ended January 3, 1999. 7

	($ mil.)	Share
Kraft	$ 429.4	32.04%
Lipton	216.9	16.19
Clorox	170.7	12.74
Other	523.0	39.03

8

Source: *Advertising Age*, April 12, 1999, p. 8, from Information Resources Inc. 9

do not have an SIC code.

4 *Title.* Third line, large type. Describes the entry with a headline.

5 *Graphic.* When a graphic is present, it follows the title. Some entries will be illustrated with a pie or bar chart. The information used to create the graphic is always shown below the pie or bar chart.

6 *Note Block.* When present, follows the title and is in italic type. The note provides contextual information about the entry to make the data more understandable. Special notes about the data, information about time periods covered, market totals, and other comments are provided. Self-explanatory entries do not have a note block.

7 *Column headers.* Follow the note block. Some entries have more than one column or the single column requires a header. In these cases, column headers are used to describe information covered in the column. In most cases, column headers are years (1999) or indicators of type and magnitude ($ mil.). Column headers are shown only when necessary for clarity of presentation.

8 *Body.* Follows the note block or the column header and shows the actual data in two or more columns. In most cases, individual rows of data in the body are arranged in descending order, with the largest market share holder heading the list. Collective shares, usually labelled "Others" are placed last.

9 *Source.* Follows the body. All entries cite the source of the table, the date of publication, and the page number (if given). In many cases, the publisher obtained the information from another source (original source); in all such cases, the original source is also shown.

Continued entries. Entries that extend over two adjacent columns on the same page are not marked to indicate continuation but continue in the second column. Entries that extend over two pages are marked *Continued on the next page.* Entries carried over from the previous page repeat the entry number, topic (followed by the word *continued*), title, and column header (if any).

Use of Names

Company Names. The editors reproduced company names as they appeared in the source unless it was clearly evident from the name and the context that a name had been misspelled in the original. Large companies, of course, tend to appear in a large number of entries and in variant renditions. General Electric Corporation may appear as GE, General Electric, General Electric Corp., GE Corp., and other variants. No attempt was made to enforce a uniform rendition of names in the entries. In the Company Index, variant renditions were reduced to a single version or cross-referenced.

Use of Numbers

Throughout *MSR*, tables showing percentage breakdowns may add to less than 100 or fractionally more than 100 due to rounding. In those cases where only a few leading participants in a market are shown, the total of the shares may be substantially less than 100.

Numbers in the note block showing the total size of the market are provided with as many significant digits as possible in order to permit the user to calculate the sales of a particular company by multiplying the market total by the market share.

In a relatively small number of entries, actual unit or dollar information is provided rather than share information in percent. In such cases, the denomination of the unit (tons, gallons, $) and its magnitude (000 indicates multiply by 1,000; mil., multiply by 1,000,000) are mentioned in the note block or shown in the column header.

Data in some entries are based on different kinds of currencies and different weight and liquid measures. Where necessary, the unit is identified in the note block or in the column header. Examples are long tons, short tons, metric tons or Canadian dollars, etc.

Graphics

Pie and bar charts are used to illustrate some of the entries. The graphics show the names of companies, products, and services when they fit on the charts. When room is insufficient to accommodate the label, the first word of a full name is used followed by three periods (...) to indicate omission of the rest of the label.

In the case of bar charts, the largest share is always the width of the column, and smaller shares are drawn in proportion. Two bar charts, consequently, should not be compared to one another.

Sources

The majority of entries were extracted from newspapers and from general purpose, trade, and technical periodicals normally available in larger public, special, or university libraries. All told, 979 sources were used; of these, 363 were primary print sources, Many more sources were reviewed but lacked coverage of the subject. These primary sources, in turn, used 616 original sources.

In many cases, the primary source in which the entry was published cites another source for the data, the original source. Original sources include other publications, brokerage houses, consultancies and research organizations, associations, government agencies, special surveys, and the like.

Many sources have also been used from the World Wide Web. The citation includes the Web address, the date the article was retrieved, and, if possible, the title of the article or report. In many cases Web pages have no title or author name. As well, it is not uncommon for Web pages to be moved or temporarity out of operation.

Since many primary sources appear as original sources elsewhere, and vice-versa, primary and original sources are shown in a single Source Index under two headings. Primary sources included in *MSR* almost always used the market share data as illustrative material for narratives covering many aspects of the subject. We hope that this book will also serve as a guide to those articles.

Indexes

Market Share Reporter features five indexes and three appendices.

- **Source Index.** This index holds 979 references in two groupings. *Primary sources* (363) are publications where the data were found. *Original sources* (616) are sources cited in the primary sources. Each item in the index is followed by one or more entry numbers arranged sequentially, beginning with the first mention of the source.

- **Place Names Index.** This index provides references to cities, states, parks and regions in North

America and elsewhere. References are to entry numbers.

- **Products, Services, Names and Issues Index.** This index holds more than 1,980 references to products, personal names and services in alphabetical order. The index also lists subject categories that do not fit the definition of a product or service but properly belong in the index. Examples include *budgets, conglomerates, crime, defense spending, economies, lotteries,* and the like. Some listings are abbreviations for chemical substances, computer software, etc. which may not be meaningful to those unfamiliar with the industries. Wherever possible, the full name is also provided for abbreviations commonly in use. Each listing is followed by one or more references to entry numbers.

- **Company Index.** This index shows references to nearly 4,000 company names by entry number. Companies are arranged in alphabetical order. In some cases, the market share table from which the company name was derived showed the share for a combination of two or more companies; these combinations are reproduced in the index.

- **Brand Index.** The Brand Index shows references to more than 1,250 brands by entry number. The arrangement is alphabetical. Brands include names of publications, computer software, operating systems, etc., as well as the more conventional brand names (Coca Cola, Maxwell House, Budweiser, etc.)

- **Appendix I - SIC Coverage.** The first appendix shows SICs covered by *Market Share Reporter*. The listing shows major SIC groupings at the 2-digit level as bold-face headings followed by 4-digit SIC numbers, the names of the SIC, and a *page* reference (rather than a reference to an entry number, as in the indexes). The page shows the first occurrence of the SIC in the book. *MSR*'s SIC coverage is quite comprehensive, as shown in the appendix. However, many 4-digit SIC categories are further divided into major product groupings. Not all of these have corresponding entries in the book.

- **Appendix II - NAICS/SIC Conversion Guide.** The SIC system is presently being revised, with SIC codes being replaced with North American Industry Classification System (NAICS) codes. NAICS is a six digit classification system that covers 20 sectors and 1,170 industries. The first two digits indicate the sector, the third indicates the subsector, the fourth indicates the industry group, the fifth indicates the NAICS industry,and the sixth indicates the national industry. This book is organized around the "old" SIC system because so many still use it. The appendix has both a SIC to NAICs and a NAICS to SIC look-up facility. More information on NAICS can be obtained form the Census Bureau web site at: http://www.census.gov/naics.

- **Appendix III - Annotated Source List.** The third appendix provides publisher names, addresses, telephone and fax numbers, and publication frequency of primary sources cited in *Market Share Reporter*, 10th Edition.

What's New

Several changes have been made to *Market Share Reporter*. Beginning with the previous edition, titles of periodicals, movies and software are rendered in italics. Personal names have been moved to the *Products, Services, Names and Issues Index.* Amusement parks and state parks will now be found in the

Places Index. With the increasing use of the North American Industrial Classification System (NAICS), we have included SIC/NAICS and NAICS/SIC conversion tables. We hope the readers find these additions of use.

Available in Electronic Formats

Diskette/Magnetic Tape. *Market Share Reporter* is available for licensing on magnetic tape or diskette in a fielded format. The complete database may be ordered. The database is available for internal data processing and nonpublishing purposes only.

Online. *Market Share Reporter* is accessible online as File MKTSHR through LEXIS-NEXIS and as part of the MarkIntel service offered by Thomson Financial Services' I/PLUS Direct. For more information, contact LEXIS-NEXIS, P.O. Box 933, Dayton, OH 45401-0933, phone (937)865-6800, toll-free (800)227-4908, website: http://www.lexis-nexis.com; or Thomson Financial Services, 22 Pittsburgh St., Boston, MA 02210, phone: (617)345-2701, toll-free: (800)662-7878.

CD-ROM. *Market Share Reporter* is available on CD-ROM as part of *Market Share Reporter and Business Ranking Worldwide*. For more information call 1-800-877-GALE.

Acknowledgements

Market Share Reporter is something of a collective enterprise which involves not only the editorial team but also many users who share comments, criticisms, and suggestions over the telephone. Their help and encouragement is very much appreciated. *MSR* could not have been produced without the help of many people in and outside of Gale Research. The editors would like to express their special appreciation to Mr. Terry Peck (Coordinating Editor, Gale Research) and to the staff of Editorial Code and Data, Inc.

Comments and Suggestions

Comments on *MSR* or suggestions for improvement of its usefulness, format, and coverage are always welcome. Although every effort is made to maintain accuracy, errors may occasionally occur; the editors will be grateful if these are called to their attention. Please contact:

Editors
Market Share Reporter
Gale Research Inc.
27500 Drake Road
Farmington Hills, Michigan 48331-3535
Phone: (248)699-GALE or (800)347-GALE
Fax: (248) 699-8069

General Interest and Broad Topics

★1★

Catastrophes

Costliest Disasters

Data show estimated losses in billions of dollars.

Hurricane Andrew (1992)	$ 15.5
Earthquake (Cal. - 1994)	12.5
Hurrican Hugo	4.1
Hurricane Georges (1998)	2.9
Hurricane Opal	2.1

Source: *Chicago Tribune*, May 7, 1999, p. 1, from Property Claim Service, Insurance Services Office.

★2★

Consumer Spending

Checkout Stand Sales

Total sales of products at checkout reached $4.3 billion.

Magazines	33.5%
Gum/mints	17.7
Candy	15.5
Soft drinks	11.8
Batteries	7.6
Film/cameras	5.7
Razors/blades	4.2
Salty snacks	0.9
Cookies/crackers	0.7
Lip care	0.6
Oral care	0.6
Other	1.2

Source: *Supermarket Business*, May 1999, p. 28, from Front End Focus Phase II.

★3★

Consumer Spending

Consumer Spending

Spending is estimated in billions of dollars.

	2000	2005
Personal checks	$ 2,265	$ 2,118
Credit cards	1,288	1,983
Debit cards	364	962

Source: *Banking Strategies*, Janaury/February 1998, p. 60, from Nilson Report.

★4★

Consumer Spending

How We Pay For Goods

Data show volume of transactions.

	(bil.)	Share
Paper checks	65.0	75.0%
Credit cards	16.0	19.0
Electronic	3.0	3.5
Debit cards	2.6	3.0
Wire transfers	0.1	0.0

Source: *Wall Street Journal*, November 24, 1998, p. 2A, from Bank for International Settlements.

★5★

Consumer Spending

Supermarket Payments - 1997

Cash	59.3%
Checks	22.1
Credit	6.1
Debit	3.2
Other	9.3

Source: *Stores*, February 1999, p. 23, from FMI Annual Payment Survey.

★ 6 ★

Corporations

Canada's Corporate Assets

Data show the assets of the top 1,000 public and 300 private companies. Figures are in assets in millions of dollars.

Ontario	$ 1,274,689
Quebec	717,153
Alberta	149,665
Manitoba	132,773
British Columbia	87,061
Saskatchewan	17,951
Newfoundland	3,145
Nova Scotia	2,289
New Brunswick	1,052
Prince Edward Island	131

Source: *Globe and Mail*, November 2, 1998, p. B1, from Globe Information Services.

★ 7 ★

Gardening

Largest Vegetable Garden Markets

Data show that one in four households have a vegetable garden.

Glendive, Montana	41.0%
Bangor, Maine	38.0
Bluefield-Beckley-Oak Hill, West Virginia	38.0
Minot-Bismarck-Dickenson, ND	38.0
Twin Falls, Idaho	38.0
Clarksburg-Weston, West Virginia	37.0
Ottumwa, Iowa-Kirksville, MO	37.0

Source: *USA TODAY*, April 22, 1999, p. D1, from The Polk Company.

★ 8 ★

Gifts

Gift Market by Region - 1997

	($ bil.)	Share
South Atlantic	$ 9.1	19.16%
EN Central	8.1	17.05
Pacific	7.2	15.16
Mid-Atlantic	6.4	13.47
WS Central	5.0	10.53
WN Central	3.5	7.37
Mountain	3.0	6.32
ES Central	$ 2.7	5.68%
New England	2.5	5.26

Source: *Gifts & Decorative Accessories*, January 1999, p. 136.

★ 9 ★

Gifts

Gift Market by Segment - 1997

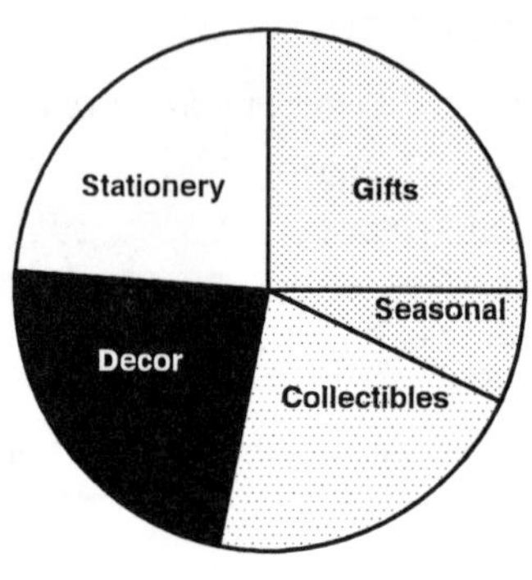

The total market for gifts and decorative accessories. including greeting cards, reached $47.11 billion.

	($ bil.)	Share
Gifts	$ 11.9	25.0%
Stationery	11.4	24.0
Decor	10.8	23.0
Collectibles	10.0	21.0
Seasonal	3.3	7.0

Source: *Gifts & Decorative Accessories*, January 1999, p. 136.

★ 10 ★

Homefurnishings

Houseware Sales - 1997

Sales are shown at discount stores and supercenters.

Electrics	16.3%
Cook and bakeware	13.8
Tabletop	12.6
Decorative accessories	11.6
Furniture	8.3
Space organizers	7.7

Continued on next page.

★ 10 ★ *Continued*

Homefurnishings

Houseware Sales - 1997

Sales are shown at discount stores and supercenters.

Cleaning products/stick goods	7.3%
Bathroom and personal care	6.3
Outdoor and hardware	5.6
Other	10.5

Source: *Discount Store News*, October 26, 1998, p. 27, from National Housewares Manufacturers Association.

★ 11 ★

Homefurnishings

Houseware Sales by Segment - 1997

Total supermarket sales for the category reached $3.015 billion.

Cookware, bakeware	$ 400.87
Plastics, rubberware	279.63
Appliances	217.91
Sponges	209.30
Gadgets	205.69
Foilware	191.03
Brooms, mops & accessories	172.84
Coffee filters	172.06
Hardware	116.27
Glassware, china	111.18

Source: *Progressive Grocer*, August 1998, p. 55, from Information Resources Inc.

★ 12 ★

Insulation

Insulation Demand - 2002

Fiberglass	55.0%
Foamed plastics	30.0
Cellulose/other	15.0

Source: *Plastics News*, September 21, 1998, p. 2, from Freedonia Group.

★ 13 ★

Leisure Activities

Popular Art Activities - 1997

Data show the events that adults attended at least once in a year. Approximately 50% attended an arts activity in 1997.

Art museum	35.0%
Musical play	25.0
Classical music concert	16.0
Nonmusical play	16.0
Dance	12.0
Jazz performance	12.0
Ballet	6.0
Opera	5.0

Source: *USA TODAY*, May 13, 1999, p. D1, from Westat for the National Endowment for the Arts.

★ 14 ★

Leisure Activities

Popular Forms of Entertainment

Interactive games	34.0%
TV	18.0
Going to movies	16.0
Surfing the Net	13.2
Reading books	11.9
Renting movies	7.4

Source: *Investor's Business Daily*, May 17, 1999, p. A2, from Interactive Digital Software Association.

★ 15 ★

Licensed Merchandise

Licensed Merchandise Sales - 1997

Retail sales reached $73.23 billion in the United States and Canada.

Entertainment	22.0%
Trademarks/brands	22.0
Sports	19.0
Fashion	18.0
Art	7.0
Other	12.0

Source: *New York Times*, June 12, 1998, p. C1, from *The Licensing Letter*.

★ 16 ★

Mailing Supplies

Mailing Supplies Market - 1997

Total retail sales reached $189 million.

Packaging tapes	58.9%
Mailers	16.3
Mail accessories	9.4
Bubble wrap	7.6
Boxes, tubes	5.0
Other	2.9

Source: *Discount Store News*, June 22, 1998, p. 49, from Manco Inc., A.C. Nielsen, and Information Resources Inc.

★ 17 ★

Media

Largest Media Buying Firms in Canada - 1998

Data show estimated billings in millions of dollars.

OMD Canada	$ 905
Media Buying Services/Media Company/ Retail Media Inc./Publicite/Le Gro	475
Initiative Media	407
The Media Edge/The Young & Rubicam Group	330
Cossette Media	321
WPP Alliance	290
Optimedia Canada	180
Leo Burnett Company Ltd.	152

Source: *Marketing Magazine*, November 30, 1998, p. 29.

★ 18 ★

Office Products

Office Product Shipments - 1997

Manufacturer shipments are shown in billions of dollars.

Microcomputers	$ 67.0
Supplies	35.7
Computer software	30.0
Machines	28.6
Furniture	11.0
Business forms	6.3

Source: *Purchasing*, May 20, 1999, p. 96, from Business Products Industry Association.

★ 19 ★

Packaging

Converted Flexible Packaging - 2002

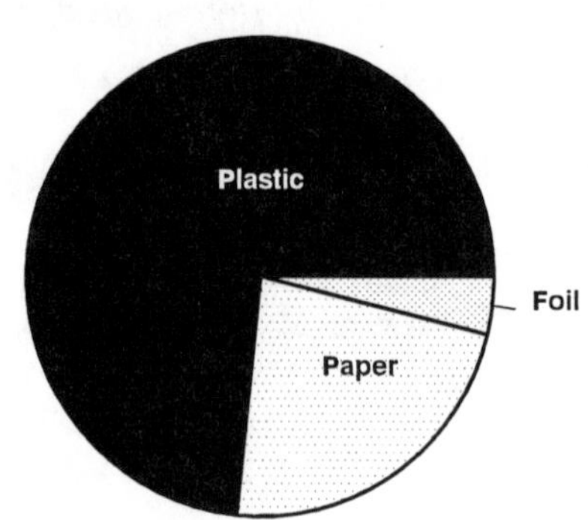

Plastic	73.5%
Paper	22.9
Foil	3.6

Source: *Plastics News*, September 7, 1998, p. 2, from Freedonia Group.

★ 20 ★

Packaging

Drug Packaging Demand - 2002

Total demand reached $4.2 billion.

Primary containers	69.0%
Secondary containers	10.8
Closures	9.5
Packaging accessories	6.8
Prescription containers	3.9

Source: *Plastics News*, September 28, 1998, p. 29, from Freedonia Group.

★ 21 ★

Packaging

Medical Packaging Demand

The demand for sterile packaging is expected to increase from $134 million in 1997 to $173 million in 2002.

	1997	2002
Thermoformed trays	26.82%	27.72%
Pouches	23.18	23.58
Bags	10.55	10.74
Plastic IV containers	10.00	9.26
Vials	9.82	8.49
Blister packs/clamshells	7.45	8.07
Other	12.18	12.14

Source: *Packaging Technology & Engineering*, April 1999, p. 10, from Freedonia Group.

★ 22 ★

Packaging

U.S. Container Shipments - 1997

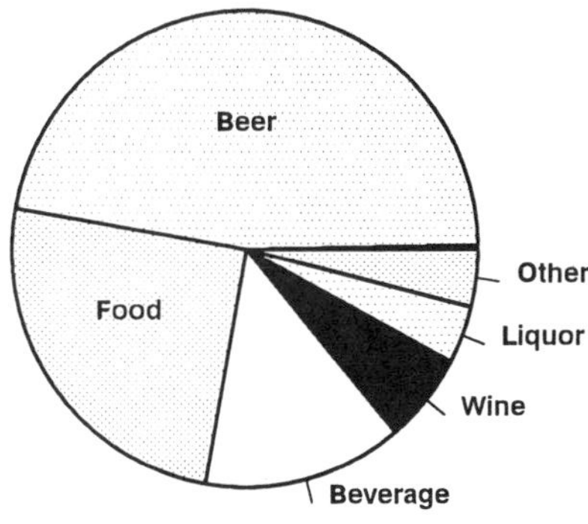

The market is shown in percent.

Beer	47.0%
Food	25.0
Beverage	14.0
Wine	6.0
Liquor	4.0
Other	4.0

Source: *Ceramic Industry*, August 1998, p. 66, from Glass Packaging Institute.

★ 23 ★

Private Label

Top Private Label Categories

Supermarket sales are shown in millions of dollars. Supermarkets have a 16.1% share of private label sales.

Milk	$ 6,200.0
Fresh bread and rolls	2,100.0
Cheese	2,000.0
Fresh eggs	1,600.0
Ice cream/sherbert	984.0
Carbonated beverages	895.3
Frozen plain vegetables	719.4
Sugar	673.6
Juices/beverages, refrigerated	672.1
Vegetables	669.3

Source: *Food Processing*, August 1998, p. 80, from Information Resources Inc.

★ 24 ★

Real Estate

Vacation Homes by State

Florida	417,500
Michigan	223,500
New York	212,000
California	195,400
Texas	151,900
Wisconsin	150,500
Pennsylvania	144,400
Minnesota	105,100
New Jersey	100,600

Source: *New York Times*, July 19, 1998, p. 8, from Economic Research Associates and U.S. Bureau of the Census.

★ 25 ★

Seasonal Items

Popular Seasonal Items - 1998

Data show sales for the quarter ended June 20, 1998.

Ice cream	$ 1,060.0
Salad dressing	495.0
Frankfurters	448.8
Suntan preparations	220.0
Pickles	219.4
Charcoal	152.0
Barbeque sauce	116.0

Source: *Advertising Age*, April 26, 1999, p. 16, from A.C. Nielsen.

★ 26 ★

Transportation

Transportation Industry in Mexico

	1996	1997	Share
Highway	383.3	402.1	59.43%
Sea	208.6	213.6	31.57
Railroad	58.8	60.6	8.96
Air	0.3	0.3	0.04

Source: *National Trade Data Bank*, November 5, 1998, p. ISA980901, from Secretariat of Communications and Transport.

★ 27 ★

Windows

Window & Door Demand

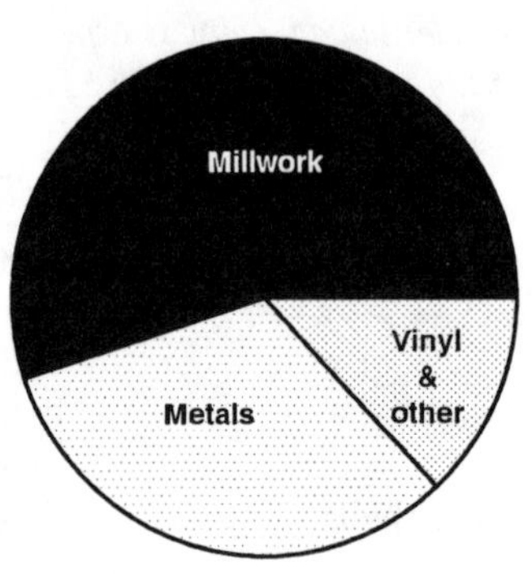

Sales are shown in millions of dollars.

	1996	2001	Share
Millwork	$ 12,050	$ 14,520	54.69%
Metals	7,884	8,505	32.03
Vinyl & other	2,359	3,525	13.28

Source: *Do-It-Yourself Retailing*, March 1998, p. 91, from Freedonia Group.

SIC 01 - Agricultural Production - Crops

★ 28 ★

Crops (SIC 0110)

Crop Acreage

Data are in millions of acres.

	1998	1999
Corn	80.2	78.8
Soybeans	72.4	73.4
Wheat	65.9	62.7
Cotton	13.4	13.5

Source: *Ag Lender*, March 1999, p. 5.

★ 29 ★

Grain (SIC 0110)

Coarse Grain Use 1997-98

Market shares are shown in percent.

Dometic feed use	60.0%
Exports	20.0
Other domestic use	20.0

Source: *Farm Journal*, April 1999, p. 30.

★ 30 ★

Grain (SIC 0110)

Largest Grain Processors - 1999

Data show the storage capacity of the 10 largest grain elevator, mill and processing companies. Figures are in millions of bushels.

ADM	611
Cargill	463
ConAgra/Peavey	198
Farmland Grain	178
Bunge	170
Continental Grain	169
Cenex Harvest States Coop.	146
Riceland Foods	102
The Andersons	80
General Mills	72

Source: *Feedstuffs*, February 2, 1999, p. 20, from *Milling & Baking News Grain and Milling Annual, 1999* and Structural Change and Performance of the U.S. Grain and Marketing Industry.

★ 31 ★

Produce (SIC 0110)

U.S. Produce Imports

An estimated 85% of fresh and frozen produce imports comes from the Americas.

Mexico	51.0%
Canada	15.0
Chile	12.0
Costa Rica	4.0
Netherlands	3.0
Guatemala	2.0

Source: *Food Management*, June 1999, p. 12.

★ 32 ★

Soyabeans (SIC 0116)

Soyabean Market Leaders

Market shares are shown in percent.

Roundup	32.0%
Pursuit	7.0
Other	61.0

Source: *Financial Times*, June 3, 1999, p. 15.

★ 33 ★

Cotton (SIC 0131)

Cotton Production by Region - 1998

Production is shown in thousands of bales.

Mid-South	4,210
Southeast	3,683
Southwest	3,653
West	1,820

Source: *ATI*, May 1999, p. 144.

★ 34 ★

Potatoes (SIC 0134)

Potato Production in Canada - 1998

Production is shown in percent.

Prince Edward Island	30.2%
Manitoba	18.0
New Brunswick	15.6
Quebec	11.1

Source: Retrieved May 31, 1999 from the World Wide Web: http:// www.agr.ca/misb/hort/potato.html.

★ 35 ★

Vegetables (SIC 0161)

Top Vegetable Growers in the North - 1998

Companies are ranked by acreage devoted to the growth of vegetables.

R.D. Offutt Co.	53,000
Hartung Brothers Inc.	19,864
Heartland Farms Inc.	11,100
A&W Farms	8,253
Paramount Farms Inc.	8,100
Black Gold Farms	7,500
Wysocki Produce Farms Inc.	6,735
Charles H. West Farms Inc.	6,714
Okray Family Farms Inc.	6,034
Empire Farms Inc.	5,832

Source: *American Vegetable Grower*, October 1998, p. 12.

★ 36 ★

Vegetables (SIC 0161)

Top Vegetable Growers in the Southeast - 1998

Companies are ranked by acreage devoted to the growth of vegetables.

A. Duda & Sons Inc.	24,000
Six L's Packing Co. Inc.	16,638
Pacific Tomato Growers Ltd.	16,473
Thomas Produce Co.	12,200
Hundley Farms Inc.	11,316
Zellwin Farms Co.	7,950
Gargiulo Inc.	7,700
Pero Family Farms Inc.	6,288
Dimare-Homestead	6,140
Long Farms Inc.	6,040

Source: *American Vegetable Grower*, October 1998, p. 12.

★ 37 ★

Vegetables (SIC 0161)

Top Vegetable Growers in the Southwest - 1998

Companies are ranked by acreage devoted to the growth of vegetables.

Navajo Agricultural Products Industry	14,670
Martori Farms	10,300
Rousseau Farming Co.	7,164
Greer Farms	5,953
Pasquinelli Produce Co.	5,499
Sharyland Plantation	4,975
Waymon Farms	3,730
Starr Produce Co.	3,695
Sakata Farms Inc.	3,200
Everkrisp Vegetables Inc.	3,060

Source: *American Vegetable Grower*, October 1998, p. 12.

★ 38 ★

Vegetables (SIC 0161)

Top Vegetable Growers in the West - 1998

Companies are ranked by acreage devoted to the growth of vegetables.

Grimmway Farms	42,700
Tanimura & Antle	37,998
D'Arrigo Bros. of California Inc.	24,367
Larsen Farms	22,300
P.J. Taggares Co.	19,725
Bruce Church Inc.	19,534
Boskovich Farms Inc.	17,200
Ocean Mist/Boutonnet Farms	14,632
Nunes Vegetables Inc.	14,164
Dresick Farms Inc.	13,393

Source: *American Vegetable Grower*, October 1998, p. 12.

★ 39 ★

Berries (SIC 0171)

Largest Berry Growers

Companies are ranked by total acreage devoted to berry production.

Cherryfield Foods	9,250
Jasper Wyman & Son	6,616
Northland Cranberries	2,548
Merrill Blueberry Farms	2,300
A.D. Makepeace	1,764
Atlantic Blueberry	1,320
Haines & Haines	1,166
Coastal Berry	1,000
Beaton's Cranberry Grower's Service	848
Reiter Bros.	820

Source: *Fruit Grower*, August 1998, p. 9.

★ 40 ★

Grapes (SIC 0172)

Largest Grape Producers - 1998

Companies are ranked by total acreage devoted to grape production.

E & J Gallo Winery	16,000
Giumarra Vineyards	10,000
Golden State Vintners	9,500
Delicato Vineyards/San Bernabe Vineyard	9,020
The McCarty Co.	7,500
Sun World International	7,407
Vino Farms	7,353
Dole Food Company	7,000
Sunmet	6,375
John Kautz Farms	5,500

Source: *Fruit Grower*, August 1998, p. 10.

★ 41 ★

Nuts (SIC 0173)

Hazelnut Production by State

	Tons	Share
Oregon	46,850	99.68%
Washington	150	0.32

Source: "Hazelnut Forecast Down 65%." Retrieved January 1, 19999 from the World Wide Web: http://www.oda.state.or.us/hazel898.htm.

★ 42 ★

Nuts (SIC 0173)

Top Nut Producers - 1998

Companies are ranked by total acreage devoted to nut production.

Parmount Farming/Paramount Citrus	48,077
Farmland Management Services	13,828
Diamond Agraindustires	8,619
Dole Food Company	8,300
Premiere Partners c/o Westchester Group	7,330
Lassen Land	7,317
Farmers Investment	7,181
Ka'U Agribusiness	6,604
Braden Farms	6,523
Capital Agricultural Property Services	5,129

Source: *Fruit Grower*, August 1998, p. 10.

★ 43 ★

Fruit (SIC 0175)

Largest Apple/Pear Producers - 1998

Companies are ranked by total acreage devoted to apple/pear production.

Stemilt Management	6,384
Naumes	6,120
Brewster Heights Packing	5,650
Evans Fruit Farm	4,482
Broetje Orchards	4,000
Fruit Hill Orchard	3,028
Borton & Sons	2,961
Northwestern Fruit and Produce	2,909
Bowman Agricultural Enterprises	2,866
Kropf Orchards & Storage	2,500

Source: *Fruit Grower*, August 1998, p. 10.

★ 44 ★

Fruit (SIC 0175)

Top Stone Fruit Producers - 1998

Companies are ranked by total acreage devoted to stone fruit production.

Gerawan Farming	4,650
Lane Packing	4,000
Sun World International	3,190
California Prune Packing	3,162
Fowler Packing	2,975
ITO Packing	2,906
Evans Farms	2,750
Taylor Orchards	2,690
Thiara Brothers Orchards	2,500
R.W. DuBose & Son	2,300

Source: *Fruit Grower*, August 1998, p. 10.

★ 45 ★

Floriculture (SIC 0181)

Canada's Floriculture Industry

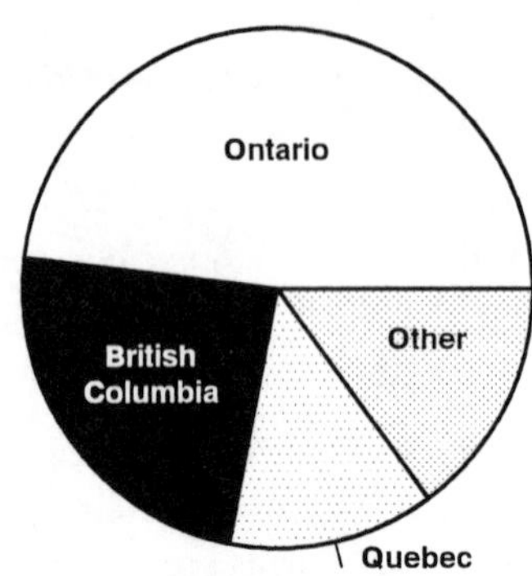

There were 4,844 floriculture farms and 4,430 nursery farms in Canada in 1996. Data show share of production.

Ontario	48.0%
British Columbia	24.0
Quebec	13.0
Other	15.0

Source: "All About Canada's Floriculture." Retrieved May 21, 1999 from the World Wide Web: http://www.agr.ca/cb/factsheets/facindxe.html.

★ 46 ★

Floriculture (SIC 0181)

Green Good Sales - 1998

Sales are shown in billions of dollars.

	($ bil.)	Share
Evergreens	$ 7.47	37.16%
Bedding/ground plants	3.75	18.66
Shade/flowering trees	3.44	17.11
Flowering plants	2.47	12.29
Fruit/nut plants	1.45	7.21
Foliage plants	0.98	4.88
Bulbs	0.54	2.69

Source: *Nursery Retailer*, February/March 1999, p. 59.

★ 47 ★

Floriculture (SIC 0181)

Green Retail Market - 1998

The $12 billion market is shown in percent.

Trees, shrubs, nursery, turfgrass, etc.	62.8%
Bedding & garden plants	17.6
Potted flowering plants	7.6
Potted foliage plants	6.6
Cut flowers & cult. greens	5.3

Source: *Agricultural Outlook*, January-February 1999, p. 4, from Economic Research Service.

★ 48 ★

Floriculture (SIC 0181)

Landscape Tree Shipments

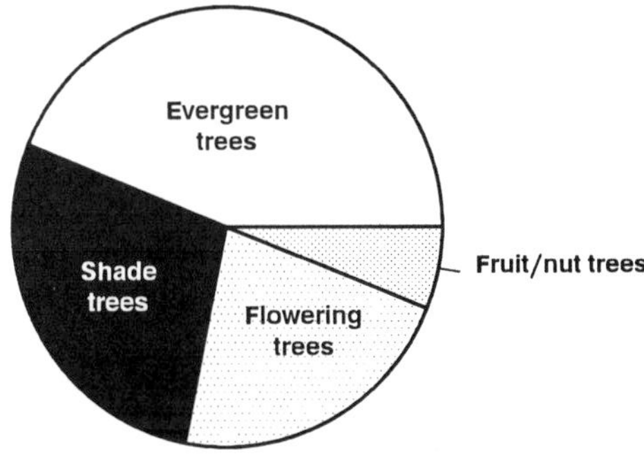

Data are in thousands of trees.

	1996-97	1997-98	Share
Evergreen trees	62,708	76,782	43.99%
Shade trees	38,521	48,547	27.81
Flowering trees	31,318	37,946	21.74
Fruit/nut trees	10,063	11,288	6.47

Source: *Grounds Maintenance*, March 1999, p. 10, from *U.S. Landscape Tree Planting Survey*.

★ 49 ★

Floriculture (SIC 0181)

Plant Sales at Garden Centers

Data are based on a survey. The primary item sold at garden centers was plant materials, with chemicals and fertilizers being the next most popular items.

Bedding plants	23.0%
Coniferous and broadleaf shrubs	23.0
Perrenials and groundcovers	18.0
Container trees	11.0%
Container flowers and flowering baskets	9.0
B&B trees	7.0
Tropical foliage	7.0
Turf	2.0

Source: *American Nurseryman*, July 15, 1998, p. 87, from Tifton.

★ 50 ★

Farms (SIC 0191)

Canada's Farms by Type

There were a total of 234,360 farms in Canada.

Grain & oilseed	45.1%
Cattle	23.9
Dairy	9.6
Hogs	3.7
Fruit & vegetables	3.3
Poultry & egg	1.9
Greenhouse & nursery	1.4
Livestock combination	0.9
Tobacco	0.7
Potato	0.6
Other	8.9

Source: *Globe and Mail*, December 28, 1998, p. B3, from Statistics Canada.

SIC 02 - Agricultural Production - Livestock

★ 51 ★

Cattle (SIC 0211)

Largest Cattle Feedlots

Companies are ranked by capacity.

Continental Grain Cattle Feeding	405,000
Cactus Feeders Inc.	350,000
ConAgra Cattle Feeding	320,000
National Farms Inc.	274,000
Caprock Industries	263,000

Source: *Small Farm Today Supplement - Consolidation in the Food and Agriculture System*, April 1999, p. 9, from *Beef Today*.

★ 52 ★

Cattle (SIC 0212)

Cow Production by State - 1998

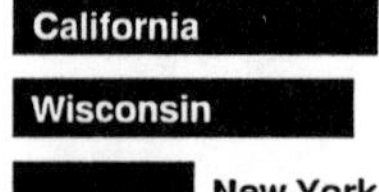

Data show number of milk cows, in thousands.

	(000)	Share
California	1,420	15.51%
Wisconsin	1,369	14.95
New York	701	7.65
Pennsylvania	623	6.80
Minnesota	551	6.02
Other	4,494	49.07

Source: *Hoard's Dairyman*, March 25, 1999, p. 228, from U.S. Bureau of the Census.

★ 53 ★

Cattle (SIC 0212)

Largest Bull Sellers

Data show the number of bulls sold in 1998. There were a total of 228 auction sales last year, with the North Central region generating the most sales. The average bull was $2,027 and the average female was $1,508.

Upstream Ranch	126.00
Jamison Herefords	122.75
Shaw Herefords	122.75
Ochs Bros.	108.00
Courtney Herefords	103.75

Source: *Hereford World*, February 1999, p. 51.

★ 54 ★

Hogs (SIC 0213)

Hog Production by State - 1999

Data show thousands of heads.

Iowa	1,220
North Carolina	1,000
Minnesota	590
Illinois	470
Indiana	420
Nebraska	420
Missouri	400
Ohio	195
Kansas	165

Source: *Pork*, May 1999, p. 61, from *Hogs and Pigs Report*.

★ 55 ★

Pork (SIC 0213)

Largest Pork Producers - 1998

Data show the number of sows. Shares are shown based on the top 50 firms.

	No.	Share
Murphy Family Farms	337,000	14.33%
Carroll's Foods	183,600	7.81
Continental Grain Company	162,000	6.89
Smithfield Foods	152,000	6.47
Seaboard Corporation	125,500	5.34
Prestage Farms	125,000	5.32
Tyson Foods	123,500	5.25
Cargill	123,000	5.23
DeKalb Swine Breeders	97,000	4.13
Iowa Select Farms	90,000	3.83
Other	832,500	35.41

Source: *Successful Farming*, October 1998, p. 21.

★ 56 ★

Livestock (SIC 0219)

Beef Semen Sales

Data show unit sales by breed.

Angus	598,690
Simmental	86,343
Red Angus	65,720
Polled Hereford	56,489
Brahman	22,454
Charolais	19,549

Source: *Angus Journal*, August 1998, p. 195.

★ 57 ★

Farms (SIC 0241)

Largest Dairy Farms

Data show number of cows owned.

Progressive Dairies	18,500
Joseph Gallo Farms	14,000
Hettinga Dairies	13,000
Braum's Dairy Farm	12,000
Larson Dairy	12,000
Las Uvas Dairy	11,000
Rockview Dairy	10,900
Bos/Bouma Partners	10,000
Arie de Jong	9,340
Den Dulk Enterprises	9,000

Source: *Successful Farming*, November 1998, p. 15.

★ 58 ★

Eggs (SIC 0250)

Largest Egg Producers - 1998

Data show millions of layers in production as of December 31, 1998. Shares are shown based on the top 61 companies.

	(mil.)	Share
Cal-Maine Foods Inc.	15.9	8.15%
Rose Acre Farms	15.7	8.05
Michaels Foods	15.0	7.69
Buckeye Egg Farm	10.0	5.13
Fort Recovery Equity	7.8	4.00
DeCoster Egg Farms	6.5	3.33
Midwest Poultry Services	5.1	2.62
ISE America	5.0	2.56
Mahard Egg Farms	4.8	2.46
Moark Productions Inc.	4.5	2.31
Other	104.7	53.69

Source: *Egg Industry*, January 1999, p. 4.

★ 59 ★

Eggs (SIC 0252)

Egg Production by State - 1998

Ohio	9.3%
California	8.3
Indiana	7.5
Pennsylvania	7.5
Indiana	7.3
Georgia	6.4
Texas	5.3
Arkansas	4.1
Minnesota	4.0
Other	40.4

Source: *Egg Industry*, March 1999, p. 4, from United States Department of Agriculture.

★ 60 ★

Eggs (SIC 0252)

Egg Production in Canada - 1997

There were 1,275 registered commercial egg producers.

Ontario	38.5%
Quebec	17.4
British Columbia	12.7
Saskatchewan	4.4
Other	27.0

Source: "All About Canada's Egg Industry." Retrieved May 21, 1999 from the World Wide Web: http:// www.agr.ca/cb/factsheets/facindxe.html, from Statistics Canada.

★ 61 ★

Turkeys (SIC 0253)

Largest Turkey Processors

Jennie-O Turkeys
Butterball
Wampler Turkeys
Cargill Turkeys
Shady Brook

Companies are ranked by capacity in millions of live pounds.

Jennie-O Turkeys	891
Butterball (ConAgra)	846
Wampler Turkeys	650
Cargill Turkeys	514
Shady Brook	489

Source: *Small Farm Today Supplement - Consolidation in the Food and Agriculture System*, April 1999, p. 10, from *Turkey World*.

★ 62 ★

Turkeys (SIC 0253)

Turkey Production by State

Data are in millions.

	(mil.)	Share
North Carolina	49.5	17.37%
Minnesota	44.5	15.61
Arkansas	27.0	9.47
Virginia	26.0	9.12
Missouri	23.0	8.07
California	19.0	6.67
Other	96.0	33.68

Source: *USA TODAY*, November 25, 1998, p. A1, from National Agricultural Statistics Service.

★ 63 ★

Dogs (SIC 0271)

Popular Dog Breeds

A total of 1,277,039 breeds were registered in 1995.

	No.	Share
Labrador retriever	132,051	10.34%
Rottweiler	93,656	7.33
Golden retriever	84,801	6.64
German shepard	78,088	6.11
Beagle	57,063	4.47
Poodle	54,784	4.29
Cocker spaniel	48,065	3.76
Dachshund	44,680	3.50
Pomeranian	37,894	2.97
Yorkshire terrier	36,881	2.89
Other	609,076	47.69

Source: Retrieved May 31, 1999 from the World Wide Web: http:// www.ndesign.ndirect.co.ticles/ information/breed_list_ranking.htm.

★ 64 ★

Horses (SIC 0272)

Horse Population by Segment

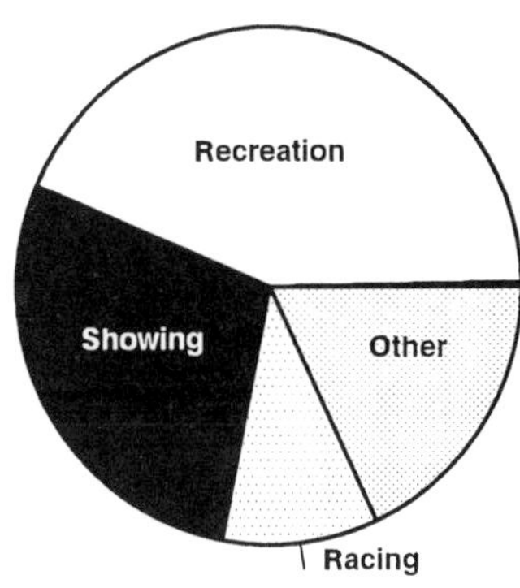

There are a total of 6.9 million horses in the United States. The horse industry employs 1.4 million on a full-time basis and has an economic impact of $112.1 billion on the gross domestic product.

	(000)	Share
Recreation	2,970	42.85%
Showing	1,974	28.48
Racing	725	10.46
Other	1,262	18.21

Source: "Horse Industry Statistics." Retrieved May 28, 1999 from the World Wide Web: http://www.horsecouncil.org/ahcstats.html, from *The Economic Impact of the Horse Industry in the United States*.

★ 65 ★

Horses (SIC 0272)

Horse Population by State

Data are in thousands.

Texas	600
California	240
Tennessee	190
Florida	170
Pennsylvania	170
Ohio	160
Kentucky	155
Minnesota	155
New York	155

Source: *Wall Street Journal*, May 7, 1999, p. C6, from U.S. Department of Agriculture.

★ 66 ★

Honey (SIC 0279)

Honey Production in Canada

Production is shown in millions of pounds. Canada's 10,870 beekeepers maintained 520,000 beehives.

Alberta	22.0
Saskatchewan	15.4
Manitoba	12.3

Source: "All About Canada's Honey Industry." Retrieved May 21, 1999 from the World Wide Web: http://www.agr.ca/cb/factsheets/facindxe.html, from Statistics Canada.

SIC 07 - Agricultural Services

★ 67 ★

Farm Management (SIC 0762)

Largest Farm Management Firms

Firms are ranked by total acres managed.

NationsBank	2,114,346
Banc One Farm and Ranch Management	1,600,000
Farmers National Co.	1,079,315
Texas Pacific Land Trust	1,067,000
Norwest Bank	1,063,790
U.S. Bank	740,000
Am South Bank	558,480
Hall and Hall Inc.	530,925
Capital Agricultural Property Services Inc.	451,366
Northeast Agri Service	425,000

Source: *Ag Lender*, November 1998, p. 3.

★ 68 ★

Lawn Care Services (SIC 0782)

Lawn Care Service Market - 1996

Market shares are shown in percent.

TruGreen-Chemlawn	18.0%
Barefoot	3.6
Orkin Lawn Care and Plantscaping	2.8
Mom & pops	75.6

Source: *Investext,* Thomson Financial Networks, July 17, 1998, p. 21, from company disclosures, Professional Lawn Care Association of America, and Morgan Stanley Dean Witter Analysis.

★ 69 ★

Trees (SIC 0831)

Christmas Tree Production in Canada

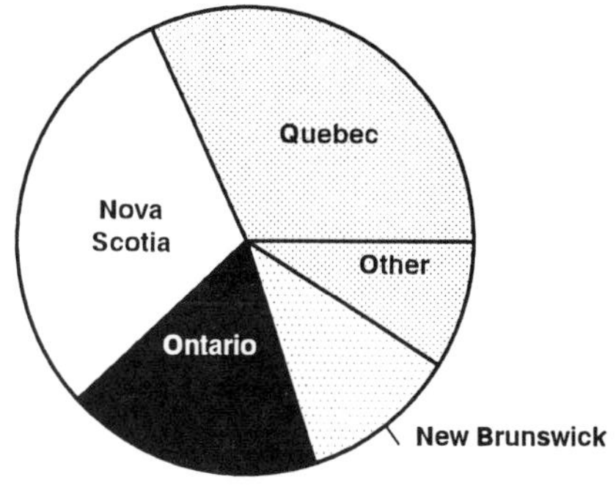

The most popular forms of balsam firs, fraser firs and scotch pine.

Quebec	32.0%
Nova Scotia	30.0
Ontario	18.0
New Brunswick	11.0
Other	9.0

Source: "All About Canada's Floriculture." Retrieved May 21, 1999 from the World Wide Web: http://www.agr.ca/cb/factsheets/facindxe.html, from Statistics Canada.

SIC 10 - Metal Mining

★ 70 ★

Mining (SIC 1000)

Largest Mining Firms in Canada - 1997

Firms are ranked by revenues in billions of dollars.

Noranda Inc.	6,409
Inco Ltd.	3,384
Potash Corp. of Saskatchewan	3,326
Boliden Ltd.	2,379
Suncor Energy Inc.	2,154
Syncrude Canada ltd.	2,107
Falconbridge ltd.	2,095
Rio Algom Ltd.	1,834
Placer Dome Inc.	1,807
Cominco Ltd.	1,652

Source: *Canadian Mining Journal*, August 1998, p. 9.

★ 71 ★

Copper (SIC 1021)

Largest Copper Mines in Arizona - 1997

Production is shown in millions of pounds.

Morenci	1,080
Ray	304
Mission	252
San Manuel	251
Bagdad	246
Sierrita	246

Source: *Mining Engineering*, April 1999, p. 8.

★ 72 ★

Copper (SIC 1021)

Leading Copper Mines

Capacity is shown in thousands of metric tons.

Morenci	475
Bingham Canyon	320
Chino	160
Ray	160
Sierrita	135
San Manuel	130
Mission Complex	120
Baghdad	110
Pinto Valley	85
Tyrone	70

Source: *Minerals Yearbook*, 1996, p. 287.

★ 73 ★

Silver (SIC 1044)

Silver Production in North America

Production is shown in millions of ounces.

	1997	1999
Mexico	81	86
United States	59	62
Canada	38	47

Source: *Engineering & Mining Journal*, April 1999, p. 24.

★ 74 ★

Uranium (SIC 1094)

Leading Uranium Producers - 1998

Data are in millions of pounds.

Highland (Wyoming)	1.1
Smith Ranch (Wyoming)	0.8
Crow Butte (Nebraska)	0.7
Uncle Sam (Louisiana)	0.6
Kingsville Dome (Texas)	0.5

Continued on next page.

★ 74 ★ *Continued*

Uranium (SIC 1094)

Leading Uranium Producers - 1998

Data are in millions of pounds.

Irigaray/Christensen (Wyoming)	0.4
White Mesa (Utah)	0.4
Donaldsonville (Louisiana)	0.3
Ambrosia Lake (New Mexico)	0.2
Rosita (Texas)	0.2

Source: *Engineering & Mining Journal*, March 1999, p. 62.

SIC 12 - Coal Mining

★ 75 ★

Coal (SIC 1200)

Coal Consumption - 1999

Electric utilities	87.88%
Industrial/retail	6.95
Coking coal	2.63
Nonutilities	2.54

Source: *Mining Engineering*, March 1999, p. 14, from National Mining Association.

★ 76 ★

Coal (SIC 1200)

Largest Coal Mines in West Virginia - 1998

Data are in millions of short tons.

Mountaineer	7.4
McElroy	6.6
UBBMC Montcoal Eagle	5.7
Robinson Run No. 95	5.6
Loveridge	5.4
Samples	4.9
Federal No. 2	4.8
No. 50	4.8
Shoemaker	4.8

Source: *Mining Engineering*, May 1999, p. 105.

★ 77 ★

Coal (SIC 1200)

Largest Coal Producers

Data are in millions of short tons. Figures are for North America.

Peabody	155
Arch	99
Kennecott	83
Consol	72
Cyprus Amax	65
Luscar	45
A.T. Massey	34
Zeigler	32
Texas Utilities	28
North American	27

Source: *Globe and Mail*, August 31, 1998, p. B1, from Luscar.

★ 78 ★

Coal (SIC 1200)

Top Coal Producers - 1998

Market shares are shown for the first six months of the year.

Peabody Holding	13.8%
Arch Coal	9.7
Kennecott Energy	9.6
Consol Energy	7.6
Cyprus Amax Coal	6.1
AEI Holding	4.4
A.T. Massey Coal	3.4
Texas Utilities	2.5
North American Coal	2.3
Pacificorp	2.0
Other	38.6

Source: *New York Times*, February 21, 1999, p. 4, from Arch Coal and Resource Data International.

SIC 13 - Oil and Gas Extraction

★ 79 ★

Natural Gas (SIC 1311)

Largest Natural Gas Producers

Companies are ranked by gas reserves in billions of cubic feet.

Amoco Corp.	847.0
Exxon Corp.	831.0
Chevron Corp.	675.0
Texaco Inc.	643.0
Shell Oil Co.	630.0
Burlington Resources Inc.	583.0
Mobil Corp.	423.0
Union Pacific Resources Group Inc.	407.0
ARCO	389.0

Source: *Oil & Gas Journal*, December 21, 1998, p. 65.

★ 80 ★

Natural Gas (SIC 1311)

Largest Natural Gas Reserve Holders

Companies are ranked by gas reserves in billions of cubic feet.

Exxon Corp.	9,689.0
Amoco Corp.	9,097.0
Burlington Resources Inc.	5,884.0
Shell Oil Co.	5,143.0
Chevron Corp.	4,991.0
ARCO	4,988.0
Texaco Inc.	4,022.0
Mobil Corp.	3,931.0
Philips Petroleum Co.	3,790.0

Source: *Oil & Gas Journal*, December 21, 1998, p. 65.

★ 81 ★

Natural Gas (SIC 1311)

Natural Gas Production in Canada

	1997	2015
Alberta	83.30%	74.34%
British Columbia	12.97	18.11
Other	3.73	7.55

Source: *Oil & Gas Journal*, August 10, 1998, p. 27, from Canadian Energy Research Institute.

★ 82 ★

Oil (SIC 1311)

Largest Oil Firms

The largest U.S. firms are shown based on worldwide liquid production, in thousands of barrels a day.

Exxon/Mobil	2,536
Chevron	1,001
Texaco	765
Amoco	660
Atlantic Richfield	650

Source: *Wall Street Journal*, December 2, 1998, p. A3, from PriceWaterhouse LLP and Petroleum Intelligence Weekly.

★ 83 ★

Oil & Gas (SIC 1311)

Largest Oil/Gas Firms in Denver, CO - 1997

Companies are ranked by total revenues in millions of dollars.

K N Energy Inc.	$ 5,200
Western Gas Resources Inc.	2,385
TransMontalgne Inc.	1,968
Gulf Canada	1,677
Ultramer Diamond Shamrock	385

Source: *Denver Business Journal*, September 25, 1998, p. 35A.

★ 84 ★

Natural Gas Liquids (SIC 1321)

Largest Natural Gas Liquid Holders

Companies are ranked by liquid reserves in millions of barrels.

BP	2,840.0
Exxon Corp.	2,377.0
ARCO	2,131.0
Shell Oil Co.	1,965.0
Texaco Inc.	1,767.0
Chevron Corp.	1,196.0
Amoco Corp.	1,080.0
Mobil Corp.	935.0
USX-Marathon Group	609.0

Source: *Oil & Gas Journal*, December 21, 1998, p. 56.

★ 85 ★

Natural Gas Liquids (SIC 1321)

LPG Consumption by Sector - 1997

LPG stands for liquid petroleum gas.

Chemicals	42.33%
Domestic	22.48
Refinery	18.33
Industry	9.18
Agriculture	5.38
Transport	2.30

Source: *Gas Engineering & Management*, January/February 1999, p. 28, from MCH Oil & Gas Consultancy.

★ 86 ★

Natural Gas Liquids (SIC 1321)

LPG Consumption by Sector in Canada - 1997

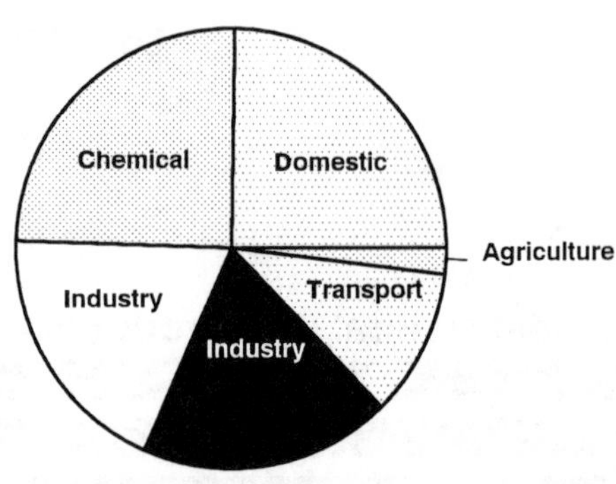

LPG stands for liquid petroleum gas.

Domestic	24.93%
Chemical	24.60
Industry	18.72
Industry	18.72
Transport	11.03
Agriculture	2.00

Source: *Gas Engineering & Management*, January/February 1999, p. 28, from MCH Oil & Gas Consultancy.

★ 87 ★

Natural Gas Liquids (SIC 1321)

LPG Consumption by Sector in Mexico - 1997

LPG stands for liquid petroleum gas.

Domestic	85.15%
Transport	14.55
Agriculture	0.29

Source: *Gas Engineering & Management*, January/February 1999, p. 28, from MCH Oil & Gas Consultancy.

★ 88 ★

Natural Gas Liquids (SIC 1321)

Top Natural Gas Liquid Producers

Companies are ranked by liquid production in millions of barrels.

ARCO	204.0
Exxon Corp.	204.0
BP	202.0
Shell Oil Co.	179.0
Texaco Inc.	145.0
Chevron Corp.	125.0
Mobil Corp.	89.0
Amoco Corp.	89.0
USX-Marathon Group	42.0

Source: *Oil & Gas Journal*, December 21, 1998, p. 56.

★ 89 ★

Oil Wells (SIC 1381)

Land Drilling Leaders

Market shares are shown based on land drilling.

NBR/BDI	27.3%
Grey Wolf	8.8
Patterson Energy	8.0
UTI Energy	7.6
Key Energy	5.1
Helmerich & Payne	2.6
Ensign/Caza	2.5
Unit	2.4
Union	1.4
Timber Sharp	1.2
Norton Drilling	1.1
Parker Drilling	1.0
Other	31.0

Source: *Investext,* Thomson Financial Networks, October 22, 1998, p. 2, from company reports, Morgan Stanley Dean Witter Research, *Land Rig Newsletter*, and Reed Rig Census.

SIC 14 - Nonmetallic Minerals, Except Fuels

★ 90 ★

Nonfuel Mining (SIC 1400)

Nonfuel Mining in California - 1997

	($ mil.)	Share
Cement, portland	$ 641.0	22.38%
Construction sand & gravel	634.0	22.14
Boron minerals	520.0	18.16
Crushed stone	308.0	10.76
Gold	264.5	9.24
Clays	59.5	2.08
Industrial sand & gravel	42.3	1.48
Lime	18.0	0.63
Masonry cement	15.0	0.52
Other	361.3	12.62

Source: *Mining Engineering*, May 1998, p. 76, from U.S. Geological Survey.

★ 91 ★

Nonfuel Mining (SIC 1400)

Nonfuel Mining in Indiana - 1997

Crushed stone	43.0%
Cement, portland	25.0
Sand and gravel	13.0
Dimension limestone	4.0
Other	15.0

Source: *Mining Engineering*, May 1998, p. 85, from U.S. Geological Survey.

★ 92 ★

Crushed Stone (SIC 1420)

Crushed Stone Market by Region

Data show millions of tons of crushed stone crushed or used from third quarter 1996 - second quarter 1998.

South Atlantic	658,200
E. North Central	534,500
E. South Central	333,100
Middle Atlantic	325,200
W. North Central	324,200
W. South Central	294,800
Pacific	176,100
Mountain	81,300
New England	56,200

Source: *Pit & Quarry*, December 1998, p. 26, from U.S. Geological Survey.

★ 93 ★

Sand and Gravel (SIC 1440)

Sand & Gravel Market by Region

Data show millions of tons of sand and gravel sold or used from third quarter 1996 - second quarter 1998.

E. North Central	401,100
Pacific	347,500
Mountain	330,400
W. North Central	218,500
W. South Central	186,900
South Atlantic	147,400
Middle Atlantic	123,800
New England	99,200
E. South Central	90,100

Source: *Pit & Quarry*, December 1998, p. 26, from U.S. Geological Survey.

★ 94 ★

Sand and Gravel (SIC 1440)

Silica Market by Glass End Use - 1997

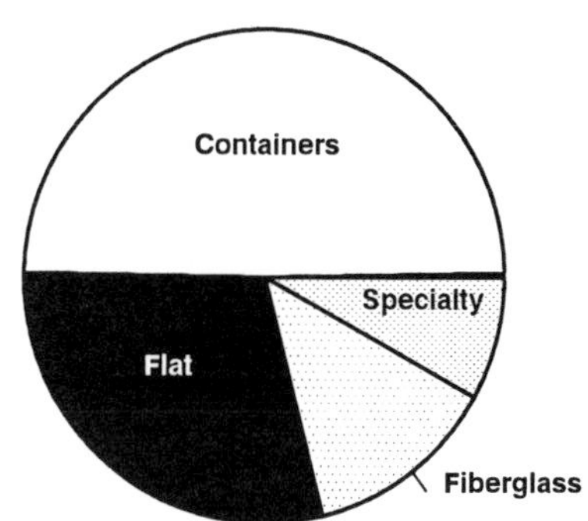

The United States is the world's largest producer of silica at over 28 million tons in 1997.

Containers	49.3%
Flat	29.3
Fiberglass	13.2
Specialty	8.2

Source: *Ceramic Industry*, January 1999, p. 63.

★ 95 ★

Clays (SIC 1455)

Clay Production by End Use - 1997

Brick	91.00%
Refractories	4.39
Floor and wall tile	2.66
Ceramics and glass	1.12
Flue linings	0.42
Drain tile and sewer pipe	0.40

Source: *Ceramic Industry*, January 1999, p. 63.

★ 96 ★

Clays (SIC 1455)

Clay Production by State - 1996

Production is shown in thousands of tons.

	(000)	Share
Georgia	10,500	23.87%
Alabama	3,360	7.64
Wyoming	3,210	7.30
Texas	2,600	5.91
North Carolina	2,440	5.55
Ohio	2,170	4.93
California	1,780	4.05%
South Carolina	1,690	3.84
Other	16,230	36.90

Source: *The American Ceramic Society Bulletin*, June 1998, p. 6/00/98.

★ 97 ★

Potash (SIC 1474)

Largest Caustic Potash Makers

Companies are ranked by capacity in thousands of short tons.

OxyChem	405
Ashta	74
Vulcan	70

Source: *Chemical Market Report*, October 5, 1998, p. 37.

★ 98 ★

Potash (SIC 1474)

Largest Potash Consumers 1996-97

Consumption is shown in thousands of tons.

	(000)	Share
Illinois	444	9.22%
Iowa	320	6.65
Minnesota	294	6.11
Texas	242	5.03
Nebraska	212	4.40
California	208	4.32
Indiana	202	4.20
Kansas	196	4.07
Missouri	187	3.88
North Dakota	183	3.80
Other	2,327	48.33

Source: *Better Crops*, vol 83, 1999, p. 5, from Association of American Plant Food Control Officials and Fertilizer Institute.

★ 99 ★

Soda Ash (SIC 1474)

Largest Soda Ash Producers - 1998

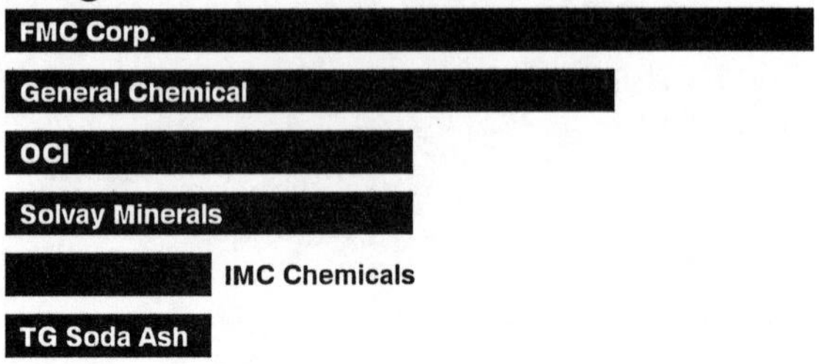

FMC Corp.
General Chemical
OCI
Solvay Minerals
IMC Chemicals
TG Soda Ash

Companies are ranked by nameplate capacities in millions of short tons.

FMC Corp.	3.55
General Chemical	2.50
OCI	2.30
Solvay Minerals	2.30
IMC Chemicals	1.40
TG Soda Ash	1.30

Source: *Engineering & Mining Journal*, April 1999, p. 24.

★ 100 ★

Gemstones (SIC 1499)

U.S. Gemstone Production - 1996

Production is shown in thousands of dollars.

	($ 000)	Share
Shell	$ 22,800	52.29%
Gem feldspar	4,980	11.42
Sapphires and rubies	2,030	4.66
Quartz	1,880	4.31
Turqoise	1,410	3.23
Other	10,500	24.08

Source: *Minerals Yearbook*, 1996, p. 369, from U.S. Bureau of Mines.

SIC 15 - General Building Contractors

★ 101 ★

Construction (SIC 1500)

Construction by Segment

Data are in millions of square feet.

	1997	1999
Stores	238	239
Warehouses	198	189
Manufacturing	187	152
Hotels	87	79

Source: *The Construction Specifer*, January 1999, p. 14, from Outlook Executive 1999 Conference.

★ 102 ★

Construction (SIC 1500)

Construction Spending by Segment - 1999

Spending is shown in billions of dollars.

	1998	1999
Retail	$ 48.0	$ 47.5
Office	36.8	37.9
Industrial	29.3	29.9
Hotel	13.9	12.9

Source: *Building Design & Construction*, January 1999, p. 31, from Cahners Economics.

★ 103 ★

Residential Construction (SIC 1521)

Housing Resales in Canada - 1998

Total house sales reached 218,662.

	Units	Share
Toronto	55,344	25.31%
Montreal	28,683	13.12
Calgary	20,554	9.40
Vancouver	19,612	8.97
Edmonton	13,727	6.28
Other	80,742	36.93

Source: *Globe and Mail*, March 6, 1999, p. B7, from The Canadian Real Estate Association.

★ 104 ★

Residential Construction (SIC 1521)

Largest Home Builders - 1998

Firms are ranked by gross revenues in millions of dollars,

Centex Corp.	$ 4,749
Pulte Home Corp.	3,005
Kaufman and Broad Home Corp.	2,449
D.R. Horton	2,421
Lennar Corp.	2,417
The Ryland Group	1,765
NVR	1,560
U.S. Home Corp.	1,500
Del Webb Corp.	1,274
M.D.C. Holdings	1,263

Source: *Builder*, March 1999, p. 151.

★ 105 ★

Residential Construction (SIC 1521)

Top Builders in Albuquerque, NM

Market shares are shown in percent.

Artistic Homes	9.3%
Kaufman and Broad Home Corp.	7.4
AMREP Southwest	7.3
Sivage-Thomas Homes	6.3
Longford Homes	6.0
Other	63.7

Source: *Builder*, May 1999, p. 238.

★ 106 ★

Residential Construction (SIC 1521)

Top Builders in Arizona - 1998

Companies are ranked by billings in millions of dollars.

Huber Hunt & Nichols Inc.	$ 412.0
The Chanene Corp.	405.4
Sundt Corp.	243.4
Kitchell Contractors Inc.	174.0
McCarthy	165.0

Source: *The Business Journal Serving Phoenix and the Valley of the Sun*, September 4, 1998, p. 44.

★ 107 ★

Residential Construction (SIC 1521)

Top Builders in Atlanta, GA - 1998

Market shares are shown in percent.

Torrey Homes/D.R. Horton	3.3%
Pulte Home Corp.	3.2
Colony Homes	2.0
John Wiedland Homnes & Neighborhoods	2.0
The Ryland Group	1.1
Other	88.4

Source: *Builder*, May 1999, p. 217, from American Metro/Study Corp.

★ 108 ★

Residential Construction (SIC 1521)

Top Builders in Austin, TX - 1998

Market shares are shown in percent.

Milburn Homes/D.R. Horton	15.1%
Kaufman and Broad Home Corp.	7.8
Wilshire Homes/The Fortress Group	7.2
Centex Corp.	6.0
Main Street Homes	5.7
Other	58.2

Source: *Builder*, May 1999, p. 228, from American Metro/Study Corp.

★ 109 ★

Residential Construction (SIC 1521)

Top Builders in Baltimore, MD - 1998

Market shares are shown in percent.

Ryan Homes/NVR	7.5%
The Ryland Group	2.9
Patriot Homes	2.5
Pulte Home Corp.	2.4
NV Homes/NVR	2.1
Other	82.6

Source: *Builder*, May 1999, p. 228, from American Metro/Study Corp.

★ 110 ★

Residential Construction (SIC 1521)

Top Builders in Boston, MA - 1998

Market shares are shown in percent.

Pulte Home Corp.	2.9%
Toll Brothers	1.7
Modern Continental Enterprises	1.5
Commons Development Group	1.1
Robert M. Hicks	0.9
Other	91.9

Source: *Builder*, May 1999, p. 232.

★ 111 ★

Residential Construction (SIC 1521)

Top Builders in Cecil County, Maryland - 1998

Market shares are shown for the first 11 months of the year.

Gemcraft Homes	23.0%
Dawitt-Simmons	12.7
Ryan Homes Inc.	8.2
McKee Group	7.7
Tiffin Builders	7.0
Hess Family Builders	5.2
G&S Contracting	4.3
Headwater Homes	3.6
Justice Builders Inc.	3.6
Clark Turner Communities	3.4
Other	21.3

Source: *The Baltimore Sun*, January 24, 1999, p. L1, from *Meyers Housing Data Reports*, Cecil County Permits and Inspection Office, and Metropolitan Regional Information Systems.

★ 112 ★

Residential Construction (SIC 1521)

Top Builders in Chicago, IL - 1998

Market shares are shown in percent.

Cambridge Homes	2.4%
Sundance Homes	1.6
Lakewood Homes	1.6
Kimball Hill Homes	1.5
Town & Country Homes	1.4
Other	91.5

Source: *Builder*, May 1999, p. 218, from The Meyers Group.

★ 113 ★

Residential Construction (SIC 1521)

Top Builders in Cincinnati, OH - 1998

M/I Schottenstein Homes

The Drees Co.

Zaring National Corp.

Crossmann Communities

Fischer Homes

Other

Market shares are shown in percent.

M/I Schottenstein Homes	4.1%
The Drees Co.	4.0
Zaring National Corp.	3.7
Crossmann Communities	3.0
Fischer Homes	2.3
Other	82.9

Source: *Builder*, May 1999, p. 228, from Robert Binns Associates.

★ 114 ★

Residential Construction (SIC 1521)

Top Builders in Columbus, OH - 1998

Market shares are shown in percent.

M/I Schottenstein Homes	15.2%
Dominion Homes	13.1
Homewood Corp.	4.2
Crossmann Communities	3.6
Maronda Homes	2.9
Other	61.0

Source: *Builder*, May 1999, p. 232, from Robert Binns Associates.

★ 115 ★

Residential Construction (SIC 1521)

Top Builders in Dallas, TX - 1998

Market shares are shown in percent.

Centex Corp.	5.5%
Highland Homes	5.4
Choice Homes	5.0
Pulte Home Corp.	3.7
Lennar Corp.	3.0
Other	77.4

Source: *Builder*, May 1999, p. 218, from Residential Strategies.

★ 116 ★

Residential Construction (SIC 1521)

Top Builders in Denver, CO - 1998

Market shares are shown in percent.

Richmond American Homes	13.8%
Melody Homes/Schuler Homes	7.7
Kaufman and Broad Home Corp.	7.5
U.S. Home Corp.	6.1
Continental Home/D.R. Horton	4.5
Other	60.4

Source: *Builder*, May 1999, p. 222, from The Meyers Group.

★ 117 ★

Residential Construction (SIC 1521)

Top Builders in Detroit, MI - 1998

Pulte Home Corp.
MJC Cos.
Tri Mount-Vincenti Cos.
Crosswinds Communities
Silverman Cos.
Other

Market shares are shown in percent.

Pulte Home Corp.	5.1%
MJC Cos.	3.1
Tri Mount-Vincenti Cos.	2.6
Crosswinds Communities	2.3
Silverman Cos.	1.7
Other	75.2

Source: *Builder*, May 1999, p. 220, from Housing Consultants.

★ 118 ★

Residential Construction (SIC 1521)

Top Builders in Fort Lauderdale, FL - 1998

Market shares are shown in percent.

Arvida/JMB Partners	10.0%
Lennar Corp.	6.7
Transeastern Properties	5.6
Westbrooke	5.4
Continental Homes/D.R. Horton	4.9
Other	67.4

Source: *Builder*, May 1999, p. 228, from The Meyers Group.

★ 119 ★

Residential Construction (SIC 1521)

Top Builders in Greensboro, NC - 1998

Market shares are shown in percent.

Westminster Homes/Washington Homes	3.1%
Shugart Enterprises	2.9
Arrapco Homes/D.R. Horton	2.8
New Fortis Corp./Hovanian Enterprises	2.7
Old South Home Co.	1.3
Other	88.2

Source: *Builder*, May 1999, p. 228, from The Meyers Group.

★ 120 ★

Residential Construction (SIC 1521)

Top Builders in Greenville-Spartanburg, SC - 1998

Market shares are shown in percent.

Pulte Home Corp.	5.5%
The Ryland Group	3.7
Torrey Homes/D.R. Horton	3.5
Seppela Homes	2.7
Centex Corp.	2.1
Other	82.5

Source: *Builder*, May 1999, p. 232, from Market Opportunity Research Enterprises.

★ 121 ★

Residential Construction (SIC 1521)

Top Builders in Houston, TX - 1998

Market shares are shown in percent.

MHI	5.6%
Perry Homes	5.1
Royce Homes	4.9
Village Builders	4.6
The Ryland Group	3.6
Other	76.2

Source: *Builder*, May 1999, p. 220, from American Metro/Study Corp.

★ 122 ★

Residential Construction (SIC 1521)

Top Builders in Indianapolis, MD - 1998

Market shares are shown in percent.

Crossmann Communities	14.7%
Davis Homes	6.7
C.P. Morgan	6.4
The Ryland Group	5.1
Dura Builders	4.2
Other	62.9

Source: *Builder*, May 1999, p. 224, from Permits Plus.

★ 123 ★

Residential Construction (SIC 1521)

Top Builders in Kansas City, MO - 1998

Market shares are shown in percent.

Brown Midwest/Parkwood Hills	1.8%
Don Bell Homes	1.7
Miller Enterprises	1.4
Prieb Homes	1.3
Pulte Home Corp.	1.3
Other	92.5

Source: *Builder*, May 1999, p. 226, from HBA of Kansas City.

★ 124 ★

Residential Construction (SIC 1521)

Top Builders in Las Vegas, NV - 1998

Market shares are shown in percent.

Lewis Homes Group of Cos.	8.6%
Kaufman and Broad Home Corp.	6.2
Del Webb Corp.	5.5
Pulte Home Corp.	5.1
Pardee Construction/Weyerhaeuser Real Estate Co.	3.6
Other	71.0

Source: *Builder*, May 1999, p. 218, from The Meyers Group.

★ 125 ★

Residential Construction (SIC 1521)

Top Builders in Los Angeles, CA - 1998

Market shares are shown in percent.

Kaufman and Broad Home Corp.	4.3%
S&S Construction	3.8
Centex Corp.	3.7
Shea Homes	3.4
Pacific Bay Homes	3.3
Other	81.5

Source: *Builder*, May 1999, p. 232, from The Meyers Group.

★ 126 ★

Residential Construction (SIC 1521)

Top Builders in Louisville, KY - 1998

Market shares are shown in percent.

Mareli Development Co./D.R. Horton	2.1%
Monsour Builders	1.3
Zaring National Corp.	1.3
VBD & Associates	1.2
Peter Built Homes	0.9
Other	93.2

Source: *Builder*, May 1999, p. 232, from HBA of Louisville.

★ 127 ★

Residential Construction (SIC 1521)

Top Builders in Memphis, TN - 1998

Market shares are shown in percent.

Bowden Building Co.	5.5%
Summit Homes	1.8
FaxonGillis Homes	1.2
Paragon Properties/Crossman Communities	1.2
Vintage Homes	1.2
Other	89.1

Source: *Builder*, May 1999, p. 232, from *Chandler Reports*.

★ 128 ★

Residential Construction (SIC 1521)

Top Builders in Nashville, TN - 1998

Market shares are shown in percent.

Fox Ridge Homes	4.5%
Phillips Builders/Beazer Homes USA	4.4
Pulte Home Corp.	3.4
Zaring National Corp.	2.3
Jerry Butler Builder	2.0

Source: *Builder*, May 1999, p. 224, from MarketGraphics.

★ 129 ★

Residential Construction (SIC 1521)

Top Builders in Norfolk/Virginia Beach - 1998

Market shares are shown in percent.

Terry Peterson Residential	3.1%
Centex Corp.	2.8
The Francisus Co.	2.8
Affordable Homes	2.5
Napolitano Enterprises	2.2
Other	86.6

Source: *Builder*, May 1999, p. 232.

★ 130 ★

Residential Construction (SIC 1521)

Top Builders in North Carolina

Companies are ranked by number of closings.

Pulte Home Corp.	1,026
Centex Homes	721
Square Homes Inc.	670
New Fortis Corp.	648
DR Horton Inc.	626
Westminster Homes Inc.	467
Ryland Homes Inc.	458

Source: *Business North Carolina*, December 1998, p. 64, from Market Opportunity Research Enterprises.

★ 131 ★

Residential Construction (SIC 1521)

Top Builders in Orlando, FL - 1998

Market shares are shown in percent.

Centex Corp.	4.3%
Maronda Homes	3.6
American Heritage Homes	3.4
Engle Homes	3.2
Morrison Homes	2.5
Other	83.0

Source: *Builder*, May 1999, p. 220, from Residential Marketing Reports and Charles Wayne Consulting.

★ 132 ★

Residential Construction (SIC 1521)

Top Builders in Philadelphia, PA - 1998

Market shares are shown in percent.

Toll Brothers	6.0%
Ryan Homes/NVR	3.0
Homes on Parade	2.8
Hovanian Enterprises	2.3
The Quaker Group	2.3
Other	83.6

Source: *Builder*, May 1999, p. 222, from The Meyers Group.

★ 133 ★

Residential Construction (SIC 1521)

Top Builders in Phoenix, AZ - 1998

Market shares are shown in percent.

Shea Homes	7.5%
Continental Homes/D.R. Horton	6.1
Beazer Homes USA	4.1
Del Webb Corp.	3.4
Kaufman and Broad Home Corp.	3.4
Other	75.5

Source: *Builder*, May 1999, p. 217, from The Meyers Group.

★ 134 ★

Residential Construction (SIC 1521)

Top Builders in Portland, OR - 1998

Market shares are shown in percent.

Arbor Custom Homes	5.3%
Marshall Grimburg Group	4.6
Centex Corp.	3.6
New Tradition Homes	2.8
Aho Construction	2.7
Other	81.0

Source: *Builder*, May 1999, p. 224, from The Meyers Group.

★ 135 ★

Residential Construction (SIC 1521)

Top Builders in Salt Lake City, Utah - 1998

Market shares are shown in percent.

Ivory Homes	6.4%
Woodside Homes	3.2
Perry Homes	2.2
Kaufman and Broad Home Corp.	1.9
Mark Higley Construction	1.7
Other	84.6

Source: *Builder*, May 1999, p. 228, from *Construction Monitor.*

★ 136 ★

Residential Construction (SIC 1521)

Top Builders in Seattle, WA - 1998

Market shares are shown in percent.

Centex Corp.	2.8%
Murray Franklyn Cos.	2.0
D.L.B. Johnson Construction	1.9
Stafford Homes	1.9
Geonerco	1.6
Other	89.8

Source: *Builder*, May 1999, p. 226, from *New Home Trends.*

★ 137 ★

Residential Construction (SIC 1521)

Top Builders in St. Louis, MO - 1998

Market shares are shown in percent.

Whitaker Homes/The Fortress Group	5.3%
The Jones Co.	4.1
McBride & Son	2.6
Mayer Homes	2.3
Taylor Morley Homes	1.8
Other	83.9

Source: *Builder*, May 1999, p. 224, from HBA of Greater St. Louis.

★ 138 ★

Residential Construction (SIC 1521)

Top Home Builders - 1998

Firms are ranked by housing revenues in billions of dollars.

Pulte Corp.	$ 2.9
Centex Corp.	2.5
Kaufman and Broad Home Corp.	2.3
D.R. Horton Inc.	2.3
Lennar Corp.	2.0
The Ryland Group Inc.	1.6
NVR Inc.	1.5
U.S. Home Corp.	1.4
Shea Homes	1.2
M.D.C. Holdings Inc.	1.2
Toll Brothers Inc.	1.2

Source: *Professional Builder*, April 1999, p. 70.

★ 139 ★

Residential Construction (SIC 1521)

Top Home Closers - 1998

Firms are ranked by number of closings.

Pulte Corp.	20,359
Kaufman and Broad Home Corp.	15,213
D.R. Horton Inc.	15,168
Centex Corp.	14,063
Lennar Corp.	10,777
Lincoln Property Co.	9,213
The Ryland Group Inc.	8,994
Trammell Crow Residential	8,758
U.S. Home Corp.	8,258
A.G. Spanos Cos.	7,630

Source: *Professional Builder*, April 1999, p. 70.

★ 140 ★

Residential Construction (SIC 1522)

Largest Multifamily Markets - 1998

Data show number of units permitted through October. Figures refer to buildings with 5 or more units.

Houston	17,363
Dallas	13,846
Atlanta	9,656
Orlando	9,102
Seattle	8,626
Las Vegas	8,597
Phoenix	8,256
Washington D.C.	8,040
Denver	5,716
New York City	5,506

Source: *Building Design & Construction*, February 1999, p. 27, from U.S. Department of Commerce.

★ 141 ★

Residential Construction (SIC 1522)

Largest Multifamily Rental Builders

Companies are ranked by number of rental starts.

A.G. Spanos Cos.	11,260
JPI	9,935
Lincoln Property Co.	9,213
Trammell Crow Residential	8,758
Colson & Colson Construction Co.	5,125

Source: *Builder*, May 1999, p. 142.

★ 142 ★

Residential Construction (SIC 1522)

Leading Multi-Unit Residential Construction Firms

Firms are ranked by revenues in millions of dollars.

Wimberly Allison Tong & Goo Inc.	$ 15.6
Huitt-Zollars Inc.	9.1
Parsons Brinckerhoff Inc.	8.0
Schoor DePalma Inc.	7.2
RTKL Associates Inc.	4.9
Fugleberg Koch Architects	4.0
Hellmuth, Obata + Kassabaum	3.0

Source: *ENR*, September 1998, p. 50.

★ 143 ★

Nonresidential Construction (SIC 1541)

Largest Auto Plant Design Firms

Firms are ranked by revenues in millions of dollars.

Golder Associates Corp.	$ 35.7
SSOE Inc.	24.7
Albert Kahan Associates Inc.	19.2
Fluor Daniel Inc.	19.0
Giffels Associates Inc.	14.3
Ghafari Associates Inc.	11.0
O'Neal Inc.	8.3

Source: *ENR*, September 1998, p. 65.

★ 144 ★

Nonresidential Construction (SIC 1541)

Largest Food Plant Design Firms

Firms are ranked by revenues in millions of dollars.

Fluor Daniel Inc.	$ 34.0
Raytheon Engineers & Constructors Intl.	26.0
A. Epstein and Sons International Inc.	24.2
Simons Engineering Inc.	18.3
Morrison Knudsen Corp.	16.0
Day & Zimmerman International Inc.	13.0
Burns & McDonnell Engrs-Archts-Consultant	10.8

Source: *ENR*, September 1998.

★ 145 ★

Nonresidential Construction (SIC 1541)

Largest Pulp/Paper Mill Design Firms

Firms are ranked by revenues in millions of dollars.

Brown & Root Inc.	$ 42.0
Raytheon Engineers & Constructors Intl.	29.0
Simons Engineering Inc.	23.5
Harris Group Inc.	15.7
URS Grenier Woodward-Clyde	9.1
Fluor Daniel Inc.	8.0
Industra Service Corp.	8.0

Source: *ENR*, September 1998.

★ 146 ★

Nonresidential Construction (SIC 1542)

Largest Design Firms - 1998

Firms are ranked by total revenues in millions of dollars.

Fluor Daniel Inc.	$ 1,698.0
Bechtel Group Inc.	1,209.0
Jacobs Sverdrup	1,094.0
Kellogg Brown & Root	1,084.0
Parsons Corp.	944.0
URS Greiner Woodward-Clyde	925.0
Foster Wheeler Corp.	917.7
CH2M Hill Cos. Ltd.	773.6
Parsons Brinckerhoff Inc.	742.7
ABB Lummus Global Inc.	710.1

Source: *ENR*, April 19, 1999, p. 63.

★ 147 ★

Nonresidential Construction (SIC 1542)

Leading Airport Design Firms

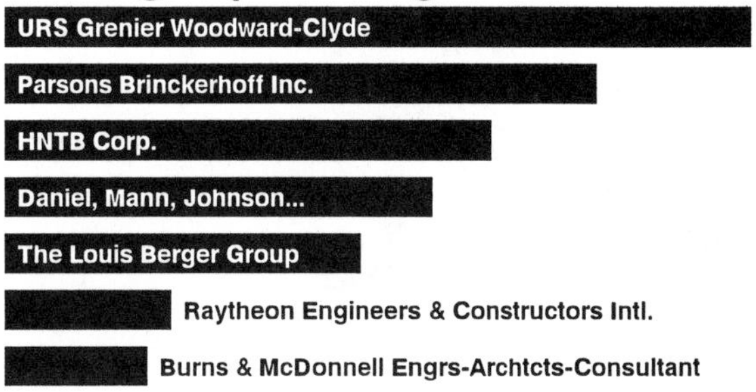

Firms are ranked by revenues in millions of dollars.

URS Grenier Woodward-Clyde	$ 63.2
Parsons Brinckerhoff Inc.	49.6
HNTB Corp.	41.0
Daniel, Mann, Johnson & Mendenhall	36.0
The Louis Berger Group	30.2
Raytheon Engineers & Constructors Intl.	14.0
Burns & McDonnell Engrs-Archtcts-Consultant	11.6

Source: *ENR*, September 1998, p. 61.

★ 148 ★

Nonresidential Construction (SIC 1542)

Leading Commercial Office Construction Firms

Firms are ranked by revenues in millions of dollars.

Gensier	$ 139.7
Hellmuth, Obata + Kassabaum	66.9
The Hillier Group	35.0
HKS Inc.	30.9
Parsons Brinckerhoff Inc.	29.0
Daniel, Mann, Johnson & Mendenhall	28.0
Kohn Pedersen Fox Associates	24.0

Source: *ENR*, September 1998, p. 50.

★ 149 ★

Nonresidential Construction (SIC 1542)

Leading Correctional Facility Designers

Firms are ranked by revenues in millions of dollars.

Firm	($ mil.)
Daniel, Mann, Johnson, & Mendenhall	$ 30.0
DLR Group Inc.	19.1
Hellmuth, Obata + Kassabaum	19.0
URS Grenier Woodward-Clyde	10.1
NBBJ	8.7
Payette Associates Inc.	8.2
HDR Inc.	8.0

Source: *ENR*, September 1998, p. 55.

★ 150 ★

Nonresidential Construction (SIC 1542)

Leading Entertainment Facility Designers

Holmes & Narver
Morris Architects
Hellmuth, Obata + Kassabaum
Tetra Tech Inc.
Lawn Engineering...
Arrowstreet Inc.
RTKL Associates Inc.

Firms are ranked by revenues in millions of dollars.

Firm	($ mil.)
Holmes & Narver	$ 10.0
Morris Architects	8.8
Hellmuth, Obata + Kassabaum	7.5
Tetra Tech Inc.	6.5
Lawn Engineering & Environ. Services Inc.	6.0
Arrowstreet Inc.	5.9
RTKL Associates Inc.	5.8

Source: *ENR*, September 1998, p. 55.

★ 151 ★

Nonresidential Construction (SIC 1542)

Leading General Building Construction Firms

Firms are ranked by revenues in millions of dollars.

Firm	($ mil.)
Hellmuth, Obeta + Kassabaum	$ 264.8
Gensier	165.3
URS Grenier Qoodward-Clyde	121.7
NBBJ	110.0
Holmes & Narver	105.0
Daniel, Mann, Johnson & Mendenhall	91.0
Ellerbe Becket	86.0

Source: *ENR*, September 1998, p. 49.

★ 152 ★

Nonresidential Construction (SIC 1542)

Leading Government Office Construction Firms

Firms are ranked by revenues in millions of dollars.

Firm	($ mil.)
Holmes & Narver	$ 75.0
Hellmuth, Obata + Kaassabaum	36.1
URS Grenier Woodward-Clyde	25.9
Daniel, Mann, Johnson & Mendenhall	25.0
Carlson Design/Construct Corp.	24.0
Parsons Brinckerhoff Inc.	20.5
Sverdrup Corp.	18.1

Source: *ENR*, September 1998, p. 49.

★ 153 ★

Nonresidential Construction (SIC 1542)

Leading Hotel/Convention Center Designers

Firms are ranked by revenues in millions of dollars.

Firm	($ mil.)
Hellmuth, Obata + Kassabaum	$ 22.0
Edward D. Stone Jr. & Associates	9.2
NBBJ	8.6
HKS Inc.	7.9
Smallwood, Reynolds, Stewart, Stewart	7.7
The Hillier Group	7.5
CDI Engineering Group Inc.	5.2

Source: *ENR*, September 1998, p. 55.

★ 154 ★

Nonresidential Construction (SIC 1542)

Leading Retail Construction Firms

Firms are ranked by revenues in millions of dollars.

RTKL Associates Inc.	$ 24.6
Hellmuth, Obata + Kassabaum	21.3
Casco Corp.	18.2
BSW International Inc.	17.7
FRCH Design Worldwide	16.8
URS Grenier Woodward-Clyde	14.5
Law Engineering & Environ. Services Inc.	14.3

Source: *ENR*, September 1998, p. 49.

★ 155 ★

Nonresidential Construction (SIC 1542)

Leading Retail Contractors - 1998

Firms are ranked by millions of square feet.

Fisher Development Inc.	19.2
EMJ Corp.	18.8
The Whiting-Turner Contracting Co.	15.0
R.A.S. Builders Inc.	13.7
Walbridge Aldinger	12.4
Miller Building Corp.	11.8
Vratsinas Construction Co.	9.9
Shrader & Martinez Construction Inc.	9.2
S.D. Deacon Corp.	9.0
Gallant Construction Co.	8.7

Source: *Shopping Center World*, July 1998, p. 56.

★ 156 ★

Nonresidential Construction (SIC 1542)

Leading Sports Facility Designers

Firms are ranked by revenues in millions of dollars.

Hellmuth, Obata + Kassabaum	$ 48.8
NBBJ	19.0
Ellerbe Becket	17.2
Wimberly Allison Tong & Goo Inc.	15.8
HNTB Corp.	7.0
Heery International Inc.	6.1
URS Grenier Woodward-Clyde	5.1

Source: *ENR*, September 1998, p. 54.

★ 157 ★

Nonresidential Construction (SIC 1542)

Top Hotel Design Firms - 1997

Companies are ranked by lodging fees in millions of dollars.

Wimberly Allison Tong Goo	$ 42.3
Hirsch Bedner Assoc.	23.4
Wilson & Associates	22.1
Arthur Shuster	16.0
DiLeonardo International	14.5
Brennan Beer Gorman Monk	12.7
RTKL	7.6
Daroff Design	6.0
Concepts 4	3.4
BSW International	3.3

Source: *Hotel & Motel Management*, November 2, 1998, p. 56.

SIC 16 - Heavy Construction, Except Building

★ 158 ★

Contracting (SIC 1600)

Top Contractors in Canada - 1997

Companies are ranked by sales in millions of dollars.

PCL Construction Group Inc.	$ 1,747.8
Ellis-Don Construction Ltd.	689.4
BFC Construction Corporation	606.8
AGRA Inc.	604.5
Ledcor Industries Ltd.	460.0
Axor Group Inc.	350.0
Vanbots Construction Corporation	350.0
Eastern Construction Co. Ltd.	280.0

Source: *Heavy Construction News*, June 1998, p. 16.

★ 159 ★

Heavy Construction (SIC 1600)

Heavy Construction Industry

Data are in billions of dollars.

	1997
Highways/bridges	$ 34.0
Sewers	8.1
Water	6.8
Dams/rivers	5.2

Source: *Civil Engineering*, December 1998, p. 16, from McGraw-Hill Construction Information Group.

★ 160 ★

Street and Highway Construction (SIC 1611)

Leading Highway Design Firms

Firms are ranked by revenues in millions of dollars.

Parsons Brinckerhoff Inc.	$ 246.3
The Louis Berger Group	221.8
URS Grenier Woodward-Clyde	93.5
HNTB Corp.	88.5
Law Engineering & Environ. Services Inc.	81.6
Sverdrup Corp.	74.7
Morrison Knudsen Corp.	61.0

Source: *ENR*, September 1998, p. 57.

★ 161 ★

Bridge Construction (SIC 1622)

Leading Bridge Design Firms

Firms are ranked by revenues in millions of dollars.

URS Grenier Woodward-Clyde	$ 64.8
Parsons Brinckerhoff Inc.	63.9
HNTB Corp.	53.4
The Louis Berger Group	18.0
HDR Inc.	17.8
STV Group	15.2
Daniel, Mann, Johnson, & Mendenhall	14.2

Source: *ENR*, September 1998, p. 57.

★ 162 ★

Mass Transit (SIC 1622)

Leading Mass Transit Light Rail Design Firms

Firms are ranked by revenues in millions of dollars.

Parsons Brinckerhoff Inc.	$ 127.2
Daniel, Mann, Johnson & Mendenhall	63.0
STV Group	37.9
Law Engineering & Environ. Services Inc.	28.3
Sverdrup Corp.	26.5
The Louis Berger Group	16.8
Burns and Roe Enterprises Inc.	14.9

Source: *ENR*, September 1998, p. 57.

★ 163 ★

Heavy Construction (SIC 1623)

Leading Dam/Reservoir Design Firms

Firms are ranked by revenues in millions of dollars.

Camp Dresser & McKee Inc.	$ 16.0
Harza Engineering Co.	14.5
URS Grenier Woodward-Clyde	13.7
Law Engineering	11.5
Montgomery Watson Inc.	11.0
Golder Associates Corp.	7.6
Parsons Brinckerhoff Inc.	5.9

Source: *ENR*, September 1998, p. 91.

★ 164 ★

Heavy Construction (SIC 1623)

Leading Hazardous Waste Design Firms

Firms are ranked by revenues in millions of dollars.

Fluor Daniel Inc.	$ 372.0
ICF Kaiser International Inc.	364.9
ERM Group	229.3
URS Grenier Woodward-Clyde	205.3
Tetra Tech Inc.	189.1
International Technology Corp.	140.0
Roy F. Weston Inc.	105.8

Source: *ENR*, September 1998, p. 81.

★ 165 ★

Heavy Construction (SIC 1623)

Leading Hydropower Design Firms

Firms are ranked by revenues in millions of dollars.

Harza Engineering Co.	$ 41.8
Stone & Webster	11.0
Parsons Brinckerhoff Inc.	3.2
Law Engineering & Environ. Services Inc.	3.1
Golder Associates Corp.	2.9
HDR Inc.	2.5
R.W. Beck Inc.	2.5

Source: *ENR*, September 1998, p. 81.

★ 166 ★

Heavy Construction (SIC 1623)

Leading Nuclear Waste Design Firms

Firms are ranked by revenues in millions of dollars.

Fluor Daniel Inc.	$ 216.0
Morrison Knudsen Corp.	63.0
URS Grenier Woodward-Clyde	10.5
Tetra Tech Inc.	10.3
Burns and Roe Enterprises Inc.	7.5
Stone & Webster	7.0
Golder Associates Corp.	6.6

Source: *ENR*, September 1998, p. 85.

★ 167 ★

Heavy Construction (SIC 1623)

Leading Sewerage/Solid Waste Design Firms

Montgomery Watson Inc.
Camp Dresser & McKee Inc.
Black & Veatch
Brown & Caldwell
Earth Tech Inc.
Roy F. Weston Inc.
Rust Environmental & Infrastructure

Firms are ranked by revenues in millions of dollars.

Montgomery Watson Inc.	$ 193.0
Camp Dresser & McKee Inc.	127.0
Black & Veatch	109.0
Brown & Caldwell	71.5
Earth Tech Inc.	66.0
Roy F. Weston Inc.	61.6
Rust Environmental & Infrastructure	54.2

Source: *ENR*, September 1998, p. 88.

★ 168 ★

Heavy Construction (SIC 1623)

Leading Utility Design Firms

Firms are ranked by revenues in millions of dollars.

Stone & Webster	$ 261.0
Black & Veatch	220.0
Raytheon Engineers & Constructors International	184.0
Burns and Roe Enterprises Inc.	140.9
Foster Wheeler Corp.	76.3
McDermott International Inc.	58.6
Harza Engineering Co.	57.5

Source: *ENR*, September 1998, p. 80.

★ 169 ★

Heavy Construction (SIC 1623)

Leading Water Supply Design Firms

Firms are ranked by revenues in millions of dollars.

Black & Veatch	$ 164.0
Montgomery Watson Inc.	121.5
Camp Dresser & McKee Inc.	106.0
Law Engineering & Environ. Services Inc.	32.9
HDR Inc.	29.0
URS Grenier Woodward-Clyde	28.1
Earth Tech Inc.	21.9

Source: *ENR*, September 1998, p. 91.

★ 170 ★

Nonresidential Construction (SIC 1623)

Largest Petroleum Facility Design Firms

Firms are ranked by revenues in millions of dollars.

ABB Lummus Global Inc.	$ 639.1
Brown & Root Inc.	614.0
Fluor Daniel Inc.	445.0
Foster Wheeler Corp.	442.8
Raytheon Engineers & Constructors Intl.	255.0
McDermott International Inc.	166.2
The M.W. Kellogg Co.	145.0

Source: *ENR*, September 1998, p. 75.

★ 171 ★

Pipeline Construction (SIC 1623)

Largest Pipeline Design Firms

Firms are ranked by revenues in millions of dollars.

Fluor Daniel Inc.	$ 93.0
Raytheon Engineers & Constructors Intl.	15.0
Wilson & Co.	8.0
Mustang Engineering Inc.	7.0
Michael Baker Corp.	5.9
Corrpro Cos. Inc.	5.2
Golder Associates Corp.	5.0

Source: *ENR*, September 1998, p. 76.

★ 172 ★

Heavy Construction (SIC 1629)

Leading Asbestos/Lead Abatement Firms

Firms are ranked by revenues in millions of dollars.

Law Engineering & Environ. Services Inc.	$ 17.0
URS Grenier Woodward-Clyde	5.8
Michael Baker Corp.	5.1
Roy F. Weston Inc.	3.3
Apex Environmental Inc.	2.9
Spotts, Stevens & McCoy Inc.	2.5
Sverdrup Corp.	2.3

Source: *ENR*, September 1998, p. 86.

★ 173 ★

Heavy Construction (SIC 1629)

Leading Chemical Treatment/Soil Remediation Design Firms

URS Grenier Woodward-Clyde
ERM Group
International Technology Corp.
Fluor Daniel Inc.
Foster Wheeler Corp.
Camp Dessier & McKee Inc.
Roy F. Weston Inc.

Firms are ranked by revenues in millions of dollars.

URS Grenier Woodward-Clyde	$ 132.6
ERM Group	128.1
International Technology Corp.	113.0
Fluor Daniel Inc.	101.0
Foster Wheeler Corp.	73.3
Camp Dessier & McKee Inc.	72.5
Roy F. Weston Inc.	69.8

Source: *ENR*, September 1998, p. 86.

★ 174 ★

Heavy Construction (SIC 1629)

Leading Telecommunications Design Firms

Firms are ranked by revenues in millions of dollars.

Fluor Daniel Inc.	$ 56.0
Bechtel Group Inc.	40.0
Tetra Tech Inc.	16.6
Michael Baker Corp.	15.4
David Evans and Associates Inc.	14.2
ARCADIS Geraghty & Miller Inc.	14.0
Edwards and Kelcey Inc.	11.0

Source: *ENR*, September 1998, p. 97.

SIC 17 - Special Trade Contractors

★ 175 ★

Contracting (SIC 1700)

Leading Specialty Contractors

Companies are ranked by revenues in millions of dollars.

EMCOR Group Inc.	$ 897.00
The Poole and Kent Organization	379.90
Limbach Constructors Inc.	258.60
MMC Corp.	255.78
Air Conditioning Co. Inc.	167.00

Source: *Building Design & Construction*, July 1998, p. 68.

★ 176 ★

Contracting - Heating and Cooling (SIC 1711)

Largest HVAC Contractors

Companies are ranked by sales in millions of dollars. HVAC stands for heating, ventillation and air conditioning.

EMCOR Group	$ 312.51
Group Maintenance America Corp.	243.46
American Residential Services	237.27
ACCO - Air Conditioning Co.	168.10
Southland Industries	119.04
The Poole & Kent Co.	113.96
MMC Corp.	94.23
Chas Roberts Air Conditioning	79.22
Limbach Constructors	77.58
TDIndustries	74.14

Source: *Contractor*, May 1998, p. 34.

★ 177 ★

Contracting - Painting (SIC 1721)

Leading Painting Contractors - 1997

Companies are ranked by revenues in millions of dollars.

Cannon Sline Inc.	$ 44.7
J.L. Manta Inc.	33.4
Techno Coatings Inc.	32.6
Prothern Services Group	30.0
M.L. McDonald Co. Inc.	29.2
Swanson & Youngdale Inc.	26.9
Robison-Prezioso Inc.	21.1
F.D. Thomas Inc.	18.5
Ascher Brothers Co. Inc.	17.9
Multiple Plant Services Inc.	16.5

Source: *ENR*, October 12, 1998, p. 65.

★ 178 ★

Contracting - Electrical (SIC 1731)

Largest Electrical Contractors in Sacramento, CA - 1997

Rex Moore Electrical Contractors & Engineers
Interstate Construction Inc.
Royal Electric Co.
Sasco Electric
Schetter Electric

Firms are ranked by gross local billings in millions of dollars.

Rex Moore Electrical Contractors & Engineers	$ 72.75
Interstate Construction Inc.	26.20
Royal Electric Co.	26.14
Sasco Electric	17.76
Schetter Electric	14.00

Source: *Sacramento Business Journal*, November 27, 1998, p. 20.

★ 179 ★

Contracting - Electrical (SIC 1731)

Leading Electrical Contractors - 1997

Companies are ranked by revenues in millions of dollars.

Company	$ mil.
EMCOR Group Inc.	$ 1,053.5
Building One Electrical Inc.	591.7
Integrated Electrical Services Inc.	558.0
MYR Group Inc.	409.7
SASCO Group	381.8
Mass. Electric Construction Co.	272.7
Motor City Electric Co.	176.3
Quanta Services Inc.	173.8
Rosendin Electric Inc.	168.0
Cupertino Electric Inc.	157.0

Source: *ENR*, October 12, 1998, p. 54.

★ 180 ★

Contracting - Mechanical (SIC 1731)

Leading Mechanical Contractors - 1997

Companies are ranked by revenues in millions of dollars.

Company	$ mil.
EMCOR Group Inc.	$ 858.4
The Kinetics Group Inc.	430.0
Poole and Kent Organization	379.9
MMC Corp.	269.2
Limbach Constructors Inc.	258.6
Comfort Systems USA	240.0
Philip Services Corp.	220.0
Scott Co. of California	220.0
Air Conditioning Co. Inc.	168.0
Southland Industries	156.4

Source: *ENR*, October 12, 1998, p. 54.

★ 181 ★

Contracting - Concrete (SIC 1741)

Leading Concrete Contractors - 1997

Companies are ranked by revenues in millions of dollars.

Company	$ mil.
Baker Concrete Construction Inc.	$ 202.0
Ceco Concrete Construction Corp.	105.9
Miller & Long Co. Inc.	90.3
Capform Inc.	70.7
The Western Group	62.0
Structural Preservation Systems Inc.	$ 61.4
T.A.S. Construction Inc.	56.5
McHugh Concrete Construction	56.0
Strescon Industries Inc.	44.1
Bomel Construction Co. Inc.	43.8

Source: *ENR*, October 12, 1998, p. 58.

★ 182 ★

Contracting - Masonry (SIC 1741)

Leading Masonry Contractors - 1997

Companies are ranked by revenues in millions of dollars.

Company	$ mil.
The Western Group	$ 46.6
Seedorff Masonry Inc.	35.0
Pyramid Masonry Contractors Inc.	33.5
Dee Brown Inc.	32.5
J.D. Long Masonry Inc.	29.7
Sun Valley Masonry Inc.	28.8
WASCO Inc.	25.6
Leonard Masonry Inc.	24.7
Masonry Arts Inc.	20.3
John J. Smith Masonry Co.	19.8

Source: *ENR*, October 12, 1998, p. 58.

★ 183 ★

Contracting - Wall and Ceiling (SIC 1742)

Leading Wall/Ceiling Contractors - 1997

Companies are ranked by revenues in millions of dollars.

Company	$ mil.
Performance Contracting Group Inc.	$ 182.1
Cleveland Construction Inc.	125.0
National Construction Enterprises Inc.	121.0
Nastasi & Associates Inc.	81.3
Ellason & Knuth Cos. Inc.	76.2
F.L. Crane & Sons Inc.	63.4
Midwest Drywall Co. Inc.	60.6
Nastasi-White Inc.	59.0
Anson Industries Inc.	58.5
Wyatt Inc.	39.1

Source: *ENR*, October 12, 1998, p. 65.

★ 184 ★

Contracting - Roofing (SIC 1761)

Leading Roofing Contractors - 1997

Companies are ranked by revenues in millions of dollars.

Centimark Corp.	$ 188.3
The Hartford Roofing Co. Inc.	58.5
Birdair Inc.	42.0
W.R. Kelso Co. Inc.	39.2
Baker Roofing Co.	32.8
Seyforth Roofing Co. Inc.	31.1
Schreiber Corp.	28.8
Western Roofing Services	27.6
The Campbell Cos.	27.2
General Roofing Industries Inc.	26.8

Source: *ENR*, October 12, 1998, p. 60.

★ 185 ★

Contracting - Sheet Metal (SIC 1761)

Largest Sheet Metal Contractors

Companies are ranked by sales in millions of dollars.

EMCOR Group	$ 89.29
Kirk & Blum	61.75
Hill Mechanical	41.46
Limbach Constructors	38.79
The Egan Cos.	27.63
Ivey Mechanical Co.	23.31
MacDonald-Miller Co.	20.75
Natkin Contracting	19.74
Colonial Mechanical Corp.	16.02
Doody Mechanical	14.85

Source: *Contractor*, May 1998, p. 34.

★ 186 ★

Contracting - Sheet Metal (SIC 1761)

Leading Sheet Metal Contractors - 1997

Companies are ranked by revenues in millions of dollars.

Kirk & Blum	$ 64.6
Hill Mechanical Group	52.5
Comfort Systems USA	45.0
Apex Industries Inc.	43.0
EMCOR Group Inc.	39.0
Crown Corr Inc.	$ 34.3
Martin Petersen Co. Inc.	27.5
Cal-Air Inc.	27.0
Anson Industries Inc.	25.8
Holaday-Parks Inc.	25.1

Source: *ENR*, October 12, 1998, p. 60.

★ 187 ★

Contracting - Steel Erection (SIC 1791)

Leading Steel Erection Contractors - 1997

Companies are ranked by revenues in millions of dollars.

Midwest Steel Inc.	$ 143.0
Schuff Steel Co.	138.2
The Williams Group Inc.	60.4
The Broad Group	59.4
National Riggers & Erectors Inc.	43.0
Adams & Smith Inc.	38.5
Allstate Steel Co.	36.5
Sowles Co.	35.5
J.L. Davidson Co.	34.8
Interstate Iron Works Corp.	34.4

Source: *ENR*, October 12, 1998, p. 58.

★ 188 ★

Contracting - Glazing & Curtain Wall (SIC 1793)

Leading Glazing/Curtain Wall Contractors - 1997

Companies are ranked by revenues in millions of dollars.

Harmon Ltd.	$ 88.7
Walters & Wolf	62.7
Harmon Inc.	60.8
Flour City Arch. Metals Inc.	35.2
MTH Industries	21.3
Cartner Glass Systems Inc.	20.5
Masonry Arts Inc.	19.5
Elward Construction Co.	17.5
Zephyr Aluminum Inc.	14.9
Ajay Glass & Mirror Co. Inc.	13.9

Source: *ENR*, October 12, 1998, p. 60.

★ 189 ★

Contracting - Excavation (SIC 1794)

Leading Excavation/Foundation Contractors - 1997

Companies are ranked by revenues in millions of dollars.

Ryan Inc.	$ 79.9
Hayward Baker Inc.	79.2
Malcolm Drilling Co.	76.9
McKinney Drilling Co.	63.4
Philip Services Corp.	60.0
Independence Excavating Inc.	58.9
AGRA Foundations Inc.	57.2
Case Foundation Co.	53.5
The Beaver Excavating Co.	51.5
Berkel & Co. Contractors Inc.	50.0

Source: *ENR*, October 12, 1998, p. 60.

★ 190 ★

Contracting - Demolition (SIC 1795)

Leading Demolition/Wrecking Contractors - 1997

Companies are ranked by revenues in millions of dollars.

Penhall International Inc.	$ 79.8
Philip Services Corp.	40.0
Cleveland Wrecking Co.	38.7
Bierlein Demolition Contractors	34.7
North American Site Developers	31.8
Diamond Dismantling Inc.	29.7
Mainline Contracting Corp.	24.3
Mercer Wrecking Recycling Corp.	24.0
Concrete Cutting & Breaking Inc.	23.2
Midwest Cutting & Breaking Inc.	23.2

Source: *ENR*, October 12, 1998, p. 68.

★ 191 ★

Contracting - Fire Protection (SIC 1799)

Largest Fire Protection Contractors

Companies are ranked by sales in millions of dollars.

S.A. Communale Co.	$ 49.31
Virginia Sprinkler Corp.	48.83
J.F. Ahern Co.	35.62
McDaniel Fire Systems	32.42
COSCO Fire Protection	$ 31.00
Atlantic Coast Fire Protection	28.88
Shambaugh & Son	28.41
Great Lakes Plumbing & Heating	12.06
John E. Green Co.	11.02
Scott Co. of California	10.01

Source: *Contractor*, May 1998, p. 34.

★ 192 ★

Contracting - Utility (SIC 1799)

Leading Utility Contractors - 1997

Companies are ranked by revenues in millions of dollars.

Henkels & McCoy Inc.	$ 342.4
Insituform Technologies Inc.	320.6
Quanta Services Inc.	97.8
UTILX Corp.	77.6
Kearney Development Co. Inc.	59.5
RCI Construction Group	44.5
Garney Cos. Inc.	44.0
Davis H. Elliot Co. Inc.	42.3
Kimmins Contracting Corp.	38.4
Super Excavators Inc.	24.6

Source: *ENR*, October 12, 1998, p. 65.

★ 193 ★

Food (SIC 2000)

Best-Selling Private Label Products in Canada - 1997

Sales are shown in millions of dollars.

Frozen dinners and entrees	$ 246.5
Flavored soft drinks	215.5
Butter and dairy blends	170.1
Cookies	116.4
Bathroom tissue	112.5
Ice cream and related products	101.8
Roast and ground coffee	93.5
Snack foods	84.4
Prepackaged cheddar	79.9

Source: *Globe and Mail*, November 30, 1998, p. B3, from A.C. Nielsen.

★ 194 ★

Food (SIC 2000)

Canada's Food Industry - 1998

Meat and meat products

Dairy products

Fruit and vegetables

Bakery products

Fish products

Poultry products

Sales are shown in billions of dollars.

	($ bil.)	Share
Meat and meat products	$ 7.5	34.09%
Dairy products	5.7	25.91
Fruit and vegetables	2.7	12.27
Bakery products	2.1	9.55
Fish products	2.0	9.09
Poultry products	2.0	9.09

Source: *National Trade Data Bank*, April 7, 1999, p. ISA990301.

★ 195 ★

Food (SIC 2000)

Honey Product Sales - 1998

Data show sales of products with honey content for the year ended September 1998.

Honey RTE cereals	14.2%
Honey breads	10.9
Honey lunch meats	5.2
Honey mustards	3.9
Honey salad dressings	2.1
Honey peanut butter	1.5

Source: Retrieved May 31, 1999 from the World Wide Web: http:// www.nhb.org/data/sept98nd.html, from A.C. Nielsen.

★ 196 ★

Food (SIC 2000)

Kid's Food Market

Sales are expected to reach $10 billion.

Cereal	35.0%
Lunch food/snacks	29.0
Beverages	18.0
Meals/entrees	12.0
Ice cream/frozen novelties	6.0

Source: Retrieved May 30, 1999 from the World Wide Web: http:// news.foodonline.com/industry-news/ 19980415-1915html, from FIND/SVP.

★ 197 ★

Food (SIC 2000)

Prepared Food Sales - 1997

Sales are shown in thousands of dollars. Figures include both retail and institutional markets.

Dinners/entrees	$ 5,988,190
Meat	3,819,673
Poultry	2,865,805
Pizza	2,827,915
Desserts/toppings	1,619,604
Breakfast foods	1,472,614
Pies/shells	1,142,542

Source: *Quick Frozen Foods International*, October 1998, p. A15, from Information Resources Inc.

★ 198 ★

Food (SIC 2000)

Takeout Food Market

Data show where consumers get their takeout food. New York City leads the nation with 4.32 meals out per week per capita.

Fast-food restaurants	52.0%
Carryout places	10.0
Deli, bagel and donut shops	9.0
Delivery from foodservice outlet	8.0
Full-service restaurants	4.0
Grocery stores	4.0
Ice cream, snacks and gourmet coffee shops	4.0

Source: *Food Processing*, February 1999, p. 42, from National Restaurant Association.

★ 199 ★

Food (SIC 2000)

Takeout Food Sales

	1997	2007
Fast-food restaurants	61.2%	57.6%
Supermarkets	11.7	14.9
Full-service	11.4	13.2
B&I	6.0	5.2
C-stores	5.2	4.1
College/univ	1.9	2.2
Hybrid stores	1.0	1.4
Others	1.6	1.4

Source: *Food Merchandiser*, November 1998, p. 14, from International Dairy Deli-Bakery Association.

★ 200 ★

Meat Packing (SIC 2011)

Largest Beef Packers

IBP Inc.

ConAgra Beef Companies

Excel Corporation

Farmland National Beef Pkg Co.

Packerland Packing Co.

Companies are ranked by capacity per day.

IBP Inc.	38,800
ConAgra Beef Companies	23,600
Excel Corporation	21,800
Farmland National Beef Pkg Co.	8,700
Packerland Packing Co.	4,750

Source: *Small Farm Today Supplement - Consolidation in the Food and Agriculture System*, April 1999, p. 9, from *Beef Today*.

★ 201 ★

Meat Packing (SIC 2011)

Leading Meat/Poultry Firms

Sales are shown in billions of dollars.

ConAgra	$ 24.0
IBP	13.3
Cargill	9.0
Tyson	6.4
Sara Lee	4.5
Smithfield	3.8
Hormel	3.2
Oscar Mayer	2.5
Gold Kist	2.3
Perdue	2.0

Source: Retrieved May 27, 1999 from the World Wide Web: http:// www.stagnito.com/np.html.

★ 202 ★

Hot Dogs (SIC 2013)

Hot Dog Market

Shares are shown for the year ended June 21, 1998.

Ball Park	14.9%
Oscar Mayer	12.1
Other	73.0

Source: *Advertising Age*, August 3, 1998, p. 8, from Information Resources Inc.

★ 203 ★

Lunch Meat (SIC 2013)

Lunch Meat Market

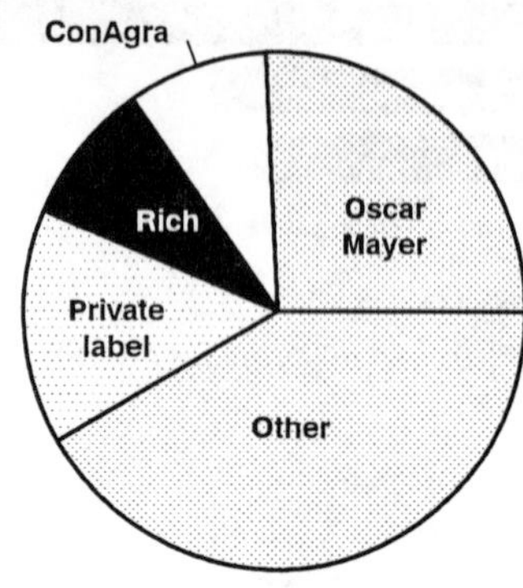

Shares are shown based on $233 million in supermarket sales.

Oscar Mayer	26.0%
ConAgra	9.0
Rich	8.5
Private label	15.0
Other	41.5

Source: *Chicago Tribune*, November 17, 1998, p. 3, from Information Resources Inc.

★ 204 ★

Meat Products (SIC 2013)

Best-Selling Meats

Sales are shown in percent.

Beef	40.2%
Poultry	22.9
Cold cuts, packaged	8.9
Pork	7.5
Sausage, cooked	6.1
Bacon	4.2
Ham, cured	4.1
Frankfurters	3.8
Lamb	1.0
Veal	0.8
Sausage, uncooked	0.5

Source: *Supermarket Business*, April 1999, p. 94.

★ 205 ★

Meat Products (SIC 2013)

Meat Sales in Canada

Sales are shown in millions of dollars.

	($ mil.)	Share
Ontario	$ 2,130	32.77%
Alberta	2,000	30.77
Quebec	1,260	19.38
British Columbia	419	6.45
Saskatchewan	248	3.82
Manitoba	239	3.68
Atlantic Canada	204	3.14

Source: *National Trade Data Bank*, April 7, 1999, p. ISA990301.

★ 206 ★

Meat Products (SIC 2013)

Meat Snack Market - 1997

Shares are shown based on supermarket sales for the year ended December 27, 1997.

	Sales ($ mil.)	Share
Oh Boy! Oberto Sausage Co.	$ 25.1	28.75%
GoodMark Foods Inc.	20.9	23.94
Bridgford Foods	10.3	11.80
Jerome Foods Inc.	5.3	6.07
Old Wisconsin Sausage	3.8	4.35
Jack Link's	3.4	3.89
Other	18.5	21.19

Source: *Snack Food & Wholesale Bakery*, June 1998, pp. S-70, from A.C. Nielsen.

★ 207 ★

Meat Products (SIC 2013)

Popular Meat Snack Brands - 1998

Market shares are shown for the year ended June 21, 1998.

Bridgford Dried Meat Snacks	18.7%
Slim Jim Dried Meat Snacks	18.3
Oh Boy Oberto Dried Meat Snacks	10.0
Armour Dried Meat Snacks	7.1
Lowreys Big Beef Dried Meat Snacks	4.5
Jack Links Dried Meat Snacks	4.4
Super Slim Dried Meat Snacks	4.2
Pemmican Dried Meat Snacks	3.2
Oberto Dried Meat Snacks	3.0

Continued on next page.

★ 207 ★ *Continued*

Meat Products (SIC 2013)

Popular Meat Snack Brands - 1998

Market shares are shown for the year ended June 21, 1998.

Old Wisconsin Dried Meat Snacks	2.0%
Other	24.6

Source: *U.S. Distribution Journal*, September/October 1998, p. 34, from Information Resources Inc.

★ 208 ★

Poultry (SIC 2015)

Largest Broiler Companies - 1998

Data show ready-to-cook production in millions of pounds. The top 47 companies had a total production of 595.83 million pounds.

	(mil.)	Share
Tyson Foods Inc.	141.60	23.77%
Gold Kist Inc.	57.70	9.68
Perdue Farms Inc.	46.57	7.82
Pilgrim's Pride Corporation	36.83	6.18
ConAgra Poultry Company	33.91	5.69
Wayne Farms	24.56	4.12
Cagle's Inc.	16.41	2.75
Sanderson Farms Inc.	15.29	2.57
Foster Farms	14.75	2.48
Townsends Inc.	14.10	2.37
Seaboard Farms Inc.	14.09	2.36
Wampler Foods Inc.	13.00	2.18
Other	167.02	28.03

Source: *Broiler Industry*, January 1999, p. 20C.

★ 209 ★

Dairy Foods (SIC 2020)

Largest Dairy Product Makers

Firms are ranked by sales in millions of dollars. Data refer to the United States and Canada.

Kraft Foods	$ 4,200
Land O' Lakes Inc.	1,810
Dean Foods Co.	1,781
Suiza Foods Corp.	1,740
Mid-America Dairymen Inc.	1,700
Parmalat Canada Ltd.	1,400
Kroger Dairy Div.	1,300

Source: *Dairy Foods*, July 1998, p. 11.

★ 210 ★

Dairy Foods (SIC 2020)

Private Label Dairy Food Sales

Data show private label's share of total sales.

Milk	67.1%
Butter	43.9
Cheese	30.2
Ice cream	25.5
Refrigerated juice	19.1
Yogurt	15.3
Margarine	8.4
Refrigerated desserts	2.8

Source: *Dairy Foods*, May 1999, p. 13, from Information Resources Inc. and Private Label Manufacturers Association.

★ 211 ★

Butter (SIC 2021)

Canada's Margarine Market

Shares of the $600 million market are shown in percent.

Unilever	$ 60.0
Other	40.0

Source: *Globe and Mail*, May 27, 1999, p. B3.

★ 212 ★

Butter (SIC 2021)

Top Butter Makers in Canada - 1999

Market shares are shown in percent for the year ended March 1999.

Parmalat	12.5%
Dairy World	5.7
Gay Lea	5.7
Private label	67.3
Others	8.8

Source: "Report on Market Share." Retrieved June 1, 1999 from the World Wide Web: http://www.marketingmag.ca/index.cgi?, from industry sources.

★ 213 ★

Cheese (SIC 2022)

Cheese Slice Market

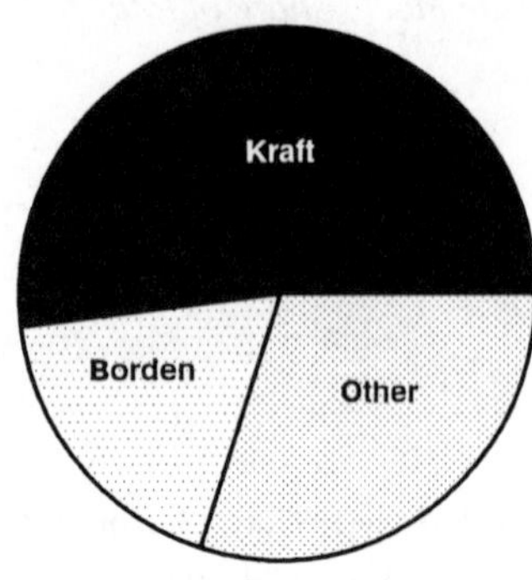

Market shares are shown in percent.

Kraft	52.0%
Borden	18.0
Other	30.0

Source: *Forbes*, May 3, 1999, p. 67.

★ 214 ★

Cheese (SIC 2022)

Top Natural Cheese Brands - 1998

Shares are shown based on sales of $1.98 billion.

	($ mil.)	Share
Kraft	$ 423.1	21.37%
Tillamook	110.4	5.58
Pollio	76.2	3.85
Sorrento	70.8	3.58
Beatrice	55.9	2.82
Frigo	47.2	2.38
Lake to Lake	43.9	2.22
Sargento	38.8	1.96
Land O'Lakes	38.4	1.94
Private label	674.2	34.05
Other	401.1	20.26

Source: *Dairy Foods*, April 1999, p. D, from Information Resources Inc.

★ 215 ★

Cheese (SIC 2022)

Top Shredded Cheese Brands - 1998

Shares are shown based on sales of $1.38 billion.

	($ mil.)	Share
Kraft	$ 401.2	29.07%
Sargento	178.7	12.95
Healthy Choice	43.3	3.14
Crystal Farms	39.2	2.84
Sorrento	20.0	1.45
Churny Provincia	16.9	1.22
Kraft Free	16.7	1.21
Sargento Double Cheese	12.7	0.92
Sargento Preferred Light	12.3	0.89
Private label	559.7	40.56
Other	79.3	5.75

Source: *Dairy Foods*, April 1999, p. D, from Information Resources Inc.

★ 216 ★

Cheese (SIC 2023)

Popular Processed Cheese Brands - 1997

Shares are shown for the year ended December 27, 1997.

Cheese Whiz	22.8%
Easy Cheese	22.3
Kaukauna	6.4
Price's	4.4
Private label	9.6
Other	34.5

Source: *Snack Food & Wholesale Bakery*, June 1998, pp. S-70, from A.C. Nielsen.

★ 217 ★

Macaroni & Cheese (SIC 2023)

Macaroni & Cheese Market - 1998

Shares are shown of the $638 million market as of December 6, 1998.

	($ mil.)	Share
Kraft	$ 499.8	78.34%
Private label	103.4	16.21
Other	34.8	5.45

Source: *Advertising Age*, January 25, 1999, p. 8.

★ 218 ★

Macaroni & Cheese (SIC 2023)

Macaroni & Cheese Market in Canada

Market shares are estimated in percent.

Kraft	73.0%
Other	27.0

Source: *Globe and Mail*, January 13, 1999, p. B29.

★ 219 ★

Potatoes (SIC 2023)

Instant Potato Market

Market shares are shown for the four weeks ended October 10, 1998.

Betty Crocker	35.0%
Lipton	22.0
Idahoan	21.1
Oetker	11.9
McCain	3.2
Nestle	1.8
Other	5.0

Source: *Globe and Mail*, November 4, 1998, p. B29, from A.C. Nielsen.

★ 220 ★

Frozen Desserts (SIC 2024)

Frozen Dairy Market - 1998

Regular fat ice cream	75.5%
Reduced fat ice cream	10.3
Frozen yogurt	6.0
Nonfat ice cream	3.6
Sherbert	3.5
Sorbet	0.5
Other	0.6

Source: *Dairy Foods*, March 1999, p. 68, from International Ice Cream Association.

★ 221 ★

Frozen Desserts (SIC 2024)

Frozen Dessert Market - 1997

Shares are shown based on supermarket sales for the year ended December 27, 1997.

Good Humor-Breyers	26.38%
Nestle Food Co.	17.49
Eskimo Pie Corp.	5.84%
Mars Inc.	5.15
Well's Dairy Inc.	4.42
The Haagen Dazs Co.	3.15
Dreyer's Grand Ice Cream Inc.	2.74
Blue Bell Creameries Inc.	2.44
Other	32.39

Source: *Snack Food & Wholesale Bakery*, June 1998, pp. S-54, from A.C. Nielsen.

★ 222 ★

Frozen Desserts (SIC 2024)

Frozen Novelty Market - 1998

Shares are shown based on 182 million units sold for the year ended May 23, 1998.

Frozen ices	26.5%
Ice cream sandwiches	16.0
Non-premium ice cream bars	11.5
Fruit/juice bars	10.1
Fudge bars	8.9
Other	27.0

Source: *Dairy Foods*, September 1998, p. 13, from *Ice Cream Market Research Project-Retail Sales Report*.

★ 223 ★

Frozen Desserts (SIC 2024)

Top Frozen Dessert Brands - 1998

Shares are shown based on a $1.66 billion market for the year ended December 6, 1998.

	($ mil.)	Share
Klondike	$ 105.9	6.38%
Popsicle	99.7	6.01
Drumstick	90.3	5.44
Haagen-Dazs	54.8	3.30
Dole	46.7	2.81
Eskimo Pie	43.1	2.60
Dove Bar	39.7	2.39
Blue Bell	36.2	2.18
Wells' Blue Bunny	36.0	2.17
Private label	276.9	16.68
Other	830.7	50.04

Source: *Dairy Foods*, March 1999, p. 70, from Information Resources Inc.

★ 224 ★

Frozen Desserts (SIC 2024)

Top Frozen Yogurt Brands - 1998

Shares are shown based on sales for the year ended October 11, 1998.

Dreyer's/Edys	17.5%
Ben & Jerry's	11.7
Turkey Hill	6.9
Haagen-Dazs	6.7
Breyer's	5.8
Kemps	5.5
Mayfield	2.4
Blue Bell	2.2
Blue Bunny	1.9
Private label	17.7
Other	21.7

Source: *Supermarket Business*, January 1999, p. 37, from Information Resources Inc.

★ 225 ★

Ice Cream (SIC 2024)

Best-Selling Ice Cream Brands in Canada - 1999

Data show millions of units sold for the 12 weeks ended February 28, 1999.

Breyer's	24.7
Dreyer's/Edy's Grand	18.5
Blue Bell	11.9
Haagen Dazs	10.7
Private label	64.7

Source: "Dinners Post 4.8% Gain; Dept. Dips 0.5%" Retrieved June 2, 1999 fromt he World Wide Web: http:// www.frozenfoodage.com/jun99-4.htm, from Information Resources Inc.

★ 226 ★

Ice Cream (SIC 2024)

Ice Cream Sales

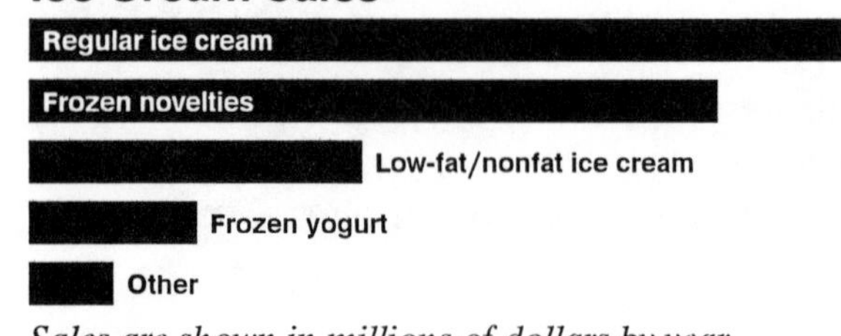

Sales are shown in millions of dollars by year. Others includes sherbert, sorbet, tofu-based products, and mellorine.

	1999	2002	Share
Regular ice cream	$ 4,350	$ 4,750	38.93%
Frozen novelties	3,775	4,000	32.79
Low-fat/nonfat ice cream	1,880	1,975	16.19
Frozen yogurt	1,000	1,000	8.20
Other	430	475	3.89

Source: *Progressive Grocer*, February 1999, p. 34, from Kalorama Information.

★ 227 ★

Ice Cream (SIC 2024)

Top Ice Cream Brands - 1998

Shares are shown for the year ended April 26, 1998.

Breyers	11.9%
Dreyers Edy's Grand	10.7
Blue Bell	5.3
Haagen-Dazs	4.6
Ben & Jerry's	3.5
Healthy Choice	3.0
Dreyer's Edy's Grand Light	2.6
Turkey Hill	2.3
Wells Bluebenny	2.0
Store brands	24.1
Other	30.0

Source: *U.S. Distribution Journal*, July/August 1998, p. 54, from Information Resources Inc.

★ 228 ★

Ice Cream (SIC 2024)

Top Ice Cream Markets

Sales are shown for the year ended October 11, 1998.

New York City	$ 215.3
Los Angeles	195.1
Chicago	115.4

Source: *Supermarket Business*, January 1999, p. 37, from Information Resources Inc.

★ 229 ★

Ice Cream (SIC 2024)

Top Sherbert/Sorbet/Ice Brands - 1998

Shares are shown based on a $196.6 million market for the year ended December 6, 1998.

	($ mil.)	Share
Hadden-Dazs	$ 28.7	14.60%
Dreyer's/Edy's Whole Fruit	16.9	8.60
Ben & Jerry's	13.2	6.71
Dreyer's/Edy's	10.5	5.34
Blue Bell	8.9	4.53
Kemps	6.8	3.46
Breyer's	4.2	2.14
Wells' Blue Bunny	3.0	1.53
Prairie Farms	2.5	1.27
Private label	53.8	27.37
Other	48.1	24.47

Source: *Dairy Foods*, March 1999, p. 70, from Information Resources Inc.

★ 230 ★

Cottage Cheese (SIC 2026)

Cottage Cheese Sales - 1997

Regular fat	46.3%
Low fat	38.3
Nonfat	15.4

Source: *Dairy Foods*, June 1998, p. 24, from A.C. Nielsen.

★ 231 ★

Cottage Cheese (SIC 2026)

Top Cottage Cheese Brands - 1998

Knudsen
Breakstone
Light 'n Lively
Dean's
Friendship
Private label
Other

Sales are shown in millions of dollars for the year ended December 6, 1998.

	($ mil.)	Share
Knudsen	$ 61.6	8.14%
Breakstone	58.3	7.70
Light 'n Lively	24.3	3.21
Dean's	21.4	2.83
Friendship	18.8	2.48
Private label	297.3	39.27
Other	275.4	36.38

Source: *Dairy Foods*, February 1999, p. 37, from Information Resources Inc.

★ 232 ★

Milk (SIC 2026)

Largest Milk Processors

Firms are ranked by estimated sales in millions of dollars.

Suiza Foods Corp.	$ 2,000
Dean Foods Co.	1,600
Kroger	1,100
Prairie Farms	1,100
Southern Foods	800

Source: *Dairy Foods*, April 1999, p. 13, from Beverage Marketing Corp.

★ 233 ★

Milk (SIC 2026)

Milk Production by State - 1998

Output is shown in millions of pounds.

	(mil.)	Share
California	27,607	17.53%
Wisconsin	22,842	14.51
New York	11,740	7.46
Pennsylvania	10,847	6.89
Minnesota	9,275	5.89
Other	75,130	47.72

Source: *Hoard's Dairyman*, March 25, 1999, p. 228, from U.S. Bureau of the Census.

★ 234 ★

Milk (SIC 2026)

Organic Milk Market

The market is shown in percent.

Horizon	78.0%
Other	22.0

Source: *Investor's Business Daily*, March 30, 1999, p. A10.

★ 235 ★

Sour Cream (SIC 2026)

Non-Flavored Sour Cream Sales - 1998

Volume shares are shown in percent.

Regular-fat	69.9%
Low-fat	16.9
Nonfat	13.0

Source: *Dairy Foods*, May 1999, p. 34, from A.C. Nielsen.

★ 236 ★

Yogurt (SIC 2026)

Refrigerated Yogurt Sales - 1998

Volume shares are shown in percent.

Low-fat	51.7%
Nonfat	44.1
Regular-fat	4.2

Source: *Dairy Foods*, May 1999, p. 34, from A.C. Nielsen and *Cultured Dairy Products Report* by the International Dairy Foods Association.

★ 237 ★

Yogurt (SIC 2026)

Yogurt Market Leaders - 1998

Shares are shown for the year ended July 19, 1998.

General Mills	28.5%
Dannon	26.9
Other	44.6

Source: *Advertising Age*, August 24, 1998, p. 8.

★ 238 ★

Canned Food (SIC 2032)

Canned Bean Sales

Sales are shown in millions of dollars.

New York City	$ 45.7
Los Angeles	43.1
Boston	24.5
Chicago	22.9
Detroit	22.6
Philadelphia	22.5
Dallas	22.2
San Francisco	21.2
Houston	21.1
Miami	20.9

Source: *USA TODAY*, August 13, 1998, p. D1, from A.C. Nielsen.

★ 239 ★

Canned Food (SIC 2032)

Canned Pasta Market

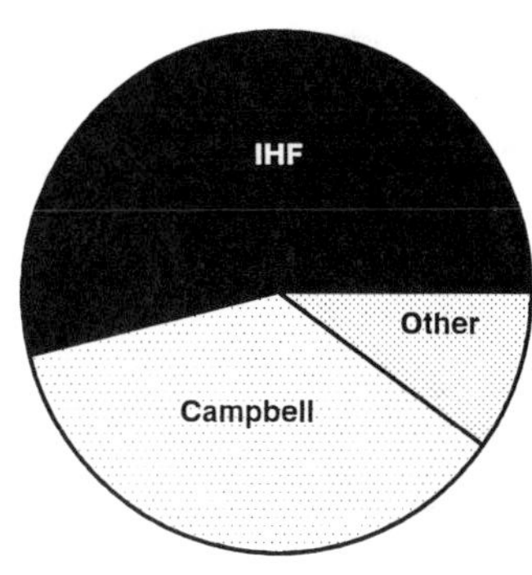

Shares are shown based on $558 million in sales for the year ended December 27, 1998.

	($ mil.)	Share
IHF	$ 300.7	53.89%
Campbell	200.0	35.84
Other	57.3	10.27

Source: *Brandweek*, April 12, 1999, p. 6, from Information Resources Inc.

★ 240 ★

Canned Food (SIC 2033)

Canned Fruit Market

Del Monte	42.0%
Private label	40.0
Other	18.0

Source: *Forbes*, November 30, 1998, p. 191.

★ 241 ★

Canned Food (SIC 2033)

Canned Pineapple Market

Dole

Del Monte

Other/private label

Market shares are shown in percent.

Dole	46.0%
Del Monte	14.0
Other/private label	40.0

Source: *Investext,* Thomson Financial Networks, October 1, 1998, p. 5, from A.C. Nielsen, WDR estimates, and company estimates.

★ 242 ★

Canned Food (SIC 2033)

Canned Vegetable Market

Del Monte	20.0%
Private label	44.0
Other	36.0

Source: *Forbes*, November 30, 1998, p. 191.

★ 243 ★

Canned Food (SIC 2033)

Canned Vegetable Market

Market shares are shown in percent.

Del Monte	20.0%
Green Giant	13.0
Dean Foods	8.0
Other/private label	59.0

Source: *Investext,* Thomson Financial Networks, October 1, 1998, p. 5, from A.C. Nielsen, WDR estimates, and company estimates.

★ 244 ★

Canned Food (SIC 2033)

Popular Canned Desserts - 1997

Shares are shown for the year ended December 27, 1997.

Hunt's	31.8%
Del Monte	23.8
Mott's	17.2
Kraft Handi-Snacks	8.6
Private label	8.5
Other	10.1

Source: *Snack Food & Wholesale Bakery*, June 1998, pp. S-70, from A.C. Nielsen.

★ 245 ★

Juices (SIC 2033)

Bottled Juice Sales - 1998

Sales are shown in millions of dollars for the year ended September 13, 1998.

Fruit drinks	$ 750.8
Cranberry cocktail/drink	743.2
Apple juice	529.1
Tomato/vegetable jucie/cocktail	241.1

Continued on next page.

★ 245 ★ *Continued*

Juices (SIC 2033)

Bottled Juice Sales - 1998

Sales are shown in millions of dollars for the year ended September 13, 1998.

Grapefruit cocktail	$ 196.3
Grape juice	189.7
Cranberry juice	127.6
Cider	74.3
Lemonade	72.0
Orange juice	53.8

Source: *Beverage Industry*, November 1998, p. 16, from Information Resources Inc.

★ 246 ★

Juices (SIC 2033)

Canada's Not From Concentrate Orange Juice Market

Shares of the orange juice not from concentrate market are shown in percent.

Tropicana	77.9%
Oasis	4.1
Minute Maid	0.1
Private label	14.4
Other	3.5

Source: *Globe and Mail*, July 21, 1998, p. B6.

★ 247 ★

Juices (SIC 2033)

Canada's Orange Juice Market

Shares of the orange juice from concentrate market are shown in percent.

Tropicana	60.3%
Minute Maid	7.1
Beatrice	5.1
Oasis	3.4
Private label	15.3
Other	8.8

Source: *Globe and Mail*, July 21, 1998, p. B6.

★ 248 ★

Juices (SIC 2033)

Chilled Orange Juice Market

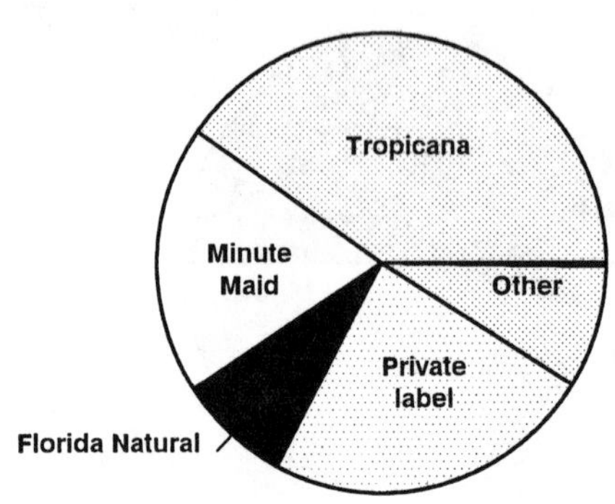

Market shares are shown in percent.

Tropicana	40.6%
Minute Maid	19.0
Florida Natural	7.8
Private label	23.6
Other	9.0

Source: *Washington Post*, July 21, 1998, p. C3, from PepsiCo. and Bloomberg News.

★ 249 ★

Juices (SIC 2033)

Frozen Concentrate Orange Juice Sales

Shares are shown based on supermarket sales for the year ended May 24, 1998.

Minute Maid	44.4%
Tropicana	5.4
Private label	39.4
Other	10.8

Source: *Wall Street Journal*, July 21, 1998, p. B6, from Information Resources Inc.

★ 250 ★

Juices (SIC 2033)

Frozen Juice Sales - 1998

Total sales reached $1.12 billion for the year ended September 13, 1998.

	($ mil.)	Share
Orange juice concentrate	$ 533.7	47.65%
Drink/cocktail drink concentrate	215.8	19.27
Lemonade/limeade concentrate	90.7	8.10
Blended fruit juice concentrate	85.7	7.65
Apple juice concentrate	80.5	7.19
Cocktail mixes	38.6	3.45
Other	75.0	6.70

Source: *Beverage Industry*, November 1998, p. 16, from Information Resources Inc.

★ 251 ★

Juices (SIC 2033)

Fruit Juice Sales by Segment

Retail	76.6%
Vending	16.3
Foodservice	7.1

Source: *Beverage World*, June 1998, p. 90, from Beverage Marketing Corporation.

★ 252 ★

Juices (SIC 2033)

Orange Juice Market - 1998

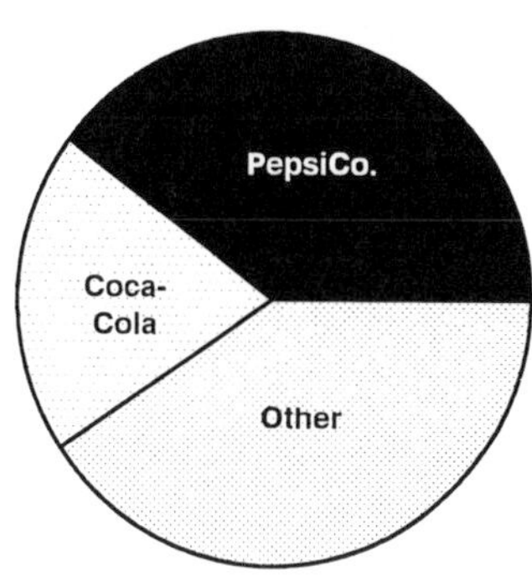

Shares are shown based on sales of $2.59 billion for the year ended January 31, 1999.

PepsiCo.	39.8%
Coca-Cola	19.5
Other	40.7

Source: *New York Times*, May 19, 1999, p. C1, from *Beverage Digest* and Information Resources Inc.

★ 253 ★

Juices (SIC 2033)

Refrigerated Juice Sales - 1998

Sales are shown in millions of dollars for the year ended September 13, 1998.

Orange juice	$ 2,498.0
Fruit drink	648.0
Grape juice	488.5
Blended fruit juice	199.8
Grapefruit juice	110.3
Lemonade	59.6
Cider	41.0

Source: *Beverage Industry*, November 1998, p. 16, from Information Resources Inc.

★ 254 ★

Juices (SIC 2033)

Shelf-Stable Juice Market

Shares are shown based on food sales for the year ended September 13, 1998.

Welch Foods Inc.	43.9%
Ocean Spray Cranberries Inc.	37.0
Motts Inc.	9.8
Procter & Gamble	4.6
Daily Juice Products Inc.	1.4
Other	3.3

Source: "Surveys and Stats." Retrieved May 9, 1999 from the World Wide Web: http:// www.just-drinks.com/ surveys_detail.asp?art16, from Information Resources Inc.

★ 255 ★

Juices (SIC 2033)

Top Orange Juice Brands - 1998

Market shares are shown for the year ended September 13, 1998.

Tropicana Pure Premium	34.0%
Minute Maid Premium	19.3
Floridas Natural	7.5
Tropicana Seasons Best	5.5
Florida Gold	1.2
Sunkist Premium	0.8
Floridas Natural Growers Pride	0.7
Citrus World Donald Duck	0.6
Private label	22.1
Other	8.3

Source: *Beverage Industry*, November 1998, p. 11, from Information Resources Inc.

★ 256 ★

Prunes (SIC 2034)

Prune Sales - 1997

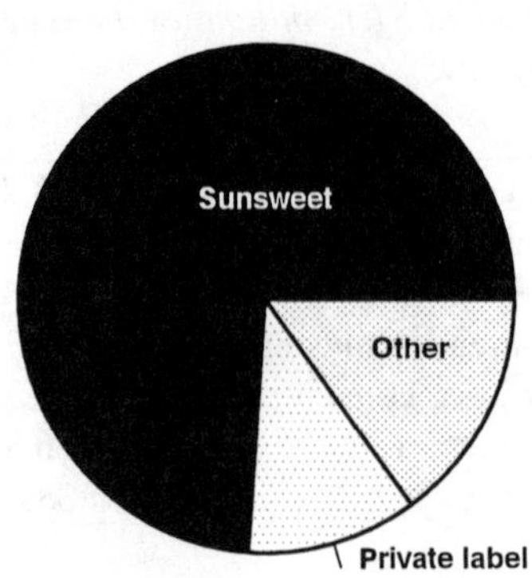

Shares are shown based on sales of $190 million.

Sunsweet	74.0%
Private label	11.0
Other	15.0

Source: *Advertising Age*, September 28, 1998, p. 8.

★ 257 ★

Soups (SIC 2034)

Top Dry Soup Brands - 1998

Shares are shown based on sales for the year ended July 21, 1998.

Lipton Recipe Secrets	20.7%
Knorr Dry Soup	12.7
Lipton Soup Secrets	10.0
Wylers Soup Starter	7.2
Lipton Cup A Soup	6.1
Mrs. Grass	4.9
Hurst Ham Beens	3.0
Nile Spice	2.7
Campbell's	2.6
Private label	5.7
Other	24.4

Source: *Supermarket Business*, October 1998, p. 24, from Information Resources Inc.

★ 258 ★

Soups (SIC 2034)

Top Soup Markets - 1998

Sales are shown in millions of dollars for the year ended July 19, 1998.

New York City	$ 158.0
Los Angeles	115.0
Baltimore/Washington	73.3
Philadelphia	72.1
San Francisco/Oakland	61.6
Detroit	55.9
Boston	54.0
Harrisburg/Scranton	42.8
Miami/Ft. Lauderdale	41.6

Source: *Supermarket Business*, October 1998, p. 24, from Information Resources Inc.

★ 259 ★

Soups (SIC 2034)

Top Wet Soup Brands - 1998

Sales are shown for the year ended July 21, 1998.

Brand	Share
Campbell's	45.7%
Campbell's Chunky	10.6
Progresso	8.8
Campbell's Healthy Request	6.3
Capbell's Home Cookin'	6.0
Healthy Choice	3.6
Swanson	3.5
College Inn	1.6
Campbell's Simply Home	1.5
Other	12.4

Source: *Supermarket Business*, October 1998, p. 24, from Information Resources Inc.

★ 260 ★

Soups (SIC 2034)

Wet Soup Market Leaders - 1998

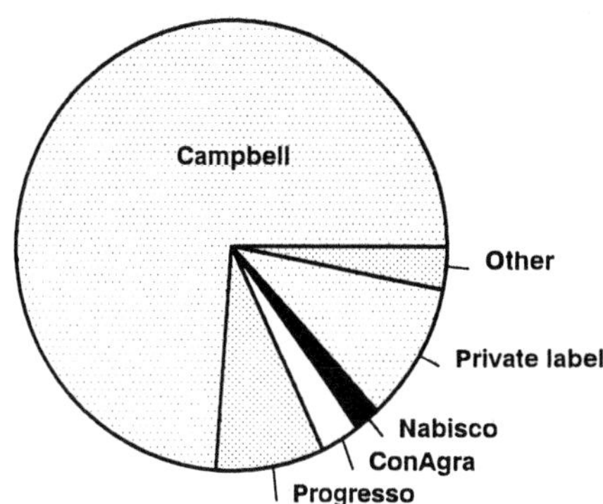

Shares of the $2.92 billion market are shown in percent.

Campbell	73.5%
Progresso	7.9
ConAgra	2.9
Nabisco	2.2
Private label	10.3
Other	3.2

Source: *Advertising Age*, February 15, 1999, p. 42, from Salomon Smith Barney.

★ 261 ★

Dips (SIC 2035)

Popular Mexican Sauce Brands - 1998

Shares of the $779.1 milllion market are shown for the year ended July 19, 1998.

Brand	Share
Pace	25.7%
Tostitos	23.8
Old El Paso	11.2
Chi-Chi's	6.7
Taco Bell	3.8
Ortega	2.5
Las Palmas	2.3
La Victoria	1.9
Herdez	1.2
Private label	6.1
Other	14.8

Source: *Snack Food & Wholesale Bakery*, September 1998, p. 18, from Information Resources Inc.

★ 262 ★

Dips (SIC 2035)

Popular Refrigerated Dip Brands - 1998

Shares of the $280.4 milllion market are shown for the year ended July 19, 1998.

T. Marzetti	18.3%
Dean's	11.8
Kraft	7.6
Heluva Good	4.8
Private label	15.9
Other	41.6

Source: *Snack Food & Wholesale Bakery*, August 1998, p. 18, from Information Resources Inc.

★ 263 ★

Dips (SIC 2035)

Popular Shelf-Stable Dip Brands - 1998

Shares of the $130.7 milllion market are shown for the year ended July 19, 1998.

Frito-Lay	61.6%
Ruffles	8.1
Old El Paso	2.3
Classic Guacamole	2.1
Private label	3.0
Other	22.9

Source: *Snack Food & Wholesale Bakery*, September 1998, p. 18, from Information Resources Inc.

★ 264 ★

Ketchup (SIC 2035)

Top Ketchup Makers

Heinz

ConAgra Inc.

Other

Market shares are shown in percent.

Heinz	55.0%
ConAgra Inc.	19.0
Other	26.0

Source: *Investext,* Thomson Financial Networks, October 9, 1998, p. 3, from Information Resources Inc. and Schroder.

★ 265 ★

Peanut Butter (SIC 2035)

Top Peanut Butter Brands - 1998

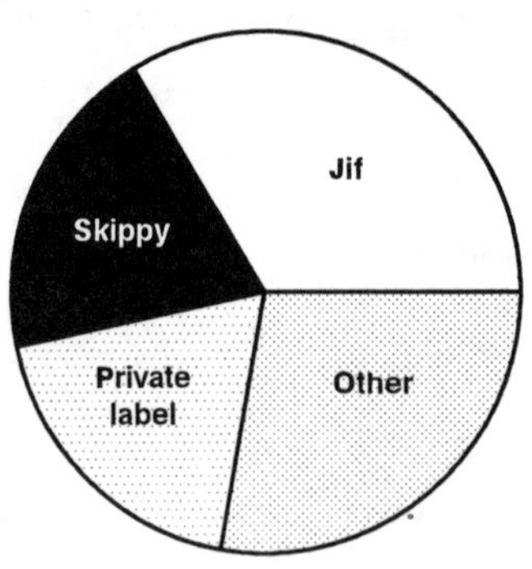

Shares are shown based on sales of $810 million for the year ended March 28, 1999.

	Sales ($ mil.)	Sare
Jif	$ 271.9	33.57%
Skippy	158.6	19.58
Private label	153.5	18.95
Other	226.0	27.90

Source: *Wall Street Journal*, May 7, 1999, p. A24, from Information Resources Inc.

★ 266 ★

Pickles (SIC 2035)

Pickle Market Leaders - 1997

Data show supermarket sales. Claussen's share is estimated.

Vlasic	32.0%
Claussen	17.0
Other	51.0

Source: *Forbes*, March 8, 1999, p. 84.

★ 267 ★

Salad Dressings (SIC 2035)

Mayo/Spoonable Dressing Market

Selected shares are shown in percent.

Bestfoods	38.0%
Philip Morris	28.0
Other	34.0

Source: *Investext,* Thomson Financial Networks, October 9, 1998, p. 3, from Information Resources Inc.

★ 268 ★

Salad Dressings (SIC 2035)

Salad Dressing Market - 1998

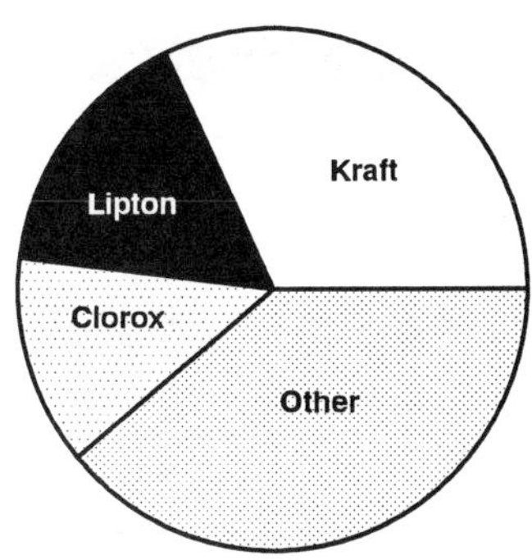

Shares are shown based on $1.34 billion in sales for the year ended January 3, 1999.

	($ mil.)	Share
Kraft	$ 429.4	32.04%
Lipton	216.9	16.19
Clorox	170.7	12.74
Other	523.0	39.03

Source: *Advertising Age*, April 12, 1999, p. 8, from Information Resources Inc.

★ 269 ★

Frozen Fruit (SIC 2037)

Frozen Fruit Sales - 1997

Sales are shown in thousands of dollars. Figures include both retail and institutional markets.

Strawberries	$ 598,542
Blueberries	292,918
Peaches	167,524
Apples	72,620
Cherries, sweet	55,391

Source: *Quick Frozen Foods International*, October 1998, p. A15, from American Frozen Food Institute, U.S. Department of Commerce, U.S. Department of Agriculture, and American Institute of Food Distribution.

★ 270 ★

Frozen Vegetables (SIC 2037)

Best-Selling Frozen Vegetables - 1999

Data show sales in millions of dollars for the 12 weeks ended February 28, 1999.

Green Giant Create a Meal!	$ 34.1
Birdseye	16.4
Birdseye Farm Fresh	12.0
Pictsweet	7.6
Private label	48.1

Source: "Dinners Post 4.8% Gain; Dept. Dips 0.5%" Retrieved June 2, 1999 from the World Wide Web: http:// www.frozenfoodage.com/jun99-4.htm, from Information Resources Inc.

★ 271 ★

Frozen Vegetables (SIC 2037)

Frozen Vegetable Sales - 1997

Sales are shown in thousands of dollars. Figures include both retail and institutional markets.

Potato products	$ 5,522,702
Corn products	1,090,912
Green peas	438,089
Green beas	367,184
Carrots	263,735
Spinach	213,903
Mixed vegetables	198,278
Lima beans	143,824
Onions	109,164

Source: *Quick Frozen Foods International*, October 1998, p. A15.

★ 272 ★

Frozen Foods (SIC 2038)

Best-Selling Frozen Chicken - 1999

Data show millions of units sold for the 12 weeks ended February 28, 1999.

Banquet	15.2
Tyson	14.9
Weaver	2.9
Cagles	1.3
Private label	12.8

Source: "Dinners Post 4.8% Gain; Dept. Dips 0.5%" Retrieved June 2, 1999 fromt he World Wide Web: http:// www.frozenfoodage.com/jun99-4.htm, from Information Resources Inc.

★ 273 ★

Frozen Foods (SIC 2038)

Best-Selling Frozen Dinners/Entrees - 1999

Data show millions of units sold for the 12 weeks ended February 28, 1999.

Stouffer's	39.4
Healthy Choice	37.7
Weight Watchers	27.5
Stouffer's Lean Cuisine	24.1
Marie Callender's	18.9

Source: "Dinners Post 4.8% Gain; Dept. Dips 0.5%" Retrieved June 2, 1999 fromt he World Wide Web: http:// www.frozenfoodage.com/jun99-4.htm, from Information Resources Inc.

★ 274 ★

Frozen Foods (SIC 2038)

Best-Selling Handheld Entrees - 1999

Data show sales in millions of dollar for the 12 weeks ended February 28, 1999.

Hot Pockets	$ 46.9
Lean Pockets	19.2
Croissant Pockets	14.0
Hot Pockets Toaster Breaks	11.6
Red Baron Pouches	9.7

Source: "Dinners Post 4.8% Gain; Dept. Dips 0.5%" Retrieved June 2, 1999 from the World Wide Web: http:// www.frozenfoodage.com/jun99-4.htm, from Information Resources Inc.

★ 275 ★

Frozen Foods (SIC 2038)

Best-Selling Pizza Brands - 1999

Data show millions of units sold for the 12 weeks ended February 28, 1999.

Totino's Pizza Party	31.0
Tombstone	19.4
DiGiorno	15.8
Red Baron	12.9
Tony's	12.4

Source: "Dinners Post 4.8% Gain; Dept. Dips 0.5%" Retrieved June 2, 1999 from the World Wide Web: http:// www.frozenfoodage.com/jun99-4.htm, from Information Resources Inc.

★ 276 ★

Frozen Foods (SIC 2038)

Best-Selling Potato/Fries/Hashbrown Brands - 1999

Data show sales in millions of dollar for the 12 weeks ended February 28, 1999.

Ore-Ida	$ 39.2
Ore-Ida Golden Crinkles	18.0
Ore-Ida Tater Tots	14.9
Ore-Ida Golden Fries	7.0
Private label	53.1

Source: "Dinners Post 4.8% Gain; Dept. Dips 0.5%" Retrieved June 2, 1999 from the World Wide Web: http:// www.frozenfoodage.com/jun99-4.htm, from Information Resources Inc.

★ 277 ★

Frozen Foods (SIC 2038)

Frozen Food Consumption in Canada

Consumption is shown in percent.

Ontario	41.8%
Quebec	20.9
British Columbia	12.1
Alberta	10.7
Other	14.5

Source: *Marketing Magazine*, April 5, 1999, p. 22, from A.C. Nielsen.

★ 278 ★

Frozen Foods (SIC 2038)

Frozen Food Market - 1998

Shares of the $4.5 billion dinner market are shown for the year ended June 21, 1998.

Nestle	26.4%
ConAgra	19.8
Heinz	9.3
Vlasic (Swanson)	9.0
Tyson	1.5
Other	34.0

Source: *New York Times*, July 25, 1998, p. C1, from Information Resources Inc., Prudential Securities, and Vlasic.

★ 279 ★

Frozen Foods (SIC 2038)

Frozen Pizza Market - 1998

Market shares are shown in percent.

Kraft Foods	37.4%
Schwann	27.4
Other	35.2

Source: *Advertising Age*, November 2, 1998, p. 10, from Information Resources Inc.

★ 280 ★

Frozen Foods (SIC 2038)

Frozen Waffle Market - 1997

Kellogg

Diageo

Aurora Foods

Store brands

Other

Market shares are shown based on supermarket sales.

Kellogg	65.0%
Diageo	17.0
Aurora Foods	9.0
Store brands	7.0
Other	2.0

Source: *Investext,* Thomson Financial Networks, September 1, 1998, p. 16.

★ 281 ★

Frozen Foods (SIC 2038)

Pot Pie Market - 1999

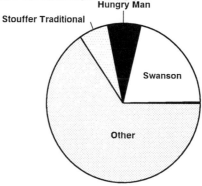

Hungry Man

Stouffer Traditional

Swanson

Other

Shares are shown based on sales of $289 million for the year ended February 28, 1999.

	($ mil.)	Share
Swanson	$ 62.0	21.45%
Hungry Man	21.0	7.27
Stouffer Traditional	17.5	6.06
Other	188.5	65.22

Source: *Brandweek*, April 5, 1999, p. 14.

★ 282 ★

Frozen Foods (SIC 2038)

Top Dinner Markets - 1998

Sales are shown in millions of dollars. The West Texas/New Mexico area has the largest growth rate in the country.

Los Angeles	$ 238.5
New York City	194.3
Baltimore/Washington	134.1
Chicago	130.3
San Francisco/Oakland	121.0

Source: *Supermarket Business*, February 1999, p. 36, from Information Resources Inc.

★ 283 ★

Frozen Foods (SIC 2038)

Top Frozen Dinner Brands - 1998

Shares are shown based on sales for the year ended December 6, 1998.

Stouffer's	14.3%
Healthy Choice	10.3

Continued on next page.

★ 283 ★ *Continued*

Frozen Foods (SIC 2038)

Top Frozen Dinner Brands - 1998

Shares are shown based on sales for the year ended December 6, 1998.

Stouffer's Lean Cuisine	7.9%
Marie Callender's	5.7
Weight Watchers Smart Ones	4.4
Swanson	4.3
Banquet	3.8
Swanson Hungry Man	3.7
Budget Gourmet	2.9
Michelina's	2.9
Other	39.8

Source: *Supermarket Business*, February 1999, p. 36, from Information Resources Inc.

★ 284 ★

Frozen Foods (SIC 2038)

Top Frozen Pizza Brands - 1999

Shares are shown based on a $2.1 billion market for the year ended January 3, 1999.

DiGiorno	13.9%
Tombstone	13.1
Tony's	8.3
Red Baron	8.1
Totino's Party Pizza	7.6
Freschetta	5.2
Stouffer's	3.6
Jack's	3.4
Celeste Pizza For One	3.1
Tombstone Oven Rising	2.6
Red Baron Super Singles	2.5
Jeno's Crisp 'N' Tasty	2.1
Red Baron Bake to Rise	2.1
Private label	4.9
Other	19.5

Source: *Snack Food & Wholesale Bakery*, March 1999, p. 20, from Information Resources Inc.

★ 285 ★

Frozen Foods (SIC 2038)

Top Veggie Burger Makers

Shares are shown for the four weeks ended June 14, 1998.

Gardenburger	48.0%
Morningstar Farms	28.0
Other	24.0

Source: "Where's the Beef?" Retrieved May 7, 1999 from the World Wide Web: http:// more.abcnews.go.com/ sections/business/DailyNews/veggieburgers.

★ 286 ★

Flour (SIC 2041)

Flour Market in Mexico

Market shares are shown in percent.

	1997	1999
Maseca	71.6%	70.0%
Minsa	25.5	28.5

Source: *Investext,* Thomson Financial Networks, January 4, 1999, p. 3, from DBS estimates.

★ 287 ★

Flour (SIC 2041)

Largest Flour Millers

Companies are ranked by daily capacity in hundredweights.

ADM Milling Co.	311,300
ConAgra Inc.	264,900
Cargill Food Flour Milling	223,000
Cereal Food Processors Inc.	82,900

Source: *Small Farm Today Supplement - Consolidation in the Food and Agriculture System*, April 1999, p. 10, from *1997 Grain & Milling Annual*.

★ 288 ★

Cereals (SIC 2043)

Kids Cereal Market

Market shares are shown in percent.

General Mills	20.0%
Kellogg	14.0
Post	9.0
Quaker Oats	8.0
Other	50.0

Source: *Investext,* Thomson Financial Networks, December 10, 1998, p. 20, from Merrill Lynch, Kellogg, and Information Resources Inc. InfoScan.

★ 289 ★

Cereals (SIC 2043)

Oatmeal Market - 1998

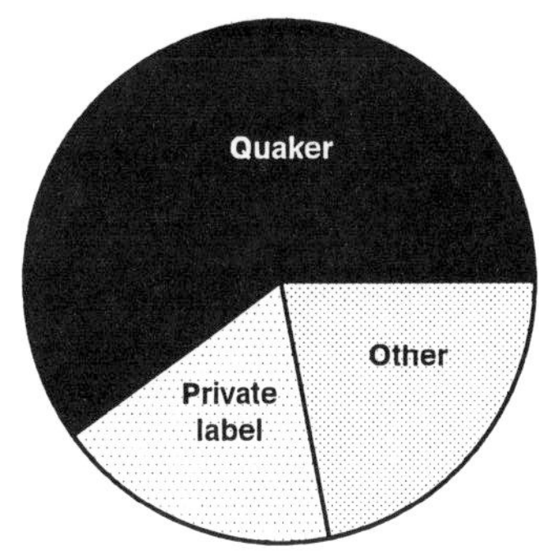

Shares of the $683.9 million market are shown in percent for the year ended July 19, 1998.

	($ mil.)	Share
Quaker	$ 410.5	60.02%
Private label	121.6	17.78
Other	151.8	22.20

Source: *Advertising Age,* August 17, 1998, p. 42, from Information Resources Inc.

★ 290 ★

Cereals (SIC 2043)

Ready-to-Eat Cereal Market - 1998

Shares are shown based on unit sales.

Kellogg	31.39%
General Mills	27.73
Post	16.55
Quaker Oats	9.59
Malt-O-Meal	3.22
Store brands	10.39
Other	1.13

Source: *Investor's Business Daily,* February 4, 1999, p. A3, from Information Resources Inc.

★ 291 ★

Cereals (SIC 2043)

Top Breakfast Cereals - 1998

Sales are shown in millions of dollars. Figures are for food stores.

General Mills Cheerios	$ 320.0
Kellogg's Frosted Flakes	259.0
General Mills Honey Nut Cheerios	204.0
Kellogg's Corn Flakes	192.0
Kellogg's Raisin Bran	189.0
Kellogg's Froot Loops	146.0
General Mills Lucky Charms	142.0
General Mills Rice Krispies	142.0
Kellogg's Special K	133.0

Source: *Discount Merchandiser,* May 1999, p. 110, from Information Resources Inc.

★ 292 ★

Cereals (SIC 2043)

Top Cereal Brands - 1997

Shares are shown based on supermarket sales.

Cheerios	9.8%
Frosted Flakes	4.2
Corn Flakes	4.1
Frosted Mini-Wheets	3.0
Rice Krispies	2.9
Raisin Bran	2.6
Froot Loops	2.3

Continued on next page.

★ 292 ★ *Continued*

Cereals (SIC 2043)

Top Cereal Brands - 1997

Shares are shown based on supermarket sales.

Lucky Charms	2.1%
Special K	2.0
Corn Pops	1.8
Other	65.2

Source: *Advertising Age*, September 28, 1998, p. S10, from Information Resources Inc.

★ 293 ★

Cereals (SIC 2043)

Top Cereal Brands - 1998

Market shares are shown for the second quarter of the year. Figures are based on volume.

Frosted Flakes	4.3%
Raisin Bran	3.8
Quaker Bags	3.6
Cheerios	3.5
Frosted Mini Wheats	3.3
Corn Flakes	3.2
Honey Nut Cheerios	2.3
Grape Nuts	2.0
Oat Life	1.9
Cap n Crunch	1.8
Other	70.3

Source: *Investext,* Thomson Financial Networks, September 1, 1998, p. 14, from Information Resources Inc. and Schroder.

★ 294 ★

Cereals (SIC 2043)

Top Cereal Makers in Canada - 1999

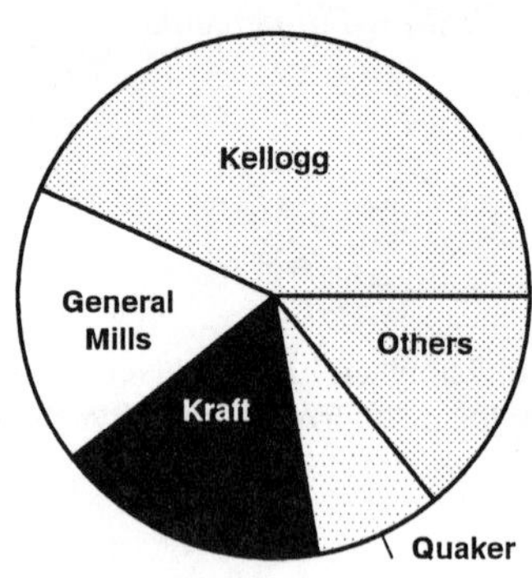

Market shares are shown in percent for the year ended March 28, 1999.

Kellogg	43.2%
General Mills	17.3
Kraft	16.7
Quaker	8.4
Others	14.4

Source: "Report on Market Share." Retrieved June 1, 1999 from the World Wide Web: http://www.marketingmag.ca/index.cgi?, from A.C. Nielsen MarketTrack.

★ 295 ★

Cereals (SIC 2043)

U.S. Cereal Producers - 1998

Market shares are shown in percent for the year ended October 4, 1998.

Kellogg	32.0%
General Mills/Ralston	31.4
General Foods	16.3
Quaker	8.9
Malt O Meal	2.6
Store brands	7.8

Source: *Chicago Tribune*, November 1, 1998, p. C1, from Information Resources Inc.

★ 296 ★

Cake Mixes (SIC 2045)

Top Cake Mix Brands

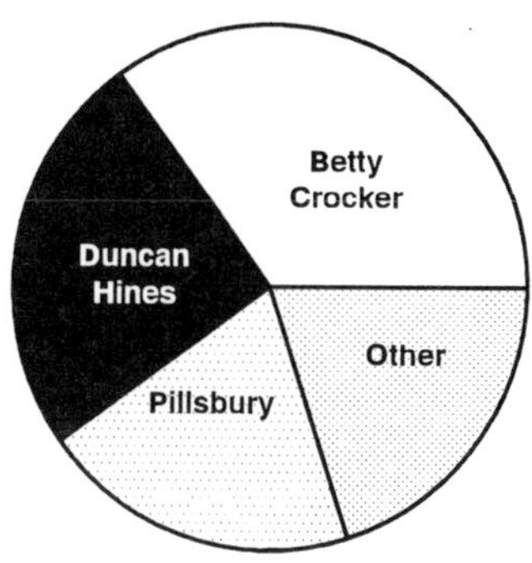

Market shares are shown in percent.

Betty Crocker	35.0%
Duncan Hines	25.0
Pillsbury	20.0
Other	20.0

Source: "Duncan Hines for Sale." Retrieved May 7, 1999 from the World Wide Web: http://more.abcnews.go.com/sections/business/duncanhines830/index.ht.

★ 297 ★

Corn Milling (SIC 2046)

Largest Corn Millers

Companies are ranked by daily capacity.

Bunge (Lauhoff Grain)	120,000
Cargill (Illinois Cereal Mills)	95,000
ADM (Krause Milling)	70,000
ConAgra (Lincoln Grain)	52,000
QuakerOats	45,000

Source: *Small Farm Today Supplement - Consolidation in the Food and Agriculture System*, April 1999, p. 10, from *Corn: Chemistry & Technology*.

★ 298 ★

Pet Food (SIC 2047)

Largest Cat Food Markets - 1998

Data show supermarket sales in millions of dollars for the year ended August 16, 1998.

New York City	$ 133.3
Los Angeles	115.3
Philadelphia	50.9
Boston	50.8
Baltimore/Washington	48.2

Source: *Supermarket Business*, November 1998, p. 32, from Information Resources Inc.

★ 299 ★

Pet Food (SIC 2047)

Largest Dog Food Markets - 1998

Data show supermarket sales in millions of dollars for the year ended August 16, 1998.

New York City	$ 137.9
Los Angeles	136.5
San Antonio/Corpus Christi	71.2
South Carolina	70.4
Philadelphia	59.2

Source: *Supermarket Business*, November 1998, p. 32, from Information Resources Inc.

★ 300 ★

Pet Food (SIC 2047)

Largest Pet Food Makers - 1998

Market shares are shown in perdent.

Ralston Purina	15.4%
Friskies PetCare (Nestle)	12.4
Heinz Pet Food	12.3
Hill's	7.9
Other	52.0

Source: *Feedstuffs*, January 4, 1999, p. 12, from *Maxwell Report*.

★ 301 ★

Pet Food (SIC 2047)

Largest Pet Food Vendors

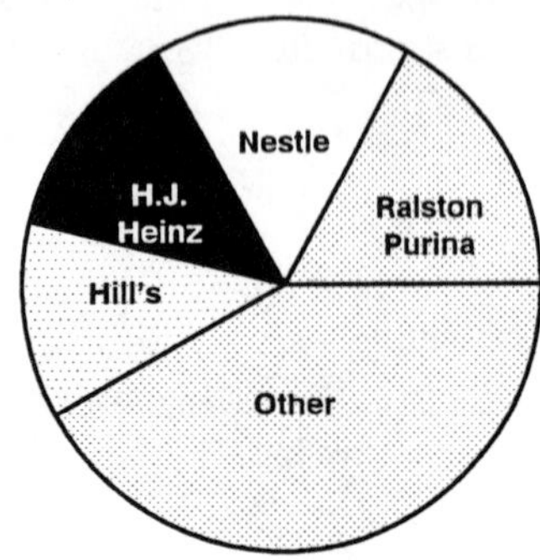

Market shares are shown in percent. Figures are shown based on grocery sales.

Ralston Purina	17.0%
Nestle	16.0
H.J. Heinz	13.0
Hill's	12.0
Other	42.0

Source: *Food Technology*, October 1998, p. 6.

★ 302 ★

Pet Food (SIC 2047)

Pet Food Market by Segment

The $9.9 billion market is shown in percent.

Dog food	56.0%
Cat food	37.0
Other	7.0

Source: "Why Pet Food?" Retrieved June 1, 1999 from the World Wide Web: http:// www.cspmarketlink.com/ Pages/kalkan18/whypet.htm.

★ 303 ★

Pet Food (SIC 2047)

Top Canned Cat Food Brands - 1998

Market shares are shown in percent for the year ended August 16, 1998.

Friskies	16.9%
9 Lives	15.6
Fancy Feast	13.4
Friskies Fancy Feast	8.7
Private label	12.0
Other	33.4

Source: *Supermarket Business*, November 1998, p. 32, from Information Resources Inc.

★ 304 ★

Pet Food (SIC 2047)

Top Canned Dog Food Brands - 1998

Market shares are shown in percent for the year ended August 16, 1998.

Pedigree	16.5%
Alpo Prime Cuts	13.6
Kal Kan Pedigree Choice Cuts	13.1
Mighty Dog	6.1
Private label	12.0

Source: *Supermarket Business*, November 1998, p. 32, from Information Resources Inc.

★ 305 ★

Pet Food (SIC 2047)

Top Dry Cat Food Brands - 1998

Market shares are shown in percent for the year ended August 16, 1998.

Purina Cat Chow	12.2%
Purina Meow Mix	11.1
Friskies	8.7
Purina One	5.2
Private label	14.0
Other	48.8

Source: *Supermarket Business*, November 1998, p. 32, from Information Resources Inc.

★ 306 ★

Pet Food (SIC 2047)

Top Dry Dog Food Brands - 1998

Market shares are shown in percent for the year ended August 16, 1998.

Kal Kan Pedigree Mealtime	13.7%
Purina Dog Chow	10.8
Purina One	8.5
Purina Puppy Chow	6.0
Private label	19.7
Other	41.3

Source: *Supermarket Business*, November 1998, p. 32, from Information Resources Inc.

★ 307 ★

Pet Food (SIC 2047)

Top Semi-Moist Cat Food Brands - 1998

Market shares are shown in percent.

Purina Tender Vittles	67.9%
Purina Happy Cat	21.4
Purina Alley Cat	2.2
Private label	7.8
Generic	2.2

Source: *Supermarket Business*, November 1998, p. 32, from Information Resources Inc.

★ 308 ★

Pet Food (SIC 2047)

Top Semi-Moist Dog Food Brands - 1998

Purina Moist & Meaty
Purina Butchers Burger
Reward Special Cuts
Ken L Ration Moist & Beefy
Private label
Other

Market shares are shown in percent for the year ended August 16, 1998.

Purina Moist & Meaty	51.1%
Purina Butchers Burger	6.1
Reward Special Cuts	4.6
Ken L Ration Moist & Beefy	3.9
Private label	27.8
Other	6.5

Source: *Supermarket Business*, November 1998, p. 32, from Information Resources Inc.

★ 309 ★

Bakery Products (SIC 2050)

Bakery Product Sales - 1998

Sales are shown in percent. The bread segment leader was white bread with a 10.7% share. The cake segment leader was decorated cakes with a 11.5% share.

Bread	27.7%
Cakes	25.9
Doughnuts	13.8
Muffins/croissants/bagels	9.5
Cookies	7.5
Pies	7.0
Sweet rolls/danish	4.9
Other	3.7

Source: *Progressive Grocer*, March 1999, p. 40.

★ 310 ★

Bakery Products (SIC 2050)

Largest Bakery Product Makers

Companies are ranked by sales in millions of dollars.

Nabisco Biscuit Co.	$ 3,700
Interstate Brands Corp.	3,300
Keebler Co.	2,100
The Earthgrains Co.	1,719
Bestfoods Baking Co	1,600

Source: *Bakery Production and Marketing*, July 15, 1998, p. 40.

★ 311 ★

Bagels (SIC 2051)

Top Fresh Bagel Brands - 1997

Shares are shown based on supermarket sales for the year ended December 27, 1997.

	($ mil.)	Share
Thomas'	$ 71.7	19.0%
Lender's Bagel Shop	61.5	16.3
Sara Lee	34.9	16.6
Lender's N.Y. Style	19.9	13.6
Earth Grains	17.3	13.6

Source: *Snack Food & Wholesale Bakery*, June 1998, p. 51, from A.C. Nielsen.

★ 312 ★

Bakery Products (SIC 2051)

Largest Breakfast Cakes/Sweet Roll Brands - 1997

Shares are shown based on supermarket sales for the year ended December 27, 1997.

Entenmann's	31.5%
Little Debbie	8.1
Svenhard's	7.7
Hostess	2.7
Private label	14.4
Other	35.6

Source: *Snack Food & Wholesale Bakery*, June 1998, pp. S-22, from A.C. Nielsen.

★ 313 ★

Bakery Products (SIC 2051)

Snack Cake Market - 1997

Shares are shown based on supermarket sales for the year ended December 27, 1997.

McKee Foods Corp.	24.63%
Interstate Bakeries	15.71
Bestfoods Baking Co.	10.11
Tasty Baking	4.97
Drake Bakeries Inc.	3.91
Nabisco	2.09
Private label	19.77
Other	18.81

Source: *Snack Food & Wholesale Bakery*, June 1998, pp. S-22, from A.C. Nielsen.

★ 314 ★

Bakery Products (SIC 2051)

Toaster Pastry Market - 1997

Market shares are shown based on supermarket sales.

Kellogg	69.0%
Nabisco	12.0
Store brands	14.0
Other	4.0

Source: *Investext,* Thomson Financial Networks, September 1, 1998, p. 16, from Information Resources Inc. and Schroder.

★ 315 ★

Bakery Products (SIC 2051)

Top Fresh Pie Brands - 1999

Brands are ranked by sales in millions of dollars.

	Sales ($ mil.)	Share
Entenmann's	$ 15.5	9.2%
Our Special Touch	6.3	3.7
Western Country Crust	5.2	3.1
Gardner	3.0	1.8
Private label	95.0	56.4

Source: *Snack Food & Wholesale Bakery*, May 1999, p. 18, from Information Resources Inc.

★ 316 ★

Bakery Products (SIC 2051)

Top Pastry Brands - 1998

Shares are shown of the $528 million market for the year ended December 27, 1998

Entenmann's	29.1%
Svenhard's	8.0
Little Debbie	7.2
Drake	2.5
Blue Bird	2.4
Dolly Madison	1.5
Mrs. Baird's	1.5
Other	20.7

Source: *Snack Food & Wholesale Bakery*, February 1999, p. 19, from Information Resources Inc.

★ 317 ★

Bakery Products (SIC 2051)

Top Refrigerated Pie Brands - 1999

Shares are shown based on sales of $22.7 million for the year ended March 28, 1999.

Gordon's	10.4%
Cyrus O'Leary's	9.8
Flaherty's	9.2
Western Country Crust	3.5
Private label	62.9
Other	4.2

Source: *Snack Food & Wholesale Bakery*, May 1999, p. 19, from Information Resources Inc.

★ 318 ★

Bakery Products (SIC 2051)

Top Snack Cake Brands - 1998

Shares are shown of the $646.1 million market for the year ended December 27, 1998

Hostess	32.3%
Little Debbie	31.3
Tastykake	10.4
Drake	7.7
Nabisco Snackwell's	2.0
Entenmann's	1.9
Dolly Madison	1.7
Break Cake	1.6%
Betty Crocker Sweet Rewards	1.3
Private label	6.1
Other	3.7

Source: *Snack Food & Wholesale Bakery*, February 1999, p. 18, from Information Resources Inc.

★ 319 ★

Bakery Products (SIC 2051)

Top Snack Pie Brands - 1998

Shares are shown of the $90.5 million market for the year ended December 27, 1998.

Hostess	13.4%
Table Talk	9.2
Tastykake	8.8
Home Run	7.0
JJ's	6.5
Drake	4.5
Entenmann's	4.4
Private label	13.1
Other	33.1

Source: *Snack Food & Wholesale Bakery*, February 1999, p. 19, from Information Resources Inc.

★ 320 ★

Bread (SIC 2051)

Top Fresh Bread Brands - 1998

Market shares are shown based on sales of $5.11 billion for the year ended May 31, 1998.

Wonder	6.2%
Pepperidge Farm	4.4
Oroweat	3.4
Nature's Own	3.2
Sunbeam	2.9
Home Pride	2.8
Merita	2.0
Roman Meal	1.8
Stroehmann	1.8
Private label	26.9
Other	44.6

Source: *Snack Food & Wholesale Bakery*, July 1998, p. 16, from Information Resources Inc.

★ 321 ★

Bread (SIC 2051)

Top Frozen Bread Brands - 1997

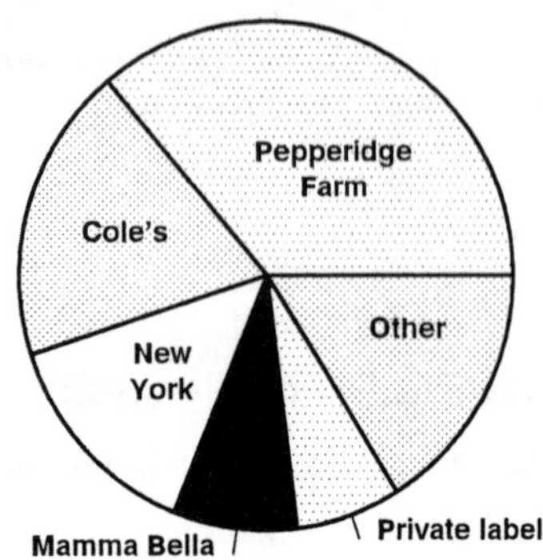

Shares are shown based on supermarket sales for the year ended December 27, 1997.

Pepperidge Farm	36.0%
Cole's	18.6
New York	14.1
Mamma Bella	8.0
Private label	6.9
Other	16.4

Source: *Snack Food & Wholesale Bakery*, June 1998, pp. S-40, from A.C. Nielsen.

★ 322 ★

Cookies (SIC 2052)

Best-Selling Cookies

Market shares are shown in percent.

Nabisco	10.1%
Nabisco Chips Ahoy!	8.5
Archway	4.2
Keebler Chips Deluxe	4.2
Nabisco Newtons	4.1
Nabisco SnackWells	4.0
Pepperidge Farm Distinctive Cookies	2.6
Keebler Fudge Shoppe	2.4
Murray's Cookies	2.1
Other	57.8

Source: *Washington Post*, August 26, 1998, p. C11, from Information Resources Inc.

★ 323 ★

Cookies (SIC 2052)

Best-Selling Girl Scout Cookies - 1998

Thin mints	26.0%
Samoas/caramel de Lites	19.0
Tagalongs/peanut butter patties	13.0
Do-Si-Dos/peanut butter sandwich	12.0
Trefolls/short-bread	11.0
Other	19.0

Source: *USA TODAY*, January 26, 1999, p. D1.

★ 324 ★

Cookies (SIC 2052)

Largest Cookie Makers - 1997

Market shares are shown based on supermarket sales.

Nabisco	29.0%
Keebler	13.0
McKee Baking Co.	12.0
President Baking	6.0
Archway	3.0
Mothers	3.0
Store brands	17.0
Other	15.0

Source: *Investext*, Thomson Financial Networks, September 1, 1998, p. 24, from Information Resources Inc. and Schroder.

★ 325 ★

Crackers (SIC 2052)

Top Cracker Brands

Shares are shown for the year ended March 1, 1998.

Nabisco	44.5%
Keebler	22.4
Pepperidge Farm	6.6
Private label	8.5
Other	18.0

Source: *Wall Street Journal*, June 10, 1998, p. B1.

★ 326 ★

Crackers (SIC 2052)

Top Cracker Makers - 1997

Shares are shown based on supermarket sales for the year ended December 27, 1997.

	Sales ($ mil.)	Share
Nabisco	$ 1,266.9	45.79%
Keebler Brands	663.9	23.99
Pepperidge Farm	163.0	5.89
Private label	239.8	8.67
Other	433.3	15.66

Source: *Snack Food & Wholesale Bakery*, June 1998, pp. S-17, from A.C. Nielsen.

★ 327 ★

Frozen Bakery Products (SIC 2053)

Frozen Bagel Market - 1997

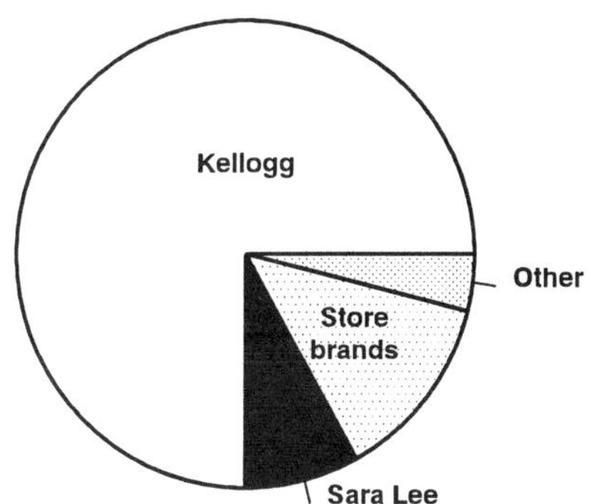

Market shares are shown based on supermarket sales.

Kellogg	75.0%
Sara Lee	8.0
Store brands	13.0
Other	4.0

Source: *Investext,* Thomson Financial Networks, September 1, 1998, p. 16, from Information Resources Inc. and Schroder.

★ 328 ★

Frozen Bakery Products (SIC 2053)

Frozen Cake Market - 1997

Shares are shown based on supermarket sales for the year ended December 27, 1997.

Sara Lee	42.7%
Pepperidge Farm	40.2
Oregon Farms	6.9
Other	10.2

Source: *Snack Food & Wholesale Bakery*, June 1998, pp. S-22, from A.C. Nielsen.

★ 329 ★

Frozen Bakery Products (SIC 2053)

Top Frozen Pie Brands - 1999

Shares are shown based on sales of $262.3 million for the year ended March 28, 1999.

Mrs. Smith's	39.5%
Sara Lee	19.8
Edwards	8.8
Mrs. Smith's Special Recipe	7.0
Mountain Top	5.4
Mrs. Smith's Restaurant Classics	4.2
Banquet	3.1
Marie Callender's	2.4
Pet Ritz	2.4
Christopher Edwards	1.8
Other	5.6

Source: *Snack Food & Wholesale Bakery*, May 1999, p. 18, from Information Resources Inc.

★ 330 ★

Sugar (SIC 2061)

Sugar Market in Florida

Market shares are shown in percent.

Flo-Sun	40.0%
US Sugar	40.0
Other	20.0

Source: *The Economist*, June 5, 1999, p. 63.

★ 331 ★

Confectionery Products (SIC 2064)

Best-Selling Candy Bars - 1998

Shares are shown based on sales of $710.1 million for the year ended January 3, 1999. Figures refer to bars less than 3.5 oz.

M&Ms	16.6%
Hershey's	11.1
Reese's	9.1
Snickers	8.9
York Peppermint Patty	3.9
Butterfinger	3.3
Nestle Crunch	3.0
Three Musketeers	3.0
Russell Stover	2.5
Peter Paul Almond Joy	2.5
Other	37.1

Source: *The Manufacturing Confectioner*, April 1999, p. 28, from Information Resources Inc.

★ 332 ★

Confectionery Products (SIC 2064)

Best-Selling Candy Holidays

Easter	27.0%
Halloween	27.0
Christmas	26.0
Valentine's Day	20.0

Source: *U.S. Distribution Journal*, May/June 1998, p. 36, from National Confectioners Association.

★ 333 ★

Confectionery Products (SIC 2064)

Canada's Confectionery Market

Chocolate bars	38.0%
Boxed/bulk chocolates	24.0
Soft candies	22.0
Chewing gum	19.0

Source: "All About Canada's Confectionery Industry." Retrieved May 28, 1999 from the World Wide Web: http:// www.agr.ca/cb/factsheets/cone.html.

★ 334 ★

Confectionery Products (SIC 2064)

Confectionery Product Sales - 1998

Sales are shown in millions of dollars for the year ended January 4, 1998.

Chocolate candy box/bag 3.5 oz	$ 1,354.4
Chocolate candy bar 3.5 oz	705.5
Chocolate candy snack size	608.1
Non-chocolate chewy box/bag 3.5 oz	482.0
Hard sugar candy/pkg & roll	392.7
Novelty candy	265.0
Breath fresheners	259.6
Gift box chocolates	237.0
Non-chocolate chewy candy bar 3.5 oz	163.8
Chocolate covered cookie/wafer	132.4

Source: *Discount Merchandiser*, June 1998, p. 116, from Information Resources Inc.

★ 335 ★

Confectionery Products (SIC 2064)

Seasonal Candy Sales

Sales are shown in millions of dollars.

Halloween	$ 1,767
Easter	1,670
Christmas	1,525
Valentine's Day	1,033

Source: *Discount Merchandiser*, February 1999, p. 42, from National Confectioners Association.

★ 336 ★

Confectionery Products (SIC 2064)

Specialty Nut Candy Market - 1998

Market shares are shown based on sales of $20.67 million for the second quarter of the year.

Leaf Pay Day	26.9%
Brach's	17.8
Pearsons	4.8
Sophie Mae	4.1
Russell Stover	3.9
Planters	3.1
Lance	3.0

Continued on next page.

★ 336 ★ *Continued*

Confectionery Products (SIC 2064)

Specialty Nut Candy Market - 1998

Market shares are shown based on sales of $20.67 million for the second quarter of the year.

Brown & Haley Almond Roca	2.8%
Standard	2.7
Private label	4.9
Other	26.0

Source: *The Manufacturing Confectioner*, September 1998, p. 38, from Information Resources Inc.

★ 337 ★

Confectionery Products (SIC 2064)

Top Bagged/Boxed Candy Makers - 1998

Hershey Chocolate USA
Mars Inc.
Nestle USA Inc.
Brach & Brock Confections
Leaf North America
Other

Shares are shown based on sales of $1.32 billion for the year ended January 3, 1999. Figures refer to boxed/bagged candy larger than 3.5 oz.

Hershey Chocolate USA	42.9%
Mars Inc.	27.1
Nestle USA Inc.	5.5
Brach & Brock Confections	4.8
Leaf North America	2.3
Other	18.4

Source: *The Manufacturing Confectioner*, April 1999, p. 28, from Information Resources Inc.

★ 338 ★

Confectionery Products (SIC 2064)

Top Bagged/Boxed Candy Vendors - 1998

Shares are shown based on sales of $1.32 billion for the year ended January 3, 1999. Figures refer to boxed/bagged candy smaller than 3.5 oz.

Hershey Chocolate USA	39.9%
Mars Inc.	33.6
Nestle USA Inc.	14.1
Russell Stover Candies	2.5
Ferrero USA Inc.	1.3
Tootsie Roll Inds. Inc.	1.3
Other	7.3

Source: *The Manufacturing Confectioner*, April 1999, p. 28, from Information Resources Inc.

★ 339 ★

Confectionery Products (SIC 2064)

Top Bagged/Boxed Licorice Makers - 1998

Shares are shown based on sales of $174.9 million for the year ended January 3, 1999. Figures refer to bagged/boxed licorice larger than 3.5 oz.

Hershey Chocolate USA	61.1%
American Licorice Co.	17.6
Leaf North America	7.6
Mars Inc.	4.6
Wilkinson-Spitz Ltd.	2.9
Kenny's Candy Co.	1.5
Brach & Brock Confections	0.6
Tootise Roll Industries	0.6
Panda Choc-Finnfoods	0.3
Private label	1.2
Others	2.0

Source: *The Manufacturing Confectioner*, April 1999, p. 30, from Information Resources Inc.

★ 340 ★

Confectionery Products (SIC 2064)

Top Hard Sugar Candy Brands - 1998

Shares are shown based on sales of $382.2 million for the year ended January 3, 1999.

LifeSavers	13.0%
Jolly Rancher	12.9

Continued on next page.

★ 340 ★ *Continued*

Confectionery Products (SIC 2064)

Top Hard Sugar Candy Brands - 1998

Shares are shown based on sales of $382.2 million for the year ended January 3, 1999.

Werthers	11.0%
Tootsie Roll Pops	7.7
Hershey's TastTations	6.6
Pearson Nips	5.7
Charms Blow Pop	5.4
Farley's	2.8
Sprangler Dum Dum Pops	2.5
Private label	5.3
Others	27.1

Source: *The Manufacturing Confectioner*, April 1999, p. 30, from Information Resources Inc.

★ 341 ★

Confectionery Products (SIC 2064)

Top Hard Sugar Candy Makers - 1998

Shares are shown based on sales of $382.2 million for the year ended January 3, 1999.

Nabisco Foods Group	14.6%
Leaf North America	12.9
Storck USA	11.8
Tootsie Roll Inds Inc.	8.2
Charms Inc.	8.2
Hershey Chocolate USA	6.6
Brach & Brock Confections	5.7
Nestle USA Inc.	5.7
Others	26.3

Source: *The Manufacturing Confectioner*, April 1999, p. 30, from Information Resources Inc.

★ 342 ★

Confectionery Products (SIC 2064)

Top Nonchocolate Chewy Candy Bar Makers - 1998

Shares are shown based on sales of $565.6 million for the year ended January 3, 1999. Figures refer to boxed or bagged candy smaller than 3.5 oz.

Mars Inc.	28.8%
Van Melle USA Inc.	17.3
Nabisco Foods Group	12.1
Hershey Chocolate USA	8.8
Tootsie Roll Industries	4.1%
Leaf North America	3.9
Sathers Inc.	3.0
Amer Licorice Co.	2.1
Sunmark Inc.	2.0
Private label	2.5
Other	15.4

Source: *The Manufacturing Confectioner*, April 1999, p. 30, from Information Resources Inc.

★ 343 ★

Confectionery Products (SIC 2064)

Top Nonchocolate Chewy Candy Makers - 1998

Shares are shown based on sales of $565.6 million for the year ended January 3, 1999. Figures refer to boxed or bagged candy larger than 3.5 oz.

Mars Inc.	17.5%
Brach & Brock Confections	11.4
Farley Candy Co.	9.5
Hersey Chocolate USA	7.7
Tootsie Roll Inds. Inc.	6.8
Leaf North America	4.2
Nabisco Foods Group	4.0
Others	38.9

Source: *The Manufacturing Confectioner*, April 1999, p. 30, from Information Resources Inc.

★ 344 ★

Confectionery Products (SIC 2064)

Top Novelty Candy Brands - 1998

Shares are shown based on sales of $313.2 million for the year ended January 3, 1999.

Pez	6.8%
Tootsie Roll Child's Play	6.5
Farley's	6.3
Sweet Tarts	6.0
M&Ms	4.5
Ce De Smarties	4.4
Mega Warheads	4.0
Hot Tamales	3.5
Sunmark Spree	3.2
Willy Wonka Nerds	3.1
Others	50.7

Source: *The Manufacturing Confectioner*, April 1999, p. 33, from Information Resources Inc.

★ 345 ★

Confectionery Products (SIC 2064)

Top Novelty Candy Makers - 1998

Shares are shown based on sales of $313.2 million for the year ended January 3, 1999.

Sunmark Inc.	22.6%
Pez Candy	6.8
Farley Candy Co.	6.5
Tootsie Roll Industries	6.5
The Topps Company Inc.	6.0
Cap Toys Inc.	5.8
Mars Inc.	5.8
Ce De Candy Inc.	4.4
Foreign Candy Co. Inc.	4.2
Just Born Inc.	3.8
Others	27.6

Source: *The Manufacturing Confectioner*, April 1999, p. 33.

★ 346 ★

Confectionery Products (SIC 2064)

Top Specialty Nut Candy Makers - 1998

Shares are shown based on sales of $88.3 million for the year ended January 3, 1999.

Leaf North America	29.3%
Brach & Brock Confections	17.4
Sophie Mae Candy Corp.	5.8
Pearson Candy Co.	4.1
Russell Stover Candies Inc.	3.4
Standard Candy Co. Inc.	3.3
Nabisco Foods Group	3.0
Brown & Haley	2.5
Lance Inc.	2.5
Private label	5.2
Other	24.5

Source: *The Manufacturing Confectioner*, April 1999, p. 28, from Information Resources Inc.

★ 347 ★

Confectionery Products (SIC 2064)

Top Sugarfree Candy Brands - 1998

Shares are shown based on sales of $313.2 million for the year ended January 3, 1999.

Sweet'N Low	13.5%
LifeSavers Delites	11.6
Estee	11.1
Sorbee	6.9
Fifty50	6.3
Bobs	4.9
GoLightly	4.9
Russell Stover	4.8
Square Shooters	4.4
Private label	7.1
Others	24.5

Source: *The Manufacturing Confectioner*, April 1999, p. 32.

★ 348 ★

Confectionery Products (SIC 2064)

Top Sugarfree Candy Makers - 1998

Shares are shown based on sales of $72.8 million for the year ended January 3, 1999.

Simply Lite	20.8%
Nabisco Foods Group	11.6
Estee Corp.	11.2
Sorbee Intl. Ltd.	6.9
Fifty50	6.3
Bobs Candies Inc.	4.9
GoLightly Candy Co.	4.9
Russell Stover	4.8
Squareshooter Co.	4.4
Others	24.2

Source: *The Manufacturing Confectioner*, April 1999, p. 32.

★ 349 ★

Cough Drops (SIC 2064)

Top Cough Drop Brands - 1998

Shares are shown based on sales of $449.1 million for the year ended January 3, 1999.

Halls	26.6%
Cold Eeze	12.4
Ricola	9.7
Ludens	6.8

Continued on next page.

★ 349 ★ *Continued*

Cough Drops (SIC 2064)

Top Cough Drop Brands - 1998

Shares are shown based on sales of $449.1 million for the year ended January 3, 1999.

Robitussin	6.2%
Halls Zinc Defense	3.5
Sucrets	3.5
Halls Plus	3.1
Celestial Seasonings	3.0
Private label	9.8
Other	15.4

Source: *The Manufacturing Confectioner*, April 1999, p. 33, from Information Resources Inc.

★ 350 ★

Cough Drops (SIC 2064)

Top Cough Drop Makers - 1998

Warner-Lambert
Quigley Corporation
Ricola Inc.
Whitehall-Robins
Ludens Inc.
Smithkline Beecham
Private label
Other

Shares are shown based on sales of $449.1 million for the year ended January 3, 1999.

Warner-Lambert	34.0%
Quigley Corporation	12.4
Ricola Inc.	9.7
Whitehall-Robins	7.5
Ludens Inc.	6.8
Smithkline Beecham	6.8
Private label	9.8
Other	13.0

Source: *The Manufacturing Confectioner*, April 1999, p. 33, from Information Resources Inc.

★ 351 ★

Mints (SIC 2064)

Top Breath Freshener Brands - 1998

Market shares are shown for the year ended July 19, 1998.

Tic Tac	27.5%
Breathsavers	24.7
Altoids	18.1
Certs	9.9
Certs Cool Mint Drops	8.2
Certs Powerful Mints	3.9
Extra Flavor Certs	3.4
Velamints	1.0
Smint	0.9
Blitz	0.5
Other	1.9

Source: *U.S. Distribution Journal*, September/October 1998, p. 22, from Information Resources Inc.

★ 352 ★

Mints (SIC 2064)

Top Breath Freshener Makers - 1998

Shares are shown based on sales of $301.7 million for the year ended January 3, 1999.

Ferrero USA Inc.	26.5%
Warner-Lambert	25.3
Nabisco Foods Group	23.2
Callard & Bowser-Suchard	20.7
Chupa Chups U.S.A.	1.0
Ragold Inc.	1.0
Blitz Design Corp.	0.9
Others	1.4

Source: *The Manufacturing Confectioner*, April 1999, p. 33, from Information Resources Inc.

★ 353 ★

Mints (SIC 2064)

Top Mint Brands - 1998

Shares are shown based on sales of $185.89 million for the year ended January 3, 1999.

LifeSavers	36.5%
Van Melles Mentos	14.1
Brock	9.0
Brach's	7.6
Farley's	5.7
Richardson After Dinner	3.2

Continued on next page.

★ 353 ★ *Continued*

Mints (SIC 2064)

Top Mint Brands - 1998

Shares are shown based on sales of $185.89 million for the year ended January 3, 1999.

Sathers	2.8%
Brach's Star Brites	2.5
Bobs	1.5
Private label	7.9
Other	9.2

Source: *The Manufacturing Confectioner*, April 1999, p. 33, from Information Resources Inc.

★ 354 ★

Mints (SIC 2064)

Top Mint Makers - 1998

Nabisco Foods Group

Brach & Brock Confections

Van Melle USA Inc.

Farley Candy Co.

Richardson Brands Inc.

Private label

Others

Shares are shown based on sales of $185.89 million for the year ended January 3, 1999.

Nabisco Foods Group	37.3%
Brach & Brock Confections	19.1
Van Melle USA Inc.	14.1
Farley Candy Co.	5.7
Richardson Brands Inc.	3.2
Private label	7.9
Others	12.7

Source: *The Manufacturing Confectioner*, April 1999, p. 33, from Information Resources Inc.

★ 355 ★

Snack Bars (SIC 2064)

Best-Selling Fruit Roll Bars

Shares are shown of the $427 million market for the year ended December 6, 1998.

Fruit Roll Ups	18.17%
Fruit by the Foot	13.98
Gushers	11.19
New Rugrats	6.96
Other	49.70

Source: *Brandweek*, January 18, 1999, p. 2, from Information Resources Inc.

★ 356 ★

Snack Bars (SIC 2064)

Cereal Bar Market - 1997

Market shares are shown based on supermarket sales.

Kellogg	26.0%
McKee Baking	14.0
Quaker Oats	14.0
Nabisco	13.0
General Mills	5.0
Mars	5.0
Bestfoods	3.0
Store brands	3.0
Other	13.0

Source: *Investext*, Thomson Financial Networks, September 1, 1998, p. 21, from Information Resources Inc. and Schroder.

★ 357 ★

Snack Bars (SIC 2064)

Leading Energy Bars - 1999

Shares are shown based on sales of $500 million for the year ended February 21, 1999.

Power Bar	6.02%
Balance	3.80
Clif	2.46
Ultra Slim Fast	1.94
Met Rx	1.56
Health Valley	1.52
Other	82.70

Source: *Snack Food & Wholesale Bakery*, April 1999, p. 18, from Information Resources Inc.

★ 358 ★

Snack Bars (SIC 2064)

Top Selling Energy Bars - 1998

PowerBar
Balance
Met Rx
Clif

Sales are shown in millions of dollars for the year ended March 22, 1998.

PowerBar	$ 29.9
Balance	7.6
Met Rx	7.4
Clif	6.4

Source: *Los Angeles Times*, May 14, 1998, p. D6, from Information Resources Inc.

★ 359 ★

Snack Bars (SIC 2064)

Top Snack/Granola Bar Makers - 1998

Shares are shown based on sales of $929.1 million for the year ended January 3, 1999.

Kellogg USA	27.1%
Quaker	17.7
Nabisco	11.3
General Mills	9.2
McKee Baking Co.	5.2
Mars Inc.	5.0
Powerfood	3.9
Entemanns	2.3
Bio-Foods Inc.	1.9
Store brands	6.6
Other	9.8

Source: *The Manufacturing Confectioner*, April 1999, p. 33, from Information Resources Inc.

★ 360 ★

Snack Bars (SIC 2064)

Top Snack/Granola Brands - 1998

Shares are shown based on sales of $929.1 million for the year ended January 3, 1999.

Kelloggs	16.3%
Chewy	13.0
Kelloggs Rice Krispies Treats	10.7
Snackwells	8.4%
Kudos	5.0
Nature Valley	4.4
Fruit & Oatmeal	4.0
Sunbelt	3.7
Power Bar	3.3
Other	31.2

Source: *The Manufacturing Confectioner*, April 1999, p. 33, from Information Resources Inc.

★ 361 ★

Chocolate (SIC 2066)

Chocolate Boxed/Bagged Candy Leaders - 1998

Market shares are shown for the year ended July 19, 1998. Figures refer to 3.5 oz brands.

M&Ms	15.7%
Hersheys	11.0
Hersheys Kisses	7.1
Snickers	5.9
Reeses	5.6
Hersheys Nuggets	4.2
York Peppermint Patty	3.3
Hersheys Sweet Escapes	2.9
Milky Way	1.9
Brachs	1.8
Private label	2.1
Other	38.5

Source: *Discount Merchandiser*, October 1998, p. 51, from Information Resources Inc.

★ 362 ★

Chocolate (SIC 2066)

Chocolate Candy Leaders - 1998

Market shares are shown for the year ended July 19, 1998. Figures refer to 3.5 oz bars.

	Sales ($ mil.)	Share
M&Ms	$ 121.0	16.7%
Hershey's	77.0	10.6
Reeses	64.0	8.8
Snickers	63.0	8.7
York Peppermint Patty	27.0	3.8
Butterfinger	25.0	3.5
Nestle Crunch	22.0	3.1

Source: *Discount Merchandiser*, October 1998, p. 51, from Information Resources Inc.

★ 363 ★

Chocolate (SIC 2066)

Chocolate Snack Candy Market - 1998

Market shares are shown based on sales of $78.9 million for the second quarter of the year.

Hershey Chocolate USA	41.7%
Mars Inc.	37.9
Nestle USA Inc.	18.6
Russell Stover	0.8
Leaf North America	0.6
D L Clark Company	0.2
Whitman's Chocolates	0.2

Source: *The Manufacturing Confectioner*, September 1998, p. 38.

★ 364 ★

Chocolate (SIC 2066)

Top Chocolate Candy Bars - 1998

Market shares are shown for the year ended March 29, 1998. Figures refer to bars 3.5 oz.

M&Ms	16.4%
Hershey's	10.7
Reeses	8.9
Snickers	8.6
York Peppermint Patty	3.7
Butterfinger	3.4
Nestle Crunch	3.0
Three Musketeers	2.9%
Russell Stover	2.8
Reeses Nutrageous	2.3
Other	37.3

Source: *Discount Merchandiser*, June 1998, p. 119.

★ 365 ★

Chocolate (SIC 2066)

Top Chocolate Candy Markets

New York City

Los Angeles

Chicago

Baltimore/Washington

Philadelphia

Sales are shown in millions of dollars. Figures are at food channels only.

New York City	$ 88.2
Los Angeles	73.3
Chicago	53.0
Baltimore/Washington	44.6
Philadelphia	32.6

Source: *Supermarket Business*, June 1999, p. 28.

★ 366 ★

Chocolate (SIC 2066)

Top Chocolate Snack Candy Bar Brands - 1998

Market shares are shown for the year ended July 19, 1998. Figures refer to 3.5 oz brands.

Snickers	15.8%
Reeses	14.4
Kit Kat	10.9
Milky Way	7.1
Butterfinger	6.1
Three Musketeers	6.1
M&Ms	5.5
Nestle Crunch	5.3
Baby Ruth	3.5
Peter Paul Almond Joy	3.5
Other	21.8

Source: *Discount Merchandiser*, October 1998, p. 51, from Information Resources Inc.

★ 367 ★

Chocolate (SIC 2066)

Top Snack Chocolate Candy Makers - 1998

Shares are shown based on sales of $683.1 million for the year ended January 3, 1999.

Hershey Chocolate USA	38.7%
Mars Inc.	38.6
Nestle USA Inc.	17.9
Leaf North America	2.7
Russell Stover Candies Inc.	0.9
Other	1.2

Source: *The Manufacturing Confectioner*, April 1999, p. 28, from Information Resources Inc.

★ 368 ★

Chewing Gum (SIC 2067)

Chewing Gum Sales - 1998

Sales are shown in millions of dollars for the year ended January 4, 1998.

Regular gum	$ 531.5
Sugarless gum	440.7

Source: *Discount Merchandiser*, June 1998, p. 116.

★ 369 ★

Chewing Gum (SIC 2067)

Top Gum Brands - 1998

Market shares are shown for the year ended March 29, 1998.

Double Mint	11.7%
Winterfresh	11.6
Freedent	9.0
Big Red	8.3
Juicy Fruit	7.2
Wrigleys Spearmint	7.2
Bubblicious	5.1
Bubble Yum	4.6
Cinn A Burst	3.9
Dentyne	3.1
Other	28.3

Source: *Discount Merchandiser*, June 1998, p. 119.

★ 370 ★

Nuts (SIC 2068)

Popular Bagged Nut Brands - 1997

Shares are shown based on supermarket sales for the year ended December 27, 1997.

Planters	16.3%
Diamond	15.7
Azar	6.8
David	5.4
Harrell	2.6
Evon's	2.3
Sunshine Country	2.3
Sunkist	1.9
Crescent	1.7
Private label	12.8
Other	32.2

Source: *Snack Food & Wholesale Bakery*, June 1998, pp. S-54, from A.C. Nielsen.

★ 371 ★

Nuts (SIC 2068)

Popular Canned Nut Brands - 1997

Shares are shown based on supermarket sales for the year ended December 27, 1997.

Planters	52.5%
Diamond	3.4
Blue Diamond	3.2
Fisher	2.0
River Queen	1.9
Planters Select Mix	1.8
Nutcracker	0.9
Evon's	0.6
Beer Nuts	0.5
Private label	28.6
Other	4.6

Source: *Snack Food & Wholesale Bakery*, June 1998, pp. S-54, from A.C. Nielsen.

★372★

Nuts (SIC 2068)

Top Nut Makers - 1997

Shares are shown based on supermarket sales for the year ended December 27, 1997.

Planters Co.	21.55%
Sun-Diamond Growers of California	6.85
John B. Sanfilippo & Sons Inc.	3.38
Azar Nut Co.	2.12
David	1.61
Private label	15.16
Other	49.34

Source: *Snack Food & Wholesale Bakery*, June 1998, pp. S-54, from A.C. Nielsen.

★373★

Fats and Oils (SIC 2070)

Shortening Leaders

Market shares are shown in percent.

Crisco	68.0%
Other	32.0

Source: *USA TODAY*, September 10, 1998, p. B1, from Procter & Gamble and Information Resources Inc.

★374★

Beverages (SIC 2080)

Alcohol Consumption

	1996	1998
Beer	87.7%	86.8%
Wine	7.1	8.1
Distilled spirits	5.1	5.0

Source: *Beverage Industry*, May 1999, p. 19.

★375★

Beverages (SIC 2080)

Beverage Retail Receipts - 1997

Receipts are in billions of dollars.

Soft drinks	$ 53.4
Beer	53.2
Spirits	34.1
Fruit beverages	15.2
Wine	13.0
Bottled water	4.7
RTD tea	$ 3.2
Sports drinks	2.1

Source: *Beverage World*, May 1998, p. 54.

★376★

Beverages (SIC 2080)

Soy Beverage Market in Canada

Market shares are shown for the year ended January 30, 1999.

So Good	25.3%
Sunrise	23.2
Sensational Soy	9.5
Other	42.0

Source: *Marketing Magazine*, March 15, 1999, p. 3, from A.C. Nielsen MarketTrack.

★377★

Beer (SIC 2082)

Beer Consumption by Type - 1998

Light	40.2%
Premium	25.9
Popular	13.0
Specialty	4.4
Malt liquor	4.0
Ice	3.9
Dry	0.1
Imported	8.5

Source: *Investor's Business Daily*, March 9, 1999, p. A10, from Adams Business Media.

★ 378 ★

Beer (SIC 2082)

Beer Sales by Region - 1997

Sales are in millions of dollars.

	($ mil.)	Share
South	$ 12,289.2	23.10%
Northeast	10,427.2	19.60
East Central	10,108.0	19.00
Pacific	7,607.6	14.30
Southwest	6,862.8	12.90
West Central	3,777.2	7.10
West	2,128.0	4.00

Source: *Beverage World*, May 1998, p. 54, from Beverage Marketing Corp., The Beer Institute, and Adams Business Media.

★ 379 ★

Beer (SIC 2082)

Beer Sales in Canada - 1997

Sales are shown in hectoliters.

	Sales	Share
Ontario	6,764,835	39.38%
Quebec	5,179,725	30.15
British Columbia	2,441,778	14.22
Manitoba	664,907	3.87
Saskatchewean	565,022	3.29
Nova Scotia	564,445	3.29
New Brunswick	464,351	2.70
Newfoundland	384,801	2.24
Prince Edward Island	81,526	0.47
Yukon Territories	34,587	0.20
Northwest Territories	31,094	0.18

Source: Retrieved May 21, 1999 from the World Wide Web: http:// brewers.ca/enter.statistics.htm.

★ 380 ★

Beer (SIC 2082)

Canada's Beer Market

Market shares are shown in percent.

Molson	46.0%
Labatt	46.0
Regional brewers	5.0
Microbreweries	1.5
Brew pubs	0.5

Source: *Toronto Star*, July 26, 1998, p. D1.

★ 381 ★

Beer (SIC 2082)

Imported Beer Leaders

Market shares are shown in percent.

Corona Extra	22.9%
Heineken	18.5
Labatt's Blue	5.8
Becks	4.4
Molson Ice	4.0
Foster	3.6
Amstel Light	2.6
Molson Golden	2.4
Tecate	2.4
Guinness	2.3
Other	31.1

Source: *Beverage Industry*, April 1999, p. 20, from *The Maxwell Consumer Report*.

★ 382 ★

Beer (SIC 2082)

Imported Beer Market

Volume is shown in millions of cases.

Corona	39.3
Heineken	39.3
Molson	20.7
Labatt	13.0
Beck's	9.2
Foster's	7.6
Guinness Stout	7.0
Tecate	6.0
Bass Ale	5.7
Amstel	5.5

Source: *Forbes*, October 5, 1998, p. 140, from *Modern Brewery Age*.

★ 383 ★

Beer (SIC 2082)

Largest Brewers - 1998

Data show estimated millions of barrels.

Anheuser-Busch	94.4
Miller	40.9
Coors	21.0
Stroh	13.1
S&P Industries (Pabst)	4.5
Genesse	1.5
Boston Beer	1.3

Source: *Supermarket Business*, April 1999, p. 44, from Information Resources Inc.

★ 384 ★

Beer (SIC 2082)

Largest Brewers in Drug Stores

Market shares are shown in percent for the year ended November 2, 1997.

Anheuser-Busch Inc.	40.5%
Miller brewing Co.	26.8
Adolph Coors Co.	8.5
Stroh/Heileman Brewing	6.9
Barton Brands Ltd.	3.0
Heineken	2.6
Pabst General Brewing Co.	1.7
Molson Breweries USA	1.6
Boston Beer Co.	1.2
Dribeck Import Co.	1.1

Source: *Beverage Industry*, August 1998, p. 20, from Information Resources Inc.

★ 385 ★

Beer (SIC 2082)

Largest Brewers in Supermarkets

Market shares are shown in percent for the year ended November 2, 1997.

Anheuser-Busch Inc.	40.1%
Miller Brewing Co.	22.0
Adolph Coors Co.	10.9
Stroh/Heileman Brewing	7.0
Barton Brands Ltd.	3.4
Pabst/General Brewing Co.	2.1
Heineken USA	2.0
Molson Breweries USA	1.7
Guinness Import Co.	1.3
Boston Beer Co.	1.2%
Other	8.3

Source: *Beverage Industry*, August 1998, p. 20, from Information Resources Inc.

★ 386 ★

Beer (SIC 2082)

Top Beer Brands - 1998

Shares are shown based on a total of 193.3 million barrels.

Budweiser	18.7%
Bud Light	13.4
Miller Lite	8.2
Coors Light	7.7
Busch	4.5
Natural Light	3.7
Miller Genuine Draft	3.1
Miller High Life	2.8
Busch Light	2.5
Corona Extra	2.0
Other	33.1

Source: *Beverage World*, April 1999, p. 51, from Beverage Marketing Corp.

★ 387 ★

Beer (SIC 2082)

Top Beer Brands in Drug Stores

Market shares are shown in percent for the year ended November 2, 1997.

Budweiser	16.1%
Bud Light	9.6
Miller Lite	9.4
Miller Genuine Draft	5.2
Coors Light	4.3
Busch	4.0
Natural Light	3.4
Miller High Life	2.9
Corona Extra	2.5
Heineken	2.3
Other	40.3

Source: *Beverage Industry*, August 1998, p. 20.

★ 388 ★

Beer (SIC 2082)

Top Beers in Supermarkets - 1998

Shares are shown based on supermarket sales for the 12 months ended July 12, 1998.

Budweiser	12.8%
Bud Light	10.8
Miller Lite	7.3
Coors Light	6.7
Natural Light	4.9
Busch	3.6
Miller Genuine Draft	3.3
Miller High Life	3.0
Busch Light	2.7
Milwaukee's Best	2.6
Other	42.3

Source: *Advertising Age*, August 31, 1998, p. 31, from Information Resources Inc.

★ 389 ★

Beer (SIC 2082)

Top Brewers - 1998

Market shares are shown in percent.

Anheuser-Busch	46.6%
Miller	21.1
Coors	10.5
Stroh	6.7
Pabst	2.0
Other	13.1

Source: *USA TODAY*, February 9, 1999, p. 6B, from *Beer Marketers's Insights*.

★ 390 ★

Beer (SIC 2082)

Top States for Canned Beer Sales

A total of 52% of all beer sales are packaged in cans. Data show the states which had the largest sales of beer in a can. Figures are for the first six months of 1997.

Delaware	68.0%
Alabama	67.0
Arizona	66.0
Mississippi	65.0
New Hampshire	65.0

Source: *Beverage World*, June 1998, p. 54, from Beer Institute estimates.

★ 391 ★

Wine (SIC 2084)

Largest Wine Producers in the Bay Area, CA - 1997

Companies are ranked by millions of cases produced. Figures refer to companies in the Bay Area, San Francisco.

Sutter Home Winery Inc.	10.0
United Distillers	8.0
Robert Mondavi	6.4
Beringer Wine Estates	5.0
Kendall-Jakson Winery	2.7

Source: *San Francisco Business Times*, October 30, 1998, p. 30.

★ 392 ★

Wine (SIC 2084)

Wine Production by State - 1997

Production is shown in thousands of gallons.

	(000)	Share
California	422,560	90.57%
New York	23,180	4.97
Washington	5,200	1.11
Oregon	1,860	0.40
Vermont	1,550	0.33

Source: *New York Times*, August 15, 1998, p. B1, from Motto, Kryla & Fisher.

★ 393 ★

Wine (SIC 2084)

Wine Sales by Region

Sales are in millions of dollars.

	($ mil.)	Share
Northeast	$ 3,432.0	26.40%
Pacific	3,250.0	25.00
South	2,418.0	18.60
East Central	1,833.0	14.10
Southwest	949.0	7.30
West Central	572.0	4.40
West	546.0	4.20

Source: *Beverage World*, May 1998, p. 60, from Beverage Marketing Corp., The Beer Institute, and Adams Business Media.

★ 394 ★

Wine (SIC 2084)

Wine Shipments by Class

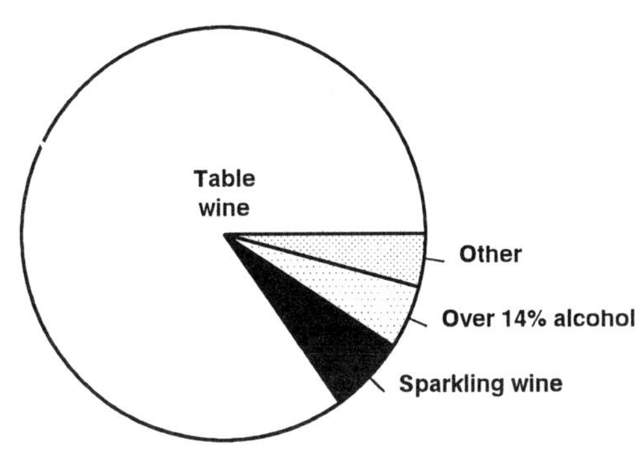

	1998	1999
Table wine	84.59%	84.45%
Sparkling wine	5.64	6.15
Over 14% alcohol	5.64	5.42
Other	4.14	3.98

Source: *Wines & Vines*, February 1999, p. 14, from Comberg, Fredrikson & Associates.

★ 395 ★

Liquor (SIC 2085)

Bloody Mary Mix Market

Mr. and Mrs. T	66.0%
Other	34.0

Source: *Fortune*, May 24, 1999, p. 52.

★ 396 ★

Liquor (SIC 2085)

Canadian Whiskey Market

Market shares are shown in percent.

Brown-Forman	58.1%
Canadian LTD	15.0
Other	26.9

Source: "The Future for Premium Canadian Whiskey." Retrieved May 25, 1999 from the World Wide Web: http:// beveragebusiness.com/art-arch/brad02.html.

★ 397 ★

Liquor (SIC 2085)

Irish Whiskey Market

Market shares are shown in percent.

Jameson	43.5%
Bushmills	36.8
Tullamore Dew	5.2
John Powers	4.8
Kilbeggan	2.2
Other	7.5

Source: "Irish Whiskies Lorded Over Their Scotch." Retrieved May 25, 1999 from the World Wide Web: http:// beveragebusiness.com/art-arch/bouc03.html.

★ 398 ★

Liquor (SIC 2085)

Largest Spirits Firms

Market shares are shown in percent.

	1997	1998
UDV/Diageo	18.2%	22.1%
Seagram Co. Ltd.	12.3	13.4
Jim Beam (Fortune Brands)	11.5	11.0
Bacardi-Martini USA	8.5	10.1
Brown Forman Corp.	8.5	8.0
Other	41.0	35.4

Source: *Beverage Industry*, May 1999, p. 18.

★ 399 ★

Liquor (SIC 2085)

Liquor Market in Mexico

The market is shown by segment.

Rum	33.0%
Brandy	31.0
Tequila	26.0
Other	10.0

Source: *National Trade Data Bank*, May 18, 1998, p. ISA980301.

★ 400 ★

Liquor (SIC 2085)

Premium Vodka Market

Absolut	64.0%
Other	36.0

Source: "Vodka Heating Up." Retrieved May 25, 1999 from the World Wide Web: http://beveragebusiness.com/art-arch/bradfd08.html.

★ 401 ★

Liquor (SIC 2085)

Spirit Sales by Region - 1997

Sales are in millions of dollars.

Northeast	$ 7,877.8
South	7,809.6
East Central	6,036.2
Pacific	5,320.1
Southwest	3,035.2
West Central	2,353.1
West	1,671.0

Source: *Beverage World*, May 1998, p. 54, from Beverage Marketing Corp., The Beer Institute, and Adams Business Media.

★ 402 ★

Liquor (SIC 2085)

Top Cooler Brands in Canada

Market shares are shown in percent for the year ended March 31, 1999.

Mike's Hard Lemonade	29.9%
Mike's Hard Cranberry Lemonade	18.2
Seagram's Wildberry Vodka Cool	6.1
Mike's Hard Lemon Ice Tea	5.0
Captain Morgan Spiked Cherry	3.0
Bacardi Breezer Carribean Key	2.8
Wildberry Xtra	2.5
Other	32.5

Source: "Report on Market Share." Retrieved June 1, 1999 from the World Wide Web: http://www.marketingmag.ca/index.cgi?, from industry sources.

★ 403 ★

Liquor (SIC 2085)

Top Liquor Brands - 1998

Market shares are shown based on estimated number of case depletions.

Bacardi	4.8%
Smirnoff	4.1
Absolut	3.2
Jack Daniels	2.4
Seagram's Gin	2.4
Jim Beam	2.3
Bacardi Breezer	2.1
Jose Cuervo	2.0
7 Crown	1.9
Canadian Mist	1.9
Other	72.9

Source: *Beverage Industry*, May 1999, p. 17.

★ 404 ★

Bottled Water (SIC 2086)

Bottled Water Brand Leaders - 1998

Shares are shown of the $1.17 billion market for the year ended March 29, 1998.

Evian	8.0%
Poland Spring	7.0
Arrowhead	5.5
Zephyrills	3.6
Deer Park	3.5
Dannon	3.4
Aquafina	3.1
Sparkletts	3.0
Naya	2.6
Private label	23.3
Other	37.0

Source: *Beverage World*, July 1998, p. 12, from Information Resources Inc.

★ 405 ★

Bottled Water (SIC 2086)

Bottled Water Market in Mexico

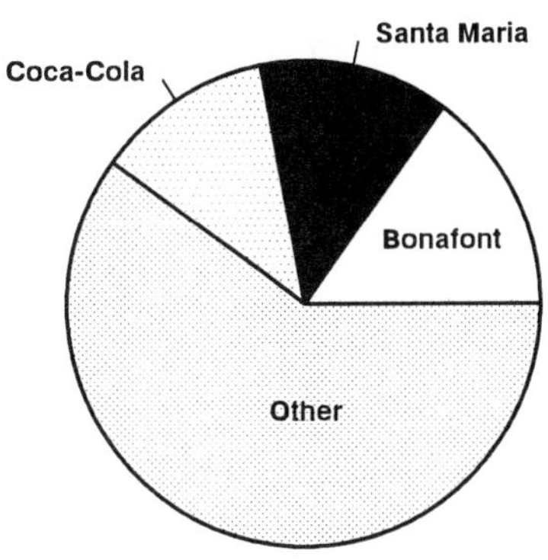

Market shares are shown in percent.

Bonafont	15.0%
Santa Maria	13.0
Coca-Cola	12.0
Other	60.0

Source: *Latin Trade*, May 1999, p. 32.

★ 406 ★

Bottled Water (SIC 2086)

Bottled Water Sales

Retail	55.5%
Home	19.6
Commercial	17.9

Source: *Beverage World*, September 1998, p. 90, from Beverage Marketing Corporation.

★ 407 ★

Bottled Water (SIC 2086)

Bottled Water Sales by State

Sales are in millions of gallons.

California	854.4
Texas	196.5
Florida	196.4
New York	179.9
Arizona	119.5

Source: *Financial Gleaner*, October 16, 1998, p. 19, from International Bottled Water Association.

★ 408 ★

Bottled Water (SIC 2086)

Bottled Water Sales by Type

Non-sparkling	86.1%
Sparkling	9.6
Imported	4.4

Source: *Beverage World*, September 1998, p. 90.

★ 409 ★

Bottled Water (SIC 2086)

Top Bottled Water Brands - 1998

Shares are shown based on total sales of $4.33 billion.

Poland Spring	8.1%
Arrowhead	6.5
Sparkletts	4.7
Evian	4.6
Aquafina	3.8
Zephyrills	3.1
Hinckley & Schmitt	3.0
Deer Park	2.9
Ozarka	2.8
Crystal Geyser	2.6
Other	57.8

Source: *Beverage World*, April 1999, p. 60, from Beverage Marketing Corp.

★ 410 ★

Bottled Water (SIC 2086)

Top Bottled Water Brands in Canada - 1999

Market shares are shown in percent for the year ended April 24, 1999.

Evian	24.4%
Volvic	9.8
MontClair	9.3
Aquafina	8.6
Naya	8.0
Crystal Springs	5.4
Labrador	2.9

Continued on next page.

★ 410 ★ *Continued*

Bottled Water (SIC 2086)

Top Bottled Water Brands in Canada - 1999

Market shares are shown in percent for the year ended April 24, 1999.

Aberfoyle	1.3%
Capilano Spring	0.7
Private label	21.8
Others	7.8

Source: "Report on Market Share." Retrieved June 1, 1999 from the World Wide Web: http://www.marketingmag.ca/index.cgi?, from industry sources.

★ 411 ★

Bottled Water (SIC 2086)

Top Bottled Water Makers - 1997

Market shares are shown in percent.

Perrier Group	27.9%
Suntory	9.2
McKesson	7.1
Groupe Danone	5.8
Crystal Geyser	2.4
Other	47.6

Source: *Wall Street Journal*, November 3, 1998, p. A7, from Beverage Marketing Corp.

★ 412 ★

Bottled Water (SIC 2086)

Top Carbonated Water Brands - 1998

Shares are shown of the $506.8 million market for the year ended March 29, 1998.

Canada Dry	12.5%
Schweppes	9.7
Vintage	5.8
Perrier	5.1
Clearly Canadian	3.6
Calistoga	2.6
Polar	2.3
Poland Spring	2.3
Adirondack	2.1
Private label	32.0
Other	22.0

Source: *Beverage World*, July 1998, p. 12.

★ 413 ★

Soft Drinks (SIC 2086)

Best-Selling Soda Brands - 1998

Volume shares are shown in percent.

Coca-Cola Classic	16.4%
Pepsi-Cola	15.0
Diet Coke	7.4
Diet Pepsi	5.1
Mountain Dew	4.9
Sprite	5.0
Dr. Pepper	4.2
Caffeine Free Diet Coke	3.0
7Up	2.3
Caffeine Free Diet Pepsi	1.9
Other	34.8

Source: *Beverage Industry*, March 1999, p. 14, from Information Resources Inc.

★ 414 ★

Soft Drinks (SIC 2086)

Canada's Soft Drink Consumption

Consumption is shown in kiloliters.

	Kiloliters	Share
Ontario	1,375,265	38.86%
West	1,069,761	30.23
Quebec	766,670	21.66
Atlantic	327,085	9.24

Source: "Ontario/Quebec Power Canadian Soft Drink Industry." Retrieved April 29, 1999 from the World Wide Web; http://www.softdrink.ca/st1998en.htm, from Statistics Canada.

★ 415 ★

Soft Drinks (SIC 2086)

Fountain Soft Drink Market

Data show the largest fountain accounts as of May 1998.

Account	Number
McDonald's	12,000
Subway	10,800
Pizza Hut	8,900
Burger King	6,900
Taco Bell	6,000
Dairy Queen	5,800
KFC	5,100
7-Eleven	5,000

Continued on next page.

★ 415 ★ *Continued*

Soft Drinks (SIC 2086)

Fountain Soft Drink Market

Data show the largest fountain accounts as of May 1998.

Wendy's	4,600
Domino's Pizza	4,300

Source: *Wall Street Journal*, August 24, 1998, p. A3, from *Beverage Digest*.

★ 416 ★

Soft Drinks (SIC 2086)

Fountain Soft Drink Sales

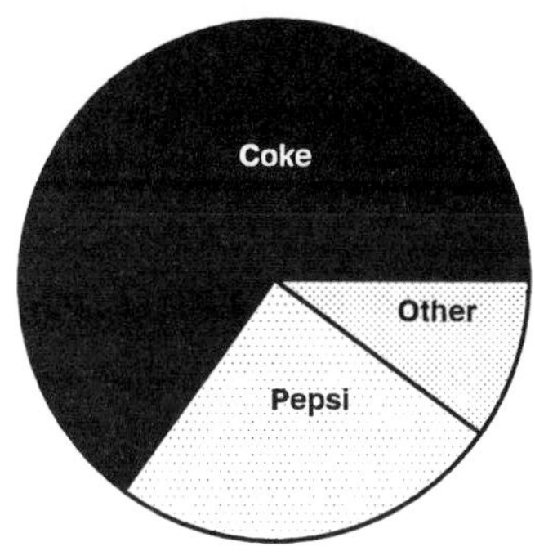

Market shares are shown in percent.

Coke	65.0%
Pepsi	25.0
Other	10.0

Source: *Time*, April 26, 1999, p. 46.

★ 417 ★

Soft Drinks (SIC 2086)

Largest Soft Drink Markets - 1998

Sales are shown in millions of dollars.

Los Angeles	$ 637.3
New York City	609.0
Chicago	446.2
Baltimore/Washington D.C.	276.8
Philadelphia	241.1
Dallas/Ft. Worth	236.6

Source: *Beverage Industry*, March 1999, p. 14, from Information Resources Inc.

★ 418 ★

Soft Drinks (SIC 2086)

Non-Cola Market Leaders - 1997

Market shares are shown in percent.

Dr. Pepper/SevenUp	35.2%
Coca-Cola	21.5
PepsiCo.	21.5
Other	21.7

Source: *Financial Times*, November 13, 1998, p. 21, from *Beverage Digest* and Information Resources Inc. InfoScan.

★ 419 ★

Soft Drinks (SIC 2086)

Ontario's Soft Drink Sales by Packaging - 1998

Cans	54.9%
Bottles	30.3
Fountain	14.8

Source: "Ontario/Quebec Power Canadian Soft Drink Industry." Retrieved April 29, 1999 from the World Wide Web; http:// www.softdrink.ca/st1998en.htm, from Statistics Canada.

★ 420 ★

Soft Drinks (SIC 2086)

Quebec's Soft Drink Sales by Packaging - 1998

Bottles	54.7%
Cans	33.3
Fountain	12.0

Source: "Ontario/Quebec Power Canadian Soft Drink Industry." Retrieved April 29, 1999 from the World Wide Web; http:// www.softdrink.ca/st1998en.htm, from Statistics Canada.

★ 421 ★

Soft Drinks (SIC 2086)

Soft Drink Market - 1998

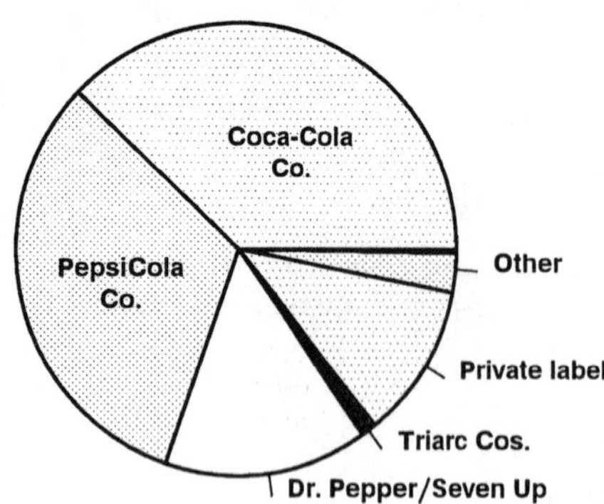

Volume shares are shown in percent.

Coca-Cola Co.	37.7%
PepsiCola Co.	32.0
Dr. Pepper/Seven Up	14.6
Triarc Cos.	1.4
Private label	11.1
Other	3.2

Source: *Beverage Industry*, March 1999, p. 14, from Information Resources Inc.

★ 422 ★

Soft Drinks (SIC 2086)

Soft Drink Market in Los Angeles, CA - 1997

Market shares are shown in percent.

Coca-Cola Classic	19.0%
Pepsi	18.0
Diet Coke	7.0
Diet Sprite	5.0
Sprite	5.0
7 Up	5.0
Dr. Pepper	3.0
Mountain Dew	2.0
Others	36.0

Source: *Beverage World*, July 1998, p. 42, from industry contacts.

★ 423 ★

Soft Drinks (SIC 2086)

Soft Drink Sales by Flavor - 1997

Market shares are shown in percent. Neon includes Mountain Dew, Mello Yello and Surge. Pepper-type includes Dr. Pepper and Mr. Pib.

Cola	62.5%
Lemon-lime	11.2
Neon	9.3
Pepper-type	8.0

Source: *USA TODAY*, July 14, 1998, p. 14B.

★ 424 ★

Soft Drinks (SIC 2086)

Sports Drink Market

The $1.5 billion market is shown in percent.

Gatorade	80.0%
Powerade	11.0
All Sport	7.0
Other	2.0

Source: *Fortune*, November 23, 1998, p. 44, from *Beverage Digest*.

★ 425 ★

Soft Drinks (SIC 2086)

Supermarket Soft Drink Sales

Shares are shown based on supermarket sales.

Coke	37.0%
Pepsi	31.0
Other	32.0

Source: *Time*, April 26, 1999, p. 46.

★ 426 ★

Soft Drinks (SIC 2086)

Top Diet Brands

Market shares are shown in percent.

Diet Coke	33.2%
Diet Pepsi	19.9
Caffeine Free Diet Coke	6.9
Caffeine Free Diet Pepsi	4.0
Diet Dr. Pepper	3.5
Diet Mountain Dew	2.9
Diet 7Up	2.3

Continued on next page.

★ 426 ★ *Continued*

Soft Drinks (SIC 2086)

Top Diet Brands

Market shares are shown in percent.

Diet Sprite	1.9%
Diet Rite	1.2
Fresca	1.1
Other	23.1

Source: *USA TODAY*, October 18, 1998, p. 26A, from *Beverage World* and Beverage Marketing Corp.

★ 427 ★

Soft Drinks (SIC 2086)

Top Soft Drink Brands - 1998

Market shares are shown in percent.

Coca-Cola	20.6%
Pesi-Cola	14.5
Diet Coke	8.6
Mountain Dew	6.7
Sprite	6.5
Dr.Pepper	5.9
Diet Pepsi	5.0
7Up	2.1
Caffeine Free Diet Coke	1.8
Minute Maid	1.2
Other	27.1

Source: *Beverage World*, March 1999, p. 37, from Beverage Marketing Corp.

★ 428 ★

Soft Drinks (SIC 2086)

Top Soft Drink Makers - 1998

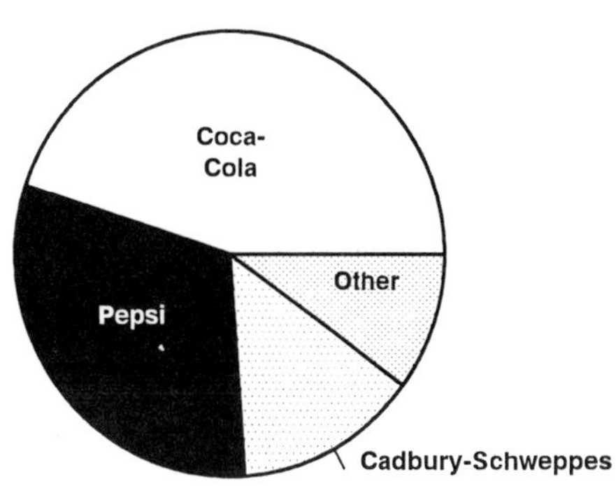

Market shares are shown in percent.

Coca-Cola	44.5%
Pepsi	31.4
Cadbury-Schweppes	14.4
Other	9.7

Source: *Wall Street Journal*, March 8, 1999, p. B1, from Davenport & Company/LLC.

★ 429 ★

Powdered Drinks (SIC 2087)

Top Fruit Drink Mix Brands - 1998

Shares are shown of the $618.4 million market for the year ended March 29, 1998.

Kool-Aid	33.9%
Crystal Light	15.1
Country Time	11.8
Kool-Aid Mega Mountain Twists	8.6
Kool-Aid Island Twists	7.5
Crystal Light Tropical Passions	6.0
CountryTime Lem 'N' Berry Sippers	3.9
Crystal Light Teas	1.9
Private label	6.2
Other	5.1

Source: *Beverage World*, July 1998, p. 10, from Information Resources Inc.

★ 430 ★

Powdered Drinks (SIC 2087)

Top Instant Tea Brands - 1998

Shares are shown of the $271.9 million market for the year ended March 29, 1998.

Lipton	38.8%
Nestea	16.7
Crystal Light	5.3
4C	4.0
Tetley	2.4
Nestea Decaf	1.4
Nestea Free	0.9
Private label	27.5
Other	4.0

Source: *Beverage World*, July 1998, p. 10, from Information Resources Inc.

★ 431 ★

Seafood (SIC 2091)

Seafood Sales in Supermarkets

Fish	38.0%
Shrimp	32.0
Prepared entrees, uncooked	12.0
Prepared entrees, cooked	11.0
Clams, other shellfish	3.0
Lobsters	2.0
Scallops	1.0

Source: *Supermarket Business*, November 1998, p. 89.

★ 432 ★

Seafood (SIC 2091)

Top Tuna Brands - 1998

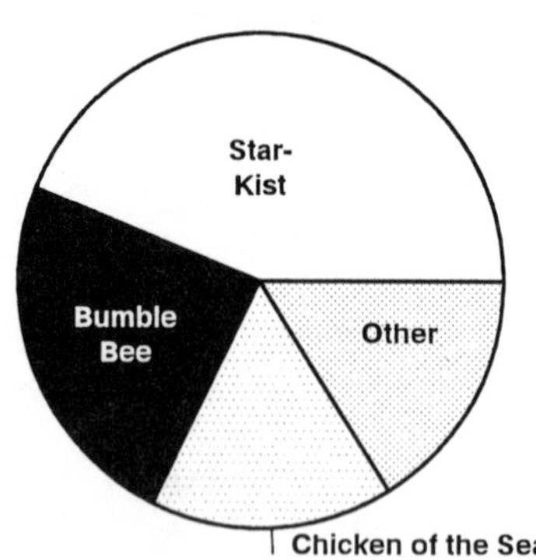

Market shares are shown based on sales for the year ended March 28, 1999.

Star-Kist	44.0%
Bumble Bee	24.2
Chicken of the Sea	15.5
Other	16.3

Source: *Advertising Age*, May 31, 1999, p. 32.

★ 433 ★

Seafood (SIC 2092)

Best-Selling Frozen Seafood Brands - 1999

Data show millions of units sold for the 12 weeks ended February 28, 1999.

Gorton's	12.5%
Van de Kamp's	9.2
Mrs. Paul's	7.3
SeaPak	3.0
Private label	8.7

Source: "Dinners Post 4.8% Gain; Dept. Dips 0.5%" Retrieved June 2, 1999 from the World Wide Web: http:// www.frozenfoodage.com/jun99-4.htm, from Information Resources Inc.

★ 434 ★

Coffee (SIC 2095)

Top Coffee Bean Brands - 1998

Shares are shown based on supermarket sales. The number of gourmet coffee drinkers has jumped from 7.5 million to 11.5 million.

Eight O'Clock	44.0%
Millstone	8.3
Brothers	6.4
Starbucks	4.4
Private label	14.2
Other	22.7

Source: *Fortune*, May 24, 1999, p. 208.

★ 435 ★

Coffee (SIC 2095)

Top Ground Coffee Brands - 1998

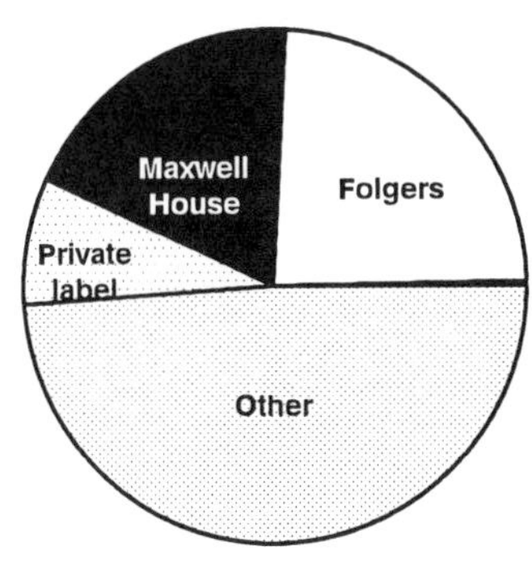

Brands are ranked by grocery sales in millions of dollars. Total grocery sales reached $2,010.2 million.

	($ mil.)	Share
Folgers	$ 480.8	23.92%
Maxwell House	383.6	19.08
Private label	165.4	8.23
Other	980.4	48.77

Source: *Supermarket Business*, December 1998, p. 33, from Information Resources Inc.

★ 436 ★

Coffee (SIC 2095)

Top Instant Coffee Brands - 1998

Brands are ranked by grocery sales in millions of dollars. Total grocery sales reached $562.4 million.

	($ mil.)	Share
Folgers	$ 119.1	21.18%
General Foods International	113.5	20.18
Maxwell House	92.9	16.52
Other	236.9	42.12

Source: *Supermarket Business*, December 1998, p. 33, from Information Resources Inc.

★ 437 ★

Coffee (SIC 2095)

Top Whole Bean Coffee Brands - 1998

Brands are ranked by grocery sales in millions of dollars. Total grocery sales reached $234.6 million.

	($ mil.)	Share
Eight O'Clock	$ 108.2	46.12%
Millstone	18.6	7.93
Private label	34.6	14.75
Other	73.2	31.20

Source: *Supermarket Business*, December 1998, p. 33, from Information Resources Inc.

★ 438 ★

Snacks (SIC 2096)

Hot Snack Market - 1997

Shares are shown based on supermarket sales for the year ended December 6, 1997. Figures include frozen hors d'oeuvres, snacks, frozen breaded vegetables, breaded onions, corn dogs, cocktail franks and frozen potatoes. Data do not include frozen sandwiches or pizza.

H.J. Heinz Co.	36.57%
Sara Lee Corp.	7.81
The Pillsbury Co.	7.68
ConAgra Inc.	4.74
Private label	14.59
Other	28.61

Source: *Snack Food & Wholesale Bakery*, June 1998, pp. S-56, from A.C. Nielsen.

★ 439 ★

Snacks (SIC 2096)

Largest Corn/Tortilla Chip Makers - 1997

Shares are shown based on supermarket sales for the year ended December 27, 1997.

Frito-Lay Inc.	80.95%
Mission Foods Corp.	1.69
Granny Goose Foods	1.22
Private label	5.83
Other	10.32

Source: *Snack Food & Wholesale Bakery*, June 1998, pp. S-40, from A.C. Nielsen.

★ 440 ★

Snacks (SIC 2096)

Largest Pretzel Makers - 1997

Shares are shown based on supermarket sales for the year ended December 27, 1997.

Frito-Lay Inc.	31.18%
Snyder's of Hanover	23.07
Bachman	4.70
Utz	2.96
Herr's	2.62
Nestle	2.51
Nabisco	2.37
M&M Mars	2.31
Gardetto's	2.23
Other	26.07

Source: *Snack Food & Wholesale Bakery*, June 1998, pp. S-40, from A.C. Nielsen.

★ 441 ★

Snacks (SIC 2096)

Salted Snack Sales

Unit sales are shown for the year ended December 6, 1998.

	(mil.)	Share
Potato chips	146.0	20.27%
Tortilla/tostada chips	134.1	18.62
Cheese snacks	68.1	9.45
Corn snacks (not tortilla chips)	61.0	8.47
Ready-to-eat popcorn/caramel corn	48.6	6.75
Pretzels	34.1	4.73
Other salted snacks (no nuts)	228.4	31.71

Source: *Discount Merchandiser*, March 1999, p. 64.

★ 442 ★

Snacks (SIC 2096)

Snacks Market - 1997

Market shares are shown based on volume.

Potato chips	31.0%
Tortilla chips	22.8
Pretzels	11.5
Snack nuts	7.0
Microwavable popcorn	6.8
Extruded snacks	5.7
Corn chips	3.8
Ready-to-eat popcorn	2.7
Party mix	2.0
Unpopped popcorn	1.8
Variety packs	1.4
Meat snacks	1.1
Other	2.4

Source: *Discount Merchandiser*, October 1998, p. 3, from Snack Food Association.

★ 443 ★

Snacks (SIC 2096)

Top Potato Chip Brands - 1998

Shares of the $2.23 billlion market are shown for the year ended September 13, 1998.

Lay's	34.0%
Ruffles	17.2
Lay's WOW	4.3
Wavy Lay's	4.1
Ruffles WOW!	3.0

Continued on next page.

★ 443 ★ *Continued*

Snacks (SIC 2096)

Top Potato Chip Brands - 1998

Shares of the $2.23 billion market are shown for the year ended September 13, 1998.

Utz	2.4%
Wise	2.3
Ruffles the Works	2.2
Herr's	1.9
Private label	7.5
Other	21.1

Source: *Snack Food & Wholesale Bakery*, November 1998, p. 19, from Information Resources Inc.

★ 444 ★

Snacks (SIC 2096)

Top Pretzel Brands - 1998

Shares are shown based on a $590.9 million market for the year ended November 8, 1998.

Rold Gold	25.1%
Snyder's of Hanover	18.9
Bachman	3.8
Gardetto's	3.0
Combos	2.9
Snyder's of Hanover Olde Tyme	2.8
Herr's	2.4
Rold Gold Crispy's	2.2
Nabisco Pretzel Air Crisps	2.0
Private label	11.8
Other	25.1

Source: *Snack Food & Wholesale Bakery*, January 1999, p. 20, from Information Resources Inc.

★ 445 ★

Diet Foods (SIC 2099)

Top Diet Aids - 1998

Market shares are shown for the year ended July 19, 1998. Total sales reached $65.3 million, with food stores winning 51.5% of the retail market.

Ultra Slim Fast	38.2%
Ensure	15.2
Ensure Plus	9.2
Boost	5.6
Nestle Sweet Success	5.2
Pedia Sure Weight	3.5
Slim Fast Jump Start	3.1
Slim Fast	2.5%
Ensure Light	2.0
Private label	6.4
Other	9.1

Source: *Supermarket Business*, October 1998, p. 69, from Information Resources Inc.

★ 446 ★

Salads (SIC 2099)

Prepackaged Salad Market - 1998

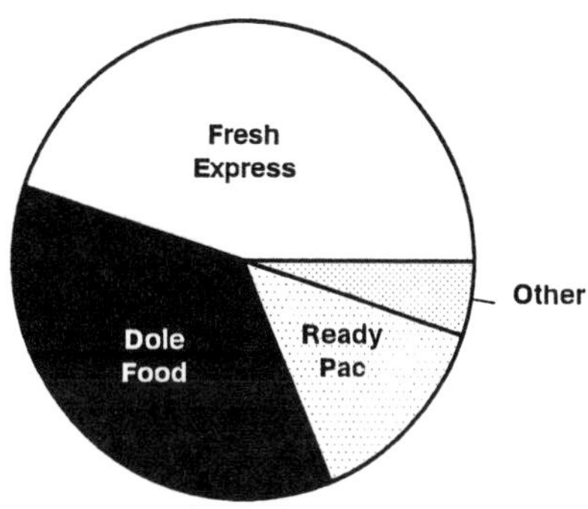

Sales are shown for the year ended September 1998.

	($ mil.)	Share
Fresh Express	$ 460.5	44.97%
Dole Food	368.8	36.02
Ready Pac	144.7	14.13
Other	50.0	4.88

Source: *Washington Post*, December 26, 1998, p. C4, from Information Resources Inc.

★ 447 ★

Spices (SIC 2099)

Largest Spice Makers

Market shares are shown in percent.

McCormick's	45.0%
Burns Philip	12.0
Other	43.0

Source: *Investext*, Thomson Financial Networks, January 5, 1999, p. 2, from Information Resources Inc. InfoScan.

★ 448 ★

Syrup (SIC 2099)

Maple Syrup Production in Canada - 1997

Annual production reached 25,455 tons.

Quebec	92.0%
Ontario	4.0
New Brunswick	3.0
Nova Scotia	1.0

Source: "All About Canada's Maple Syrup Industry." Retrieved May 21, 1999 from the World Wide Web: http://www.agr.ca/cb/factsheets/facindxe.html, from Statistics Canada.

★ 449 ★

Tea (SIC 2099)

Tea Market Leaders

Shares are shown for the year ended March 29, 1998 based on sales of bagged and loose tea.

	($ mil.)	Share
Lipton	$ 190.8	31.83%
Celestial Seasonings	71.2	11.88
Other	337.4	56.29

Source: *Brandweek*, May 18, 1998, p. 8, from Information Resources Inc.

★ 450 ★

Tortillas (SIC 2099)

Largest Tortilla Makers

Market shares are shown in percent.

Gruma	24.0%
Tyson Foods	5.0
Bimbo	3.0
ConAgra	3.0
Other	65.0

Source: *Latin Trade*, April 1999, p. 23.

★ 451 ★

Tortillas (SIC 2099)

Largest Tortilla Makers in Texas

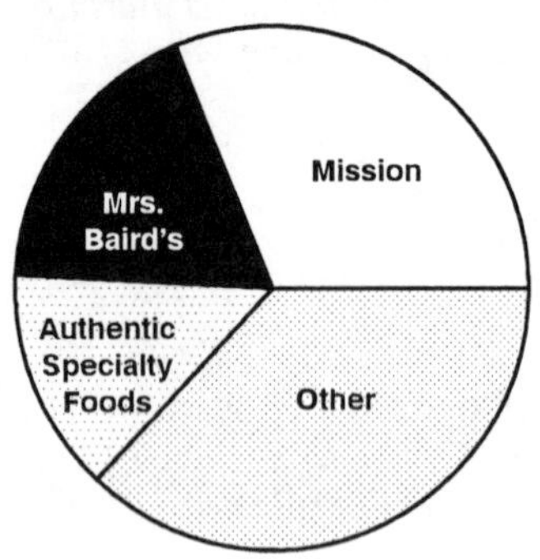

Market shares are shown in percent.

Mission	31.0%
Mrs. Baird's	18.0
Authentic Specialty Foods	14.0
Other	37.0

Source: *Latin Trade*, April 1999, p. 23.

★ 452 ★

Tortillas (SIC 2099)

Leading Refrigerated Tortilla Brands

Shares of the $179.5 milllion market are shown for the year ended May 24, 1998.

Azteca	14.7%
Pepito	6.0
La Banderita	4.7
Guerrero	4.1
Resers	3.9
Tyson	3.9
Pinata	3.8
Mission	3.5
Lynn Wilson	3.3
Private label	5.5
Other	46.6

Source: *Snack Food & Wholesale Bakery*, August 1998, p. 18, from Information Resources Inc.

SIC 21 - Tobacco Products

★ 453 ★

Cigarettes (SIC 2111)

Cigarette Industry Leaders - 1998

Unit shares are shown in percent for the second quarter of the year.

Philip Morris	48.4%
R.J. Reynolds	24.2
Brown & Williamson	15.7
Lorillard	9.2
Liggett	1.3
Other	1.2

Source: *Advertising Age*, October 26, 1998, p. 53, from *Maxwell Report*.

★ 454 ★

Cigarettes (SIC 2111)

Largest Cigarette Makers in Canada

Market shares are shown in percent.

Imperial Tobacco	64.8%
Rothmans, Benson & Hedges	23.7
RJR-Macdonald	11.5

Source: *Globe and Mail*, January 12, 1999, p. A1, from company reports.

★ 455 ★

Cigarettes (SIC 2111)

Top Cigarette Brands in Canada - 1998

Market shares are shown in percent for the year ended Decemebr 31, 1998.

Player's Light Regular	12.3%
Du Maurier King Size	9.1
Du Maurier Regular	5.7
Player's Light King Size	4.7
Du Maurier Light King Size	4.1
Player's Regular	4.1
Export A Regular	3.4%
Du Maurier Light Regular	3.2
Export A Medium Regular	2.7
Rothmans King Size	2.7
Others	48.0

Source: "Report on Market Share." Retrieved June 1, 1999 from the World Wide Web: http://www.marketingmag.ca/index.cgi?, from Canadian Tobacco Manufacturers Council.

★ 456 ★

Cigarettes (SIC 2111)

Top Cigarette Firms - 1998

Market shares are shown in percent.

Philip Morris	49.4%
RJR Nabisco	24.0
Brown & Williamson	15.0
Other	11.6

Source: *Wall Street Journal*, March 8, 1999, p. B1, from Salomon Smith Barney.

★ 457 ★

Cigarettes (SIC 2111)

Top Cigarette Firms in Mexico

Market shares are shown in percent.

Grupo Caruso	40.0%
Philip Morris Latin America	49.8
Others	0.2
Other	10.0

Source: *Investext,* Thomson Financial Networks, December 1, 1998, p. 33, from Morgan Stanley Dean Witter Research.

★ 458 ★

Cigars (SIC 2121)

Cigar Imports by Country - 1997

Data are in thousands.

Dominican Republic	268,374
Honduras	117,355
Nicaragua	43,557
Mexico	26,226
Jamaica	18,110
Netherlands	14,350
Germany	7,091
Canary Islands/Spain	5,205
Switzerland	4,277
Indonesia	2,855

Source: "Premium Cigar Imports Up 77% in 1997." Retrieved March 17, 1999 from the World Wide Web: http:// www.gosmokeshop.com/0498/signal3.htm.

★ 459 ★

Cigars (SIC 2121)

Top Cigar Vendors - 1996

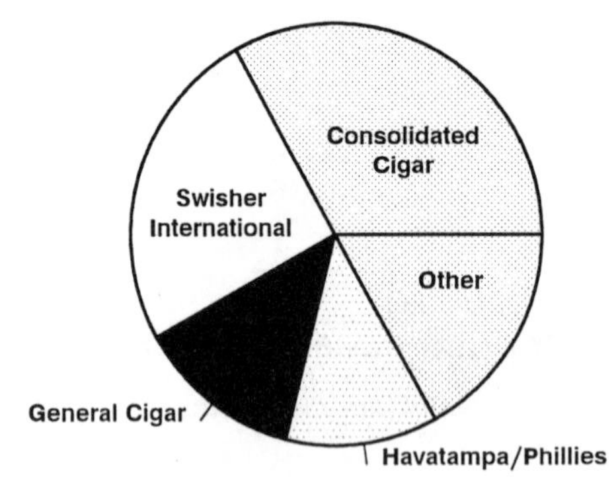

Market shares are shown based on supermarkets.

Consolidated Cigar	33.0%
Swisher International	25.0
General Cigar	13.0
Havatampa/Phillies	12.0
Other	17.0

Source: *U.S. Distribution Journal*, May/June 1998, p. 20, from Packaged Facts.

★ 460 ★

Smokeless Tobacco (SIC 2131)

Loose Leaf Market - 1997

Market shares are shown in percent.

Pinkerton	43.0%
Conwood	28.0
National	20.0
Swisher	8.0

Source: "Smokeless Slides." Retrieved May 18, 1999 from the World Wide Web: http:// tobaccos.net/ october1998feature2.asp.

★ 461 ★

Smokeless Tobacco (SIC 2131)

Smokeless Tobacco Market - 1997

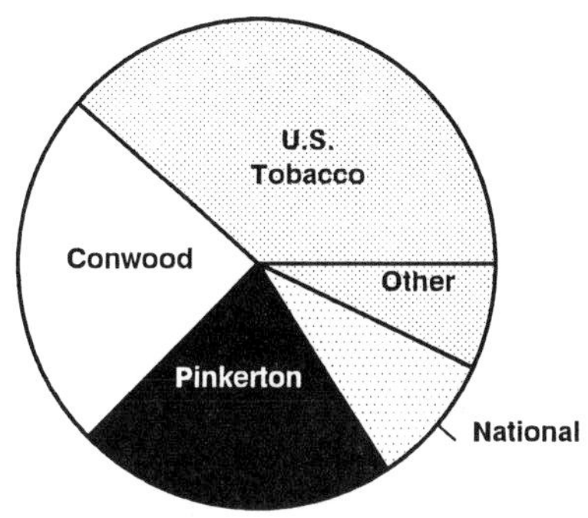

Market shares are shown in percent.

U.S. Tobacco	39.0%
Conwood	24.0
Pinkerton	21.5
National	8.9
Other	6.6

Source: "Smokeless Slides." Retrieved May 18, 1999 from the World Wide Web: http:// tobaccos.net/ october1998feature2.asp, from *Tobacco Reporter*.

★ 462 ★

Smokeless Tobacco (SIC 2131)

Snuff Market Leaders - 1997

Market shares are shown in percent.

U.S. Tobacco	79.0%
Conwood	13.0
Swisher	5.0
Other	3.0

Source: "Smokeless Slides." Retrieved May 18, 1999 from the World Wide Web: http:// tobaccos.net/ october1998feature2.asp, from *Tobacco Reporter*.

SIC 22 - Textile Mill Products

★ 463 ★

Textiles (SIC 2200)

Largest Apparel Exporters

Data show the largest shippers of apparel to the United States.

Mexico	11.8%
China	10.5
Hong Kong	9.2
Domincan Republic	5.2
Taiwan	4.8
Honduras	3.9
Indonesia	3.7
Philippines	3.7
South Korea	3.5

Source: *The Asian Wall Street Journal*, March 12, 1998, p. 5, from U.S. Department of Commerce.

★ 464 ★

Textiles (SIC 2200)

Leading Textile Firms - 1998

Firms are ranked by sales in thousands of dollars. Figures are for the first nine months of the year.

Springs Industries	$ 1,672,130
Burlington Industries	1,528,711
Unifi	1,033,486
Galey & Lord	775,504
Wellman	761,400
Cone Mills	574,834
Delta Woodside	402,013
Dan River	358,128
Dyersburg	325,625

Source: *WWD*, November 17, 1998, p. 9.

★ 465 ★

Textiles (SIC 2200)

Textile Market by Segment

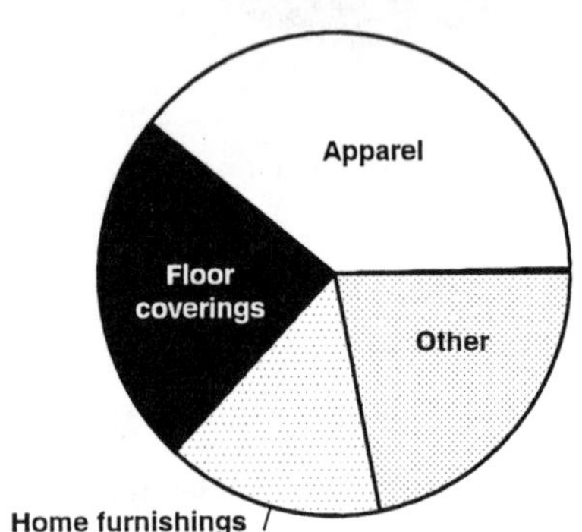

Apparel	39.0%
Floor coverings	24.0
Home furnishings	15.0
Other	22.0

Source: *Textile World*, January 1999, p. 55, from Fiber Organon.

★ 466 ★

Apparel (SIC 2211)

Largest Terry Makers

Companies are ranked by sales in millions of dollars.

WestPoint Stevens	$ 700
Pillowtex	690
Springs Industries	220
Santens of America	45
Blair Mills	39

Source: *Textile World*, May 1999, p. 30, from company information and stock analysts.

★ 467 ★

Apparel (SIC 2250)

U.S. Knit Apparel Imports - 1998

Shares are shown for the first six months of the year. Total imports reached $9.34 billion.

Sweaters, pullovers, vests	32.5%
T-shirts, singlets	15.5
Men's & boy's shirts	12.2
Women's & girl's slips & pajamas	7.7
Women's & girl's suits & ensembles	7.5
Women's & girl's shirts & blouses	5.3
Infants garments and accessories	5.0
Hosiery	3.2
Men's & boy's underwear & pajamas	2.9
Other	8.2

Source: *Textile Asia*, November 1998, p. 128.

★ 468 ★

Hosiery (SIC 2252)

Hosiery Production - 1997

Data are in dozens of pairs.

	(000)	Share
Socks	286,404	67.01%
Sheer hosiery	120,298	28.15
Tights/opaques	20,694	4.84

Source: *Textile World*, October 1998, p. 74.

★ 469 ★

Hosiery (SIC 2252)

Hosiery Sales by Segment

Figures are based on dollar volume.

	1997	1998
Casual socks	42.04%	41.35%
Athletic socks	34.63	34.35
Dress socks	11.76	12.07
Other	11.57	12.24

Source: *Discount Merchandiser*, January 1999, p. 98, from NPD American Shoppers Panel.

★ 470 ★

Hosiery (SIC 2252)

Men's Sock Market - 1997

Sales are shown in billions of dollars.

	($ bil.)	Share
Athletic	$ 1.00	53.48%
Dress/casual	0.87	46.52

Source: *Discount Merchandiser*, August 1998, p. 3, from NPD Group Inc. and Kayser-Roth.

★ 471 ★

Hosiery (SIC 2252)

U.S. Legwear Market - 1997

Sales are shown in billions of dollars.

	($ bil.)	Share
Women's	$ 4.3	55.13%
Men's	2.0	25.64
Children's	1.5	19.23

Source: *Discount Merchandiser*, August 1998, p. 3, from NPD Group Inc. and Kayser-Roth.

★ 472 ★

Carpets (SIC 2273)

Top Carpet Makers - 1997

Market shares are shown in percent.

Shaw Industries	34.0%
Mohawk Industries	19.0
Beaulieu of America	11.0
Interface	8.0
World Carpet	4.6
Other	23.4

Source: *Wall Street Journal*, August 19, 1998, p. B4, from *Floor Focus* and Baseline.

★ 473 ★

Yarn and Thread (SIC 2280)

U.S. Yarn/Thread Imports

Market shares are shown by country for the first eight months of the year.

Canada	27.4%
Mexico	10.7
Korea	7.3
Germany	6.5
Japan	5.1
Italy	4.0
Other	29.0

Source: *Textile Asia*, December 1998, p. 122.

★ 474 ★

Homefurnishings (SIC 2299)

Largest Home Textile Makers - 1997

Shipments are shown in millions of dollars.

WestPoint Stevens	$ 1,670
Springs	1,662
Pillowtex	1,630
Burlington	307
Crown Crafts	306
Dan River	256

Source: *ATI*, October 1998, p. 46.

SIC 23 - Apparel and Other Textile Products

★ 475 ★

Apparel (SIC 2300)

Jeans Market - 1998

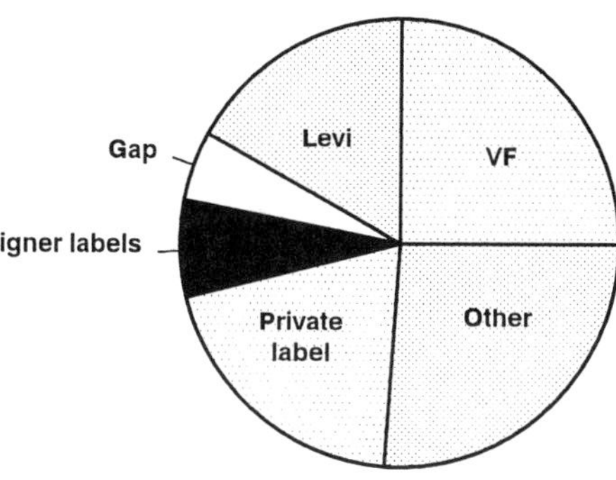

Shares are shown for the first half of the year. Gap includes Gap, Banana Republic, and Old Navy. VF includes Lee and Wrangler.

VF	25.3%
Levi	16.9
Gap	4.9
Designer labels	7.0
Private label	20.2
Other	25.7

Source: *Los Angeles Times*, November 17, 1998, p. C2, from Tactical Retail Monitor.

★ 476 ★

Apparel (SIC 2300)

Largest Apparel Firms - 1997

Firms are ranked by sales in billions of dollars.

Sara Lee Personal Products	$ 7.3
VF Corp.	5.2
Nike Inc.	2.8
Liz Claiborne Inc.	2.4
Fruit of the Loom Inc.	2.1
Kellwood Co.	1.7
Ralph Lauren	1.4
Warnaco Group	$ 1.4
Jones Apparel Group	1.3
Phillips-Van Heusen Corp.	1.3

Source: *Bobbin*, June 1998, p. 58.

★ 477 ★

Apparel (SIC 2300)

Largest Beach Apparel Makers - 1997

Companies are ranked by sales in millions of dollars.

Quiksilver	$ 151
No Fear	95
Big Dog	86
Hang Ten	81
Gotcha	74
Ocean Pacific	72
Mossimo	71
Rusty	58

Source: *Sportstyle*, May 1998, p. 22.

★ 478 ★

Apparel (SIC 2300)

Largest Bodywear Makers - 1997

Companies are ranked by sales in millions of dollars.

Jacques Moret	$ 98.0
Danskin	82.0
Rainbeau/Flyte	80.0
Marika	35.0
S.F. City Lights	20.0

Source: *Sportstyle*, May 1998, p. 22.

★ 479 ★

Apparel (SIC 2300)

Largest Branded Activewear Makers - 1997

Companies are ranked by sales in millions of dollars.

Nike	$ 1,431
Adidas	465
Reebok	432
Russell Athletic	260
Sara Lee Casualwear	250
Fila	177
Champion	150

Source: *Sportstyle*, May 1998, p. 22.

★ 480 ★

Apparel (SIC 2300)

Largest Licensed Apparel Makers - 1997

Companies are ranked by sales are in millions of dollars.

VF Corp. Licensing	$ 326
Starter	270
Logo 7	262
Fruit of the Loom Sports & Licensing	230
Champion	185
Nike	140
Russell Licensed Products	122
Haddad (Mighty Mac)	100

Source: *Sportstyle*, May 1998, p. 20.

★ 481 ★

Apparel (SIC 2300)

Largest Licensed Apparel Properties - 1997

Sales are shown in millions of dollars.

NFL	$ 2,865
Collegiate Licensing Company	2,500
NBA	2,400
MLB	1,740
NHL	1,150
NASCAR	800
IMS Properties	79
WNBA	40

Source: *Sportstyle*, May 1998, p. 20.

★ 482 ★

Apparel (SIC 2300)

Largest Outdoor Apparel Makers - 1997

Companies are ranked by sales are in millions of dollars.

Columbia	$ 250.3
Timberland	144.6
Woolrich	130.0
Patagonia	99.0
The North Face	77.5
Pacific Trail	75.0
Helly-Hansen	40.5
Gramicci	24.0
Marmot Mountain	23.0
Royal Robbins	23.0

Source: *Sportstyle*, May 1998, p. 20.

★ 483 ★

Apparel (SIC 2300)

Largest Performance Apparel Makers - 1997

Companies are ranked by sales in millions of dollars.

Speedo/Authentic Fitness	$ 200
Champion Jogbra	77
Pearl Izumi	30
Tyr	28
Insport	18

Source: *Sportstyle*, May 1998, p. 22.

★ 484 ★

Apparel (SIC 2300)

Largest Ski/Snowboard Apparel Makers - 1997

Companies are ranked by sales are in millions of dollars.

Burton	$ 40.7
Snowmass Apparel	35.0
Sport Obermeyer	34.2
Bogner	20.0
The North Face	15.5
Roffe	13.0
Spyder	11.1

Continued on next page.

★ 484 ★ *Continued*

Apparel (SIC 2300)

Largest Ski/Snowboard Apparel Makers - 1997

Companies are ranked by sales are in millions of dollars.

Nordica	$ 11.0
Nils	9.5

Source: *Sportstyle*, May 1998, p. 20.

★ 485 ★

Apparel (SIC 2300)

Sports Logo Market - 1997

T-shirts	37.0%
Fleece tops	22.6
Jackets	13.5
Knit shirts	12.0
Caps/hats	7.4
Shorts	3.0
Warm-up suits	2.7
Fleece bottoms	1.8

Source: *Stores*, July 1998, p. 16, from National Sporting Goods Association.

★ 486 ★

Apparel (SIC 2300)

Sports Logo Sales - 1997

	($ mil.)	Share
T-shirts	$ 1,040	36.98%
Fleece tops	635	22.58
Jackets	381	13.55
Knit shirts	338	12.02
Caps/hats	208	7.40
Shorts	84	2.99
Warm-up suits	75	2.67
Fleece bottoms	51	1.81

Source: *Sporting Goods Business*, June 22, 1998, p. 20, from National Sporting Goods Association.

★ 487 ★

Apparel (SIC 2300)

Uniform Apparel Market - 1998

Total sales in key categories reached $904.63 million.

	($ mil.)	Share
Tops	$ 408.9	45.0%
Bottoms	239.2	26.0
Jumpers/dresses/skirts/shorts	88.4	10.0
Hosiery	82.5	9.0
Sweats and warmups	49.6	6.0
Sweaters/sportscoats	35.8	4.0

Source: *Discount Merchandiser*, April 1999, p. 122, from NPD American Shoppers Panel.

★ 488 ★

Apparel (SIC 2320)

Men's and Boy's Clothing Sales

Sales are shown in billions of dollars.

Chicago, IL	$ 2.34
New York, NY	2.17
Los Angeles-Long Beach, CA	1.89
Washington D.C.	1.45
Philadelphia, PA	1.33

Source: *Sales & Marketing Management*, August 1998, p. 194.

★ 489 ★

Apparel (SIC 2325)

Men's Jeans Sales - 1998

Sales refer to men 16 and older.

Lee and Wrangler	31.9%
Levi's	25.0
Private label	20.4
Other	22.7

Source: *Fortune*, April 12, 1999, p. 85, from Tactical Retail Monitor.

SIC 24 - Lumber and Wood Products

★ 490 ★

Lumber (SIC 2411)

Southern Pine Lumber Sales - 1997

Decks	40.7%
Landscaping	16.4
Fences	11.7
Marine	11.0
Highway	9.0
Other	11.4

Source: *Building Material Dealer*, October 1998, p. 20.

★ 491 ★

Paneling (SIC 2421)

Canada's Panel Production - 1996

Data are in millions of feet. OSB stands for oriented-strand board.

OSB	4,684
Particleboard	2,072
Construction plywood	1,814
Fiberboard	468

Source: *Wood Technology*, October 1998, p. 46, from Statistics Canada.

★ 492 ★

Paneling (SIC 2421)

U.S. Panel Production - 1996

Data are in millions of feet.

Structural panels	28,495
Hardboard	5,279
Particleboard	4,367
Medium-density fiberboard	1,200

Source: *Wood Technology*, October 1998, p. 46, from American Particleboard Association, Composite Panel Association, and American Hardboard Association.

★ 493 ★

Hardwood (SIC 2426)

Hardwood Plywood Sales - 1995

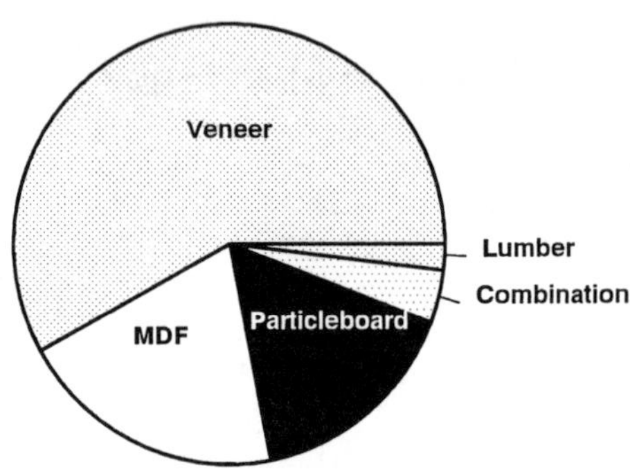

Sales are shown in percent. MDF stands for medium-density fiberboard.

Veneer	58.0%
MDF	20.0
Particleboard	16.0
Combination	4.0
Lumber	2.0

Source: *Forest Products Journal*, no. 5, 1998, p. 23.

★ 494 ★

Hardwood (SIC 2426)

Popular Hardwood Species - 1997

Oak	55.0%
Maple	51.0
Poplar	34.0
Cherry	29.0
Mahogany	14.0
Birch	10.0

Continued on next page.

★ 494 ★ *Continued*

Hardwood (SIC 2426)

Popular Hardwood Species - 1997

Walnut	8.0%
Ash	7.0
Alder	4.0
Hickory	4.0

Source: *Wood & Wood Products*, December 1998, p. 47, from Vance Research Services.

★ 495 ★

Lumber (SIC 2426)

Softwood Lumber Demand

Data are in billion board feet.

	1998	1999
United States	52.30	50.60
Canada	6.45	5.90

Source: *Wood Technology*, January/February 1999, p. 22, from National Association of Home Builders, APA-The Engineered Wood Association, Western Wood Products Association, and *World Wood Review*.

★ 496 ★

Paneling (SIC 2426)

Structural Panel Production

Data are in billion square feet.

	1998	1999
United States	29.06	28.64
Canada	9.55	9.62

Source: *Wood Technology*, January/February 1999, p. 22, from National Association of Home Builders, APA-The Engineered Wood Association, Western Wood Products Association, and *World Wood Review*.

★ 497 ★

Wood Products (SIC 2426)

Wood I-Joist Production

Data are in millions of linear feet.

	1998	1999
United States	680	775
Canada	105	120

Source: *Wood Technology*, January/February 1999, p. 22, from National Association of Home Builders, APA-The Engineered Wood Association, Western Wood Products Association, and *World Wood Review*.

★ 498 ★

Cabinets (SIC 2434)

Popular Cabinet Materials

Data refer to both kitchens and bathrooms.

Maple	40.0%
Cherry	20.0
Oak	20.0
Laminate	10.0
Pine	10.0

Source: *Do-It-Yourself Retailing*, April 1999, p. 90.

★ 499 ★

Paneling (SIC 2435)

Industrial Panel Market - 1997

The market is shown by end use.

Furniture	44.0%
Cabinets/vanities/countertops	21.0
Doors	12.0
Moulding & millwork	8.0
Wall paneling	4.0
Flooring	2.0

Source: *Wood & Wood Products*, January 1999, p. 106.

★ 500 ★

Paneling (SIC 2436)

U.S. Paneling Market

The market is shown by end use.

Furniture	44.0%
Moulding & millwork	21.0
Doors	9.0
Wall paneling	9.0
Cabinets	8.0
Displays	6.0
Flooring	2.0

Source: *Wood Digest*, March 1999, p. 117.

★ 501 ★

Manufactured Homes (SIC 2451)

Largest Manufactured Housing Makers

Companies are ranked by revenues in millions of dollars.

Champion Enterprises Inc.	$ 1,898.5
Fleetwood Enterprises Inc.	1,547.9
Oakwood Homes Corp.	1,404.4
Clayton Homes Inc.	880.8
Palm Harbor Homes Inc.	637.2

Source: *Professional Builder*, April 1999, p. 108.

★ 502 ★

Manufactured Homes (SIC 2451)

Manufactured Homes Market - 1997

Market shares are shown in percent.

Fleetwood	18.1%
Champion	17.7
Clayton	7.8
Cavalier	7.5
Oakwood	7.3
Other	41.6

Source: "Manufactured Housing." Retrieved February 18, 1999 from the World Wide Web: http://www.fleetwoodhomes.com/annualpg.html, from *Manufactured Home Merchandiser*.

★ 503 ★

Manufactured Homes (SIC 2451)

Manufactured Housing Shipments

Data show unit shipments.

	No.	Share
Texas	37,154	10.75%
North Carolina	33,318	9.64
Georgia	21,412	6.20
South Carolina	20,062	5.81
Florida	18,971	5.49
Alabama	17,323	5.01
Tennessee	15,393	4.45
Michigan	11,836	3.42
Kentucky	11,723	3.39
Other	158,402	45.83

Source: *Builder*, September 1998, p. 86, from Manufactured Housing Institute.

★ 504 ★

Manufactured Homes (SIC 2451)

Top Manufactured Housing Shippers

Data show unit shipments.

Fleetwood Enterprises	63,869
Champion Enterprises	62,543
Clayton Homes	27,543
Cavalier Homes	26,583
Oakwood Homes	25,793
Skyline Corp.	17,033
Palm Harbor Homes	14,122
Horton Homes	10,696
Southern Energy Homes	9,166
Fairmont Homes	9,141

Source: *Builder*, September 1998, p. 86, from *Manufactured Home Merchandiser.*

★ 505 ★

Mobile Homes (SIC 2451)

Mobile Home Supply Market

Data refer to the market for roof trusses and floor joists.

Company	Share
Universal Forest Products Inc.	65.0%
Other	35.0

Source: *Investor's Business Daily*, May 6, 1999, p. A10.

SIC 25 - Furniture and Fixtures

★ 506 ★

Furniture (SIC 2500)

Canada's Furniture Industry

The market has experienced growth from an increase in construction, low rates and strong consumer confidence.

Household furniture	45.1%
Office furniture	25.8
Hotel, restaurant and institutional	18.3
Other furniture/fixtures	10.8

Source: *National Trade Data Bank*, May 18, 1998, p. ISA990301.

★ 507 ★

Furniture (SIC 2500)

Largest Contract Furniture Makers

Companies are ranked by sales in millions of dollars.

Steelcase Inc.	$ 2,760.0
Herman Miller Inc.	1,720.0
Hon Industries	1,700.0
Haworth Inc.	1,540.0
The Global Group	1,200.0
Knoll Inc.	948.7
Kimball Intl.	647.6
Krueger Intl.	550.0
Virco Mfg. Corp.	273.6
Flexsteel Industries Inc.	236.1

Source: *Wood & Wood Products*, May 1999, p. 64.

★ 508 ★

Furniture (SIC 2500)

Largest Furniture Makers

Companies are ranked by sales in millions of dollars.

Life Style Furnishings Intl.	$ 1,959.0
Furniture Brands Intl.	1,808.0
La-Z-Boy Inc.	1,000.0
Ethan Allen Interiors	571.8
LADD Furniture Inc.	525.5
Sauder Woodworking	500.0
Bassett Furniture	446.8
Dorel Industries Inc.	384.1
Bush Industries	325.2
O'Sullivan Ind. Holdings	321.5

Source: *Wood & Wood Products*, June 1998, p. 56.

★ 509 ★

Furniture (SIC 2500)

Leading RTA Furniture Firms

Sales are shown in millions of dollars. RTA stands for ready-to-assemble.

Sauder	$ 530.0
Bush	384.3
O'Sullivan	362.2

Source: *Furniture Today*, May 10, 1999, p. 16, from company reports.

★ 510 ★

Furniture (SIC 2500)

Top Furniture/Bedding Markets - 2002

Sales are shown in millions of dollars.

Chicago, IL	$ 2,779.6
Washington	2,019.0
Atlanta	1,577.8
New York City	1,530.1
Detroit	1,401.0
Los Angeles-Long Beach	1,287.0
Phoenix-Mesa	1,098.8
Dallas	1,064.6
Philadelphia	973.4
Minneapolis-St. Paul	952.8

Source: *Furniture Today Retail Planning Guide*, 1999, p. 34.

★ 511 ★

Furniture (SIC 2511)

Upholstered Wood Frame Seats

Shipments are shown in thousands of dollars.

Italy	$ 276,201
Mexico	97,622
Canada	69,639
China	13,157
Taiwan	4,922

Source: *Furniture Today*, May 3, 1999, p. 27, from U.S. International Trade Commission.

★ 512 ★

Furniture (SIC 2511)

Wood Bedroom Furniture Imports - 1998

Shipments are shown in thousands of dollars.

Canada	$ 253,539
Mexico	122,174
Italy	74,439
China	52,634
Indonesia	37,477

Source: *Furniture Today*, May 3, 1999, p. 27, from U.S. International Trade Commission.

★ 513 ★

Furniture (SIC 2511)

Wood Dining Table Imports - 1998

Shipments are shown in thousands of dollars.

China	$ 60,339
Malaysia	59,631
Taiwan	34,282
Italy	19,229
Canada	15,005

Source: *Furniture Today*, from U.S. International Trade Commission.

★ 514 ★

Furniture (SIC 2514)

Metal Household Furniture Imports

Shipments are shown in thousands of dollars.

China	$ 232,315
Taiwan	130,944
Mexico	112,755
Philippines	35,740
Canada	32,727

Source: *Furniture Today*, May 3, 1999, p. 27, from U.S. International Trade Commission.

★ 515 ★

Furniture (SIC 2519)

Rattan Furniture Imports - 1998

Shipments are shown in thousands of dollars.

China	$ 36,572
Philippines	22,595
Indonesia	12,350
Hong Kong	3,620
Thailand	796

Source: *Furniture Today*, May 3, 1999, p. 27, from U.S. International Trade Commission.

★ 516 ★

Office Furniture (SIC 2520)

Home Office Sales

Sales are shown at electronic specialty stores for the first two months of the year.

Desk/workcenters	62.8%
Computer carts	17.2
Armoire	12.5
Printer/utility carts	5.4
Other	2.1

Source: *HFN*, April 12, 1999, p. 88, from NPD's Hometrack.

★ 517 ★

Office Furniture (SIC 2520)

Largest Office Furniture Makers in Dallas, TX - 1997

Sales are shown in millions of dollars.

Business Interiors	$ 83.0
Goldsmith's Inc. of Texas	55.0
Wilson Office Interiors	54.9
Furniture Marketing Group Inc.	40.0
BKM Total Office of Texas Inc.	31.5

Source: *Dallas Business Journal*, July 24, 1998, p. C11.

★ 518 ★

Office Furniture (SIC 2520)

Office Product Shipments - 1998

Systems	36.8%
Seating	24.5
Files	12.9
Desks	10.2
Tables	6.5
Storage	5.3
Other	3.8

Source: "The U.S. Office Furniture Market." Retrieved June 1, 1999 from the World Wide Web: http://www.bifma.com/statover.html, from Business and Institutional Furniture Manufacturers Association.

★ 519 ★

Fixtures (SIC 2541)

Top Fixture Makers - 1997

Companies are ranked by fixture sales in millions of dollars.

OSF Inc.	$ 192
Madix Store Fixtures	160
Oklahoma Fixture Co.	78
Hamilton Fixture	65
Ready Fixtures	60
MII Inc. Fixture Group	50
Goer Manufacturing Co.	48
Econoco Corporation	43
Dan Dee Display Fixtures	42
J.D. Store Equipment Inc.	42

Source: *VM+SD*, October 1998, p. 39.

SIC 26 - Paper and Allied Products

★ 520 ★

Paper (SIC 2600)

Largest Paper Companies in Canada

Companies are ranked by net sales of pulp, paper and converted products in millions of dollars. Shares of the group are shown in percent.

	($ mil.)	% of Group
Abitibi-Consolidated Inc.	$ 3,577	23.87%
Cascades Inc.	2,208	14.73
Domlar Inc.	1,750	11.68
Avanor Inc.	1,604	10.70
Fletcher Challenge Canada Ltd.	1,350	9.01
Noranda Forest Inc.	1,280	8.54
Donohue Inc.	1,207	8.05
MacMillan Bloedel Ltd.	1,009	6.73
Kruger Inc.	1,000	6.67

Source: *PIMA's Papermaker*, June 1998, p. 63.

★ 521 ★

Paper (SIC 2600)

Largest U.S. Paper Companies

Companies are ranked by net sales of pulp, paper and converted products in millions of dollars. Shares of the group are shown in percent.

	($ mil.)	% of Group
International Paper Co.	$ 15,190	19.56%
Kimberly-Clark Corp.	12,600	16.22
Procter & Gamble Co.	10,113	13.02
Fort James Corp.	7,439	9.58
Unisource Worldwide Inc.	7,108	9.15
Georgia-Pacific Corp.	5,556	7.15
The Mead Corp.	$ 5,335	6.87%
Stone Container Corp.	4,849	6.24
Champion International Corp.	4,767	6.14
Weyerhaeuser Co.	4,704	6.06

Source: *PIMA's Papermaker*, June 1998, p. 63.

★ 522 ★

Pulp (SIC 2611)

Top Pulp Makers in North America

Market shares are shown based on total capacity of 17.945 million metric tons.

Weyerhaeuser	12.1%
Georgia-Pacific	9.5
Stone Container	6.3
International Paper	6.1
Parsons & Whittemore	6.1
Avenor	4.7
Champion	4.3
Fletcher Challenge Canada	4.0
Canfor	3.7
Skeena Cellulose	2.3
Other	40.9

Source: *Pulp & Paper*, August 1998, p. 11.

★ 523 ★

Paper (SIC 2621)

Largest Newsprint Makers

Market shares are shown based on total capacity. Figures are for North America.

Abitibi-Consolidated	21.9%
Bowater	17.0
Donohue	12.8
Kruger	6.2
Fletcher Challenge Canada	4.5
North Pacific Paper	4.3
Smurfit Newsprint	4.3
Other	29.0

Source: *Wall Street Journal*, January 28, 1999, p. B14, from *Pulp & Paper Week*, Canadian Pulp and Paper Association, and American Forest & Paper Association.

★ 524 ★

Paper (SIC 2621)

Largest Semi-Chemical Corrugating Medium Producers - 1999

Market shares are estimated in percent.

Smurfit-Stone Container	13.0%
Weyerhaeuser	10.0
Georgia-Pacific	9.0
Mead	8.0
International Paper	6.0
Temple-Inland	5.0
Willamette	4.0
Other	43.0

Source: *Investext,* Thomson Financial Networks, December 10, 1998, p. 48.

★ 525 ★

Paper (SIC 2621)

Uncoated Free Sheet Producers - 1999

Market shares are estimated in percent.

International Paper	21.0%
Georgia-Pacific	15.0
Boise Cascade	10.0
Union Camp	9.0
Champion International	8.0
Weyerhaeuser	8.0
Fort James	3.0
Mead	1.0
Other	25.0

Source: *Investext,* Thomson Financial Networks, December 10, 1998, p. 59.

★ 526 ★

Paper (SIC 2621)

Uncoated Groundwood Market

Shares are shown based on annual capacity. Figures are for North America.

Abitibi-Consolidated	28.4%
Bowater	7.3
Stora North America	7.0
Alliance	6.8
Pacifica Papers	5.1
Champion	4.4
Consolidated (LSPI)	4.4
Daishowa	4.4
St. Mary's	4.1
Madison Paper	4.0
Other	26.0

Source: *Pulp & Paper*, September 1998, p. 13.

★ 527 ★

Paperboard (SIC 2650)

Bleached Paperboard Market

Shares are shown based on total capacity of 7.2 million tons. Figures are for North America.

International Paper	34.1%
Westvaco	13.2
Temple-Inland	10.1
Potlatch	8.5
Georgia-Pacific	5.7

Continued on next page.

★ 527 ★ *Continued*

Paperboard (SIC 2650)

Bleached Paperboard Market

Shares are shown based on total capacity of 7.2 million tons. Figures are for North America.

Champion Intl.	4.1%
Gulf States Paper	3.7
James River	3.1
Weyerhaeuser	3.1
Gilman Paper	2.8
Other	11.6

Source: *Pulp & Paper*, October 1998, p. 13.

★ 528 ★

Paperboard (SIC 2650)

Largest Linerboard Makers - 1998

Market shares are shown based on total capacity.

Smurfit Stone	19.0%
Georgia-Pacific	9.0
International Paper	9.0
Temple-Inland	8.0
Union Camp	7.0
Weyerhaeuser	6.0
Tenneco	.0
Other	37.0

Source: *Paperboard Packaging*, December 1998, p. 24, from Merrill Lynch.

★ 529 ★

Paperboard (SIC 2650)

Largest Linerboard Makers - 1999

Market shares are estimated in percent.

International Paper	16.0%
Smurfit-Stone Container	16.0
Georgia-Pacific	10.0
Temple-Inland	8.0
Weyerhaeuser	7.0
Willamette	5.0
Gaylord	4.0
Boise Cascade	2.0
Other	30.0

Source: *Investext,* Thomson Financial Networks, December 10, 1998, p. 48.

★ 530 ★

Paperboard (SIC 2650)

Largest Paperboard Producers - 1999

Market shares are estimated in percent.

International Paper	36.0%
Westvaco	14.0
Temple-Inland	10.0
Potlatch	8.0
Champion International	4.0
Fort James	4.0
Union Camp	4.0
Smurfit-Stone Container	3.0
Weyerhaeuser	3.0
Other	14.0

Source: *Investext,* Thomson Financial Networks, December 10, 1998, p. 36.

★ 531 ★

Paperboard (SIC 2650)

Largest Recycled Paperboard Firms - 1999

Market shares are estimated in percent.

Caraustar	13.0%
Rock Tenn	13.0
Sonoco	12.0
Smurfit-Stone Container	10.0
Fort James	4.0
International Paper	2.0
Other	45.0

Source: *Investext,* Thomson Financial Networks, December 10, 1998, p. 54.

★ 532 ★

Paperboard (SIC 2650)

Unbleached Kraft Producers - 1999

Market shares are estimated in percent.

International Paper	24.0%
Smurfit-Stone Container	24.0
Longview Fiber	22.0
Georgia-Pacific	12.0
Other	19.0

Source: *Investext,* Thomson Financial Networks, December 10, 1998, p. 57.

★ 533 ★
Boxes (SIC 2652)

Rigid Box Shipments - 1998

Total shipments reached $519 million.

	($ mil.)	Share
Confections	$ 85.9	16.55%
Jewelry, silverware	66.1	12.74
Drugs, chemicals, pharmaceuticals	48.4	9.33
Stationery, office supplies	42.7	8.23
Toys and games	29.9	5.76
Other	246.0	47.40

Source: *Paperboard Packaging*, January 1999, p. 33.

★ 534 ★
Containers (SIC 2653)

Corrugated Container Market - 1999

Data show share of total square footage.

Food, meat, dairy, bakery, etc.	40.2%
Paper, allied products	23.4
Toys and sporting goods	5.7
Chemical & allied products	4.9
Rubber products	4.2
Stone, clay, glass	4.1
Electrical machinery, radios, etc.	3.8
Other	13.7

Source: *Paperboard Packaging*, January 1999, p. 20, from Paperboard Packaging Council.

★ 535 ★
Paperboard (SIC 2653)

Container Market Sales - 1999

Sales are shown in millions of dollars.

	($ mil.)
Corrugated/solid fiber	$ 19,862
Folding cartons	5,223
Sanitary food containers	3,686
Fibre cans/tubes/drums	1,646
Rigid boxes	526

Source: *Paperboard Packaging*, January 1999, p. 20, from Paperboard Packaging Council.

★ 536 ★
Containers (SIC 2656)

Food Container Sales - 1997

Paperboard	39.0%
Metal	26.0
Plastic	21.0
Glass	12.0

Source: *Chemical & Engineering News*, June 15, 1998, p. 27, from Freedonia Group.

★ 537 ★
Cartons (SIC 2657)

Folding Carton Shipments - 1998

Total shipments reached $5.1 billion.

	($ mil.)	Share
Dry food	$ 825.8	16.11%
Wet foods	610.0	11.90
Carriers	445.6	8.69
Paper goods	436.0	8.51
Medicinals	411.6	8.03
Other	2,397.0	46.76

Source: *Paperboard Packaging*, January 1999, p. 33.

★ 538 ★
Paper (SIC 2672)

Largest Coated Groundwood Producers

Market shares are shown in percent.

Consolidated Papers	18.3%
Champion International	12.4
International Paper	10.1
Mead	10.1
Bowater	8.8
Repap	8.8
Blandin	8.5
Crown Vantage	5.5
Pacifica Papers	3.7
Weyerhaeuser	3.6
Other	10.2

Source: *Pulp & Paper*, May 1999, p. 13.

★ 539 ★

Diapers (SIC 2676)

Diaper Market Leaders

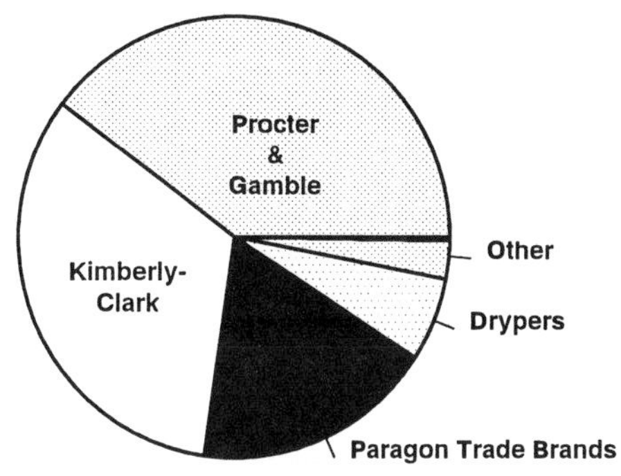

Market shares are shown in percent.

Procter & Gamble	40.0%
Kimberly-Clark	33.0
Paragon Trade Brands	18.0
Drypers	6.0
Other	3.0

Source: "Diaper Business Turns Dirty." Retrieved May 7, 1999 from the World Wide Web: http://more.abcnews.go.com/sections/business/diaper_wars.

★ 540 ★

Diapers (SIC 2676)

Top Diaper Brands - 1998

Shares are shown of the $3.8 billion market for the year ended August 23, 1998.

Huggies	40.7%
Pampers	26.0
Luvs	12.3
Drypers	3.5
Fitti	0.8
Baby Choice	0.1
Comfees	0.1
Cuddles	0.1
Snuggems	0.1
Other	16.3

Source: *Discount Merchandiser*, November 1998, p. 114, from Information Resources Inc.

★ 541 ★

Diapers (SIC 2676)

Top Diaper Makers - 1998

Market shares are shown based on both diapers and training paints.

Kimberly-Clark	40.7%
Procter & Gamble	37.9
Other	21.4

Source: *Advertising Age*, April 5, 1999, p. 14, from Salomon Smith Barney and Information Resources Inc.

★ 542 ★

Stationery (SIC 2678)

Stationery Product Sales - 1997

Total supermarket sales for the category reached $1.02 billion.

	($ mil.)	Share
School/office supplies	$ 343.10	33.61%
Writing instruments	261.17	25.59
Tapes	105.57	10.34
Tablets	64.79	6.35
Crayons, chalk, markers	56.75	5.56
Paste and glue	34.30	3.36
Playing cards, chips	23.32	2.28
Other	131.78	12.91

Source: *Progressive Grocer*, August 1998, p. 55, from Information Resources Inc.

SIC 27 - Printing and Publishing

★ 543 ★

Printing (SIC 2700)

Largest In-Plant Printers

Sales are shown in millions of dollars. Shares of the group are shown in percent.

	($ mil.)	% of Group
U.S. Government Printing Office	$ 195.9	51.07%
California Office of State Publishing	58.1	15.15
Boeing	19.1	4.98
USAA	18.1	4.72
Cigna Printing & Distribution	16.0	4.17
Pitney Bowles	16.0	4.17
University of Washington	15.8	4.12
Spartan Stores	15.1	3.94
Allstate Print Communications Center	15.0	3.91
Bankers Systems	14.5	3.78

Source: *In-Plant Graphics*, December 1998, p. 31.

★ 544 ★

Printing (SIC 2700)

Largest Metro Printing Markets - 1997

Shipments are shown in billions of dollars.

	($ bil.)	Share
Chicago, IL	$ 6.5	4.58%
New York, NY	4.7	3.31
Los Angeles, CA	4.5	3.17
Boston, MA	4.3	3.03
Philadelphia, PA	4.0	2.82
Minneapolis, MN	3.5	2.46
Atlanta, GA	2.3	1.62
Dallas, TX	2.1	1.48
Newark, NJ	2.0	1.41
Milwaukee, WI	$ 1.9	1.34%
Other	106.2	74.79

Source: *American Ink Maker*, October 1998, p. 10, from Printing Industries of America.

★ 545 ★

Printing (SIC 2700)

Largest Printing Markets - 1999

Data show the printing potential in billions of dollars. The potential of the top 25 catgeories show $125.1 billion.

Telecommunications equipment/services	$ 13.1
Computer software	11.8
Publishing/newspapers	11.8
Automotive	7.3
Beverages	7.2
Banking/insurance	6.7
Packaged foods	6.0
Fashion	5.9
Healthcare	5.9
Home improvement	5.9

Source: *American Printer*, December 1998, p. 43, from PB/BA International.

★ 546 ★

Printing (SIC 2700)

Largest Printing Markets by State - 1997

Shipments are shown in billions of dollars.

	($ bil.)	Share
California	$ 13.1	9.23%
New York	10.7	7.54
Illinois	10.5	7.39
Pennsylvania	8.6	6.06
New Jersey	6.9	4.86

Continued on next page.

★ 546 ★ *Continued*

Printing (SIC 2700)

Largest Printing Markets by State - 1997

Shipments are shown in billions of dollars.

	($ bil.)	Share
Ohio	$ 6.7	4.72%
Texas	6.4	4.51
Wisconsin	5.4	3.80
Massachusetts	4.8	3.38
Michigan	4.8	3.38
Other	64.1	45.14

Source: *American Ink Maker*, October 1998, p. 10, from Printing Industries of America.

★ 547 ★

Printing (SIC 2700)

Printing Sales by Region - 1998

Sales are shown in billions of dollars.

	($ mil.)	Share
North Central	$ 19.9	24.24%
Mid-Atlantic	17.9	21.80
Southern	17.2	20.95
Pacific	10.3	12.55
Plains	8.9	10.84
New England	4.9	5.97
Mountain	3.0	3.65

Source: *American Printer*, December 1998, p. 35.

★ 548 ★

Printing (SIC 2700)

Top Catalog Printers - 1997

Companies are ranked by catalog revenues in millions of dollars.

R.R. Donnelley & Sons	$ 1,320.0
Quebecor	525.0
Quad/Graphics	479.3
World Color	443.1
Banta Corp.	216.8
Arandell	141.2
Brown Printing	125.0

Source: *Catalog Age*, June 1998, p. 218, from *Printing Impressions*.

★ 549 ★

Newspapers (SIC 2711)

Canada's Newspaper Market - 1998

Market shares are shown in percent.

Southam	29.5%
Hollinger	24.8
Sun Media	14.8
Thomson	7.6
Power Corp.	3.8
Quebecor	3.8
Independents	16.2

Source: *Globe and Mail*, July 28, 1998, p. B1, from Canadian Newspaper Association.

★ 550 ★

Newspapers (SIC 2711)

Largest Daily Newspapers in Canada

Figures are as of March 1997.

Toronto Star	461,337
Globe and Mail	307,990
Journal de Montreal	261,574
Toronto Sun	229,750
Vancouver Sun	176,303

Source: *New York Times*, July 21, 1998, p. C6, from Canadian Newspaper Association.

★ 551 ★

Newspapers (SIC 2711)

Largest Newspaper Media Firms - 1997

Companies are ranked by newspaper revenues in millions of dollars.

Gannett Co.	$ 3,582.0
Knight Ridder	2,770.0
New York Times Co.	2,557.1
Advance Publications	2,385.7
Times Mirror Co.	2,196.1
Dow Jones & Co.	1,601.0
Tribune Co.	1,437.0
Cox Enterprises	1,050.0
McClatchy Co.	998.9
Hearst Corp.	949.8

Source: *Advertising Age*, August 17, 1998, p. S10.

★ 552 ★

Newspapers (SIC 2711)

Largest Spanish Language Dailies

Data show circulation.

El Nuevo Herald	102,000
La Opinion	102,000
Diario las Americas	72,000
El Diario La Prensa	68,000
El Vocero del Puerto Rico	45,000

Source: *Advertising Age*, April 26, 1999, p. S20, from Western Publication Research and Audit Bureau of Circulations.

★ 553 ★

Newspapers (SIC 2711)

Largest U.S. Newspapers - 1998

Data show circulation for the six months ended September 1998.

Wall Street Journal	1,740
USA TODAY	1,653
Los Angeles Times	1,068
New York Times	1,067
Washington Post	759
New York Daily News	723
Chicago Tribune	652
Newsday	572
Houston Chronicle	551
Chicago Sun-Times	486

Source: *New York Times*, November 3, 1998, p. C7, from Audit Bureau of Circulations.

★ 554 ★

Newspapers (SIC 2711)

Newspaper Market in Canada

Owners are shown by share of total daily circulation.

Southam and Hollinger	40.70%
Sun Media	16.40
Thomson	10.75
Torstar	10.60
Other	21.60

Source: *Wall Street Journal*, October 26, 1998, p. A12, from Canadian Newspaper Association.

★ 555 ★

Newspapers (SIC 2711)

Top Sunday Newspapers - 1998

Figures are for the six months ended September 1998.

New York Times	1,627,099
Los Angeles Times	1,361,202
Washington Post	1,080,082
Chicago Tribune	1,019,458
Philadelphia Inquirer	880,918
New York Daily News	810,295

Continued on next page.

★ 555 ★ *Continued*

Newspapers (SIC 2711)

Top Sunday Newspapers - 1998

Figures are for the six months ended September 1998.

Detroit News & Free Press	805,405
Dallas Morning News	780,084
Houston Chronicle	752,190
Boston Globe	751,021

Source: *Chicago Tribune*, November 3, 1998, p. 3, from Audit Bureau of Circulations.

★ 556 ★

Comic Books (SIC 2721)

Comic Book Market - 1997

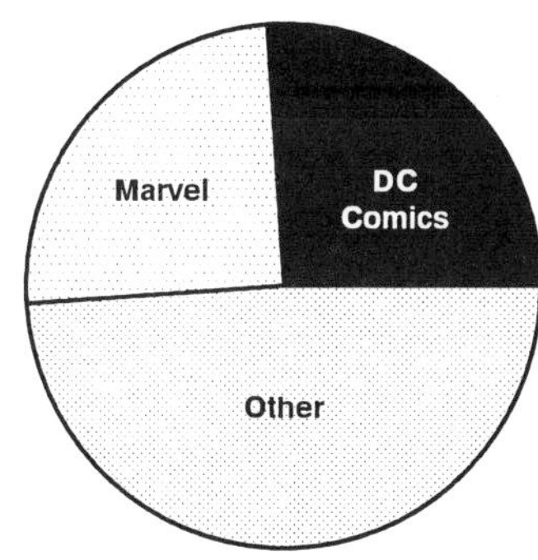

Market shares are shown based on sales at specialty stores.

DC Comics	25.78%
Marvel	24.81
Other	49.41

Source: "DC Announces 1997 Market Share." Retrieved October 28, 1998 from the World Wide Web: http://www.comicbookresources.com/news/0198.

★ 557 ★

Magazines (SIC 2721)

Largest Magazine Media Firms - 1997

Companies are ranked by magazine revenues in millions of dollars.

Time Warner	$ 3,070.9
Hearst Corp.	1,460.3
Advance Publications	1,283.0
Reed Elsevier	1,268.6
Thomson Corp.	$ 937.0
Primedia	859.1
Reader's Digest Association	811.1
International Data Group	786.5
Ziff-Davis Publishing Co.	747.6
News Corp.	673.2

Source: *Advertising Age*, August 17, 1998, p. S10.

★ 558 ★

Magazines (SIC 2721)

Popular Magazines in Canada - 1997

Data show the ad revenues for the leading English-language publications. Figures are in millions of dollars.

Maclean's	$ 43.3
Chatelaine	40.1
Canadian Living	28.9
TV Guide	24.1
Time	22.4
Reader's Digest	21.3
Flare	14.5

Source: *Marketing Magazine*, September 21, 1998, p. 27, from INA Canada.

★ 559 ★

Magazines (SIC 2721)

Top English-Language Magazines in Canada

Readership is shown in thousands.

Reader's Digest	3,367
TV Times	2,433
Chatelaine	2,055
Canadian Living	2,023
Time	1,899

Source: *Marketing Magazine*, April 26, 1999, p. 33.

★ 560 ★

Magazines (SIC 2721)

Top French-Language Magazines in Canada

Readership is shown in thousands.

7 Jours	1,076
TV 7 Jours/TV Hebdo	978
Tele-Plus	674
Primeurs	671
Selection du Reader's Digest	662

Source: *Marketing Magazine*, April 26, 1999, p. 33, from Print Measurement Bureau.

★ 561 ★

Magazines (SIC 2721)

Top Magazine Publishers - 1998

Companies are ranked by ad revenues in millions of dollars.

Time Inc.	$ 2,935.4
Conde Nast	1,215.1
Hearst Magazines	1,140.0
Hachette Filipacchi	960.7
Meredith Corp.	808.2
Gruner + Jahr	593.3
Parade Publications	517.1
Ziff-Davis	468.1
News America Corp.	461.7
Newsweek Inc.	400.0

Source: *Mediaweek*, March 8, 1999, p. 42, from PIB/ Competitive Media Reporting.

★ 562 ★

Magazines (SIC 2721)

Top Magazines - 1998

Circulation is shown for the second half of the year.

Modern Maturity	20,534,357
Reader's Digest	13,767,575
TV Guide	12,579,912
National Geographic	8,612,102
Better Homes & Gardens	7,613,249
Family Circle	5,004,902
Good Housekeeping	4,584,879
Ladies' Home Journal	4,575,996
Woman's Day	4,242,097
McCall's	4,202,809
Time	4,060,074
People	3,635,146
Playboy	3,336,213
Sports Illustrated	3,264,345
Newsweek	3,153,281

Source: *Advertising Age*, February 22, 1999, p. 32, from Audit Bureau of Circulations.

★ 563 ★

Magazines (SIC 2721)

Top Magazines in Ad Revenues - 1998

Figures are in millions of dollars.

People's Weekly	$ 626.6
Time	561.7
Sports Illustrated	554.9
Parade	517.1
TV Guide	453.5
Better Homes and Gardens	410.1
Newsweek	400.0
Business Week	361.6
PC Magazine	314.2
USA Weekend	274.5

Source: *Mediaweek*, March 8, 1999, p. 40, from Publishers Information Bureau and Competitive Media Reporting.

★ 564 ★

Magazines (SIC 2721)

Top Magazines in Quebec

Magazines are ranked by total readership.

7 Jours	1,076,000
TV 7 Jours/TV HEBDO	978,000
Selection du Reader's Digest	622,000
Le Lundi	594,000
L'Actualite	558,000
Coup de Pouce	505,000
Chatelaine	503,000
Derniere Heure	494,000
Le Bel Age	384,000
Elle Quebec	364,000

Source: *Globe and Mail*, June 7, 1999, p. B3, from Print Measurement Bureau.

★ 565 ★

Magazines (SIC 2721)

Top Music Magazines - 1998

Data show circulation.

Rolling Stone	1,200,000
Vibe	606,237
Spin	535,392
The Source	402,042

Source: *USA TODAY*, December 30, 1998, p. 2B, from Audit Bureau of Circulations.

★ 566 ★

Books (SIC 2731)

Book Sales - 1998

Data show estimated sales in millions of dollars.

	($ mil.)	Share
Professional	$ 4,404.6	20.32%
Adult	4,160.0	19.19
Elhi	3,102.4	14.31
College	2,852.8	13.16
Mass market	1,480.3	6.83
Juvenile	1,437.6	6.63
Book clubs	1,207.2	5.57
Religious	1,178.0	5.43
Sub. reference	766.9	3.54
Mail order	504.7	2.33
University press	382.1	1.76
Stand. tests	204.3	0.94

Source: *Publishers Weekly*, July 27, 1998, p. 8, from *Book Industry Study Group Trends, 1998.*

★ 567 ★

Books (SIC 2731)

Book Sales by Type - 1997

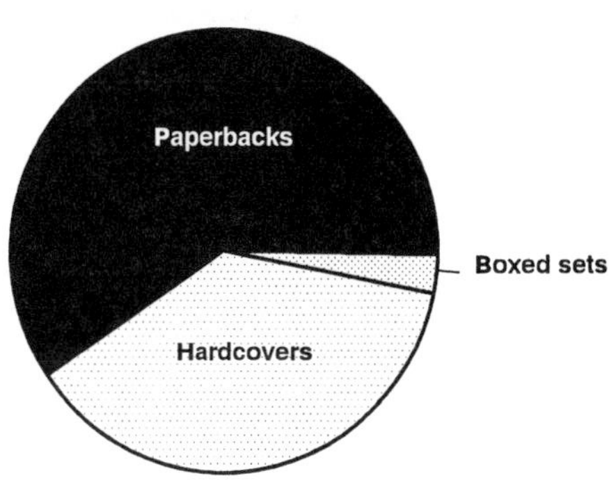

Paperbacks	59.0%
Hardcovers	37.0
Boxed sets	3.0

Source: *Publishers Weekly*, June 8, 1998, p. 12, from 1997 Consumer Research Study on Book Publishing.

★ 568 ★

Books (SIC 2731)

Canada's Publishing Market

Market shares are shown based on revenues. Figures are based on a survey.

Law	45.0%
Medical	25.0
Business	14.0
Gen. reference	10.0
Computer science	3.0
Eng. & arch.	2.0
Science	2.0

Source: Retrieved May 21, 1999 from the World Wide Web: http:// www.pubcouncil.ca/prof-ref-rev.html.

★ 569 ★

Books (SIC 2731)

Largest Children's Publishers - 1997

Companies are ranked by sales in millions of dollars.

Golden Books	$ 166
Penguin Putnam	130
Random House	128
Scholastic	103

Continued on next page.

★ 569 ★ *Continued*

Books (SIC 2731)

Largest Children's Publishers - 1997

Companies are ranked by sales in millions of dollars.

HarperCollins	$ 101
Simon & Schuster	92
Disney Publishing	75
Landoll Inc.	71
Bantam Doubleday Dell	55
Hearst Book Group	46

Source: *New York Times*, August 10, 1998, p. C6, from Simba Information.

★ 570 ★

Books (SIC 2731)

Where Men Get Books

Figures are based on a survey.

Bookstore	60.0%
Library	33.0
Family/friend	17.0
Dept./discount store	7.0
Secondhand bookstore	5.0
Book club	4.0
Supermarket	4.0
Internet	3.0

Source: *USA TODAY*, May 5, 1999, p. D1, from Maritz AmeriPoll.

★ 571 ★

Books (SIC 2731)

Where Women Get Books

Figures are based on a survey.

Bookstore	49.0%
Library	33.0
Friend/family	25.0
Dept./discount store	11.0
Secondhand bookstore	7.0
Bookclub	7.0
Garage sale	5.0
Supermarkets	5.0

Source: *USA TODAY*, May 5, 1999, p. D1, from Maritz AmeriPoll.

★ 572 ★

Sports Cards (SIC 2741)

Sports Grading Market

This market refers to the authentication of collectible sports cards. This niche market is experiencing significant growth as trades take place online. Figures show the company's estimated share.

Professional Sports Authenticator	90.0%
Other	10.0

Source: *Inc.*, April 1999, p. 36.

★ 573 ★

Trading Cards (SIC 2741)

Trading Card Market

Sales have fallen from $1.2 billion in 1991 to $400 million in 1997. Top companies include Topps and Upper Deck Co. The game segment is performing rather well, lead by Wizards of the Coast Inc.

Baseball cards	37.0%
Football cards	34.0
Game, role-playing	5.0
Other	24.0

Source: Retrieved April 30, 1999 from the World Wide Web: http:// www-cgi.cnnfn.com/hottories/companies/9712/30/topps/index.htm.

★ 574 ★

Business Forms (SIC 2761)

Largest Label Producers

Firms are ranked by sales in millions of dollars.

American Business Forms	$ 161.5
Precept	157.9
SFI	127.0
ProForma	118.0
GBS	103.7

Source: "Riding High." Retrieved February 22, 1999 from the World Wide Web: http:// www.napco.com/bfls/1198200dist.html.

★ 575 ★

Greeting Cards (SIC 2771)

Greeting Card Market

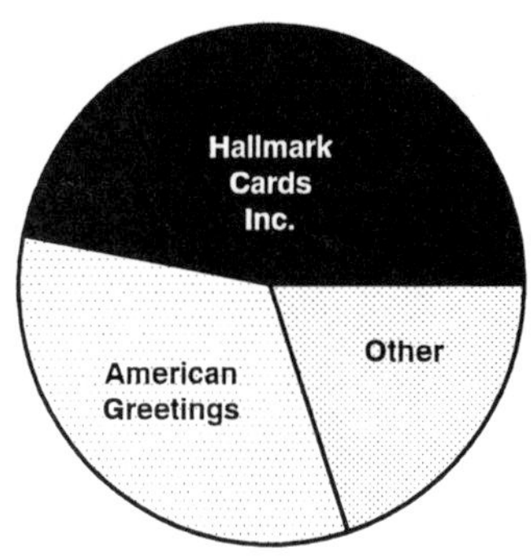

Market shares are shown in percent.

Hallmark Cards Inc.	47.0%
American Greetings	33.0
Other	20.0

Source: *Wall Street Journal*, March 3, 1999, p. A8.

★ 576 ★

Greeting Cards (SIC 2771)

Popular Greeting Card Holidays - 1998

Data show the millions of cards sold. A total of 6.8 billion cards are expected to be sold, generating retail sales of $7.5 billion.

Christmas	2,600
Valentine's Day	900
Mother's Day	150
Easter	120
Father's Day	95
Graduation	60
Thanksgiving	30
Halloween	25
St. Patrick's Day	15
Jewish New Year	10
Chanukah	10

Source: "GCA Industry Fact Sheet." Retrieved October 28, 1998 from the World Wide Web. http://www.greetingcard.org/gca/facts.htm.

SIC 28 - Chemicals and Allied Products

★ 577 ★

Chemicals (SIC 2800)

Aerosol Use - 1998

Sales are shown in millions of units.

	(mil.)	Share
Personal care products	811.6	35.63%
Household products	757.4	33.25
Paints/varnishes	393.0	17.25
Food products	158.2	6.94
Insect sprays	132.1	5.80
Animal products	2.5	0.11
Other	23.2	1.02

Source: *Spray Technology & Marketing*, June 1999, p. 23.

★ 578 ★

Chemicals (SIC 2800)

Auto Catalyst Market

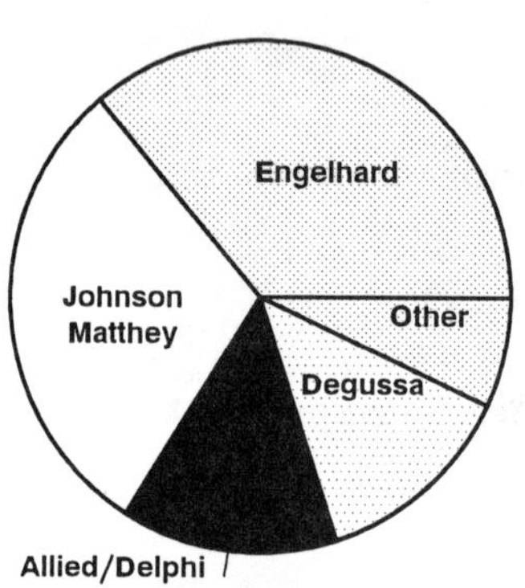

Market shares are shown in percent.

Engelhard	36.0%
Johnson Matthey	30.0
Allied/Delphi	14.0
Degussa	13.0
Other	7.0

Source: *Investext,* Thomson Financial Networks, January 19, 1999, p. 2, from company reports and Merrill Lynch.

★ 579 ★

Chemicals (SIC 2800)

Bleaching Chemicals Market

The North American market is shown in percent.

Sodium chlorate	55.0%
Chlorine	20.0
Hydrogen peroxide	10.0
Oxygen	10.0
Other	5.0

Source: *Chemical Week*, February 17, 1999, p. 46, from Consulting Resources.

★ 580 ★

Chemicals (SIC 2800)

Chemical Catalyzer Market - 1998

Chemicals	27.0%
Refining	27.0
Polymers	24.0
Environmental	22.0

Source: *Chemical Week*, May 5, 1999, p. 30, from The Catalyst Group.

★ 581 ★

Chemicals (SIC 2800)

Fine Chemicals Market - 1998

Sales are shown in billions of dollars.

	($ bil.)	Share
Industrial coatings	$ 10.0	11.36%
Agricultural chemicals	8.6	9.77
Adhesives & sealants	7.0	7.95
Electronic cleaners	6.1	6.93
I&I cleaners	6.1	6.93
Specialty polymers	4.9	5.57
Construction chemicals	4.2	4.77
Food ingredients	3.8	4.32
Plastic additives	3.1	3.52
Other	34.2	38.86

Source: *Chemical Week*, January 6, 1999, p. 27, from Kline & Co.

★ 582 ★

Chemicals (SIC 2800)

Food Additives Market - 1998

The $5.25 billion market is shown in percent.

Flavors	24.0%
Nonnutritive sweeteners	18.0
Bulking agents	11.0
Gums & thickeners	11.0
Fat replacements	9.0
Emulsifiers	8.0
Colorants	7.0
Acidulants	5.0
Preservatives	4.0
Other	2.0

Source: *Chemical Week*, June 10, 1998, p. 30, from Frost & Sullivan.

★ 583 ★

Chemicals (SIC 2800)

Hydrogen Peroxide Market

Pulp & paper	55.0%
Environmental	15.0
Chemicals	12.0
Textiles	8.0
Other	10.0

Source: *Chemical Week*, November 18, 1998, p. 15, from Kline & Co.

★ 584 ★

Chemicals (SIC 2800)

Largest Chemical Producers

Firms are ranked by chemical sales in billions of dollars.

DuPont	$ 26.20
Dow Chemical	17.71
Exxon	10.50
General Electric	6.63
Union Carbide	5.65
Huntsman Chemical	5.20
ICI Americas	4.90
Praxair	4.83
Eastman Chemical	4.48
BP Amoco	4.47

Source: *Chemical & Engineering News*, May 3, 1999, p. 20.

★ 585 ★

Chemicals (SIC 2800)

Largest Hydrogen Peroxide Makers

Companies are ranked by capacity in millions of pounds.

Solvay Interox	443
FMC	325
DuPont	240
Degussa	176
Degussa Canada	176

Source: *Chemical Market Report*, August 24, 1998, p. 49.

★ 586 ★

Chemicals (SIC 2800)

Largest Industrial Chemical Makers - 1997

Firms are ranked by sales in millions of dollars.

Dow Chemical	$ 20,065.0
Monsanto	7,514.0
Union Carbide	6,502.0
Praxair	4,735.0
Eastman Chemical	4,678.0

Source: *Chemical Week*, May 20, 1998, p. 43.

★ 587 ★

Chemicals (SIC 2800)

Largest Specialty Chemical Makers

Companies are ranked by sales in millions of dollars.

Sherwin-Williams	$ 1,378.0
Engelhard	1,076.0
Avery Dennison	871.5
M.A. Hanna	595.6
Crompton & Knowles	474.3

Source: *Chemical Week*, July 29, 1998, p. 11, from company reports.

★ 588 ★

Chemicals (SIC 2800)

Paper Chemicals Market

Spending is shown in millions of dollars. Figures are for North America.

	1998 ($ mil.)	2004 ($ mil.)	Share
Coatings	$ 2,039	$ 2,424	33.69%
Bleaching	1,193	1,580	21.96
Starch	832	993	13.80
Pulping	592	598	8.31
Retention and drainage aids	301	419	5.82
Internal size	247	321	4.46
Synthetic surface size	46	63	0.88
Other	653	796	11.06

Source: *Chemical Week*, February 17, 1999, p. 44, from Frost & Sullivan.

★ 589 ★

Chemicals (SIC 2800)

Personal Care Chemical Market - 1998

Total sales reached $810 million.

Conditioning polymers	29.0%
Specialty surfactants	15.0
Thickeners	13.0
Specialty emolients	12.0
Antimicrobals	9.0
UV absorbers	9.0
Fixative polymers	7.0
Actives	6.0

Source: *Chemical Week*, December 9, 1998, p. 38, from Kline & Co.

★ 590 ★

Chemicals (SIC 2800)

Photographic Chemicals Market - 2002

Total sales are expected to reach $2.04 billion.

Photoprocessing	49.0%
Medical and dental imaging	24.0
Commercial and industrial imaging	15.0
Home darkroom and other markets	12.0

Source: *Chemical Week*, October 14, 1998, p. 64, from Freedonia Group.

★ 591 ★

Chemicals (SIC 2800)

Plant-Derived Chemicals Market

Demand is shown in percent.

	1998	2008
Essential oils	38.07%	32.45%
Botanical extracts	19.54	18.49
Other	42.39	49.06

Source: *Chemical & Engineering News*, April 12, 1999, p. 21, from Freedonia Group.

★ 592 ★

Chemicals (SIC 2800)

Specialty Biocide Consumption - 1998

Recreational water	20.0%
Wood preservation	20.0
Cosmetics	10.0
Disinfectants	10.0
Paints & coatings	10.0
Other	30.0

Source: *Chemical Market Report*, September 14, 1998, p. 38, from Kline & Co.

★ 593 ★

Chemicals (SIC 2800)

Wet Chemicals Market - 1997

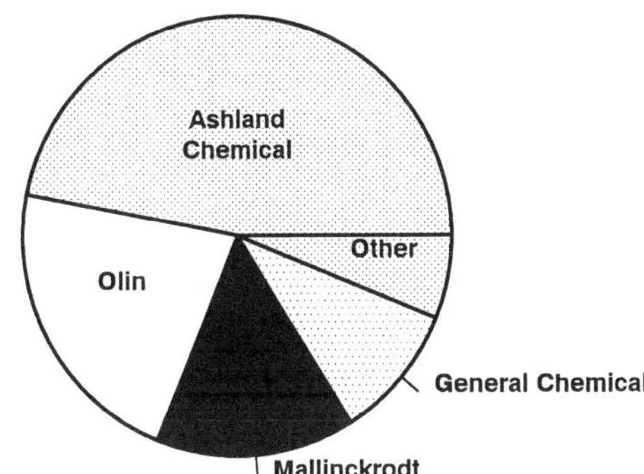

Ashland Chemical	47.0%
Olin	22.0
Mallinckrodt	15.0
General Chemical	10.0
Other	6.0

Source: *Chemical Week*, July 15, 1998, p. 24, from Information Network.

★ 594 ★

Chemicals (SIC 2800)

Wet Chemicals Market by Segment - 1997

The $223.5 million market is shown in percent.

Hydrogen peroxide	27.0%
Etchants	18.0
Sulfuric acid	18.0
Solvents	12.0
Nitric acid	6.0%
Ammonium hydroxide	5.0
Hydrochloric acid	3.0
Acetic acid	2.0

Source: *Chemical Week*, August 19, 1998, p. 64, from Information Network.

★ 595 ★

Alkalies and Chlorine (SIC 2812)

Largest Caustic Soda Producers

Companies are ranked by capacity in thousands of short tons.

Dow	4,500
OxyChem	3,182
PPG	1,863
Olin	1,115
Formosa	985

Source: *Chemical Market Report*, June 1, 1998, p. 37.

★ 596 ★

Industrial Gases (SIC 2813)

U.S. Helium Consumption - 1996

Cryogenics	24.4%
Pressure/purge	19.9
Welding	18.2
Controlled atmosphere	16.0
Breathing mixtures	3.1
Other	12.8

Source: *Minerals Yearbook*, 1996, p. 419.

★ 597 ★

Inorganic Chemicals (SIC 2819)

Bicarb Market Leaders - 2000

Market shares are shown in percent.

Church & Dwight	74.1%
IMC	23.8
Natrium	2.1

Source: *Chemical Market Report*, December 28, 1998, p. 16, from Church & Dwight.

★ 598 ★

Inorganic Chemicals (SIC 2819)

Largest Adipic Acid Makers - 1998

Companies are ranked by capacity in millions of pounds.

DuPont	1,210
Solutia	670
DuPont Canada	330
AlliedSignal	50

Source: *Chemical Market Report*, June 15, 1998, p. 33.

★ 599 ★

Inorganic Chemicals (SIC 2819)

Largest Calcium Chloride Makers

Companies are ranked by capacity in thousands of short tons.

Dow	700
General	469
Tetra Technologies	375
Ambar	300
Great Lakes	150

Source: *Chemical Market Report*, February 1, 1999, p. 49.

★ 600 ★

Inorganic Chemicals (SIC 2819)

Largest Hydrogen Cyanide Makers

Companies are ranked by capacity in millions of pounds.

DuPont	1,000
Rohm and Haas	200
BP Chemicals	145
Ciba	90
Degussa	76
Sterling	75
Cytec Indsutries	65

Source: *Chemical Market Report*, November 23, 1998, p. 61.

★ 601 ★

Inorganic Chemicals (SIC 2819)

Largest Sodium Silicate Producers

Companies are ranked by capacity in thousands of short tons.

PQ	500
OxyChem	280
PPG	200
J.M. Huber	140

Source: *Chemical Market Report*, January 18, 1999, p. 53.

★ 602 ★

Inorganic Chemicals (SIC 2819)

Largest Sodium Sulfite Makers

Companies are ranked by capacity in thousands of short tons.

Southern Ionics	75
Indspec	40
Solvay	55
General	36
Calabrian	15
Olympic	7

Source: *Chemical Market Report*, January 25, 1999, p. 37.

★ 603 ★

Inorganic Chemicals (SIC 2819)

Sodium Sulfate Market

Companies are ranked by capacity in thousands of short tons.

Penoles	660
Saskatchewan Minerals	300
IMC Chemicals	220
Cooper Resources	165
OxyChem	125

Source: *Chemical Market Report*, August 17, 1998, p. 37.

★ 604 ★

Plastics (SIC 2821)

Auto Plastic Sales - 2002

Data are for North America.

Interior	39.47%
Exterior	27.48
Powertrain/thermal	9.42
Electrical/electronic	8.01
Fuel	6.30
Chassis	0.59
Other	8.73

Source: *Automotive Engineering International*, February 1999, p. 103, from *Automotive Plastics Report*.

★ 605 ★

Plastics (SIC 2821)

Blends/Alloys Compounding Market

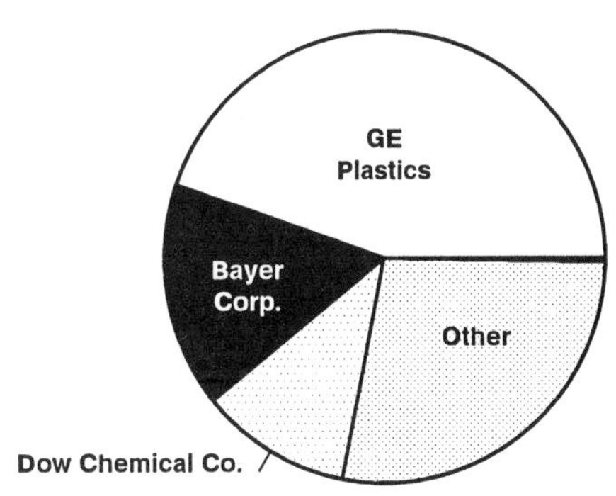

Market shares are estimated based on sales.

GE Plastics	45.0%
Bayer Corp.	16.0
Dow Chemical Co.	11.0
Other	28.0

Source: *Plastics News*, July 20, 1998, p. 18, from Frost & Sullivan.

★ 606 ★

Plastics (SIC 2821)

Filled/Reinforced Resin Market

Market shares are estimated based on sales.

DuPont Co.	12.0%
GE Plastics	10.0
Ferro Corp.	9.0
Other	69.0

Source: *Plastics News*, July 20, 1998, p. 18, from Frost & Sullivan.

★ 607 ★

Plastics (SIC 2821)

HDPE by End Market - 1998

The high-density polyethylene market is shown by end use.

	(mil.)	Share
Blow molding	4,190	30.07%
Extrusion	4,091	29.36
Injection molding	2,280	16.36
Other	3,372	24.20

Source: *Modern Plastics*, January 1999, p. 72.

★ 608 ★

Plastics (SIC 2821)

HDPE Market by End Use

The market is shown for high-density polyethylene.

Blow molding	34.0%
Film and sheet	21.0
Injection molding	19.0
Pipe and conduit	10.0
Wire and cable	1.0
Other	15.0

Source: *Chemical Week*, April 14, 1999, p. 31, from Chemical Market Associates.

★ 609 ★

Plastics (SIC 2821)

Injection Molding Industry

Sales are shown in percent.

Consumer & institutional	27.5%
Transportation	17.6
Electrical/electronic	14.3

Continued on next page.

★ 609 ★ *Continued*

Plastics (SIC 2821)

Injection Molding Industry

Sales are shown in percent.

Building & construction	9.1%
Industrial/machinery	6.5
Furniture & furnishings	5.1
Medical	4.9
Packaging	3.4
Toys	3.2
Other	8.0

Source: *Injection Molding*, December 1998, p. 24.

★ 610 ★

Plastics (SIC 2821)

Largest Plastic Compounders - 1997

Market shares are estimated based on sales.

Geon Co.	9.0%
GE Plastics	7.0
M.A. Hanna Co.	6.0
DuPont Co.	4.0
Ferro Corp.	4.0
Georgia Gulf Corp.	4.0
K-Bin	4.0
A. Schulman Inc.	4.0
Other	58.0

Source: *Plastics News*, July 20, 1998, p. 18, from Frost & Sullivan.

★ 611 ★

Plastics (SIC 2821)

Largest Plastics Markets in Canada - 1997

Auto parts
Synthetic fibers
Bags
Other bags
Others

Shipments are shown in millions of dollars.

	($ mil.)	Share
Auto parts	$ 2,810	31.75%
Synthetic fibers	1,630	18.42
Bags	1,420	16.05
Other bags	1,200	13.56
Others	1,790	20.23

Source: *Globe and Mail*, October 20, 1998, p. B16, from Industry Canada.

★ 612 ★

Plastics (SIC 2821)

Largest Polycarbonate Makers

Companies are ranked by capacity in thousands of short tons.

GE Plastics	955
Bayer	396
Dow	175

Source: *Chemical Market Report*, January 11, 1999, p. 37.

★ 613 ★

Plastics (SIC 2821)

Largest Polystyrene Makers

Shares are shown based on 3.8 million metric tons per year. Data are for North America.

Nova Chemicals	32.0%
Dow Chemical	20.0
BASF	13.0
Fina Oil & Chemical	13.0
Chevron Chemical	10.0
Deltech Polymers	2.0
Others	10.0

Source: *Chemical Week*, August 12, 1998, p. 32, from company reports and Chemical Market Associates.

★ 614 ★

Plastics (SIC 2821)

LDPE Market by End Use

The market is shown for low-density polyethylene.

Film and sheet	56.0%
Extrusion coating	15.0
Injection molding	5.0
Wire and cable	3.0
Blow molding	2.0
Other	15.0

Source: *Chemical Week*, April 14, 1999, p. 31, from Chemical Market Associates.

★ 615 ★

Plastics (SIC 2821)

LLDPE Market by End Use

The market is shown for linear low-density polyethylene.

Film and sheet	58.0%
Injection molding	8.0
Rotomolding	6.0
Wire and cable	2.0
Blow molding	1.0
Other extrusion	4.0
Other	21.0

Source: *Chemical Week*, April 14, 1999, p. 31, from Chemical Market Associates.

★ 616 ★

Plastics (SIC 2821)

PVC Compounding Market

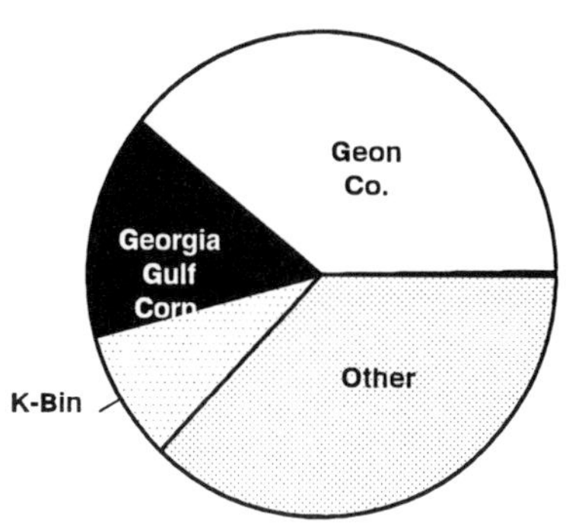

Market shares are estimated based on sales. PVC stands for polyvinyl chloride.

Geon Co.	39.0%
Georgia Gulf Corp.	15.0
K-Bin	9.0
Other	37.0

Source: *Plastics News*, July 20, 1998, p. 18, from Frost & Sullivan.

★ 617 ★

Synthetic Rubber (SIC 2822)

Largest Rubber Makers - 1997

Firms are ranked by rubber sales in millions of dollars.

Goodyear Tire & Rubber Co.	$ 12,153.7
Bridgestone-Firestone Inc.	5,970.0
Michelin North America Inc.	4,700.0
Cooper Tire & Rubber Co.	1,815.0
Tomkins (Gates & Stanat/Trico)	1,800.0
Mark IV Industries Inc.	1,487.0
Continental General Tire Inc.	1,360.0
Standard Products Co.	831.0
Dunlop Tire Corp.	750.0
Bandag Inc.	714.7

Source: *Rubber & Plastics News*, June 29, 1998, p. 12.

★ 618 ★

Fibers (SIC 2823)

Manmade Staple Fiber Shipments

Data are in millions of pounds.

	1997	1998
Industrial	1,209	1,217
Apparel	1,042	942
Home textiles	458	459

Source: *ATI*, March 1999, p. 105, from Fiber Economics Bureau.

★ 619 ★

Fibers (SIC 2824)

Polypropylene Fiber Shipments

Nonwovens	57.54%
Carpet face yarns	34.04
Broadwoven	8.07
Other	0.35

Source: *ATI*, February 1999, p. 56, from Fiber Economics Bureau.

★ 620 ★

Medicinals (SIC 2833)

Best-Selling Herbs

Sales are shown in millions of dollars.

Echinecea	$ 310
Ginseng	270
Ginko biloboa	240
Garlic	200
St. John's wort	200
Goldenseal	150
Saw palmetto	130
Aloe	120
Cat's claw	90
Astragalus	80

Source: *Entrepeneur*, January 1999, p. 14, from *Nutrition Business Journal*.

★ 621 ★

Medicinals (SIC 2833)

Best-Selling Supplements

Figures are based on a survey.

Multi-vitamins	51.2%
Vitamin C	28.8
Vitamin E	27.1
Calcium	24.7
Garlic	11.1

Source: *Grocery Headquarters*, November 1998, p. 48, from Hartman & New Hope.

★ 622 ★

Medicinals (SIC 2833)

Creatine Market - 1997

EAS had a 90% share in 1995, but the share has fallen as Met-Rx, GNC, Weider and MLD products entered the market.

EAS	50.0%
Other	50.0

Source: "Scoring Big With Creatine Sales." Retrieved May 18, 1999 from the World Wide Web: http://nbj.net/news6.htm.

★ 623 ★

Medicinals (SIC 2833)

Top Selling Herbs

Shares are shown based on unit sales.

Gingko	8.8%
Garlic	8.7
St. John's Wort	7.7
Ginseng	6.9
Glucosamine	6.0
Other	61.9

Source: *Washington Post*, February 6, 1999, p. E1, from Hartman Group.

★ 624 ★

Vitamins (SIC 2833)

Best-Selling Vitamins

Shares are shown based on unit sales.

Multivitamins	37.8%
Vitamin E	11.9
Calcium	11.3
Vitamin C	9.9
Children's vitamins	6.9
Other	22.2

Source: *Washington Post*, February 6, 1999, p. E1, from Hartman Group.

★ 625 ★

Vitamins (SIC 2833)

Vitamin Sales by Segment

Unit sales are shown for the year ended January 3, 1999.

Mineral supplements	207.8
1 & 2 Letter vitamins	131.9
Multivitamins	113.5
Liquid vitamins/minerals	10.2

Source: *Supermarket Business*, April 1999, p. 76, from Information Resources Inc.

★ 626 ★

Drugs (SIC 2834)

ADHD Drug Remedies - 1997

Shares of the $550 million market are shown in percent. ADHD stands for attention deficit hyperactivity disorder.

Ritalin	47.6%
Dexedrine	10.3
Adderall	9.9
Ritalin-SR	8.7
Clonidine HCL	3.6
Others	19.9

Source: *Investor's Business Daily*, November 20, 1998, p. A4, from IMS Health.

★ 627 ★

Drugs (SIC 2834)

Allergy Drug Market - 1998

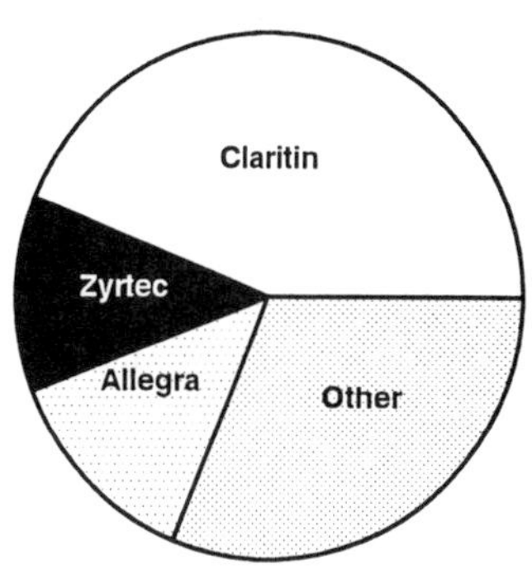

Market shares are shown in percent for November 1998.

Claritin	43.9%
Zyrtec	12.0
Allegra	12.7
Other	31.4

Source: *Investext*, Thomson Financial Networks, December 16, 1998, p. 6.

★ 628 ★

Drugs (SIC 2834)

Antibiotic Drug Market

Market shares are shown in percent for September 1998. Data refer to the oral, cephalosprorin category.

Cefzil	12.0%
Ceftin	9.0
Lorabid	4.0
Suprax	3.0
Vantin	2.0
Other	70.0

Source: *Investext*, Thomson Financial Networks, November 12, 1998, p. 27, from IMS America.

★ 629 ★

Drugs (SIC 2834)

Antibiotic Macrolide Market

Market shares are shown in percent for September 1998.

Zithromax	50.0%
Biaxin	25.0
Other	25.0

Source: *Investext*, Thomson Financial Networks, November 12, 1998, p. 28, from IMS America.

★ 630 ★

Drugs (SIC 2834)

Antidepressant Drug Market - 1999

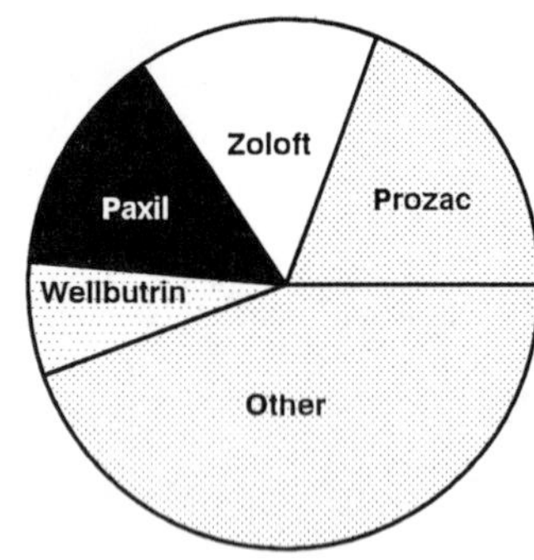

Market shares are shown for February 1999.

Prozac	19.1%
Zoloft	15.2
Paxil	14.3
Wellbutrin	7.2
Other	44.2

Source: *Wall Street Journal*, April 20, 1999, p. A3, from company reports and Baseline.

★ 631 ★

Drugs (SIC 2834)

Antifungal Drug Market - 1998

Market shares are shown in percent for September 1998.

Diflucan	19.0%
Terazol	12.0
Lamisil	9.0
Nizoral	8.0

Source: *Investext*, Thomson Financial Networks, December 16, 1998, p. 14, from IMS America.

★ 632 ★

Drugs (SIC 2834)

Antipsychotic Drug Market - 1998

Market shares are shown in percent for November 1998.

Risperdal	34.0%
Zyprexa	28.3
Haloperidol	16.0
Clozaril	6.5
Seroguel	5.5
Other	9.6

Source: *Investext*, Thomson Financial Networks, December 16, 1998, p. 6.

★ 633 ★

Drugs (SIC 2834)

Antiviral (HIV) Drug Market - 1998

Market shares are shown in percent for November 1998.

Zerit	15.9%
3TC	15.2
Combivir	12.2
Viracept	11.6
Crixivan	10.4
AZT	4.9
Sustiva	4.9
Other	25.0

Source: *Investext*, Thomson Financial Networks, December 16, 1998, p. 6.

★ 634 ★

Drugs (SIC 2834)

Arthritis Drug Market

Market shares are shown in percent for September 1998.

Relafen	9.0%
Daypro	6.0
Arthrotec	4.0
Oruvail	2.0
Naprelan	1.0
Generics	29.0
Other	48.0

Source: *Investext,* Thomson Financial Networks, November 12, 1998, p. 60.

★ 635 ★

Drugs (SIC 2834)

Best-Selling Drugs - 1997

Sales are shown in millions of dollars.

Prilosec	$ 2,300
Prozac	1,900
Zocor	1,400
Epogen	1,200
Zoloft	1,200
Zantac	1,100
Paxil	949
Norvasc	915
Claritin	908
Vasotec	843

Source: *USA TODAY,* July 20, 1998, p. 3B, from IMS America.

★ 636 ★

Drugs (SIC 2834)

Best-Selling Drugs - 1998

Data show the number of prescriptions written in U.S. community pharmacies.

Premarin tabs	41,316
Synthroid	34,709
Trimox	31,281
Hydrocodone/APAP	30,747
Prozac	23,835
Prilosec	23,586
Zithromax	22,965
Lipitor	21,575
Norvasc	20,838
Claritin	20,031

Source: *Medical Tribune,* February 18, 1999, p. 16, from Scott-Levin.

★ 637 ★

Drugs (SIC 2834)

Calcium Channel Blockers - 1998

Monthly shares are shown in percent.

Norvasc	25.9%
Cadizem CD	14.2
Procardia XL	13.0
Verapamil SR	13.0

Source: *Drug Topics,* July 20, 1998, p. 17, from Scott-Levin.

★ 638 ★

Drugs (SIC 2834)

Calcium Channel Drug Market - 1998

Market shares are shown in percent for November 1998.

Norvasc	28.2%
Cadizem	15.0
Procardia XL	11.9
Adalat CC	7.4
Plendil	3.5
Other	34.0

Source: *Investext,* Thomson Financial Networks, December 16, 1998, p. 9.

★ 639 ★

Drugs (SIC 2834)

Cardiovascular Drug Market in Canada - 1998

Shares are for September 1997 - August 1998.

Merck Frosst	21.7%
Pfizer	9.9
Apotex	7.9
Bayer	7.8
Hoechst Rouseel	6.5
Other	46.1

Source: *Globe and Mail,* October 20, 1998, p. C6, from IMS Health Canada.

★ 640 ★

Drugs (SIC 2834)

Cholesterol Reducing Drug Market

Market shares are shown in percent for September 1998.

Lipitor	36.0%
Zocor	22.0
Pravachol	16.0
Leschol	8.0
Mevacor	5.0
Other	13.0

Source: *Investext,* Thomson Financial Networks, November 12, 1998, p. 37, from IMS America.

★ 641 ★

Drugs (SIC 2834)

Depression Drug Market - 1998

Market shares are shown in percent for November 1998.

Prozac	16.9%
Zoloft	15.4
Paxil	14.4
Effexor	5.0
Serzone	3.4
Celexa	1.9
Other	42.9

Source: *Investext,* Thomson Financial Networks, December 16, 1998, p. 11.

★ 642 ★

Drugs (SIC 2834)

Enlarged Prostate Drug Market - 1998

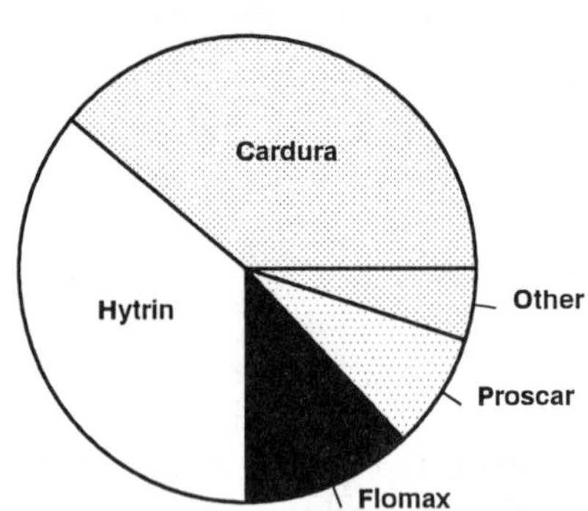

Market shares are shown in percent for November 1998.

Cardura	39.2%
Hytrin	36.1
Flomax	11.7
Proscar	8.3
Other	4.7

Source: *Investext,* Thomson Financial Networks, December 16, 1998, p. 12.

★ 643 ★

Drugs (SIC 2834)

Largest Antidepressant Makers

Market shares are shown in percent.

Eli Lilly	18.0%
Pfizer	15.0
SmithKline Beecham	15.0
Glaxo-Wellcome	6.0
Organon	2.0
Other	44.0

Source: *Investext,* Thomson Financial Networks, December 7, 1998, p. 139, from IMS Health.

★ 644 ★

Drugs (SIC 2834)

Largest U.S. Drug Makers - 1997

Companies are ranked by sales in billions of dollars.

Bristol-Myers Squibb	$ 5.70
Johnson & Johnson	5.66
Merck	5.65

Continued on next page.

★ 644 ★ *Continued*

Drugs (SIC 2834)

Largest U.S. Drug Makers - 1997

Companies are ranked by sales in billions of dollars.

Glaxo Wellcome	$ 5.54
American Home Products	5.33
Pfizer	4.95
Eli Lilly	4.39
SmithKline Beecham	4.02
Novartis	3.99
Schering-Plough	3.81

Source: *Wall Street Journal*, November 16, 1998, p. 14A, from IMS Health.

★ 645 ★

Drugs (SIC 2834)

Leading Hair Growth Products

Sales are shown in millions of dollars.

Rogaine	$ 71
Propecia	45

Source: *New York Times*, November 11, 1998, p. C1, from Information Resources Inc.

★ 646 ★

Drugs (SIC 2834)

Leading Migraine Remedies - 1998

Market shares are shown in percent.

Imitrex	83.0%
Zomig	7.0
Amerge	3.0
Maxalt	1.0
Other	7.0

Source: *New York Times*, December 29, 1998, p. C1, from IMS Health.

★ 647 ★

Drugs (SIC 2834)

Leading Smoke Cessation Products

Nicorette
Nicoderm
Zyban
Nicotrol

Sales are shown in millions of dollars.

Nicorette	$ 318
Nicoderm	216
Zyban	84
Nicotrol	33

Source: *New York Times*, November 11, 1998, p. C1, from Information Resources Inc.

★ 648 ★

Drugs (SIC 2834)

Medical Product Sales - 1999

Data show supermarket sales in selected categories. Figures are in millions of dollars. Sales of cold products reached $1.2 billion.

Analgesics	$ 1,027.91
Allergy & sinus remedies	780.04
Diet aids	504.96
Antacids	498.02
Eye care	340.33
Laxatives	168.19
Cough medications	129.06
Nasal drops and inhalers	94.08
Sedatives and stimultants	65.75
Hemorrhoidals	64.40
Asthmatic remedies	19.17
Ear care	15.00
Wart removers	12.21
Motion sickness	10.80
Diuretics	4.91

Source: *Progressive Grocer*, August 1998, p. 56.

★ 649 ★

Drugs (SIC 2834)

Pain Reliever Market

Tylenol
Advil
Excedrin
Aleve
Bayer
Private label
Other

Shares of the $2.58 billion market are shown for the year ended August 16, 1998.

Tylenol	22.2%
Advil	13.8
Excedrin	5.5
Aleve	5.4
Bayer	4.4
Private label	24.3
Other	24.4

Source: *Los Angeles Times*, September 24, 1998, p. D1, from Information Resources Inc.

★ 650 ★

Drugs (SIC 2834)

Popular Drug Brands - 1998

Ad spending for prescription drugs reached $1.2 billion in 1998. Claritin and Zyrtec are for allergy relief, Propecia is for hair loss, and Pravachol is for cholesterol relief. Figures are in millions of dollars.

Claritin	$ 136
Propecia	91
Zyrtec	75
Pravachol	60
Zyban	55

Source: *USA TODAY*, April 20, 1999, p. B1, from Competitive Media Reporting.

★ 651 ★

Drugs (SIC 2834)

Popular Vaccine Products

Market shares are shown in percent.

Engerix-B	13.0%
Recombivax HB	7.0
Vavivax	7.0
M-M-R-II	6.0%
Omminue Trivalent	6.0
Havrix	4.0
FluShield	3.0
HibTITER	3.0
Tetramune	3.0
Acel Imune	2.0
Pnu-Imune	2.0
Other	47.0

Source: *Chemical Market Report*, November 23, 1998, p. 30, from *Health Industries Handbook* and SRI Consulting.

★ 652 ★

Drugs (SIC 2834)

Psychotherapeutic Drug Market in Canada - 1998

Shares are for September 1997 - August 1998.

SmithKline Beecham	18.1%
Pfizer	15.0
Eli Lilly	12.5
Johnson & Johnson	7.8
American Home Products	7.4
Other	39.2

Source: *Globe and Mail*, October 20, 1998, p. C6, from IMS Health Canada.

★ 653 ★

Drugs (SIC 2834)

Schizophrenia/Tranquilizer Drug Market

Market shares are shown in percent for September 1998.

Risperdal	24.0%
Zyprexa	22.0
Seroquel	4.0
Generics	5.0
Other	44.0

Source: *Investext*, Thomson Financial Networks, November 12, 1998, p. 43, from IMS America.

★ 654 ★

Drugs (SIC 2834)

Seizure Relief Market

Market shares are shown in percent for September 1998. Data include seizures, Parkinson's and Alzheimer's.

Depakote	16.0%
Dilantin/phenytoin	12.0
Neurontin	11.0
Lamictal	1.0
Seizure generics	33.0

Source: *Investext,* Thomson Financial Networks, November 12, 1998, p. 45, from IMS America.

★ 655 ★

Drugs (SIC 2834)

Smoking Cessation Market

Shares of the $567 million market are shown in percent.

Nicorette	56.9%
NicoDerm	37.3
Other	5.8

Source: *Advertising Age*, December 21, 1998, p. 4, from Information Resources Inc.

★ 656 ★

Drugs (SIC 2834)

Statin Market Leaders - 1999

Statins are cholesterol lowering drugs. Figures are as of January 15, 1999.

Lipitor	42.9%
Zocor	26.0
Pravachol	16.8
Lescol	8.0
Mevacor	4.3
Baycol	2.0

Source: *Investext,* Thomson Financial Networks, January 25, 1999, p. 1, from IMS.

★ 657 ★

Drugs (SIC 2834)

Top Antidepressant Drugs - 1998

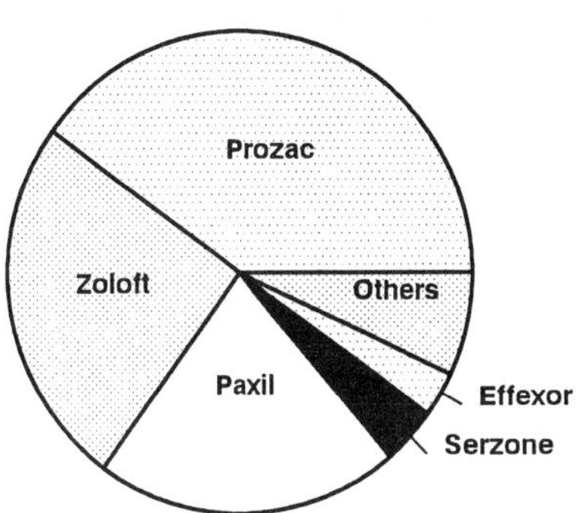

Data show sales as of August 31, 1998.

	($ mil.)	Share
Prozac	$ 1,429	40.0%
Zoloft	901	25.0
Paxil	754	21.0
Serzone	133	4.0
Effexor	122	3.0
Others	269	7.0

Source: *New York Times*, October 11, 1998, p. 8, from IMS Health.

★ 658 ★

Drugs (SIC 2834)

Top Birth Control Pill Brands - 1998

Data show the market share of oral contraceptives. Figures are for the year-to-date ending June 1998.

Ortho Tri-Cyclen	12.1%
Triphasil 28	10.4
Ortho-Novum 7/7/7 28	9.7
Other	67.8

Source: *Wall Street Journal*, September 28, 1998, p. B1, from IMS Health.

★ 659 ★

Drugs (SIC 2834)

Top Cough/Cold Remedies

Market shares are shown in percent.

Tylenol	10.8%
Robitussen	8.6
Benadryl	6.9

Continued on next page.

★ 659 ★ *Continued*

Drugs (SIC 2834)

Top Cough/Cold Remedies

Market shares are shown in percent.

Sudafed	6.8%
NyQuil	5.7
Alka Seltzer	5.0
Private label	30.6
Other	25.6

Source: *Discount Merchandiser*, June 1999, p. 54, from Information Resources Inc.

★ 660 ★

Drugs (SIC 2834)

Top Drug Firms in Canada - 1998

Market shares are shown in percent.

Merck Frosst	7.6%
Johnson & Johnson	5.7
Glaxo Wellcome	5.5
Astra Pharma	5.0
Novartis	4.9
Apotex	4.6
Bristol-Myers	4.5
Pfizer	4.1
American Home Products	3.9
Abbott	3.8
Other	50.4

Source: *Globe and Mail*, October 20, 1998, p. C6, from IMS Health Canada.

★ 661 ★

Drugs (SIC 2834)

Top Prescribed Drugs in Canada - 1998

Market shares are shown in percent for the year ended August 1998.

Premarin	1.8%
Tylenol with codeine 3	1.8
Synthroid	1.7
Novamoxin	1.4
Novasen	1.2
Vasotec	1.2
Losec	1.1
Triphasil	1.0
Ativan	0.9
Apo-amoxin	0.8%
Other	87.1

Source: *Globe and Mail*, October 20, 1998, p. C6, from IMS Health Canada.

★ 662 ★

Drugs (SIC 2834)

Top Stomach Remedies

Market shares are shown in percent.

PepcidAC	14.1%
Tums	11.4
Zantac75	10.7
Mylanta	8.3
Imodium	8.0
Pepto Bismol	6.3
Tagamet	5.0
Maalox	4.8
Alka Seltzer	4.0
Private label	10.8
Other	16.6

Source: *Discount Merchandiser*, June 1999, p. 59, from Information Resources Inc.

★ 663 ★

Drugs (SIC 2834)

Ulcer Drug Market - 1998

Market shares are shown in percent for November 1998.

Prilosec	32.4%
Prevacid	18.0
Ranitidine	16.7
Pepcid	11.0
Axid	4.7
Zantac	3.7
Other	13.5

Source: *Investext*, Thomson Financial Networks, December 16, 1998, p. 14.

★ 664 ★

Biotechnology (SIC 2836)

Agricultural Biotech Product Sales

	1997	2002
Transgenic seeds and plants	46.29%	70.36%
Animal growth hormones	25.71	14.04
Biopesticides	7.43	3.81
Other	20.57	11.79

Source: *Chemical & Engineering News*, April 19, 1999, p. 28, from Freedonia Group.

★ 665 ★

Biotechnology (SIC 2836)

Largest Biotech Firms

Firms are ranked by sales in millions of dollars.

Amgen	$ 2,401.0
Chiron	1,162.1
Genentech	947.6
Genzyme	608.8
Alza	464.4

Source: *Chemical Week*, May 20, 1998, p. 43.

★ 666 ★

Detergents (SIC 2841)

Dishwasher Detergent Market

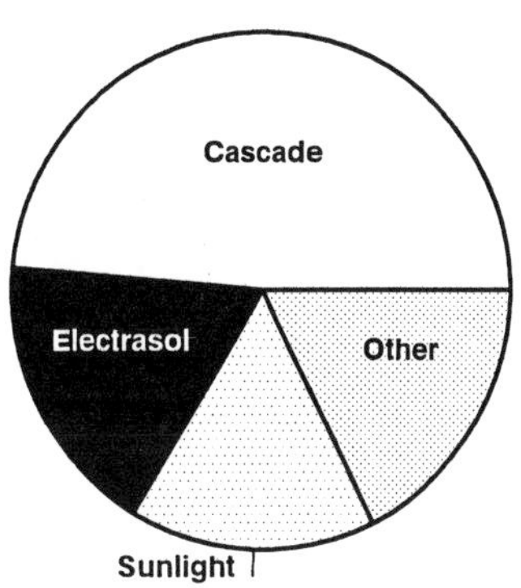

Shares of the $522 million market are shown in percent for September 27, 1998.

	($ mil.)	Share
Cascade	$ 254.8	48.81%
Electrasol	92.5	17.72
Sunlight	83.1	15.92
Other	91.6	17.55

Source: *Advertising Age*, November 30, 1998, p. 4, from Information Resources Inc.

★ 667 ★

Detergents (SIC 2841)

Largest Liquid Detergent Brands - 1998

Shares are shown based on sales of $2.3 billion for the year ended September 27, 1998.

Tide	33.2%
All	11.3
Wisk	10.1
Purex	7.3
Era	6.6
Cheer	5.6
Xtra	4.9
Surf	3.6
Arm & Hammer	3.4
Private label	2.5
Other	11.5

Source: *Household and Personal Products Industry*, January 1999, p. 82, from Information Resources Inc.

★ 668 ★

Detergents (SIC 2841)

Laundry Detergent Market - 1998

Shares are shown for the year ended November 11, 1998.

	($ mil.)	Share
Tide	$ 785.7	33.4%
All	260.0	11.1
Wisk	233.1	9.9
Purex	178.4	7.6
Era	156.3	6.6
Cheer	134.4	5.7
Xtra	114.3	4.9

Source: *Chemical Week*, January 27, 1999, p. 27, from Information Resources Inc.

★ 669 ★

Detergents (SIC 2841)

Top Detergent Makers - 1998

Shares are shown based on a $4.4 billion market for the year ended November 22, 1998.

Procter & Gamble	58.0%
Unilever	19.0
Dial	7.0
Church & Dwight	5.0
Colgate Palmolive	4.0
USA Detergents	3.0
Others	4.0

Source: *Chemical Week*, January 27, 1999, p. 28, from Information Resources Inc.

★ 670 ★

Detergents (SIC 2841)

Top Dish Detergent Brands in Canada - 1999

Market shares are shown in percent for the year ended January 2, 1999.

Sunlight	36.4%
Palmolive	27.8
Ivory	10.7
Excel	1.1
Mir	0.8%
Dove	0.2
Private label	22.0
Others	1.0

Source: "Report on Market Share." Retrieved June 1, 1999 from the World Wide Web: http://www.marketingmag.ca/index.cgi?, from industry sources.

★ 671 ★

Detergents (SIC 2841)

Top Powdered Detergent Brands - 1998

Shares are shown based on sales of $2.3 billion for the year ended September 27, 1998.

Tide	43.8%
Cheer	9.3
Gain	8.8
Surf	7.3
Arm & Hammer	3.8
Purex	3.8
Wisk	3.5
All	2.4
Fab	2.3
Private label	2.7
Other	12.3

Source: *Household and Personal Products Industry*, January 1999, p. 82, from Information Resources Inc.

★ 672 ★

Detergents (SIC 2841)

U.S. Bleach Market

The color-safe bleach market was valued at $226 million.

Clorox	59.7%
Other	40.3

Source: *Advertising Age*, July 27, 1998, p. 4, from Information Resources Inc.

★ 673 ★

Soaps (SIC 2841)

Body Wash Market - 1998

Shares are shown of the $451 million market for the year ended November 22, 1998.

Olay	18.0%
Dove	12.0
Herbal Essence	10.0
Caress	8.0
Softsoap	8.0
Lever 2000	6.0
Jergens	5.0
Suave	5.0
Dial	4.0
Neutrogena	2.0
White Rain	2.0
Others	20.0

Source: *Chemical Week*, January 27, 1999, p. 30, from Information Resources Inc.

★ 674 ★

Soaps (SIC 2841)

Hand Sanitizer Market - 1998

Sales are shown in millions of dollars.

	($ mil.)	Share
Purell	$ 20.4	53.13%
Softsoap	6.5	16.93
Dial	6.0	15.63
Lysol	4.2	10.94
Other	1.3	3.39

Source: *Advertising Age*, October 26, 1998, p. 22, from Information Resources Inc.

★ 675 ★

Soaps (SIC 2841)

Institutional Soap Market

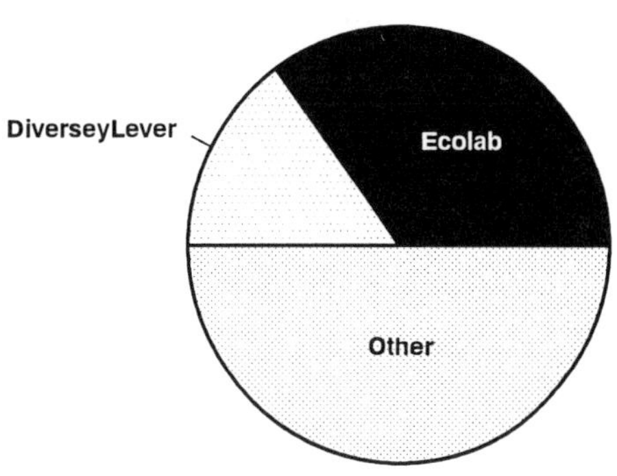

Data show the estimated market shares of detergents and rinses to the institutional food service market.

Ecolab	35.0%
DiverseyLever	15.0
Other	50.0

Source: *Forbes*, March 8, 1999, p. 95.

★ 676 ★

Soaps (SIC 2841)

Largest Cleaning Material Makers

Firms are ranked by sales in millions of dollars.

Procter & Gamble	$ 35,764.0
Colgate-Palmolive	9,056.7
Clorox	2,541.0
Ecolab	1,640.4
NCH	766.8

Source: *Chemical Week*, May 20, 1998, p. 50.

★ 677 ★

Soaps (SIC 2841)

Largest Soap Makers - 1998

Shares are shown based on a $2.18 billion market for the year ended November 22, 1998.

Unilever	31.0%
Procter & Gamble	22.0
Dial	15.0
Colgate Palmolive	14.0
Kao	4.0
Brimyesq	2.0
Others	12.0

Source: *Chemical Week*, January 27, 1999, p. 28, from Information Resources Inc.

★ 678 ★

Soaps (SIC 2841)

Top Bar Soap Brands - 1999

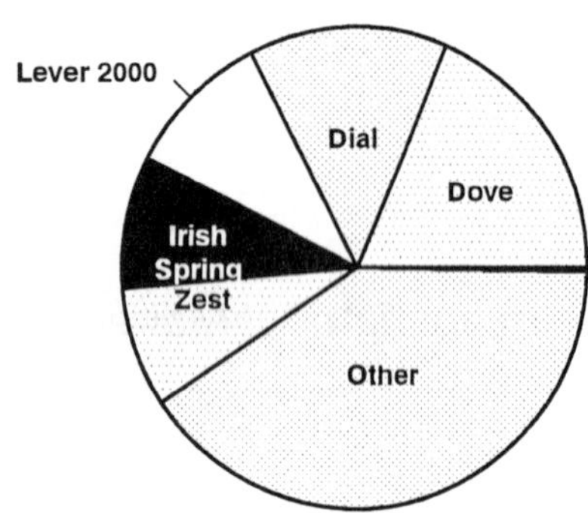

Market shares are shown in percent.

Dove	19.2%
Dial	13.6
Lever 2000	9.7
Irish Spring	8.6
Zest	8.3
Other	40.6

Source: *Household and Personal Products Industry*, December 1998, p. 102, from Information Resources Inc.

★ 679 ★

Soaps (SIC 2841)

Top Liquid Soap Brands - 1998

Market shares are shown for the year ended November 22, 1998.

Softsoap	42.3%
Dial 1	21.0
Clean & Smooth	8.8
Ivory	5.0
Jergens	4.5
Suave	2.4
Private label	10.4
Other	5.6

Source: *Chemical Market Report*, February 1, 1999, p. 16, from Information Resources Inc.

★ 680 ★

Cleaning Preparations (SIC 2842)

Cleaning Product Sales

Sales are shown in millions of dollars.

Counters/windows	$ 492.2
Floors/walls	401.2
Bath	395.9
Sinks/cleaners	167.3

Source: *Household and Personal Products Industry*, December 1998, p. 62, from Information Resources Inc.

★ 681 ★

Cleaning Preparations (SIC 2842)

Counter/Window Cleaner Market

Shares are shown of the $492 million market for the year ended August 23, 1998.

	($ mil.)	Share
Windex	$ 164.6	33.46%
Formula 409	88.3	17.95
Fantastik	34.8	7.07
Lysol Kitchen & Bath	33.0	6.71
Other	171.3	34.82

Source: *Advertising Age*, October 12, 1998, p. 4.

★ 682 ★

Cleaning Preparations (SIC 2842)

Leading Cleaning Product Makers - 1998

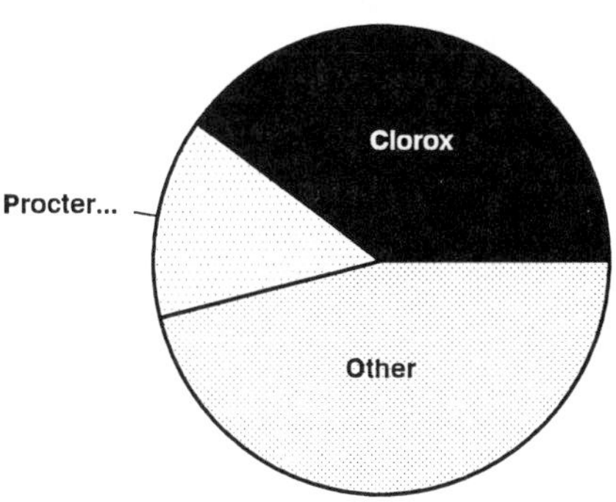

Market shares are shown for the first quarter of 1998.

Clorox	39.9%
Procter & Gamble Co.	14.0
Other	46.1

Source: *Advertising Age*, August 3, 1998, p. 43, from Salomon Smith Barney.

★ 683 ★

Waxes (SIC 2842)

Car Wax Market

Market shares are shown in percent.

Turtle Wax	56.4%
Meguiar's	12.7
NuFinish	8.1
Other	22.8

Source: *Discount Store News*, October 26, 1998, p. 24, from NPD Autopost.

★ 684 ★

Baby Care (SIC 2844)

Baby Care Market - 1997

Total supermarket sales for the category reached $512 million.

	($ mil.)	Share
Disposable towelettes	$ 243.45	47.55%
Cotton swabs	110.83	21.65
Oils, lotion, creams	56.39	11.01
Baby powder	37.66	7.36
Soaps and shampoos	31.37	6.13
Other	32.30	6.31

Source: *Progressive Grocer*, August 1998, p. 56, from Information Resources Inc.

★ 685 ★

Baby Care (SIC 2844)

Baby Lotion Market

Shares are shown of the $42 million market for the year ended May 24, 1998. Unit sales reached 18.3 million. First aid products was the top category in the baby care market with sales reaching $434.4 million.

Johnson & Johnson	50.8%
Mennen	38.8
Other	10.4

Source: *Household and Personal Products Industry*, August 1998, p. 58, from Information Resources Inc.

★ 686 ★

Baby Care (SIC 2844)

Top Baby Powder Brands - 1998

Shares are shown based on sales for the year ended May 24, 1998.

Johnson's	57.3%
Gold Bond	5.2
Mennen Baby Magic	4.0
Diaparene	3.0
Caldesene	2.2
Suave	2.2
Desitin	1.6
Lander	0.4
Generic	1.8
Private label	22.0
Other	0.3

Source: *Household and Personal Products Industry*, August 1998, p. 58, from Information Resources Inc.

★ 687 ★

Cosmetics (SIC 2844)

Canada's Cosmetics Market - 1998

Total sales at drugstores reached $280.6 million for the year ended January 30, 1999.

	($ mil.)	Share
Eye makeup	$ 81.2	28.94%
Lip makeup	80.4	28.65
Face makeup	78.3	27.90
Nail color	37.0	13.19
Nail kits and sets	3.5	1.25
Other	0.2	0.07

Source: *Marketing Magazine*, May 12, 1999, p. 12, from A.C. Nielsen.

★ 688 ★

Cosmetics (SIC 2844)

Cosmetics Market - 1998

Shares are shown based on $3.2 billion in sales for the year ending February 21, 1999.

Revlon	20.6%
Cover Girl	19.1
Maybelline	16.8
L'Oreal	12.7
Almay	7.0
Max Factor	4.2
Other	19.6

Source: *Wall Street Journal*, April 12, 1999, p. B1, from Information Resources Inc.

★ 689 ★

Cosmetics (SIC 2844)

Leading Face Makeup Brands

Unit shares are shown in percent for the 52 weeks ended October 25, 1998.

Cover Girl	42.1%
Maybelline	14.5
Revlon	11.3
L'Oreal	7.2
Almay	6.2
Max Factor	6.1
Jane	2.0
Physicians Formula	1.8%
Cornsilk	1.4
Coty	1.4
Other	6.0

Source: *Discount Store News*, January 4, 1999, p. 58.

★ 690 ★

Cosmetics (SIC 2844)

Popular Girl's Makeup Brands

Figures are based on a survey of teens 13 - 17 for the last six months.

Cover Girl	24.0%
Clinique	17.0
MAC	6.0
Revlon	6.0
Maybelline	4.0
Jane	2.0
L'Oreal	2.0

Source: *Household and Personal Products Industry*, August 1998, p. 53, from Zandl Group.

★ 691 ★

Cosmetics (SIC 2844)

Top Color Cosmetic Brands - 1998

Market shares are shown in percent.

	1Q 1998	2Q 1998
Revlon	22.0%	22.5%
Cover Girl	20.0	18.7
Maybelline	17.1	17.0
L'Oreal	12.2	12.7
Almay	8.5	8.3
Max Factor	5.3	4.8
Others	14.9	15.9

Source: *Investext*, Thomson Financial Networks, August 3, 1998, p. 3, from Nielsen.

★ 692 ★

Cosmetics (SIC 2844)

Women's Cosmetics Sales in Mexico - 1996

Sales are in millions of dollars.

	($ mil.)	Share
Lips	$ 58.467	32.57%
Face	48.519	27.03
Eyes	47.508	26.47
Nail	18.860	10.51
Other	6.148	3.43

Source: *National Trade Data Bank*, November 4, 1998, p. ISA980901, from Mexican Chamber of Perfumes and Cosmetics.

★ 693 ★

Deodorants (SIC 2844)

Best-Selling Deodorants - 1998

Unit shares are shown for the year ended March 29, 1998.

Secret	14.6%
Mennen	9.8
Right Guard	9.5
Degree	7.7
Lady Mennen	6.5
Sure	6.5
Arrid	5.7
Other	39.7

Source: *Supermarket Business*, June 1998, p. 65, from Information Resources Inc.

★ 694 ★

Deodorants (SIC 2844)

Top Deodorant Brands - 1998

Market shares are shown for the year ended December 27, 1998.

Secret	14.6%
Right Guard	9.9
Mennen	9.0
Degree	8.2
Sure	6.8
Other	51.5

Source: *Advertising Age*, March 8, 1999, p. 54, from Information Resources Inc.

★ 695 ★

Foot Care (SIC 2844)

Athlete's Foot Remedies - 1998

Lotrimin
Tinactin
Desenex
Micatin
Private label
Other

The $280 million market is shown in percent.

	($ mil.)	Share
Lotrimin	$ 57.8	20.64%
Tinactin	43.4	15.50
Desenex	32.8	11.71
Micatin	15.4	5.50
Private label	29.0	10.36
Other	101.6	36.29

Source: *Advertising Age*, May 10, 1999, p. 8, from Information Resources Inc.

★ 696 ★

Foot Care (SIC 2844)

Top Foot Care Medication Brands - 1998

Market shares are shown for the year ended October 11, 1998.

Lotrimin AF	20.6%
Tinactin	15.5
Desenex	11.7
Dr. Scholl	10.1
Micatin	5.8
Johnson Odor Eaters	3.5
Freeman Bare Foot	2.8
Fungi Care	2.2
Dr. Scholl Odor Destroyers	2.0
Private label	10.3
Other	17.7

Source: *Discount Merchandiser*, December 1998, p. 51, from Information Resources Inc.

★ 697 ★

Foot Care (SIC 2844)

Top Foot Care Product Brands - 1998

Market shares are shown for the year ended October 11, 1998.

Dr. Scholl	36.1%
Dr. Scholl Dynastep	7.2
Dr. Scholl Air Pillow	5.5
Dr. Scholl Maximum Comfort	5.5
Dr. Scholl Flexo	3.0
Dr. Scholl Advanced Pain Relief	2.9
Dr. Scholl One Step	2.9
Dr. Scholl Double Air Pillow	2.5
Sof Comfort	2.3
Private label	5.0
Others	27.1

Source: *Discount Merchandiser*, December 1998, p. 51, from Information Resources Inc.

★ 698 ★

Foot Care (SIC 2844)

Top Foot Care Product Makers

Market shares are shown for the year ended October 11, 1998.

Schering-Plough	74.3%
ProFoot Care	4.3
Combe Inc.	3.3
Implus Corp.	3.1
Johnson & Johnson	2.2
Footsply	1.8
Spenco Medc Corp.	1.4
Del Labs Inc.	0.6
LaLoren Inc.	0.6
Private label	5.0
Others	3.4

Source: *Discount Merchandiser*, December 1998, p. 51, from Information Resources Inc.

★ 699 ★

Fragrances (SIC 2844)

Fragrance Market in Mexico

Sales are in millions of dollars.

Women's fragrances	$ 95.276
Men's fragrances	82.458

Source: *National Trade Data Bank*, November 4, 1998, p. ISA980901, from Mexican Chamber of Perfumes and Cosmetics.

★ 700 ★

Fragrances (SIC 2844)

Popular Boy's Colognes

Tommy
Michael Jordan
Cool Water
Brut
CK One

Figures are based on a survey of teens 13 - 17 for the last six months.

Tommy	15.0%
Michael Jordan	8.0
Cool Water	7.0
Brut	4.0
CK One	4.0

Source: *Household and Personal Products Industry*, August 1998, p. 53, from Zandl Group.

★ 701 ★

Fragrances (SIC 2844)

Popular Men's Fragrances - 1997

Market shares are shown in percent.

Tommy	9.7%
Eternity for Men	5.9
Obsession for Men	5.5
Polo Sport	5.3
Pleasures for Men	4.2
Cool Water	4.1
Hugo	3.7

Continued on next page.

★ 701 ★ *Continued*

Fragrances (SIC 2844)

Popular Men's Fragrances - 1997

Market shares are shown in percent.

Aramis	3.5%
Drakkar Noir	3.4
Escape	3.4
Other	51.3

Source: *Household and Personal Products Industry*, November 1998, p. 94, from NPD BeautyTrends.

★ 702 ★

Fragrances (SIC 2844)

Popular Women's Fragrances - 1997

Market shares are shown in percent.

Pleasures	5.8%
Beautiful	5.5
Tommy Girl	4.3
Tresor	3.0
Eternity	2.9
Chanel No. 5	2.6
White Linen	2.3
Obsession	2.2
Aromatics Elixir	2.0
White Diamonds	2.0
Other	67.40

Source: *Household and Personal Products Industry*, November 1998, p. 94, from NPD BeautyTrends.

★ 703 ★

Fragrances (SIC 2844)

Top Fragrance Makers - 1997

Sales are shown in millions of dollars.

	($ mil.)	Share
Estee Lauder	$ 1,000.0	56.81%
Cosmair	385.2	21.88
Chanel	88.2	5.01
Unilever	57.6	3.27
Fashion Fair	55.8	3.17
LVMH	46.8	2.66
Princess Marcella Borghese	30.6	1.74
Shiseido	23.4	1.33
Clarins	14.4	0.82
Others	58.4	3.32

Source: *Household and Personal Products Industry*, August 1998, p. 70, from NPD BeautyTrends.

★ 704 ★

Hair Care (SIC 2844)

Hair Care Market

Sales are shown in millions of units.

Hair spray/spritz	309.4
Coloring	191.5
Styling aids	188.8
Perms	7.5

Source: *Household and Personal Products Industry*, December 1998, p. 116, from Information Resources Inc.

★ 705 ★

Hair Care (SIC 2844)

Hair Care Product Sales in Mexico - 1996

Sales are in millions of dollars.

	($ mil.)	Share
Shampoo	$ 195.744	55.91%
Dye, peroxide, bleach	67.213	19.20
Fixatives	58.117	16.60
Conditioners	18.175	5.19
Special treatments	7.891	2.25
Permanents	2.967	0.85

Source: *National Trade Data Bank*, November 4, 1998, p. ISA980901.

★ 706 ★

Hair Care (SIC 2844)

Hair Spray Market - 1998

Shares are shown for the year ended July 26, 1998.

Rave	12.8%
Pantene	11.9
Clairol	7.4
Aussie	6.9
Salon Selectives	6.8
Aquanet	6.5
Suave	6.3
White Rain	5.0
Finesse	4.0
Vidal Sasson	2.7
Other	29.7

Source: *Household and Personal Products Industry*, December 1998, p. 118, from Information Resources Inc.

★ 707 ★

Hair Care (SIC 2844)

Hair Styling Market

Unit shares are shown for the year ended December 27, 1998.

Suave	10.9%
Studio Line	7.9
LA Looks	7.7
Clairol	7.4
Salon Select	6.4
Other	59.7

Source: *Household and Personal Products Industry*, May 1999, p. 57, from Information Resources Inc.

★ 708 ★

Hair Care (SIC 2844)

Largest Shampoo Makers - 1998

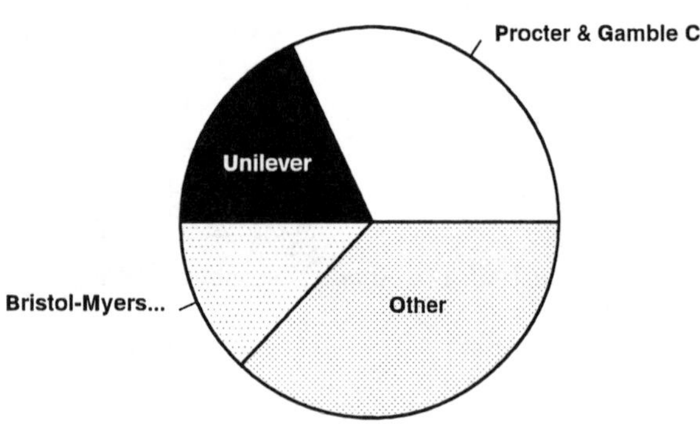

Market shares are shown for the second quarter of the year.

Procter & Gamble Co.	32.4%
Unilever	17.7
Bristol-Myers Squibb Co.	13.2
Other	36.7

Source: *Advertising Age*, October 19, 1998, p. 4, from Information Resources Inc.

★ 709 ★

Hair Care (SIC 2844)

Popular Boy's Shampoos

Figures are based on a survey of teens 13 - 17 for the last six months.

Head & Shoulders	13.0%
Suave	13.0
Pantene	9.0
Pert Plus	7.0
Clairol Herbal Essences	5.0
Salon Selectives	3.0
VO5	3.0

Source: *Household and Personal Products Industry*, August 1998, p. 53, from Zandl Group.

★ 710 ★

Hair Care (SIC 2844)

Styling Aids Market - 1998

Shares are shown for the year ended July 26, 1998.

L'Oreal Studio Line	9.6%
Clairol	7.3
LA Look	6.3
Suave	5.9
Pantene	5.6
Salon Select	5.5
Dep	4.1
Aussie	3.1
Softsheen	2.5
Vitacare	2.5
Other	47.6

Source: *Household and Personal Products Industry*, December 1998, p. 118, from Information Resources Inc.

★ 711 ★

Hair Care (SIC 2844)

Top Ethnic Hair Care Brands - 1997

Market shares are shown in percent.

Shades of You	23.3%
Revlon Color Style	18.1
Posner	13.0
Black Radiance	10.3
Tropez	5.3
Darker Tones	3.9
Cover Girl Ethnic	3.0
Wet &Wild	2.4
Zuri	2.3

Continued on next page.

★ 711 ★ *Continued*

Hair Care (SIC 2844)

Top Ethnic Hair Care Brands - 1997

Market shares are shown in percent.

Solo Para Ti	2.0%
Zhen Cosmetics	1.9
Simply Satin	0.5
Other	14.0

Source: *DCI*, October 1998, p. 58, from Datamonitor.

★ 712 ★

Hair Care (SIC 2844)

Top Hair Coloring Brands - 1998

Sales are shown for the 52 weeks ended January 3, 1999.

	($ mil.)	Share
L'Oreal Preference	$ 158.6	13.49%
Clairol Nice 'N Easy	122.7	10.44
L'Oreal Excellence	108.3	9.21
Just For Men	72.1	6.13
Clairol Natural Instincts	67.9	5.78
Clairol Hydrience	62.3	5.30
Clairol Loving Care	45.0	3.83
Clairol Ultress	43.7	3.72
Revlon Colorstay	40.2	3.42
Other	454.8	38.69

Source: *Advertising Age*, February 15, 1999, p. 4, from Information Resources Inc.

★ 713 ★

Hair Care (SIC 2844)

Top Hair Styling Aid Brands - 1998

Market shares are shown in percent.

L'Oreal	9.4%
Clairol	7.4
LA Looks	6.3
Suave	5.8
Pantene	5.4
Salon Selectives	5.3
DEP	4.0
Aussie	3.1
ThermaSilk	2.8%
Soft Sheen	2.4
Vidal Sassoon	2.4
Other	45.7

Source: *Spray Technology & Marketing*, May 1999, p. 12, from Information Resources Inc.

★ 714 ★

Oral Care (SIC 2844)

Mouthwash Unit Sales

Unit shares are shown in percent.

Listerine	32.6%
Scope	30.0
Plax	5.4
Act	2.3
Cepacol	1.6
Targon	1.6
Private label	30.0

Source: *Discount Merchandiser*, June 1999, p. 56, from Information Resources Inc.

★ 715 ★

Oral Care (SIC 2844)

Oral Care Market in Canada

Toothpaste	43.0%
Oral antiseptics	23.0
Toothbrushes	22.0
Denture cleansers	7.0
Dental floss	5.0

Source: *National Trade Data Bank*, March 30, 1998, p. IMI980330.

★ 716 ★

Oral Care (SIC 2844)

Oral Care Sales - 1997

Total supermarket sales reached $1.713 billion.

Toothpaste	$ 871.90
Toothbrushes	311.63
Mouthwashes, dental rinses	303.52
Denture needs	133.47
Dental floss and tape	62.76
Breath fresheners	18.69
Other	11.63

Source: *Progressive Grocer*, August 1998, p. 56, from Information Resources Inc.

★ 717 ★

Oral Care (SIC 2844)

Top Dental Hygiene Product Makers - 1998

Market shares are shown in percent.

Procter & Gamble	19.7%
Colgate-Palmolive	17.5
Warner Lambert	10.4
Elida Faberge	8.6
SmithKline Beecham	6.8
Johnson & Johnson	5.8
Gillette	5.6
Stafford Miller	5.4
Private label	7.0
Others	13.2

Source: *Chemical Market Report*, April 5, 1999, p. 12, from Euromonitor.

★ 718 ★

Oral Care (SIC 2844)

Top Dentifrices - 1999

Market shares are shown in percent.

Colgate	27.7%
Crest	25.3
Aquafresh	10.5
Mentadent	9.5
Arm & Hammer	5.9
Sensodyne	3.4
Rembrandt	3.0
Closeup	1.9
Listerine	1.9
Ultra Brite	1.5%
Other	9.4

Source: *Discount Merchandiser*, June 1999, p. 54, from Information Resources Inc.

★ 719 ★

Oral Care (SIC 2844)

Top Mouthwash Brands - 1998

Market shares are shown based on sales for the year ended February 28, 1998.

Listerine	40.7%
Scope	17.2
Plax	6.9
Act	2.6
Mentadent	1.9
Cepacol	1.6
Peroxyl	1.3
Actfrkid	1.0
Viadent	0.9
Targon	0.8
Private label	20.4
Other	4.7

Source: *Chemical Market Report*, May 11, 1998, p. 18, from Datamonitor.

★ 720 ★

Oral Care (SIC 2844)

Top Toothpaste Brands in Canada - 1999

Market shares are shown in percent for the year ended January 2, 1999.

Colgate	39.2%
Crest	25.2
Aquafresh	15.3
Sensodyne	8.7
Arm & Hammer	4.2
Close-Up	2.5
Macleans	1.1
Aim	0.8
Pepsodent	0.4
Others	2.6

Source: "Report on Market Share." Retrieved June 1, 1999 from the World Wide Web: http://www.marketingmag.ca/index.cgi?, from Canadian Tobacco Manufacturers Council.

★ 721 ★

Personal Care Products (SIC 2844)

Cosmetics/Toiletries Market

Makeup
Fragrances
Hair care
Personal hygiene
Oral hygiene
Shaving products
Other

Makeup	23.0%
Fragrances	18.4
Hair care	14.5
Personal hygiene	13.5
Oral hygiene	10.5
Shaving products	5.6
Other	14.5

Source: *DCI*, June 1998, p. 26, from Datamonitor.

★ 722 ★

Personal Care Products (SIC 2844)

Ethnic Products Market

	1998
Hair care	$ 1,268
Cosmetics	432
Skin care	107

Source: *Soap/Cosmetics/Chemical Specialties*, September 1998, p. 42, from Packaged Facts.

★ 723 ★

Personal Care Products (SIC 2844)

Health & Beauty Care Product Sales

OTC stands for over-the-counter.

OTC remedies	29.3%
Hair care	12.7
Oral hygiene	11.6
Feminine hygiene	8.2
Cosmetics & nail care	7.1
Vitamins/supplements	5.0
Personal deodorants	4.6%
Shaving needs	4.4
Skin/sun tan products	4.0
Other	13.1

Source: *Supermarket Business*, May 1999, p. 118.

★ 724 ★

Personal Care Products (SIC 2844)

Men's Toiletries Market - 1997

Data show supermarket sales in millions of dollars.

	($ mil.)	Share
Razors and blades	$ 403.92	48.32%
Disposable shavers	188.56	22.56
Shaving creams	132.04	15.79
Pre- and after-shave lotions	59.88	7.16
Hair care products	26.55	3.18
Colognes	19.31	2.31
Other	5.74	0.69

Source: *Progressive Grocer*, August 1998, p. 56.

★ 725 ★

Personal Care Products (SIC 2844)

Personal Care Industry in Canada - 1996

Sales are shown in millions of dollars for the year ended November/December 1996.

Cough, cold and allergy remedies	$ 298.75
Headache remedies	231.90
Deodorants	138.84
Dentifrices	102.66
Upset stomach remedies	84.42
Contact lens preparations	77.61
Multiple vitamins	65.82
Laxatives	55.11
Oral antiseptics	51.61
Topical wound care	44.68

Source: "About the Industry." Retrieved May 21, 1999 from the World Wide Web: http:// www.ndmac.ca/ industry/P-index.html, from A.C. Nielsen MarketTrack HABC.

★ 726 ★

Personal Care Products (SIC 2844)

Personal Care Product Sales

Sales are shown in billions of dollars for health and beauty aid products.

New York, NY	$ 3.66
Chicago, IL	3.64
Philadelphia, PA	3.17
Los Angeles-Long Beach, CA	3.14
Washington, D.C.	2.54

Source: *Sales & Marketing Management*, August 1998, p. 192.

★ 727 ★

Shaving Preparations (SIC 2844)

Top Shaving Cream Brands - 1998

Shares are shown based on a $331 million market for the year ended October 11, 1998.

Edge	27.3%
Skintimate	20.6
Gillette Foamy	9.7
Gillette Satin Care	9.4
Colgate	9.4
Gillette Series	7.8
Barbasol	6.6
Noxzema	2.6
Aveeno	1.2
Soft Shave	0.8
Private label	0.7
Other	3.9

Source: *Discount Merchandiser*, January 1999, p. 80, from Information Resources Inc.

★ 728 ★

Skin Care (SIC 2844)

Skin Care Market in Canada

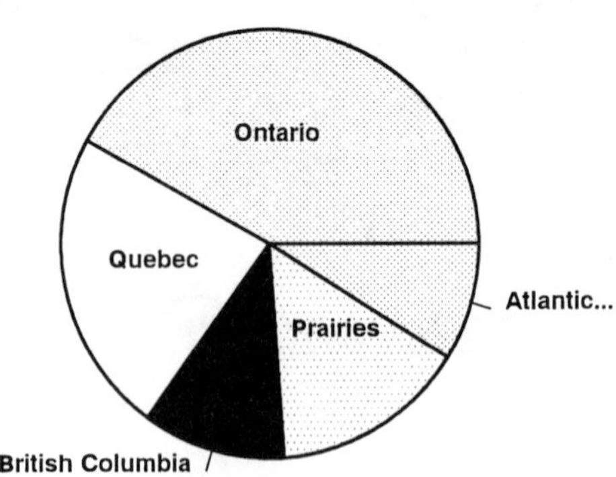

The market is shown in percent.

Ontario	42.0%
Quebec	23.0
British Columbia	11.0
Prairies	15.0
Atlantic Provinces	9.0

Source: *National Trade Data Bank*, October 22, 1998, p. ISA980901.

★ 729 ★

Skin Care (SIC 2844)

Skin Care Market in Mexico - 1996

Sales are shown in millions of dollars.

Moisturizing	$ 106.994
All-purpose	106.994
Cold cream	42.405
Night cream	41.983
Lotion-toner	15.251

Source: *National Trade Data Bank*, November 4, 1998, p. ISA980901, from Mexican Chamber of Perfumes and Cosmetics.

★ 730 ★

Skin Care (SIC 2844)

Skin Care Sales - 1997

Total supermarket sales reached $777.7 million.

	($ mil.)	Share
Hand and body preparations	$ 222.31	28.59%
Face creams and cleansers	209.48	26.94
Sun care	108.03	13.89

Continued on next page.

★ 730 ★ *Continued*

Skin Care (SIC 2844)

Skin Care Sales - 1997

Total supermarket sales reached $777.7 million.

	($ mil.)	Share
Acne preparations	$ 80.13	10.30%
Bath and shower products	57.97	7.45
Colognes, women's	26.23	3.37
Talcum powder	22.84	2.94
Specialty bar soaps	17.74	2.28
Depilatories	15.07	1.94
Other	17.90	2.30

Source: *Progressive Grocer*, August 1998, p. 56, from Information Resources Inc.

★ 731 ★

Skin Care (SIC 2844)

Top Face Moisturizer Brands

Market shares are shown in percent.

Olay	27.8%
L"Oreal Plenitude	16.5
Ponds	12.3
Neutrogena	11.0
Alpha Hydroxy	4.0
Visage	3.9
Almay	3.5
Sudden Change	1.9
University Medical	1.8
Private label	2.3
Other	25.0

Source: *Discount Merchandiser*, June 1999, p. 54, from Information Resources Inc.

★ 732 ★

Sun Care (SIC 2844)

Top Baby Sun Care Brands - 1998

The $60.2 million market is shown in percent.

Coppertone Water Babies	33.6%
Hawaiian Tropic Baby Faces	5.2
Neutrogena Kids	3.0
Banana Boat	1.5
NO-AD Solar Babies	1.5
Private label	12.5
Others	42.7

Source: *Chemical Market Report*, April 5, 1999, p. 8, from Euromonitor.

★ 733 ★

Sun Care (SIC 2844)

Top Suntan Lotion Brands

Coppertone	14.0%
Banana Boat	11.8
Neutrogena	9.0
Hawaiian Tropic	5.5
Bain De Soleil	4.7
Coppertone Sport	4.6
No Ad	4.3
Private label	7.8
Other	38.3

Source: *Discount Merchandiser*, June 1999, p. 59, from Information Resources Inc.

★ 734 ★

Paints and Coatings (SIC 2851)

Exterior Coatings Market

Epoxies	30.0%
Urethanes	16.0
Alkyds	15.0
Acrylics	12.0
Other	27.0

Source: *Chemical & Engineering News*, October 12, 1998, p. 61, from WEH Corp.

★ 735 ★

Paints and Coatings (SIC 2851)

Largest Coatings Producers - 1997

Shares of the $17.5 billion market are shown in percent.

Sherwin-Williams	20.0%
PPG Industries	12.0
ICI	9.0
Akzo Nobel	8.0
BASF	6.0
RPM	6.0
DuPont	5.0
Courtaulds	4.0
H. B. Fuller	4.0
Valspar	4.0
Other	22.0

Source: *Chemical & Engineering News*, October 12, 1998, p. 56, from Frost & Sullivan.

★ 736 ★

Paints and Coatings (SIC 2851)

Largest Paint/Coating Makers

Firms are ranked by sales in millions of dollars.

Sherwin Williams	$ 4,881.1
RPM	1,350.5
Valspar	1,017.3
Benjamin Moore	666.3
Lilly Industries	601.3

Source: *Chemical Week*, May 20, 1998, p. 48.

★ 737 ★

Paints and Coatings (SIC 2851)

Paint Sales by End Use - 1997

OEM stands for original equipment manufacturer.

Architectural	37.0%
OEM	30.0
Special purpose	27.0
Powder	5.0
Radiation cured	1.0

Source: *Chemistry & Engineering News*, October 12, 1998, p. 42, from Frost & Sullivan.

★ 738 ★

Paints and Coatings (SIC 2851)

Popular Colors for Full-Intermediate Vehicles

Data are for North American vehicles.

Medium/dark green	16.4%
White	15.6
Light brown	14.1
Silver	11.0
Black	8.9
Medium red	6.5
Medium/dark red	6.5
Other	21.0

Source: *WARD's Auto World*, March 1999, p. 30, from DuPont Automotive.

★ 739 ★

Paints and Coatings (SIC 2851)

Popular Colors for Luxury Vehicles

Data are for North American vehicles.

Light brown	17.7%
Black	12.3
White met.	12.3
White	11.3
Med./dark green	10.0
Silver	9.2
Medium red	7.5
Other	19.7

Source: *WARD's Auto World*, March 1999, p. 30, from DuPont Automotive.

★ 740 ★

Paints and Coatings (SIC 2851)

Popular Colors for Sport/Compact Vehicles

Data are for North American vehicles.

Medium/dark green	15.9%
Black	15.0
White	14.7
Silver	10.4
Bright red	9.5
Light brown	7.0
Medium red	6.4
Other	21.1

Source: *WARD's Auto World*, March 1999, p. 30, from DuPont Automotive.

★ 741 ★

Paints and Coatings (SIC 2851)

Popular Colors for Trucks/SUVs/ Vans

Data are for North American vehicles.

White	22.5%
Medium/dark green	15.5
Black	11.5
Medium red	7.2
Bright red	7.1
Silver	6.2

Source: *WARD's Auto World*, March 1999, p. 30, from DuPont Automotive.

★ 742 ★

Organic Chemicals (SIC 2865)

Benzene Demand by End Use - 2000

Styrene	50.0%
Cumene/phenol	24.0
Cyclohexane	12.0
Aniline	6.0
Alkylbenzene	2.0
Chlorobenzene	1.0
Other	5.0

Source: *Chemical Market Report*, March 15, 1999, p. 29, from Chem Systems.

★ 743 ★

Organic Chemicals (SIC 2865)

Ethylene Glycol Sales

The market is shown by end use.

Antifreeze	30.0%
Polyester fiber	27.0
PET botlle grade resins	25.0
Industrial	10.0
Polyester film	4.0
Other	4.0

Source: *Chemical Market Report*, November 2, 1998, p. 37.

★ 744 ★

Organic Chemicals (SIC 2865)

Fatty Acid Demand - 1997

Personal care products
Lubricants & corrosion inhibitors
Plastics additives
Household & industrial cleaners
Coatings & adhesives
Fabric softeners
Others

Consumption is shown in percent.

Personal care products	17.0%
Lubricants & corrosion inhibitors	11.0
Plastics additives	11.0
Household & industrial cleaners	10.0
Coatings & adhesives	9.0
Fabric softeners	9.0
Others	33.0

Source: *Chemical & Engineering News*, April 26, 1999, p. 13, from SRI Consulting.

★ 745 ★

Organic Chemicals (SIC 2865)

Largest Alpha Olefin Producers

Companies are ranked by capacity in millions of pounds.

Shell	1,335
Amoco	1,036
Chevron	750

Source: *Chemical Market Report*, November 7, 1998, p. 49.

★ 746 ★

Organic Chemicals (SIC 2865)

Largest Analine Producers

Companies are ranked by capacity in millions of pounds.

Rubicon	500
First Chemical	490
DuPont	280
BASF	230
Aristech	150

Source: *Chemical Market Report*, November 7, 1998, p. 49.

★ 747 ★

Organic Chemicals (SIC 2865)

Largest Cumene Producers

Companies are ranked by capacity in millions of pounds.

Georgia Gulf	1,500
Koch Petroleum	1,500
Citgo Petroleum	1,115
Shell Chemical	1,100
Chevron Chemical	1,000

Source: *Chemical Market Report*, March 22, 1999, p. 33.

★ 748 ★

Organic Chemicals (SIC 2865)

Largest MIBT Producers

Companies are ranked by capacity in millions of pounds. MIBT stands for methyl isobutyl ketone.

Shell	100
Union Carbide	75
Eastman	35

Source: *Chemical Market Report*, March 8, 1999, p. 37.

★ 749 ★

Organic Chemicals (SIC 2865)

Largest Nonylphenol Makers

Companies are ranked by capacity in millions of pounds.

Schenectady	140
Huntsman	70
GE	60
Dover Chemical	48
BFG Kalama	20

Source: *Chemical Market Report*, September 28, 1998, p. 37.

★ 750 ★

Organic Chemicals (SIC 2865)

Largest Phenol Producers

Companies are ranked by capacity in millions of pounds.

Sun	1,000
Aristech	700
GE Plastics	700
Shell	700
Georgia Gulf	660

Source: *Chemical Market Report*, March 29, 1999, p. 33.

★ 751 ★

Organic Chemicals (SIC 2865)

Organic Chemical Production - 1997

Data are in millions of pounds.

Ethylene	51,078
Propylene	27,533
Ethylene dichloride	26,294
Urea	15,530
Ethylbenzene	12,691
Ethylene oxide	8,241

Source: *Chemical & Engineering News*, June 29, 1998, p. 42, from National Petroleum Refiners Association and U.S. Bureau of the Census.

★ 752 ★
Organic Chemicals (SIC 2865)

Phenol Production Leaders - 2000

Shell	18.0%
Sun	17.0
Aristech	14.0
Phenolchemie	14.0
Georgia Gulf	10.0
Mt. Vernon	10.0
Dow	8.5
Solutia/JLM	5.0
Others	3.5

Source: *European Chemical News*, April 6, 1998, p. 9, from ICIS-LOR.

★ 753 ★
Organic Chemicals (SIC 2865)

Titanium Dioxide Market - 1998

Market shares are shown based on capacity.

DuPont	23.0%
Millennium	16.0
Tioxide	14.0
Kerr-McGee	10.0
Kronos	9.0
Kemira	7.0
Others	21.0

Source: *Chemical Week*, January 13, 1999, p. 7, from BT Alex. Brown.

★ 754 ★
Organic Chemicals (SIC 2869)

Artificial Sweetener Market

	2000	2005
Aspartame	69.7%	63.3%
Saccharin	18.5	15.2
Acesulfame-K	5.4	10.4

Source: *Chemical Engineering*, September 1998, p. 43, from Freedonia Group.

★ 755 ★
Organic Chemicals (SIC 2869)

Largest Acrylamide Producers

Companies are ranked by capacity in millions of pounds.

Dow	105
Cytec Industries	90
Nalco	35
Ciba Specialties	33

Source: *Chemical Market Report*, March 15, 1999, p. 45.

★ 756 ★
Organic Chemicals (SIC 2869)

Largest Ethylbenzene Makers

Companies are ranked by capacity in millions of pounds.

Arco	3,000
Cos-Mar	2,200
Sterling	2,000
Chevron	1,900
Huntsman	1,650

Source: *Chemical Market Report*, April 27, 1998, p. 57.

★ 757 ★

Organic Chemicals (SIC 2869)

Largest Ethylene Oxide Producers

Companies are ranked by capacity in millions of pounds.

Union Carbide	2,385
Shell	1,260
Huntsman	997
Equistar	750
PD Glycol	640

Source: *Chemical Market Report*, November 9, 1998, p. 53.

★ 758 ★

Organic Chemicals (SIC 2869)

Largest Methanol Makers

Companies are ranked by capacity in millions of gallons. Figures are for North America.

Methanex	535
Borden Chemicals & Plastics	330
Terra	320
Celanese Canada	254

Source: *Chemical Market Report*, August 3, 1998, p. 33.

★ 759 ★

Agrichemicals (SIC 2870)

DIY Lawn Chemical Market

Market shares are shown in percent. DIY stands for do-it-yourself. Scott Co. also has a 35% share of the consumer grass seed market, 52% share of the garden fertilizer market, 33% share of the indoor plant foods, and 48% share of the consumer potting soil market.

Scott Co.	58.0%
Other	42.0

Source: *Forbes*, November 16, 1998, p. 90.

★ 760 ★

Fertilizers (SIC 2879)

Largest Fertilizer Makers - 1997

Firms are ranked by sales in millions of dollars. Figures are for North America.

Farmland Industries	$ 9,417.5
IMC Global	2,988.6
Terra Industries	2,506.8
Potsdh Corp. of Saskatchewan	2,325.9
Scotts	902.8

Source: *Chemical Week*, May 20, 1998, p. 45.

★ 761 ★

Herbicides (SIC 2879)

U.S. Herbicide Market

The market is shown by crop.

Corn	30.0%
Soybeans	25.0
Noncrop uses	16.0
Small grains	8.0
Cotton	5.0
Other crops	16.0

Source: *Chemical & Engineering News*, April 19, 1999, p. 32, from SRI Consulting.

★ 762 ★

Adhesives (SIC 2891)

Sealant & Caulk Demand - 1997

Type	Share
Polyurethanes	28.0%
Silicones	23.0
Bituminous	15.0
Synthetic elastomers	12.0
Acrylics	5.0
Polysulfides	4.0
Other	13.0

Source: *Adhesives Age*, October 1998, p. 58, from Freedonia Group.

★ 763 ★

Adhesives (SIC 2891)

Sealant & Caulk Unit Sales - 1998

Sales are shown at hardware stores and home improvement chains for the year ended August 1998.

Latex	62.0%
Silicone	23.0
Aerosol foam	9.0
Other	6.0

Source: *Do-It-Yourself Retailing*, February 1999, p. 92, from Vista Sales and Marketing.

★ 764 ★

Explosives (SIC 2892)

Explosives Sales by State

Data are in metric tons.

	Tons	Share
Kentucky	356,000	15.89%
West Virginia	243,000	10.85
Wyoming	189,000	8.44
Virginia	148,000	6.61
Pennsylvania	142,000	6.34
Other	1,162,000	51.88

Source: *Minerals Yearbook*, 1996, p. 321, from Institute of Makers of Explosives.

★ 765 ★

Printing Ink (SIC 2893)

Ink Industry by Segment

	1997	2002
Lithographic	47.20%	47.67%
Flexo	19.81	22.07
Gravure	17.72	16.29
Letterpress	2.91	1.68
Other	12.35	12.29

Source: *American Printer*, October 1998, p. 12.

★ 766 ★

Printing Ink (SIC 2893)

Leading Printing Ink Producers - 1997

Companies are ranked by sales in millions of dollars. Figures are for North America.

Sun Chemical	$ 3,000
Flink Ink Corp.	900
INX Intl. Ink Co.	290
Alper Group	125
The Ink Company	125
Nazdar Company	85
Siegwerk Inc.	80
Superior Printing Ink Co. Inc.	70
Wickoff Color	65
Van Son Holland Ink Corp. of America	61
Color Converting Industries Co.	60
Sicpa Securink	60

Source: *American Ink Maker*, October 1998, p. 24.

★ 767 ★

Printing Ink (SIC 2893)

Printing Ink Market by End Use

	($ mil.)	Share
Publishing	$ 1,630	38.0%
Packaging	1,415	33.0
Commercial	815	19.0
Other	430	10.0

Source: *Paperboard Packaging*, January 1999, p. 34, from Impact Marketing Consultants and Official Board Markets.

SIC 29 - Petroleum and Coal Products

★ 768 ★

Fuels (SIC 2911)

Gasoline Consumption by State - 1997

Consumption is shown in billions of gallons. Total consumption is 118.32 billion.

	(bil.)	Share
California	13.72	13.72%
Texas	9.57	9.57
New York	5.64	5.64
Pennsylvania	4.87	4.87
Illinois	4.79	4.79
Other	61.41	61.41

Source: *National Petroleum News*, July 1998, p. 90, from Federal Highway Administration.

★ 769 ★

Fuels (SIC 2911)

Gasoline Market - 1997

Market shares are shown in percent.

Mobil	10.25%
Shell	10.10
Exxon	9.81
Citgo	9.79
Amoco	8.28
Texaco	8.21
Chevron	7.42
Marathon	5.67
Other	30.47

Source: *National Petroleum News*, July 1998, p. 151.

★ 770 ★

Fuels (SIC 2911)

Leading Propane Retailers - 1998

Data show millions of retail gallons.

AmeriGas Partners L.P.	785.30
Ferrellgas Partners L.P.	659.93
Suburban Propane Partners L.P.	530.00
Cornerstone Propane Partners L.P.	304.40
Thermogas Company	262.64
Heritage Propane Partners L.P.	170.44
National Propane Partners L.P.	155.00
Star Gas Partners L.P.	110.73

Source: *LP/GAS*, January 1999, p. 22.

★ 771 ★

Fuels (SIC 2911)

Top Propane Producers in Canada - 1997

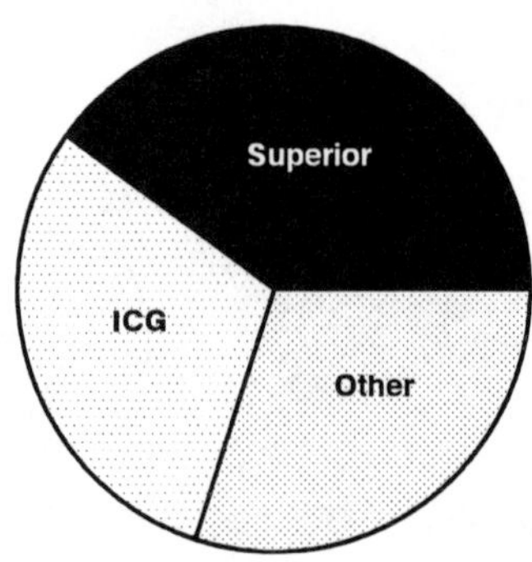

Market shares are shown in percent.

Superior	40.0%
ICG	30.0
Other	30.0

Source: *Globe and Mail*, July 17, 1998, p. B1.

★ 772 ★

Petroleum Refining (SIC 2911)

Largest Petroleum Refiners

Companies are ranked by crude capacity in barrels of crude daily.

Exxon Co. USA	1,119.5
Chevron USA Products Co.	1,049.0
Amoco Oil Co.	1,016.6
Marathon Ashland Petroleum LLC	935.0
Tosco Refining Co.	909.5
Equilon Enterprises LLC	834.3
Motiva Enterprises LLC	825.0
Sun Company Inc.	697.0
Mobil Oil Corp.	696.7
Citgo Petroleum Corp.	607.3

Source: *Oil & Gas Journal*, December 21, 1998, p. 46.

★ 773 ★

Petroleum Refining (SIC 2911)

Petroleum Refining Market

Market shares are shown in percent.

Exxon/Mobil	14.5%
Chevron	7.6
Shell	7.6
Amoco	7.3
Tosco	6.3
Sun Refining & Marketing	5.0
Other	51.7

Source: *Wall Street Journal*, December 3, 1998, p. A10, from *Oil & Gas Journal* and *National Petroleum News*.

★ 774 ★

Lubricants (SIC 2992)

Motor Oil Market

Shares are shown in percent.

Brand	Share
Pennzoil	21.5%
Quaker State	14.5
Valvoline	14.0
Castrol	13.2
Havoline	11.3
Others	25.1

Source: *Wall Street Journal*, July 1, 1998, p. B4, from NPD Group Inc. and Baseline.

★ 775 ★

Lubricants (SIC 2992)

Multipurpose Lubricant Market

"Other" is composed of approximately 200 brands.

Brand	Share
WD-40	70.0%
Other	30.0

Source: *Forbes*, March 8, 1999, p. 76.

SIC 30 - Rubber and Misc. Plastics Products

★ 776 ★

Tires (SIC 3011)

Light Truck Tire Market

Goodyear	15.0%
B.F. Goodrich	10.0
Firestone	9.0
Michelin	8.0
Cooper	6.0
Kelly-Springfield	6.0
Bridgestone	5.0
General	5.0
Other	36.0

Source: *Tire Business*, December 7, 1998, p. 12.

★ 777 ★

Tires (SIC 3011)

Tire Market Leaders - 1997

Goodyear
Michelin/Uniroyal Goodrich
Bridgestone/Firestone
Continental General Tire
Cooper
Others

Sales of tires in the United States and Canada reached $21 billion.

Goodyear	29.1%
Michelin/Uniroyal Goodrich	21.9
Bridgestone/Firestone	21.0
Continental General Tire	6.5
Cooper	6.4
Others	15.1

Source: *Tire Business*, December 7, 1998, p. 12.

★ 778 ★

Tires (SIC 3011)

Tire Production by State

Data show daily production.

Oklahoma	139,500
North Carolina	134,750
Alabama	110,800
Tennessee	86,350
Illinois	81,300
South Carolina	74,000
Mississippi	50,000

Source: *Tire Business*, December 7, 1998, p. 12, from Rubber Manufacturers Association.

★ 779 ★

Athletic Footwear (SIC 3021)

Athletic Footwear Sales - 1997

Sales are shown in billions of dollars.

Basketball	$ 2.985
Cross training	2.475
Running	2.332
Athleisure	1.814
Walking	1.216
Hiking	0.858
Tennis	0.825
Aerobic	0.478
Sport sandals	0.340

Source: *Sporting Goods Business*, July 24, 1998, p. 23, from Athletic Footwear Association and NPD Group Inc.

★ 780 ★

Athletic Footwear (SIC 3021)

Top Sports Shoe Makers - 1997

Companies are ranked by sales in millions of dollars.

Nike	$ 3,585
Reebok	1,229
Fila	488
Adidas	468
Converse	285
New Balance	265
Asics Tiger	129
K-Swiss	92
Etonic	80
Spalding	75
Avia	70
L.A. Gear	70
Saucony	56

Source: *Sportstyle*, May 1998, p. 22.

★ 781 ★

Athletic Footwear (SIC 3021)

Top Sports Shoe Makers - 1998

Market shares are shown in percent.

Nike	34.0%
Reebok	13.0
Adidas	6.0
New Balance	5.0
Easy Spirit	2.0
Other	40.0

Source: Retrieved April 30, 1999 from the World Wide Web: http:// www.npd.com/corp/press/ press_9903222.htm, from NPD Group Inc.

★ 782 ★

Athletic Footwear (SIC 3021)

Top Sports Shoes for Juniors - 1998

Market shares are shown in percent. Juniors refer to children 4-11.

Nike	39.0%
Reebok	9.0
Adidas	6.0
Converse	3.0
Fila	3.0
Other	40.0

Source: Retrieved April 30, 1999 from the World Wide Web: http:// www.npd.com/corp/press/ press_9903222.htm, from NPD Group Inc.

★ 783 ★

Athletic Footwear (SIC 3021)

Top Sports Shoes for Men - 1998

Market shares are shown in percent.

Nike	37.0%
Reebok	12.0
Adidas	6.0
New Balance	5.0
Rockport	2.0
Other	38.0

Source: Retrieved April 30, 1999 from the World Wide Web: http:// www.npd.com/corp/press/ press_9903222.htm, from NPD Group Inc.

★ 784 ★

Athletic Footwear (SIC 3021)

Top Sports Shoes for Women - 1998

Market shares are shown in percent.

Nike	29.0%
Reebok	16.0
Adidas	6.0
Easy Spirit	5.0
New Balance	5.0
Other	39.0

Source: Retrieved April 30, 1999 from the World Wide Web: http:// www.npd.com/corp/press/ press_9903222.htm, from NPD Group Inc.

★ 785 ★

Footwear (SIC 3021)

Retail Footwear Sales

Sales are shown in millions of dollars.

New York, NY	$ 1,242
Chicago, IL	1,170
Los Angeles-Long Beach, CA	1,020
Washington D.C.	762
Philadelphia, PA	735

Source: *Sales & Marketing Management*, August 1998, p. 195.

★ 786 ★

Belts and Hoses (SIC 3052)

Largest Industrial Flat Belting Markets in the Mid- Atlantic States

Sales are in millions of dollars.

Grocery stores	$ 6.5
U.S. Postal Service	2.5
Pharmaceutical preparations	2.4
Blast furnaces and steel mills	2.1
Industrial buildings and warehouse	2.0

Source: *Industrial Distribution*, September 1998, p. 77, from Industrial Market Information Inc.

★ 787 ★

Packaging (SIC 3080)

Plastic Packaging Sales - 1997

Total sales reached $4.5 billion.

Strapping	53.8%
Drum, bin & box liners	20.7
Intermediate bulk containers	11.1
Other	14.4

Source: *Plastics News*, November 16, 1998, p. 3, from Freedonia Group.

★ 788 ★

Plastic Containers (SIC 3080)

Plastic Container Market in Mexico

Packaging and bottling	45.0%
Electronics industry	20.0
Household items, including toys	16.0
Automotive parts	11.0
Electrical consumer goods	6.0
Others	2.0

Source: *National Trade Data Bank*, October 28, 1998, p. ISA980701.

★ 789 ★

Plastic Products (SIC 3080)

Largest Plastic Sheet/Film Makers

Firms are ranked by film and sheet sales in millions of dollars.

DuPont	$ 1,600
Bemis Co. Inc.	1,100
Cryovac Division	990
Printpack Inc.	850
Huntsman Packaging Corp.	767
Tyco Plastics & Adhesives Group	700

Source: *Plastics News*, September 14, 1998, p. 1.

SIC 31 - Leather and Leather Products

★ 790 ★

Luggage (SIC 3100)

Luggage Sales - 1997

Suitcases 24 inches or larger

Suitcases less than 24 inches

Soft carry-ons

Garment bags

Sales are shown in millions of items. Figures do not include backpacks/daypacks, business/computer cases and personal leather goods.

Suitcases 24 inches or larger	5.6
Suitcases less than 24 inches	3.0
Soft carry-ons	2.4
Garment bags	1.9

Source: *USA TODAY*, October 9, 1998, p. B1, from Luggage and Leather Goods Manufacturers of America.

★ 791 ★

Footwear (SIC 3140)

Largest Casual Footwear Makers

Companies are ranked by sales in millions of dollars. Shares of the group are shown in percent.

	($ mil.)	Group % of
Rockport	$ 405.0	17.42%
Easy Spirit	360.0	15.48
Dexter	300.0	12.90
Skechers	240.0	10.32
Airwalk	210.0	9.03
Hush puppies	175.0	7.53
Keds	175.0	7.53
Vans	120.4	5.18
Lugz	90.0	3.87
Birkenstock	$ 75.0	3.23%
Tommy Hilfiger	75.0	3.23
Natural Sport	50.0	2.15
Sperry	50.0	2.15

Source: *Sportstyle*, May 1998, p. 24.

★ 792 ★

Footwear (SIC 3140)

Largest Rugged Footwear Makers

Companies are ranked by sales are in millions of dollars. Shares of the group are shown in percent.

	($ mil.)	Group % of
Timberland	$ 434.0	34.19%
Nike ACG	210.0	16.54
Wolverine	200.0	15.76
Rocky	91.0	7.17
Lacrosse	88.0	6.93
Hi-Tec USA	57.0	4.49
Reebok	42.0	3.31
Adidas	37.0	2.91
Vasque	34.0	2.68
Merrell	30.0	2.36
Danner	25.0	1.97
Columbia	21.4	1.69

Source: *Sportstyle*, May 1998, p. 24.

★ 793 ★

Footwear (SIC 3140)

Top Footwear Producing States in Mexico

Total footwear production is expected to reach 210 million pairs in 1998. The typical Mexican family devotes 4.6% of its total expenditures to apparel and footwear.

Guanajuato	39.0%
Mexico, D.F.	22.0
Jalisco	17.0
Estado de Mexico	8.0
Nuevo Leon	6.0

Source: *National Trade Data Bank*, October 23, 1998, p. ISA980701, from National Chamber of the Footwear Industry.

SIC 32 - Stone, Clay, and Glass Products

★ 794 ★

Glassware (SIC 3229)

Retail Crystal Sales - 1997

Total sales were $699.53 million.

Giftware	69.0%
Stemware	25.0
Barware	6.0

Source: *HFN*, September 14, 1998, p. 8.

★ 795 ★

Glassware (SIC 3229)

Retail Glassware Sales - 1997

Total sales were $1.067 billion.

Beverageware	46.5%
Serveware, tabletop accessories	21.0
Ovenware	15.0
Storageware	8.5
Decorative accessories	8.0

Source: *HFN*, September 14, 1998, p. 8.

★ 796 ★

Tableware (SIC 3229)

Tabletop Market by Segment - 1997

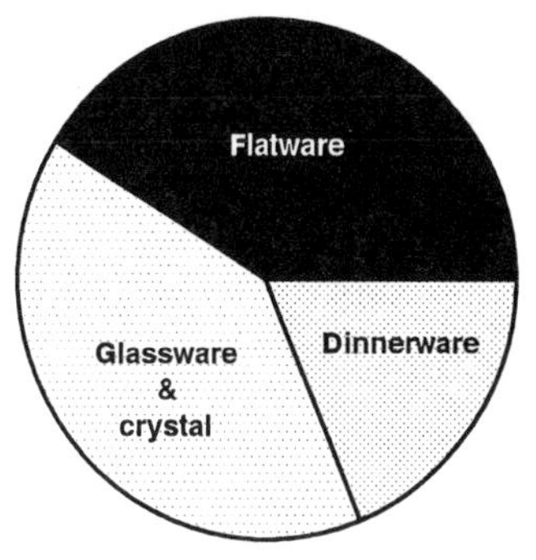

	($ mil.)	Share
Flatware	$ 1,766.0	40.9%
Glassware & crystal	1,719.0	39.8
Dinnerware	835.6	19.3

Source: *HFN*, September 14, 1998, p. 4.

★ 797 ★

Ceramics (SIC 3250)

Advanced Ceramics Market - 2001

The market is estimated.

Electronic	68.1%
Chemical & environmental	17.9
Coatings	8.1
Structural	5.9

Source: *Ceramic Industry*, August 1998, p. 35, from Business Communications Co. Inc.

★ 798 ★

Ceramics (SIC 3250)

High-Performance Ceramic Coatings - 2002

Data are for North America.

Thermal spray	51.7%
CVD	22.1
PVD	18.8
Others	7.4

Source: *Ceramic Bulletin*, March 1999, p. 71, from Business Communications Co.

★ 799 ★

Ceramics (SIC 3250)

Smart Materials Market

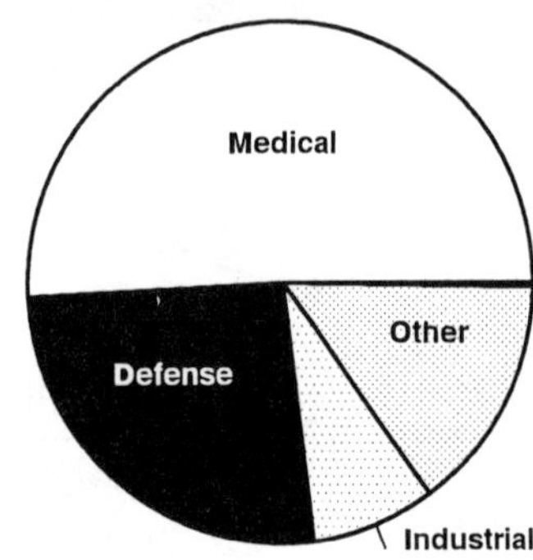

	1998	2003
Medical	44.26%	50.81%
Defense	39.09	25.95
Industrial	8.96	7.85
Other	7.69	15.39

Source: *Ceramic Bulletin*, January 1999, p. 25, from Business Communications Co.

★ 800 ★

Plumbing Fixtures (SIC 3261)

Plumbing Fitting Shipments - 1997

Sink fittings	21.0%
Single-lever controls	18.0
Bathtub/shower fittings	11.0
Other	50.0

Source: *Do-It-Yourself Retailing*, May 1999, p. 95, from Freedonia Group.

★ 801 ★

Plumbing Fixtures (SIC 3261)

Plumbing Fixture Sales - 1997

Sales are shown in percent.

Fiberglass/plastics	48.0%
Vitreous china	27.0
Metal/other	25.0

Source: *Ceramic Industry*, August 1998, p. 43.

★ 802 ★

Plumbing Fixtures (SIC 3261)

Showerhead Sales by Type

Sales are shown at hardware stores and home improvement chains.

	Share Unit	Share Dollar
Fixed head	79.0%	68.0%
Handheld	16.0	29.0
Add on	6.0	3.0

Source: *Do-It-Yourself Retailing*, April 1999, p. 28, from Vista Sales and Marketing.

★ 803 ★

Plumbing Fixtures (SIC 3261)

Toilet Repair Parts Market

Unit sales are shown for the year ended January 1999.

Tank repair kits	47.0%
Tank flapper	28.0
Tank fill valve	20.0
Tank ball	5.0

Source: *Do-It-Yourself Retailing*, May 1999, p. 95, from Vista Sales and Marketing.

★ 804 ★

Gypsum (SIC 3275)

Largest Gypsum Wallboard Makers

Market shares are shown based on capacity.

USG	32.0%
National Gypsum	21.0
Georgia-Pacific	19.0
Hardie Gypsum	7.0
Centex Construction Products	4.0

Continued on next page.

★ 804 ★ *Continued*

Gypsum (SIC 3275)

Largest Gypsum Wallboard Makers

Market shares are shown based on capacity.

Celotex	4.0%
Temple-Inland	4.0
Lafarge	3.0
Pabco	3.0
Other	3.0

Source: *Investext,* Thomson Financial Networks, July 6, 1998, p. 3, from companies, Gypsum Association, and A&SB.

SIC 33 - Primary Metal Industries

★ 805 ★

Metals (SIC 3300)

Largest Metal Firms in North America - 1997

Companies are ranked by metals sales in billions of dollars.

Aluminum Co. of America	$ 8.2
Alcan Aluminum Ltd.	7.0
U.S. Steel Group of USX Corp.	6.7
Reynolds Metals Co.	5.7
Inland Steel Industries Inc.	5.0
Bethlehem Steel Corp.	4.6
LTV Corp.	4.4
Nucor Corp.	4.1
Noranda Inc.	4.1
National Steel Corp.	3.1

Source: *American Metal Market*, June 18, 1998, p. 3A.

★ 806 ★

Metals (SIC 3300)

Largest Metal Service Centers - 1998

Firms are ranked by sales in billions of dollars.

Ryerson Tull Inc.	$ 2.8
Thyssen Inc.	2.5
Metals USA Inc.	1.5
Reliance Steel & Aluminum Co.	1.4
MacSteel Service Centers USA	1.2
Ruseell Metals Inc.	1.2

Source: *Purchasing*, May 6, 1999, p. 40B, from Analystical Computer.

★ 807 ★

Steel (SIC 3312)

Largest Steel Makers - 1998

Sales are shown in thousands of dollars.

U.S. Steel	$ 6.2
Bethlehem	4.4
LTV	4.2
Nucor	4.1
Allegheny Teledyne	3.8
National	2.8
Timken	2.6
Commercial Metals	2.3
AK Steel	2.3
Armco	2.3

Source: *New Steel*, March 1999, p. 54, from company reports.

★ 808 ★

Steel (SIC 3312)

U.S. Steel Mill Product Imports - 1999

Figures show thousands of net tons for the first quarter of the year.

	(000)	Share
European Union	1,468	18.85%
Canada	1,254	16.10
Japan	929	11.93
South Korea	876	11.25
Brazil	781	10.03
Mexico	751	9.64
China	155	1.99
Other	1,573	20.20

Source: *Financial Times*, May 14, 1999, p. 2, from American Iron & Steel Institute.

★ 809 ★

Steel (SIC 3316)

U.S. Steel Use - 1999

Data are in thousands of net tons. OCTG stands for oil country tubular goods.

	(000)	Share
Mechanical tube	5,052	39.67%
Standard pipe	2,157	16.94
Structural tube	1,941	15.24
Line pipe	1,809	14.20
OCTG pipe	1,311	10.29
Structural pipe	321	2.52
Pressure tube	85	0.67
Stainless pipe & tube	59	0.46

Source: *Purchasing*, March 11, 1999, p. 42B.

★ 810 ★

Aluminum (SIC 3334)

Aluminum Product Shipments - 1997

The market is shown in percent.

Transportation	29.0%
Packaging	22.0
Construction	13.0
Durables	7.0
Electrical	7.0
Machinery	6.0
Exports	13.0
Other	3.0

Source: *Purchasing*, November 5, 1998, p. 34B, from Aluminum Association.

★ 811 ★

Wiring (SIC 3351)

Insulated Wire & Cable

	1997	2002
Building	3,055%	3,850%
Electronics	2,780	3,800
Telephones	2,205	2,600
Fiber optics	1,640	2,525
Power	1,840	2,450
Magnets	1,070%	1,350%
Transportation equipment	1,015	1,325
Apparatus	985	1,150
Other	665	875

Source: *Purchasing*, September 15, 1998, p. 93, from Freedonia Group.

★ 812 ★

Aluminum Foil (SIC 3353)

Aluminum Foil Market in Canada

Shares are shown of the $38 million market are shown for the year ended August 15, 1998.

Alcan/Reynolds	50.0%
Private label	50.0

Source: *Marketing Magazine*, October 5, 1998, p. 3.

★ 813 ★

Castings (SIC 3364)

Steel Casting Shipments

Shipments are shown in thousands of tons.

	1998	2008
Carbon & low alloy	46.93%	45.95%
Railroad	28.17	23.83
Corrosion resistant	2.62	3.64
Manganese	1.29	1.77
Heat resistant	1.09	1.40
Other C & LA	18.76	22.12
Other steel	1.13	1.29

Source: *Modern Casting*, January 1999, p. 37.

★ 814 ★

Metal Cans (SIC 3410)

Metal Can Makers

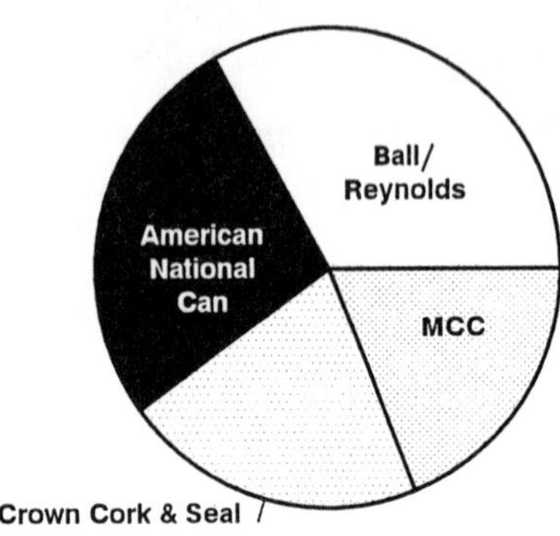

Ball/Reynolds	33.3%
American National Can	26.7
Crown Cork & Seal	21.0
MCC	19.0

Source: *Beverage World*, June 1998, p. 64, from industry reports.

★ 815 ★

Razor Blades (SIC 3421)

Best-Selling Disposable Razors

Unit shares are shown in percent.

Bic	19.3%
Schick Slim Twin	11.1
Gillette Good News	9.8
Gillette Good News Plus	9.2
Gillette Custom Plus	7.3
Private label	10.2
Other	33.1

Source: *Discount Merchandiser*, June 1999, p. 54, from Information Resources Inc.

★ 816 ★

Razor Blades (SIC 3421)

Top Razor Blade Brands - 1998

Shares are shown based on a $137.5 million market for the year ended October 11, 1998.

Gillette Mach 3 Razors	24.7%
Gillette Sensor Excel Razors	12.3
Gillette Sensor Excel Women Razors	10.7
Schick Silk Effects Razors	8.2
Schick Tracer FX Razors	7.6
Gillette Sensor Razors	6.9
Gillette Sensor For Women Razors	6.5
Schick Protector Razors	6.2
Gillette ATRA Plus Razors	4.1
Gillette Trac II Plus Razors	4.0
Personal TouchRazors	3.3
Other	5.5

Source: *Discount Merchandiser*, January 1999, p. 80, from Information Resources Inc.

★ 817 ★

Guns (SIC 3484)

Largest Gun Makers - 1997

Data show the number of automatics and revolvers produced.

Smith & Wesson	380,516
Sturm Ruger	293,363
Lorcin	92,033
Colts Mfg.	89,915
Beretta	75,156

Source: *USA TODAY*, March 9, 1999, p. 3B, from U.S. Bureau of Alcohol, Tobacco and Firearms.

★ 818 ★

Valves (SIC 3491)

Industrial Valve Market in Mexico

The demand for PVC (polyvinyl chloride) pipe is shown in percent. CFE stands for Federal Electricity Commission.

Water, wastewater, irrigation	14.0%
PEMEX	13.0
Construction	11.0
Plastics	8.0
Pharmaceuticals	7.0
Food & beverages	6.0
CRE	5.0
Automobiles	4.0
Iron & steel	4.0
Mining	4.0
Other	9.0

Source: *National Trade Data Bank*, October 19, 1998, p. ISA980801.

★ 819 ★

Powdered Metal (SIC 3499)

Iron Oxide Powder Use - 1997

The $244.2 million market is shown in percent.

Pigments	54.0%
Magnetic uses	32.0
Ferrites	9.0
Other	5.0

Source: *Ceramic Industry*, January 1999, p. 30, from Business Communications Co.

SIC 35 - Industry Machinery and Equipment

★ 820 ★

Farm Equipment (SIC 3523)

Farm Wheel Tractor Sales in Canada - 1999

Unit sales are for the first two months of the year.

2 WD 0-40 HP	424
2WD 40-49	865
2 WD 100+ HP	370
4WD	99

Source: *Implement & Tractor*, March/April 1999, p. 17.

★ 821 ★

Farm Equipment (SIC 3523)

Tractor Sales by Type

Retail sales are shown by year.

	1998	1999	Share
Under 40 HP	59,542	55,944	45.04%
40-100 HP	49,715	45,430	36.58
100 HP +	22,084	19,374	15.60
4WD	4,182	3,460	2.79

Source: *Implement & Tractor*, January/February 1999, p. 32, from Equipment Manufacturers Institute.

★ 822 ★

Lawn and Garden Equipment (SIC 3524)

Lawn & Garden Retail Sales - 1998

Retail sales are shown in billions of dollars.

	($ bil.)	Share
Green goods	$ 20.1	26.80%
Chemicals	11.4	15.20
Power equipment	9.6	12.80
Fertilizers	8.4	11.20
Watering equipment	7.9	10.53
Lawn furniture	6.4	8.53
Accessories	5.3	7.07
Trim-a-tree	$ 4.2	5.60%
Snow removal	1.7	2.27

Source: *Nursery Retailer*, February/March 1999, p. 59.

★ 823 ★

Lawn and Garden Equipment (SIC 3524)

Lawn/Garden Sales by State - 1998

	($ mil.)	Share
California	$ 8,154	10.3%
New York	6,338	8.0
Texas	4,800	6.1
Pennsylvania	4,197	5.3
Illinois	4,015	5.1
Ohio	3,855	4.9
Michigan	3,289	4.2
Florida	3,194	4.0

Source: *Nursery Retailer*, February/March 1999, p. 59.

★ 824 ★

Lawn and Garden Equipment (SIC 3524)

Outdoor Appliance Shipments - 1998

Data show unit shipments, in thousands.

Outdoor grills, gas	6,539
Power mowers, walk behind	5,829
Outdoor grills, charcoal	4,951
Trimmers/brushcutters, gasoline	4,004
Chain saws, gasoline	2,119
Leaf blowers, hand-held, gasoline	1,614
Riding mowers and lawn tractors, front engine	1,198

Source: *Appliance*, April 1999, p. 54.

★ 825 ★

Lawn and Garden Equipment (SIC 3524)

Top Electric String Trimmer Makers - 1997

Shares are shown based on shipments of 2,800,000 units.

Frigidaire Home Products	42.0%
Black & Decker	24.0
Toro	24.0
McCulloch	5.0
Ryobi	3.0
Others	2.0

Source: *Appliance Manufacturer*, May 1998, p. 23.

★ 826 ★

Lawn and Garden Equipment (SIC 3524)

Top Leaf Blower Makers - 1997

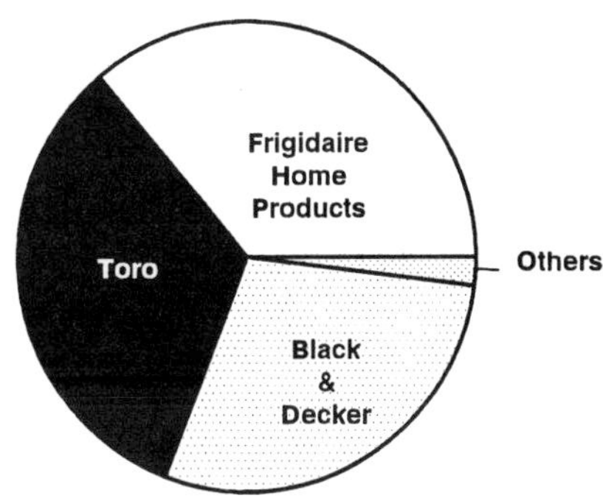

Shares are shown based on shipments of 1,600,000 units.

Frigidaire Home Products	36.0%
Toro	33.0
Black & Decker	29.0
Others	2.0

Source: *Appliance Manufacturer*, May 1998, p. 23.

★ 827 ★

Lawn and Garden Equipment (SIC 3524)

Top Riding Mower Makers - 1997

Shares are shown based on shipments of 110,800 units.

American Yard Products	21.0%
Murray	17.0
MTD	14.0%
John Deere	9.0
Snapper	4.0
Toro	4.0
Ariens	1.0
Others	30.0

Source: *Appliance Manufacturer*, May 1998, p. 23.

★ 828 ★

Lawn and Garden Equipment (SIC 3524)

Top Snowblower Makers - 1997

Shares are shown based on shipments of 1,030,000 units.

MTD	23.0%
Toro	22.0
Murray	12.0
Ariens	6.0
John Deere	4.0
Honda	3.0
Simplicity	3.0
Others	27.0

Source: *Appliance Manufacturer*, May 1998, p. 23.

★ 829 ★

Lawn and Garden Equipment (SIC 3524)

Top Walk-Behind Mower Makers - 1997

Shares are shown based on shipments of 5,557,000 units.

American Yard Products	23.0%
Murray	20.0
MTD Products	18.0
Toro	9.0
Snapper	2.0
Others	28.0

Source: *Appliance Manufacturer*, May 1998, p. 23.

★ 830 ★

Construction Equipment (SIC 3531)

Skid Steer Market

Construction	28.0%
Landscaping	22.0
Agriculture	17.0
Spec trades	13.0
Concrete	9.0
Other	11.0

Source: *ENR*, February 1, 1999, p. 29, from Caterpillar Inc.

★ 831 ★

Construction Equipment (SIC 3536)

Compact Wheel Loader Market by Segment

Agriculture	26.0%
Infrastructure	15.0
Dealer rental fleet	13.0
Building construction	10.0
Manufacturing	9.0
Other	27.0

Source: *ENR*, September 21, 1998, p. 89, from Caterpillar Inc.

★ 832 ★

Construction Equipment (SIC 3536)

Mini-Excavator Market by Segment

Building construction	60.0%
Specialty trade	20.0
Concrete	7.0
Landscaping	7.0
Heavy/indus. construction	3.0
Agriculture	1.0
Other	2.0

Source: *ENR*, September 21, 1998, p. 89, from Caterpillar Inc.

★ 833 ★

Machine Tools (SIC 3540)

Machine Tool Consumption by Region

	($ mil.)	Share
Midwest	$ 165.82	39.0%
Central	80.51	19.0
West	68.12	16.0
Northeast	59.15	14.0
South	46.31	11.0

Source: *American Machinist*, July 1998, p. 30, from Association for Manufacturing Technology and American Machine Tool Distributors Association.

★ 834 ★

Machine Tools (SIC 3540)

Machine Tool Demand - 1998

Consumption is shown for the first nine months of the year.

	($ mil.)	Share
Metal cutting	$ 3,484.20	84.25%
Metal forming	410.38	9.92
Other	241.06	5.83

Source: *Assembly*, January 1999, p. 9, from Association for Manufacturing Technology.

★ 835 ★

Machine Tools (SIC 3540)

Top CNC EDM Machinery Vendors in Canada - 1997

CNC stands for computer numerically controlled. EDM stands for electrical discharge machinery.

Charmilles	43.9%
Agie	16.7
Mitsubishi	12.1
Sodick	9.0
Other	18.3

Source: *National Trade Data Bank*, May 15, 1998, p. IMI980507.

★ 836 ★

Machine Tools (SIC 3540)

Top CNC Machinery Vendors in Canada - 1997

CNC stands for computer numerically controlled.

Mazak	10.6%
Okuma	9.2
Fadal	7.8
Mori Seiki	5.2
Matsuura	4.5
Nakamura	4.1
Toshiba	3.9
Other	54.7

Source: *National Trade Data Bank*, May 15, 1998, p. IMI980507.

★ 837 ★

Machine Tools (SIC 3540)

Top Fabricating Equipment Vendors in Canada - 1997

Market shares are shown in percent.

Cincinnati	21.5%
Trumpf	19.6
Messer	11.7
Peddinghaus	8.6
Mazak	6.8
Other	33.6

Source: *National Trade Data Bank*, May 15, 1998, p. IMI980507, from *CNC Census, 1998*.

★ 838 ★

Machine Tools (SIC 3540)

Top Machining Center Vendors in Canada - 1997

Market shares are shown in percent.

Fadal	21.5%
Matsuura	12.4
Mazak	10.2
OKK	8.6
Toshiba	5.5
Other	41.8

Source: *National Trade Data Bank*, May 15, 1998, p. IMI980507, from *CNC Census, 1998*.

★ 839 ★

Machine Tools (SIC 3540)

Top Milling Center Vendors in Canada - 1997

Market shares are shown in percent.

Trak	26.7%
Correa	10.5
Takumi Seiki	7.0
Milltronics	5.8
Tree	5.8
Other	44.2

Source: *National Trade Data Bank*, May 15, 1998, p. IMI980507.

★ 840 ★

Assembly Equipment (SIC 3549)

Automated Assembly Demand

Vehicles and parts	33.6%
Electronics	24.1
Electrical	13.6
Medical and pharmaceutical	9.7
Appliance	7.4
Other	11.7

Source: *Assembly*, August 1998, p. 14, from Advanced Technology Advisors.

★ 841 ★

Textile Machinery (SIC 3552)

Textile Machinery Market

Data show shuttleless looms in place for the third quarter of the year.

Air jet	29.0%
Projectile	27.0
Rapier	23.0
Water jet	8.0
Pile/plush	1.0
Other	12.0

Source: *ATI*, February 1999, p. 50, from ATMI Textile HiLights.

★ 842 ★

Textile Machinery (SIC 3552)

U.S. Textile Machinery Imports - 1998

Market shares are shown for the first eight months of the year.

Germany	33.0%
Japan	26.0
Italy	11.0
France	6.0
Switzerland	6.0
Belgium	5.0
Other	13.0

Source: *Textile Asia*, December 1998, p. 9.

★ 843 ★

Food Machinery (SIC 3556)

Who Uses Meat Processing Equipment in Canada

Industrial packers/processors	45.0%
Grocery stores	30.0
Independent delis/meat shops	25.0

Source: *National Trade Data Bank*, April 7, 1999, p. ISA990301.

★ 844 ★

Plastics Machinery (SIC 3559)

Blow Molding Market

Packaging	24.0%
Consumer/industrial	20.0
Transportation	10.0
Other	46.0

Source: *Plastics News*, October 17, 1998, p. 2, from Freedonia Group.

★ 845 ★

Packaging Machinery (SIC 3565)

Canning/Labeling Equipment Market in Canada

The import market is shown in percent.

Germany	13.0%
Italy	11.0
France	4.8
United Kingdom	2.2
Sweden	1.6
Other	7.1

Source: *National Trade Data Bank*, August 4, 1998, p. ISA980701.

★ 846 ★

Power Equipment (SIC 3568)

Power Transmission Equipment Sales in Northeast Central States

Data show sales by market in millions of dollars.

Construction machinery	$ 64.6
Paper mills	59.0
Blast furnaces and steel mills	41.3
Electrical work	41.0
Internal combustion engines	40.5

Source: *Industrial Distribution*, April 1999, p. 77, from Industrial Market Information.

★ 847 ★

Power Equipment (SIC 3568)

Power Transmission Equipment Sales in South- Atlantic States

Data show sales by market in millions of dollars.

Electrical work	$ 61.0
Highway and street construction	56.4
Paper mills	45.6
Broadwoven fabric mills	37.9
Plumbing, heating & air conditioning	32.8

Source: *Industrial Distribution*, April 1999, p. 77, from Industrial Market Information.

★ 848 ★

Power Equipment (SIC 3568)

Power Transmission Equipment Sales in Southwest Central States

Data show sales by market in millions of dollars.

Petroleum refining	$ 39.4
Heavy construction	33.6
Chemical & fertilizer mining	31.4
Electrical work	31.3
Highway and street construction	25.4

Source: *Industrial Distribution*, April 1999, p. 77, from Industrial Market Information.

★ 849 ★

Robotics (SIC 3569)

Robotics Market by Segment - 1997

The North American market is shown in percent.

Automotive	45.0%
Food and beverage	13.0
Electronics	8.0
Aerospace	5.0
Appliance	2.0
Other	27.0

Source: *Electronic Design*, June 22, 1998, p. 64E, from Robotics Industries Association.

★ 850 ★

Office Products (SIC 3570)

Largest Office Product Makers

Data show revenues in millions of dollars. Figures include copiers, scanners and calculators.

Xerox	$ 13,526.0
Pitney Bowes	2,460.3
Harris	1,220.5
Eastman Kodak	919.2
Texas Instruments	487.5

Source: *Electronic Business*, July 1998, p. 95.

★ 851 ★

Postage Meters (SIC 3570)

Postage Meter Market

Shares are shown in percent.

Pitney Bowles	84.3%
Other	15.7

Source: *Wall Street Journal*, July 6, 1998, p. A17, from Pitney Bowles.

★ 852 ★

Computers (SIC 3571)

Computer Industry in Canada

The computer industry is composed of 300 companies and employs an estimated 14,000 people. Sales are shown by region.

Ontario	70.0%
Quebec	20.0
Other	10.0

Source: *National Trade Data Bank*, June 18, 1998, p. ISA980601.

★ 853 ★

Computers (SIC 3571)

Computer Mainframe Market - 1998

IBM	76.0%
Hitachi	14.0
Amdahl	10.0

Source: *Computerworld*, March 15, 1999, p. 70, from Meta Group Inc.

★ 854 ★

Computers (SIC 3571)

Computer Sales by Price

	1998	2003
$0 to $599	3.0%	27.0%
$600 to $999	31.0	38.0
$1,000 to $1,999	51.0	34.0
$2,000 and over	15.0	1.0

Source: *Forbes*, May 31, 1999, p. 50, from International Data Corp.

★ 855 ★

Computers (SIC 3571)

Corporate Dealer PC Market

Market shares are shown in percent.

IBM	34.0%
Compaq	28.0
Hewlett-Packard	13.0
Apple	7.0
Toshiba	4.0
Other	14.0

Source: *Investor's Business Daily*, April 5, 1999, p. A6, from ZD StoreBoard.

★ 856 ★

Computers (SIC 3571)

Desktop PC Sales by Processor

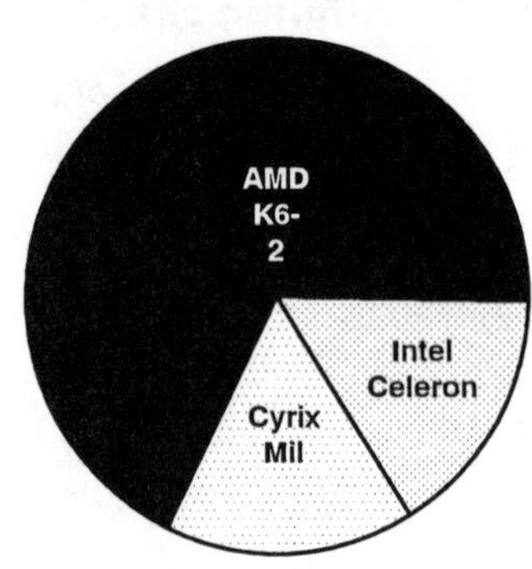

Data show sales for September 1998. Figures refer to PCs costing less than $1,000.

AMD K6-2	68.0%
Cyrix Mil	16.0
Intel Celeron	16.0

Source: *PC Magazine*, January 5, 1999, p. 10, from ZD Market Intelligence.

★ 857 ★

Computers (SIC 3571)

Hand Held Computer Vendors in Mexico

Market shares are shown in percent.

Hewlett-Packard	60.0%
Sharp	20.0
Casio	8.0
Others	12.0

Source: *National Trade Data Bank*, August 5, 1998, p. ISA980601.

★ 858 ★

Computers (SIC 3571)

Handheld Computer Market - 1998

Palm	40.2%
Windows CE	25.0
EPOC32	13.0
Proprietary/others	21.8

Source: *Computer Reseller News*, April 19, 1999, p. 14, from Dataquest Inc.

★ 859 ★

Computers (SIC 3571)

Handheld Device Market in Mexico

3Com	60.0%
Palm Pilot	40.0

Source: *National Trade Data Bank*, August 5, 1998, p. ISA980601.

★ 860 ★

Computers (SIC 3571)

Handheld Market by Platform - 1998

Data are for the fourth quarter of the year.

Palm OS	69.0%
Windows CE	20.0
Other	11.0

Source: *WINDOWS Magazine*, April 1999, p. 147.

★ 861 ★

Computers (SIC 3571)

Largest Desktop PC Vendors - 1998

Market shares are shown in percent.

Compaq	13.6%
Dell	10.1
Hewlett-Packard	7.5
IBM	7.2
Other	61.6

Source: *Forbes*, October 19, 1998, p. 132, from Dataquest Inc.

★ 862 ★

Computers (SIC 3571)

Largest Portable Computer Makers in Mexico - 1997

Market shares are shown based on units sold. Data include laptops, notebooks and subnotebooks.

Toshiba	33.0%
Acer/TI	25.0
IBM	16.0
Compaq	15.8
Dell	2.8
Digital	0.6
Other	6.8

Source: *National Trade Data Bank*, August 5, 1998, p. ISA980601.

★ 863 ★

Computers (SIC 3571)

Largest Portable Computer Vendors in Mexico - 1997

Market shares are shown based on dollar sales. Data include laptops, notebooks and subnotebooks.

Toshiba	35.0%
IBM	19.0
Acer/TI	18.1
Compaq	16.6
Dell	4.3
Other	7.0

Source: *National Trade Data Bank*, August 5, 1998, p. ISA980601.

★ 864 ★

Computers (SIC 3571)

Network Computer Shipments

Data show shipments of network computers and Window-based terminals as of June 1998.

IBM	33.0%
Wyse	24.5
Tektronix	10.6
NCD	10.4
Boundless	6.2
Other	15.3

Source: *Computerworld*, November 16, 1998, p. 26, from International Data Corp.

★ 865 ★

Computers (SIC 3571)

Office PC Market

Data show the top computers in the office superstore market.

Company	Share
Compaq	38.0%
Hewlett-Packard	18.0
IBM	15.0
Emachines	13.0
Packard Bell	8.0
Others	8.0

Source: *Investor's Business Daily*, March 30, 1999, p. A6, from ZD Market Intelligence.

★ 866 ★

Computers (SIC 3571)

PC Industry by Segment

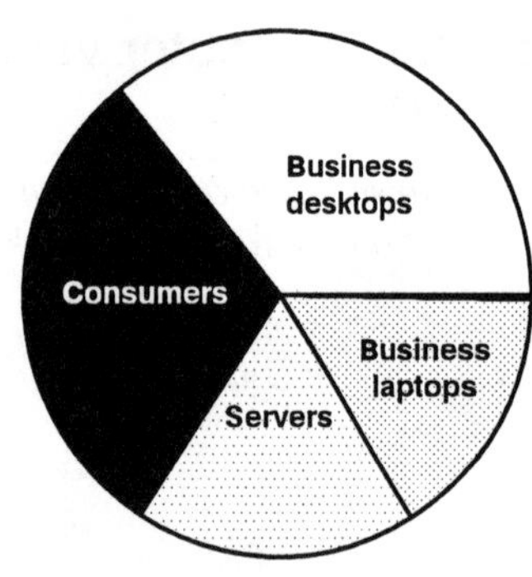

	1999	2001
Business desktops	44.02%	35.62%
Consumers	20.83	30.43
Servers	17.75	17.63
Business laptops	17.39	16.33

Source: *Computer Reseller News*, November 30, 1998, p. 115, from Forrester Research Inc.

★ 867 ★

Computers (SIC 3571)

Personal Digital Assistant Market in Mexico - 1997

Market shares are shown in percent.

Company	Share
3Com	40.0%
Hewlett-Packard	20.0
Rolodex	12.5
Casio	10.0
Sharp	10.0
Others	7.5

Source: *National Trade Data Bank*, August 5, 1998, p. ISA980601.

★ 868 ★

Computers (SIC 3571)

Retail Notebook Market

Company	Share
Compaq	36.0%
Toshiba	35.2
IBM	11.9
Other	16.9

Source: *Advertising Age*, December 14, 1998, p. 6, from ZD Market Intelligence.

★ 869 ★

Computers (SIC 3571)

Retail PC Market

Market shares are shown in percent.

Company	Share
Compaq	34.0%
Hewlett-Packard	16.0
IBM	11.0
Packard Bell	7.0
Toshiba	7.0
Apple	6.0
Emachines	6.0
Other	13.0

Source: *Investor's Business Daily*, April 5, 1999, p. A6, from ZD StoreBoard.

★ 870 ★

Computers (SIC 3571)

Small-Business PC Market - 1998

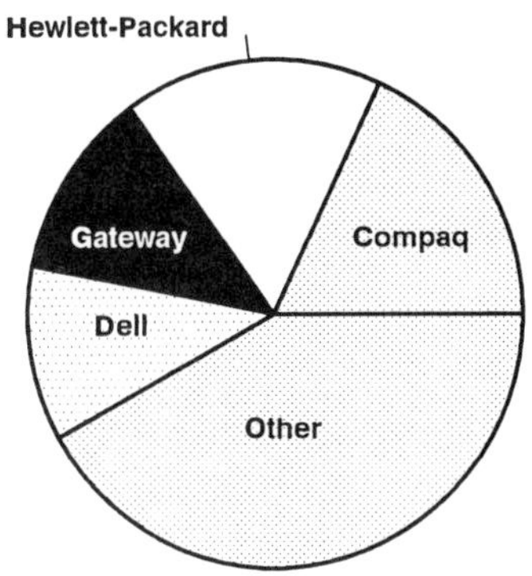

Data show the preferred brands.

Compaq	18.0%
Hewlett-Packard	17.0
Gateway	12.0
Dell	11.0
Other	42.0

Source: *Investor's Business Daily*, March 16, 1999, p. A6, from Access Media International Inc.

★ 871 ★

Computers (SIC 3571)

Top Computer Makers in Canada - 1998

Shares are shown based on 605,000 units shipped in the third quarter of the year.

IBM Canada	21.3%
Compaq Canada	20.9
Dell	9.3
Hewlett-Packard	8.0
Toshiba	5.7
Other	34.8

Source: *Globe and Mail*, November 25, 1998, p. B8, from International Data Corp.

★ 872 ★

Computers (SIC 3571)

Top PC Firms in Canada - 1998

Market shares are shown in percent for the year ended December 31, 1998.

Compaq	21.5%
IBM	19.6
Dell	10.2
Hewlett-Packard	7.0
Toshiba	4.7
Apple	4.0
Packard Bell NEC	3.3
Others	29.7

Source: "Report on Market Share." Retrieved June 1, 1999 from the World Wide Web: http://www.marketingmag.ca/index.cgi?, from Evans Research Corp.

★ 873 ★

Computers (SIC 3571)

Top PC Makers - 1999

Market shares are shown for the first quarter of the year.

Compaq	16.1%
Dell	14.8
Gateway	9.3
Hewlett-Packard	8.6
IBM	8.0
Others	43.2

Source: *Investor's Business Daily*, April 28, 1999, p. A6, from International Data Corp.

★ 874 ★

Workstations (SIC 3571)

Largest High-End Workstation Makers - 1998

Firms are ranked by sales in millions of dollars. Market shares are shown in percent.

	($ mil.)	Share
Hewlett-Packard	$ 699.4	26.4%
Sun	659.3	24.9
IBM	437.5	16.5
Compaq	240.6	9.1
Silicon Graphics	215.7	8.1
Others	394.0	15.0

Source: *Investor's Business Daily*, April 6, 1999, p. A6, from Dataquest Inc.

★ 875 ★

Workstations (SIC 3571)

NT Workstation Market - 1997

Market shares are shown in percent.

Hewlett-Packard	18.0%
Compaq	17.0
Dell	11.0
IBM	9.0
Digital	5.0
Intergraph	4.0
Others	36.0

Source: Retrieved May 18, 1999 from the World Wide Web: http:// www.sonic.net/cgi-bin/cif/cif/search-free.pl.

★ 876 ★

Workstations (SIC 3571)

Unix Workstation Market - 1997

Market shares are shown in percent.

Sun	45.0%
Hewlett-Packard	16.0
Silicon Graphics	12.0
IBM	11.0
Digital	5.0
Other	11.0

Source: Retrieved May 18, 1999 from the World Wide Web: http:// www.sonic.net/cgi-bin/cif/cif/search-free.pl.

★ 877 ★

Computer Data Storage (SIC 3572)

CD/DVD-ROM Market Leaders - 1998

Figures are for the fourth quarter of the year.

LGE	15.0%
Toshiba	13.0
Panasonic	11.0
TEAC	8.0
Lite-On	7.0
Mitsumi	7.0
Samsung	7.0
Acer	5.0
Other	27.0

Source: *E-Media Professional*, June 1999, p. 14, from International Data Corp.

★ 878 ★

Computer Data Storage (SIC 3572)

Computer Storage Device Sales

Shares are shown based on $4.2 billion in sales.

Half inch cartridges	28.0%
Digital audio tape	24.0
Digital linear tape	23.0
8 mm wide drives	12.0
Quarter inch cartridges	9.0
Other	4.0

Source: Retrieved May 18, 1999 from the World Wide Web: http:// www.sonic.net/cgi-bin/cif/cif/search-free.pl.

★ 879 ★

Computer Data Storage (SIC 3572)

Largest CD/DVD-ROM Makers - 1998

Market shares are shown for the first quarter of the year.

Panasonic	14.5%
Toshiba	13.8
Mitsumi	9.4
Goldstar	9.2
Samsung	6.9
Acer	6.6
Sony	6.6
Hitachi	6.1
NEC	5.9
Others	35.5

Source: *E-Media Professional*, October 1998, p. 11.

★ 880 ★

Computer Data Storage (SIC 3572)

Removable Rigid Disk Storage Vendors - 1998

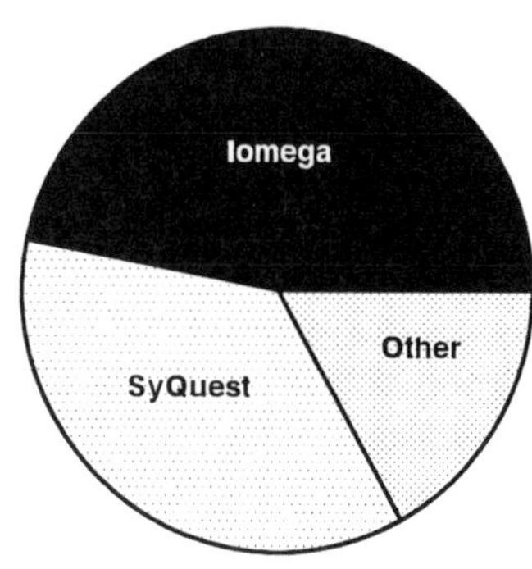

Market shares are shown in percent.

Iomega	47.0%
SyQuest	36.0
Other	17.0

Source: Retrieved May 18, 1999 from the World Wide Web: http:// www.sonic.net/cgi-bin/cif/cif/search-free.pl.

★ 881 ★

Computer Data Storage (SIC 3572)

Servo Drive Hardware Shipments

Shipments are shown by drive command interface.

Proprietary	52.4%
Analog	36.6
Drive network	9.0
Device network	2.0

Source: *Control Engineering*, August 1998, p. 41, from Automation Research Corp.

★ 882 ★

Computer Data Storage (SIC 3572)

Top DVD-ROM Drive Makers

Market shares are shown in percent.

Hitachi	38.0%
Toshiba	28.5
Panasonic	28.2
Others	5.3

Source: Retrieved May 18, 1999 from the World Wide Web: http:// www.sonic.net/cgi-bin/cif/cif/search-free.pl.

★ 883 ★

Computer Peripherals (SIC 3577)

Canada's Motherboard Market

Multinationals	60.0%
Canadian	37.0
Other	3.0

Source: *Computing Canada*, May 14, 1999, p. 19, from Evans Research Corp.

★ 884 ★

Computer Peripherals (SIC 3577)

Desktop Mouse Market

Market shares are shown in percent.

Microsoft	30.0%
Logitech	25.0
Kensington	17.0
Other	28.0

Source: "Hardware & Mouseware." Retrieved May 28, 1999 from the World Wide Web: http:// www.userwww.stsu.edu/~magpie5/mshare/ hardware.html, from PC Data Inc.

★ 885 ★

Computer Peripherals (SIC 3577)

Largest Computer Hardware Makers

Data show revenues in millions of dollars.

IBM	$ 25,907.6
Compaq Computer	24,584.0
Hewlett-Packard	16,310.4
Dell Computer	8,628.9
Sun Microsystems	6,905.0

Source: *Electronic Business*, July 1998, p. 95.

★ 886 ★

Computer Peripherals (SIC 3577)

Trackball Market Vendors

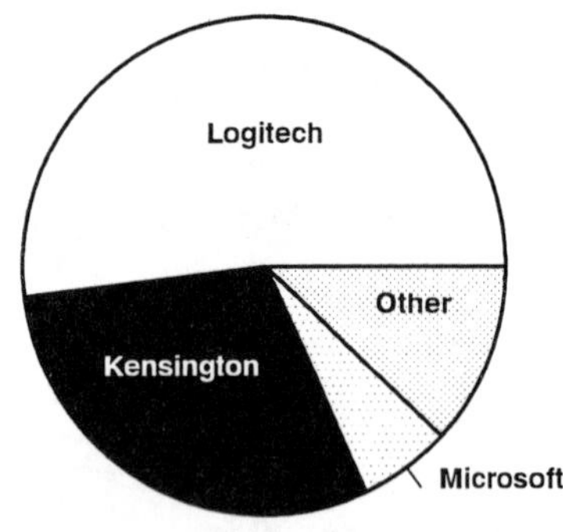

Market shares are shown in percent.

Logitech	52.0%
Kensington	30.0
Microsoft	6.0
Other	12.0

Source: "Hardware & Mouseware." Retrieved May 28, 1999 from the World Wide Web: http://www.userwww.stsu.edu/~magpie5/mshare/hardware.html, from PC Data Inc.

★ 887 ★

Computer Printers (SIC 3577)

Business Printer Market - 1997

Market shares are shown in percent.

Hewlett-Packard	37.2%
Textronix	37.2
Lexmark	6.6
Apple	5.6
Xerox	5.1
Other	8.3

Source: *Investor's Business Daily*, October 14, 1998, p. A10, from International Data Corp.

★ 888 ★

Computer Printers (SIC 3577)

Largest Multi-Function Printer Makers

Market shares are shown based on revenues.

Canon	37.6%
Xerox	30.9
Hewlett-Packard	15.2
Brother	6.5
Sharp	6.2
Panasonic	3.6
Other	37.7

Source: *Investext,* Thomson Financial Networks, July 2, 1998, p. 6, from International Data Corp. and Morgan Stanley Dean Witter Research.

★ 889 ★

Computer Printers (SIC 3577)

U.S. Printer Shipments

	1997 (000)	2002 (000)	Share
Inkjet	12,222.72	18,000.00	82.88%
Monochrome laser	3,070.36	3,046.29	14.03
Color laser	80.56	672.00	3.09

Source: *Purchasing*, December 10, 1998, p. 90, from International Data Corp.

★ 890 ★

Automated Teller Machines (SIC 3578)

ATM Market Leaders - 1996

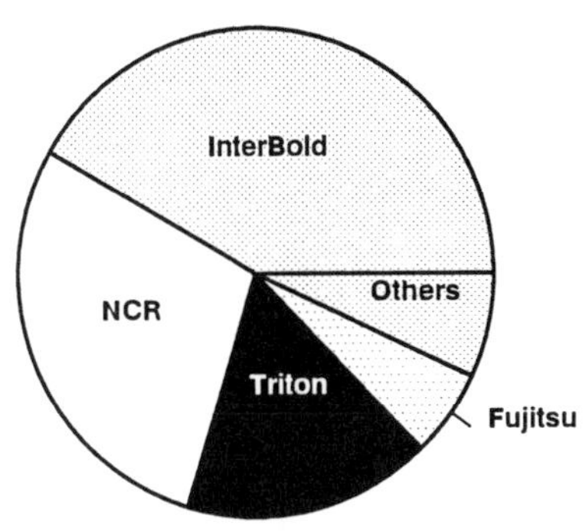

Data show shipments.

InterBold	42.0%
NCR	28.5
Triton	16.7
Fujitsu	6.3
Others	6.5

Source: "ATM Manufacturers' Market Share." Retrieved May 10, 1999 from the World Wide Web: http:// www.tritonsystemsinc.com/mktshare.htm.

★ 891 ★

Automated Teller Machines (SIC 3578)

Largest ATM Managers

Firms are ranked by number of ATMs serviced.

Access Cash	4,800
Card Capture Services	4,000
McLane FSP	3,000
Hanco Inc.	2,000
Intl. Merchant Services	1,615
North American	1,200
XtraCash ATM	1,200
ATM International	1,100
Nationwide Money Services	1,000
Momentum Cash Systems	900

Source: *Financial Service Online*, October 1998, p. 42, from *Bank Network News*.

★ 892 ★

Automated Teller Machines (SIC 3578)

Largest Regional ATM Networks

Data show number of ATMs.

Honor	42,000
MAC	40,000
Star	36,720
PULSE	30,000
NYCE	19,600

Source: *Bank Systems & Technology*, October 1998, p. 8, from network figures.

★ 893 ★

Vending Machines (SIC 3581)

Refrigerated Vending Machine Market

Shares are estimated.

Dixie-Narco	42.0%
Vendo	23.0
Royal Vendors	20.0
Others	15.0

Source: Retrieved May 28, 1999 from the World Wide Web: http:// www.bnp.com/thenews/stat-rfg.html, from Arthur D. Little.

★ 894 ★

Heating and Cooling (SIC 3585)

Central Heating Industry

Shipments are estimated in thousands of units.

	2000	2002
Replacement/modernization	3,699	3,722
Warm air furnaces	3,527	3,451
New residential installations	1,608	1,396
Heat pumps	1,195	1,102
Boilers	340	325

Source: *Contractor*, January 1999, p. 46, from Honeywell Home & Building Control.

★ 895 ★

Heating and Cooling (SIC 3585)

Heating & Cooling Leaders

Market shares are estimated. Data do not include rooftop or packaged equipment, room units, heat pumps or related cooling equipment.

Carrier	22.0%
Goodman Manufacturing	18.0
Rheem Manufacturing	13.0
The Trane Company	12.0
International Comfort Products	11.0
York International	10.0
Lennox Industries	10.0
Other	4.0

Source: *Air Conditioning, Heating & Refrigeration News*, April 12, 1999, p. 8.

★ 896 ★

Heating and Cooling (SIC 3585)

Heating Market in Indianapolis, IN

Data show share of heating replacement permits for single-family homes.

ARS	20.5%
Service Experts	13.8
Modern HAC	7.5
DIAL ONE Hoosier	6.8
Airtron/GroupMAC	5.8
Others	45.6

Source: *Air Conditioning, Heating & Refrigeration News*, June 29, 1998, p. 3, from Citizen Gas.

★ 897 ★

Heating and Cooling (SIC 3585)

Largest Heat and Air Conditioning Markets - 1997

The market is shown in billions of dollars.

	($ bil.)	Share
Unitary and close control air conditioning	$ 5,392	29.19%
Central plant air conditioning	3,591	19.44
Space heaters	3,468	18.77
Water heating	2,221	12.02
Residential and specialty air conditioning	2,136	11.56
Central ducted furnaces	1,667	9.02

Source: *Contractor*, June 1998, p. 7, from Building Services Research.

★ 898 ★

Heating and Cooling (SIC 3585)

Reach-In Refrigeration Equipment Market

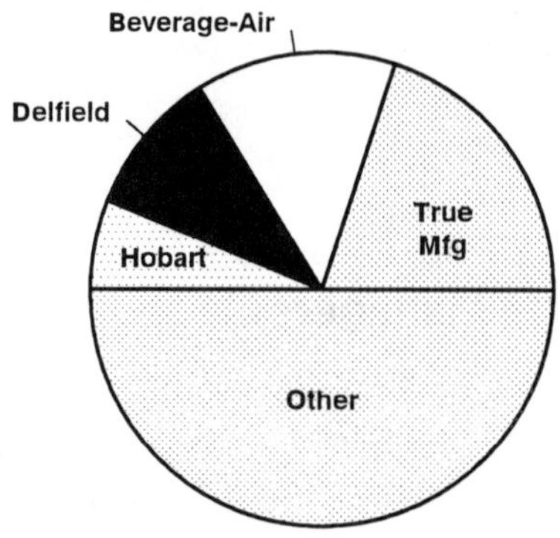

True Mfg	20.0%
Beverage-Air	14.0
Delfield	10.0
Hobart	6.0
Other	50.0

Source: Retrieved May 28, 1999 from the World Wide Web: http:// www.bnp.com/thenews/stat-rfg.html, from Arthur D. Little.

★ 899 ★

Heating and Cooling (SIC 3585)

Room Air Conditioner Sales by State - 1996

	Units	Share
New York	440,700	9.69%
Florida	298,400	6.56
Georgia	242,700	5.34
California	231,900	5.10
Illinois	203,500	4.47
Other	3,131,392	68.84

Source: "Industry Statistics." Retrieved May 28, 1999 from the World Wide Web: http:// www.aham.org/ mfrs/statys/refdist.htm, from U.S. Bureau of the Census.

★ 900 ★

Heating and Cooling (SIC 3585)

Top Air Purifier Makers - 1997

Holmes
Honeywell
Sunbeam
Duracraft
Norelco
Rival
Others

Shares are shown based on shipments of 3,800,000 units.

Holmes	35.0%
Honeywell	16.0
Sunbeam	9.0
Duracraft	8.0
Norelco	8.0
Rival (Bionaire)	6.0
Others	18.0

Source: *Appliance Manufacturer*, May 1998, p. 22.

★ 901 ★

Heating and Cooling (SIC 3585)

Top Electric Room Heater Makers - 1997

Shares are shown based on shipments of 7,300,000 units.

Holmes	30.0%
Honeywell/Duracraft	22.0
Rival (Patton)	13.0
Arvin	10.0
DeLonghi	8.0
Lakewood	8.0
Others	9.0

Source: *Appliance Manufacturer*, May 1998, p. 22.

★ 902 ★

Heating and Cooling (SIC 3585)

Top Electric Water Heater Makers - 1997

Shares are shown based on shipments of 4,804,000 units.

Rheem	28.0%
State	27.0
A.O. Smith	16.0
American	15.0
Bradford-White	11.0
Others	3.0

Source: *Appliance Manufacturer*, May 1998, p. 22.

★ 903 ★

Heating and Cooling (SIC 3585)

Top Gas Furnace Makers - 1997

Shares are shown based on shipments of 2,779,086 units.

Carrier	21.0%
Goodman	17.0
Rheem	14.0
Lennox	11.0
International Comfort Products	10.0
Trane	10.0
Others	17.0

Source: *Appliance*, September 1998, p. 68.

★ 904 ★

Heating and Cooling (SIC 3585)

Top Gas Water Heater Makers - 1997

Shares are shown based on shipments of 4,196,000 units.

Rheem	28.0%
State	28.0
A.O. Smith	16.0
American	15.0
Bradford-White	12.0
Others	1.0

Source: *Appliance Manufacturer*, May 1998, p. 22.

★ 905 ★

Heating and Cooling (SIC 3585)

Top Heat Pump Makers - 1997

Shares are shown based on shipments of 1,130,718 units.

United Technologies	21.0%
Goodman	16.0
American Standard	12.0
Rheem	12.0
York	10.0
International Comfort Products	9.0
Lennox	9.0

Source: *Appliance Manufacturer*, May 1998, p. 22.

★ 906 ★

Heating and Cooling (SIC 3585)

Top Humidifer Makers - 1997

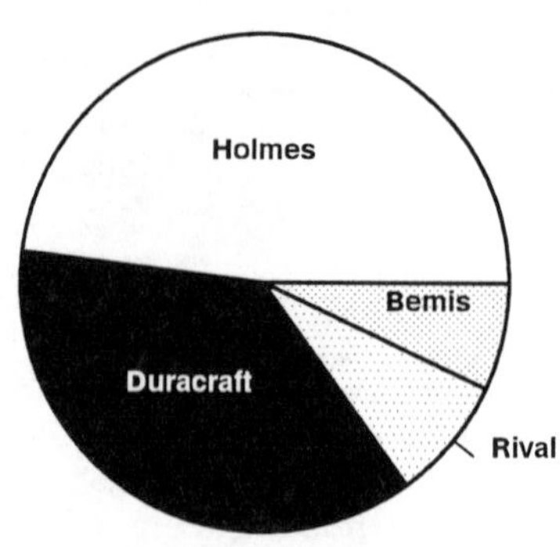

Shares are shown based on shipments of 2,160,000 units. Figures refer to console or tapletop models.

Holmes	48.0%
Duracraft	37.0
Rival	8.0
Bemis	7.0

Source: *Appliance Manufacturer*, May 1998, p. 22.

★ 907 ★

Heating and Cooling (SIC 3585)

Top Icemaker Producers - 1997

Shares are shown based on shipments of 155,000 units.

Manitowoc	35.0%
Scotsman	24.0
Hoshizaki	20.0
Welbilt (Mile High)	12.0
Cornelius	3.0
Crystal Tips	3.0
Others	3.0

Source: *Appliance Manufacturer*, May 1998, p. 23.

★ 908 ★

Heating and Cooling (SIC 3585)

Top Refrigerated Display Case Makers - 1997

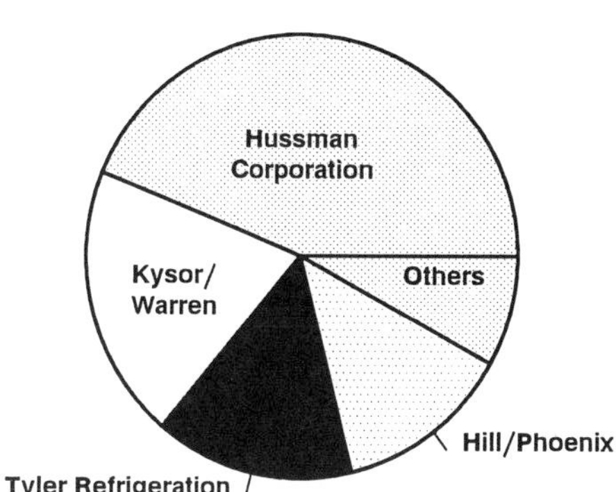

Shares are shown based on shipments of 324,000 units.

Hussman Corporation	44.0%
Kysor/Warren	20.0
Tyler Refrigeration	15.0
Hill/Phoenix	13.0
Others	8.0

Source: *Appliance*, September 1998, p. 69.

★ 909 ★

Heating and Cooling (SIC 3585)

Top Residential Air Conditioner Makers - 1997

Shares are shown based on shipments of 9,014,700 units.

United Technologies	20.0%
Goodman	19.0
American Standard	13.0
Rheem	12.0
International Comfort Products	9.0
Lennox	9.0
York	7.0
Nordyne	4.0
Others	7.0

Source: *Appliance Manufacturer*, May 1998, p. 22.

★ 910 ★

Heating and Cooling (SIC 3585)

Top Residential Furnace Makers - 1997

Shares are shown based on shipments of 124,008 units.

Lennox	23.0%
Ducane	13.0
Thermo-Products	13.0
International Comfort Products	8.0
Rheem	8.0
Williamson	7.0
Bard	3.0
Nordyne	3.0
Other	22.0

Source: *Appliance Manufacturer*, May 1998, p. 22.

★ 911 ★

Heating and Cooling (SIC 3585)

Top Room Air Conditioner Makers - 1997

Shares are shown based on shipments of 4,122,600 units.

Whirlpool	27.0%
Fedders	25.0
Electrolux	20.0
Friedrich	6.0
Matsushita	6.0
Goodman	5.0
United Technologies	5.0
Sharp	2.0
Others	4.0

Source: *Appliance Manufacturer*, May 1998, p. 22.

★ 912 ★

Heating and Cooling (SIC 3585)

Top Water Heater Makers - 1997

Shares are shown based on shipments of 8,670,220 units.

State Industries	28.0%
Rheem Manufacturing	27.0
Southcorp	17.0
A.O. Smith	15.0
Bradford-White	13.0

Source: *Appliance*, September 1998, p. 69.

★ 913 ★
Ice Machines (SIC 3585)
Ice Machine Market

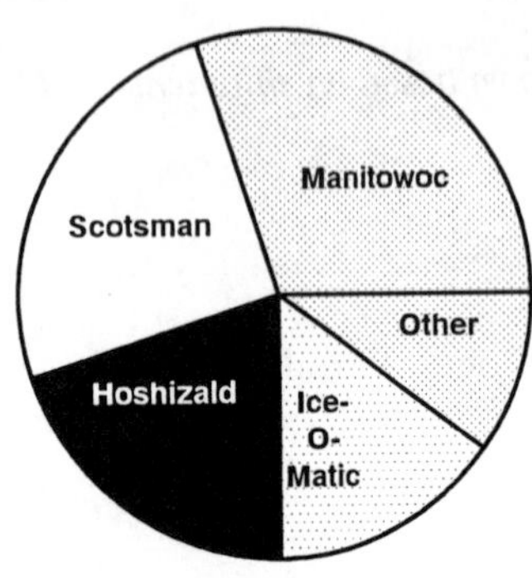

Shares are estimated.

Manitowoc	30.0%
Scotsman	25.0
Hoshizald	20.0
Ice-O-Matic	15.0
Other	10.0

Source: Retrieved May 28, 1999 from the World Wide Web: http:// www.bnp.com/thenews/stat-rfg.html, from Arthur D. Little.

★ 914 ★
Extractors (SIC 3589)
Top Extractor Makers - 1997

Shares are shown based on shipments of 2,932,500 units.

Hoover	52.0%
Bissell	37.0
Eureka	5.0
Others	6.0

Source: *Appliance Manufacturer*, May 1998, p. 23.

★ 915 ★
Floor Polishers (SIC 3589)
Top Floor Polisher Makers - 1997

Shares are shown based on shipments of 175,000 units.

Hoover	70.0%
Thorne Electric	20.0
Electrolux	10.0

Source: *Appliance Manufacturer*, May 1998, p. 23.

★ 916 ★
Water Filters (SIC 3589)
Faucet/Sink Filter Market

PUR	85.0%
Other	15.0

Source: *Forbes*, April 19, 1999, p. 118.

SIC 36 - Electronic and Other Electric Equipment

★ 917 ★

Electronics (SIC 3600)

Factory Electronic Sales - 1998

Sales are shown in millions of dollars for the six months ended June 1998.

	($ mil.)	Share
Electronic components	$ 74,156	30.61%
Computers and peripherals	49,423	20.40
Telecommunications	36,902	15.23
Industrial electroncis	18,607	7.68
Defense communications	15,792	6.52
Electromedical equipment	6,169	2.55
Consumer electronics	4,808	1.98
Other related products	36,400	15.03

Source: *Electronic Servicing & Technology*, October 1998, p. 4, from U.S. Department of Commerce and Electronic Industries Alliance Market Research.

★ 918 ★

Electronics (SIC 3600)

Largest Contract Manufacturers

Data show revenues in billions of dollars.

SCI Systems	$ 6.3
IBM	4.7
Solectron	4.0
Hewlett-Packard	1.2
Jabil Circuit	1.0

Source: *Electronic Business*, July 1998, p. 97.

★ 919 ★

Electronics (SIC 3600)

Mexico's Electronics Plants by State

Data show number of maquiladora plants.

	No.	Share
Baja California	203	46.24%
Chihuahua	79	18.00
Sonora	56	12.76
Tamaulipas	48	10.93
Nuevo Leon	18	4.10
Others	35	7.97

Source: *National Trade Data Bank*, October 28, 1998, p. ISA980901.

★ 920 ★

Electronics (SIC 3600)

Small Device Market - 2001

The market is estimated by segment.

Hand-held devices	56.0%
Screen phones	13.0
Online game consoles	12.0
Net TV boxes	8.0
Other	11.0

Source: *Investor's Business Daily*, August 6, 1998, p. A8, from Dain Rauscher Wessels and International Data Corp.

★ 921 ★

Household Appliances (SIC 3600)

Appliance Shipments

Shipments are shown in thousands of units for year to date.

Microwaves	2,219.7
Refrigerators	1,882.6
Washers	1,823.2
Dryers	1,508.1

Continued on next page.

★ 921 ★ *Continued*

Household Appliances (SIC 3600)

Appliance Shipments

Shipments are shown in thousands of units for year to date.

Disposals	1,300.1
Dishwashers	1,272.7
Room air conditioners	1,180.8
Electric ranges	1,146.6
Gas ranges	713.0
Freezers	364.9
Dehumidifiers	222.5
Compactors	27.0

Source: *HFN*, April 26, 1999, p. 66, from Association of Home Appliance Manufacturers.

★ 922 ★

Household Appliances (SIC 3630)

Canada's Appliance Industry

Cooking stoves, ovens, ranges	35.8%
Refrigerators	14.9
Dishwashers	6.5
Electric cooking top mountings	1.1
Other	41.7

Source: "Profile of the Canadian Appliance Industry." Retrieved May 21, 1999 from the World Wide Web: http:// strategis.ic.gc.ca/SSG/mb03098e.html.

★ 923 ★

Household Appliances (SIC 3630)

Home Appliance Market - 1998

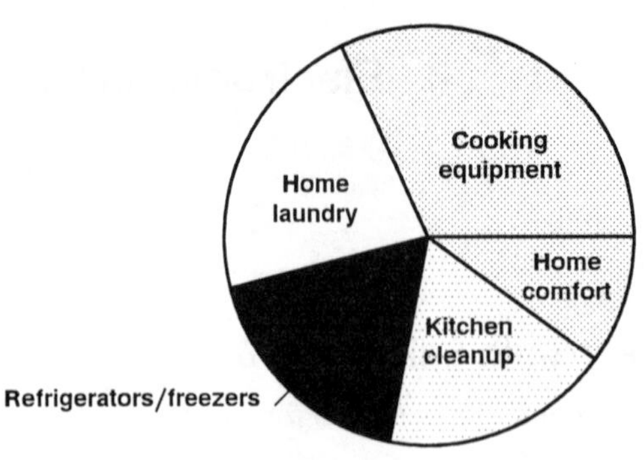

Shipments are shown in millions of dollars.

	(mil.)	Share
Cooking equipment	17.953	31.72%
Home laundry	12.624	22.30
Refrigerators/freezers	10.400	18.38
Kitchen cleanup	10.186	18.00
Home comfort	5.435	9.60

Source: *Purchasing*, April 8, 1999, p. 62, from Association of Home Appliance Manufacturers.

★ 924 ★

Household Appliances (SIC 3630)

Household Appliance Sales

Sales are shown in millions of dollars.

Los Angeles-Long Beach, CA	$ 761.6
Chicago, IL	723.1
New York, NY	532.3
Detroit, MI	436.5
Philadelphia, PA	404.6

Source: *Sales & Marketing Management*, August 1998, p. 195.

★ 925 ★

Cooking Equipment (SIC 3631)

Built-In Gas Range Sales by State

	Units	Share
California	19,500	26.93%
New York	7,300	10.08
Texas	5,800	8.01
New Jersey	5,300	7.32
Illinois	4,500	6.22
Other	30,000	41.44

Source: "Industry Statistics." Retrieved May 28, 1999 from the World Wide Web: http:// www.aham.org/ mfrs/stats/cookdistgas.htm, from U.S. Bureau of the Census.

★ 926 ★

Cooking Equipment (SIC 3631)

Gas Range Sales by State

Data refer to free-standing units.

	Units	Share
California	300,100	12.81%
New York	237,200	10.12
Texas	158,600	6.77
Illinois	156,200	6.67
New Jersey	138,400	5.91
Other	1,352,500	57.73

Source: "Industry Statistics." Retrieved May 28, 1999 from the World Wide Web: http:// www.aham.org/ mfrs/stats/cookdistgas.htm.

★ 927 ★

Cooking Equipment (SIC 3631)

Gas Surface Cooking Unit Sales by State

	Units	Share
California	74,900	27.58%
Texas	29,400	10.82
New York	14,000	5.15
Illinois	11,600	4.27
Maryland	10,600	3.90
Other	131,100	48.27

Source: "Industry Statistics." Retrieved May 28, 1999 from the World Wide Web: http:// www.aham.org/ mfrs/stats/cookdistgas.htm, from U.S. Bureau of the Census.

★ 928 ★

Cooking Equipment (SIC 3631)

Top Electric Range Makers - 1997

Shares are shown based on shipments of 4,379,800 units.

GE	45.0%
Whirlpool	20.0
Maytag	15.0
Electrolux	10.0
Goodman	5.0
Brown	2.0
Peerless Premier	2.0
Others	1.0

Source: *Appliance*, September 1998, p. 69.

★ 929 ★

Cooking Equipment (SIC 3631)

Top Gas Grill Makers - 1997

Shares are shown based on shipments of 6,361,102 units.

Char-Broil	40.0%
Sunbeam	30.0
Weber-Stephen	8.0
Ducane	2.0
Others	20.0

Source: *Appliance Manufacturer*, May 1998, p. 23.

★ 930 ★

Cooking Equipment (SIC 3631)

Top Gas Range Producers - 1997

Shares are shown based on shipments of 2,860,300 units.

GEA	38.0%
Maytag	25.0
Electrolux	19.0
Goodman	13.0
Whirlpool	5.0

Source: *Appliance Manufacturer*, May 1998, p. 21.

★ 931 ★

Cooking Equipment (SIC 3631)

Top Microwave Oven Producers - 1997

Shares are shown based on shipments of 9,622,300 units.

Sharp	31.0%
Samsung	20.0
Matsushita	15.0
LG Electronics	11.0
Sanyo Fisher	10.0
Whirlpool	4.0
Other	9.0

Source: *Appliance Manufacturer*, May 1998, p. 21.

★ 932 ★

Cooking Equipment (SIC 3631)

Top Range Hood Makers - 1997

Shares are shown based on shipments of 2,850,000 units.

Broan	60.0%
Nutone	27.0
Watertown Metal Products	8.0
Others	5.0

Source: *Appliance*, September 1998, p. 69.

★ 933 ★

Refrigerators and Freezers (SIC 3632)

Chest Freezer Sales by State - 1996

	Units	Share
Texas	70,400	8.96%
Florida	63,000	8.02
Georgia	36,700	4.67
California	35,000	4.45
Michigan	34,800	4.43
Other	546,000	69.47

Source: "Industry Statistics." Retrieved May 28, 1999 from the World Wide Web: http:// www.aham.org/ mfrs/statys/refdist.htm, from U.S. Bureau of the Census.

★ 934 ★

Refrigerators and Freezers (SIC 3632)

Refrigerator Sales by State - 1996

	Units	Share
California	841,400	10.64%
Texas	617,100	7.81
Florida	578,200	7.31
Ohio	375,100	4.74
Illinois	338,100	4.28
Other	5,156,200	65.22

Source: "Industry Statistics." Retrieved May 28, 1999 from the World Wide Web: http:// www.aham.org/ mfrs/statys/refdist.htm, from U.S. Bureau of the Census.

★ 935 ★

Refrigerators and Freezers (SIC 3632)

Top Compact Refrigerator Makers - 1997

Shares are shown based on shipments of 1,110,000 units.

Sanyo	58.0%
GE/Mabe	18.0
Haier	15.0
Wanbao	5.0
Whirlpool/Consul	2.0
Others	2.0

Source: *Appliance*, September 1998, p. 69.

★ 936 ★

Refrigerators and Freezers (SIC 3632)

Top Compact/Built-In/Undercounter Refrigerator Makers - 1997

Shares are shown based on shipments of 131,000 units.

U-Line	60.0%
Marvel industries	28.0
Sub-Zero Freezer	11.0
Others	1.0

Source: *Appliance*, September 1998, p. 69.

★ 937 ★

Refrigerators and Freezers (SIC 3632)

Top Freezer Makers - 1997

Shares are shown based on shipments of 1,701,300 units.

Electrolux (Frigidaire)	72.0%
W.C. Wood	25.0
Sanyo	1.0
Others	2.0

Source: *Appliance*, September 1998, p. 69.

★ 938 ★

Refrigerators and Freezers (SIC 3632)

Top Reach-In Refrigerator/Freezer Makers - 1997

Shares are shown based on shipments of 300,000 units.

True	45.0%
Beverage Air	24.0
Traulsen	8.0
Delfield	5.0
Hobart	5.0
Randell	5.0
Other	8.0

Source: *Appliance Manufacturer*, May 1998, p. 23.

★ 939 ★

Refrigerators and Freezers (SIC 3632)

Top Refrigerator Makers - 1997

Shares are shown based on shipments of 9,014,700 units.

GEA	37.0%
Whirlpool	29.0
Electrolux	16.0
Maytag	11.0
Goodman	7.0

Source: *Appliance Manufacturer*, May 1998, p. 21.

★ 940 ★

Refrigerators and Freezers (SIC 3632)

Upright Freezer Sales by State - 1996

	Units	Share
California	49,800	7.58%
Texas	64,600	9.83
Maryland	35,300	5.37
Florida	33,900	5.16
Michigan	31,500	4.79
Other	442,100	67.27

Source: "Industry Statistics." Retrieved May 28, 1999 from the World Wide Web: http:// www.aham.org/ mfrs/statys/refdist.htm, from U.S. Bureau of the Census.

★ 941 ★

Laundry Equipment (SIC 3633)

Automatic Washer Sales by State - 1996

	Units	Share
California	593,800	9.58%
Texas	515,800	8.32
Florida	500,300	8.07
New York	297,700	4.80
Ohio	285,600	4.61
Other	4,008,300	64.63

Source: "Industry Statistics." Retrieved May 28, 1999 from the World Wide Web: http:// www.aham.org/ mfrs/stats/laundist.htm, from U.S. Bureau of the Census.

★ 942 ★

Laundry Equipment (SIC 3633)

Electric Dryer Sales by State - 1996

	Units	Share
Texas	359,500	9.13%
Florida	321,400	8.16
California	214,400	5.45
Ohio	208,900	5.31
North Carolina	156,200	3.97
Units	2,676,600	67.99

Source: "Industry Statistics." Retrieved May 28, 1999 from the World Wide Web: http:// www.aham.org/ mfrs/stats/laundist.htm, from U.S. Bureau of the Census.

★ 943 ★

Laundry Equipment (SIC 3633)

Gas Dryer Sales by State - 1996

	Units	Share
California	271,400	22.69%
Illinois	134,100	11.21
Michigan	101,400	8.48
New York	86,500	7.23
New Jersey	85,400	7.14
Other	517,400	43.25

Source: "Industry Statistics." Retrieved May 28, 1999 from the World Wide Web: http:// www.aham.org/ mfrs/stats/laundist.htm, from U.S. Bureau of the Census.

★ 944 ★

Laundry Equipment (SIC 3633)

Top Dryer Makers - 1997

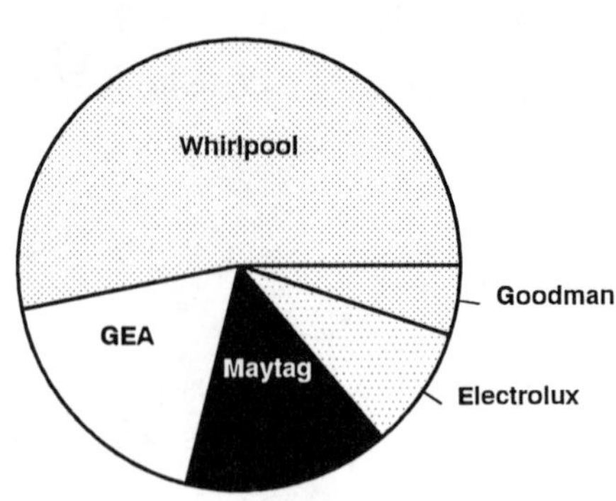

Shares are shown based on shipments of 5,776,100 units. Figures include both electric and gas.

Whirlpool	53.0%
GEA	18.0
Maytag	15.0
Electrolux	9.0
Goodman	5.0

Source: *Appliance Manufacturer*, May 1998, p. 21.

★ 945 ★

Laundry Equipment (SIC 3633)

Top Electric Dryer Makers - 1997

Shares are shown based on shipments of 4,828,100 units.

Whirlpool	54.0%
GE	19.0
Maytag	15.0
Electrolux (Frigidaire)	7.0
Goodman (Speed Queen)	5.0

Source: *Appliance*, September 1998, p. 69.

★ 946 ★

Personal Care Appliances (SIC 3634)

Men's Shaver Makers - 1997

Shares are shown based on shipments of 6,760,000 units.

Norelco Consumer Products	49.0%
Remington	22.0
Braun	18.0
Matsushita (Panasonic)	8.0
Others	3.0

Source: *Appliance*, September 1998, p. 68.

★ 947 ★

Personal Care Appliances (SIC 3634)

Personal Care Appliance Shipments - 1998

Data show unit shipments.

Curlin irons and styling combs	15,700
Hair dryers, euro (rear entry fan)	11,000
Hair dryers, side fan system	7,500
Hair clippers	6,500
Shaver's, men	6,489
Hair setters	4,925
Heating pads	4,700
Toothbrushes/plaque removers	2,750
Trimmers, beard & moustache	2,600

Source: *Appliance*, April 1999, p. 54.

★ 948 ★

Personal Care Appliances (SIC 3634)

Top Beard/Mustache Trimmer Makers - 1997

Shares are shown based on shipments of 2,400,000 units.

Wahl	39.0%
Norelco Consumer Products	26.0
Windmere	8.0
Remington	6.0
Conair	5.0
Oster	3.0
Others	13.0

Source: *Appliance*, September 1998, p. 69.

★ 949 ★

Personal Care Appliances (SIC 3634)

Top Curling Iron Makers - 1997

Shares are shown based on shipments of 15,700,000 units.

Conair	36.0%
Helen of Tory	21.0
Windmere	15.0
Revlon	13.0
Remington/Clairol	3.0
Others	12.0

Source: *Appliance*, September 1998, p. 69.

★ 950 ★

Personal Care Appliances (SIC 3634)

Top Hair Dryer Makers - 1997

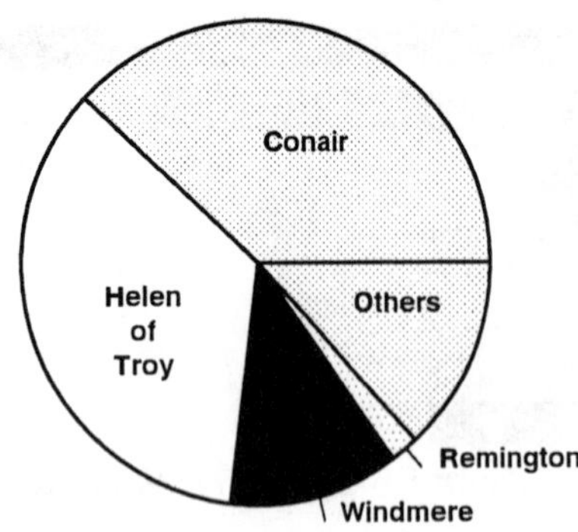

Shares are shown based on shipments of 22,933,955 units.

Conair	38.0%
Helen of Troy	35.0
Windmere	12.0
Remington	2.0
Others	13.0

Source: *Appliance Manufacturer*, May 1998, p. 23.

★ 951 ★

Personal Care Appliances (SIC 3634)

Top Hair Setter Makers - 1997

Shares are shown based on shipments of 21,972,902 units.

Remington	40.0%
Conair	20.0
Helen of Troy	20.0
Windmere	10.0
Others	10.0

Source: *Appliance Manufacturer*, May 1998, p. 23.

★ 952 ★

Personal Care Appliances (SIC 3634)

Top Lighted Make-up Mirror Makers - 1997

Shares are shown based on shipments of 745,000 units.

Conair	23.0%
Windmere	22.0
Hartman	12.0
Remington/Clairol	11.0
Revlon	2.0
Others	30.0

Source: *Appliance*, September 1998, p. 69.

★ 953 ★

Personal Care Appliances (SIC 3634)

Top Women's Shaver Makers - 1997

Shares are shown based on shipments of 2,493,512 units.

Remington	34.0%
Norelco	30.0
Matsushita	25.0
Conair	5.0
Others	6.0

Source: *Appliance Manufacturer*, May 1998, p. 23.

★ 954 ★

Small Appliances (SIC 3634)

Electric Houseware Shipments - 1998

Data show shipments in thousands of units for selected products.

Smoke detectors	16,475
Coffee makers, automatic drip	15,820
Clocks, alarm	15,800
Irons, steam and spray	14,500
Toasters	11,150
Clocks, kitchen wall	8,000
Can openers	7,983
Blenders, stand-type	6,400
Carbon monoxide detectors	5,950
Mixers, food, portable hand	5,562
Electric blankets	4,000
Slow cookers	3,395

Source: *Appliance*, April 1999, p. 53.

★ 955 ★

Small Appliances (SIC 3634)

Top Blender Makers - 1997

Shares are shown based on shipments of 7,590,000 units.

Hamilton Beach/Proctor Silex	52.0%
Oster/Sunbeam	26.0
Braun	7.0
Waring	7.0
Appliance Corp.	5.0
Others	3.0

Source: *Appliance*, September 1998, p. 69.

★ 956 ★

Small Appliances (SIC 3634)

Top Breadmaker Producers - 1997

Welbilt
Regal Ware
Sunbeam Oster
West Bend
Toastmaster
Hitachi
Sanyo Fisher
Matsushita

Shares are shown based on shipments of 2,826,240 units.

Welbilt	31.0%
Regal Ware	12.0
Sunbeam Oster	12.0
West Bend	12.0
Toastmaster	11.0
Hitachi	8.0
Sanyo Fisher	4.0
Matsushita	3.0

Source: *Appliance Manufacturer*, May 1998, p. 23.

★ 957 ★

Small Appliances (SIC 3634)

Top Can Opener Makers - 1997

Shares are shown based on shipments of 7,291,699 units.

Hamilton Beach/Proctor-Silex	31.0%
Rival	28.0
Black & Decker	13.0
Sunbeam-Oster	12.0
Betty Crocker	8.0
Presto	4.0

Source: *Appliance Manufacturer*, May 1998, p. 23.

★ 958 ★

Small Appliances (SIC 3634)

Top Coffee Machine Makers - 1997

Shares are shown based on shipments of 15,897,000 units.

Mr. Coffee	32.0%
Hamilton Beach/Proctor Silex	27.0
Black & Decker	8.0
West Bend	7.0
Krups	6.0
Braun	5.0
Appliance Corp.	4.0
Bunn	2.0
Regal	2.0
Others	7.0

Source: *Appliance*, September 1998, p. 69.

★ 959 ★

Small Appliances (SIC 3634)

Top Dehumidifer Makers - 1997

Shares are shown based on shipments of 819,900 units.

Whirlpool	25.0%
MCD	20.0
Holmes	19.0
Electrolux	18.0
GEA	5.0
Other	13.0

Source: *Appliance Manufacturer*, May 1998, p. 22.

★ 960 ★

Small Appliances (SIC 3634)

Top Electric Knive Makers - 1997

Shares are shown based on shipments of 1,470,000 units.

Hamilton Beach/Proctor Silex	34.0%
Black & Decker	26.0
Toastmaster	19.0
Appliance Corp.	7.0
Oster/Sunbeam	5.0
Regal	4.0
Others	5.0

Source: *Appliance*, September 1998, p. 69.

★ 961 ★

Small Appliances (SIC 3634)

Top Food Chopper Makers - 1997

Shares are shown based on shipments of 1,600,000 units.

Black & Decker	30.0%
Hamilton Beach/Proctor Silex	17.0
Cuisinart	14.0
Toastmaster	14.0
Appliance Corp.	7.0
Oster/Sunbeam	4.0
Others	14.0

Source: *Appliance*, September 1998, p. 69.

★ 962 ★

Small Appliances (SIC 3634)

Top Food Processor Makers - 1997

Shares are shown based on shipments of 5,033,176 units.

Hamilton Beach/Proctor-Silex	40.0%
Cuisinart	19.0
Black & Decker	9.0
Sunbeam-Oster	7.0
Betty Crocker	6.0
Braun	5.0
KitchenAid	5.0
Regal	5.0
West Bend	4.0

Source: *Appliance Manufacturer*, May 1998, p. 23.

★ 963 ★

Small Appliances (SIC 3634)

Top Iron Makers - 1997

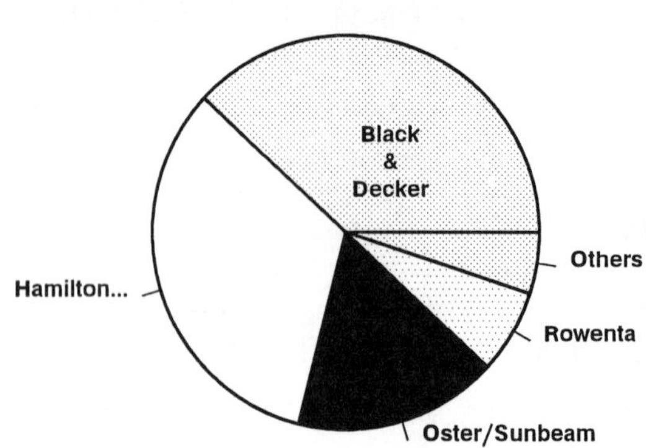

Shares are shown based on shipments of 13,600,000 units.

Black & Decker	38.0%
Hamilton Beach/Proctor Silex	33.0
Oster/Sunbeam	17.0
Rowenta	7.0
Others	5.0

Source: *Appliance*, September 1998, p. 69.

★ 964 ★

Small Appliances (SIC 3634)

Top Percolator Makers - 1997

Shares are shown based on shipments of 2,636,134 units.

Regal Ware	31.0%
Westbilt	26.0
West Bend	15.0
Betty Crocker	14.0
Presto	8.0
Others	6.0

Source: *Appliance Manufacturer*, May 1998, p. 23.

★ 965 ★

Small Appliances (SIC 3634)

Top Rice Cooker Makers - 1997

Shares are shown based on shipments of 1,660,000 units.

Black & Decker	25.0%
Aroma Manufacturing	16.0
Oster/Sunbeam	15.0

Continued on next page.

★ 965 ★ *Continued*

Small Appliances (SIC 3634)

Top Rice Cooker Makers - 1997

Shares are shown based on shipments of 1,660,000 units.

Hitachi	10.0%
Rival	9.0
Salton	9.0
Sanyo	5.0
Zojirushi	4.0
West End	3.0
Others	4.0

Source: *Appliance*, September 1998, p. 69.

★ 966 ★

Small Appliances (SIC 3634)

Top Small Electrics Makers - 1997

Shares are shown based on shipments.

Hamilton Beach Proctor Silex	38.0%
Black & Decker	17.0
Sunbeam-Oster	10.0
Rival	6.2
Signature Brands USA (Mr. Coffee)	5.8
Betty Crocker	4.7
Toastmaster	4.4
Braun	2.5
Cuisinart	1.4
West Bend	1.2
Rowenta	1.1
Others	7.7

Source: *Appliance Manufacturer*, May 1998, p. 23.

★ 967 ★

Small Appliances (SIC 3634)

Top Waffle Iron Makers - 1997

Toastmaster
Hamilton Beach/Proctor Silex
Salton
Oster/Sunbeam
Appliance Corp.
Dazey
Others

Shares are shown based on shipments of 1,470,000 units.

Toastmaster	23.0%
Hamilton Beach/Proctor Silex	22.0
Salton	16.0
Oster/Sunbeam	6.0
Appliance Corp.	5.0
Dazey	5.0
Others	23.0

Source: *Appliance*, September 1998, p. 69.

★ 968 ★

Vacuum Cleaners (SIC 3635)

Top Hand-Held Vacuum Cleaner Makers - 1997

Shares are shown based on shipments of 6,250,000 units.

Royal	42.0%
Black & Decker	27.0
Hoover	14.0
Eureka	6.0
Bissell	5.0
Others	6.0

Source: *Appliance Manufacturer*, May 1998, p. 23.

★ 969 ★

Vacuum Cleaners (SIC 3635)

Top Vacuum Cleaner Makers - 1997

Hoover
Eureka
Royal
Matsushita
Kirby
Other

Shares are shown based on shipments of 15,692,420 units.

Hoover	37.0%
Eureka	23.0
Royal	12.0
Matsushita	10.0
Kirby	5.0
Other	13.0

Source: *Appliance Manufacturer*, May 1998, p. 23.

★ 970 ★

Vacuum Cleaners (SIC 3635)

Top Wet/Dry Vacuum Makers - 1997

Shares are shown based on shipments of 2,700,000 units.

Shop Vac	43.0%
Sears/Kenmore	35.0
Genie	8.0
Hoover	5.0
Royal	5.0
Eureka	3.0
Others	1.0

Source: *Appliance*, September 1998, p. 68.

★ 971 ★

Dishwashers (SIC 3639)

Built-In Dishwasher Sales by State - 1996

	Units	Share
California	430,700	9.82%
Texas	394,300	8.99
Florida	305,000	6.95
New York	190,100	4.33
Ohio	169,000	3.85
Other	2,896,800	66.05

Source: "Industry Statistics." Retrieved May 28, 1999 from the World Wide Web: http:// www.aham.org/ mfrs/stats/cleandist.htm, from U.S. Bureau of the Census.

★ 972 ★

Dishwashers (SIC 3639)

Portable Dishwasher Sales by State - 1996

	Units	Share
Ohio	12,500	6.66%
California	11,000	5.86
Pennsylvania	10,800	5.76
Michigan	10,700	5.70
New York	10,400	5.54
Illinois	9,400	5.01
Other	122,800	65.46

Source: "Industry Statistics." Retrieved May 28, 1999 from the World Wide Web: http:// www.aham.org/ mfrs/stats/cleandist.htm, from U.S. Bureau of the Census.

★ 973 ★

Dishwashers (SIC 3639)

Top Dishwasher Makers - 1997

Shares are shown based on shipments of 5,124,200 units.

GEA	39.0%
Whirlpool	38.0
Maytag	15.0
Electrolux	8.0

Source: *Appliance Manufacturer*, May 1998, p. 21.

★ 974 ★

Garbage Disposals (SIC 3639)

Top Disposal Makers - 1997

Shares are shown based on shipments of 4,828,100 units.

In-Sink-Erator	76.0%
Anaheim Manufacturing	18.0
Watertown Metal Products	5.0
Maytag	1.0

Source: *Appliance*, September 1998, p. 69.

★ 975 ★

Trash Compactors (SIC 3639)

Compactor Sales by State - 1996

	Units	Share
California	19,300	19.90%
Texas	9,000	9.28
Florida	4,100	4.23
Massachusetts	3,300	3.40
Tennessee	2,900	2.99
Other	58,400	60.21

Source: "Industry Statistics." Retrieved May 28, 1999 from the World Wide Web: http:// www.aham.org/ mfrs/stats/cleandist.htm, from U.S. Bureau of the Census.

★ 976 ★

Trash Compactors (SIC 3639)

Top Compactor Makers - 1997

Shares are shown based on shipments of 105,400 units.

Whirlpool	89.0%
Broan	11.0

Source: *Appliance Manufacturer*, May 1998, p. 21.

★ 977 ★

Consumer Electronics (SIC 3651)

Consumer Electronics Market - 1999

The market is shown in percent.

Home information products	44.9%
Video products	18.8
Mobile electronics	10.6
Electronic gaming	9.2
Home & portable audio	7.5%
Accessories & batteries	5.6
Home security	2.0
Blank media	1.4

Source: *Electronic Business*, February 1999, p. 11, from Consumer Electronics Manufacturers Association.

★ 978 ★

Consumer Electronics (SIC 3651)

DVD Player Market in Canada - 1999

Market shares are shown in percent for the year ended March 31, 1999.

Toshiba	23.2%
Panasonic	22.0
Pioneer	20.5
Sony	17.8
RCA	8.4
Proscan	3.2
Other	4.9

Source: "Report on Market Share." Retrieved June 1, 1999 from the World Wide Web: http:// www.marketingmag.ca/index.cgi?, from industry sources.

★ 979 ★

Consumer Electronics (SIC 3651)

Home Information Products - 1997

PCs	50.0%
Computer printers	12.0
Software	11.0
Cordless phones	5.0
Modem	4.0
PC peripherals	4.0
Fax machines	3.5
Others	10.5

Source: *Investor's Business Daily*, July 14, 1998, p. A8, from Consumer Electronics Manufacturers Association.

★ 980 ★

Consumer Electronics (SIC 3651)

Largest Consumer Electronics Firms

Data show revenues in millions of dollars.

Zenith Electronics	$ 1,173.1
Eastman Kodak	919.2
Audiovox	536.2
Recoton	502.0
Harman Intl. Industries	498.7

Source: *Electronic Business*, July 1998, p. 95.

★ 981 ★

Consumer Electronics (SIC 3651)

Top Camcorder Makers - 1997

Shares are shown based on shipments of 3,649,667 units.

Sony	33.0%
Thomson	21.0
Matsushita	18.0
JVC	13.0
Sharp	7.0
Hitachi	4.0
Others	4.0

Source: *Appliance Manufacturer*, May 1998, p. 23.

★ 982 ★

Consumer Electronics (SIC 3651)

Top CD Player Makers - 1997

Shares are shown based on shipments of 33,000,000 units.

Sony	43.0%
Matsushita	11.0
Pioneer	10.0
JVC	7.0
Kenwood	7.0
Sanyo Fisher	7.0
Thomson	5.0
Sharp	4.0

Source: *Appliance Manufacturer*, May 1998, p. 23.

★ 983 ★

Consumer Electronics (SIC 3651)

Top DVD Player Makers - 1997

Shares are shown based on shipments of 12,500,000 units.

Sony	29.0%
Toshiba	20.0
Matsushita (Panasonic)	14.0
Thomson (RCA)	8.0
Others	29.0

Source: *Appliance*, September 1998, p. 68.

★ 984 ★

Consumer Electronics (SIC 3651)

Top DVD Player Makers - 1998

Shares are shown for July 1998.

Sony	40.0%
Matsushita	25.0
Toshiba	11.0
Pioneer	10.0
Philips/Magnavox	4.0
Thomson/RCA	4.0
Other	6.0

Source: *Investor's Business Daily*, September 23, 1998, p. A10, from NPD Group Inc., Consumer Electronics Manufacturers Association, and InfoTech Inc.

★ 985 ★

Consumer Electronics (SIC 3651)

Top TV Makers - 1998

Market shares are shown based on shipments for July 1997 - June 1998.

Thomson	21.4%
Philips/Magnavox	12.4
Sony	11.1
Zenith	10.9
Sanyo	7.1
Panasonic	5.4
Toshiba	5.3
Sharp	4.8
JVC	3.5
Samsung	2.9
Mitsubishi	1.9
Other	13.3

Source: *Investor's Business Daily*, February 1, 1999, p. A6, from company reports and *Television Digest*.

★ 986 ★

Consumer Electronics (SIC 3651)

Top VCR Makers - 1997

Shares are shown based on shipments of 16,673,202 units.

Thomson	17.0%
NAP	12.0
Matsushita	10.0
Emerson	7.0
JVC	6.0
Sanyo Fisher	5.0
Sharp	5.0
Sony	5.0
Zenith	5.0
Others	28.0

Source: *Appliance Manufacturer*, May 1998, p. 23.

★ 987 ★

Consumer Electronics (SIC 3651)

TV Shipments by Segment

Shipments are shown in thousands of units. Data are for the year ended April 1999. Digital television shipments are for the first quarter of the year.

Color TV	5,730
Projection TVs	261
35-inch or larger	215
Digital	12

Source: *Investor's Business Daily*, May 17, 1999, p. A6, from Consumer Electronics Manufacturers Association.

★ 988 ★

Consumer Electronics (SIC 3651)

Video Product Sales - 1997

The value of factory sales reached $14.2 billion.

Color TVs	43.0%
VCR decks	18.0
Camcorders	13.0
Projection TVs	10.0
Home satellite systems	7.0
TV/VCR combos	5.0
Other	4.0

Source: *Investor's Business Daily*, July 15, 1998, p. A8, from Consumer Electronics Manufacturers Association.

★ 989 ★

Electronics (SIC 3651)

Consumer Electronics Market - 1998

PCs, information devices	44.0%
Televisions	19.0
Mobile electronics	11.0
Home audio	8.0
Video games	8.0
Others	10.0

Source: *Investor's Business Daily*, February 9, 1999, p. A6, from Consumer Electronics Manufacturers Association.

★ 990 ★

Prerecorded Music (SIC 3651)

Best-Selling Record Artists

The top artists are ranked by unit sales.

The Beatles	106.0
Garth Brooks	89.0
Led Zeppelin	80.3
The Eagles	64.0
Barbara Streisand	61.8
Elton John	61.6
Billy Joel	61.0
Aerosmith	54.4
Pink Floyd	52.6
Van Halen	50.5

Source: *Detroit Free Press*, January 11, 1999, p. F1, from Recording Industry Association of America.

★ 991 ★

Prerecorded Music (SIC 3651)

U.S. Latin Music Sales - 1998

Total shipments reached 49.3 billion units and $570.84 million.

CDs	$ 426,765
Cassettes	142,011
Music videos	2,073

Source: *Billboard*, March 20, 1999, p. 81, from Recording Industry Association of America.

★ 992 ★

Prerecorded Music (SIC 3652)

Best-Selling Albums - 1998

Sales are shown in millions of albums.

Titanic Soundtrack	9.2
Let's Talk About Love	5.6
Backstreet Boys	4.9
Come on Over	4.2
City of Angels Soundtrack	3.8
Big Willie Style	3.2
'N Sync	3.2
Savage Garden	3.1
Yourself Or Someone Like You	3.0
Hello Nasty	2.9

Source: *Wall Street Journal*, December 23, 1998, p. A4, from SoundScan.

★ 993 ★

Prerecorded Music (SIC 3652)

Largest Music Publishers - 1998

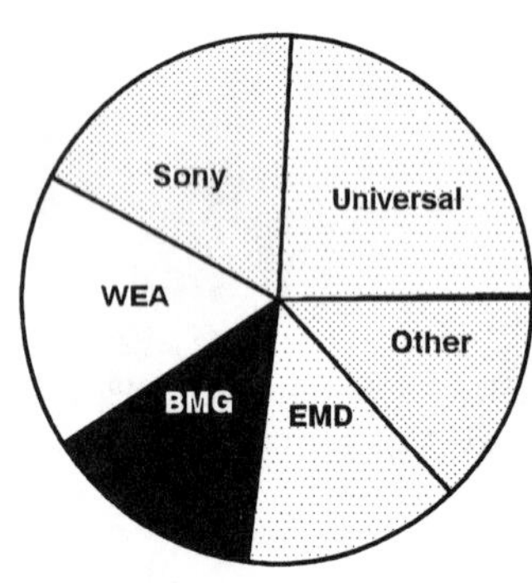

Market shares are shown as of December 27, 1998.

Universal	24.05%
Sony	17.50
WEA	17.30
BMG	14.40
EMD	13.60
Other	13.15

Source: *Los Angeles Times*, December 31, 1998, p. C5, from SoundScan.

★ 994 ★

Prerecorded Music (SIC 3652)

Largest Singles Distributors - 1998

Market shares are shown for the first nine months of the year.

BMG	24.6%
WEA	19.3
Sony	18.2
PGD	17.0
EMD	8.6
Universal	6.5
Indies	5.9

Source: *Billboard*, October 17, 1998, p. 75, from Soundscan.

★ 995 ★

Prerecorded Music (SIC 3652)

Music Sales by Format

CDs	81.7%
Cassettes	13.6
Cassette singles	2.3
CD singles	1.8

Source: *Discount Merchandiser*, October 1998, p. 60, from National Association of Recording Merchandisers.

★ 996 ★

Prerecorded Music (SIC 3652)

Music Sales by Genre - 1997

Rock	32.5%
Country	14.4
R&B	11.2
Rap	10.1
Pop	9.4
Gospel	4.5
Classical	2.8
Jazz	2.8
Soundtracks	1.2
Children's	0.9
Oldies	0.8
New age	0.8
Other	5.7

Source: *Discount Merchandiser*, October 1998, p. 60, from National Association of Recording Merchandisers.

★ 997 ★

Prerecorded Music (SIC 3652)

New Age Music Market

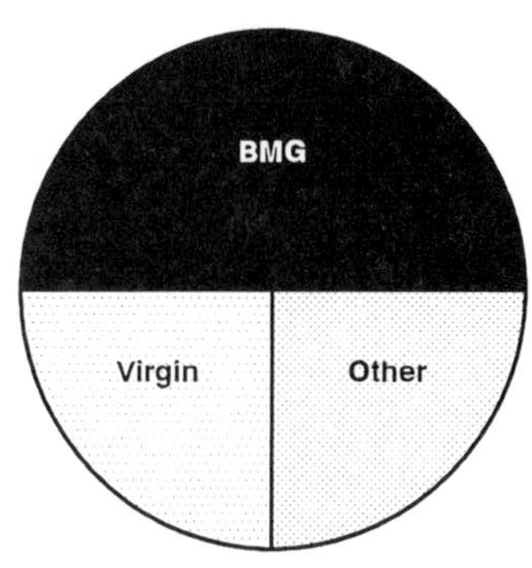

Market shares are shown in percent.

BMG	50.0%
Virgin	25.0
Other	25.0

Source: *Forbes*, August 10, 1998, p. 62.

★ 998 ★

Prerecorded Music (SIC 3652)

U.S. Online Music Market

Sales are shown in millions of dollars.

	1999	2001
Email order	$ 236	$ 870
Digital	8	101

Source: *Financial Times*, May 7, 1999, p. 7, from Jupiter Communications.

★ 999 ★

Fax Machines (SIC 3661)

Fax Machine Leaders - 1997

Sharp	25.0%
Brother	24.0
Panasonic	17.0
Hewlett-Packard	13.0
Canon	11.0
Xerox	2.0
Muratec	1.0%
Pitney Bowles	1.0
Ricoh	1.0
Other	5.0

Source: "Market Share Information." Retrieved January 14, 1999 from the World Wide Web: http:// www.sharp-usa.com/products/business/mrktsfax.html, from Dataquest Inc.

★ 1000 ★

Fax Machines (SIC 3661)

Largest LASER/LED Fax Vendors - 1997

Canon	17.0%
Sharp	13.0
Brother	10.0
Panasonic	10.0
Ricoh	10.0
Pitney Bowles	8.0
Okidata	6.0
Xerox	6.0
Lanier	4.0
Mita	3.0
Other	13.0

Source: Retrieved May 27, 1999 from the World Wide Web: http:// www.usa-canon.com/corpoffice/faxmach/ mktshare/fax1share.html, from International Data Corp./ Link.

★ 1001 ★

Fax Machines (SIC 3661)

Multifunction Fax Machine Leaders - 1997

Sharp	26.5%
Lanier	16.1
Canon	13.6
Pitney Bowles	7.2
Other	24.6

Source: "Market Share Information." Retrieved January 14, 1999 from the World Wide Web: http:// www.sharp-usa.com/products/business/mrktsfax.html, from Dataquest Inc.

★ 1002 ★

Fiber Optics (SIC 3661)

Fiber Optics Market in Canada

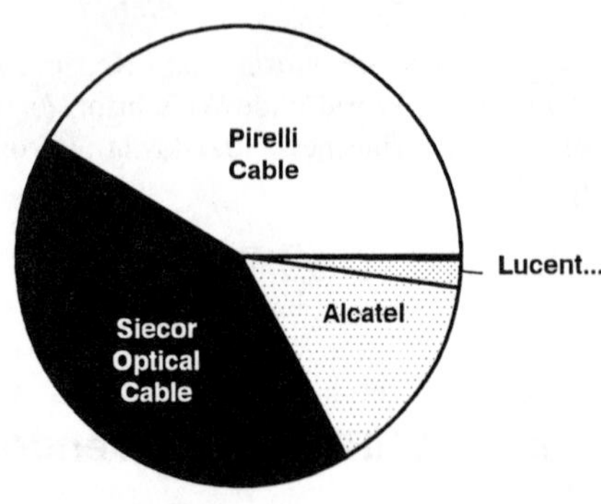

Market shares are shown in percent. The market is experiencing growth from the telecom service industry.

Pirelli Cable	40.0%
Siecor Optical Cable	40.0
Alcatel	14.0
Lucent Technologies	2.0

Source: *National Trade Data Bank*, October 23, 1998, p. ISA980901.

★ 1003 ★

Modems (SIC 3661)

ADSL Modem Leaders - 1998

Shares are shown for the fourth quarter of the year. ADSL stands for asymmetric digital subscriber line.

Cisco	32.0%
Nortel	15.0
Alcatel	13.0
Paradyne	5.0
Other	35.0

Source: *Business Communications Review*, May 1999, p. 14.

★ 1004 ★

Modems (SIC 3661)

Analog Modem Vendors - 1997

Market shares are shown in percent.

3Com	32.9%
MaxTech/GVC	6.8
CIS/Wisecom	4.1
Diamond	3.4%
Hayes	3.4
Askey	3.2
Archtek	2.8
Boca	2.7
Other	40.7

Source: Retrieved May 18, 1999 from the World Wide Web: http:// www.sonic.net/cgi-bin/cif/cif/search-free.pl.

★ 1005 ★

Modems (SIC 3661)

Cable Modem Leaders - 1998

Shares are shown in percent.

Motorola	40.0%
Bay Networks	24.0
Com21	8.0
Terayon	6.0
Other	22.0

Source: *Business Communications Review*, May 1999, p. 14.

★ 1006 ★

Modems (SIC 3661)

Cable Modem Service Market - 1998

An estimated 16 million homes are expected to have broadband cable modem or digital subscriber line Net access by 2002. ATHome is backed by AT&T. Road Runner is backed by Time Warner.

ATHome	47.0%
Road Runner	29.0
Other	24.0

Source: *Investor's Business Daily*, November 30, 1998, p. A8, from Forrester Research Inc.

★ 1007 ★

Modems (SIC 3661)

Modem Shipments by Type - 1998

Analog	97.9%
Cable	1.8
ADSL	0.3

Source: *Electronic News*, March 22, 1999, p. 14, from Cahners In-Stat Group.

★ 1008 ★

Scanners (SIC 3661)

Top Scanner Producers

Vendors are ranked by revenues in millions of dollars.

	($ mil.) Rev.	Share
Hewlett-Packard	$ 230	16.7%
Umax	229	16.7
Epson	30	2.2
Kodak	9	0.7
Polaroid	5	0.4
Other	870	63.3

Source: *Investext,* Thomson Financial Networks, July 2, 1998, p. 6, from International Data Corp. and Morgan Stanley Dean Witter Research.

★ 1009 ★

Telephones (SIC 3661)

Top Cordless Telephone Makers - 1997

Shares are shown based on shipments of 26,900,000 units.

AT&T	17.0%
GE	15.0
BellSouth	12.0
Uniden	11.0
Sony	10.0
Panasonic	6.0
Radio Shack	4.0
Southwestern Bell	4.0
Others	21.0

Source: *Appliance*, September 1998, p. 68.

★ 1010 ★

Cellular Phones (SIC 3663)

Cell Phone Market - 1998

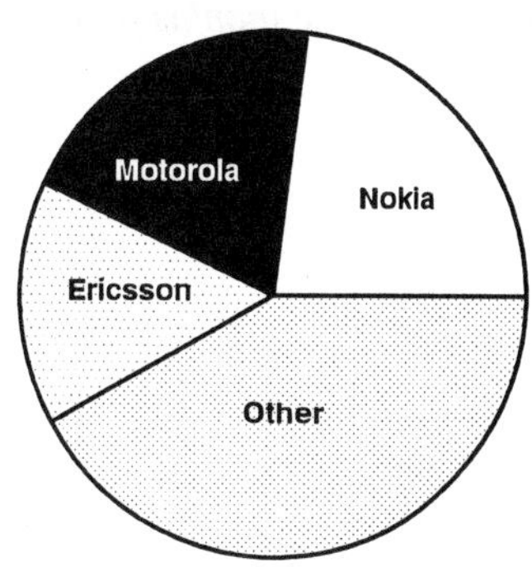

Market shares are shown in percent.

Nokia	23.0%
Motorola	20.0
Ericsson	15.0
Other	42.0

Source: *Investor's Business Daily*, May 4, 1999, p. A6, from Dataquest Inc. and Thomas Weisel Partners Inc.

★ 1011 ★

Cellular Phones (SIC 3663)

Top Cellular Phone Markets

Data show the cities with the highest percentage of adults living in households that have at least one cell phone.

Detroit, MI	48.0%
Greensboro, NC	47.7
Atlanta, GA	47.4
Charlotte, NC	45.6
Chicago, IL	45.3
Birmingham, AL	44.9
Washington	44.5
Raleigh, NC	43.5
Greenville, SC	43.4
Sacramento, CA	43.0

Source: *Christian Science Monitor*, July 31, 1998, p. 2, from Scarborough Research.

★ 1012 ★

Cellular Phones (SIC 3663)

Top Digital Cell Phone Makers - 1998

Figures are for the first nine months of the year.

Nokia	40.3%
Ericsson	20.6
Motorola	11.5
Qualcomm	8.2
Sony	7.1
Samsung	6.2
Other	6.1

Source: *Investor's Business Daily*, January 20, 1999, p. A6, from Dataquest inc.

★ 1013 ★

Cellular Phones (SIC 3663)

Top Wireless Telephone Makers - 1997

Shares are shown based on shipments of 12,500,000 units.

Motorola	38.0%
Nokia-Mobira	16.0
GE/Ericsson	7.0
Audiovox	5.0
NEC	5.0
Sony	4.0
Others	25.0

Source: *Appliance*, September 1998, p. 68.

★ 1014 ★

Data Communications (SIC 3669)

Access Concentrator Market - 1997

Market shares are shown in percent.

3Com/US Robotics	32.5%
Ascend	26.7
Cisco	21.2
Livingston (Lucent)	6.0
Other	13.6

Source: *Telecommunications*, June 1998, p. 25, from Dell'Oro Group.

★ 1015 ★

Data Communications (SIC 3669)

Fast Ethernet PC Card Market - 1998

Market shares are shown in percent.

Xircom	50.0%
3Com	40.0
Other	10.0

Source: *Investext,* Thomson Financial Networks, January 19, 1999, p. 2, from International Data Corp. and Xircom.

★ 1016 ★

Data Communications (SIC 3669)

Fast Ethernet Switching Market

Shares are shown for the first quarter of the year.

3Com	31.0%
Bay Networks	25.0
Other	44.0

Source: Retrieved May 28, 1999 from the World Wide Web: http:// www.itweb.co.za/office/3com/ 9806181125.htm, from Dell'Oro Group.

★ 1017 ★

Data Communications (SIC 3669)

Gigabit Ethernet Market - 1998

Market shares are shown for the second quarter of the year.

Bay Networks	28.2%
3Com	14.6
Extreme Networks	11.2
Lucent	11.2
Cabletron	2.1
Other	32.7

Source: *Investor's Business Daily*, October 21, 20'9, p. A10, from Dell'Oro Group.

★ 1018 ★

Data Communications (SIC 3669)

LAN Hub Market - 1998

Shares are shown for the first quarter of the year.

3Com	27.2%
Bay	12.6
Cisco	11.8

Source: "LAN Hub, Switch Market Grew 9% in Q1." Retrieved June 1, 1999 from the World Wide Web: http:// www2.idg.com.au/nwwdb.NSF/Home+pag, from In-Stat.

★ 1019 ★

Data Communications (SIC 3669)

LAN+Modem PC Card Market - 1998

Market shares are shown in percent.

Xircom	50.0%
3Com	35.0
Other	15.0

Source: *Investext,* Thomson Financial Networks, January 19, 1999, p. 2, from International Data Corp. and Xircom.

★ 1020 ★

Data Communications (SIC 3669)

Managed Shared Ethernet Market - 1998

Shares are shown for the first quarter of the year. Data refer to fixed configuration.

3Com	31.0%
Bay Networks	16.0
Other	53.0

Source: Retrieved May 28, 1999 from the World Wide Web: http:// www.itweb.co.za/office/3com/ 9806181125.htm, from Dell'Oro Group.

★ 1021 ★

Data Communications (SIC 3669)

Managed Shared Fast Ethernet Market - 1998

Shares are shown for the first quarter of the year. Data refer to fixed configuration.

3Com	67.0%
Bay Networks	9.0
Other	24.0

Source: Retrieved May 28, 1999 from the World Wide Web: http:// www.itweb.co.za/office/3com/ 9806181125.htm, from Dell'Oro Group.

★ 1022 ★

Data Communications (SIC 3669)

Memory Card Makers - 1997

Market shares are shown in percent.

SanDisk	45.0%
Hitachi	17.0
Toshiba	9.0
Samsung	5.0
Intel	4.0
SiliconTech	4.0
Advanced Micro Devices	2.0
Other	14.0

Source: *Investor's Business Daily*, December 3, 1998, p. A10, from International Data Corp.

★ 1023 ★

Data Communications (SIC 3669)

Network Market Leaders - 1998

Market shares are shown based on sales.

Cisco	29.2%
3Com	16.4
Nortel Networks	10.5
Ascend Communications Inc.	4.0
Cabletron Systems Inc.	3.9
Other	36.0

Source: *PC Week*, April 5, 1999, p. 99, from In-Stat.

★ 1024 ★

Data Communications (SIC 3669)

Networking Equipment Leaders

Market shares are shown in percent.

Cisco	33.0%
Ascend	23.0
3Com	12.0
Nortel	10.0
Lucent	3.0
Other	19.0

Source: *Investor's Business Daily*, January 14, 1999, p. A7, from International Data Corp.

★ 1025 ★

Data Communications (SIC 3669)

PC Card Market - 1998

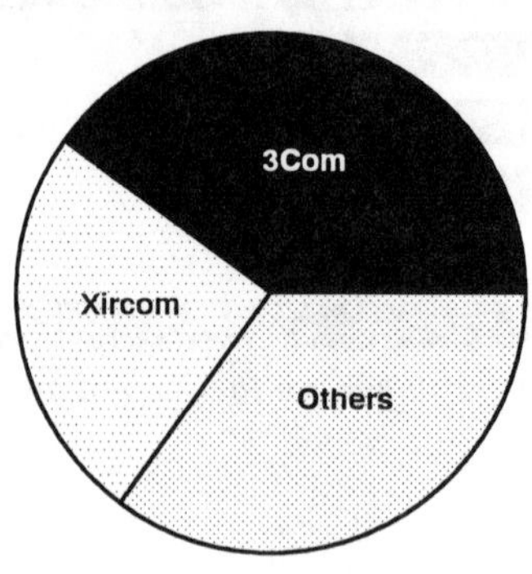

Market shares are shown in percent.

3Com	40.0%
Xircom	25.0
Others	35.0

Source: *Investext,* Thomson Financial Networks, January 19, 1999, p. 2, from International Data Corp. and Xircom.

★ 1026 ★

Data Communications (SIC 3669)

Physical Library Market - 1997

According to the source, physical libraries are collections of electronic parts used by design engineers to create silicon intellectual property cores. Cores are combined to create systems on a chip.

Synopsys	40.0%
Avant!	22.0
Artisan Components	20.0
Aspec Technology	11.0
Other	7.0

Source: *Electronic News*, November 30, 1998, p. 24.

★ 1027 ★

Data Communications (SIC 3669)

Private Branch Exchange Market - 1998

Lucent
Nortel
Siemens BCS
NEC
Mitel
Others

Data show total shipments in the 101-to-400 station segment. Figures are in thousands of systems.

	(000)	Share
Lucent	4.46	39.8%
Nortel	2.38	21.3
Siemens BCS	1.30	11.6
NEC	1.05	9.4
Mitel	0.91	8.2
Others	1.09	14.3

Source: *Computer Reseller News*, May 31, 1999, p. 113, from Dataquest Inc.

★ 1028 ★

Data Communications (SIC 3669)

Shared Media Hub Market - 1998

Shares are shown for the first quarter of the year.

3Com	31.8%
Bay Networks	21.4
Cabletron	5.7
Hewlett-Packard	4.5
IBM	4.2
Other	32.4

Source: *Investor's Business Daily*, August 3, 1998, p. A8, from Dataquest Inc.

★ 1029 ★

Data Communications (SIC 3669)

Switched Ethernet Market - 1997

Market shares are shown based on $4.7 billion.

Cisco	37.8%
3Com	15.7
Cabletron	13.8
Bay	10.4
Others	22.8

Source: *Network World*, July 13, 1998, p. 28, from Dell'Oro Group.

★ 1030 ★

Data Communications (SIC 3669)

Token Ring Hub Market - 1998

Figures are for the third quarter of the year.

IBM	32.0%
Nortel Networks	22.0
Madge Networks	14.0
3Com	13.0
Other	19.0

Source: "IBM Token Ring Products Named Market Leader." Retrieved June 1, 1999 from the World Wide Web: http:// thesource.dwpub.com/frames/2122.html, from Dell'Oro Group.

★ 1031 ★

Data Communications (SIC 3669)

Top NIC Makers - 1998

Market shares are shown in percent. NIC stands for network interface card.

3Com	38.0%
Intel	19.0
IBM	9.0
Other	34.0

Source: *Investext*, Thomson Financial Networks, December 3, 1998, p. 1, from Dell'Oro Group.

★ 1032 ★

Data Communications (SIC 3669)

Top Remote Access Device Makers - 1998

Market shares are shown in percent.

3Com	25.0%
Ascend	25.0
Cisco	20.0
Others	30.0

Source: *Wall Street Journal*, May 12, 1999, p. A3, from company reports and Dell'Oro Group.

★ 1033 ★

Data Communications (SIC 3669)

Top Router Makers - 1998

Market shares are shown in percent.

Cisco	67.0%
Nortel/Bay	12.0
3Com	3.0
Other	18.0

Source: *Investext*, Thomson Financial Networks, December 3, 1998, p. 1, from Dell'Oro Group.

★ 1034 ★

Data Communications (SIC 3669)

Top Switch/Hub Makers - 1998

Market shares are shown in percent.

Cisco	33.0%
3Com	16.0
Nortel/Bay Networks	14.0
Others	37.0

Source: *Wall Street Journal*, May 12, 1999, p. A3.

★ 1035 ★

Data Communications (SIC 3669)

Touch Screen Market

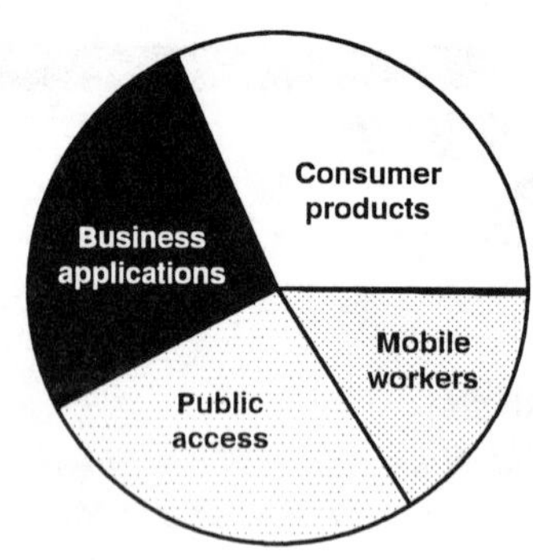

	1998	2004
Consumer products	13.0%	32.0%
Business applications	33.0	26.0
Public access	40.0	26.0
Mobile workers	14.0	16.0

Source: *Investor's Business Daily*, June 8, 1999, p. A6, from MicroTouch Systems Inc.

★ 1036 ★

Data Communications (SIC 3669)

Unmanaged Shared Fast Ethernet Market - 1998

Shares are shown for the first quarter of the year. Data refer to fixed configuration.

3Com	23.0%
Allied Telysyn	21.0
Other	56.0

Source: Retrieved May 28, 1999 from the World Wide Web: http:// www.itweb.co.za/office/3com/ 9806181125.htm, from Dell'Oro Group.

★ 1037 ★

Data Communications (SIC 3669)

Virtual Private Networks - 2000

The market is expected to reach $6.34 billion. PSTN stands for public switched telephone network.

PSTN-based	52.0%
IP-based	42.3
Satellite	3.0
Hardware	2.0
Software	0.7

Source: *PC Week*, December 7, 1998, p. 141, from Frost & Sullivan.

★ 1038 ★

Data Communications (SIC 3669)

Voice Messaging Leaders - 1997

Shares are shown based on a $2.33 billion market.

Octel Communications	20.2%
Lucent Technologies	17.2
Nortel	11.9
Active Voice	5.8
Comverse Technology	5.5
Centigram Communications	4.9
Siemens	3.8
Other	30.8

Source: *Electronic News*, September 14, 1998, p. 10.

★ 1039 ★

Phone Cards (SIC 3669)

Phone Card Market - 1997

Retail	44.0%
Promotional	40.0
Fund-raising	12.0
Collectible	4.0

Source: *Supermarket Business*, September 1998, p. 136, from Atlantic ACM.

★ 1040 ★

Security Equipment (SIC 3669)

Security Equipment Sales

Sales are shown in millions of dollars. EAS stands for electronic article surveillance systems. CCTV stands for closed circuit television.

	1997	2002	Share
Alarms	$ 2,930	$ 3,875	58.71%
EAS	730	1,280	19.39
CCTV	485	830	12.58
Bomb/metal detection	280	485	7.35
Other	80	130	1.97

Source: *Security Management*, December 1998, p. 12, from Freedonia Group.

★ 1041 ★

Security Equipment (SIC 3669)

Top Carbon Monoxide Detector Makers - 1997

Shares are shown based on shipments of 5,850,000 units.

First Alert	49.0%
American Sensors (Dicon)	15.0
Jameson (Maple Chase)	3.0
Others	33.0

Source: *Appliance*, September 1998, p. 69.

★ 1042 ★

Security Equipment (SIC 3669)

Top Smoke Detector Makers - 1997

Shares are shown based on shipments of 16,650,000 units.

First Alert	60.0%
Jameson (Maple Chase)	32.0
American Sensors (Dicon)	5.0
Others	3.0

Source: *Appliance*, September 1998, p. 69.

★ 1043 ★

Circuit Boards (SIC 3672)

Printed Circuit Board Makers - 1998

Data show the largest makers in North America ranked by sales in millions of dollars.

Viasystems	$ 1,200
Sanmina	984
Hadco	856
Johnson Matthey	455
IBM Micro	430
Tyco Group + AMC	414
Photocircuits	385

Source: *Electronic News*, January 4, 1999, p. 46, from Fabfile Systems.

★ 1044 ★

Microprocessors (SIC 3674)

Desktop 3D Graphics Chip Market - 1998

Shares are shown based on 88 million units.

ATI Technologies	37.0%
S3	18.0
Matrox Electronic	10.0
Nvidia	10.0
3Dfx Interactive	6.0
Other	19.0

Source: *Investor's Business Daily*, March 29, 1998, p. A10, from Mercury Research.

★ 1045 ★

Microprocessors (SIC 3674)

EEPROM Market - 2001

Market shares are shown based on bus protocol. EEPROM stands for electrically erasable, programmable, read-only memory.

I2C	57.0%
SPI	23.0
Microwire	18.0
Other	2.0

Source: *Computer Design*, June 1998, p. 92, from In-Stat.

★ 1046 ★

Microprocessors (SIC 3674)

Embedded Microprocessor Market

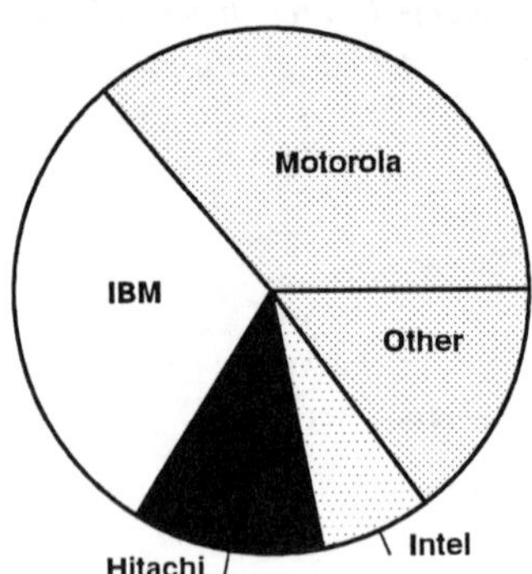

Motorola	36.0%
IBM	30.0
Hitachi	12.0
Intel	7.0
Other	15.0

Source: *Forbes*, May 31, 1999, p. 52, from Cahner's In-Stat Group.

★ 1047 ★

Microprocessors (SIC 3674)

Graphics Chip Market - 1998

Shares are shown for the first quarter of the year.

S3 Inc.	29.0%
ATI Technologies Inc.	20.0
Cirrus Logic Inc.	11.0
Trident Microsystems Inc.	9.0
Nvdia Inc.	6.0
Other	25.0

Source: *Wall Street Journal*, July 2, 1998, p. 4B, from company reports and Mercury Research.

★ 1048 ★

Microprocessors (SIC 3674)

Non-PC Device Market - 1997

Shares are shown based on 98 million units. Data refer to 32-bit RISC microprocessors.

MIPS	48.0%
Hitachi	24.3
ARM	10.0
Intel	9.6
Power PC	3.9
Other	3.2

Source: *Business Week*, August 17, 1998, p. 63, from *Inside the New Computer Industry*.

★ 1049 ★

Microprocessors (SIC 3674)

Portable Graphics Market - 1998

Market shares are shown based on units. Figures are for the second quarter of the year.

NeoMagic	46.0%
Intel	27.0
Trident	13.0
Other	14.0

Source: *Investor's Business Daily*, December 8, 1998, p. A4, from company reports.

★ 1050 ★

Microprocessors (SIC 3674)

RISC Microprocessor Market - 1997

Market shares are shown for 32-bit RISC microprocessors in low end non-PC devices. RISC stands for random instruction set computer.

MIPS	49.0%
Hitachi	24.0
ARM	10.0
Intel	10.0
Other	7.0

Source: Retrieved May 18, 1999 from the World Wide Web: http:// www.sonic.net/cgi-bin/cif/cif/search-free.pl.

★ 1051 ★

Semiconductors (SIC 3674)

Digital Signal Processing Market - 1997

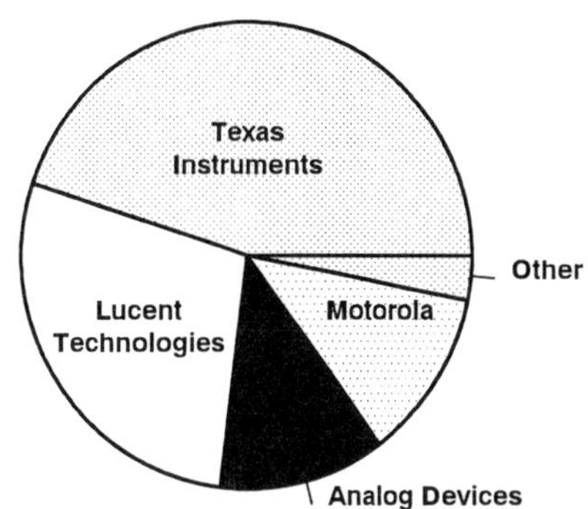

Market shares are shown in percent.

Texas Instruments	45.0%
Lucent Technologies	28.0
Analog Devices	12.0
Motorola	12.0
Other	3.0

Source: *Investor's Business Daily*, September 3, 1998, p. A8, from World Semiconductor Trade Statistics and A.G. Edwards & Sons Inc.

★ 1052 ★

Semiconductors (SIC 3674)

Disk Drive Chip Market - 1998

The $2.8 billion market is shown for chips for hard disk-drives.

Texas Instruments	31.0%
IBM	12.0
Lucent Technologies	11.0
Cirrus Logic	10.0
STMicrosystems	8.0
Mitsubishi	5.0
Hitachi	4.0
NEC	3.0
Other	16.0

Source: *Electronic Business*, February 1999, p. 68, from International Data Corp.

★ 1053 ★

Semiconductors (SIC 3674)

Largest Semiconductor Makers

Data show revenues in millions of dollars.

Intel	$ 21,309.5
Texas Instruments	8,092.5
Motorola	7,150.6
Applied Materials	4,546.2
IBM	3,925.4

Source: *Electronic Business*, July 1998, p. 95.

★ 1054 ★

Semiconductors (SIC 3674)

Semiconductor Market - 1999

The $140.4 billion market is shown in percent.

Computers	50.0%
Communications	20.0
Consumer	14.0
Industrial	9.0
Automotive	6.0
Government	1.0

Source: *Purchasing*, May 20, 1999, p. 38, from WSTS and IC Insights.

★ 1055 ★

Connectors (SIC 3679)

Connector Sales in North America

Multimode	$ 522
Singlemode	487
Cables & cable assemblies	256
Application specific	122

Source: *Electronic News*, March 29, 1999, p. 35, from Fleck Research.

★ 1056 ★

CPI Equipment (SIC 3679)

Largest CPI Equipment Producers

Sales are shown in millions of dollars. CPI stands for chemical process industry.

Fluor	$ 3,295
Foster Wheeler	1.394
Jacobs Engineering Group	555
Stone & Webster	287
Blount International	200
Millipore	179

Source: *Chemical Week*, March 3, 1999, p. 42.

★ 1057 ★

Flat Panel Displays (SIC 3679)

Flat Panel Shipments - 1999

Figures are based on revenues for the first quarter of the year.

NEC	26.3%
Fujitsu	14.8
Mitsubishi	6.9
Compaq	4.7
Samsung	4.3
Other	43.0

Source: *Investor's Business Daily*, June 3, 1999, p. A6, from DisplaySearch.

★ 1058 ★

Flat Panel Displays (SIC 3679)

Top Flat Panel Brands - 1999

Figures are based on revenues for the first quarter of the year.

NEC	21.3%
Viewsonic	16.0
Compaq	11.0
IBM	6.6
Philips	6.1
Other	39.0

Source: *Investor's Business Daily*, June 3, 1999, p. A6, from DisplaySearch.

★ 1059 ★

Liquid Crystal Displays (SIC 3679)

Liquid Crystal Display Market - 1998

Market shares are shown for North America.

Toshiba	13.2%
Sharp	11.9
NEC	8.7
IBM	8.3
Optrex	7.3
Seiko Epson	6.3
Samsung	5.9
Hitachi	2.8
LG	2.6
Sanyo	2.3
Hyundai	1.6
Fujitsu	1.3
Other	27.8

Source: *Investor's Business Daily*, June 17, 1999, p. A4, from Stanford Resources Inc.

★ 1060 ★

Liquid Crystal Displays (SIC 3679)

Liquid Crystal Display Market Leaders - 1998

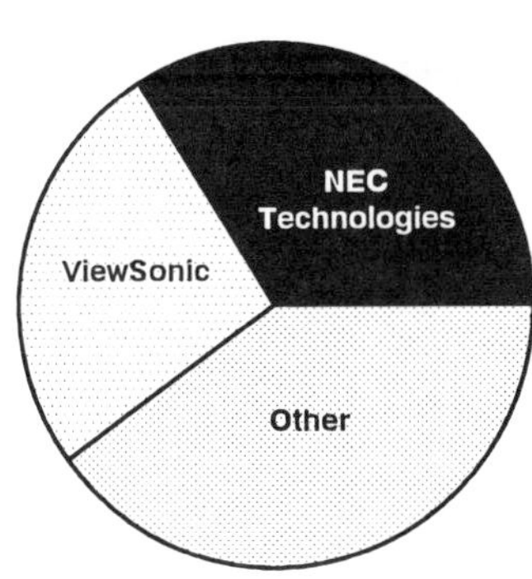

Market shares are shown for the third quarter of the year. Figures are for North America.

NEC Technologies	34.0%
ViewSonic	26.0
Other	40.0

Source: Retrieved May 18, 1999 from the World Wide Web: http:// www.sonic.net/cgi-bin/cif/cif/search-free.pl.

★ 1061 ★

Personal Displays (SIC 3679)

Personal Display Market

Data show thousands of units.

	1999	2001
Notebooks and wearables	19,052	23,472
Handheld PCs	8,949	16,198
Smart phones	3,264	8,792
Digital cameras	3,500	7,000

Source: *Semiconductor International*, September 1998, p. 92.

★ 1062 ★

Switches (SIC 3679)

ATM Backbone Switch Market

Market shares are shown in percent.

Newbridge	29.6%
Cisco	21.2
Nortel	17.2
Ascend	8.3
Alcatel	7.6
FORE	4.6
General DataComm	2.6
Other	8.9

Source: *Telecommunications*, June 1998, p. 25, from Dataquest Inc.

★ 1063 ★

Switches (SIC 3679)

ATM LAN Switch Makers - 1998

Market shares are shown in percent.

Fore	33.0%
Cisco	28.0
Nortel/Bay	11.0
Other	28.0

Source: *Investext*, Thomson Financial Networks, December 3, 1998, p. 1, from Dell'Oro Group and InStat.

★ 1064 ★

Switches (SIC 3679)

ATM Network Switch Producers

Market shares are shown in percent.

Fore Systems	25.0%
Cisco Systems	24.0
Bay Networks	21.0
3Com	12.0
Other	18.0

Source: *Investor's Business Daily*, September 3, 1998, p. A4, from International Data Corp.

★ 1065 ★

Switches (SIC 3679)

ATM WAN Switch Makers - 1998

Market shares are shown in percent.

Cisco	25.0%
Newbridge	21.0
Ascend	18.0
Other	36.0

Source: *Investext,* Thomson Financial Networks, December 3, 1998, p. 1, from Dell'Oro Group and InStat.

★ 1066 ★

Switches (SIC 3679)

LAN Switch Makers - 1998

Market shares are shown in percent.

Cisco	44.0%
3Com	13.0
Cabletron	12.0

Source: *Investext,* Thomson Financial Networks, December 3, 1998, p. 1, from Dell'Oro Group and InStat.

★ 1067 ★

Batteries (SIC 3691)

Battery Market Leaders

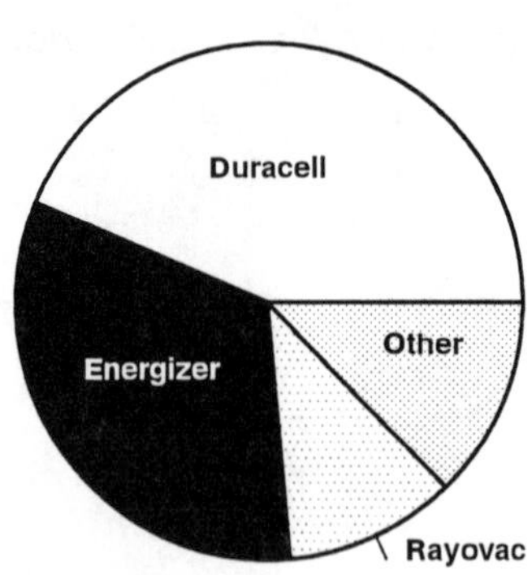

Shares are shown for the year ended March 28, 1999.

Duracell	43.6%
Energizer	32.5
Rayovac	11.1
Other	12.8

Source: *Wall Street Journal*, June 11, 1999, p. A3, from Information Resources Inc.

★ 1068 ★

Batteries (SIC 3691)

U.S. Battery Market

Market shares are shown in percent.

Duracell	42.0%
Eveready	36.0
Other	22.0

Source: "Ante Up in Battle With Duracell." Retrieved May 7, 1999 from the World Wide Web: http://www.more.abcnews.go.com/sections/business, from A.C. Nielsen.

★ 1069 ★

Lasers (SIC 3699)

Industrial Laser Shipments - 1998

CO_2	62.35%
CW Nd:YAG	30.10
Pulsed Nd:YAG/Excimer	7.55

Source: *Photonics Spectra*, May 1999, p. 80, from Association for Manufacturing Technology.

SIC 37 - Transportation Equipment

★ 1070 ★

Autos (SIC 3711)

Auto Market Leaders - 1999

GM	29.0%
Ford	25.0
DaimlerChrysler	17.0
Toyota	9.0
Honda	6.0
Nissan	4.0
VW	2.0
Other	8.0

Source: *Automotive Industries*, February 1999, p. 15, from Autofacts.

★ 1071 ★

Autos (SIC 3711)

Auto Sales Leaders in Canada

Data show sales for the year ended January 6, 1999.

GM	225,025
Honda	98,586
Ford	94,544
Toyota	91,528
Chrysler	86,148
Volkswagen	40,583
Hyundai	23,136
Mazda	22,650
Nissan	20,036
Volvo	9,011

Source: *Globe and Mail*, January 6, 1999, p. B4.

★ 1072 ★

Autos (SIC 3711)

Best-Selling Cars - 1998

Data show unit sales.

Toyota Camry	429,575
Honda Accord	401,071
Ford Taurus	371,074
Honda Civic	334,562
Ford Escort	219,936
Chevrolet Cavalier	256,099
Toyota Corolla	250,051
Saturn	231,522
Chevrolet Malibu	223,703
Pontiac Grand Am	180,428

Source: *WARD'S Auto World*, February 1999, p. 29, from WARD's AutoInfobank.

★ 1073 ★

Autos (SIC 3711)

Best-Selling Cars in Los Angeles County, CA - 1998

Toyota Camry
Honda Accord
Honda Civic
Ford Explorer
Toyota Corolla

Toyota Camry	23,302
Honda Accord	19,178
Honda Civic	18,585
Ford Explorer	17,304
Toyota Corolla	15,435

Source: *Detroit Free Press*, March 2, 1999, p. A1, from R.L. Polk Co.

★ 1074 ★

Autos (SIC 3711)

Best-Selling Light Trucks - 1998

Data show unit sales.

Ford F-series	767,552
Chevrolet CK Pickup	533,177
Ford Explorer	431,488

Continued on next page.

★ 1074 ★ *Continued*

Autos (SIC 3711)

Best-Selling Light Trucks - 1998

Data show unit sales.

Dodge Ram	410,130
Ford Ranger	328,136
Dodge Caravan	293,819
Jeep Grand Cherokee	229,135
Chevrolet S-10 Pickup	228,093
Ford Expedition	225,703
Chevrolet S Blazer	219,710
Nissan Frontier	68,113
GMC Sonoma	42,191

Source: *WARD'S Auto World*, February 1999, p. 29, from WARD's AutoInfobank.

★ 1075 ★

Autos (SIC 3711)

Best-Selling Minivans - 1998

Unit sales are shown for the first nine months of the year.

Dodge Caravan	227,709
Ford Windstar	152,191
Plymouth Voyager	123,448
Chevrolet Venture	76,284
Chevrolet Astro	73,185
Toyota Sienna	59,013
Chrysler Town & Country	54,901
Pontiac Trans Sport	44,217
Mercury Villager	30,667
Oldsmobile Silhouette	27,723

Source: *WARD's Dealer Business*, November 1998, p. 13.

★ 1076 ★

Autos (SIC 3711)

Best-Selling Pickups - 1998

Unit sales are shown for the first nine months of the year.

Ford F-series	587,601
Chevrolet CK	396,138
Dodge Ram	298,952
Ford Ranger	250,811
Chevrolet S-10	179,925
GMC Sierra	120,329
Dodge Dakota	115,790
Toyota Tacoma	115,241

Source: *WARD's Dealer Business*, November 1998, p. 13.

★ 1077 ★

Autos (SIC 3711)

Best-Selling Sports Utilities - 1998

Figures are as of November 1998.

Ford Expedition	203,412
Jeep Grand Cherokee	181,908
Dodge Durango	139,811
Ford Explorer	93,710
Chevrolet Suburban	48,982
Chevrolet Tahoe	47,103

Source: *USA TODAY*, December 9, 1998, p. 3B, from Autodata.

★ 1078 ★

Autos (SIC 3711)

Best-Selling Vehicles in Canada - 1998

Ford F-series	74,859
Honda Civic	54,066
Chrysler Caravan	51,646
Ford Windstar	48,300
GM Chevrolet Pick-up	44,851
GM Cavalier	43,942
GM Sunfire	40,797
Toyota Corolla	40,773
GM GMC Pick-up	39,790
Chrysler Voyager	38,553

Source: *Globe and Mail*, January 7, 1999, p. 4, from company reports.

★ 1079 ★

Autos (SIC 3711)

Canada's Car Market - 1998

Market shares are shown in percent for the year ended December 31, 1998.

Honda Civic	7.3%
GM Chevrolet Cavalier	5.9
GM Pontiac Sunfire	5.5
Toyota Corolla	5.5

Continued on next page.

★ 1079 ★ *Continued*

Autos (SIC 3711)

Canada's Car Market - 1998

Market shares are shown in percent for the year ended December 31, 1998.

Chrysler Neon	4.2%
Honda Accord	3.4
GM Chevrolet Malibu	3.3
Other	64.9

Source: "Report on Market Share." Retrieved June 1, 1999 from the World Wide Web: http://www.marketingmag.ca/index.cgi?, from *Canadian Auto World*.

★ 1080 ★

Autos (SIC 3711)

Canada's Vehicle Market - 1997

GM
Ford
Chrysler
Toyota
Other

Market shares are shown in percent.

GM	31.7%
Ford	20.4
Chrysler	19.6
Toyota	8.6
Other	19.6

Source: *Globe and Mail*, July 14, 1998, p. B1.

★ 1081 ★

Autos (SIC 3711)

Car Market in Canada - 1998

Data show the market share of the "Big 3" (Ford, Chrysler, GM) auto firms in the provinces.

Saskatchewan	86.4%
Alberta	83.4
Manitoba	82.6
New Brunswick	78.7
Prince Edward Island	73.4
Ontario	71.7
Newfoundland	71.1
Nova Scotia	70.8
British Columbia	66.1%
Quebec	57.0

Source: *Globe and Mail*, February 8, 1999, p. B4, from DesRosiers Automotive Consultants Inc.

★ 1082 ★

Autos (SIC 3711)

Car Production in North America

Data are in thousands. Figures are estimated for 1999.

	1997	1999
United States	5,922	5,640
Canada	1,376	1,505
Mexico	855	941

Source: *Financial Times*, May 27, 1999, p. 6, from Marketing Systems.

★ 1083 ★

Autos (SIC 3711)

Car Sales by Segment - 1998

Mid-size	54.9%
Large	20.0
Small	16.7
Sports	6.8
Prestige	1.5

Source: *Automotive Industries*, February 1999, p. 15, from Autofacts.

★ 1084 ★

Autos (SIC 3711)

Convertible Registrations by Market Area - 1998

New York City	18,351
Los Angeles	14,267
San Francisco/Oakland/San Jose	8,127
Chicago	7,696
Philadelphia	6,583

Source: *USA TODAY*, June 1, 1999, p. B1, from The Polk Company.

★ 1085 ★

Autos (SIC 3711)

Large Van Market

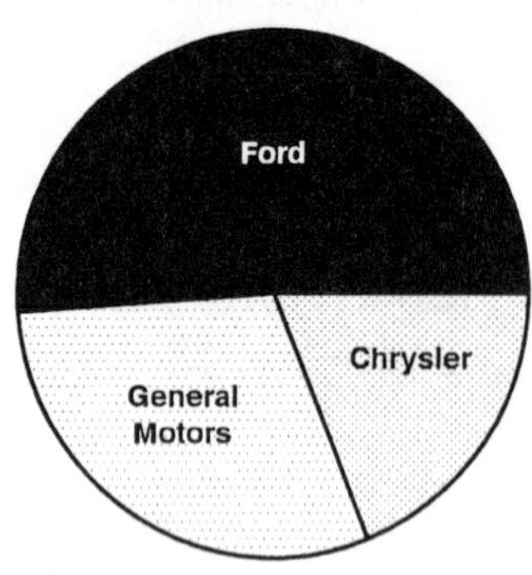

Market shares are shown in percent.

	1997	1999
Ford	49.4%	50.6%
General Motors	31.2	30.4
Chrysler	19.4	19.0

Source: *Investext,* Thomson Financial Networks, November 16, 1998, p. 16, from PaineWebber estimates and industry sources.

★ 1086 ★

Autos (SIC 3711)

Light Truck Sales - 1998

The market is shown by segment.

Pickups	40.2%
Sport utility vehicles	37.8
Vans	22.1

Source: *Automotive Industries*, February 1999, p. 15, from Autofacts.

★ 1087 ★

Autos (SIC 3711)

Light Truck Sales in Canada

Data show sales for the year ended January 6, 1999.

GM	203,662
Chrysler	183,048
Ford	176,935
Toyota	36,847
Honda	18,430

Source: *Globe and Mail*, January 6, 1999, p. B4.

★ 1088 ★

Autos (SIC 3711)

Light Vehicle Sales - 1999

Shares are shown for the first two months of the year.

GM	28.9%
Ford	24.2
DaimlerChrysler	17.2
Toyota	8.5
Honda	6.5
Nissan	3.7
VW	1.6
Mitsubishi	1.4
Mazda	1.3
Other	6.7

Source: *Christian Science Monitor*, March 16, 1999, p. 24, from Autodata and Reuters.

★ 1089 ★

Autos (SIC 3711)

Mini-Pickup Market

Market shares are shown in percent.

	1997	1999
Ford	30.1%	30.2%
General Motors	23.6	28.6
Chrysler	13.3	13.8
Other	33.0	27.5

Source: *Investext,* Thomson Financial Networks, November 16, 1998, p. 16, from PaineWebber estimates and industry sources.

★ 1090 ★

Autos (SIC 3711)

Minivan Market in Canada - 1998

Market shares are shown in percent for the year ended December 31, 1998.

Dodge Caravan	22.7%
Ford Windstar	21.2
GM FWD Minivans	17.5
Plymouth Voyager	16.9
GM Astro/Safari	8.8
Toyota Sienna	6.6
Other	5.4

Source: "Report on Market Share." Retrieved June 1, 1999 from the World Wide Web: http://www.marketingmag.ca/index.cgi?, from *Canadian Auto World*.

★ 1091 ★

Autos (SIC 3711)

Minivan Market Leaders

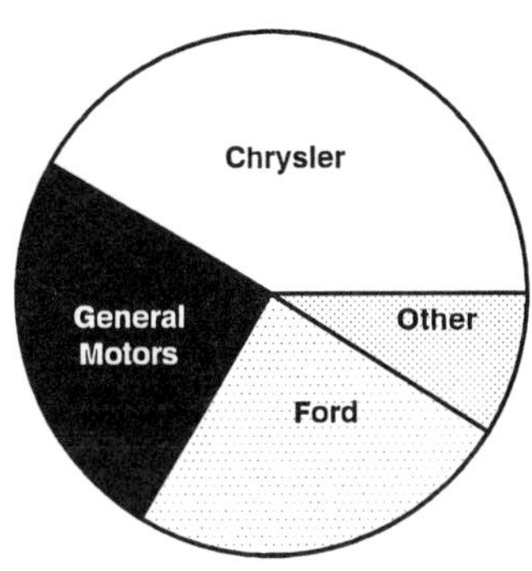

Market shares are shown in percent.

	1997
Chrysler	42.1%
General Motors	24.5
Ford	24.8
Other	8.6

Source: *Investext,* Thomson Financial Networks, November 16, 1998, p. 16, from PaineWebber estimates and industry sources.

★ 1092 ★

Autos (SIC 3711)

New Car Registrations in North America

Data are in thousands. Figures are estimated for 1999.

	1997	1999
United States	8,273	8,172
Canada	738	739
Mexico	303	432

Source: *Financial Times*, May 27, 1999, p. 6, from Marketing Systems.

★ 1093 ★

Autos (SIC 3711)

Sport Utility Market

Market shares are shown in percent.

	1997	1999
Ford	27.5%	25.6%
General Motors	27.5	24.6
Chrysler	20.2	24.4
Other	24.8	25.4

Source: *Investext,* Thomson Financial Networks, November 16, 1998, p. 16, from PaineWebber estimates and industry sources.

★ 1094 ★

Autos (SIC 3711)

Sports Utility Vehicle Sales in Canada - 1998

Market shares are shown in percent for the year ended December 31, 1998.

GM Blazer/Jimmy	12.5%
Ford Explorer	12.4
Chrysler Jeep Grand Cherokee	9.9
Honda CR-V	9.0
GM Tahoe/Yukon	6.3
Nissan Pathfinder	5.5
Toyota RAV4	5.5
Chrysler Jeep Cherokee	4.9
Chrysler Dodge Durango	4.7
Toyota 4Runner	4.5
Other	24.8

Source: "Report on Market Share." Retrieved June 1, 1999 from the World Wide Web: http://www.marketingmag.ca/index.cgi?, from *Canadian Auto World*.

★ 1095 ★

Autos (SIC 3711)

Top Pickup Truck Brands in Canada - 1998

Market shares are shown in percent for the year ended December 31, 1998.

GM Silverado/Sierra	36.4%
Ford F-series	32.2
Dodge Ram	14.7
Dodge Dakota	6.1
Ford Ranger	3.6
GM S-Series/Sonoma	3.2
Other	3.8

Source: "Report on Market Share." Retrieved June 1, 1999 from the World Wide Web: http://www.marketingmag.ca/index.cgi?, from *Canadian Auto World*.

★ 1096 ★

Autos (SIC 3711)

U.S. Car Market - 1998

Data show sales.

	Units	Share
General Motors	4,552,789	29.2%
Ford Motor	3,885,351	24.9
DaimlerChrysler	2,510,011	16.1
Toyota	1,361,025	8.7
Honda	1,009,600	6.5
Nissan	621,528	4.0
Mazda	240,546	1.5
Volkswagen	219,679	1.4
Mitsubishi	190,515	1.2
Mercedes-Benz	170,245	1.1

Source: *USA TODAY*, January 7, 1999, p. 2B, from Autodata.

★ 1097 ★

Autos (SIC 3713)

Best-Selling Trucks in Los Angeles County, CA - 1998

Model	Units
Chevy Cavalier	10,547
Ford Expedition	9,960
Toyota 4Runner	9,136
Ford Taurus	8,755
Ford F150 pickup	8,567

Source: *Detroit Free Press*, March 2, 1999, p. A1, from R.L. Polk Co.

★ 1098 ★

Trucks (SIC 3713)

Class 6 Truck Leaders - 1998

Market shares are shown in percent.

Ford	33.9%
Freightliner	30.7
GMC	9.5
Navistar	7.5
Chevrolet	6.5
Nissan Diesel	2.8
Mack	2.7
Mitsubishi Fuso	2.6
Other	3.8

Source: *Commercial Carrier Journal*, March 1999, p. 41, from Ward's Communications.

★ 1099 ★

Trucks (SIC 3713)

Class 7 Truck Leaders - 1998

Market shares are shown in percent.

Navistar	53.4%
Freightliner	15.5
GMC	12.1
Ford	9.5
Chevrolet	5.1
Kenworth	1.1
Sterling	0.9
Peterbilt	0.8
Other	1.6

Source: *Commercial Carrier Journal*, March 1999, p. 41, from Ward's Communications.

★ 1100 ★

Trucks (SIC 3713)

Class 8 Truck Makers - 1997

Market shares are shown in percent.

Freightliner	28.2%
Navistar	19.3
Mack	12.5
Peterbilt	11.3
Kenworth	10.1
Volvo	9.7
Ford	7.1
Western Star	1.3
Other	0.5

Source: *Commercial Carrier Journal*, July 1998, p. 61.

★ 1101 ★

Trucks (SIC 3713)

Heavy Truck Leaders - 1998

Figures are for trucks weighing over 33,000 lbs.

Freightliner (Daimler/Chrysler)	30.6%
Kenworth, Peterbuilt (PACCAR)	20.8
Navistar	18.4
Mack (Renault)	12.8
Volvo	11.5
Other	5.9

Source: *Chicago Tribune*, February 16, 1999, p. 1, from company reports, Hoover's, *Market Guide*, and Reuter's.

★ 1102 ★

Trucks (SIC 3713)

Heavy Truck Leaders - 1998

Shares are shown for class 4-8 for the first 10 months of the year.

International	25.2%
Freightliner	21.8
Ford	15.5
Mack	6.4
Volvo	5.9
GMC	5.4
Kenworth	5.4
Other	14.4

Source: *Traffic World*, December 14, 1998, p. 27, from American Automobile Management Association.

★ 1103 ★

Trucks (SIC 3713)

Heavy Truck Market in Mexico

Market shares are shown in percent.

Mercedes-Benz de Mexico	34.0%
Kenworth Mexicana SA	16.5
Grupo Consorcio Dina SA	15.2
Other	34.3

Source: "Mercedes Benz Sees Truck Sales Rising." Retrieved May 28, 1999 from the World Wide Web: http:// businessjournal.net/stories/020698/mexico.

★ 1104 ★

Auto Parts (SIC 3714)

Bumper Fascia Market - 1998

The market is for North America.

Polypropylene	76.0%
Polyurethane	20.0
Other	4.0

Source: *Plastics News*, October 5, 1998, p. 2, from Freedonia Group.

★ 1105 ★

Auto Parts (SIC 3714)

Heavy-Duty Diesel Engine Market - 1998

Market shares are shown in percent for the first eight months of the year.

CUM	32.9%
DDC	28.5
CAT	22.3
Mack	14.6
Other	1.7

Source: *Investext*, Thomson Financial Networks, October 20, 1998, p. 18, from Motor Vehicle Manufacturers Association of America.

★ 1106 ★

Auto Parts (SIC 3714)

Instrument Panel Market - 1997

Shares are for North America.

Textron	26.0%
Delphi	25.0

Continued on next page.

★ 1106 ★ *Continued*

Auto Parts (SIC 3714)

Instrument Panel Market - 1997

Shares are for North America.

Visteon	19.0%
Honda	5.0
Goodyear	4.0
Toyota	4.0
UTA	4.0
Other	11.0

Source: *WARD's Auto World*, January 1999, p. 17, from The ITB Group.

★ 1107 ★

Auto Parts (SIC 3714)

Largest Auto Parts Suppliers in North America

Companies are ranked by auto parts sales in millions of dollars.

Delphi Automotive Systems	$ 20,635
Visteon Automotive Systems	14,489
Johnson Controls Inc.	5,590
Dana Corp.	5,542
Lear Corp.	5,369
Magna International Inc.	3,780
TRW Inc.	3,528
Robert Bosch Corp.	3,458
Eaton Corp.	2,380
Cummins Engine Co.	2,344

Source: *Automotive News*, April 12, 1999, p. 21.

★ 1108 ★

Auto Parts (SIC 3714)

Leaf Spring Market

Market shares are shown for North America.

Sanluis Rassini	62.0%
Other	38.0

Source: *Financial Times*, May 22, 1999, p. 23.

★ 1109 ★

Auto Parts (SIC 3714)

Rearview Mirror Market

Market shares are shown in percent.

Donnelly	95.0%
Other	5.0

Source: *Forbes*, March 8, 1999, p. 110.

★ 1110 ★

Motor Homes (SIC 3716)

Motorized RV Market - 1997

Market shares are shown in percent.

Fleetwood	28.1%
Winnebago	15.8
Coachmen	13.2
Thor	7.3
Monaco	6.6
National RV	5.7
SMC (Safari)	3.8
Damon	3.5
Gulf Stream	3.4
Tiffin	3.0
Other	9.6
Other	9.6

Source: *RV Business*, April 1998, p. 20, from Statistical Surveys Inc.

★ 1111 ★

Motor Homes (SIC 3716)

Towable RV Market - 1997

Market shares are shown in percent.

Fleetwood	25.6%
Thor	13.5
Jayco	10.8
Coachmen	7.3
Forest River	7.1
Skyline	4.8
Starcraft	3.7
Damon	2.4
Kit	2.1
Gulf Stream	1.8
Other	20.9

Source: *RV Business*, April 1998, p. 20, from Statistical Surveys Inc.

★ 1112 ★

Aircraft (SIC 3721)

Aircraft Sales by Type - 1998

Unit sales are shown by type.

Single-engine piston	64.60%
Turbofan	18.80
Turboprop	12.19
Multiengine piston	4.41

Source: *Business & Commercial Aviation*, March 1999, p. 31, from General Aviation Manufacturers Association.

★ 1113 ★

Aircraft (SIC 3721)

U.S. Fleet - 2002

Large jets	35.9%
Narrowbody jets	22.5
Turboprops	11.3
Jumbo jets	10.9
Regional jets	8.2
Large regional jets	3.6
Turboprops	2.6
Micro jets	1.2

Source: *Business & Commercial Aviation*, December 1998, p. 76, from *1998 Boyd Group Global Aircraft Forecast*.

★ 1114 ★

Oxygen Equipment (SIC 3728)

Oxygen Mask Market

Market shares are shown in percent. the company also controls 50% of the oxygen market for fire departments.

Scott Technologies	60.0%
Other	40.0

Source: *Forbes*, December 14, 1998, p. 79.

★ 1115 ★

Boats (SIC 3732)

Boat Accessory Sales by State - 1998

Sales are shown in millions of dollars.

Florida	$ 109.1
Michigan	76.6
Texas	69.3
Minnesota	68.8
California	67.2

Source: *Boating Industry*, February 1999, p. 13.

★ 1116 ★

Boats (SIC 3732)

Boat Equipment Sales - 1998

Data show units, in thousands.

Outboard motors	314.0
Outboard boats	200.9
Trailers	174.0
Personal watercraft	130.0
Canoes	107.8
Sterndrive	91.0

Source: *Boating Industry*, February 1999, p. 3, from National Marine Manufacturers Association Annual Sailing Busness Review.

★ 1117 ★

Boats (SIC 3732)

Boat Sales by State - 1998

Sales are shown in millions of dollars.

Florida	$ 475.7
Michigan	334.3
Texas	302.4
Minnesota	300.0
California	293.0

Source: *Boating Industry*, February 1999, p. 13.

★ 1118 ★

Boats (SIC 3732)

Popular Aluminum Boat Brands - 1998

Data show unit sales based on data from the 34 states that compose 88% of the industry.

Tracker	12,486
Lowe	11,244
Alumacraft	7,041
Lund	5,681
Smoker-Craft	5,075

Source: *Boating Industry*, February 1999, p. 25, from Statistical Surveys Inc.

★ 1119 ★

Boats (SIC 3732)

Popular Fiberglass Boat Brands - 1998

Data show unit sales based on data from the 34 states that compose 88% of the industry. Figures refer to 14 feet or larger.

BayLiner	12,831
Sea Ray	10,629
Four Winns	3,935
Tracker	3,491
Sea-Doo	3,191

Source: *Boating Industry*, February 1999, p. 25, from Statistical Surveys Inc.

★ 1120 ★

Boats (SIC 3732)

Sailboat Production in North America

Distribution is shown by boat size.

Size	Units
Under 11'	5,564
12'-19'	8,815
20'-29'	2,683
30'-35'	994
36'-40'	696
41'-45'	510
46'-59'	169
60'+	31

Source: *Boating Industry*, February 1999, p. 10.

★ 1121 ★

Personal Watercraft (SIC 3732)

Popular Personal Watercraft Brands - 1998

Data show unit sales based on data from the 34 states that compose 88% of the industry. Figures refer to 13 feet or under.

Sea-Doo	44,237
Wave Runner	26,133
Jet Ski	17,784
Polaris	6,083
Tigershark	5,067

Source: *Boating Industry*, February 1999, p. 25, from Statistical Surveys Inc.

★ 1122 ★

Railroad Equipment (SIC 3743)

Railcar Deliveries - 1999

Type	Units
Covered hopper	22,500
Flat car	13,000
Tank	11,000
Gondola	10,750
Open hopper	6,000
Boxcar	3,000
Other	500

Source: *Railway Age*, October 1998, p. 23, from American Railway Car Institute and Economic Planning Associates.

★ 1123 ★

Railroad Equipment (SIC 3743)

Railway Car Purchases - 1998

Data show number of cars.

Toronto (TTC)	158
Philadelphia (SEPTA)	94
NY City (LIRR)	57
Chicago (METRA)	42
Amtrak	41
Los Angeles (LACMTA)	26
San Francisco (MUNI)	26

Source: *Railway Age*, January 1999, p. 48.

★ 1124 ★

Bicycles (SIC 3751)

Bicycle Accessories Market - 1998

Market shares are shown for the first seven months of the year.

Bell Sports	57.0%
Protective Technologies	19.7
Troxel	3.4
Circle Express	2.0
Other	17.9

Source: *Playthings*, October 1998, p. 22, from NPD Group TRSTS.

★ 1125 ★

Bicycles (SIC 3751)

Bicycle Market Producers - 1998

Huffy
Dynacraft
Pacific Cycle
Murray
Roadmaster
Other

Market shares are shown for the first seven months of the year.

Huffy	33.9%
Dynacraft	21.2
Pacific Cycle	12.7
Murray	11.4
Roadmaster	11.1
Other	9.7

Source: *Playthings*, October 1998, p. 22, from NPD Group TRSTS.

★ 1126 ★

Bicycles (SIC 3751)

Bike Sales by Segment - 1998

Sales are shown for the third quarter of the year. Figures are based on sales of 350 specialty bicycle retailers.

Mountain bikes	52.0%
Youth bikes	26.0
Hybrids	12.6
Comfort bikes	4.0
Road bikes	2.3
Cruisers	2.0

Source: "Retail Data Capture." Retrieved June 1, 1999 from the World Wide Web: http:// www.bikebiz.com/ rdc.htm, from Natioanl Bicycle Dealers Association.

★ 1127 ★

Motorcycles (SIC 3751)

Motorcycle Market Leaders - 1998

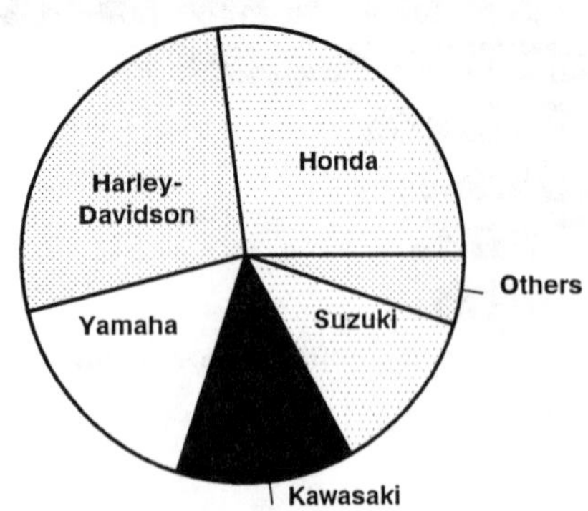

Market shares are shown for the first six months of the year. Figures refer to all sizes.

Honda	27.3%
Harley-Davidson	26.6
Yamaha	15.8
Kawasaki	12.6
Suzuki	12.3
Others	5.4

Source: *New York Times*, May 15, 1999, p. B1, from Motorcycle Industry Council.

★ 1128 ★

Motorcycles (SIC 3751)

Motorcycle Ownership by Age - 1998

Under 35	36.5%
40-49	26.2
50 and older	18.4
35-49	15.6

Source: *USA TODAY*, May 7, 1999, p. 2B, from Motorcycle Industry Council.

★ 1129 ★

Defense (SIC 3761)

Defense Sales by State - 1998

Total defense spending for contract grants, payroll and pensions was $226 billion in fiscal year 1998.

	($ bil.)	Share
California	$ 29.0	12.83%
Virginia	23.0	10.18
Texas	16.0	7.08
Florida	12.0	5.31
Maryland	9.0	3.98
Other	137.0	60.62

Source: *USA TODAY*, April 16, 1999, p. A1.

★ 1130 ★

Defense (SIC 3761)

Top Defense Contractors - 1998

Firms are ranked by contract value in billions of dollars.

Lockheed Martin	$ 12.3
Boeing	10.9
Raytheon	5.7
General Dynamics	3.7
Northrop Grumman	2.7
United Technologies	2.0
Textron	1.8
Litton Industries	1.6
Newport News Shipbuilding	1.5
TRW	1.3

Source: *USA TODAY*, March 10, 1999, p. A1, from U.S. Department of Defense.

SIC 38 - Instruments and Related Products

★ 1131 ★

Sensors (SIC 3812)

Biosensor Sales by Market

	1998 ($ mil.)	2003 ($ mil.)	Share
Medical	$ 692	$ 1,555	92.73%
Research	44	55	3.28
Industrial	10	40	2.39
Environmental	8	14	0.83
Government	11	13	0.78

Source: *The American Ceramic Society Bulletin*, April 1999, p. 30, from Business Communications Co. Inc.

★ 1132 ★

Instrumentation (SIC 3820)

Largest Industrial System Makers

Honeywell
Rockwell International
Eaton
Emerson
Johnson Controls

Data show revenues in billions of dollars. Figures refer to automation, control and security information.

Honeywell	$ 6.0
Rockwell International	4.5
Eaton	4.0
Emerson	3.3
Johnson Controls	3.1

Source: *Electronic Business*, July 1998, p. 97.

★ 1133 ★

Instrumentation (SIC 3820)

Largest Test/Measuring Equipment Makers

Data show revenues in billions of dollars.

Hewlett-Packard	$ 4.2
Thermo Electron	1.8
Perkin-Elmer	1.4
KLA-Tencor	1.1
Teradyne	1.0

Source: *Electronic Business*, July 1998, p. 97.

★ 1134 ★

Testing Equipment (SIC 3820)

Testing Equipment Market - 2002

Sales are shown in millions of dollars.

	($ mil.)	Share
Radiography	$ 231.9	27.62%
Ultrasonics	199.1	23.71
Visual and optical	152.6	18.17
Eddy current	115.9	13.80
Infrared and thermal	68.8	8.19
Liquid penetrant	26.0	3.10
Magnetic particle	22.3	2.66
Acoustic emission	23.1	2.75

Source: *R&D Magazine*, February 1999, p. 9, from Business Communications Co. Inc.

★ 1135 ★

Control Equipment (SIC 3823)

Advanced Industrial Controls Market

The market is shown by year. PLC stands for programmable logic control.

	1997	2002
PLCs	30.71%	30.04%
Adjustable speed drives	22.72	21.91
Software	17.22	18.73
Other	29.36	29.33

Source: *Control Engineering*, August 1998, p. 13, from Freedonia Group.

★ 1136 ★

Holography (SIC 3827)

Holographic Market - 1998

The $1.7 billion market is shown in percent.

Scanning	60.0%
Testing	29.0
Holographic optical elements	6.0
Holographic CAD, TV and other uses	3.0
Holographic data	2.0

Source: *R&D Magazine*, January 1999, p. 9, from Business Communications Co. Inc.

★ 1137 ★

Instrumentation (SIC 3829)

EDS Market by Application

Sales are shown in millions of dollars. EDS stands for electrostatic discharge.

	1998	2003	Share
Manufacturing	$ 642.8	$ 1,132.5	75.77%
Communications and office	208.7	362.2	24.23

Source: *Electronic Packaging & Production*, May 1999, p. 9, from *The Maturing ESD Market.*

★ 1138 ★

Logistics (SIC 3829)

Top Third-Party Logistics Vendors

Sea-Land
C.H. Robinson
Air Express International
Fritz Companies
Ryder Integrated Logistics
Expeditors International
Schneider Logistics
Penske Logisitcs

Firms are ranked by revenues in millions of dollars.

Sea-Land	$ 4,500
C.H. Robinson	1,500
Air Express International	1,300
Fritz Companies	1,200
Ryder Integrated Logistics	1,100
Expeditors International	730
Schneider Logistics	710
Penske Logisitcs	650

Source: *Financial Times*, December 1, 1998, p. 11, from Armstrong & Associates.

★ 1139 ★

Bandages (SIC 3841)

Top Bandage Brands

Band Aid	23.5%
Johnson & Johnson	16.3
3M Active Strips	3.6
Curad	2.9
3M Comfort Strip	2.7
Private label	14.5
Other	36.5

Source: *Discount Merchandiser*, June 1999, p. 56.

★ 1140 ★

Diagnostics Equipment (SIC 3841)

Automated Chemistry Analyzer Market

Market shares are shown based on total placements.

Dade Intl.	25.0%
Beckman	22.0
J&J Clinical Diagnostics	18.0

Continued on next page.

★ 1140 ★ *Continued*

Diagnostics Equipment (SIC 3841)

Automated Chemistry Analyzer Market

Market shares are shown based on total placements.

Boehringer Mannheim	9.0%
Roche	9.0
Abbott	5.0
Bayer Diag	3.0
Others	8.0

Source: *American Clinical Laboratory*, June 1998, p. 18, from IMV Ltd.

★ 1141 ★

Diagnostics Equipment (SIC 3841)

Coagulation Analyzer Market

Market shares are shown based on total placements.

Hemoflance	41.0%
Il	18.0
BD	13.0
OT	7.0
Sysmex	6.0
Others	15.0

Source: *American Clinical Laboratory*, June 1998, p. 18, from IMV Ltd.

★ 1142 ★

Diagnostics Equipment (SIC 3841)

Hemotology Analyzer Market

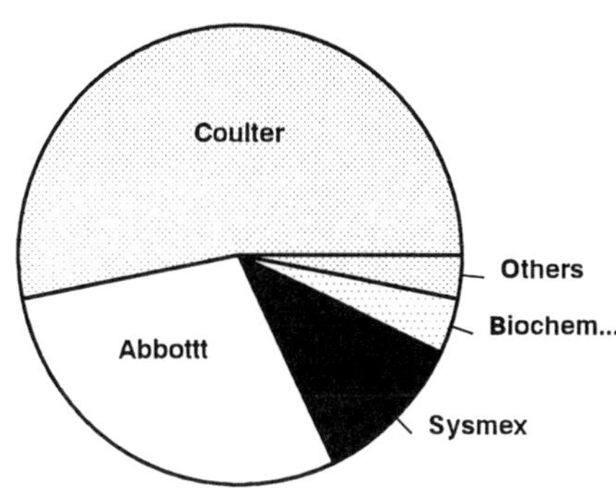

Market shares are shown based on total placements.

Coulter	53.0%
Abbottt	29.0
Sysmex	11.0
Biochem Immuno.	4.0
Others	3.0

Source: *American Clinical Laboratory*, May 1998, p. 12, from IMV Ltd.

★ 1143 ★

Diagnostics Equipment (SIC 3841)

Immunochemistry Analyzer Market

Market shares are shown based on total placements.

Abbott	67.0%
Dade Behring	15.0
Beckman	3.0
Chiron	3.0
Others	12.0

Source: *American Clinical Laboratory*, April 1998, p. 18, from IMV Ltd.

★ 1144 ★

Diagnostics Equipment (SIC 3841)

Veterinary Medicine Market

Market shares are shown in percent.

Idexx Laboratories	73.0%
Synbiotics	6.0
Other	21.0

Source: *Forbes*, September 7, 1998, p. 92.

★ 1145 ★

First Aid Kits (SIC 3841)

First Aid Supply Sales - 1997

Total supermarket sales for the category reached $477.8 million.

	($ mil.)	Share
Antiseptics, sprays and ointments	$ 197.57	41.34%
Adhesive bandages	107.65	22.53
Absorbent products	44.67	9.35
Surgical dressings	36.33	7.60
Wets and drys	34.44	7.21
Petroleum jelly	24.45	5.12
Adhesive tapes	15.14	3.17
Other	17.62	3.69

Source: *Progressive Grocer*, August 1998, p. 56, from Information Resources Inc.

★ 1146 ★

Medical Instruments (SIC 3841)

Insulin Pump Market

Market shares are shown in percent.

MiniMed	80.0%
Other	20.0

Source: *Forbes*, July 27, 1998, p. 24.

★ 1147 ★

Medical Instruments (SIC 3841)

Largest Biotech/Drug/Medical Device Vendors in Massachusetts

Companies are ranked by revenues in millions of dollars.

Boston Scientific Corp.	$ 2,233.6
Genzyme Corp.	673.3
Biogen Inc.	557.6
Haemonetics Corp.	271.0
Millennium Pharmaceuticals inc.	133.7

Source: *The Boston Globe*, May 18, 1999, p. D36, from Nordby International Inc.

★ 1148 ★

Medical Instruments (SIC 3841)

Largest Medical Equipment Makers

Data show revenues in millions of dollars.

Medtronic	$ 1,862.1
Hewlett-Packard	1,287.7
Beckman Coulter	1,198.0
Varian Associates	478.0
Acuson	437.8

Source: *Electronic Business*, July 1998, p. 95.

★ 1149 ★

Medical Instruments (SIC 3841)

Sleep Apnea Market - 2000

Market shares are estimated in percent.

Respironics	53.0%
ResMed	22.0
Mallinckrodt	18.0
Sunrise	3.0
Other	4.0

Source: *Investor's Business Daily*, September 9, 1998, p. A4, from company reports and William Blair & Co.

★ 1150 ★

Orthopedic Appliances (SIC 3842)

Knee/Hip Replacement Market - 1998

Market shares are estimated in percent. The global market for orthopedic devices reached $9 billion.

Bristol Myers	18.0%
DePuy	13.0
Pfizer	13.0
Biomet	12.0
Johnson & Johnson	11.0
Stryker	9.0
Sulzer Medica	8.0

Source: *Wall Street Journal*, July 22, 1998, p. A3, from NationsBanc Montgomery Securities.

★ 1151 ★

Surgical Implants (SIC 3842)

Coronary Stent Market

Shares of the estimated $1.3 billion market are shown in percent.

Arterial Vascular Engineering Inc.	40.0%
Guidant Corp.	40.0
Cordis (J&J)	15.0
Other	5.0

Source: *Wall Street Journal*, August 13, 1998, p. A13, from SBC Warburg Dillon Read.

★ 1152 ★

Surgical Implants (SIC 3842)

Microelectronic Implant Market

	1998	2003
Cardiovascular	89.58%	81.17%
Neurological	5.27	12.15
Cancer	2.30	1.94
Diabetics	0.00	0.27
Hearing impairment	2.84	4.46

Source: *Electronic Packaging & Production*, April 1999, p. 9, from Business Communications Co.

★ 1153 ★

Surgical Implants (SIC 3842)

U.S. Stent Sales - 1999

Market shares are estimated in percent.

BSX	43.0%
Guidant	30.0
AVEI	21.0
Johnson & Johnson	5.0
Other	2.0

Source: *Investext,* Thomson Financial Networks, October 20, 1998, p. 9, from industry data and PaineWebber estimates.

★ 1154 ★

Surgical Supplies (SIC 3842)

Custom Procedure Pack Providers - 1997

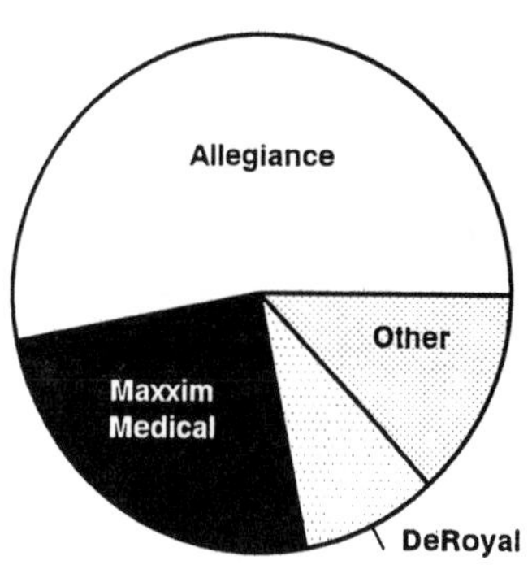

Shares are shown of the $1.2 billion market

Allegiance	53.0%
Maxxim Medical	25.0
DeRoyal	9.0
Other	13.0

Source: *Investext,* Thomson Financial Networks, October 1, 1998, p. 12, from Allegiance Corporation.

★ 1155 ★

Surgical Supplies (SIC 3842)

Exam Glove Market - 1998

Shares are shown for the first quarter of the year.

Safeskin	25.0%
Allegiance	17.0
Ansell Perry	12.0
Other	46.0

Source: *Health Industry Today*, October 1998, p. 11, from IMS America.

★ 1156 ★

Surgical Supplies (SIC 3842)

Medical Instrumentation Market - 1997

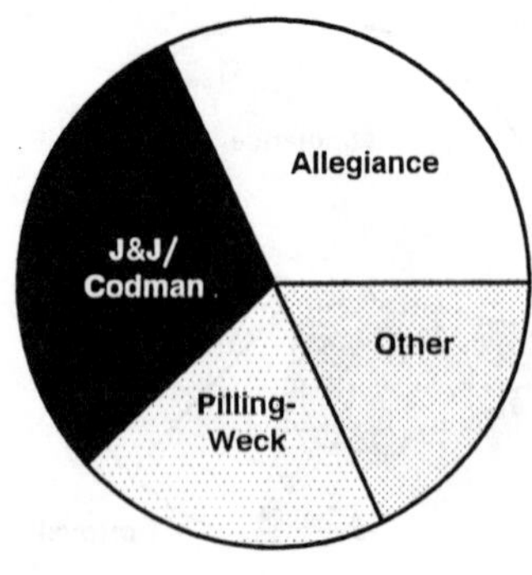

Shares of the $450 million market are shown in percent.

Allegiance	32.0%
J&J/Codman	30.0
Pilling-Weck	20.0
Other	18.0

Source: *Investext,* Thomson Financial Networks, October 1, 1998, p. 12, from Allegiance Corporation.

★ 1157 ★

Surgical Supplies (SIC 3842)

Medical Supplies Market - 1997

Shares of the $1.0 billion market are shown in percent. Figures include acute care and alternate site.

Allegiance	20.0%
Safeskin	19.0
Johnson & Johnson	13.0
Other	48.0

Source: *Investext,* Thomson Financial Networks, October 1, 1998, p. 12, from Allegiance Corporation.

★ 1158 ★

Surgical Supplies (SIC 3842)

Respiratory Therapy Care Market - 1997

Shares of the $550 million market are shown in percent.

Allegiance	25.0%
Hudson/RCI	20.0
SIMS	10.0
Other	45.0

Source: *Investext,* Thomson Financial Networks, October 1, 1998, p. 12, from Allegiance Corporation.

★ 1159 ★

Surgical Supplies (SIC 3842)

Standard Packs/Gowns Market - 1997

Shares are shown of the $450 million market.

Allegiance	45.0%
Kimberly Clark	28.0
Johnson & Johnson	20.0
Other	17.0

Source: *Investext,* Thomson Financial Networks, October 1, 1998, p. 12, from Allegiance Corporation.

★ 1160 ★

Surgical Supplies (SIC 3842)

Suction/Collection Systems Market - 1997

Shares of the $350 million market are shown in percent.

Allegiance	30.0%
CR Bard Davol	20.0
Sherwood Medical	10.0
Other	40.0

Source: *Investext,* Thomson Financial Networks, October 1, 1998, p. 12, from Allegiance Corporation.

★ 1161 ★

Surgical Supplies (SIC 3842)

Surgical Glove Market - 1998

Shares are shown for the first quarter of the year.

Allegiance	30.0%
Johnson & Johnson	21.0
Regent	21.0
Other	28.0

Source: *Health Industry Today*, October 1998, p. 11, from IMS America.

★ 1162 ★

Surgical Supplies (SIC 3842)

Synthetic Exam Glove Market - 1998

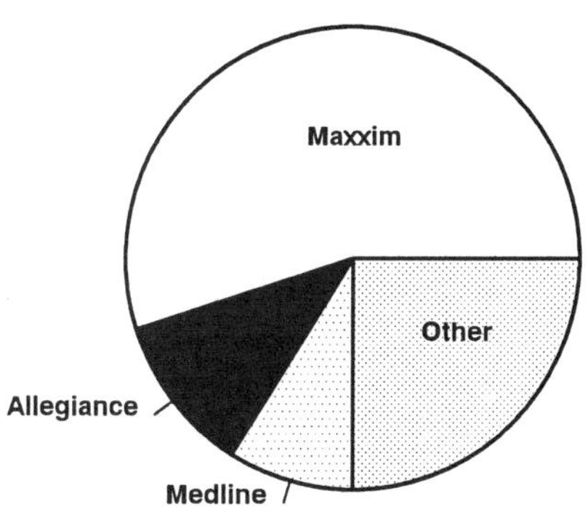

Shares are shown for the first quarter of the year.

Maxxim	55.0%
Allegiance	11.0
Medline	9.0
Other	25.0

Source: *Health Industry Today*, October 1998, p. 11, from IMS America.

★ 1163 ★

Surgical Supplies (SIC 3842)

Tissue Technology Market - 2000

Shares are shown based on an estimated $699.9 million market.

Allograft	37.0%
Autograft	19.0
Bone-graft substitutes	23.0
Soft tissue	11.0
Growth factors	9.0

Source: *Investor's Business Daily*, January 27, 1999, p. A4, from company reports and Stifel, Nicolaus & Co.

★ 1164 ★

Electromedical Equipment (SIC 3845)

Cardiac Defibrillator Market

Market shares are shown in percent.

Medtronic	46.0%
Guidant	21.0
Other	33.0

Source: *New York Times*, September 22, 1998, p. C1.

★ 1165 ★

Contact Lenses (SIC 3851)

Contact Lens Leaders

The soft lens market is valued at $2.5 billion.

Johnson & Johnson	24.0%
Ciba	20.0
Bausch & Lomb	16.0
Other	40.0

Source: *Wall Street Journal*, March 18, 1999, p. B14, from Baush & Lomb.

★ 1166 ★

Cameras (SIC 3861)

Camera Sales by Segment

Total sales reached 15.45 million units. APS stands for advanced photo system.

35mm lens shutter	58.4%
APS lens shutter	15.1
Instant	12.7
110	9.9
35mm SLR	3.7
APS SLR	0.2

Source: *Discount Merchandiser*, April 1999, p. 62, from PMA Marketing Research.

★ 1167 ★

Cameras (SIC 3861)

Online Digital Camera Market

Market shares are shown in percent.

Olympus	18.0%
Kodak	14.0
Sony	13.0
Agfa	11.0
Toshiba	6.0
Casio	5.5
Ricoh	5.5
Fuji	5.0
Other	22.0

Source: *Investor's Business Daily*, March 18, 1998, p. A6, from ARS Inc.

★ 1168 ★

Photocopiers (SIC 3861)

Digital Copier Market

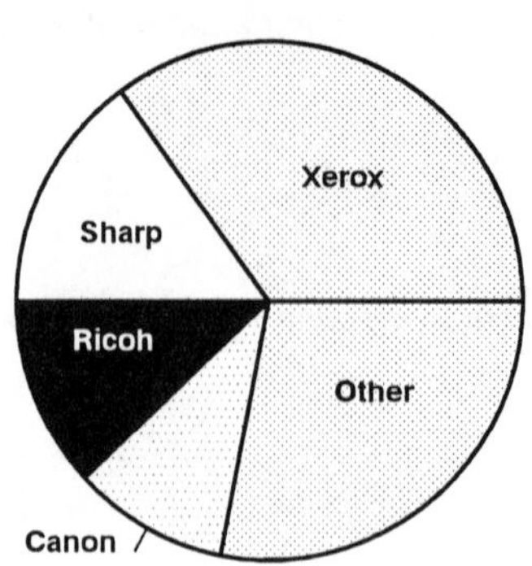

Market shares are shown in percent.

Xerox	35.0%
Sharp	15.0
Ricoh	12.0
Canon	10.0
Other	28.0

Source: *Investor's Business Daily*, April 27, 1999, p. A6, from Dataquest Inc.

★ 1169 ★

Photocopiers (SIC 3861)

Largest Copy Machine Makers - 1997

Market shares are shown in percent.

Xerox	27.3%
Canon	27.0
Sharp	10.9
Mita	5.8
Minolta	4.7
Other	24.3

Source: *USA TODAY*, December 14, 1998, p. C3, from Dataquest Inc.

★ 1170 ★
Photographic Film (SIC 3861)

35mm Film Sales - 1998

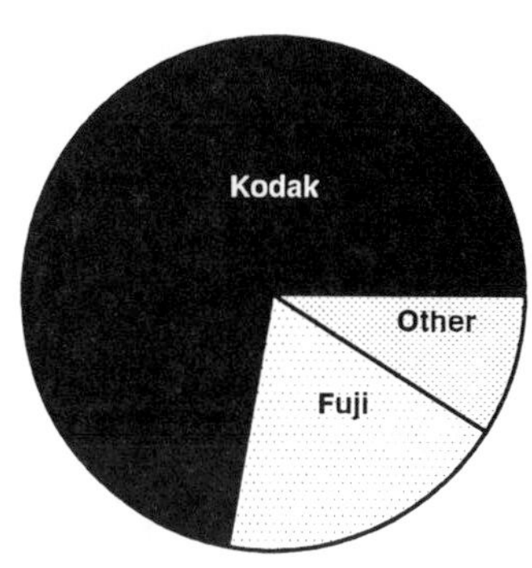

Shares are shown for December 1998.

Kodak	72.0%
Fuji	18.9
Other	9.1

Source: *Wall Street Journal*, May 28, 1999, p. A3, from Information Resources Inc.

★ 1171 ★
Photographic Film (SIC 3861)

U.S. Film Sales - 1999

Unit shares are shown for the four weeks ended April 25, 1999.

Kodak	73.4%
Fuji	22.3
Other	4.3

Source: *Wall Street Journal*, May 28, 1999, p. A3, from Information Resources Inc.

★ 1172 ★
Photographic Film (SIC 3861)

X-Ray Film Market

Market shares are shown in percent.

Kodak	43.0%
Agfa-Sterling	40.0
Fuji	14.0
Others	3.0

Source: *Modern Healthcare*, January 18, 1999, p. 12, from industry estimates.

★ 1173 ★
Scanners (SIC 3861)

Leading Scanner Makers - 1998

Market shares are shown in percent for June 1998.

Umax Technologies	29.4%
Hewlett-Packard	23.8
Visioneer	10.7
Mustek Systems	8.5
Microtek	7.0
Others	20.6

Source: *Investor's Business Daily*, August 20, 1998, p. A8.

★ 1174 ★
Sound Equipment (SIC 3861)

Theater Sound Market

Dolby	35.0%
Digital Theater Systems	30.0
Sony Dynamic Digital Sound	25.0
Other	10.0

Source: *U.S. News & World Report*, March 22, 1999, p. 52.

★ 1175 ★
Telescopes (SIC 3861)

Top Telescope Makers - 1998

Shares are shown based on sales of $155 million.

Meade	46.0%
Tasco	16.0
Bushnell	8.0
Vixen	5.0
Other	25.0

Source: *Investor's Business Daily*, June 15, 1999, p. A10, from company reports.

SIC 39 - Miscellaneous Manufacturing Industries

★ 1176 ★

Jewelry (SIC 3910)

Popular Jewelry Purchases

Yellow gold	65.0%
Silver	16.0
White good	8.0
Stainless steel	2.0
Platinum	1.0

Source: *Jewelers Circular Keystone*, May 1999, p. 76, from Taylor Nelson Sofres Intersearch.

★ 1177 ★

Jewelry (SIC 3911)

Gold Jewelry Sales - 1998

	($ mil.)	Share
Neckware (chains)	$ 5,161,179	41.44%
Earrings	1,786,890	14.35
Bracelets	1,513,086	12.15
Wedding rings	1,079,736	8.67
Charms	963,784	7.74
Neckware (all other)	370,636	2.98
Other gold jewlery	700,573	5.63
Other rings	877,743	7.05

Source: *Discount Store News*, March 22, 1999, p. A6, from Audit & Surveys Worldwide and World Gold Council.

★ 1178 ★

Jewelry (SIC 3911)

U.S. Jewelry Market - 1997

Diamonds/diamond jewelry	42.0%
Karat gold jewelry	13.0
Repairs	10.0
Colored stone jewelry	9.0
Watches	6.0
Fashion jewelry	3.0
Cultured pearls	2.0
Estate jewelry	2.0%
Appraisals	1.0
Other	9.0

Source: *Michigan Retailer*, March 1999, p. 1, from 1997 Jewelers of America survey.

★ 1179 ★

Musical Instruments (SIC 3931)

Best-Selling School Instruments - 1998

Data show unit sales.

Clarinets	145,694
Flutes	139,349
Trumpets	135,354
Violins	85,276
Alto saxs	62,657
Trombones	58,561
Tenor saxs	12,241
French horns	11,789
Euphoniums	9,315
Coronets	7,119

Source: *Music Trades*, April 1999, p. 116.

★ 1180 ★

Musical Instruments (SIC 3931)

Grand Piano Sales - 1998

Data show unit sales.

Under 5'10"	9,072
5' to 5'5"	12,268
5'6" to 5'10"	6,610
5'11 to 6'4"	3,215
6'5" to 7'10"	2,160

Source: *Music Trades*, April 1999, p. 112.

★ 1181 ★

Musical Instruments (SIC 3931)

Largest Music Industry Suppliers - 1998

Companies are ranked by estimated total revenues in millions of dollars.

Yamaha Corporation of America	$ 795.0
Harman Intl.	453.0
Telex Audio	345.0
Peavey Electronics	300.0
Steinway Musical Instruments	293.2
Shure Brothers	220.0
Fender Musical Instruments	200.7
Roland Corporation	175.0
Baldwin Piano & Organ	134.2
Kaman Music Corp.	118.3

Source: *Music Trades*, April 1999, p. 20.

★ 1182 ★

Musical Instruments (SIC 3931)

Musical Product Sales - 1998

Sales are shown in millions of dollars.

Sound reinforcement	$ 833.0
Acoustic pianos	799.2
Fretted instruments	699.1
School music products	662.2
Print music	452.9
Percussion products	345.4
Single unit amplifiers	340.2
Microphones	319.3
Electronic music products	243.3
Organs	231.7
Signal processing	221.8
Portable keyboards	173.2

Source: *Music Trades*, April 1999, p. 83.

★ 1183 ★

Toys and Games (SIC 3942)

Action Figure Market - 1999

Hasbro
Toy Biz
Bandai America
Jakks Pacific
McFarlane Toys
Other

Dollar shares are shown in percent for February 1999.

Hasbro	39.5%
Toy Biz	15.7
Bandai America	14.2
Jakks Pacific	11.1
McFarlane Toys	4.9
Other	14.6

Source: *Playthings*, May 1999, p. 18, from NPD Group TRSTS.

★ 1184 ★

Toys and Games (SIC 3942)

Action Figure Market Leaders - 1999

Unit shares are shown in percent for February 1999.

Bandai America	49.1%
Hasbro	21.6
Toy Biz	10.7
Jakks Pacific	6.7
Mattel	2.5
Other	9.4

Source: *Playthings*, May 1999, p. 18, from NPD Group TRSTS.

★ 1185 ★

Toys and Games (SIC 3942)

Plush Toy Market - 1998

Unit shares are shown in percent.

Dan-Dee Imports	18.6%
Tyco Preschool	12.3
Mattel	10.3
Hasbro	9.6
Arco	9.5
Windsor	2.9

Continued on next page.

★ 1185 ★ *Continued*

Toys and Games (SIC 3942)

Plush Toy Market - 1998

Unit shares are shown in percent.

Westlands	2.7%
Others	34.1

Source: *Playthings*, March 1999, p. 4, from NPD Group TRSTS.

★ 1186 ★

Toys and Games (SIC 3944)

Board Game Market - 1999

Dollar shares are shown for January 1999.

Milton Bradley	31.2%
Parker Brothers	24.6
Mattel	8.7
Cardinal	7.4
Pressman	6.1
U.S. Playing Card	4.4
Wizards of the Coast	2.3
Other	15.3

Source: *Playthings*, April 1999, p. 18, from NPD TRSTS Toy Service.

★ 1187 ★

Toys and Games (SIC 3944)

Largest Toy Brands - 1998

Brands are ranked by dollar share of the industry for the first six months of the year. Hot Wheels leads by unit sales.

Barbie	6.1%
Hot Wheels	2.3
Lego Basic	2.0
Star Wars	1.9
Super Soaker	1.7
Crayola	1.4%
Winnie the Pooh	1.3
Power Rangers	1.1
Micro Machines	0.8
Transformers/Beast Wars	0.7
Other	80.7

Source: *Playthings*, August 1998, p. 18, from NPD Group Inc.

★ 1188 ★

Toys and Games (SIC 3944)

Popular Interactive Games for Consoles

Figures are based on a survey.

Action	35.8%
Strategy, driving/racing	28.8
Adventure/role playing	24.3

Source: *Investor's Business Daily*, May 17, 1999, p. A2, from Interactive Digital Software Association.

★ 1189 ★

Toys and Games (SIC 3944)

Popular Interactive Games for PCs

Figures are based on a survey.

Puzzle/board/card	35.8%
Action	28.8
Learning	24.3

Source: *Investor's Business Daily*, May 17, 1999, p. A2, from Interactive Digital Software Association.

★ 1190 ★

Toys and Games (SIC 3944)

Retail Toy Sales - 1997

Data show wholesale shipments in millions of dollars.

	($ bil.)	Share
Video games	$ 4.3	21.94%
Activity toys	2.1	10.71
Dolls	2.1	10.71
Games/puzzles	1.8	9.18
Vehicles	1.5	7.65
Infant/preschool	1.4	7.14
Stuffed toys	1.4	7.14

Continued on next page.

★ 1190 ★ *Continued*

Toys and Games (SIC 3944)

Retail Toy Sales - 1997

Data show wholesale shipments in millions of dollars.

	($ bil.)	Share
Action figures	$ 1.1	5.61%
Ride-ons	0.7	3.57
Misc. toys	3.2	16.33

Source: *Washington Post*, October 24, 1998, p. D1, from Toy Manufacturers of America.

★ 1191 ★

Toys and Games (SIC 3944)

Sports Activity Makers - 1998

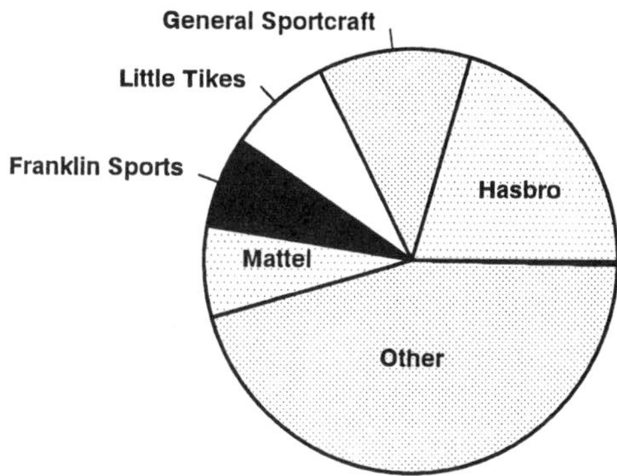

Shares are shown for May 1998.

Hasbro	20.7%
General Sportcraft	12.1
Little Tikes	8.2
Franklin Sports	6.9
Mattel	6.5
Other	45.6

Source: *Playthings*, August 1998, p. 18, from NPD Group TRSTS.

★ 1192 ★

Toys and Games (SIC 3944)

Top Gamepad Makers

Market shares are shown in percent.

Advanced Gravis Computer Technology	53.0%
Microsoft	20.0
Other	27.0

Source: "Hardware & Mouseware." Retrieved May 28, 1999 from the World Wide Web: http://www.userwww.stsu.edu/~magpie5/mshare/hardware.html, from PC Data Inc.

★ 1193 ★

Toys and Games (SIC 3944)

Top Joystick Makers

Market shares are shown in percent.

Microsoft	27.0%
Logitech	22.0
CH Products	13.0
Advanced Gravis	10.0
Other	28.0

Source: "Hardware & Mouseware." Retrieved May 28, 1999 from the World Wide Web: http://www.userwww.stsu.edu/~magpie5/mshare/hardware.html, from PC Data Inc.

★ 1194 ★

Toys and Games (SIC 3944)

Top Puzzle Makers - 1998

Market shares are shown for the first 10 months of the year.

Hasbro	48.2%
Mattel	15.0
Ceaco	11.7
Rose Art	6.9
Patch Products	5.1
Fink & Co.	2.7
Others	10.4

Source: *Playthings*, January 1999, p. 24, from NPD Group TRSTS.

★ 1195 ★

Toys and Games (SIC 3944)

Toy Shipments - 1998

Manufacturer shipments are in millions of dollars.

	($ mil.)	Share
Video games	$ 6,105	28.64%
Activity toys	2,097	9.84
Dolls	2,085	9.78
Vehicles	1,633	7.66
Plush	1,614	7.57
Games/puzzles	1,506	7.06
Infant/preschool	1,379	6.47
Action figures	907	4.25
Ride-ons	728	3.41
Other	3,265	15.31

Source: *Discount Store News*, March 8, 1999, p. 26, from NPD Group/TMA.

★ 1196 ★

Toys and Games (SIC 3944)

Video Game Console Market - 1998

Market shares are shown for October 1998. The leading segment of Playstation players were those 24 to 34.

Sony PlayStation	64.9%
Nintendo 64	34.2
Sega Saturn	0.9

Source: *Investor's Business Daily*, January 7, 1999, p. A4, from NPD Group Inc. and Sony Computer Entertainment America.

★ 1197 ★

Toys and Games (SIC 3944)

Video Game Ratings

Data show the market share of mature-rated games. The industry is experiencing enormous growth, with spending increasing 29% in 1998. Spending on movies and music jumped 10-11%. According to the source nine out of ten game buyers are over 18, but roughly two-thirds of video game households have children.

	1996	1997	1998
Everyone rating	75.0%	72.0%	72.0%
Mature rating	25.0	28.0	28.0

Source: *Forbes*, May 31, 1999, p. 54, from A.C. Nielsen, EDI, NPD Group Inc., and Recording Industry Association of America.

★ 1198 ★

Toys and Games (SIC 3944)

Video Game Sales - 1998

Shares are shown for the year to date.

Sony PlayStation	60.9%
Nintendo 64	31.9
Sega Saturn	7.2

Source: *Investor's Business Daily*, November 19, 1998, p. A8, from NPD Group Inc.

★ 1199 ★

Toys and Games (SIC 3944)

Video Games Sales by Segment

Data show sales for February 1999.

Action	35.5%
Strategy	14.6
Racing	13.9
Sports	13.5
Fighting	11.4
Shooter	8.3
Simulation	1.9
Other	0.9

Source: *Investor's Business Daily*, March 25, 1999, p. A6, from NPD Group Inc.

★ 1200 ★

Toys and Games (SIC 3944)

Water/Pool/Sand Toy Makers - 1998

Shares are shown for May 1998.

Intex	34.0%
Aqua Leisure	9.1
General Foam Plastic	8.8
Tony Trading	7.1
Kidpower	4.8
Florida Pool Products	4.2
Other	32.0

Source: *Playthings*, August 1998, p. 18, from NPD Group TRSTS.

★ 1201 ★

Sporting Goods (SIC 3949)

Exercise Equipment Sales by Region - 1996

Sales are in millions of dollars.

New York City	$ 61.4
Minneapolis/St. Paul	54.7
Atlanta	51.0
Detroit	50.5
Greensboro	50.1
Seattle	49.9
Nassau/Suffolk Counties, NY	46.7
Norfolk, VA	46.3
Chicago	45.2
Philadelphia	39.8

Source: *Wall Street Journal*, December 18, 1998, p. W12, from Market Statistics.

★ 1202 ★

Sporting Goods (SIC 3949)

Largest Inline Skate Makers - 1997

Companies are ranked by sales are in millions of dollars. Shares of the group are shown in percent.

	($ mil.)	% of Group
Rollerblade	$ 168.0	35.74%
Roller Derby	46.0	9.79
First Team	43.8	9.32
Bauer	42.5	9.04
K2	39.0	8.30
Variflex	30.0	6.38
Seneca Sports	22.9	4.87
Mission	20.0	4.26
Oxygen	16.8	3.57
Roces	16.0	3.40
National	13.0	2.77
CCM	12.0	2.55

Source: *Sportstyle*, May 1998, p. 20.

★ 1203 ★

Sporting Goods (SIC 3949)

Largest Outdoor Equipment Makers - 1997

Companies are ranked by sales are in millions of dollars.

Brunswick Outdoor Recreation Group	$ 700.0
Coleman	515.0
American Recreation	143.0
Jansport	114.5
Eastpak	66.0
Johnson Worldwide	60.0
The Outdoor Recreation Group	41.0
Eagle Creek	33.8
The North Face	26.6
Henderson Products	25.0

Source: *Sportstyle*, May 1998, p. 20.

★ 1204 ★

Sporting Goods (SIC 3949)

Largest Ski Equipment Makers - 1997

Companies are ranked by sales are in millions of dollars. Shares of the group are shown in percent.

	($ mil.)	% of Group
Salomon	$ 95.0	24.28%
Rossignol	55.5	14.19
K2	35.0	8.95
Dynastar	32.3	8.26
Tecnica	30.5	7.80
Marker	29.0	7.41
Nordica	25.9	6.62
Head USA	21.6	5.52
Volkl	15.0	3.83
Atomic	14.0	3.58
Elan	13.5	3.45
Fischer	8.2	2.10
Alpina	8.0	2.04
Volant	7.7	1.97

Source: *Sportstyle*, May 1998, p. 20.

★ 1205 ★

Sporting Goods (SIC 3949)

Largest Snowboard Equipment Makers - 1997

Companies are ranked by sales are in millions of dollars. Shares of the group are shown in percent.

	($ mil.)	% of Group
Burton	$ 62.0	30.27%
K2	27.0	13.18
Airwalk	22.0	10.74
Ride	19.4	9.47
Sims	13.6	6.64
Morrow	11.1	5.42
Mervin	10.4	5.08
Salomon	10.0	4.88
Vans	8.6	4.20
Lamar	6.4	3.13
Nitro	5.6	2.73
Rossignol	5.0	2.44
Wintersticks	2.0	0.98
Oxygen	1.7	0.83

Source: *Sportstyle*, May 1998, p. 20.

★ 1206 ★

Sporting Goods (SIC 3949)

Scuba Equipment Sales

Approximately eight percent of Americans say they are active scuba divers. Data show where they spent their money.

Buoyancy control devices	$ 33.3
Masks	32.0
Fins	31.7
Air regulators	31.4
Wet suits	26.6

Source: *USA TODAY*, August 4, 1998, p. C1, from Gallup and Leisure Trends for Diving Equipment and Marketing Association.

★ 1207 ★

Sporting Goods (SIC 3949)

Top Golf Brands - 1998

Sales are shown in millions of dollars.

Titleist	$ 400
Cobra	200
FootJoy	200

Source: Retrieved April 30, 1999 from the Worldw Wide Web: http:// www.ambrands.com/fact/golf.htm.

★ 1208 ★

Brushes (SIC 3991)

Popular Hair Care Accessories

The market is shown in percent. Ponytailers has the lead in unit sales.

Brushes	27.1%
Ponytailers	16.5
Barrettes	13.2
Fashion combs	11.5
Combs & lifts	7.2
Head bands	6.2
Rollers	6.0
Pins & clips	4.2
Caps & nets	3.7
Mirrors	3.5

Source: *Supermarket Business*, May 1999, p. 157, from Information Resources Inc.

★ 1209 ★

Brushes (SIC 3991)

Top Comb Makers - 1998

Market shares are shown for the first half of the year.

Goody	51.0%
L&N	12.5
Helen of Troy	11.6
Conair	5.6
Shalom	2.4
Fantasia	1.9
Almar	1.0
Private label	2.4
Other	11.6

Source: *Supermarket Business*, May 1999, p. 157, from Information Resources Inc.

★ 1210 ★

Toothbrushes (SIC 3991)

Best-Selling Toothbrushes - 1998

Oral-B
Colgate
Reach
Crest
Mentadent
Other

Sales are shown in millions of dollars for the year ended September 27, 1998.

	($ mil.)	Share
Oral-B	$ 163	25.08%
Colgate	122	18.77
Reach	108	16.62
Crest	71	10.92
Mentadent	58	8.92
Other	128	19.69

Source: *Wall Street Journal*, October 22, 1998, p. B1, from Information Resources Inc.

★ 1211 ★

Caskets (SIC 3995)

Burial Casket Market

Market shares are estimated in percent.

Hillenbrand	40.0%
York Group	15.0
Aurora Casket	10.0
Other	25.0

Source: *Wall Street Journal*, February 23, 1999, p. A8.

★ 1212 ★

Kitty Litter (SIC 3999)

Kitty Litter Market

Market shares are shown in percent. Ralston-Purina makes Golden Cat and Tidy Cat. First Brands includes Johnny Cat and Scoop Away. Clorox makes Fresh Step. Oil Dri makes Cat's Pride.

Ralston-Purina	27.0%
First Brands	17.0
Clorox	16.0
Oil-Dri's	8.0
Other	32.0

Source: *Chicago Tribune*, August 4, 1998, p. C3, from Information Resources Inc.

★ 1213 ★

Kitty Litter (SIC 3999)

Kitty Litter Sales

	($ mil.)	Share
Tidy Cat	$ 204.7	25.59%
Fresh Step	130.1	16.26
Other	465.2	58.15

Source: *Advertising Age*, July 20, 1998, p. 31, from Information Resources Inc.

★ 1214 ★

Swimming Pools (SIC 3999)

Swimming Pool Market

Metal	75.0%
Resin	15.0
Other	10.0

Source: *Swimming Pool/Spa Age*, February 1999, p. 61.

SIC 40 - Railroad Transportation

★ 1215 ★

Railroads (SIC 4011)

Chemical Transportation Industry

Market shares are shown by tons originated. Figures are for North America.

UP	35.0%
CP	16.0
CSX	14.0
BNSF	12.0
NS	10.0
CN	5.0
IC	5.0
KCS	3.0

Source: *Chemical Week*, January 6, 1999, p. 56, from American Association of Railroads.

★ 1216 ★

Railroads (SIC 4011)

Largest Intermodal Railroads - 1998

Data show millions of units originated.

Burlington Northern Santa Fe	2.87
Union Pacific	2.39
Conrail	1.29
Norfolk Southern	1.03
CSX Transportation	0.74

Source: *Transport Topics*, April 19, 1999, p. 8, from Association of American Railroads.

★ 1217 ★

Railroads (SIC 4011)

Railroads by State

There are 541 railroads in the United States.

	No.	Share
Pennsylvania	62	11.46%
Texas	46	8.50
Illinois	42	7.76
New York	38	7.02%
Indiana	33	6.10
Ohio	33	6.10
California	32	5.91
North Carolina	27	4.99
Arkansas	25	4.62
Michigan	23	4.25
Other	180	33.27

Source: *Business North Carolina*, June 1998, p. 60, from Association of American Railroads.

SIC 41 - Local and Interurban Passenger Transit

★ 1218 ★

Mass Transit (SIC 4131)

Largest Bus Fleets

Agencies are ranked by fleet size. The top 10 groups in the United States and Canada have approximately 24% of the entire transit bus fleet.

MTA New York City Transit	3,745
New Jersey Transit Corp.	2,970
Los Angeles County MTA	2,413
Chicago Transit Authority	1,930
Montreal Urban Community Transit Corp.	1,544
Toronto Transit Commission	1,473
Southeastern Pennsylvania Transportation Authority	1,336
Washington Metropolitan Area Transit Authority	1,285
King County Metro	1,234
Metropolitan Transit Authority of Harris County	1,179

Source: *Metro Magazine Fact Book*, 1998, p. 12.

★ 1219 ★

Mass Transit (SIC 4131)

Largest Motorcoach Fleets - 1997

Companies are ranked by fleet size. The top 10 groups in the United States and Canada have approximately 24% of the entire transit motorcoach fleet.

Greyhound Lines Inc.	1,894
Ryder-ATE	1,280
ATC/Vancom Inc.	1,241
Laidlaw Transit Services	955
Academy Bus Tours Inc.	585
Liberty Lines Transit	419
Greyhound Canada Transportation Corp.	387
Diversified Transportation Ltd.	350
Suburban Transit Corp.	333
Holland America Line-Westours Inc.	299

Source: *Metro Magazine Fact Book*, 1998, p. 12.

★ 1220 ★

Trucking (SIC 4210)

Largest Northeast/Middle Atlantic LTL Carriers - 1997

Estes Express Lines
New Penn
USF Red Star
Jevic Transportation
NEMF

Companies are ranked by revenues in thousands of dollars. LTL stands for less-than-truckload.

Estes Express Lines	$ 404,615
New Penn	203,299
USF Red Star	194,800
Jevic Transportation	190,821
NEMF	139,593

Source: *Logistics Management*, July 1998, p. 44, from Transportation Technical Services.

★ 1221 ★

Trucking (SIC 4210)

Largest Southeast/South Central LTL Carriers - 1997

Companies are ranked by revenues in thousands of dollars. LTL stands for less-than-truckload.

Averitt Express	$ 370,405
Southeastern Freight	347,024
AAA Cooper	343,619
Sala Motor Freight	311.167
Central Freight Lines	111,869

Source: *Logistics Management*, July 1998, p. 44, from Transportation Technical Services.

★ 1222 ★

Trucking (SIC 4210)

Largest Truckers in Dallas, TX

Firms are ranked by number of trucks and trailers.

Schneider National	48,000
Yellow Freight Systems Inc.	42,933
American Freightways	19,233
Fleetline Inc.	7,414
Con-Way Southern Express	7,372

Source: *Dallas Business Journal*, June 26, 1998, p. 13.

★ 1223 ★

Trucking (SIC 4210)

Largest Trucking Firms - 1996

Shares are shown based on trucking industry revenues.

Schneider National	7.9%
J.B. Hunt Transport	4.8
Werner Enterprises	2.4
Swift Transportation	2.1
Landstar Ranger	1.4
M.S. Carriers	1.3
Landstar Inway	1.2
Builders Transport	1.1
Crete Carrier	1.0
U.S. Xpress	1.0
Other	57.1

Source: *Investext,* Thomson Financial Networks, August 26, 1998, p. 21, from *Commercial Carrier Journal* and Morgan Stanley Dean Witter Research.

★ 1224 ★

Trucking (SIC 4210)

Largest Trucking Firms in Arkansas

Firms are ranked by operating revenues in millions of dollars.

J.B. Hunt Transport Inc.	$ 1,351.0
ABF Freight System Inc.	1,136.4
American Freightways Corp.	870.3
USA Truck Inc.	129.5
P.A.M. Transportation Services Inc.	127.2

Source: *Arkansas Business*, September 4, 1998, p. 22, from U.S. Department of Transportation.

★ 1225 ★

Trucking (SIC 4210)

Largest U.S. Trucking Firms - 1997

Firms are ranked by revenues in billions of dollars.

United Parcel Service	$ 15.73
Roadway Express	2.57
Schneider National	2.51
Yellow Freight System	2.50
Consolidated Freightways	2.18
RPS Inc.	1.58
Con-Way Express Carriers	1.35
J.B. Hunt Transport	1.35
Ryder Integrated Logistics	1.29
ABF Freight System	1.13

Source: *Transport Topics*, August 10, 1998, p. 12.

★ 1226 ★

Trucking (SIC 4210)

Tank Truck Market - 1997

Firms are ranked by sales in millions of dollars. Figures are for North America.

Alliance Carriers	$ 750
MTL Inc.	593
Matlack Systems	231
DSI Transports	159
Kenan	138

Source: *Chemical Week*, January 6, 1999, p. 56.

★ 1227 ★

Trucking (SIC 4210)

Top Less-than-Truckload Carriers

Firms are ranked by gross revenues in thousands of dollars.

United Parcel Service Trucking	$ 15,730,318
Roadway Express	2,577,328
Yellow Freight System	2,509,537
Consolidated Freightways	2,187,801
Con-Way Transportation	1,359,550

Source: *Commercial Carrier Journal*, August 1998, p. 49.

★ 1228 ★

Trucking (SIC 4210)

Trucking Industry in Canada

Data show the traffic for trucking for-hire industry.

Product	Share
General freight	31.9%
Forest products	19.4
Food and food products	18.5
Manufactured end products	8.3
Petroleum products	7.3
Chemical products	5.8
Non-metallic minerals	4.5
Other	4.3

Source: *National Trade Data Bank*, October 21, 1998, p. ISA980901, from *Annual Report on Transportation in Canada*.

★ 1229 ★

Trucking (SIC 4214)

Largest Household Goods Carriers - 1997

Companies are ranked by revenues in thousands of dollars. LTL stands for less-than-truckload.

Company	Revenues
United Van Lines	$ 730,261
North American Van	642,052
Allied Van Lines	486,222
Atlas Van Lines	348,410
Mayflower Transit	337,273
Bekins Van Lines	207,839

Continued on next page.

★ 1229 ★ *Continued*

Trucking (SIC 4214)

Largest Household Goods Carriers - 1997

Companies are ranked by revenues in thousands of dollars. LTL stands for less-than-truckload.

Global Van Lines	$ 75,367
Wheaton Worldwide	73,883
New World Van Lines	66,172
National Van	50,633

Source: *Logistics Management*, July 1998, p. 23.

★ 1230 ★

Courier Services (SIC 4215)

Express Package Industry

Companies are ranked by revenues in thousands of dollars.

UPS	$ 22,458,000
RPS	1,581,754

Source: *Logistics Management*, July 1998, p. 44, from Transportation Technical Services.

★ 1231 ★

Courier Services (SIC 4215)

Overnight Delivery Market - 1998

Market shares are shown as of June 1998.

FedEx	45.5%
Airborne Express	22.8
UPS	20.8
Postal Service	6.4
DHL Worldwide	2.4
Others	2.8

Source: *Wall Street Journal*, November 12, 1998, p. 4B, from Colography Group Inc.

★ 1232 ★

Courier Services (SIC 4215)

Package Delivery Market - 1997

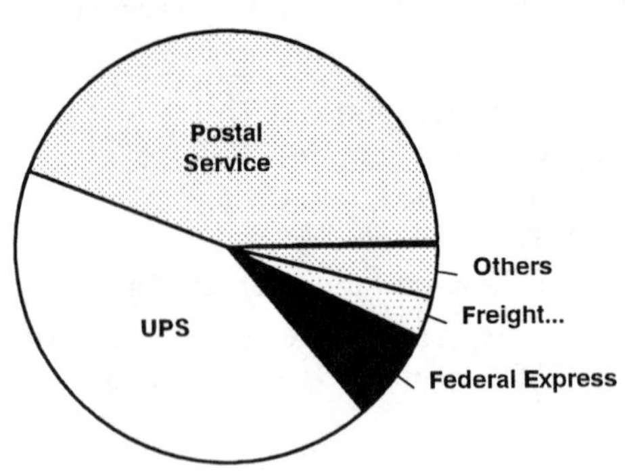

Market shares are shown in percent.

Postal Service	44.0%
UPS	42.0
Federal Express	7.0
Freight Consolidators	3.0
Others	4.0

Source: *Chicago Tribune*, August 2, 1998, p. C1, from *Dean Report*.

★ 1233 ★

Storage Facilities (SIC 4220)

Largest Warehouse Operators

Companies are ranked by millions of square feet.

Exel Logistics	25.0
DSC Logistics	10.6
USCO Distribution	9.0
Kenco Group	8.1
Tibbet & Britten	6.9
Elston-Richards	5.8
Ozburn-Hesseey	5.7
Warehouse Specialists	5.0
Metro Canada	4.9
Standard Warehouse	4.8

Source: *Logistics Management*, July 1998, p. 52, from International Warehouse Logistics Association.

SIC 43 - U.S. Postal Service

★ **1234** ★

Postal Service (SIC 4311)

Commemorative Stamp Nominations

The Postal Service recently conducted a poll for subjects for a set of stamps to commemorate the 1990s. The table shows the top vote getters, with the winner to be released April 2000.

Cellular phones	214,449
Titanic	210,154
Recovering species	193,313
World Wide Web	191,292
Jurassic Park	184,370

Source: *Detroit Free Press*, June 25, 1999, p. 2A.

SIC 44 - Water Transportation

★ 1235 ★

Shipping (SIC 4412)

Largest Ocean Shippers - 1997

Carriers are ranked by 20-foot equivalent units.

Sea-Land Service	1,355,126
Evergreen Line	1,244,734
Maersk Line	1,081,450
Hanjin Shipping Co.	827,591
Hyundai Merchant Marine	676,772
American President Line	656,185
Orient Overseas Container Line	518,773
China Ocean Shipping Co.	513,599
YangMing Marine Line	491,356
Nippon Yusen Kaisha	466,616

Source: *Logistics Management*, July 1998, p. 49, from *U.S. Global Container Report* and PIERS.

★ 1236 ★

Shipping (SIC 4412)

Largest U.S. Exporters - 1998

Companies are ranked by cargo exported in TEUs (20-foot equivalent units).

DuPont	82,000
America Chung Nam	75,300
Weyerhaeuser	64,400
Philip Morris	46,000
Westvaco	45,400
General Electric	44,600
Pacific Forest Resources	32,500
IBP	30,900
Military Sealift Command	29,800
Engelhard	27,400

Source: *Journal of Commerce*, March 29, 1999, p. 4.

★ 1237 ★

Shipping (SIC 4412)

Largest U.S. Importers - 1998

Companies are ranked by cargo imported in TEUs (20-foot equivalent units).

Dole	142,500
Chiquita Brands	82,000
Dayton Hudson	80,000
Payless Shoe Source	37,200
J.C. Penney	36,000
Michelin Tire	32,100
Mattel	31,600
Bridgestone Firestone	28,000
North American Philips	26,700
Pier One Imports	22,200

Source: *Journal of Commerce*, March 29, 1999, p. 4.

★ 1238 ★

Shipping (SIC 4412)

Shipping by State - 1996

Data are in millions of tons.

Louisiana	494.2
Texas	385.6
California	181.2
Ohio	123.5
Florida	117.4
Washington	116.9
Illinois	113.9
Pennsylvania	108.2

Source: *Plants Sites & Parks*, April/May 1998, p. 129, from U.S. Army Corps of Engineers.

★ 1239 ★

Ports (SIC 4491)

Largest Northeast Ports - 1996

Figures are in millions of short tons.

South Louisiana	189.8
Houston	148.1
New York-New Jersey	131.6
New Orleans	83.7
Baton Rouge, LA	81.0
Corpus Christi	80.4
Valdez, Alaska	77.1

Source: *Traffic World*, June 1, 1998, p. 31, from American Association of Port Authorities.

★ 1240 ★

Ports (SIC 4491)

Largest Ports - 1997

Ports are ranked by containerized cargo in thousands of twenty-foot equivalents.

Long Beach	2,667
Los Angeles	2,092
New York City	1,741
Charleston	954
Seattle	952
Oakland	841
Norfolk	768
Houston	608
Miami	624
Tacoma	550

Source: *World Trade*, June 1998, p. 70, from PIERS.

★ 1241 ★

Ports (SIC 4491)

Top Ports in North America - 1997

Data are in twenty-foot equivalent units.

Long Beach, CA	3.60
Los Angeles	2.95
New York/New Jersey	2.45
San Juan PR	1.83
Seattle	1.47
Oakland, CA	1.46
Hampton Roads, VA	1.23
Charleston, SC	1.21
Wacoma, WA	1.15

Source: *Logistics Management*, July 1998, p. 48.

★ 1242 ★

Ports (SIC 4491)

Top States for Water Traffic

Data show millions of tons, domestic and foreign.

Louisiana	494
Texas	386
California	181
Ohio	125
Florida	117
Washington	117
Illinois	114
Pennsylvania	108

Source: *Site Selection*, January 1999, p. 1168, from U.S. Army Corps of Engineers.

SIC 45 - Transportation by Air

★ 1243 ★

Airlines (SIC 4512)

Air Market in Charlotte, NC

Market shares are shown in percent.

US Airways	68.0%
Other	32.0

Source: *Philadelphia Inquirer*, May 23, 1999, p. C1, from U.S. Department of Transportation.

★ 1244 ★

Airlines (SIC 4512)

Air Market in Cincinnati, OH

Market shares are shown in percent.

Delta	72.0%
Other	28.0

Source: *Philadelphia Inquirer*, May 23, 1999, p. C1, from U.S. Department of Transportation.

★ 1245 ★

Airlines (SIC 4512)

Air Market in Philadelphia, PA

Market shares are shown in percent.

US Airways	52.0%
Other	48.0

Source: *Philadelphia Inquirer*, May 23, 1999, p. C1, from U.S. Department of Transportation.

★ 1246 ★

Airlines (SIC 4512)

Air Market in Pittsburgh, PA

Market shares are shown in percent.

US Airways	67.0%
Other	33.0

Source: *Philadelphia Inquirer*, May 23, 1999, p. C1, from U.S. Department of Transportation.

★ 1247 ★

Airlines (SIC 4512)

Airlines Leaders - 1998

Market shares are shown based on October 1998.

United Airlines	19.5%
Delta	18.4
American Airlines	17.6
Northwest Airlines	9.2
USAir	8.8
Continental	8.7
Southwest	7.6
Other	10.2

Source: *Interavia*, March 1998, p. 53.

★ 1248 ★

Airlines (SIC 4512)

Largest Air Routes - 1997

Data show millions of travelers.

New York-Los Angeles	3.7
Miami-New York	3.1
New York-Chicago	3.0
Boston-New York	2.7
Honolulu-Kahului, Maui	2.6

Source: *USA TODAY*, July 10, 1998, p. B1, from Air Transport Association.

★ 1249 ★
Airlines (SIC 4512)

Largest Airlines in Atlanta, GA - 1997

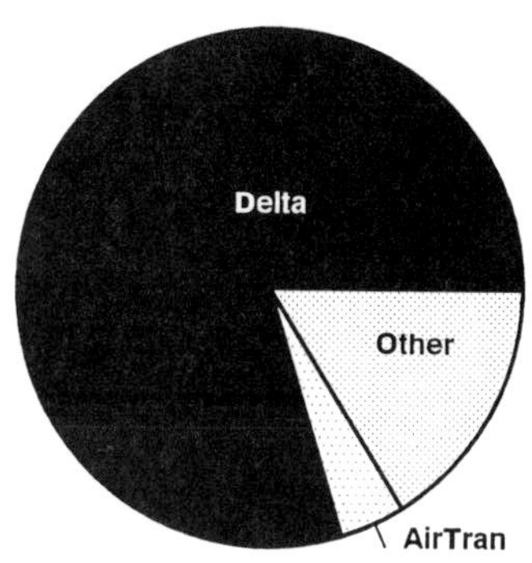

Market shares are shown based on enplanements.

Delta	79.3%
AirTran	4.4
Other	16.3

Source: *Investext,* Thomson Financial Networks, July 23, 1998, p. 3.

★ 1250 ★
Airlines (SIC 4512)

Largest Airlines in Charlotte, NC - 1997

Market shares are shown based on enplanements.

US Airways	92.3%
Delta	2.7
Other	5.0

Source: *Investext,* Thomson Financial Networks, July 23, 1998, p. 3.

★ 1251 ★
Airlines (SIC 4512)

Largest Airlines in Chicago, IL - 1997

Market shares are shown based on enplanements.

United	47.6%
American	32.3
Other	20.1

Source: *Investext,* Thomson Financial Networks, July 23, 1998, p. 3.

★ 1252 ★
Airlines (SIC 4512)

Largest Airlines in Cincinnati, OH - 1997

Market shares are shown based on enplanements.

Delta	94.1%
United	1.3
Other	4.6

Source: *Investext,* Thomson Financial Networks, July 23, 1998, p. 3.

★ 1253 ★
Airlines (SIC 4512)

Largest Airlines in Dallas, TX - 1997

Market shares are shown based on enplanements.

American	64.3%
Delta	19.6
Other	17.1

Source: *Investext,* Thomson Financial Networks, July 23, 1998, p. 3.

★ 1254 ★
Airlines (SIC 4512)

Largest Airlines in Denver, CO - 1997

Market shares are shown based on enplanements.

United	68.8%
Delta	4.9
Other	27.3

Source: *Investext,* Thomson Financial Networks, July 23, 1998, p. 3.

★ 1255 ★
Airlines (SIC 4512)

Largest Airlines in Detroit, MI - 1997

Market shares are shown based on enplanements.

Northwest	76.8%
American	4.9
Other	18.3

Source: *Investext,* Thomson Financial Networks, July 23, 1998, p. 3.

★ 1256 ★

Airlines (SIC 4512)

Largest Airlines in Houston, TX - 1997

Market shares are shown based on enplanements.

Continental	76.3%
American	7.2
Other	16.5

Source: *Investext,* Thomson Financial Networks, July 23, 1998, p. 3.

★ 1257 ★

Airlines (SIC 4512)

Largest Airlines in Las Vegas, NV - 1997

Market shares are shown based on enplanements.

Southwest	33.1%
America West	20.9

Source: *Investext,* Thomson Financial Networks, July 23, 1998, p. 3.

★ 1258 ★

Airlines (SIC 4512)

Largest Airlines in Los Angeles, CA - 1997

Market shares are shown based on enplanements.

United	28.7%
Southwest	14.7
Other	56.6

Source: *Investext,* Thomson Financial Networks, July 23, 1998, p. 3.

★ 1259 ★

Airlines (SIC 4512)

Largest Airlines in Miami, FL - 1997

Market shares are shown based on enplanements.

American	56.2%
Delta	9.5
Other	34.3

Source: *Investext,* Thomson Financial Networks, July 23, 1998, p. 3.

★ 1260 ★

Airlines (SIC 4512)

Largest Airlines in Minneapolis, MN - 1997

Market shares are shown based on enplanements.

Northwest	80.0%
United	4.0
Other	16.0

Source: *Investext,* Thomson Financial Networks, July 23, 1998, p. 3.

★ 1261 ★

Airlines (SIC 4512)

Largest Airlines in Philadelphia, PA - 1997

Market shares are shown based on enplanements.

US Airways	64.1%
American	8.0
Other	27.9

Source: *Investext,* Thomson Financial Networks, July 23, 1998, p. 3.

★ 1262 ★

Airlines (SIC 4512)

Largest Airlines in Phoenix, AZ - 1997

Market shares are shown based on enplanements.

America West	38.5%
Southwest	29.8
Other	31.7

Source: *Investext,* Thomson Financial Networks, July 23, 1998, p. 3.

★ 1263 ★

Airlines (SIC 4512)

Largest Airlines in Pittsburgh, PA - 1997

Market shares are shown based on enplanements.

US Airways	89.5%
Delta	2.5
Other	8.0

Source: *Investext,* Thomson Financial Networks, July 23, 1998, p. 3.

★ 1264 ★

Airlines (SIC 4512)

Largest Airlines in Salt Lake City, Utah - 1997

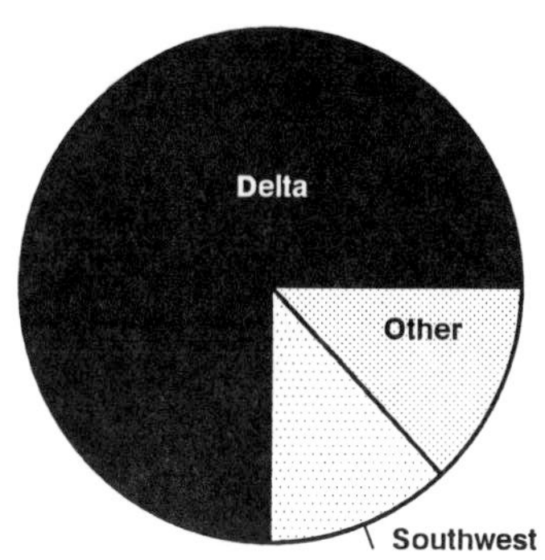

Market shares are shown based on enplanements.

Delta	74.9%
Southwest	11.9
Other	13.2

Source: *Investext,* Thomson Financial Networks, July 23, 1998, p. 3.

★ 1265 ★

Airlines (SIC 4512)

Largest Airlines in San Francisco, CA - 1997

Market shares are shown based on enplanements.

United	57.2%
American	7.4
Other	35.4

Source: *Investext,* Thomson Financial Networks, July 23, 1998, p. 3.

★ 1266 ★

Airlines (SIC 4512)

Largest Airlines in St. Louis, MO - 1997

Market shares are shown based on enplanements.

TWA	68.4%
Southwest	15.4
Other	16.2

Source: *Investext,* Thomson Financial Networks, July 23, 1998, p. 3.

★ 1267 ★

Airlines (SIC 4512)

Top Airlines in Canada - 1997

Market shares are shown in percent for the year ended December 31, 1997.

Air Canada	41.9%
Canadian Airlines	23.3
Others	34.8

Source: "Report on Market Share." Retrieved June 1, 1999 from the World Wide Web: http://www.marketingmag.ca/index.cgi?, from Statisiics Canada.

★ 1268 ★

Airlines (SIC 4512)

Top Airlines in New York City, NY - 1998

Shares are shown for three major airports serving the city.

Continental	22.2%
American	13.9
Delta	13.3
US Airways	9.6
United	8.1
TWA	4.6
Northwest	3.2
British Air	1.8
Other	23.3

Source: *Wall Street Journal*, February 9, 1999, p. 1, from BACK Associates Inc.

★ 1269 ★

Air Cargo (SIC 4513)

Air Cargo Market - 1998

Data show shipments for the first six months of the year.

FedEx	45.0%
UPS-Air	26.0
Airborne	19.8
Postal Service	4.3
DHL	1.8
Emery	0.3
BAX	0.2
Other	2.7

Source: *Air Cargo World*, March 1999, p. 63, from Colography Group Inc.

★ 1270 ★

Air Cargo (SIC 4513)

Largest Air Mail Carriers at LAX

Market shares are shown for Los Angeles International Airport.

United Airlines	20.56%
Evergreen International	12.83
American AIrlines	11.00
Delta Airlines	10.12
Emery Worldwide	7.44
Express One	7.14
Kalitta	5.49
Northwest Airlines	4.87
USAir	3.95
Southwest Airlines	3.44
Other	13.16

Source: Retrieved May 13, 1999 from the World Wide Web: http:// www.airports.ci.la.ca.us/statistics/ top_airmail98.htm.

★ 1271 ★

Air Cargo (SIC 4513)

Miami Cargo Market - 1998

Data show metric tons carried.

Atlas	208,096
American	165,650
Fine Air	144,277
Challenge	129,296
AIA	127,121
Tampa	98,799
Amerijet	74,963
Arrow	56,772

Source: *Traffic World*, March 22, 1999, p. 36, from Atlas Air and Miami International Airport.

★ 1272 ★

Airports (SIC 4581)

Denver's Airport Market

Data show share of passenger boardings at Denver International Airport.

United	65.9%
Air Wisconsin	6.8
Frontier	5.6
Delta	5.1
Others	16.6

Source: *USA TODAY*, March 30, 1999, p. 5B, from Denver International Airport.

★ 1273 ★

Airports (SIC 4581)

Largest Air Carriers at LAX - 1998

Market shares are shown for Los Angeles International Airport.

United Airlines	22.90%
Southwest Airlines	11.33
American Airlines	9.20
Delta Airlines	8.73
Northwest Airlines	3.81
Continental Airlines	3.66
Alaska Airlines	3.58
Other	36.79

Source: Retrieved May 13, 1999 from the World Wide Web: http:// www.airports.ci.la.ca.us/statistics/ top_airmail98.htm.

★ 1274 ★

Airports (SIC 4581)

Top Airlines at Chicago's O'Hare Airport - 1998

Market shares are shown for the first six months of the year.

United	47.6%
American	32.7
Simmons	4.8
Delta	3.5
Other	11.4

Source: *USA TODAY*, November 3, 1998, p. B1, from GKMG Consulting Services for *Aviation Daily*.

★ 1275 ★

Airports (SIC 4581)

Top Airlines at the New Orleans Airport - 1998

Southwest
Delta
Continental
American
US Airways
Other

Market shares are shown for the first six months of the year.

Southwest	23.04%
Delta	21.30
Continental	13.46
American	10.62
US Airways	9.80
Other	21.78

Source: *USA TODAY*, November 6, 1998, p. B1, from GKMG Consulting Services for *Aviation Daily*.

★ 1276 ★

Airports (SIC 4581)

Top Airlines at the Seattle/Tacoma Airport - 1998

Market shares are shown for the first six months of the year.

Alaska	32.21%
United	15.55
Horizon	12.32
Northwest	9.48
Delta	6.83
Southwest	5.78
Other	17.83

Source: *USA TODAY*, November 6, 1998, p. B1, from GKMG Consulting Services for Aviation Daily.

★ 1277 ★

Airports (SIC 4581)

Top Airlines in Boston's Logan Airport - 1998

Market shares are shown for the first six months of the year.

Delta	22.0%
US Airways	18.0
American	15.0
United	11.0
Commuters	8.0
Other	26.0

Source: *USA TODAY*, November 4, 1998, p. B1, from GKMG Consulting Services for *Aviation Daily*.

SIC 46 - Pipelines, Except Natural Gas

★ 1278 ★

Pipelines (SIC 4610)

Largest Gas Pipelines - 1998

Companies are ranked by gas throughput in millions of cubic feet.

ANR Pipeline Co.	4.16
PG&E Texas Pipeline	3.70
Transcontinental Gas Pipe Line Corp.	3.60
Tennessee Gas Pipeline Co.	2.33
Natural Gas Pipeline Co. of America	2.24
Tejas Energy Co.	1.65
Northern Natural Gas Co.	1.59
Texas Eastern Transmission Corp.	1.50
El Paso Natural Gas Co.	1.36
Koch Gateway Pipeline Co.	1.30

Source: *Pipeline & Gas Journal*, November 1998, p. 43.

★ 1279 ★

Tourism (SIC 4720)

Largest State Travel Budgets - 1999

Illinois
Hawaii
Texas
Florida
Pennsylvania
Maryland
New York

Budgets are shown in billions of dollars.

Illinois	$ 40.1
Hawaii	37.9
Texas	29.5
Florida	27.3
Pennsylvania	23.1
Maryland	21.4
New York	18.7

Source: *Detroit Free Press*, June 27, 1999, p. 8A, from Michigan Travel Bureau.

★ 1280 ★

Tourism (SIC 4720)

Top Destinations for Mexican Tourists

Data show the top cities visited by Mexico's tourists.

Los Angeles	17.0%
Miami	15.2
Las Vegas	9.0
New York City	8.7
Houston	8.2
Other	41.9

Source: *National Trade Data Bank*, September 14, 1998, p. ISA980601.

★ 1281 ★

Tourism (SIC 4720)

Top States for Tourism

Data show millions of trips.

California	89.3
Texas	76.0
Florida	59.1
New York	40.8
Pennsylvania	35.9
Michigan	34.6
Ohio	34.5
Illinois	33.1

Source: *Detroit Free Press*, June 27, 1999, p. 8A, from U.S. Department of Transportation.

★ 1282 ★

Tourism (SIC 4720)

Top Travel Destinations - 1998

Chicago	54.0%
New York	44.0
Atlanta	41.0
Los Angeles	40.0
Dallas	39.0

Source: *USA TODAY*, June 7, 1999, p. B1, from Runzheimer International.

★ 1283 ★

Tourism (SIC 4720)

Tourism by Foreigners in Canada - 1998

Market shares are shown in percent for the year ended September 30, 1998.

Ontario	43.4%
British Columbia	24.0
Quebec	14.7
Alberta	9.4

Continued on next page.

★ 1283 ★ *Continued*

Tourism (SIC 4720)

Tourism by Foreigners in Canada - 1998

Market shares are shown in percent for the year ended September 30, 1998.

Nova Scotia	2.6%
Manitoba	1.5
New Brunswick	1.3
Other	3.2

Source: "Report on Market Share." Retrieved June 1, 1999 from the World Wide Web: http://www.marketingmag.ca/index.cgi?, from Statistics Canada.

★ 1284 ★

Travel Agencies (SIC 4724)

Largest Travel Agencies

American Express Travel Services
Carlson Wagonlift
WorldTravel Partners
Rosenbluth
Maritz

Firms are ranked by annual air bookings in billions of dollars.

American Express Travel Services	$ 8.4
Carlson Wagonlift	5.0
WorldTravel Partners	3.3
Rosenbluth	2.0
Maritz	1.5

Source: *Atlanta Journal-Constitution*, November 26, 1998, p. G1, from WorldTravel and *Travel Weekly*.

★ 1285 ★

Travel Agencies (SIC 4724)

Largest Travel Agencies in Baltimore, MD

Sales are shown in millions of dollars.

Travel One	$ 175.5
Travel Destinations Management Group Inc.	126.0
Travel Guide	80.0
Adventure Vacations/Singer Travel	58.0
Omega World Travel	30.7

Source: *Baltimore Business Journal*, May 29, 1998, p. 19.

★ 1286 ★

Travel Agencies (SIC 4724)

Ticket Bookings by Channel

CRS stands for computer reservation system.

Travel agency/CRS	80.0%
Direct-to-vendor	19.0
Internet	1.0

Source: *Investor's Business Daily*, July 29, 1998, p. A4, from Lehman Brothers.

★ 1287 ★

Cruise Lines (SIC 4725)

Cruise Line Market - 1997

Market shares are shown in percent.

Carnival	36.0%
Royal Caribbean	26.0
Princess Cruises	11.0
Other	27.0

Source: *Time*, May 11, 1998, p. 44.

★ 1288 ★

Cruise Lines (SIC 4725)

Top Cruise Lines - 1998

Data show number of passengers.

Carnival	1,700,000
Royal Caribbean	1,440,914
Norwegian	511,015
Princess	500,000
Holland America	458,745

Source: *Consumer Reports Travel Letter*, April 1999, p. 6.

★ 1289 ★

Forwarding Services (SIC 4731)

Largest Freight Forwarders in South Florida - 1997

Companies are ranked by gross revenues in millions of dollars.

Miami International Forwarders	$ 112.4
Howard S. Reeder Inc.	41.4
Customs & Trade Services Inc.	37.1
Econocaribe Consolidators Inc.	35.0
Eagle Cos.	28.0

Source: *South Florida Business Journal*, March 13, 1998, p. 16A.

★ 1290 ★

Forwarding Services (SIC 4731)

Leading Forwarders - 1998

Companies are ranked by total revenues for the third quarter of the year.

AEI	$ 373.0
Fritz Cos.	342.2
Expeditors	289.7
Circle	191.0
Eagle USA	121.8

Source: *Air Cargo World*, January 1999, p. 62, from company reports.

★ 1291 ★

Wireless Communications (SIC 4812)

Broadband Market by Segment - 2004

MMDS stands for multichannel multipoint distribution service. LMDS stands for linear multipoint distribution service. ADSL stands for asymmetric digital subscriber line.

ADSL	36.0%
Cable modem	28.0
LMDS	14.0
ISDN	12.0
Satellite	8.0
MMDS	2.0

Source: *Telecommunications*, March 1999, p. 12, from Allied Business Intelligence.

★ 1292 ★

Wireless Communications (SIC 4812)

ISDN Leaders - 1998

AT&T
Bell Atlantic
SBC
Ameritech
BellSouth
Other

Market shares are shown for the first quarter of the year. ISDN stands for integrated services digital network.

AT&T	25.0%
Bell Atlantic	21.0
SBC	18.0
Ameritech	9.0
BellSouth	7.0
Other	20.0

Source: *Industry Standard*, August 24, 1998, p. 33, from International Data Corp.

★ 1293 ★

Wireless Communications (SIC 4812)

Largest Digital PCS Providers in Canada - 1999

Market shares are shown in percent for the year ended March 31, 1999. PCS stands for personal communications services.

Cantel AT&T	36.3%
Clearnet Communications	21.0
Microcell Telecom	20.8
Other	21.9

Source: "Report on Market Share." Retrieved June 1, 1999 from the World Wide Web: http://www.marketingmag.ca/index.cgi?, from industry sources.

★ 1294 ★

Wireless Communications (SIC 4812)

Largest PCS Carriers - 1997

Market shares are shown in percent. PCS stands for personal communications systems.

Sprint PCS	21.0%
AT&T Wireless	17.0
PrimeCo.	14.0
Southwestern Bell Mobile	13.0
Sprint Spectrum	10.0
Aerial	5.0
Omnipoint	5.0
Western Wireless	5.0
Other	10.0

Source: *Industry Standard*, August 24, 1998, p. 33, from International Data Corp.

★ 1295 ★

Wireless Communications (SIC 4812)

Largest Telecom Firms in Canada - 1998

Market shares are shown in percent,

Bell Canada	49.0%
BCT.TELUS Comm.	24.0
AT&T Canada	7.0
Call-Net Enterprises	7.0
Other	13.0

Source: *Wall Street Journal*, March 5, 1999, p. A7, from company reports and Yankee Group in Canada.

★ 1296 ★

Wireless Communications (SIC 4812)

Largest Wireless Carriers

Data show millions of carriers.

Bell Atlantic/GTE	12.9
AT&T	10.4
SBC/Ameritech	9.2
AirTouch	8.4
BellSouth	4.7

Source: *Wall Street Journal*, April 6, 1999, p. A13, from NationsBanc Montgomery Securities.

★ 1297 ★

Wireless Communications (SIC 4812)

Largest Wireless Markets - 1997

Data show millions of subscribers.

Los Angeles	2.5
New York City	1.9
Chicago	1.8
Miami/West Palm Beach	1.4
Washington D.C./Baltimore	1.3
San Francisco/San Jose	1.2
Boston	1.1
Detroit	1.1
Philadelphia	1.1
Atlanta	1.0

Source: *New York Times*, January 11, 1999, p. C4, from RCR Publications and Strategis Group.

★ 1298 ★

Wireless Communications (SIC 4812)

Largest Wireless Providers

Data show millions of customers.

GTE-Bell Atlantic	13.4
SBC-Ameritech	9.6
AirTouch	7.9
AT&T	7.2
BellSouth	4.6

Source: *Investor's Business Daily*, May 27, 1999, p. A4, from Alltel.

★ 1299 ★

Wireless Communications (SIC 4812)

Mobile Phone Services in Quebec

Bell Mobility	54.0%
Cantel	31.0
Microcell	7.0
Clearnet	4.0
Other	4.0

Source: Retrieved May 28, 1999 from the World Wide Web: http:// www.pubzone.com/pubzone/stories/ cellphones.html.

★ 1300 ★

Wireless Communications (SIC 4812)

PCS Market Leaders - 2002

Market shares are estimated in percent.

Sprint PCS	37.0%
PrimeCo PCS	16.0
Pacific Bell	13.0
AT&T Wireless	7.0
Other	27.0

Source: *Computerworld*, July 20, 1998, p. 39, from Strategis Group Inc.

★ 1301 ★

Wireless Communications (SIC 4812)

T1 Line Leaders - 1998

Market shares are shown for the second quarter of the year.

AT&T	22.0%
MCI	12.0

Continued on next page.

★ 1301 ★ *Continued*

Wireless Communications (SIC 4812)

T1 Line Leaders - 1998

Market shares are shown for the second quarter of the year.

US West	10.0%
Bell Atlantic	9.0
Ameritech	8.0
SBC	8.0
Sprint	8.0
Other	23.0

Source: *Industry Standard*, August 24, 1998, p. 33, from International Data Corp.

★ 1302 ★

Wireless Communications (SIC 4812)

Top Wireless Carriers - 1998

Data show millions of subscribers for the third quarter of the year.

Airtouch	7.46
AT&T Wireless	6.81
Bell Atlantic Mobile	5.91
Southwestern Bell	5.34
GTE Mobile	4.65
Bell South	4.54
Alltel	3.86
Ameritech Mobile Systems	3.52
Nextel	2.42
U.S. Cellular	2.02

Source: *New York Times*, January 11, 1999, p. C1, from company reports.

★ 1303 ★

Wireless Communications (SIC 4812)

Wireless Market - 2006

PCS stands for personal communications services.

Cellular	68.0%
PCS	25.0
ESMR (Nextel)	7.0

Source: *Investor's Business Daily*, July 8, 1998, p. A8, from BancAmerica Robertson Stephens.

★ 1304 ★

Call Centers (SIC 4813)

Call Centers by State 1990-98

Data show the states with the most new call centers.

Texas	113
Florida	81
Virginia	42
Arizona	31
Illinois	31
North Carolina	29
California	25
Ohio	25

Source: *Site Selection*, May 1999, p. 538, from *Site Selection News*.

★ 1305 ★

Telephone Services (SIC 4813)

CLEC Market Leaders - 1997

Shares of the $3.7 billion in revenues. CLEC stands for competitive local exchange carriers.

MFS	23.1%
TCG	12.0
MCI Local	9.0
Intermedia	6.3
ICG	4.6
Brooks	3.5
McLeodUSA	3.0
GST	2.5

Source: *Telecommunications*, September 1998, p. 27, from International Data Corp.

★ 1306 ★

Telephone Services (SIC 4813)

Largest Phone Companies - 1998

Data show millions of customers.

AT&T/TCI	80
Bell Atlantic/GTE	41
SBC/Ameritech	30
MCI WorldCom	20

Source: *Wall Street Journal*, March 8, 1999, p. B1, from companies.

★ 1307 ★

Telephone Services (SIC 4813)

Largest Telephone Companies in Canada - 1997

Revenues are shown in millions of dollars.

Bell Canada	$ 9,200
BC Tel	2,700
Telus	2,010
SaskTel	694
Manitoba Tel	620

Source: *Globe and Mail*, September 12, 1998, p. B9, from Bloomberg Financial Services, Datastream, and company reports.

★ 1308 ★

Telephone Services (SIC 4813)

Long-Distance Market in Canada - 1998

Sales are shown in millions of dollars.

Bell Canada	$ 2,480
Sprint Canada	994
AT&T Canada	800
BC Tel	650
Telus	490
Fonorola	258
ACC	172

Source: *Globe and Mail*, June 29, 1998, p. B1, from Yankee Group.

★ 1309 ★

Telephone Services (SIC 4813)

Long-Distance Service Market in Canada - 1998

Market shares are shown in percent for the year ended December 31, 1998.

Bell Canada	42.5%
Sprint Canada	13.4
AT&T Canada	11.6
BC Tel	9.7
Telus Communications	7.6
Others	15.2

Source: "Report on Market Share." Retrieved June 1, 1999 from the World Wide Web: http://www.marketingmag.ca/index.cgi?, from NBI/Michael Sone Associates.

★ 1310 ★

Telephone Services (SIC 4813)

Popular Phone Call Destinations

Data show the countries which receive the most calls from U.S. based businesses. Figures show millions of minutes.

Canada	3,461,0
Mexico	2,380.7
United Kingdom	1,178.6
Germany	780.6
Japan	698.2

Source: *World Trade*, October 1998, p. 20, from *Federal Communications Commission Report*.

★ 1311 ★

Telephone Services (SIC 4813)

Telephone Systems Leaders - 1997

The $3.0 billion market is shown in percent.

Northern Telecom	19.0%
Lucent	16.0
Toshiba	12.0
Intertel	9.0
Comdial	7.0
Others	37.0

Source: *Investor's Business Daily*, July 17, 1998, p. A3, from Phillips InfoTech.

★ 1312 ★

Internet (SIC 4822)

Auto Sales on the Internet

Market shares of auto Internet deals.

Autobytel.com	36.0%
AutoVantage.com	23.0
CarPoint.msn.com	14.0
Carsmart.com	10.0
Autoweb.com	7.0
Others	10.0

Source: *Automotive News*, November 23, 1998, p. 6, from J.D. Power & Associates.

★ 1313 ★

Internet (SIC 4822)

E-Commerce Leaders - 1997

Companies are ranked by estimated online sales in millions of dollars.

Cisco Systems	$ 3,200
Dell	1,020
Digital	950
IBM	500
Gateway 2000	360
Amazom.com	122
Computer Discount Warehouse	64
NECX	60
iQVC	36
Egghead	52

Source: *Catalog Age*, August 1998, p. 63, from *Electronic Advertising and Marketplace Report*.

★ 1314 ★

Internet (SIC 4822)

E-Commerce Market - 1998

Figures are estimated.

Computer hardware	30.1%
Travel	29.6
Books	9.2
Other	31.1

Source: *U.S. News & World Report*, December 7, 1998, p. 44, from Jupiter Communications.

★ 1315 ★

Internet (SIC 4822)

How We Access the Internet - 1998

Dial-up ISPs	95.58%
Internet-TV providers	2.54
Cabel modem providers	1.88

Source: *Industry Standard*, March 22, 1999, p. 47, from *Internactive Services Report* and Telecommunications Reports International.

★ 1316 ★

Internet (SIC 4822)

How We Access the Internet - 2000

ADSL stands for asymmetric digital subscriber line.

56K modems	65.0%
Cable modems	7.0
ISDN	5.0
ADSL	3.0
Satellite/wireless	2.0

Source: *USA TODAY*, February 2, 1999, p. 3B, from Jupiter Communications.

★ 1317 ★

Internet (SIC 4822)

Internet Access by City

Data show the cities with the most residents who have access to the Internet.

New York City	4,085,000
Los Angeles	2,900,000
San Francisco	2,900,000
Philadelphia	1,666,000
Boston	1,554,000
Chicago	1,540,000
Washington	1,483,000
Dallas-Ft. Worth	833,000
Detroit	808,000
Cleveland	726,000

Source: *Wall Street Journal*, May 14, 1999, p. C8, from Mediamark Research Inc.

★ 1318 ★

Internet (SIC 4822)

Internet Access for Small Businesses - 2002

Data show the estimated access methods for small offices and telecommuters.

Analog modem	65.0%
ISDN	15.0
Cable modem	10.0
DSL	5.0
Wireless/satellite	5.0

Source: Retrieved May 18, 1999 from the World Wide Web: http:// www.sonic.net/cgi-bin/cif/cif/search-free.pl.

★ 1319 ★

Internet (SIC 4822)

Internet Auction Market - 2003

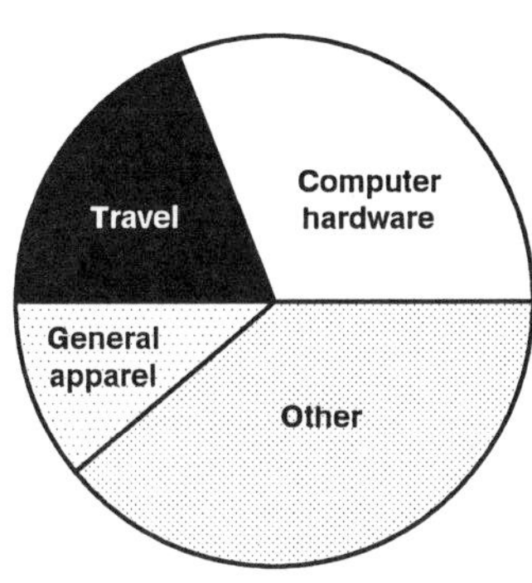

The business-to-consumer on-line auction market is estimated in percent.

Computer hardware	31.19%
Travel	19.27
General apparel	11.01
Other	38.53

Source: *USA TODAY*, May 17, 1999, p. 2B, from Forrester Research Inc.

★ 1320 ★

Internet (SIC 4822)

Internet Backbone Market

Market shares are shown in percent.

WorldCom	25.0%
IBM	20.0
PSINet	5.0
Sprint	5.0
Others	25.0

Source: *Telephony*, August 3, 1998, p. 14, from TeleChoice.

★ 1321 ★

Internet (SIC 4822)

Internet Backbone Providers

Market shares are shown in percent.

MCI	26.0%
UUNet	20.0
SprintLink	12.0
BBN	7.0
Digex	3.0
Other	32.0

Source: *Electronic Business*, November 1998, p. 56, from Price Waterhouse Coopers.

★ 1322 ★

Internet (SIC 4822)

Internet Connections by Carrier - 2000

Data show estimated market shares of business Internet connections. Top carriers refers to AT&T, MCI, Sprint, GTE and Worldcom. RBOC stands for regional bell operating company.

	($ bil.)	Share
Top U.S. carriers	$ 8.0	48.0%
RBOC	1.0	6.0
Other ISPs	7.6	46.0

Source: Retrieved May 18, 1999 from the World Wide Web: http:// www.sonic.net/cgi-bin/cif/cif/search-free.pl.

★ 1323 ★

Internet (SIC 4822)

Internet Households in Canada

By the middle of 1998 an estimated 5.2 million Canadians used the Internet on a regular basis. Approximately 40% go on the Internet daily.

Ontario	857,850
British Columbia	340,273
Quebec	308,485
Alberta	229,440
Manitoba	70,950

Continued on next page.

★ 1323 ★ *Continued*

Internet (SIC 4822)

Internet Households in Canada

By the middle of 1998 an estimated 5.2 million Canadians used the Internet on a regular basis. Approximately 40% go on the Internet daily.

Saskatchewan	44,312
Nova Scotia	43,554
New Brunswick	42,750
Prince Edward Island	4,410

Source: *National Trade Data Bank*, August 10, 1998, p. IMI980806, from CORINFO Research and Information Services.

★ 1324 ★

Internet (SIC 4822)

Internet Use in Canada

Data show share of residential and business subscribers.

	Res.	Bus.
Quebec	64.0%	36.0%
Ontario	66.0	33.0
Prairies	81.0	19.0
British Columbia/Territories	81.0	19.0
Atlantic	82.0	18.0

Source: *National Trade Data Bank*, August 10, 1998, p. IMI980806, from CORINFO Research and Information Services.

★ 1325 ★

Internet (SIC 4822)

Internet Use in the United States

Data show the share of the population that accessed the Web in the last 30 days.

San Francisco	72.0%
Miami	67.0
Houston	65.0
Seattle/Tacoma	65.0
Washington D.C.	64.0
San Diego	64.0
Cleveland/Akron	62.0
Atlanta	61.0
Dallas	60.0
Philadelphia	60.0

Source: *Industry Standard*, March 15, 1999, p. 47, from Inteco.

★ 1326 ★

Internet (SIC 4822)

Internet/Intranet Market - 1997

The $49.2 billion market is shown in percent.

Communications	65.85%
Containment	23.58
Consumption	4.27
Creation	2.64
Control	2.24
Content	1.42

Source: *Industry Standard*, November 16, 1998, p. 42, from Zona Research.

★ 1327 ★

Internet (SIC 4822)

Largest Business Internet Transactions - 1997

Sales are shown in millions of dollars.

Computers/peripherals	$ 3,800
Industrial supplies	924
Packaged software	630
Office supplies/equipment	340
Information retrieval services	300

Source: *Industry Standard*, November 2, 1998, p. 46, from Zona Research.

★ 1328 ★

Internet (SIC 4822)

Largest Web Portal Companies

Firms are ranked by market valuation in billions of dollars.

America Online	$ 70.4
Yahoo	39.7
Amazon.com	25.9
Netscape	6.4
Excite	3.9
Infoseek	2.7

Source: *Washington Post*, January 13, 1999, p. F1, from Bloomberg News.

★ 1329 ★
Internet (SIC 4822)

Leading E-Retailers - 1998

Data show sales in millions of dollars for the third quarter of the year.

Dell	$ 900
Amazon	154
Schwab	150
Gateway	109
E-Trade	69
Waterhouse	50
Ameritrade	40
Gap	20

Source: *Stores*, January 1999, p. 18, from Marketing Corp. of America.

★ 1330 ★
Internet (SIC 4822)

Leading Online Industries

Travel
Books
Apparel/accessories
Music
Health & beauty

Data show selected estimated markets in millions of dollars.

	1999	2001	2002
Travel	$ 3,900	$ 8,300	$ 11,700
Books	1,100	2,500	3,600
Apparel/accessories	641	1,800	2,800
Music	280	878	1,600
Health & beauty	65	595	1,200

Source: *WWD*, March 24, 1999, p. 25, from Jupiter Communications.

★ 1331 ★
Internet (SIC 4822)

People Using the Internet at Home

Data show the share of adults using the Internet at home. San Jose had the largest percentage of adults using the Web at work.

Austin, TX	32.4%
San Jose, CA	25.1
Denver, CO	25.0
Nashville, TN	24.8%
Oakland, CA	24.0
Washington D.C.	23.5
Baltimore, MD	21.7
Minneapolis-St. Paul, MN	21.2
Atlanta, GA	20.7
Norfolk-Virginia Beach, VA	20.6

Source: *Yahoo! Internet Life*, March 1999, p. 107, from MIDS.

★ 1332 ★
Internet (SIC 4822)

Popular Finance Web Sites

Figures show the millions of visitors. Data refer to people using office computers to visit sites that provide stock information or handle trades.

	1998 Dec.	1999 March
Yahoo Finance	2.22	2.80
Quicken Financial Network	1.23	2.00
AOL Personal Finance	1.20	1.72
Moneycentral	0.68	1.16
CBS Marketwatch	0.74	0.89

Source: *New York Times*, May 20, 1999, p. C8, from Media Metrix.

★ 1333 ★
Internet (SIC 4822)

Popular Internet Languages - 1998

English	82.3%
German	4.0
Japanese	1.6
French	1.5
Spanish	1.1
Italian	0.8
Portugese	0.7
Swedish	0.6

Source: *Control Engineering*, July 1998, p. 62, from Artis Technological the Internet Society.

★ 1334 ★

Internet (SIC 4822)

Popular Internet Products

Sales are shown in millions of dollars.

	($ mil.)	Share
PC hardware, software	$ 1,600	33.55%
Travel	1,500	31.45
Entertainment	591	12.39
Books and music	268	5.62
Gifts, flowers, greeting cards	264	5.54
Food and beverages	168	3.52
Apparel and footwear	157	3.29
Jewelry	56	1.17
Consumer electronics	34	0.71
Sporting goods	29	0.61
Tools and gardening	22	0.46
Toys and hobbies	21	0.44
Health, beauty, drugs	16	0.34
Other	43	0.90

Source: *The Boston Sunday Globe*, August 23, 1998, p. A1, from Forrester Research Inc.

★ 1335 ★

Internet (SIC 4822)

Popular Shopping Web Sites - 1998

Bluemountainarts.com
Amazon.com
Ebay.com
Barnesandnoble.com
Etoys.com

Data show millions of visitors for December 1998.

Bluemountainarts.com	12.3
Amazon.com	9.1
Ebay.com	5.5
Barnesandnoble.com	4.7
Etoys.com	3.9

Source: *Time*, February 8, 1999, p. 79, from Media Metrix.

★ 1336 ★

Internet (SIC 4822)

Top Internet Buyer States

Computer hardware and software generated the most sales.

California	10.1%
New York	5.6
Texas	4.4
Massachusetts	3.6
Florida	3.5
New Jersey	3.5
Pennsylvania	3.4
Illinois	3.1
Ohio	2.4
Michigan	2.3
Other	58.1

Source: *Security Distribution & Marketing*, September 1998, p. W, from ViaWeb.

★ 1337 ★

Internet (SIC 4822)

Top Internet Cities

Data show the top cities for Internet domain registrations. A total of 1.43 million .com, .net and .org sites were registered in the United States.

New York City	9.5%
Washington D.C.	7.2
Los Angeles-Long Beach	6.9
San Francisco	3.6
Boston-Lawrence-Lowell-Brockton	3.4
San Jose	2.9
Dallas	2.2
San Diego	2.2
Atlanta	2.1
Oakland	2.1
Other	57.9

Source: *Smart Computing*, September 1998, p. 5, from Network Solutions Inc.

★ 1338 ★

Internet (SIC 4822)

U.S. Internet Use by Region

South Atlantic	19.0%
Pacific	18.0
East North Central	16.0
Middle Atlantic	14.0

Continued on next page.

★ 1338 ★ *Continued*

Internet (SIC 4822)

U.S. Internet Use by Region

West South Central	10.0%
Mountain	7.0
New England	6.0
West North Central	6.0
East South Central	5.0

Source: *Industry Standard*, March 15, 1999, p. 47, from Inteco.

★ 1339 ★

Internet (SIC 4822)

Web Commerce Market - 2002

The market is estimated.

Midsize or large business	37.0%
Home	22.0
Small business	24.0
Education	11.0
Government	6.0

Source: *Infoworld*, December 14, 1998, p. 59, from International Data Corp.

★ 1340 ★

Online Services (SIC 4822)

Internet Service Provider Market

America Online	53.0%
Microsoft	7.7
Others	39.3

Source: *Investor's Business Daily*, December 21, 1998, p. A12, from Jupiter Communications, Acknowledge, and Dataquest Inc.

★ 1341 ★

Online Services (SIC 4822)

Largest Internet Service Providers

Data show millions of subscribers.

America Online	15,000
CompuServe	2,000
MSN Internet Access	1,500
AT&T WorldNet	1,400
EarthLink Sprint	1,000
IBM Internet Connection	1,000
GTE Internet Solutions	824
WebTV Networks	700
MindSpring	650
Prodigy	643

Source: *Industry Standard*, March 15, 1999, p. 20, from Telecommunications Reports International.

★ 1342 ★

Online Services (SIC 4822)

Largest Internet Service Providers in Canada - 1998

Market shares are shown in percent for the year ended December 31, 1998.

Sympatico	16.8%
PSINet Ltd.	4.4
Sprint Canada	4.4
AOL Canada	3.7
Internet Direct	3.7
Netcom Canada	2.5
Shaw@Home	2.0
Others	62.5

Source: "Report on Market Share." Retrieved June 1, 1999 from the World Wide Web: http://www.marketingmag.ca/index.cgi?, from Evans Research Corp.

★ 1343 ★

Online Services (SIC 4822)

Online Services at Companies

Data show share of users for March 1999.

AOL	9.6%
CompuServe	4.3
AT&T	3.6
MCI	2.7
Local providers	61.0

Source: *Wall Street Journal*, April 29, 1999, p. B4, from Ziff-Davis InfoBeads.

★ 1344 ★

Online Services (SIC 4822)

Top Internet Service Providers - 1998

Market shares are shown in percent.

America Online	42.6%
MSN	6.4

Continued on next page.

★ 1344 ★ *Continued*

Online Services (SIC 4822)

Top Internet Service Providers - 1998

Market shares are shown in percent.

AT&T WorldNet	5.0%
Regional Bells	4.3
Compuserve	4.0
Prodigy	3.2
Earthlink/Sprint Passport	3.0
IBM Global Network	2.8
GTE	2.2
Mindspring	2.2
Other	24.3

Source: *New York Times*, January 31, 1999, p. 20, from International Data Corp. and America Online.

★ 1345 ★

Online Services (SIC 4822)

Top Internet Service Providers - 1999

Market shares are estimated.

AOL/CompuServe	44.0%
AT&T WorldNet	6.0
MSN	6.0
Earthlink/Sprint	3.0
Regional bells	6.0
Cable modems	5.0
Other	30.0

Source: *Forbes*, May 3, 1999, p. 53, from International Data Corp.

★ 1346 ★

Radio Broadcasting (SIC 4832)

Canada's Radio Market - 1998

Data show share of listeners.

Adult contemporary	31.8%
News/talk	21.7
Contemporary hit radio	12.4
Album-oriented rock	7.9
Country	7.6
Classical	5.2
Fullservice	4.2
Classic rock	3.1
Gold	2.8
Others	3.3

Source: *Marketing Magazine*, August 17, 1998, p. 15, from Bohn and Associates Media.

★ 1347 ★

Radio Broadcasting (SIC 4832)

Largest Radio Groups - 1998

Companies are ranked by estimated revenues in millions of dollars.

Chancellor Media Corp.	$ 1,870.0
Infinity Broadcasting Corp.	1,660.0
Clear Channel Communications Inc.	1,118.0
ABC Radio	354.9
Cox Radio Inc.	291.9
Entercom Communications Corp.	199.3
Heftel Broadcasting Corp.	183.5
Susquehanna Radio Corp.	162.6
Emmis Communications Corp.	158.4
Citadel Communications Corp.	156.1

Source: *Chicago Tribune*, March 16, 1999, p. 1, from BIA Research.

★ 1348 ★

Radio Broadcasting (SIC 4832)

Largest Radio Media Firms - 1997

Companies are ranked by radio revenues in millions of dollars.

CBS Corp.	$ 1,187.0
Capstar Broadcasting Partners	570.0
Chancellor Media Corp.	548.9
Jacor Communications	503.4
Walt Disney Co.	450.0
Clear Channel Communications	402.9
American Radio Systems Corp.	374.1
Cox Enterprises	199.6
Sinclair Broadcast Group	66.6
Tribune Co.	65.5

Source: *Advertising Age*, August 17, 1998, p. S10.

★ 1349 ★

Radio Broadcasting (SIC 4832)

Radio Market in Buffalo/Niagara, NY

Shares are shown based on ownership.

Sinclair Communications	33.2%
Mercury Radio	32.0
Infinity Broadcasting	24.2
Palm Beach Radio	7.2
Casciani Communications	1.9
Other	1.5

Source: *Mediaweek*, April 19, 1999, p. 33, from BIA Research and Arbitron.

★ 1350 ★

Radio Broadcasting (SIC 4832)

Radio Market in Denver, CO

Shares are shown based on ownership.

Jacor Communications	42.6%
Chancellor Media Corp.	21.7
Jefferson-Pilot	16.8
Tribune Broadcasting	14.8
EXCL Communications	1.1
Other	3.0

Source: *Mediaweek*, April 26, 1999, p. 39, from BIA Research and *Duncan's Radio Market Guide, 1998.*

★ 1351 ★

Radio Broadcasting (SIC 4832)

Radio Market in Miami, FL

Shares are shown based on ownership.

Clear Channel Comm.	26.0%
Beasley Broadcasting	17.2
Heftel Broadcasting Corp.	14.6
Spanish Broadcasting System	12.0
Jefferson-Pilot	11.0
Other	19.2

Source: *Mediaweek*, April 12, 1999, p. 20, from *BIA Radio Market Report, 1999* and *Duncan's Radio Market Guide, 1998.*

★ 1352 ★

Radio Broadcasting (SIC 4832)

Radio Market in New Orleans, LA

Shares are shown based on ownership.

Clear Channel Communications	42.2%
Sinclair Communications	40.3
Centennial Broadcasting	10.0
Others	7.5

Source: *Mediaweek*, May 3, 1999, p. 44, from BIA Research and *Duncan's Radio Market Guide, 1998.*

★ 1353 ★

Radio Broadcasting (SIC 4832)

Radio Market in San Francisco, CA

Shares are shown based on ownership.

Chancellor Media	27.7%
Infinity Broadcasting	20.7
Susquehanna	19.1
ABC	12.9
Bonneville International	10.3
Other	9.3

Source: *Mediaweek*, April 5, 1999, p. 24, from BIA Research and Arbitron.

★ 1354 ★

Radio Broadcasting (SIC 4832)

Talk Radio Leaders

Data show estimated millions of weekly listeners. Figures refer to listeners 12 and older.

Dr. Laura Schlessinger	18.00
Howard Stern	17.50
Rush Limbaugh	17.25
Art Bell	8.75
Dr. Joy Browne	8.75
Don Imus	7.50

Source: *USA TODAY*, July 15, 1998, p. A1, from *Talkers.*

★ 1355 ★

Radio Broadcasting (SIC 4832)

Top Radio Stations - 1997

Owners are ranked by revenues in millions of dollars.

CBS	$ 1,529.4
Chancellor Media	996.0
Jacor Communications	602.2
Capstar Broadcasting Partners	537.7
Clear Channel Communications	452.3
ABC Radio	310.4
Cox Radio	246.9
Emmis Broadcasting	156.7
Heftel Broadcasting	155.5
Susquehanna Radio	141.4

Source: *USA TODAY*, July 7, 1998, p. 2A, from BIA Research and Duncan's American Radio.

★ 1356 ★

Radio Broadcasting (SIC 4832)

Top Radio Stations in Chicago, IL

WGN-AM
WGCI-FM
WBBM-FM
WNUA-FM
WVAZ-FM

Data show the estimated share. The market's population is 7 million.

WGN-AM	6.6%
WGCI-FM	6.4
WBBM-FM	4.8
WNUA-FM	4.2
WVAZ-FM	4.0

Source: *PR Week*, March 1, 1999, p. 19, from Arbitron.

★ 1357 ★

Radio Broadcasting (SIC 4832)

Top Radio Stations in Los Angeles, CA

Data show the estimated share. The market's population is 10 million.

KSCA-FM	6.9%
KLVE-FM	6.5
KLAX-FM	4.1
KPWR-FM	4.1
KFI-AM	3.9

Source: *PR Week*, March 1, 1999, p. 19, from Arbitron.

★ 1358 ★

Radio Broadcasting (SIC 4832)

Top Radio Stations in New York City, NY

Data show the estimated share. The market's population is 14.2 million.

WLTW-FM	5.9%
WQHT-FM	5.3
WSKQ-FM	5.2
WCBS-FM	4.7
WHTZ-FM	4.5

Source: *PR Week*, March 1, 1999, p. 19, from Arbitron.

★ 1359 ★

Radio Broadcasting (SIC 4832)

Top Radio Stations in San Francisco, CA

Data show the estimated share. The market's population is 5.6 million.

KGO-AM	7.3%
KOIT-FM	4.7
KCBS-AM	4.4
KYLD-FM	3.9
KMEL-FM	3.6

Source: *PR Week*, March 1, 1999, p. 19, from Arbitron.

★ 1360 ★
Television Broadcasting (SIC 4833)

Children's TV Leaders

Shares are shown for viewers aged 2-11 watching all children's programs.

Nickelodeon	50.0%
Cartoon Network	28.0
Fox	6.0
Fox Family	5.0
Other	11.0

Source: *New York Times*, June 17, 1999, p. C1, from Nielsen Media Research via Horizon Media.

★ 1361 ★
Television Broadcasting (SIC 4833)

English-TV Viewing in Canada - 1998

Data show share of viewing for full day in March 1998.

CTV network/baton	19.3%
WIC/CanWest Global	18.0
CBC Network plus local on O&Os	7.5
Other	50.7

Source: *Globe and Mail*, August 19, 1998, p. B1, from CBC.

★ 1362 ★
Television Broadcasting (SIC 4833)

Largest TV Groups

Data show penetration rate in the United States.

Fox Television Stations Inc.	35.3%
CBS Stations Inc.	30.8
Paxson Communications Corp.	29.2
Tribune Broadcasting	27.6
NBC	26.6
ABC Inc.	24.0
Chris Craft Television Inc./United Television Inc.	18.3
Gannett Broadcasting	16.3
Hearst Argyle Television Inc.	16.0%
USA Broadcasting	15.4

Source: *Broadcasting & Cable*, January 25, 1999, p. 44.

★ 1363 ★
Television Broadcasting (SIC 4833)

Largest TV Media Firms - 1997

Companies are ranked by television revenues in millions of dollars.

NBC TV	$ 4,803.0
Walt Disney Co.	4,122.0
CBS Corp.	3,652.0
News Corp.	2,730.0
Tribune Co.	861.0
Gannett Co.	653.1
A.H. Belo Corp.	536.7
Univision Communications	459.7
Cox Enterprises	450.0
Sinclair Broadcast Group	449.9

Source: *Advertising Age*, August 17, 1998, p. S10.

★ 1364 ★
Television Broadcasting (SIC 4833)

Popular Soap Operas

Data show the season-to-date rating for women 18-49.

General Hospital	3.4%
The Young and the Restless	3.3
All My Children	3.2
Days of Our Lives	3.2
One Life to Live	3.0
Guiding Light	2.5
The Bold and the Beautiful	2.5
As the World Turns	2.2
Port Charles	1.6
Another World	1.6
Sunset Beach	1.2

Source: *Broadcasting & Cable*, May 31, 1999, p. 23, from Nielsen Media Research.

★ 1365 ★

Television Broadcasting (SIC 4833)

Top TV Programming Spenders in Canada

Spending is shown in millions of dollars.

CBC English TV	$ 207.8
CBC French TV	146.5
Baton/CTV	147.0
WIC	84.0
CanWest Global	67.0
CHUM	25.0

Source: *Globe and Mail*, August 22, 1998, p. B5, from Canadian Association of Broadcasters and CRTC.

★ 1366 ★

Cable Broadcasting (SIC 4841)

Cable Market in Canada

Market shares are shown in percent.

Rogers	28.0%
Shaw	18.5
Videotron	16.5
Cogeco	9.0
Moffat	4.1
Fundy	2.4
Others	16.5

Source: *Globe and Mail*, July 15, 1998, p. B3, from Canadian Cable Television Association and Skyreport.com.

★ 1367 ★

Cable Broadcasting (SIC 4841)

Cable Subscribers by State

Data show millions of subscribers.

California	6.8
Florida	4.7
New York	4.6
Pennsylvania	3.5
Utah	3.5
Ohio	2.8
Illinois	2.6
New Jersey	2.3

Source: *Cablevision*, March 8, 1999, p. 50, from National Cable TV Association and Cable TV Developments.

★ 1368 ★

Cable Broadcasting (SIC 4841)

Largest Cable Media Firms - 1997

Companies are ranked by cable revenues in millions of dollars.

Time Warner	$ 10,063.0
Tele-Communications Inc.	6,429.0
MediaOne Group	2,323.0
Viacom Inc.	2,273.6
Comcast Corp.	2,073.0
Walt Disney Co.	1,950.0
Cablevision Systems Corp.	1,949.4
Cox Enterprises	1,610.4
News Corp.	1,200.0
Discovery Communications	756.0

Source: *Advertising Age*, August 17, 1998, p. S10.

★ 1369 ★

Cable Broadcasting (SIC 4841)

Largest Cable Operators - 1998

Market shares are shown based on number of total basic cable subscribers.

Time Warner Inc.	18.8%
AT&T Corp.	18.6
Comcast Corp.	16.4
Adelphia Communications Corp.	7.0
Cox Communications Inc.	5.7
Other	33.5

Source: *Chicago Tribune*, March 23, 1999, p. 1, from Hoover's and company reports.

★ 1370 ★

Cable Broadcasting (SIC 4841)

Largest Multiple System Operators

Data show millions of subscribers.

AT&T Broadband	16.20
Time Warner	12.90
Comcast	5.35
Cox	5.14
Adelphia	4.94
Charter	3.90
Cablevision	3.36
Falcon	1.11
Insight	1.04

Source: *Broadcasting & Cable*, May 24, 1999, p. 34.

★ 1371 ★

Cable Broadcasting (SIC 4841)

Top Cable Firms in Canada

Market shares are shown in percent.

Rogers	29.0%
Videotron	20.2
Shaw	18.5
Cogeco	9.0
Fundy	2.3
Videon	2.0
Access	0.9
Western	0.8
Cable Regina	0.7
Other	16.6

Source: *National Trade Data Bank*, October 23, 1998, p. ISA980901, from MediaStats.

★ 1372 ★

Cable Broadcasting (SIC 4841)

Top Cable Stations - 1998

Data show number of households.

USA	1,712
TNT	1,530
NICK	1,441
TBS	1,404
ESPN	1,217
LIFE	1,155
TOON	942
A&E	919
FAM	890
DISC	858

Source: *Broadcasting & Cable*, January 4, 1999, p. 65, from Turner Entertainment and Nielsen Media Research.

★ 1373 ★

Satellite Broadcasting (SIC 4841)

Largest Satellite Broadcasters in Canada

Shares are shown based on the small dish market.

	Units	Share
Cable	7,700,000	89.71%
Big dish	500,000	5.83
Grey market	200,000	2.33
Express Vu	93,000	1.08
Star Choice	90,000	1.05

Source: *Globe and Mail*, July 15, 1998, p. B3, from Canadian Cable Television Association and Skyreport.com.

★ 1374 ★

Satellite Broadcasting (SIC 4841)

Pay TV Market

Market shares are shown for January 1998.

DirecTV/USSB	5.8%
PrimeStar	2.9
EchoStar	2.6
SMATV	2.3
C-band	2.5
Wireless cable	1.0
Cable	82.9

Source: *Investor's Business Daily*, February 25, 1999, p. A6, from Carmel Group Inc.

★ 1375 ★

Satellite Broadcasting (SIC 4841)

Satellite Subscription Market

Data show millions of subscribers as of July 31, 1998.

Direct TV/USSB	3.86
Primestar	2.11
C-band	2.00
EchoStar	1.46

Source: "Industry Stats." Retrieved May 27, 1999 from the World Wide Web: http:// www.satbiznews.com/ jul98sat.html.

SIC 49 - Electric, Gas, and Sanitary Services

★ 1376 ★

Energy (SIC 4900)

Electricity Production

Coal	56.9%
Nuclear	20.8
Hydro	11.6
Gas	7.5
Other	3.2

Source: *New York Times*, March 6, 1999, p. B1, from Cambridge Energy Research Association, Resource Data International, and Utility Data Institute.

★ 1377 ★

Utilities (SIC 4911)

Electricity Market in Mexico - 1998

Industrial	61.0%
Residential	22.0
Commercial	7.0
Agriculture	6.0
Public services	4.0

Source: *Dallas Morning News*, March 24, 1999, p. 1D, from Mexico's Energy Ministry.

★ 1378 ★

Utilities (SIC 4911)

Largest Power Marketers

Market shares are shown in percent.

Enron Power Marketing Inc.	17.50%
Southern Co. Energy and Marketing	7.99
Dynegy	5.59
Aquila Power Corp.	5.00
Entergy Power Marketing Corp.	4.63
LG&E Energy Marketing Inc.	4.16%
Duke Energy Trading and Marketing	4.06
PacifiCorp Power Marketing	3.70
Other	47.37

Source: *Industry Week*, January 18, 1999, p. 75, from *Power Markets Week*.

★ 1379 ★

Utilities (SIC 4911)

Largest Utility Providers in Arkansas

Entergy	48.47%
Southwestern Electric Power Co.	7.45
Oklahoma Gas & Electric Co.	4.63
Municipal	11.37
Electric cooperatives	28.08

Source: *Arkansas Business*, January 18, 1999, p. 1, from Arkansas Public Service Commission.

★ 1380 ★

Refuse Systems (SIC 4950)

Largest Trash Importers

Data show millions of tons of trash received.

Pennsylvania	6.34
Virginia	2.80
Indiana	2.12
Michigan	1.69
Illinois	1.31
Wisconsin	1.16
Kansas	1.15

Source: *Christian Science Monitor*, April 28, 1999, p. 24, from *Biocycle*.

SIC 50 - Wholesale Trade - Durable Goods

★ 1381 ★

Wholesale Trade - Housing (SIC 5012)

Manufactured Housing Market

Data show shares of the wholesale market.

Champion	18.0%
Fleetwood	18.0
Skyline	5.0
Palm Harbor	4.0
American Homestar	3.0
Southern Energy	2.0
Oakwood	1.0
Other	49.0

Source: *Investext,* Thomson Financial Networks, July 14, 1998, p. 56.

★ 1382 ★

Wholesale Trade - Tires (SIC 5014)

Wholesale Tire Shipments

Independent dealers	64.0%
Mass merchandisers	18.0
Tire company stores	9.0
Wholesale club/discounters	7.0
Others	2.0

Source: *Tire Business*, December 7, 1998, p. 11.

★ 1383 ★

Wholesale Trade - Office Supplies (SIC 5044)

Office Products Industry

Data show manufacturer shipments in billions of dollars.

	($ bil.)	Share
PCs	$ 47.5	41.13%
Supplies	28.2	24.42
Machines	15.4	13.33
Furniture	9.2	7.97
Computer software	9.1	7.88
Business forms	6.1	5.28

Source: *Purchasing*, August 13, 1998, p. 85, from Business Products Industry Association.

★ 1384 ★

Wholesale Trade - Office Supplies (SIC 5044)

Office Supplies Vendors - 1997

Sales are shown in billions of dollars.

Office Depot	$ 6.72
Staples	5.18
OfficeMax	3.77
Corporate Express	3.57
U.S. Office Products	2.70
Boise Cascade Office Products	2.60
BT Office Products	1.62
Viking Office Products	1.38

Source: *Catalog Age*, May 1998, p. 36, from Brown Brothers Hartman & Co.

★ 1385 ★

Wholesale Trade - Office Supplies (SIC 5044)

Office/School Product Shipments - 1997

Office superstores	19.0%
Discount stores	15.0

Continued on next page.

★ 1385 ★ *Continued*

Wholesale Trade - Office Supplies (SIC 5044)

Office/School Product Shipments - 1997

Office product dealers	13.0%
Commercial office product wholesalers	9.0
Food stores	6.0
Specialty retailers	6.0
Drug stores	5.0
Mail order	3.0
Wholesalers/distributors to mass retail	3.0
Wholesale clubs	3.0
Office product retailers	3.0
Institutional school supply wholesalers	1.0
Other	15.0

Source: *Discount Store News*, October 26, 1998, p. 35, from School and Home Products Association.

★ 1386 ★

Wholesale Trade - Software (SIC 5045)

Largest Value Added Resellers

Companies are ranked by revenues in millions of dollars.

Ingram Micro Inc.	$ 22.08
Tech Data Corp.	11.58
CHS Electronics Inc.	8.58
Pinacor	5.08
Merisel Inc.	4.68
Synnex Information Technologies Inc.	2.48
Gates/Arrow Distributing Inc.	2.08
GE Information Technology Distribution Group	1.98

Source: *VAR Business*, May 17, 1999, p. 43.

★ 1387 ★

Wholesale Trade - Electronics (SIC 5060)

Largest Contract Manufacturing Vendors

Distributors are ranked by calendar year sales in millions of dollars.

Kent Electronics	$ 199.2
Reptron	151.4
Bell Microproducts	123.5
Coghlin	23.5
Nu Horizons	12.6

Source: *Purchasing*, May 20, 1999, p. 52.

★ 1388 ★

Wholesale Trade - Electronics (SIC 5060)

Largest Electronics Distributors

Data show revenues in billions of dollars.

Ingram Micro	$ 16.5
Arrow Electronics	7.7
Tech Data	7.0
Avnet	5.5
CHS Electronics	4.7

Source: *Electronic Business*, July 1998, p. 95.

★ 1389 ★

Wholesale Trade - Electronics (SIC 5060)

Leading Electronics Distributors

Firms are ranked by calendar year sales in millions of dollars.

Arrow Electronics Inc.	$ 5.3
Avnet Inc.	4.8
Future Electronics	2.5
VEBA Electronics	2.3
Pioneer-Standard Electronics Inc.	2.0

Source: *Purchasing*, May 20, 1999, p. 58.

★ 1390 ★

Wholesale Trade - Sporting Goods (SIC 5091)

Sporting Good Equipment Sales

Data show estimated sales in millions of dollars.

	($ mil.)	Share
Exercise machines	$ 3,100	18.18%
Golf	2,595	15.22
Camping	1,655	9.70
Water sports	490	2.87
Bowling/billiards	460	2.70
In-line skates	435	2.55
Baseball/softball	357	2.09
Archery	310	1.82
Tennis	247	1.45
Soccer	245	1.44
Other	7,160	41.98

Source: *Discount Merchandiser*, July 1998, p. 3, from Sporting Goods Manufacturers Association.

★ 1391 ★

Wholesale Trade - Drugs (SIC 5122)

Drug Distribution Industry - 1997

Shares are shown based on a $110 billion market.

McKesson	17.0%
Bergen Brunswig	12.0
Cardinal Health	12.0
AmeriSource	10.0
Direct from manufacturers	24.0
Other	25.0

Source: *Investor's Business Daily*, August 28, 1998, p. A4, from NationsBanc Montgomery Securities Inc.

★ 1392 ★

Wholesale Trade - Chemicals (SIC 5160)

Leading Chemical Distributors in North America

Sales are shown in millions of dollars.

Ashland Chemical	$ 2,650
Van Waters & Rogers	1,850
Chemcentral	875
Brenntag U.S.	773
Ellis & Everard U.S.	700
Holland Chemical	594
Chemical Logistics	366
JLM Industries	275
Great Western Chemical	250
Harcros Chemical	222

Source: *Chemical Week*, September 23, 1998, p. 42, from company reports.

★ 1393 ★

Wholesale Trade - Gasoline (SIC 5172)

Fuel Distribution Market - 1997

Direct retail	45.0%
Bulk endusers	20.0
Open dealer	20.0
Lessee dealer	10.0
Wholesalers	4.0
Other	2.0

Source: *National Petroleum News*, July 1998, p. 138, from *PMAA Marketer Profile Survey, 1998.*

★ 1394 ★

Wholesale Trade - Beverages (SIC 5180)

Largest Alcohol Wholesalers - 1999

Companies are ranked by estimated sales in billions of dollars. The top five firms have a 33.1% share of wholesaler revenues.

Southern Wine & Spirits of America	$ 2.820
Charmer Industries/Sunbelt Beverage	1.575
National Distributing Co.	1.370
Young's Market Co.	1.090
Glazer's Wholesale Distributors	1.085

Source: "Surveys and Stats." Retrieved May 9, 1999 from the World Wide Web: http:// www.just-drinks.com/ surveys_detail.asp?art54, from *Impact Newsletter*.

SIC 52 - Building Materials and Garden Supplies

★ 1395 ★

Retailing - Home Improvement (SIC 5211)

Home Renovation Spending in Canada - 1998

Spending is shown in millions of dollars. Total home renovation and repair spending was expected to grow to $17 billion in 1998. Renovation spending has taken a lead over new housing construction. This will translate to growth in the markets of building materials, hardware and housewares.

Ontario	$ 6,791
Quebec	4,143
British Columbia	2,136
Alberta	1,413
Manitoba	549
Nova Scotia	523
Saskatchewan	520
New Brunswick	333
Newfoundland	300
Prince Edward Island	71

Source: *National Trade Data Bank*, February 11, 1998, p. IMI980210, from Canadian Mortgage and Housing Corp.

★ 1396 ★

Retailing - Home Improvement (SIC 5211)

Largest Home Improvement Chains - 1997

Sales are shown in billions of dollars.

Home Depot	$ 24.1
Lowe's	10.1
Hechinger/Builders Square	4.1
Menard	3.2
Payless Cashway's	2.2
84 Lumber	1.5
Homebase	1.4
Carolina Holdings	1.3
Sears/Orchard	$ 1.2
Lanoga	0.9

Source: *Stores*, July 1998, p. S18.

★ 1397 ★

Retailing - Paint (SIC 5231)

Retail Paint/Glass/Wallpaper Sales - 1997

Distribution is shown based on total sales of $12.6 billion.

Paint/glass/wallpaper stores	43.6%
Home centers	26.6
Discount stores	15.2
Hardware stores	13.6
Variety stores	0.2
Misc. general merchandise stores	0.8

Source: *Discount Merchandiser*, July 1998, p. 53.

★ 1398 ★

Retailing - Hardware (SIC 5251)

Retail Hardware Market in Canada

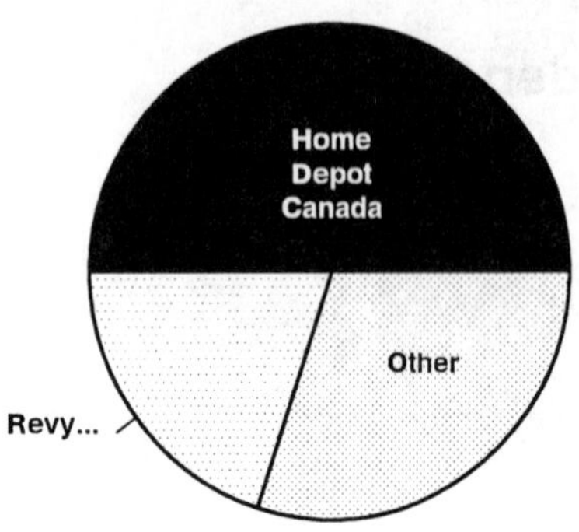

Home Depot Canada	50.0%
Revy Home and Garden	20.0
Other	30.0

Source: *National Trade Data Bank*, September 8, 1998, p. IMI980826.

★ 1399 ★

Retailing - Hardware (SIC 5251)

Retail Hardware/Tools Market - 1997

Distribution is shown based on total sales of $31.2 billion.

Hardware stores	31.5%
Home centers	26.3
Discount stores	20.3
Wholesale clubs	6.8
Department stores	3.9
Nonstore retailers	3.9
Auto/home supply stores	1.8
Other	5.5

Source: *Discount Merchandiser*, July 1998, p. 51.

★ 1400 ★

Retailing - Lawn & Garden (SIC 5261)

Retail Lawn/Garden Market - 1997

Distribution is shown based on total sales of $20.2 billion.

Garden supply stores	27.3%
Discount stores	22.3
Home centers	13.9
Florists	11.7
Hardware stores	8.0%
Non-store retailers	4.8
Supermarkets	4.2
Auto/home supply stores	2.7
Other	5.1

Source: *Discount Merchandiser*, July 1998, p. 51.

SIC 53 - General Merchandise Stores

★ 1401 ★

Retailing (SIC 5300)

Largest Retail Firms in Massachusetts - 1998

Companies are ranked by revenues in millions of dollars.

TJX Cos.	$ 7,949.1
Staples Inc.	7,123.2
BJ's Wholesale Club Inc.	3,552.2
Neiman Marcus Group Inc.	2,460.7
Talbots Inc.	1,142.2

Source: *The Boston Globe*, May 18, 1999, p. D36, from Nordby International Inc.

★ 1402 ★

Retailing (SIC 5300)

Retail Sales in Canada - 1997

Data show the leading sales categories at retail stores.

Food and beverages	24.5%
New cars	13.7
Clothing & footwear	9.6
Auto parts & access.	8.0
Home furnishings & electronics	7.1
Automotive fuels, oil	6.7
Health & personal care	6.4
Used cars	6.4
Other	17.6

Source: *Globe and Mail*, December 22, 1998, p. B15, from Statistics Canada.

★ 1403 ★

Department Stores (SIC 5311)

Largest Department Stores - 1997

Sales are shown in billions of dollars.

Sears	$ 30.7
JC Penney	19.9
Federated	15.6
May	12.3
Dillard	6.6
Montgomery Ward	5.7
Nordstrom	4.8
Proffitt's	3.5
Dayton Hudson	3.1
Mercantile	3.1

Source: *Stores*, July 1998, p. S15.

★ 1404 ★

Department Stores (SIC 5311)

Top Department Stores in Canada - 1998

Market shares are estimated in percent.

Sears	40.6%
The Bay	35.2
Eaton's	24.2

Source: *Globe and Mail*, July 15, 1998, p. B1, from CIBC Wood Gundy.

★ 1405 ★

Convenience Stores (SIC 5331)

Largest Convenience Stores

Data show number of stores.

The Southland Corp.	6,122
Mobil Oil Corp.	4,000
Tosco Corp.	3,575
Texaco Inc.	2,651
Chevron Corp.	2,437

Continued on next page.

★ 1405 ★ *Continued*

Convenience Stores (SIC 5331)

Largest Convenience Stores

Data show number of stores.

Speedway SuperAmerica	2,411
Ultramar Diamond Shamrock	2,254
Amoco Corp.	1,950
Atlantic Richfield Co.	1,682

Source: *U.S. Distribution Journal*, September/October 1998, p. 16, from *Convenience Store News*.

★ 1406 ★

Convenience Stores (SIC 5331)

Top Convenience Stores - 1999

Sales are shown in millions of dollars.

7-Eleven	$ 6,122
Mobil Mart	3,680
Circle K	3,424
76 Self Serve Mart	2,717
Chevron Food Market	2,439
Split Second	1,953
AM/PM Mini Mart	1,682
ETD/Shell Food Marts	1,590
Star Mart	1,459
Corner Store	1,404

Source: Retrieved May 28, 1999 from the World Wide Web: http:// www.c-store.com/top100.htm, from Convenience.Net C-store Database.

★ 1407 ★

Discount Merchandising (SIC 5331)

Largest Discount Store Chains

Sales are shown in billions of dollars.

Wal-Mart	$ 58.0
Kmart	27.5
Target	20.3
Dollar General	2.6
ShopKo Stores	2.5
Caldor	2.4
Ames	2.3
Family Dollar Stores	1.9
Hills Stores	1.7
Bradlees	1.3

Source: *Discount Store News*, July 13, 1998, p. 77.

SIC 54 - Food Stores

★ 1408 ★

Grocery Stores (SIC 5411)

Grocery Food Sales

Food sales are shown in billions of dollars.

Los Angeles-Long Beach, CA	$ 10.6
Chicago, IL	9.0
New York, NY	7.0
Washington D.C.	6.5
Philadelphia, PA	6.1

Source: *Sales & Marketing Management*, August 1998, p. 191.

★ 1409 ★

Grocery Stores (SIC 5411)

Grocery Store Market - 1998

Shares are shown based on total sales of the top 75 companies of $400.5 billion.

Kroger Co.	10.8%
Albertson's	8.9
Wal-Mart Supercenters	8.0
Safeway	6.2
Ahold USA	4.9
Supervalu	4.5
Fleming Cos.	3.7
Winn-Dixie Stores	3.5
Publix Super Markets	3.1
Loblaw Cos.	2.7
Other	43.7

Source: *Supermarket News*, January 25, 1999, p. 4.

★ 1410 ★

Grocery Stores (SIC 5411)

Grocery Store Market in British Columbia

Market shares are shown in percent.

Safeway	30.0%
Overwaitea	27.0
Loblaw	17.0
Other	26.0

Source: *Globe and Mail*, October 31, 1998, p. 1, from Levesque Beaubien Geoffrion and Eagle & Partners Inc.

★ 1411 ★

Grocery Stores (SIC 5411)

Grocery Store Market in Canada

Market shares are shown in percent.

Loblaw	21.0%
Oshawa Group	11.0
Provigo	11.0
Safeway	9.0
Metro-Richlieu	7.0
Sobeys	6.0
Other	35.0

Source: *Globe and Mail*, October 31, 1998, p. 1.

★ 1412 ★

Grocery Stores (SIC 5411)

Grocery Store Market in Los Angeles, CA - 1997

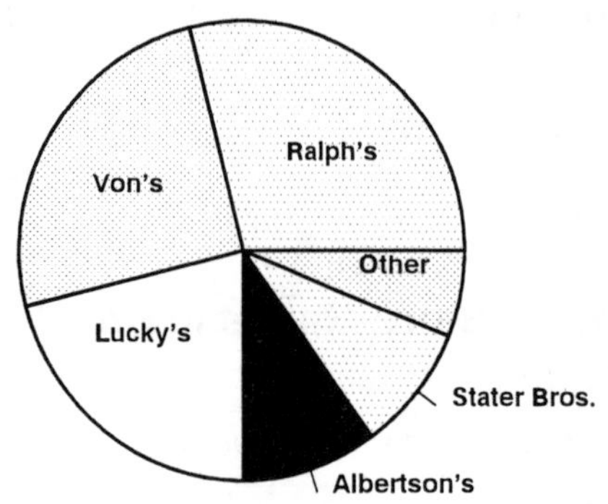

Market shares are shown in percent.

Ralph's	29.2%
Von's	25.0
Lucky's	20.8
Albertson's	9.6
Stater Bros.	9.0
Other	6.4

Source: *Beverage World*, July 1998, p. 42.

★ 1413 ★

Grocery Stores (SIC 5411)

Grocery Store Market in Ontario

Market shares are shown in percent.

Loblaw	37.0%
A&P	17.0
Oshawa	14.0
Provigo	8.0
Other	24.0

Source: *Globe and Mail*, October 31, 1998, p. 1, from Levesque Beaubien Geoffrion and Eagle & Partners Inc.

★ 1414 ★

Grocery Stores (SIC 5411)

Grocery Store Market in Quebec

Market shares are shown in percent.

Provigo	35.0%
Metro-Richelieu	34.0
Oshawa	19.0
Other	12.0

Source: *Globe and Mail*, October 31, 1998, p. 1, from Levesque Beaubien Geoffrion and Eagle & Partners Inc.

★ 1415 ★

Grocery Stores (SIC 5411)

Grocery Store Market in the Atlantic Provinces

Market shares are shown in percent.

Sobeys	41.0%
Loblaw	27.0
Oshawa	10.0
Other	22.0

Source: *Globe and Mail*, October 31, 1998, p. 1, from Levesque Beaubien Geoffrion and Eagle & Partners Inc.

★ 1416 ★

Grocery Stores (SIC 5411)

Grocery Store Market in the Prairies

Market shares are shown in percent.

Safeway	31.0%
Loblaw	25.0
Oshawa	10.0
Co-ops	19.0
Other	15.0

Source: *Globe and Mail*, October 31, 1998, p. 1, from Levesque Beaubien Geoffrion and Eagle & Partners Inc.

★ 1417 ★

Grocery Stores (SIC 5411)

Grocery Store Sales - 1997

The industry is shown by segment.

	($ mil.)	Share
Chain supermarkets	$ 262.0	60.05%
Independent supermarkets	72.5	16.62
Convenience stores	27.4	6.28
Wholesale club stores	20.3	4.65
Small stores/other	54.1	12.40

Source: *Chicago Tribune*, February 17, 1999, p. 1, from Food Marketing Institute.

★ 1418 ★

Grocery Stores (SIC 5411)

Health Food Sales - 1997

Natural food supermarkets	43.0%
Health food chains	20.0
Natural food stores	19.0
Health food stores	12.0
Natural food cooperatives	6.0

Source: *U.S. Distribution Journal*, September 1998, p. 76, from Packaged Facts.

★ 1419 ★

Grocery Stores (SIC 5411)

Largest Grocers in Baltimore, MD

Market shares are shown in percent.

Giant Food Inc.	29.3%
Metro Food Markets	9.1
Safeway	8.2
Super Fresh Stores	8.0
Mars Super Markets Inc.	5.6
Valu Food Inc.	3.6
Other	36.2

Source: *Baltimore Business Journal*, November 16, 1998, p. 1, from *Food World*.

★ 1420 ★

Grocery Stores (SIC 5411)

Largest Grocers in Boston, MA

Market shares are shown in percent.

Ahold	27.0%
De Moulas	15.0
Star Markets/Market	15.0
Hanna-Shaw's	11.0
Ford	2.0
Other	30.0

Source: *Investext*, Thomson Financial Networks, December 1, 1998, p. 3, from *Metro Market Study, 1997.*

★ 1421 ★

Grocery Stores (SIC 5411)

Largest Grocers in Chattanooga, TN

Market shares are shown in percent.

Bi-Lo	31.0%
Food Lion	12.5
Wal-Mart	10.5
Winn-Dixie	9.0
Fleming	6.5
Other	30.5

Source: Retrieved April 30, 1999 from the World Wide Web: http:// www.foodpeople.com/Market%20Share/ market.htm, from Food People Research Department.

★ 1422 ★

Grocery Stores (SIC 5411)

Largest Grocers in Columbus, OH

Market shares are shown in percent.

Kroger	54.0%
Big Bear	20.0
Other	26.0

Source: *Forbes*, April 5, 1999, p. 123, from *Columbus Dispatch*.

★ 1423 ★

Grocery Stores (SIC 5411)

Largest Grocers in Knoxville, TN

Market shares are shown in percent.

Kroger	26.0%
Mid Mountain Foods	21.5
Wal-Mart	10.5
Food Lion	9.5
Ingles	8.0
Other	25.5

Source: Retrieved April 30, 1999 from the World Wide Web: http:// www.foodpeople.com/Market%20Share/ market.htm, from Food People Research Department.

★ 1424 ★

Grocery Stores (SIC 5411)

Largest Grocers in Mexico - 1997

Data show number of outlets.

Cifra	372
Gigante	192
Comerical Mexicana	147
Casa Ley	72
Soriana	53
Chedraul	27

Source: *Traffic World*, August 31, 1998, p. 36, from Sistemas Agroindustriales en Mexico.

★ 1425 ★

Grocery Stores (SIC 5411)

Largest Grocers in Providence, RI

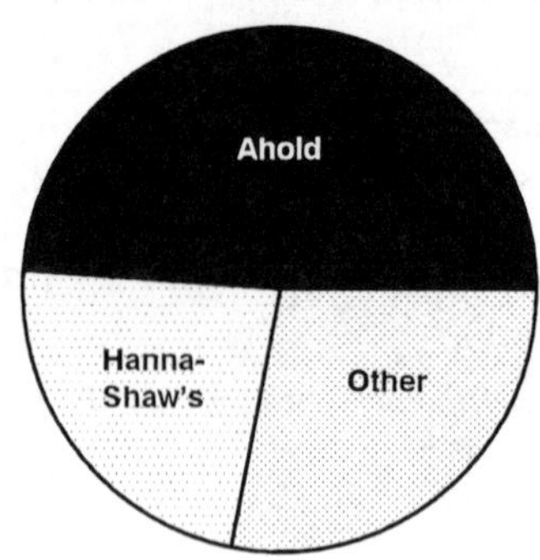

Market shares are shown in percent.

Ahold	49.0%
Hanna-Shaw's	23.0
Other	28.0

Source: *Investext,* Thomson Financial Networks, December 1, 1998, p. 3, from *Metro Market Study, 1997.*

★ 1426 ★

Grocery Stores (SIC 5411)

Largest Grocers in Tacoma, WA

Market shares are shown in percent.

Safeway	27.1%
Piggly Wiggly	17.6
Albertson's	13.3
Fred Meyer	11.8
Other	30.2

Source: *Investext,* Thomson Financial Networks, September 3, 1998, p. 11, from *Market Scope.*

★ 1427 ★

Grocery Stores (SIC 5411)

Largest Grocers in Worcester, MA

Market shares are shown in percent.

Hanna-Shaw's	17.0%
Ahold	10.0
De Moulas Basket	7.0
Ford	4.0
Star Markets/Market	2.0
Otehr	60.0

Source: *Investext,* Thomson Financial Networks, December 1, 1998, p. 3, from *Metro Market Study, 1997.*

★ 1428 ★

Grocery Stores (SIC 5411)

Top Grocery Chains in Atlanta, GA

Market shares are shown in percent.

Kroger	32.78%
Publix	19.26
Winn-Dixie	9.75
Ingles	7.02
Super Discount (Cub)	6.43
A&P	5.43
Wal-Mart	3.74
Harry's	3.01
Harris Teeter	1.73
All American Quality	1.40
Other	9.45

Source: *Atlanta Journal-Constitution*, April 27, 1999, p. D1, from Shelby Report/Trade Dimensions.

★ 1429 ★

Grocery Stores (SIC 5411)

Top Grocery Stores in Arkansas

Affiliated Foods Southwest
Kroger
Associated Wholesale Grocery
Fleming Co.
Wal-Mart Stores
Other

Market shares are shown in percent.

Affiliated Foods Southwest	45.0%
Kroger	20.0
Associated Wholesale Grocery	11.0
Fleming Co.	11.0
Wal-Mart Stores	10.0
Other	3.0

Source: *Arkansas Business*, August 31, 1998, p. 13, from *Food People*.

★ 1430 ★

Grocery Stores (SIC 5411)

Top Grocery Stores in Chicago, IL - 1997

Market shares are shown in percent.

Jewel Food Stores	35.4%
Dominick's	26.7
Club Foods	4.0
Eagle Food Centers	3.6
Aldi	1.4
Other	28.9

Source: *Chicago Tribune*, October 14, 1998, p. A1, from Dominick's, Food Marketing Institute, *Progressive Grocer*, and Reuters.

★ 1431 ★

Retailing - Food (SIC 5411)

Canada's Food Store Sales - 1997

Ontario	31.5%
Quebec	26.0
British Columbia	14.8
Alberta	11.1
Other	16.6

Source: Retrieved April 30, 1999 from the World Wide Web: http:// www.thomaslargesinger.com/ TLS_CdnMkt.html, from *Canadian Grocer.*

★ 1432 ★

Retailing - Food (SIC 5411)

Wet Soup Sales by Channel

Food stores	94.0%
Mass	4.8
Drug	1.2

Source: *Supermarket Business*, October 1998, p. 24, from Information Resources Inc.

★ 1433 ★

Retailing - Snacks (SIC 5411)

Potato Chip Sales - 1997

Total sales reached $160.5 million.

Supermarkets	46.0%
Convenience stores	13.5
Mass merchandisers	9.2
Grocery stores	8.8
Warehouse clubs	4.9
Drug stores	3.9
Other	8.3

Source: *Discount Merchandiser*, October 1998, p. 3, from Snack Food Association.

★ 1434 ★

Retailing - Confectionery (SIC 5441)

Retail Confectionery Sales - 1996

Food	19.0%
C-store	15.0
Mass	12.0
Vending	11.0
Drug	10.0
Ind. drug and grocery	8.0
Manufact. retailers	5.0

Source: *The Manufacturing Confectioner*, June 1998, p. 61.

SIC 55 - Automotive Dealers and Service Stations

★ 1435 ★

Retailing - Autos (SIC 5511)

Largest Auto Dealers - 1998

Dealers are ranked by unit sales of new vehicles.

AutoNation Inc.	286,179
United Auto Group Inc.	77,403
Asbury Automotive Group	68,000
V.T. Inc.	64,296
Hendrick Automotive Group	56,667
Group 1 Automotive Inc.	39,822
Sonic Automotive Inc.	37,674
Planet Automotive	37,000
Bill Heard Enterprises Inc.	27,895
Penske Automotive Group	24,514

Source: *Automotive News*, April 19, 1999, p. 34.

★ 1436 ★

Retailing - Autos (SIC 5511)

Leading Auto Dealers in Detroit, MI - 1998

Companies are ranked by revenues in millions of dollars.

Don Massey Cadillac Group	$ 979.9
Mel Farr Automotive Group	588.1
Troy Motors Inc.	437.9
The Suburban Collection	374.0
Tamaroff Automotive Group	284.0

Source: *Crain's Detroit Business*, May 10, 1999, p. 16.

★ 1437 ★

Aftermarket Services (SIC 5531)

Aftermarket Sales - 1997

The motor vehicle aftermarket has been estimated at $249 billion. PBE stands for paint, body & engineering.

Automotive	77.56%
PBE	16.31
Tool & equipment	3.58
Trim	2.56

Source: *Aftermarket Business*, July 1, 1998, p. 1, from Automotive Service Industry Association.

★ 1438 ★

Aftermarket Services (SIC 5531)

Auto Aftermarket in North America - 2002

The estimated $51.1 billion market is shown in percent.

Mechanical	41.49%
Tires	19.96
Electronic	16.63
Electrical	16.05
Other	5.87

Source: *Assembly*, April 1999, p. 11, from Freedonia Group.

★ 1439 ★

Aftermarket Services (SIC 5531)

Auto Battery Sales

Market shares are shown in percent.

Automotive chains	56.0%
Discount store chains	34.0
Department store chains	9.0
Non-automotive chains	1.0

Source: *Aftermarket Business*, April 1999, p. 44.

★ 1440 ★

Aftermarket Services (SIC 5531)

Auto Brake Sales

Market shares are shown in percent.

Automotive chains	73.0%
Discount store chains	16.0
Department stores	10.0
Non-automotive chains	1.0

Source: *Aftermarket Business*, April 1999, p. 44.

★ 1441 ★

Aftermarket Services (SIC 5531)

Auto Cleaning Cloth Sales

Market shares are shown in percent.

Automotive chains	40.0%
Discount store chains	38.0
Department store chains	12.0
Non-automotive chains	10.0

Source: *Aftermarket Business*, April 1999, p. 48.

★ 1442 ★

Aftermarket Services (SIC 5531)

Auto Cleaning Product Sales

Market shares are shown in percent.

Automotive chains	58.0%
Discount store chains	38.0
Department store chains	2.0
Non-automotive chains	2.0

Source: *Aftermarket Business*, April 1999, p. 42.

★ 1443 ★

Aftermarket Services (SIC 5531)

Car Cover Sales

Market shares are shown in percent.

Automotive chains	80.0%
Discount store chains	14.0
Department store chains	4.0
Non-automotive chains	2.0

Source: *Aftermarket Business*, April 1999, p. 46.

★ 1444 ★

Aftermarket Services (SIC 5531)

Engine Treatment Sales

Market shares are shown in percent.

Automotive chains	52.0%
Discount store chains	43.0
Department store chains	3.0
Non-automotive chains	2.0

Source: *Aftermarket Business*, April 1999, p. 50.

★ 1445 ★

Retailing - Auto Parts (SIC 5531)

Largest Auto Parts Chains

Data show number of stores.

AutoZone Inc.	2,657
General Parts Inc./CARQUEST	990
CSK Auto Corporation	773
Genuine Parts/NAPA	750

Source: *Aftermarket Business*, January 1999, p. 22.

★ 1446 ★

Retailing - Tires (SIC 5531)

Tire Sales Outlets by State - 1998

	No.	Share
California	3,785	9.69%
Texas	3,037	7.77
Florida	2,250	5.76
Pennsylvania	1,635	4.18
North Carolina	1,560	3.99
New York	1,554	3.98
Ohio	1,547	3.96
Georgia	1,424	3.64
Illinois	1,294	3.31

Continued on next page.

★ 1446 ★ *Continued*

Retailing - Tires (SIC 5531)

Tire Sales Outlets by State - 1998

	No.	Share
Michigan	1,090	2.79%
Other	19,905	50.93

Source: *Tire Business*, December 7, 1998, p. 13, from American Business Directories and R.L. Polk Co.

★ 1447 ★

Retailing - Tires (SIC 5531)

Top Independent Tire Retailers - 1997

Companies are ranked by sales in millions of dollars. Figures are for North America.

Tire Centers Inc.	$ 305
Kal Tire	200
Les Schwab Tire Centers Inc.	140
Treadco Inc.	128
Purcell Tire & Rubber Co.	110
Bauer Built Inc.	75
Pomp's Tire Service Inc.	74

Source: *Tire Business*, December 7, 1998, p. 22.

★ 1448 ★

Retailing - Tires (SIC 5531)

Top Tire Dealerships - 1997

Companies are ranked by number of outlets.

Penske Auto Centers	790
Discount Tire Co.	380
Heafner Group	210
Les Schwab Tire Centers	202
Morgan Tire & Auto	181

Source: *Tire Business*, December 7, 1998, p. 22.

★ 1449 ★

Retailing - Tires (SIC 5531)

Top Tire Dealerships by Sales - 1997

Companies are ranked by retail sales in millions of dollars.

Discount Tire Co.	$ 864.0
Les Schwab Tire	588.3
Penske Auto Centers	300.0
Tire Kingdom	207.0
Merchant's Inc.	170.0

Source: *Tire Business*, December 7, 1998, p. 22.

★ 1450 ★

Retailing - Tires (SIC 5531)

Top Tire Retailers - 1997

Companies are ranked by sales in millions of dollars. Figures are based on tires, wheels and auto service.

Sears/NTB	$ 2,500
Bridgestone/Firestone	1,855
Discount Tire	864
Goodyear	840
Wal-Mart/Sam's Club	750
Les Schwab network	712
Pep Boys	607
Big O Network	500

Source: *Tire Business*, December 7, 1998, p. 22.

★ 1451 ★

Gas Stations (SIC 5541)

Gas Station Market

Data show share of all stations.

Exxon	8.7%
Citgo	8.2
Star Enterprises	5.1
Amoco	5.0
Shell	4.7
Chevron	4.2
BP	3.7
Phillips	3.6
Other	57.8

Source: *New York Times*, December 3, 1998, p. C6, from *National Petroleum News* via Energy Information Administration.

★ 1452 ★

Gas Stations (SIC 5541)

Gas Station Market in Canada - 1998

Market shares are shown in percent for the year ended December 31, 1998.

Eso (Imperial Oil)	20.0%
Petro-Canada	19.3
Shell	16.9
Ultramar	5.9
Sunoco	5.2
Canadian Tire	4.4
Chevron	3.4
Mohawk	2.2
Pioneer	2.0
Irving Oil	1.8
Others	18.9

Source: "Report on Market Share." Retrieved June 1, 1999 from the World Wide Web: http://www.marketingmag.ca/index.cgi?, from *Canadian Petroleum Products Institute*.

★ 1453 ★

Gas Stations (SIC 5541)

Gas Stations by State - 1998

There were a total of 182,596 gas stations in 1998.

	No.	Share
Texas	15,074	8.21%
California	11,258	6.13
Florida	9,024	4.92
North Carolina	7,816	4.26
Louisiana	7,424	4.04
Georgia	7,356	4.01
New York	6,374	3.47
Other	119,270	64.96

Source: *National Petroleum News*, July 1998, p. 124.

★ 1454 ★

Gas Stations (SIC 5541)

Largest Gas Outlets in Canada - 1997

Data show number of outlets.

	No.	Share
Imperial Oil	2,634	22.86%
Shell Canada	1,867	16.20
Petro-Canada	1,862	16.16
Ultramar Canada	1,295	11.24
Olco Petroleum	442	3.84
Federated Co-ops	362	3.14%
Fas Gas Oil Ltd.	348	3.02
Tempo	307	2.66
Other	2,406	20.88

Source: *National Petroleum News*, July 1998, p. 84, from *Octane*.

SIC 56 - Apparel and Accessory Stores

★ 1455 ★

Retailing - Apparel (SIC 5611)

Boy's Apparel Sales - 1998

Sales are shown for the first nine months of the year.

Discount stores	38.92%
Mid-tier stores	23.86
Department stores	11.81
Off-price	7.26
Factory outlets	5.65
Other	12.50

Source: *Discount Store News*, December 14, 1998, p. A44, from NPD Group Inc.

★ 1456 ★

Retailing - Apparel (SIC 5611)

Canada's Leading Apparel Stores for Men - 1997

Stores are ranked by market penetration.

Zellers	29.0%
Sears	26.0
Wal-Mart	22.0
Bay	19.0
Mark's Work Wearhouse	19.0
Eaton's	14.0
Kmart	14.0

Source: *Marketing Magazine*, May 12, 1999, p. 12, from *J.C. Williams Group of Toronto's National Retail Report, 1997.*

★ 1457 ★

Retailing - Apparel (SIC 5611)

Men's and Boy's Apparel Market - 1997

Distribution is shown based on total sales of $62.47 billion.

Department stores	29.8%
Discount stores	23.9
Family apparel stores	14.9
Men's and boy's wear stores	13.7
Off-price apparel stores	5.7
Non-store retailers	4.8
Sporting goods stores	3.4
Other	3.8

Source: *Discount Merchandiser*, July 1998, p. 50.

★ 1458 ★

Retailing - Apparel (SIC 5611)

Men's Dress Clothing Sales - 1997

Sales are shown in percent. Wal-Mart is the leading retailer for men's athletic and casual apparel.

JC Penney	17.0%
Sears	7.4
Wal-Mart	6.1
Kmart	2.5
Target	0.9
Dept. stores	22.3
Apparel specialty stores	8.2
Off-price	6.1
Upscale dept. stores	5.5
Factory outlet	5.1
Mail order	3.0

Source: *DNR*, September 14, 1998, p. 6, from Consumer Database Management Horizons.

★ 1459 ★

Retailing - Apparel (SIC 5611)

Men's Suit Market

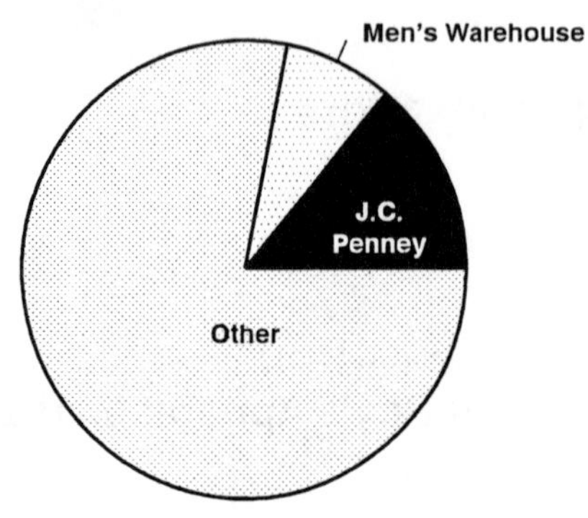

The market is highly fragmented.

J.C. Penney	14.0%
Men's Warehouse	8.0
Other	78.0

Source: *Advertising Age*, August 10, 1998, p. 4.

★ 1460 ★

Retailing - Apparel (SIC 5621)

Canada's Leading Apparel Stores for Women - 1997

Stores are ranked by market penetration.

Zellers	33.0%
Sears	29.0
Wal-Mart	24.0
Bay	21.0
Eaton's	17.0
Kmart	16.0
Reitman's	14.0
Suzy Shier	12.0

Source: *Marketing Magazine*, May 12, 1999, p. 12, from *J.C. Williams Group of Toronto's National Retail Report, 1997.*

★ 1461 ★

Retailing - Apparel (SIC 5621)

Plus-Sized Women's Apparel Market - 1998

The top brands include Just My Size, Faded Glory, White Stag and Bobbie Brooks.

J.C. Penney	8.1%
Lane Bryant	7.7
Wal-Mart	7.6
Kmart	4.8
Target	2.5
Other	69.3

Source: *Discount Merchandiser*, September 1998, p. 84, from NPD Group Inc.

★ 1462 ★

Retailing - Apparel (SIC 5632)

Intimate Apparel Sales - 1998

Sales are shown for the first nine months of the year.

Discount stores	28.50%
Specialty stores	18.50
Mid-tier stores	17.47
Department stores	17.31
Factory outlets	5.71
Off-price	3.76
Other	8.76

Source: *Discount Store News*, December 14, 1998, p. A44, from NPD Group Inc.

★ 1463 ★

Retailing - Apparel (SIC 5632)

Retail Apparel Sales in Canada

	1996	1997
Specialty stores	42.6%	41.2%
Department stores	24.4	26.1
Discount stores	22.6	22.5
Other	10.5	10.2

Source: *National Trade Data Bank*, August 20, 1998, p. IMI980819.

★ 1464 ★

Retailing - Apparel (SIC 5632)

Retail Hosiery Sales - 1998

Sales are shown by outlet.

Discount stores	36.8%
Chain stores	11.4
Department stores	9.9
Specialty stores	9.6
Food and drug	8.0
Factory outlets	6.3
Direct mail	5.4
Off price	5.2
Other	7.3

Source: *Discount Merchandiser*, January 1999, p. 98, from NPD American Shoppers Panel.

★ 1465 ★

Retailing - Apparel (SIC 5632)

Retail Pantyhose Sales - 1997

Dollar shares are shown in percent.

Mass	43.6%
Supermarkets	32.4
Drugstores	24.0

Source: *Progressive Grocer*, August 1998, p. 38, from Information Resources Inc.

★ 1466 ★

Retailing - Apparel (SIC 5632)

Sheer Hosiery Sales - 1998

Sales are shown by outlet.

Food and drug	21.4%
Discount stores	19.1
Department stores	13.8
Direct mail	10.7
Factory outlets	9.7%
Chain stores	9.7
Specialty stores	9.3
Other	16.3

Source: *Discount Merchandiser*, January 1999, p. 98, from NPD American Shoppers Panel.

★ 1467 ★

Retailing - Apparel (SIC 5632)

Women's Apparel Sales - 1997

Sales are shown by channel.

Department stores	21.0%
Specialty chains	18.0
Discount	16.0
Chains	15.0
Specialty stores	8.0
Direct mail	7.0
Off-pricers	6.0
Factory outlets	3.0
Other	5.0

Source: *Women's Wear Daily*, August 5, 1998, p. 28.

★ 1468 ★

Retailing - Apparel (SIC 5641)

Infant's Apparel Market - 1997

Distribution is shown based on total sales of $11.2 billion.

Discount stores	37.4%
Department stores	36.8
Children's/Infant's wear stores	13.1
Family apparel stores	8.2
Women's ready-to-wear stores	4.5

Source: *Discount Merchandiser*, July 1998, p. 50.

★ 1469 ★

Retailing - Apparel (SIC 5641)

Leading Children's Retailers in Canada - 1997

Figures are based on a survey.

Zeller's	48.0%
Wal-Mart	40.0
Sears	32.0
Kmart	22.0
The Bay	17.0

Source: *Discount Merchandiser*, August 1998, p. 116, from *J.C. Williams Group National Retail Report, 1998.*

★ 1470 ★

Retailing - Apparel (SIC 5641)

Retail Apparel Sales

Discount stores	36.0%
Chain	25.0
Specialty	20.0
Dept. stores	7.0
Off-price	4.0
Other	9.0

Source: *Discount Merchandiser*, April 1999, p. 120.

★ 1471 ★

Retailing - Apparel (SIC 5641)

Retail Jeans Sales - 1998

Sales are shown for the first nine months of the year.

Discount stores	27.28%
Specialty stores	23.74
Mid-tier stores	23.70
Department stores	10.55
Factory outlets	4.57
Off-price	3.39
Other	6.76

Source: *Discount Store News*, December 14, 1998, p. A44, from NPD Group Inc.

★ 1472 ★

Discount Merchandising (SIC 5651)

Largest Off-Price Apparel Chains

Sales are shown in billions of dollars.

T.J. Maxx	$ 3,549
Marshalls	3,265
Ross Stores	1,989
Burlington Coat Factory	1,777
Goody's Family Clothing	972
Kids R Us	795
Stein Mart	793
The Men's Warehouse	631
Dress Barn	555
Filene's Basement	554

Source: *Discount Store News*, July 13, 1998, p. 83.

★ 1473 ★

Retailing - Apparel (SIC 5651)

Retail Sports Apparel Sales - 1997

Data show estimated sales.

Discount stores	26.5%
Chains	15.2
Sporting goods	14.7
Department stores	12.6
Specialty stores	9.3
Other	21.7

Source: *Discount Merchandiser*, July 1998, p. 3, from Sporting Goods Manufacturers Association Sports Apparel Index by NPD.

★ 1474 ★

Retailing - Footwear (SIC 5661)

Largest Footwear Retailers - 1998

Data show estimated sales in millions of dollars.

Foot Locker	$ 2,670
Just For Feet	700
Footaction	658
The Finish Line	568
The Athlete's Foot	490

Source: *Sporting Goods Business*, May 15, 1998, p. 35.

★ 1475 ★

Retailing - Footwear (SIC 5661)

Top Sports Shoe Retailers - 1998

Market shares are shown in percent.

Athlete's Foot	5.6%
Jumbo Sports	3.0
MC Sports	1.9
Sport Chalet	1.3
Other	88.2

Source: *New York Times*, May 10, 1999, p. C4, from Global Sports.

SIC 57 - Furniture and Homefurnishings Stores

★ 1476 ★

Retailing - Furniture (SIC 5712)

Baby Furniture Sales

Data show where people shop for furniture, based on a survey.

Mass merchants	38.0%
Mid-ranged priced dept. stores	37.0
Toy stores	27.0
Infant/child specialty stores	26.0
Baby warehouses/chain	25.0
Catalog stores/showrooms	22.0
Warehouse/membership clubs	6.0

Source: *Discount Merchandiser*, October 1998, p. 46, from Bruno and Ridgeway Research Associates for *American Baby*.

★ 1477 ★

Retailing - Furniture (SIC 5712)

Canada's Furniture Sales

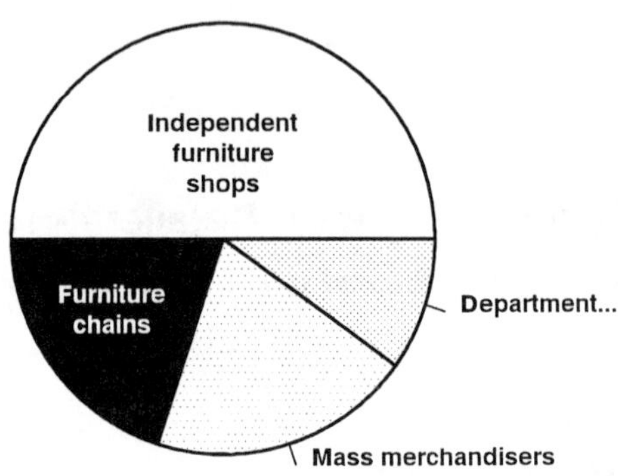

There are more than 1,500 retail stores that sell furniture in Canada. Sales are shown in percent.

Independent furniture shops	50.0%
Furniture chains	20.0
Mass merchandisers	20.0
Department stores	10.0

Source: *National Trade Data Bank*, May 18, 1998, p. ISA990301.

★ 1478 ★

Retailing - Furniture (SIC 5712)

Furniture Sales at Discount Stores

Distribution is shown based on total sales of $5.55 billion.

Office	15.50%
Juvenile	12.79
Living room	10.81
Dining	9.55
Entertainment	9.55
Decorative/accessories	6.49
Bedroom	3.24
Other	32.07

Source: *Discount Store News*, August 10, 1998, p. 72.

★ 1479 ★

Retailing - Furniture (SIC 5712)

Largest Furniture Retailers - 1997

Sales are shown in millions of dollars. Figures include furniture and bedding.

Heilig-Meyers	$ 1,693.9
Levitz	839.1
Office Depot	779.2
J.C. Penney	747.0
Federated Department Stores	742.9
Sears	737.0
Ethan Allen	735.9
Wal-Mart	673.0
Rooms To Go	549.9
Montgomery Ward	547.3

Source: *Furniture Today Retail Planning Guide*, 1999, p. 56.

★ 1480 ★

Retailing - Furniture (SIC 5712)

Largest Furniture Stores in the South - 1997

Rooms To Go
W.S. Babcock
Finger Furniture
Furnitureland South
Kane's Furniture

Sales are shown in millions of dollars.

Rooms To Go	$ 585.0
W.S. Babcock	289.5
Finger Furniture	150.8
Furnitureland South	127.0
Kane's Furniture	101.5

Source: *Furniture Today Retail Planning Guide*, 1999, p. 54.

★ 1481 ★

Retailing - Furniture (SIC 5712)

Leading Furniture Retailers - 1997

Market shares are shown in percent.

MFI	9.4%
DFS	3.5
Magnet	3.1
Argos	2.8
IKEA	2.6%
Courts	2.5
John Lewis	2.2
Limelight	2.1
Harveys	1.7
M&S	1.2
Other	68.9

Source: *Investext,* Thomson Financial Networks, October 13, 1998, p. 7, from Verdict Research.

★ 1482 ★

Retailing - Floor Coverings (SIC 5713)

Largest Floor Covering Retailers - 1997

Companies are ranked by revenues in millions of dollars. The top 10 companies cover 63% of the market.

Carpet One	$ 2,000
Home Depot	1,300
The Maxim Group	1,200
Abbey Carpet	700
Shaw Industries	600
Sears	365
Lowe's Cos.	300
Sherwin-Williams	200
Hechinger/Builders Square	150
Federated	125

Source: *HFN*, July 20, 1998, p. 35.

★ 1483 ★

Retailing - Homefurnishings (SIC 5719)

Homefurnishing Sales - 1997

Total sales reached $10.9 billion.

Bedding	21.00%
Sewing goods/fabrics	12.28
Bed covers	12.17
Bath goods	11.55
Shades/blinds	9.27
Yarns	7.91
Draperies	5.00
Curtains	4.68
Rugs	4.22

Source: *Discount Merchandiser*, June 1998, p. 50.

★ 1484 ★

Retailing - Homefurnishings (SIC 5719)

Largest Houseware Retailers - 1997

Companies are ranked by revenues in millions of dollars. The top 25 retailers account for approximately 66% of the $37.1 billion total housewares market.

Wal-Mart	$ 6,226.6
Kmart	2,719.4
Costco Wholesale	1,890.0
Sam's Club	1,777.4
Target	1,700.0
Sears	1,362.8
Service Merchandise	879.1
Williams-Sonoma	840.0
CVS	823.5

Source: *HFN*, July 20, 1998, p. 65.

★ 1485 ★

Retailing - Homefurnishings (SIC 5719)

Largest Tabletop Retailers - 1997

Companies are ranked by revenues in millions of dollars. The top 25 retailers had sales of $1.346 billion.

Service Merchandise	$ 116.0
Macy's West	114.0
Macy's East	109.2
Ross-Simons	95.0
Dayton-Hudson	78.6

Source: *HFN*, July 20, 1998, p. 65.

★ 1486 ★

Retailing - Homefurnishings (SIC 5719)

Largest Textile Retailers - 1997

Companies are ranked by revenues in millions of dollars.

J.C. Penney	$ 3,161.4
Wal-Mart	2,019.2
Kmart	1,582.7
Target	1,218.5
Sears	809.3
Bed Bath & Beyond	586.6
Mervyn's	410.3
Linens 'N Things	488.7
T.J. Maxx/Marshalls	$ 378.9
Spiegel	295.0

Source: *HFN*, July 20, 1998, p. 35.

★ 1487 ★

Retailing - Homefurnishings (SIC 5719)

Retail Dinnerware Sales - 1997

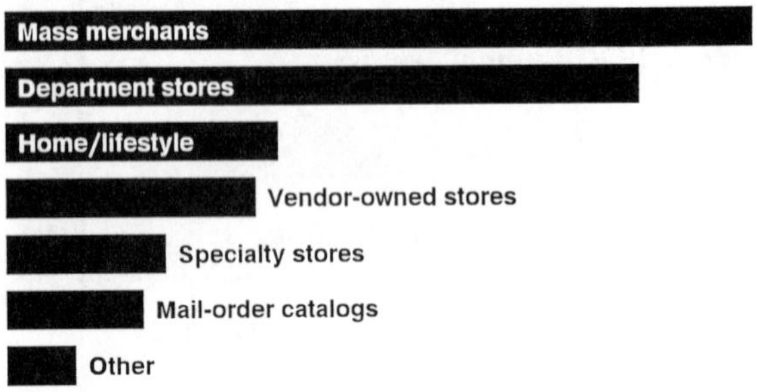

Mass merchants	33.0%
Department stores	28.0
Home/lifestyle	12.0
Vendor-owned stores	11.0
Specialty stores	7.0
Mail-order catalogs	6.0
Other	3.0

Source: *HFN*, September 14, 1998, p. 6.

★ 1488 ★

Retailing - Appliances (SIC 5722)

Largest Appliance Stores - 1997

Companies are ranked by revenues in millions of dollars.

Sears	$ 5,100.0
Circuit City	1,199.5
Best Buy	756.0
Montgomery Ward	643.7
Lowe's	611.0
Wal-Mart	386.0
Costco	270.0
P.C. Richard & Son	230.0

Source: *HFN*, July 20, 1998, p. 84.

★ 1489 ★

Retailing - Appliances (SIC 5722)

Retail Small Appliance Sales - 1997

Distribution is shown based on total sales of $11.2 billion.

Discount stores	37.7%
Wholesale clubs	15.8
Drug/proprietary stores	13.3
Department stores	11.6
Misc. general merchandise stores	4.6
Catalog showrooms	3.8
Supermarkets	3.8
Other	9.4

Source: *Discount Merchandiser*, July 1998, p. 51.

★ 1490 ★

Retailing - Electronics (SIC 5731)

Top Electronics Stores - 1997

The consumer electronics industry was valued at $72 billion.

Best Buy	10.5%
Circuit City	9.4
CompUSA	7.0
Radio Shack	4.4
Sears	4.4
Other	64.3

Source: *New York Times*, March 8, 1999, p. C6, from *Twice* and Consumer Electronics Manufacturers Association.

★ 1491 ★

Retailing - Computers (SIC 5734)

Largest Computer Hardware Retailers - 1998

Companies are ranked by sales in millions of dollars. Total hardware business for the top 100 firms reached $24.8 billion.

CompUSA	$ 3,586.0
Best Buy	3,179.8
Circuit City Stores	1,950.0
Micro Warehouse	1,884.3
CDW Computer Centers	1,395.0

Source: Retrieved May 31, 1999 from the World Wide Web: http:// www.crw.com/reports/1998/ 231topsoftware1.asp, from *Computer Retail Week*.

★ 1492 ★

Retailing - Computers (SIC 5734)

Largest Computer Vendors - 1998

Sales are estimated in millions of dollars.

CompUSA	$ 5,750.0
Best Buy	3,935.0
Office Depot	2,900.0
Micro Warehouse	2,324.0
Circuit City	2,081.5
Staples	1,910.0
CDW Computer Centers	1,675.0

Source: *Discount Merchandiser*, May 1999, p. 90, from *Computer Retail Week*.

★ 1493 ★

Retailing - Software (SIC 5734)

Largest Software Retailers - 1998

Companies are ranked by sales in millions of dollars. Total software business reached $4.6 billion.

CompUSA	$ 1,100.0
Best Buy	548.6
Wal-Mart Stores	315.0
Micro Warehouse	293.1
Office Depot	280.0

Source: Retrieved May 31, 1999 from the World Wide Web: http:// www.crw.com/reports/1998/ 231topsoftware1.asp, from *Computer Retail Week*.

★ 1494 ★

Retailing - Software (SIC 5734)

Software Distribution in Mexico

Data show distribution channels.

Wholesalers	36.0%
Developers/consultants	34.0
Direct sale	17.0
Distributors/value added resellers	10.0
OEMs	2.0
Other	1.0

Source: *National Trade Data Bank*, October 23, 1998, p. ISA980901.

★ 1495 ★

Retailing - Music (SIC 5735)

Music Sales by Channel - 1997

Record stores	51.8%
Tape and record clubs	11.6
Mail order	2.7
Internet	0.3
Other stores	31.9

Source: *New York Times*, February 1, 1999, p. C6, from Audit Bureau of Circulations.

★ 1496 ★

Retailing - Music (SIC 5735)

Music Sales Leaders in Canada - 1998

Market shares are shown in percent for the year ended December 31, 1998.

HMV	19.4%
Music World	11.0
A&B Sound	6.1
Future Shop	4.2
Archambault Musique	4.1
Sam the Record Man	3.9
Virgin Megsatore	1.0
Record clubs	16.7
Other music specialty stores	16.3
Others	1.4

Source: "Report on Market Share." Retrieved June 1, 1999 from the World Wide Web: http://www.marketingmag.ca/index.cgi?, from HMV Canada.

★ 1497 ★

Retailing - Music (SIC 5735)

Online Music Sales - 1997

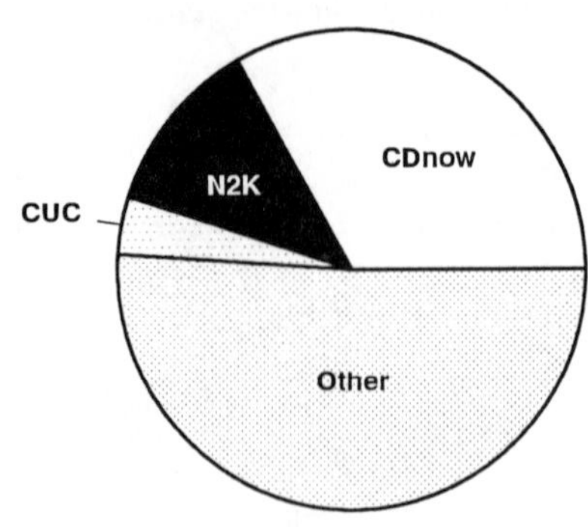

The online music industry is expected to have domestic sales of $1.1 billion and international sales of $1.6 billion in 2002.

	Rev. ($ mil.)	Share
CDnow	$ 16.4	33.0%
N2K	6.0	12.0
CUC	2.0	4.0
Other	25.0	51.0

Source: "Statistics Toolbox." Retrieved May 27, 1999 from the World Wide Web: http://www.internetworld.com/daily/stats/1998/05/1304-music.html, from Jupiter Communications.

SIC 58 - Eating and Drinking Places

★ 1498 ★

Catering (SIC 5812)

Top Catering Services in Arizona

Firms are ranked by estimated gross sales in millions of dollars.

Continental Catering Inc.	$ 8.45
The Wigwam Resort	7.50
Arizona Biltmore Resort and Spa	5.90
Radisson Resort Scottsdale	4.75
Arizona Caterers by Hyatt Regency	4.50

Source: *The Business Journal Serving Phoenix and the Valley of the Sun*, January 22, 1999, p. 28.

★ 1499 ★

Foodservice (SIC 5812)

Canada's Foodservice Industry - 1997

Total sales reached $32.2 billion.

Restaurants, licensed	35.9%
Restaurants, unlicensed	18.2
Accomodation foodservice	10.9
Take-out and delivery	10.5
Institutional foodservice	7.6
Other	16.9

Source: Retrieved May 10, 1999 from the World Wide Web: http:// www.gov.on.ca/OMAFRA/english/stats/ food/indsales.html, from Canadian Restaurant and Foodservice Association, Foodservice Facts, Statistics Canada, and CANSIM Matrix.

★ 1500 ★

Foodservice (SIC 5812)

Foodservice Sales - 1999

Sales are shown in billions of dollars.

Quick-service	$ 116.2
Full-service	104.3
Retail	29.3
Business/industry	$ 23.5
Recreation	12.7
Lodging	12.1
Schools	11.8
College/university	8.7
Hospitals	7.1
Nursing homes	5.3
Cafeteria/buffet	4.3
Others	36.3

Source: *Restaurants and Institutions*, January 1, 1999, p. 51, from Technomic Inc.

★ 1501 ★

Foodservice (SIC 5812)

Largest Food Contract Management Firms - 1998

Firms are ranked by volume in millions of dollars.

Aramark	$ 4,340
Sodexho Marriott Services	4,306
Compass Group USA	2,300
Delaware North Companies	1,285
Morrison Health Care Inc.	610
The Wood Co.	460
Volume Services America	407
Ogden Entertainment Group	400

Source: *Food Management*, April 1999, p. 61.

★ 1502 ★

Foodservice (SIC 5812)

Ontario's Foodservice Industry - 1997

Total sales reached $11.8 billion.

Restaurants, licensed	34.3%
Restaurants, unlicensed	18.1
Take-out and delivery	12.9
Accommodation foodservice	10.9
Institutional foodservice	7.6
Other	16.2

Source: Retrieved May 10, 1999 fromt he World Wide Web: http:// www.gov.on.ca/OMAFRA/english/stats/food/indsales.html, from Canadian Restaurant and Foodservice Association, Foodservice Facts, Statistics Canada, and CANSIM Matrix.

★ 1503 ★

Foodservice (SIC 5812)

Recreational Foodservice Market - 1997

Companies are ranked by food and beverage purchases in millions of dollars.

Walt Disney Co.	$ 1,018.0
Carnival Cruise Lines	331.0
Club Corp. International	270.0
AMC Entertainment	251.0
Volume Services	234.0

Source: *Restaurants and Institutions*, September 15, 1998, p. 84.

★ 1504 ★

Foodservice (SIC 5812)

School District Foodservice Market - 1997

Companies are ranked by food and beverage purchases in millions of dollars. Figures are for North America.

New York City Board of Education	$ 127.5
Los Angeles Unified School District	86.0
Chicago Public Schools	70.5
Dade County Schools, Miami	37.1
Philadelphia School District	25.2

Source: *Restaurants and Institutions*, September 15, 1998, p. 78.

★ 1505 ★

Foodservice (SIC 5812)

University Foodservice Market - 1997

Companies are ranked by food and beverage purchases in millions of dollars. Figures are for self-operated firms.

Pennsylvania State University	$ 21.7
Michigan State University	16.1
Brigham Young University	14.0
University of Notre Dame	12.0
Purdue University	9.1

Source: *Restaurants and Institutions*, September 15, 1998, p. 82.

★ 1506 ★

Restaurants (SIC 5812)

Cafeteria Restaurant Leaders - 1997

Companies are ranked by sales in millions of dollars. Total sales reached $2.28 billion.

Old Country Buffet	$ 537.8
Luby's Cafeterias	495.4
Piccadilly Cafeterias	281.6
Morrison's Fresh Cooking	250.0
HomeTown Buffet	248.0

Source: *Restaurants and Institutions*, July 15, 1998, p. 103.

★ 1507 ★

Restaurants (SIC 5812)

Fast-Food Market in Canada - 1997

Market shares are shown in percent for the year ended December 31, 1997.

McDonald's	19.6%
Cara Operations Ltd.	12.9
Tricon Global Restaurants	12.2
Subway Sandwiches and Salads	4.3
A&W Food Services of Canada	3.5
Burger King Restaurants	3.5
Wendy's Restaurants of Canada	3.4
Dairy Queen Canada	3.0
Others	37.6

Source: "Report on Market Share." Retrieved June 1, 1999 from the World Wide Web: http://www.marketingmag.ca/index.cgi?, from *Foodservice and Hospitality Magazine*.

★ 1508 ★

Restaurants (SIC 5812)

Hamburger Market Leaders - 1998

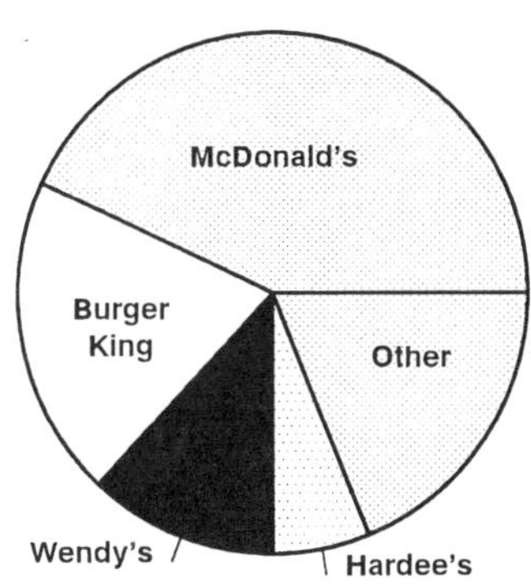

Market shares are shown in percent.

McDonald's	43.0%
Burger King	20.0
Wendy's	12.0
Hardee's	6.0
Other	19.0

Source: *USA TODAY*, June 16, 1999, p. 3B, from Technomic Inc.

★ 1509 ★

Restaurants (SIC 5812)

Hamburger Restaurant Leaders - 1997

Companies are ranked by sales in millions of dollars. Total sales reached $57.58 billion.

McDonald's	$ 33,638
Burger King	9,800
Wendy's	5,226
Hardee's	3,526
Jack in the Box	1,300
Sonic Drive-Ins	1,192
Carl's Jr.	703

Source: *Restaurants and Institutions*, July 15, 1998, p. 100.

★ 1510 ★

Restaurants (SIC 5812)

Largest Chicken Chains - 1997

Data show share of aggregate sales on the magazine's list of top 100 restaurants.

KFC	56.07%
Boston Market	16.78
Popeyes	10.09
Chick-fil-A	9.02
Churchs Chicken	8.04

Source: *Nation's Restaurant News*, June 22, 1998, p. 120.

★ 1511 ★

Restaurants (SIC 5812)

Largest Contract Chains - 1997

Data show share of aggregate sales on the magazine's list of top 100 restaurants.

Aramark Global Food/Leisure Services	23.36%
Marriott Management Services	23.22
LSG Lufthansa Service/Sky Chef	11.43
Canteen Services	6.43
Eurest Dining Services	5.89
Sodexho U.S.A.	5.86
Other	23.81

Source: *Nation's Restaurant News*, June 22, 1998, p. 148.

★ 1512 ★

Restaurants (SIC 5812)

Largest Dinner-House Chains - 1997

Data show share of aggregate sales on the magazine's list of top 100 restaurants.

Applebee's	15.37%
Red Lobster	15.37
Olive Garden	11.74
Outback Steakhouse	10.64
Chili's Grill & Bar	10.21
T.G.I. Friday's	8.42
Ruby Tuesday	5.47
Lone Star Steakhouse	4.35
Bennigan's	4.35
Other	14.08

Source: *Nation's Restaurant News*, June 22, 1998, p. 146.

★ 1513 ★

Restaurants (SIC 5812)

Largest Family Chains - 1997

Data show share of aggregate sales on the magazine's list of top 100 restaurants.

Denny's	21.20%
Shoney's	13.02
Cracker Barrel Old Country Store	9.77
Intl. House of Pancakes/IHOP	9.63
Big Boy Restaurant & Bakery	8.49
Perkins Family Restaurants	8.05
Bob Evans Restaurants	7.00
Other	22.84

Source: *Nation's Restaurant News*, June 22, 1998, p. 120.

★ 1514 ★

Restaurants (SIC 5812)

Largest Grill-Buffet Chains - 1997

Golden Corral
Ponderosa Steakhouse
Ryan's Family Steak House
Sizzler
Other

Data show share of aggregate sales on the magazine's list of top 100 restaurants.

Golden Corral	28.49%
Ponderosa Steakhouse	24.28
Ryan's Family Steak House	23.50
Sizzler	12.56
Other	11.17

Source: *Nation's Restaurant News*, June 22, 1998, p. 146.

★ 1515 ★

Restaurants (SIC 5812)

Largest Independent Restaurants - 1998

Data show food and beverage sales in millions of dollars.

Tavern on the Green	$ 34,200
Windows on the World	31,870
Smith & Wollensky	24,446
Bob Chinn's Crab House	21,708
Sparks Steakhouse	20,400
Joe's Stone Crab	19,035
21 Club	17,289
Fulton's Crab House	16,000
Four Seasons	15,083
The Lobster House	14,954

Source: *Restaurants and Institutions*, April 1, 1999, p. 50.

★ 1516 ★

Restaurants (SIC 5812)

Largest Pizza Makers - 1997

Market shares are shown in percent.

Pizza Hut Inc.	22.2%
Domino's Pizza Inc.	11.7
Little Caeser Enterprises Inc.	8.4
Papa John's International Inc.	4.1
Other	53.6

Source: *Crain's Detroit Business*, September 21, 1998, p. 1, from Technomic Inc.

★ 1517 ★

Restaurants (SIC 5812)

Mexican Restaurant Leaders - 1997

Companies are ranked by sales in millions of dollars. Total sales reached $7.28 billion.

Taco-Bell	$ 4,900.0
Chi-Chi's	245.8
Del Taco	239.0
El Torito	228.4
Don Pablo's	196.5
Taco John's	174.0

Source: *Restaurants and Institutions*, July 15, 1998, p. 100.

★ 1518 ★

Restaurants (SIC 5812)

Pizza Market Leaders - 1998

Shares are shown of the $30 billion market.

Pizza Hut	25.3%
Domino's Pizza	11.1
Little Caesars	10.2
Chucky Cheese's	1.9
Papa Joe's	0.9
Other	50.6

Source: Retrieved April 30, 1999 from the World Wide Web:http://www.detnews.com/1998/biz/9810/15/10150031.htm.

★ 1519 ★

Restaurants (SIC 5812)

Seafood Restaurant Leaders - 1997

Companies are ranked by sales in millions of dollars. Total sales reached $3.97 billion.

Red Lobster	$ 1,900.0
Long John Silver's Seafood Shoppes	846.2
Captain D's	464.4
Joe's Crab Shack	134.1
Landry's Seafood House	134.1
Legal Sea Foods	80.3

Source: *Restaurants and Institutions*, July 15, 1998, p. 103.

★ 1520 ★

Restaurants (SIC 5812)

Steak/Barbecue Restaurant Leaders - 1997

Companies are ranked by sales in millions of dollars. Total sales reached $7.99 billion.

Outback Steakhouse	$ 1,246.0
Golden Corral	770.9
Sizzler	677.9
Ryan's Family Steak House	635.6
Ponderosa	630.2
Lone Star Steakhouse & Saloon	585.3
Tony Roma's Famous for Ribs	350.9

Source: *Restaurants and Institutions*, July 15, 1998, p. 100.

★ 1521 ★

Restaurants (SIC 5812)

Sweets/Snacks Restaurant Leaders - 1997

Companies are ranked by sales in millions of dollars. Total sales reached $9.678 billion.

Dairy Queen	$ 2,540.0
Dunkin' Donuts	2,229.5
Baskin-Robbins	800.0
Tim Hortons	772.0
Starbucks Coffee	596.2

Source: *Restaurants and Institutions*, July 15, 1998, p. 100.

★ 1522 ★

Retailing - Beverages (SIC 5813)

Coffee Sales in Canada - 1998

Sales are estimated in millions of dollars.

	($ mil.)	Share
Doughnut and bagel shops	$ 900	31.52%
Grocery stores	400	14.01
Specialty coffee houses	375	13.13
Restaurants	300	10.51
Workplace	300	10.51
Mass merchants	80	2.80
Warehouse outlets	50	1.75
Other retail	50	1.75
Other	400	14.01

Source: *Globe and Mail*, March 8, 1999, p. B4, from Coffee Association of Canada.

★ 1523 ★

Retailing - Beverages (SIC 5813)

Where Soft Drinks Are Sold - 1997

Distribution is shown based on 9.6 billion cases.

Supermarkets	34.0%
Fountain	22.0
Convenience, large retail and drug stores	11.0
Vending machines	11.0
Gas stations	7.0
Small groceries	4.0
Other	11.0

Source: *New York Times*, January 21, 1999, p. C1.

★ 1524 ★

Retailing - Coffee (SIC 5813)

Largest Coffee Bars

There are nearly 7,000 coffeehouses in the United States. Starbucks has 170 outlets abroad.

Starbucks	1,830
Second Cup Ltd.	318
Caribou Coffee	124
Seattle Coffee Co.	72
Tully's Coffee	54
Peet's Coffee & Tea	44
Diedrich Coffee	43

Source: *Forbes*, February 22, 1999, p. 55, from *Fresh Cup*.

SIC 59 - Miscellaneous Retail

★ 1525 ★

Drug Stores (SIC 5912)

Drug Store Market in Los Angeles, CA

Data show share of area volume.

OSCO	44.5%
Rite Aid	21.3
Longs Drug Stores	6.6
Bergen-Brunswig	5.0
Other	22.6

Source: Retrieved May 28, 1999 from the World Wide Web: http:// metromarketstudies.com/drugsample.htm.

★ 1526 ★

Drug Stores (SIC 5912)

Largest Drug Stores - 1997

Sales are shown in billions of dollars.

Walgreen	$ 13.3
CVS	12.7
Rite Aid	11.3
Eckerd	9.6
American Stores	5.6
Longs	2.9
Medicine Shoppe	1.2
Phar-Mor	1.0
Arbor Drug	0.9
Drug Emporium	0.8

Source: *Stores*, July 1998, p. S17.

★ 1527 ★

Drug Stores (SIC 5912)

Pharmacies by Type

LTCPP stands for long term care pharmacy provider.

Independently owned	51.0%
LTCPP chains	34.0
Hospital	7.0
Nursing facility	4.0
Government	2.0
Home health agency chain	1.0
Nursing facility chain	1.0

Source: *Provider*, September 1998, p. 21, from SMG Marketing Group.

★ 1528 ★

Drug Stores (SIC 5912)

Top Drug Store Markets

Sales are shown in billions of dollars.

Chicago	$ 4.2
New York City	3.3
Philadelphia	2.5
Detroit	2.1

Source: *Michigan Retailer*, January/February 1999, p. 1, from *Chain Drug Review*.

★ 1529 ★

Retailing - Drugs (SIC 5912)

Largest Pharmacy Benefit Managers

Data show number of covered lives, in millions

PCS Health Systems	61
MMerck-Medco	52
Express-Scripts/ValueRx	30
DPS	20
WellPoint Pharmacy	16
Integrated Pharmaceutical Services	15
Advanced Paradigm	13

Continued on next page.

★ 1529 ★ *Continued*

Retailing - Drugs (SIC 5912)

Largest Pharmacy Benefit Managers

Data show number of covered lives, in millions

WHP	13
Caremark	10

Source: *Business & Health*, January 1999, p. 27, from Scott-Levin.

★ 1530 ★

Retailing - Drugs (SIC 5912)

Where Prescriptions Are Filled

Community pharmacies	60.0%
Hospitals	22.0
Mail order	8.0
Nursing homes	3.0
HMOs	2.0
Other	5.0

Source: *Wall Street Journal*, July 15, 1998, p. A4, from National Association of Chain Drug Stores and Boston Consulting Group.

★ 1531 ★

Retailing - Drugs (SIC 5912)

Who Pays for Prescriptions - 1998

Shares are shown for the second quarter of the year.

Third party	64.5%
Patient	25.0
Medicaid	10.4

Source: *Wall Street Journal*, November 16, 1998, p. 14A, from IMS Health.

★ 1532 ★

Retailing - Sporting Goods (SIC 5941)

Largest Fitness Retailers - 1998

Data show estimated sales in millions of dollars.

BusyBody Fitness Warehouse	$ 140
Gym Source	42
Omni Fitness	40
Exercise Equipment Center Inc.	28
The Fitness Experience	20

Source: *Sporting Goods Business*, May 15, 1998, p. 32.

★ 1533 ★

Retailing - Sporting Goods (SIC 5941)

Largest Golf Retailers - 1998

Data show estimated sales in millions of dollars.

Nevada Bob's	$ 500
Golf Smith	350
Pro Golf Discount	203
Edwin Watts Golf Shops	175
Golf Day	110

Source: *Sporting Goods Business*, May 15, 1998, p. 30.

★ 1534 ★

Retailing - Sporting Goods (SIC 5941)

Largest Sporting Good Retailers - 1998

Data show estimated sales in millions of dollars.

Foot Locker	$ 2,670
The Sports Authority	1,690
L.L. Bean	1,110
Gart Sports	730
Just For Feet	700
Champs	695
Footaction	658

Source: *Sporting Goods Business*, May 15, 1998, p. 29.

★ 1535 ★

Retailing - Sporting Goods (SIC 5941)

Largest Sporting Goods Chains

Companies are ranked by number of outlets.

Foot Locker	1,750
Lady Foot Locker	700
Play it Again Sports	700
Champs	675
Athlete's Foot	670
J.C. Penney	650
Footaction	550
Forzani	290
Big 5	200
The Sports Authority	185

Source: *Sportstyle*, May 1998, p. 14.

★ 1536 ★

Retailing - Books (SIC 5942)

Adult Book Sales - 1998

Sales are shown in percent.

Large chain bookstores	25.3%
Book clubs	18.0
Independent/small chain bookstores	16.6
Warehouse clubs	6.4
Mass merchandisers	5.9
Mail order	4.9
Food/drug stores	3.6
Discount stores	3.3
Used books	3.0
Internet	1.9
Multimedia	1.0

Source: *Publishers Weekly*, May 10, 1999, p. 13, from *1998 Consumer Research Study on Book Purchasing.*

★ 1537 ★

Retailing - Books (SIC 5942)

Book Sales by Outlet

Total units sold reached 1.07 billion.

Large chain bookstores	25.2%
Book clubs	20.3
Small chain/indep. bookstores	17.2
Warehouse clubs/disct. stores	14.6
Online	0.3
Other	22.3

Source: *New York Times*, April 18, 1999, p. 1, from Book Industry Study Group and J.P. Morgan Securities Inc.

★ 1538 ★

Retailing - Books (SIC 5942)

Leading Book Chains - 1998

Market shares are shown in percent.

Barnes & Noble	15.7%
Borders	12.7
Books-a-Million	1.8
Crown	1.7
Other	68.1

Source: *Washington Post*, July 20, 1998, p. 13, from Merrill Lynch.

★ 1539 ★

Retailing - Books (SIC 5942)

Leading Book Chains - 1999

Sales are estimated for the first six months of the year.

Barnes & Noble	$ 1,341.0
Borders Group	1,091.2
Books-A-Million	152.4
Crown Books	121.0

Source: *Publishers Weekly*, September 28, 1998, p. 11.

★ 1540 ★

Retailing - Greeting Cards (SIC 5943)

Greeting Card Sales - 1997

Card/gift stores	34.0%
Mass merchandisers	22.0
Drug stores	18.0
Supermarkets	15.0
Dept. stores	1.0
Variety	1.0
Other	9.0

Source: *Discount Merchandiser*, August 1998, p. 77, from American Greetings.

★ 1541 ★

Retailing - Jewelry (SIC 5944)

Retail Jewelry Sales - 1997

Distribution is shown based on total sales of $27.8 billion.

Jewelry stores	56.8%
Department stores	13.7
Discount stores	11.8
Catalog showrooms	7.5
Non-store retailers	4.2
Other	6.0

Source: *Discount Merchandiser*, July 1998, p. 53.

★ 1542 ★

Retailing - Jewelry (SIC 5944)

U.S. Jewelry Sales

Sales are estimated in percent. Chain jewelers include Wal-Mart, Zale Corp., J.C. Penney and Service Merchandise.

Independent and small jewelers	66.0%
Chain jewelers	33.0

Source: *Washington Post*, September 29, 1998, p. E1, from *National Jeweler*.

★ 1543 ★

Retailing - Hobby Products (SIC 5945)

Craft Kit Sales by Outlet

Total sales reached $302.1 million.

Discount	47.0%
National toy chains	14.0
Variety stores	4.0
Department stores	2.0
Food/drug stores	2.0
Other toy stores	3.0
Other outlets	28.0

Source: *Playthings*, September 1998, p. 44, from NPD Group Inc. Toy Market Index.

★ 1544 ★

Retailing - Toys (SIC 5945)

Sports Activity Toy Sales

A total of 90.3 million units were sold reaching total sales of $791.5 million.

Discount stores	54.0%
National toy chains	21.0
Food drug	5.0
Variety	5.0
Other	15.0

Source: *Playthings*, September 1998, p. 30, from NPD Group Inc. Toy Market Index.

★ 1545 ★

Retailing - Toys (SIC 5945)

Top Toy Retailers - 1997

Market shares are shown in percent.

Toys R Us	20.2%
Wal-Mart	12.7
Kmart	7.3
Consolidated	4.5
Service Merchandise	1.6
Hills	1.0
Target	0.3
Other	52.4

Source: *Los Angeles Times*, December 13, 1998, p. C1, from Toy Manufacturers of America.

★ 1546 ★

Retailing - Toys (SIC 5945)

Top Toy Retailers - 1998

Wal-Mart	17.4%
Toys R Us	16.8
Kmart	8.0
Target	6.9
KB Toys	4.9
Other	46.0

Source: "Wal-Mart Top Toy Retailer" Retrieved May 7, 1999 from the World Wide Web: http://more.abcnews.go.com/sections/business/DailyNews, from NPD Group Inc.

★ 1547 ★

Retailing - Toys (SIC 5945)

Water Toy Sales by Outlet

Total sales reached $457.7 million.

Discount	55.0%
Food/drug stores	11.0
Toy chains	11.0
Variety	6.0
Catalog showroom	1.0
Department stores	1.0
Other	15.0

Source: *Playthings*, September 1998, p. 32, from NPD Group Inc. Toy Market Index.

★ 1548 ★

Retailing - Cameras (SIC 5946)

Retail Camera Sales - 1997

Distribution is shown based on total sales of $11.6 billion.

Discount stores	33.2%
Drug/proprietary stores	23.3
Camera/photo supply stores	20.0
Supermarkets	14.5
Catalog showrooms	3.6
Department stores	3.5
Other	1.9

Source: *Discount Merchandiser*, July 1998, p. 55.

★ 1549 ★

Retailing - Film (SIC 5946)

Retail Film Sales - 1997

Dollar shares are shown in percent.

Mass	45.2%
Drugstores	34.5
Supermarkets	20.3

Source: *Progressive Grocer*, August 1998, p. 38, from Information Resources Inc.

★ 1550 ★

Retailing - Party Supplies (SIC 5947)

Largest Party Supply Stores - 1997

Party City

Factory Card Outlet

Paper Warehouse

Chains are ranked by sales in millions of dollars.

Party City	$ 142
Factory Card Outlet	134
Paper Warehouse	52

Source: *Chain Store Age*, October 1998, p. 66.

★ 1551 ★

Mail Order (SIC 5961)

Largest Catalogers - 1997

Firms are ranked by sales in millions of dollars.

Dell Computer Corp.	$ 11,946
Gateway 2000	6,293
J.C. Penney Co.	$ 3,880
International Business Machines	3,000
Micro Warehouse	2,126
Fingerhut Cos.	1,530
Spiegel	1,522
Henry Schein	1,518
Viking Office Products	1,383
Brylane	1,279

Source: *Catalog Age*, August 1998, p. 66.

★ 1552 ★

Mail Order (SIC 5961)

Leading Catalog Businesses

Data show the leading U.S. catalog businesses ranked by worldwide sales through mail order. Figures are in billions of dollars.

Dell Computer Corp.	$ 8.4
Gateway 2000	5.0
J.C. Penney	3.5
Hewlett-Packard Direct Marketing Division	2.1
Micro Warehouse	1.7

Source: *Direct Marketing*, September 1998, p. 27.

★ 1553 ★

Mail Order (SIC 5961)

Leading Mail Order Businesses

Data show the leading U.S. companies ranked by worldwide sales through mail order. Figures are in billions of dollars.

Dell Computer Corp.	$ 8.47
United Services Automobile Association	7.46
Time Warner	6.99
Tele-Communications Inc.	6.64
Gateway 2000	5.03
J.C. Penney	4.54
American Association of Retired Persons	4.41
Comcast	3.70
Berkshire Hathaway	3.32
Cendant	3.25

Source: *Direct Marketing*, September 1998, p. 24.

★ 1554 ★

Mail Order (SIC 5961)

Mail Order Spending - 1998

Specialty products	40.0%
Nonfinancial services	21.0
Financial services	20.0
General merchandise	10.0

Source: *Stores*, May 1999, p. 14, from National Mail Order Association.

★ 1555 ★

Vending Machines (SIC 5962)

Popular Vending Machine Items

Cold beverages in cans

Snack food

Cold beverages in cups

Hot beverages

Cigarettes

Other food

Other goods

Distribution is shown based on revenues.

Cold beverages in cans	40.0%
Snack food	19.0
Cold beverages in cups	8.0
Hot beverages	8.0
Cigarettes	2.0
Other food	10.0
Other goods	13.0

Source: *The Boston Globe*, December 30, 1998, p. F1, from National Automatic Merchandising Association.

★ 1556 ★

Vending Machines (SIC 5962)

Vending Machine Product Sales - 1998

Data show shares of unit volume.

Salty snacks	33.38%
Candy	32.87
Crackers	9.43
Cookies	9.28
Pastries	5.88
Nuts	2.39
Micro pop	1.14
Cereal bars	0.47%
Other	5.16

Source: *Vending Times*, February 1999, p. 10, from *InfoVend Trend Report*.

★ 1557 ★

Vending Machines (SIC 5962)

Vending Machine Sales - 1998

Data show share of space in vending machines.

Salty snacks	26.71%
Chocolate	26.35
Cookies	8.96
Non-chocolate	8.65
Crackers	8.47
Gum	7.60
Pastries	5.95
Other	7.30

Source: *Vending Times*, March 1999, p. 10, from InfoVend.

★ 1558 ★

Retailing - Flowers (SIC 5992)

Cut Flower Market

Data show share of all cut flower transactions.

Supermarkets	41.0%
Florists shops	35.0
Discount chains	3.0
Department stores	2.0
Garden centers	2.0
Toll-free numbers	2.0
Other	15.0

Source: *Los Angeles Times*, May 6, 1999, p. C8, from *American Floral Endowment Consumer Tracking Study 1997-98*.

★ 1559 ★

Retailing - Flowers (SIC 5992)

Flower Retail Market

Data show share of all floral transactions.

Supermarkets	22.0%
Garden centers	20.0
Discount chains	14.0
Florist shops	12.0
Home improvement chains	12.0

Continued on next page.

★ 1559 ★ *Continued*

Retailing - Flowers (SIC 5992)

Flower Retail Market

Data show share of all floral transactions.

Department stores	5.0%
Mail order catalogs	2.0
Other	13.0

Source: *Los Angeles Times*, May 6, 1999, p. C8, from American Floral Endowment Consumer Tracking Study 1997-98.

★ 1560 ★

Retailing - Flowers (SIC 5992)

Flower Sales by Outlet

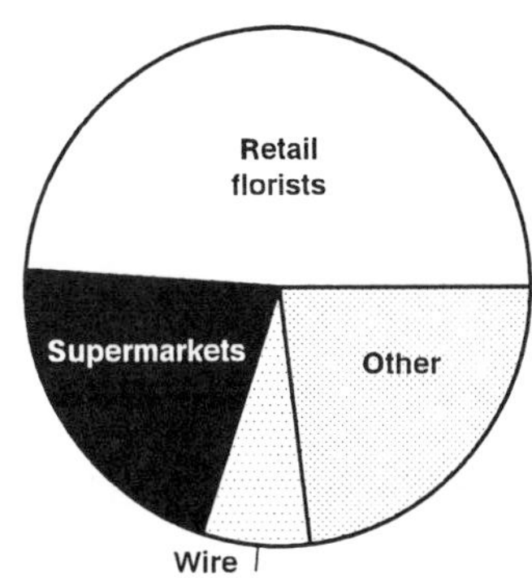

Retail florists	49.0%
Supermarkets	21.0
Wire	7.0
Other	23.0

Source: *Grocery Headquarters*, October 1998, p. 42, from Flowers & Green Profit and American Floral Endowment.

★ 1561 ★

Retailing - Tobacco (SIC 5993)

Retail Tobacco Sales - 1997

Distribution is shown based on total sales of $40.7 billion. Figures include cigars, cigarettes and tobacco.

Supermarkets	56.0%
Gas/service stations	19.1
Drug/proprietary stores	11.3
Discount stores	3.7
Automatic merchandising machines	3.1
Liquor stores	2.6%
Cigar stores	1.8
Wholesale clubs	1.5
Other	0.9

Source: *Discount Merchandiser*, July 1998, p. 55.

★ 1562 ★

Retailing - Batteries (SIC 5999)

Retail Battery Sales - 1997

Dollar shares are shown in percent.

Mass	48.9%
Drugstores	26.3
Supermarkets	24.8

Source: *Progressive Grocer*, August 1998, p. 38, from Information Resources Inc.

★ 1563 ★

Retailing - Beverages (SIC 5999)

Beer/Ale Sales by Outlet

Unit sales are shown for the year ended January 3, 1999.

	(mil.)	Share
Supermarkets	1,028.1	88.32%
Drug stores	110.9	9.53
Mass merchandisers	25.0	2.15

Source: *Progressive Grocer*, March 1999, p. 47, from Information Resources Inc.

★ 1564 ★

Retailing - Cosmetics (SIC 5999)

Cosmetics Sales by Outlet - 1997

Mass market	32.0%
Department stores	31.0
Alternative	37.0

Source: *Wall Street Journal*, July 8, 1998, p. B1, from Market View.

★ 1565 ★

Retailing - Cough/Cold Medicine (SIC 5999)

Cough/Cold Remedy Sales

Distribution is shown based on unit sales.

Drug stores	36.09%
Food	35.70
Mass	28.21

Source: *Discount Merchandiser*, June 1999, p. 54, from Information Resources Inc.

★ 1566 ★

Retailing - Deodorants (SIC 5999)

Retail Deodorant Sales

Sales are shown for the year ended March 29, 1998.

Food	40.32%
Mass	38.46
Drug	21.22

Source: *Supermarket Business*, June 1998, p. 65, from Information Resources Inc.

★ 1567 ★

Retailing - Diapers (SIC 5999)

Diaper Sales by Outlet

Food	49.07%
Mass	41.90
Drug	9.02

Source: *Discount Merchandiser*, November 1998, p. 114, from Information Resources Inc.

★ 1568 ★

Retailing - Drugs (SIC 5999)

Antihistimine Sales in Canada

The market is valued at $91 million.

Drugstores	80.0%
Foodstore pharmacies	12.5
Mass	7.0
Grocery stores	0.5

Source: Retrieved May 31, 1999 from the World Wide Web: http:// www.mhbizlink.com/content/pharmacy/ phpost/1999/03-99/ppo039907.html, from A.C. Nielsen MarketTrack.

★ 1569 ★

Retailing - Drugs (SIC 5999)

Stomach Remedy Sales

Drug	35.22%
Food	34.15
Mass	30.63

Source: *Discount Merchandiser*, June 1999, p. 59, from Information Resources Inc.

★ 1570 ★

Retailing - Feminine Hygiene Products (SIC 5999)

Retail Sanitary Napkin Sales - 1997

Dollar shares are shown in percent.

Supermarkets	46.3%
Mass	32.4
Drugstores	21.3

Source: *Progressive Grocer*, August 1998, p. 38, from Information Resources Inc.

★ 1571 ★

Retailing - Light Bulb (SIC 5999)

Retail Light Bulb Sales - 1997

Dollar shares are shown in percent.

Mass	46.6%
Supermarkets	43.4
Drugstores	10.0

Source: *Progressive Grocer*, August 1998, p. 38, from Information Resources Inc.

★ 1572 ★

Retailing - Mailing Supplies (SIC 5999)

Where We Buy Mailing Supplies - 1997

Total retail sales reached $189 million.

Office superstores	40.7%
Mass	20.2
Drug store	19.9
Food	17.1
Other	2.1

Source: *Discount Store News*, June 22, 1998, p. 49, from Manco Inc., A.C. Nielsen, and Information Resources Inc.

★ 1573 ★

Retailing - Oral Care (SIC 5999)

Dentifrice Sales by Outlet

Sales are shown in percent.

Food	46.21%
Mass	35.26
Drug	18.53

Source: *Discount Merchandiser*, June 1999, p. 54, from Information Resources Inc.

★ 1574 ★

Retailing - Oral Care (SIC 5999)

Retail Toothpaste Sales - 1997

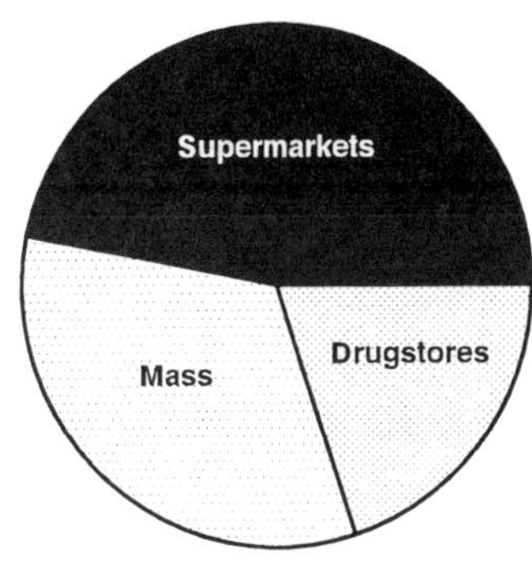

Dollar shares are shown in percent.

Supermarkets	47.3%
Mass	32.8
Drugstores	19.9

Source: *Progressive Grocer*, August 1998, p. 38, from Information Resources Inc.

★ 1575 ★

Retailing - Personal Care Products (SIC 5999)

Anti-Smoking Product Sales - 1997

Sales are shown by outlet.

Drugstores	58.3%
Mass	26.2
Supermarkets	15.5

Source: *Progressive Grocer*, August 1998, p. 40, from Information Resources Inc.

★ 1576 ★

Retailing - Personal Care Products (SIC 5999)

External Analgesic Rub Sales - 1997

Sales are shown by outlet.

Drugstores	54.2%
Mass	24.1
Supermarkets	21.7

Source: *Progressive Grocer*, August 1998, p. 40.

★ 1577 ★

Retailing - Personal Care Products (SIC 5999)

Men's Fragrance/Shaving Cream Sales - 1997

Sales are shown by outlet.

Mass	51.0%
Drugstores	35.9
Supermarkets	13.1

Source: *Progressive Grocer*, August 1998, p. 40, from Information Resources Inc.

★ 1578 ★

Retailing - Personal Care Products (SIC 5999)

Nasal Product Sales - 1997

Sales are shown by outlet.

Drugstores	48.3%
Supermarkets	27.9
Mass	23.8

Source: *Progressive Grocer*, August 1998, p. 40, from Information Resources Inc.

★ 1579 ★

Retailing - Personal Care Products (SIC 5999)

Retail Contraceptive Sales - 1997

Sales are shown by outlet.

Drugstores	59.1%
Mass	22.8
Supermarkets	18.1

Source: *Progressive Grocer*, August 1998, p. 40, from Information Resources Inc.

★ 1580 ★

Retailing - Personal Care Products (SIC 5999)

Retail Cotton Ball Sales - 1997

Sales are shown by outlet.

Supermarkets	37.5%
Mass	36.6
Drustores	25.9

Source: *Progressive Grocer*, August 1998, p. 40, from Information Resources Inc.

★ 1581 ★

Retailing - Personal Care Products (SIC 5999)

Retail Facial Tissue Sales - 1997

Sales are shown by outlet.

Supermarkets	63.6%
Mass	27.1
Drugstores	9.3

Source: *Progressive Grocer*, August 1998, p. 40, from Information Resources Inc.

★ 1582 ★

Retailing - Personal Care Products (SIC 5999)

Retail Hair Coloring Sales - 1997

Sales are shown by outlet.

Drugstores	44.0%
Mass	36.3
Supermarkets	19.6

Source: *Progressive Grocer*, August 1998, p. 40, from Information Resources Inc.

★ 1583 ★

Retailing - Personal Care Products (SIC 5999)

Retail Laxative Sales - 1997

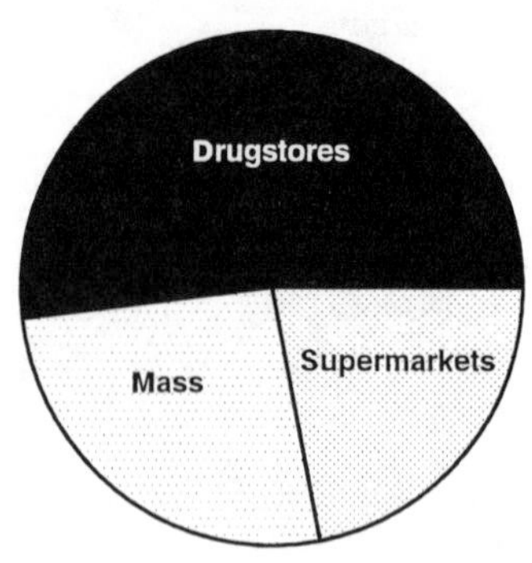

Sales are shown by outlet.

Drugstores	52.2%
Mass	26.2
Supermarkets	21.7

Source: *Progressive Grocer*, August 1998, p. 40, from Information Resources Inc.

★ 1584 ★

Retailing - Personal Care Products (SIC 5999)

Retail Moist Towelette Sales - 1997

Sales are shown by outlet.

Supermarkets	46.5%
Mass	42.7
Drugstores	10.8

Source: *Progressive Grocer*, August 1998, p. 40, from Information Resources Inc.

★ 1585 ★

Retailing - Personal Care Products (SIC 5999)

Retail Nail Product Sales - 1997

Sales are shown by outlet.

Drugstores	48.1%
Mass	37.8
Supermarkets	14.1

Source: *Progressive Grocer*, August 1998, p. 40, from Information Resources Inc.

★ 1586 ★

Retailing - Personal Care Products (SIC 5999)

Retail Razor Sales

Food	39.40%
Mass	39.25
Drug	21.36

Source: *Discount Merchandiser*, June 1999, p. 54, from Information Resources Inc.

★ 1587 ★

Retailing - Personal Care Products (SIC 5999)

Skin Care Sales by Outlet

Drug	44.11%
Mass	37.64
Food	18.25

Source: *Discount Merchandiser*, June 1999, p. 54.

★ 1588 ★

Retailing - Personal Care Products (SIC 5999)

Spa & Salon Product Sales in Mexico - 1996

Supermarkets	18.1%
Wholesale	17.0
State-owned stores	12.5
Department stores	8.4
Pharmacies	8.2
Other	35.8

Source: *National Trade Data Bank*, November 4, 1998, p. ISA980901.

★ 1589 ★

Retailing - Pet Products (SIC 5999)

Bird Maintenance Product Sales

Pet stores
Discount
Pet superstores
Supermarkets

Pet stores	53.0%
Discount	34.0
Pet superstores	24.0
Supermarkets	16.0

Source: *Discount Merchandiser*, June 1998, p. 86, from American Pet Products Manufacturers Association.

★ 1590 ★

Retailing - Pet Products (SIC 5999)

Bird Toy Sales

Discount	35.0%
Pet stores	32.0
Pet superstores	19.0
Supermarkets	9.0
Garden/feed	5.0

Source: *Discount Merchandiser*, June 1998, p. 86, from American Pet Products Manufacturers Association.

★ 1591 ★

Retailing - Pet Products (SIC 5999)

Cat Accessories Sales

Discount	35.0%
Pet stores	11.0
Pet superstores	10.0
Supermarkets	9.0
Garden/feed	2.0
Warehouse	2.0

Source: *Discount Merchandiser*, June 1998, p. 86, from American Pet Products Manufacturers Association.

★ 1592 ★

Retailing - Pet Products (SIC 5999)

Dog Toy Sales

Discount	33.0%
Pet superstores	14.0
Supermarkets	13.0
Pet stores	8.0
Garden/feed	2.0
Warehouse	1.0

Source: *Discount Merchandiser*, June 1998, p. 86, from American Pet Products Manufacturers Association.

★ 1593 ★

Retailing - Pet Products (SIC 5999)

Pet Product Sales - 1997

Litter
Food treats
Flea, tick products
Toys
Grooming products
Accessories
Other

Total sales reached $1.3 billion.

Litter	20.35%
Food treats	18.71
Flea, tick products	16.48
Toys	11.97
Grooming products	8.86
Accessories	13.36
Other	10.27

Source: *Discount Merchandiser*, June 1998, p. 50.

★ 1594 ★

Retailing - Sun Care Products (SIC 5999)

Retail Sun Care Sales - 1998

Market shares are shown in percent. Sales of sun care products reached $457.2 million.

Mass	39.6%
Drug stores	37.0
Food stores	23.4

Source: *Spray Technology & Marketing*, June 1999, p. 18, from A.C. Nielsen.

★ 1595 ★

Retailing - Sun Care Products (SIC 5999)

Sun Care Product Sales in Canada

Drug stores	50.0%
Department stores	11.5
Supermarkets	10.5
Mass	7.5
Warehouse outlets	5.5
Other	15.0

Source: *National Trade Data Bank*, March 30, 1998, p. IMI980330.

★ 1596 ★

Retailing - Vitamins (SIC 5999)

Retail Vitamin Sales - 1997

Dollar shares are shown in percent.

Drugstores	46.6%
Mass	29.2
Supermarkets	24.2

Source: *Progressive Grocer*, August 1998, p. 38, from Information Resources Inc.

SIC 60 - Depository Institutions

★ 1597 ★

Banking (SIC 6020)

Bank Deposits in Canada - 1997

Bank	Share
Royal Bank	18.0%
Bank of Montreal	13.0
Bank of Nova Scotia	12.0
CIBC	12.0
Toronto Dominion	11.0
National	4.0
Credit unions	7.0
Canada Trust	6.0
Desjardins	6.0
Alberta Treasury Branches	1.0
Province of Ontario Saving Office	1.0
Other	10.0

Source: *Toronto Star*, September 16, 1998, p. E5, from Report of the Task Force.

★ 1598 ★

Banking (SIC 6020)

In-Store Banking Leaders

Data show the number of in-store branches.

Wells Fargo Bank	936
Bank of America	278
NationsBank	278
TCF Financial Corp.	152
Bank One	129

Source: *Design-Build*, October 1998, p. 12, from Geosegment Systems Corp.

★ 1599 ★

Banking (SIC 6020)

Largest Banks in Mexico

Market shares are shown in percent.

Bank	Share
Banamex-Accival	35.8%
Bancomer	22.8
Other	49.4

Source: *Wall Street Journal*, March 22, 1999, p. A14, from Banamex, SG Cowen Securities, and Goldman Sachs & Co.

★ 1600 ★

Banking (SIC 6020)

Largest Online Bankers

Data show thousands of customers.

Wells Fargo & Co.	620
NationsBank	500
Citibank	350
Canadian Imperial Bank of Commerce	270
BankBoston	250
Chase Manhattan Bank	250
Bank of America	200
Toronto-Dominion Bank	170
Royal Bank of Canada	150

Source: *Industry Standard*, October 5, 1998, p. 41, from *Faulkner & Gray's Directory of Home Banking and Online Financial Services*.

★ 1601 ★

Banking (SIC 6020)

Largest Online Banks

NationsBank
Wells Fargo
Citibank
BankBoston
Chase Manhattan

Data show number of online subscribers. The number of households expected to pay bills or bank online is expected to reach 22 million in 2001.

NationsBank	425,000
Wells Fargo	400,000
Citibank	350,000
BankBoston	250,000
Chase Manhattan	250,000

Source: *Chicago Tribune*, November 12, 1998, p. 1, from Booz Allen & Hamilton and *Online Banking Report*.

★ 1602 ★

Banking (SIC 6020)

Largest Thrifts in Michigan

Banks are ranked by assets in millions of dollars.

Standard Federal Bank	$ 18,338.0
Flagstar Bancorp Inc.	3,046.4
D&N Financial Corp.	2,018.2
Sterling Bank & Trust F.S.B.	1,083.9
Dearborn Federal Savings Bank	239.2

Source: *Crain's Detroit Business*, May 24, 1999, p. 13.

★ 1603 ★

Banking (SIC 6020)

Largest U.S. Banks

Banks are ranked by assets in billions of dollars as of December 31, 1998.

Citigroup	$ 669
BankAmerica	618
Chase Manhattan	366
BancOne	261
J.P. Morgan & Co.	$ 261
First Union	237
Wells Fargo	202
Fleet Boston	184

Source: *Wall Street Journal*, March 15, 1999, p. A3, from bank financial statements.

★ 1604 ★

Banking (SIC 6020)

Leading Banks in Canada

Data show share of Canadian bank assets.

Canadian Imperial Bank of Commerce	21.4%
Royal Bank of Canada	20.3
Bank of Montreal	17.9
Scotiabank	17.4
Toronto Dominion Bank	16.3
Others	6.8

Source: *New York Times*, October 14, 1998, p. C1, from Canadian Bankers Association.

★ 1605 ★

Banking (SIC 6020)

Mexico's Bank Shares

Market shares are shown in percent.

Bancomer	20.76%
Banamex	20.68
Serfin	13.56
Bital	8.45
Santander Mexicano	6.37
Bilbao Viscaya	5.68
Banorte	3.22
Banpais	2.91
Centro	2.34

Source: *Mexico Business*, June 1999, p. 16, from CNBV.

★ 1606 ★

Banking (SIC 6020)

Top Banks in Canada - 1998

Market shares are shown in percent for the year ended October 31, 1998.

Royal Bank of Canada	20.1%
Scotiabank	18.6
CIBC	17.9
Bank of Montreal	16.1
Toronto Dominion Bank	13.5
National Bank of Canada	5.4
Others	8.3

Source: "Report on Market Share." Retrieved June 1, 1999 from the World Wide Web: http://www.marketingmag.ca/index.cgi?, from Canadian Bankers Association.

★ 1607 ★

Banking (SIC 6020)

Top Banks in Caswell County, NC

Market shares are shown based on deposits as of June 30, 1997.

First Union	64.49%
American National	35.51

Source: *Investext,* Thomson Financial Networks, August 25, 1998, p. 3, from SNL Securities.

★ 1608 ★

Banking (SIC 6020)

Top Banks in Danville, VA

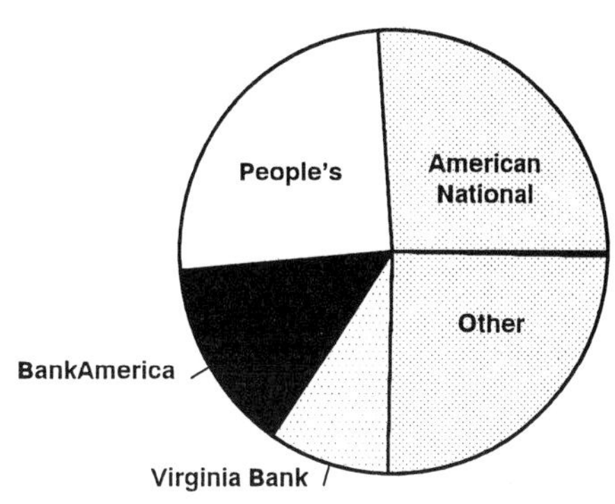

Market shares are shown based on deposits as of June 30, 1997.

American National	26.49%
People's	25.34
BankAmerica	13.87
Virginia Bank	9.40
Other	24.90

Source: *Investext,* Thomson Financial Networks, August 25, 1998, p. 3, from SNL Securities.

★ 1609 ★

Banking (SIC 6020)

Top Banks in Georgia

Market shares are shown in percent.

BankAmerica	17.20%
SunTrust Banks	12.57
Wachovia Corp.	10.54
First Union	9.14
Regions Financial Corp.	5.95
Synovus Financial Corp.	5.77
SouthTrust Corp.	5.18
First Liberty Financial	1.45
Premier Bancshares	1.23
Century South Banks Inc.	1.00
Other	29.97

Source: *Investext,* Thomson Financial Networks, December 3, 1998, p. 3, from First Liberty Financial Corp. and Interstate/Johnson Lane.

★ 1610 ★

Banking (SIC 6020)

Top Banks in Greenville, SC

Market shares are shown based on deposits as of June 30, 1997.

BB&T Corporation	15.65%
Wachovia Corporation	13.84
NationsBank Corporation	13.07
First Union Corporation	11.26
CCB Financial Corporation	8.82
Carolina First Corporation	7.10
FirstSpartan Financial Corporation	3.66
Regions Financial Corporation	3.64
First Citizen Bancorp	3.03
Other	19.93

Source: *Investext,* Thomson Financial Networks, October 28, 1998, p. 5.

★ 1611 ★

Banking (SIC 6020)

Top Banks in Jackson County, Ohio

Market shares are shown based on deposits as of June 1997.

Oak Hill Financial	36.4%
National City Corp.	21.5
First NB of Wellston	14.3
Milton Bank Co.	14.3
Ohio Valley Banc Corp.	10.0
Other	3.5

Source: *Investext,* Thomson Financial Networks, November 19, 1998, p. 4.

★ 1612 ★

Banking (SIC 6020)

Top Banks in Mexico

Banks are ranked by assets in billions of dollars as of December 31, 1997.

Banamex	$ 35,536
Bancomer	27,177
Serfin	18,292
Bital	9,196
Santander Mexicano	8,026
Bilbao Vizcaya	7,791
Promex	4,747
Mercantil del Norte	3,691
Banpais	$ 2,768
Centro	2,651

Source: *US/Mexico Business*, July/August 1998, p. 35.

★ 1613 ★

Banking (SIC 6020)

Top Banks in Norfolk, VA

Market shares are shown based on deposits.

BankAmerica	22.57%
SunTrust	21.21
BB&T	20.39
Other	35.83

Source: *Investext,* Thomson Financial Networks, January 11, 1999, p. 7.

★ 1614 ★

Banking (SIC 6020)

Top Banks in North Carolina

Market shares are shown based on deposits as of October 31, 1998.

BB&T	18.3%
Wachovia	16.8
First Union	16.6
First Citizens	8.4
BankAmerica	7.9
Centura Banks	6.5
CCB Financial	6.1
Other	19.4

Source: *Business North Carolina*, February 1999, p. 62, from SNL Securities.

★ 1615 ★

Banking (SIC 6020)

Top Banks in South Carolina - 1997

Market shares are shown in percent.

Wachovia Corp.	17.40%
NationsBank Corp.	14.00
BB&T Corp.	10.50
First Union Corp.	7.60
Carolina First Union Corp.	5.70
First Citizens Bancorp.	5.60
Synovus Corporation	3.60
First Financial Holding	3.50
CCB Financial Corp.	3.10
Regions Financial Corp.	2.80
Other	26.20

Source: *Investext,* Thomson Financial Networks, October 28, 1998, p. 4.

★ 1616 ★

Banking (SIC 6020)

Top Banks in Tampa Bay, FL

Banks are ranked by assets in thousands of dolalrs as of March 31, 1998.

Republic Bank	$ 1,839,563
First Federal Florida	423,625
Raymond James Bank	381,854
American Bank of Bradenton	376,289
Citurs and Chemical Bank	317,685

Source: *South Florida Business Journal*, August 14, 1998, p. 1, from Federal Deposit Insurance Corp.

★ 1617 ★

Banking (SIC 6020)

Top Banks in Virginia

Market shares are shown in percent.

First Union	17.2%
SunTrust	13.3
NationsBank	13.2
Wachovia	12.6
First Virginia	8.1
BB&T	4.4
F&M National	2.3
One Valley Bancorp	1.6%
Capital One Financial	1.3
United Bankshares	1.2
Other	24.8

Source: *Investext,* Thomson Financial Networks, September 1, 1998, p. 3, from SNL Securities.

★ 1618 ★

Community Banks (SIC 6029)

Largest Community Banks in the Northeast

Banks are ranked by assets in millions of dollars.

Bank of Granite (NC)	$ 577.3
The Drovers & Mechanics Bank (PA)	556.6
The Palmetto Bank (SC)	548.2
Bank of Newport (RI)	518.3
First Comm. Bank-Mercer Co. Inc. (WVA)	513.3

Source: *ABA Banking Journal*, September 1998, p. 19.

★ 1619 ★

International Banking (SIC 6082)

Foreign Banks in the United States

Data show total assets booked into the United States as of June 1998.

Japan	$ 291,192
France	153,620
Germany	134,256
Canada	117,691
United Kingdom	86,328

Source: *The Banker*, March 1999, p. 42, from U.S. Federal Reserve Bank.

★ 1620 ★

Money Orders (SIC 6099)

Money Order Market

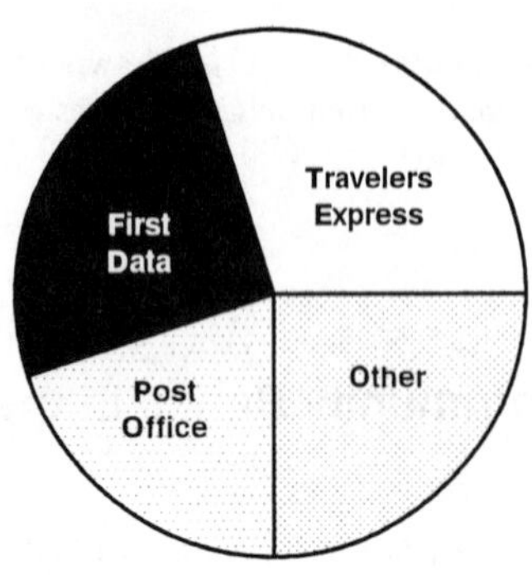

Market shares are shown in percent.

Travelers Express	30.0%
First Data (FDC)	25.0
Post Office	20.0
Other	25.0

Source: *Investext,* Thomson Financial Networks, August 13, 1998, p. 7, from PaineWebber estimates and company reports.

SIC 61 - Nondepository Institutions

★ 1621 ★

Financial Services (SIC 6100)

Largest Financial Companies - 1997

Institutions are ranked by assets in billions of dollars as of December 31, 1997.

Fannie Mae	$ 392
Chase Manhattan Corp.	366
Federal Home Loan Banks	358
Citicorp	311
NationsBank Corp.	265

Source: *Business Week*, August 17, 1998, p. 79, from Federal Home Loan Bank of Chicago.

★ 1622 ★

Financial Services (SIC 6100)

Largest Financial Groups in Mexico

Banamex/Accival	24.3%
Bancomer	19.2
Inbursa	14.4
Serfin	10.1
Bital	6.6
BBV-Probursa	5.5
Banorte	5.3
Santander Mexicano	3.3
Citibank	2.2
Others	9.1

Source: *Mexico Business*, May 1999, p. 18, from CNBV.

★ 1623 ★

Financial Services (SIC 6100)

Top Financial Service Firms in Minnesota

Companies are ranked by revenues in millions of dollars.

Norwest Corporation	$ 9,665.7
U.S. Bancorp.	6,909.8
The St. Paul Companies Inc.	6,219.3
American Express Financial Advisors	4,599.0
Lutheran Brotherhood	2,900.3

Source: *Corporate Report*, June 1998, p. 64, from *Corporate Report Fact Book*.

★ 1624 ★

Credit Cards (SIC 6141)

Credit Card Market

Market shares are shown as of June 30, 1998.

Visa	50.0%
MasterCard	25.0
American Express	18.0
Discover	5.0
Diner's Club	1.0

Source: *Wall Street Journal*, October 8, 1998, p. A3, from Visa, MasterCard, and *Nilson Report*.

★ 1625 ★
Credit Cards (SIC 6141)

Credit Card Market - 1999

Market shares are shown for the first quarter of the year.

Visa	50.8%
MasterCard	25.0
American Express	17.5
Discover	5.4
Diners Club International	1.3

Source: *Wall Street Journal*, June 11, 1999, p. B4, from Nilson Report.

★ 1626 ★
Credit Cards (SIC 6141)

Credit Card Market in Mexico

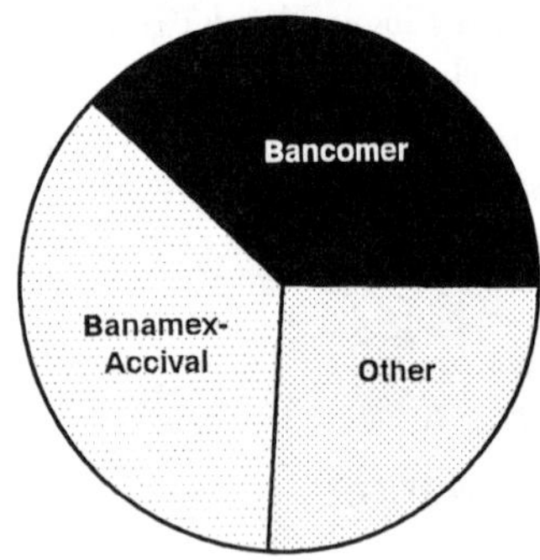

Market shares are shown in percent.

Bancomer	38.2%
Banamex-Accival	35.5
Other	26.3

Source: *Wall Street Journal*, March 22, 1999, p. A14, from Banamex, SG Cowen Securities, and Goldman Sachs & Co.

★ 1627 ★
Credit Cards (SIC 6141)

Gold Card Market

Data show millions of cards.

Visa	74.9
Mastercard	42.0
American Express	7.8

Source: *New York Times*, May 23, 1999, p. 12, from Nilson Report.

★ 1628 ★
Credit Cards (SIC 6141)

Government Card Market

Market shares are shown for new government card contracts as of December 1, 1998. Figures refer to combined purchasing, travel and vehicle fleet card use.

Nationsbank	37.0%
Citibank	33.0
U.S. Bancorp	24.0
First Chicago NBD	5.0
Not yet awarded	1.0

Source: *ABA Banking Journal*, November 1998, p. 49, from U.S. General Services Administration.

★ 1629 ★
Credit Cards (SIC 6141)

Largest Credit Card Issuers in Canada - 1997

Market shares are shown in percent.

CIBC	23.2%
Royal Bank of Canada	18.7
Bank of Montreal	13.9
Toronto-Dominion Bank	11.0
American Express	7.3
Bank of Nova Scotia	6.9
National Bank of Canada	3.8
Canada Trust	3.7
La Confederation Des Caisses	3.2
Other	8.3

Source: *Globe and Mail*, May 10, 1999, p. 7B, from Nilson Report.

★ 1630 ★
Credit Cards (SIC 6141)

Largest Credit Cards Issuers - 1998

Companies are ranked by outstanding debt in billions of dollars.

First USA	$ 69.8
Citigroup	69.6
MBNA	48.3
American Express	33.9
Discover	32.8
Chase	32.2
Bank of America	20.9

Continued on next page.

★ 1630 ★ *Continued*

Credit Cards (SIC 6141)

Largest Credit Cards Issuers - 1998

Companies are ranked by outstanding debt in billions of dollars.

Household	$ 14.4
Capital One	14.3
Fleet	14.3

Source: *Wall Street Journal*, February 11, 1999, p. A6, from Nilson Report.

★ 1631 ★

Credit Cards (SIC 6141)

Largest Gas Credit Card Programs - 1997

Data show total number of cards, in thousands.

Mobil Oil Credit Corp.	8,400
Chevron Co. U.S.A.	7,400
Citgo Petroleum Corp.	5,101
Shell Oil Co.	3,800
Tosco Corp.	3,366
BP America	2,650
Phillips 66 Co.	1,800
Sun Co. Inc.	1,610
Conoco Inc.	1,020
Gulf Oil	1,000

Source: *National Petroleum News*, July 1998, p. 129.

★ 1632 ★

Credit Cards (SIC 6141)

Leading Credit Card Issuers

Data show millions of cards.

Bank One/First USA	44.1
Citibank	40.5
Discover	38.0
American Express	29.8
MBNA	27.2
Chase Manhattan	21.0
Bank of America	17.6

Source: *New York Times*, April 25, 1999, p. 10, from CardWeb.com and listed banks.

★ 1633 ★

Loan Arrangers (SIC 6150)

Agricultural Lending Market

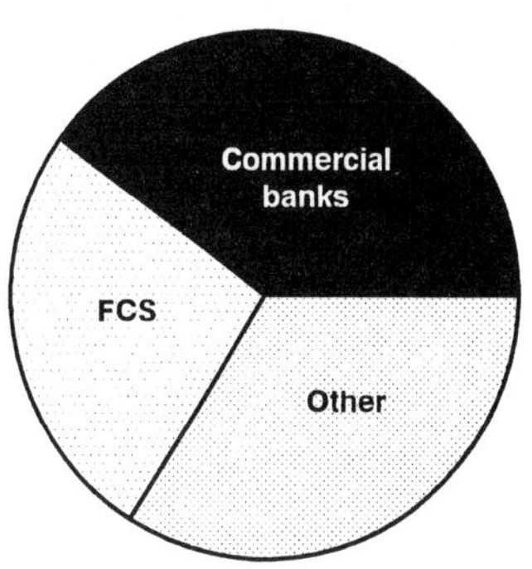

FCS stands for Farm Credit System.

Commercial banks	40.0%
FCS	26.0
Other	34.0

Source: *Ag Lender*, November 1998, p. 10.

★ 1634 ★

Loan Arrangers (SIC 6150)

Largest Agricultural Banks

Data show value of loans in thousands of dollars. Figures are for the quarter ended December 31, 1997.

Wells Fargo Bank	$ 1,913,633
Bank of America Nat Tr & SA	1,833,000
US Bank NA	1,405,144
NationsBank NA	996,513
Keybank NA	860,008
Sanwa Bank California	831,347
First Union NB	480,771
Norwest Bank SD NA	365,017

Source: *Agri Finance*, July 1998, p. 10, from Federal Reserve System.

★ 1635 ★

Loan Arrangers (SIC 6150)

Largest Small Business Lenders

Banks are ranked by size of portfolio loans in billions of dollars. Figures are as of June 30, 1998.

First Union National Bank	$ 20.8
Nationsbank	19.8
Wells Fargo Bank	15.1

Continued on next page.

★ 1635 ★ *Continued*

Loan Arrangers (SIC 6150)

Largest Small Business Lenders

Banks are ranked by size of portfolio loans in billions of dollars. Figures are as of June 30, 1998.

U.S. Bank	$ 12.0
Keybank	11.8
Southtrust Bank	9.2
Bank of America	8.3
Wachovia Bank	8.0
PNC Bank	7.6
Huntington National Bank	6.7

Source: *Wall Street Journal*, April 19, 1999, p. 4, from Federal Deposit Insurance Corp.

★ 1636 ★

Mortgage Loans (SIC 6162)

Largest Mortgage Brokers in Canada

Norlite Financial Services
Multi Prets Hypotheques
The Mortgage Group Western Canada
Hypotek Nor-bec
Complete Mortgage Services Inc.

Brokers are ranked by annual mortgage volume in millions of dollars.

Norlite Financial Services	$ 1,000
Multi Prets Hypotheques	650
The Mortgage Group Western Canada	400
Hypotek Nor-bec	300
Complete Mortgage Services Inc.	200

Source: *Canadian Business*, February 12, 1999, p. 22.

★ 1637 ★

Mortgage Loans (SIC 6162)

Largest Mortgage Loan Providers in Dallas, TX

Data show number of originated loans.

CTX Mortgage Co.	4,863
Fort Worth Mortgage	3,390
Prime Lending Inc.	3,362
FT Mortgage Cos.	3,072
North American Mortgage Co.	2,907

Source: *Dallas Business Journal*, July 17, 1998, p. C14.

★ 1638 ★

Mortgage Loans (SIC 6162)

Leading Mortgage Arrangers - 1998

Market shares are shown in percent.

Norwest Mortgage	7.0%
Countrywide Home Loans	6.1
Chase & Affiliates	5.3
BankAmerica	2.5
NationsBank & Affiliates	2.5
Washington Mutual	2.4
HomeSide Lending	2.3
Dime/North Amer Mortgage	2.2
Fleet Mortgage	2.1
ABN AMRO Mortgage	2.0
Other	34.4

Source: *Investext,* Thomson Financial Networks, August 17, 1998, p. 13, from *Inside Mortgage Finance*.

★ 1639 ★

Mortgage Loans (SIC 6162)

Leading Online Mortgage Lenders - 1998

Market shares are shown in percent.

E-Loan	29.0%
QuickenMortgage	22.0
GetSmart	14.0
Mortgage.com	11.0
HomeShark	8.0
Other	16.0

Source: *Forbes*, April 19, 1999, p. 224, from Deutsche Bank.

★ 1640 ★

Loan Arrangers (SIC 6163)

Largest Retail Lenders - 1998

Data show the amount committed in billions of dollars.

Lehman Brothers	$ 5.00
Credit Suisse First Boston	4.00
Bank of America Corp./NationsBanc Montgomery Securities LLC	2.30
TIAA	1.98
First Union	1.80

Source: *Shopping Center World*, April 1999, p. 54.

★ 1641 ★

Loan Arrangers (SIC 6163)

Largest Small Business Loan Arrangers in Iowa - 1998

Data show the value of loans arranged.

Iowa Business Growth Co. West Des Moines	$ 15,818,000
Norwest Bank	5,398,081
Firstar Bank	4,892,000
Black Hawk County Economic Development	4,073,000
NationsBank	1,804,850

Source: *Des Moines Register*, November 20, 1998, p. 14, from U.S. Small Business Adminsitration.

★ 1642 ★

Loan Arrangers (SIC 6163)

Letters of Credit Providers

Market shares are shown among the top 100 providers. Figures are as of June 30, 1998.

Citibank	18.1%
Chase Manhattan	14.4
First Union	10.8
Bank of America	10.2
Bank of New York	6.5
BankBoston	6.3
NationsBank	3.5
Other	30.2

Source: *Banking Strategies*, January/February 1999, p. 59, from SNL Securities.

SIC 62 - Security and Commodity Brokers

★ 1643 ★

Investment Banking (SIC 6211)

Largest 401(k) Plan Providers - 1997

Data show assets in billions of dollars.

Fidelity Investments	$ 175.2
Vanguard Group	87.3
State Street Global	85.2
Barclays Global Investor	49.0
Merrill Lynch	45.2
Bankers Trust	42.9
UAM	35.1

Source: *Wall Street Journal*, October 22, 1998, p. C1, from BernsteinResearch and Cerulli Associates.

★ 1644 ★

Investment Banking (SIC 6211)

Largest Bond Counsels

Data show the market shares of new tax-exempt healthcare issues for January - March 1999.

Orrick, Herrington & Sutcliffe	15.0%
Hawkins, Delafield & Wood	12.9
Jones, Day, Reavis & Pogue	11.7
Harper, Ferguson & Davis	5.4
Chapman and Cutler	5.2
Other	49.8

Source: *Modern Healthcare*, April 12, 1999, p. %, from Securities Data Co.

★ 1645 ★

Investment Banking (SIC 6211)

Largest Book Managers

Data show the top managers of syndicated loans.

Chase Manhattan	23.3%
NationsBank/BankAmerica	14.7
J.P. Morgan	13.0
Citicorp	7.8
Bankers Trust	5.5
Other	35.7

Source: *Wall Street Journal*, July 23, 1998, p. C1, from Securities Data Co.

★ 1646 ★

Investment Banking (SIC 6211)

Largest Equity Managers

State Street Global
Barclays Global
Fidelity Investments
TIAA-CREF
Bankers Trust

Companies are ranked by institutional tax-exempt assets under management in millions of dollars.

State Street Global	$ 405,332
Barclays Global	398,378
Fidelity Investments	319,100
TIAA-CREF	245,177
Bankers Trust	230,236

Source: *Pensions & Investments*, May 17, 1999, p. 26.

★ 1647 ★

Investment Banking (SIC 6211)

Largest Institutional Equity Traders in Canada

Market shares are shown for July 1998.

Nesbitt Burns	12.5%
RBC Dominion	12.5
Midland Walwyn	11.5
ScotiaMcLeod	10.7
CIBC Wood Gundy	10.0
Other	42.8

Source: *Globe and Mail*, August 19, 1998, p. B10, from TSE, ME, and VSE.

★ 1648 ★

Investment Banking (SIC 6211)

Largest IPO Book Managers - 1998

Market shares are shown in percent. IPO stands for initial public offerings.

Morgan Stanley Dean Witter	19.0%
Goldman, Sachs	18.2
Bear, Stearns	13.2
Bankers Trust	7.2
Bank of America	6.7
Salomon Smith Barney	6.7
CS First Boston	6.3
Other	22.7

Source: *The Asian Wall Street Journal*, May 17, 1999, p. 1, from Securities Data Co.

★ 1649 ★

Investment Banking (SIC 6211)

Largest Money Managers in Chicago, IL

Data show assets managed as of August 30, 1998. Figures are in billions of dollars.

Brinson Partners Inc.	$ 356.0
Northern Trust Global Investments	228.7
Scudder Kemper Investments	91.3
Van Kampen Investment	58.6
Lincoln Capital Management Co.	57.2

Source: *Crain's Chicago Business*, August 17, 1998, p. 15.

★ 1650 ★

Investment Banking (SIC 6211)

Largest Mutual Funds in Canada - 1999

Market shares are shown in percent for the year ended March 31, 1999.

Investors Group	10.9%
Royal Mutual Funds	8.8
Mackenzie Financial	7.9
Trimark Investment Management	6.9
Fidelity Investments Canda	6.3
Others	59.2

Source: "Report on Market Share." Retrieved June 1, 1999 from the World Wide Web: http://www.marketingmag.ca/index.cgi?, from Investment Funds Institute of Canada.

★ 1651 ★

Investment Banking (SIC 6211)

Largest Real Estate Equity Managers

Companies are ranked by institutional tax-exempt assets under managment in millions of dollars.

Lend Lease Real Estate	$ 11,728
Prudential Insurance	7,140
TIAA-CREF	6,877
RREEF Funds	6,815
Heitman Capital	5,985

Source: *Pensions & Investments*, May 17, 1999, p. 26.

★ 1652 ★

Investment Banking (SIC 6211)

Largest Securities Firms

Data show number of employees.

Merrill Lynch & Company Inc.	49,800
Merrill Lynch Pierce Fenner & Smith Inc.	46,000
Morgan Stanley Dean Witter Discover & Co.	45,000
Salomon Smith Barney Holdings Inc.	36,400
Smith Barney Inc.	28,000

Source: *Industry Week*, January 18, 1999, p. 48, from *Dun & Bradstreet's Business Rankings, 1998.*

★ 1653 ★

Investment Banking (SIC 6211)

Largest Telecom Deal Advisors

The top advisors to deals in the telecommunications and media industries are ranked by value of deals in billions of dollars.

Goldman, Sachs & Co.	$ 246.89
Salomon Smith Barney	159.28
Merrill Lynch & Co.	94.00
Morgan Stanley Dean Witter	91.79
Credit Suisse First Boston	84.19

Source: *New York Times*, August 17, 1998, p. C3, from Securities Data Co.

★ 1654 ★

Investment Banking (SIC 6211)

Online Trading Leaders - 1998

Market shares are shown for the fourth quarter of the year.

Schwab	27.4%
Waterhouse	12.4
E* Trade	11.8
Datek	10.0
Fidelity	9.4
Ameritrade	7.6
Others	21.4

Source: *New York Times*, February 1, 1999, p. C9, from Credit Suisse First Boston.

★ 1655 ★

Investment Banking (SIC 6211)

Online Trading Market - 1998

Shares are shown based on trades per day.

	3Q Share
Schwab	30.1%
Waterhouse	10.4
E*Trade	10.8
Datek	8.4
Fidelity	11.2
Ameritrade	7.2
DLJ Direct	4.1
Discover	3.7%
SURETRADE	2.7
NDB	1.5
Others	10.0

Source: *Network World*, April 12, 1999, p. 41.

★ 1656 ★

Investment Banking (SIC 6211)

Variable Annuity Sales - 1998

According to the source, a variable annuity is an IRA that also has an insurance policy. Contributions are generally invested in mutual funds and are tax deferred until withdrawal. Market shares are shown based on net assets reaching $778.4 billion.

TIAA-CREF	31.7%
Hartford Life Insurance Co.	8.0
Lincoln National Life Insurance Co.	4.8
Equitable Life Insurance Society of the U.S.	4.0
Nationwide Life Insurance Co.	3.9
IDS Life Insurance Co.	3.4
American General Corp.	3.0
Aetna Life Insurance and Annuity Co.	2.6
Prudential Insurance Company of America	2.4
Other	36.2

Source: *Chicago Tribune*, March 4, 1999, p. 1, from Variable Annuity Research and Data Service.

★ 1657 ★

Investment Banking (SIC 6211)

Variable Annuity Sales Leaders - 1998

Sales are shown in billions of dollars.

Hartford Life Ins. Co.	$ 9.87
TIAA-CRAF	8.18
Nationwide Life Ins. Co.	5.72
American General Corp.	5.42
Equitable Life Assurance Society	5.37
American Skandia Life Assurance	4.12
Anchor National Life Ins. Co.	3.57
Prudential Ins. Co.	3.26
Allmerica Financial	3.17
Lincoln National Life Ins. Co.	3.15

Source: *National Underwriter*, February 22, 1999, p. 1.

★ 1658 ★

Mutual Funds (SIC 6211)

Best-Selling Mutual Fund Families

Net sales are shown in billions of dollars as of November 30, 1998.

Vanguard Group	$ 44.1
Putnam Investments	11.9
Fidelity Investments	10.2
Massachusetts Financial Services	9.8
American Fund Distributors	9.6
Pimco Advisors	9.3
Blackrock Funds	8.2

Source: *New York Times*, January 10, 1999, p. 35, from Financial Research Corp.

★ 1659 ★

Mutual Funds (SIC 6211)

Largest Mutual Fund Companies

Companies are ranked by revenues in billions of dollars.

Metropolitan Life	$ 28.8
State Farm Mutual Automobile	27.7
Prudential Insurance Co. of America	27.4
Principal Mutual Life	15.5
New York Life	12.5
Northwestern Mutual	11.4
John Hancock Mutual Life	10.1

Source: *Forbes*, November 30, 1998, p. 197, from A.M. Best & Co.

★ 1660 ★

Mutual Funds (SIC 6211)

Largest Mutual Fund Groups

Market shares are as of February 1999.

Fidelity Distributors	12.84%
Vanguard Group	10.77
American Fund Distributors	7.36
Putnam Investments	5.02
Franklin Distributors Inc.	4.19
Other	59.82

Source: Retrieved April 30, 1999 from the World Wide Web: http:// www.mfcafe.com/market/msp_top50.html.

★ 1661 ★

Mutual Funds (SIC 6211)

Largest Mutual Funds - 1999

Data show assets in billions of dollars for the first quarter of the year.

Fidelity Magellan	$ 85.86
Vanguard 500 Index	78.07
Washington Mutual Inv.	51.44
Investment Co. of America	49.96
Fidelity Growth & Income	48.26

Source: *Christian Science Monitor*, April 12, 1999, p. 19, from Lipper Inc.

★ 1662 ★

Underwriting (SIC 6211)

Largest Health Care Issues Underwriters - 1998

Market shares are for new tax exempt health care issues for October - December 1998.

Salomon Smith Barney Holdings	19.6%
PaineWebber	15.7
Merrill Lynch & Co.	12.7
Morgan Stanley Dean Witter	7.4
Goldman, Sachs & Co.	7.2
Other	37.4

Source: *Modern Healthcare*, January 18, 1999, p. 37, from Securities Data Co.

★ 1663 ★

Underwriting (SIC 6211)

Largest Underwriters in Arkansas

Market shares are shown in percent. Full credit is given to book manager.

Stephens Inc.	19.6%
Goldman Sachs & Co.	15.8
PaineWebber Inc.	10.8
Morgan Keegan & Co.	10.7
Bank of Oklahoma, Tulsa	8.2
Other	35.3

Source: *Arkansas Business*, March 8, 1999, p. 11, from Securities Data Co.

★ 1664 ★

Underwriting (SIC 6211)

Leading Underwriters - 1999

Data show the leading managing underwriters of corporate securities. Shares are shown for the first quarter.

Merrill Lynch	16.0%
Salomon Smith Barney	13.5
Morgan Stanley Dean Witter	9.3
Credit Suisse First Boston	8.8
Goldman. Sachs	8.1
Lehman Brothers	8.0
Chase Manhattan	6.5
Other	29.8

Source: *New York Times*, April 1, 1999, p. C8, from Securities Data Co.

★ 1665 ★

Underwriting (SIC 6211)

Top Underwriters - 1998

Market shares are shown with full credit given to book manager.

Merrill Lynch & Co.	22.8%
Salomon Smith Barney	15.1
Morgan Stanley Dean Witter	12.0
Chase Manhattan Corp.	11.5
Goldman, Sachs & Co.	11.2
Other	27.4

Source: *US Banker*, February 1999, p. 72, from Securities Data Co.

★ 1666 ★

Underwriting (SIC 6211)

Top Underwriters in Canada - 1998

Data show all financings. Firms are ranked by bonus credit in millions of dollars.

RBC Dominion Securities Inc.	$ 11,864
CIBC Wood Gundy Securities Inc.	10,609
Nesbitt Burns Inc.	8,701
Merrill Lynch & Co.	8,314
ScotiaMcLeod Inc.	7,774
TD Securities	$ 6,295
Goldman Sachs & Co.	5,945
SBC Warburg, Dillon Read	3,809
Salomon Smith Barney	3,720

Source: *Financial Post*, January 30, 1999, p. 1.

★ 1667 ★

Venture Capital (SIC 6211)

Leading Venture Capital Firms - 1998

Data show number of deals for the third quarter of the year.

New Enterprise Associates	54
Hambrecht & Quist Venture Capital	51
St. Paul Venture Capital Inc.	51
Accel Partners	45
Brentwood Venture Capital	43
Bessemer Venture Partners	42

Source: *Industry Week*, January 18, 1999, p. 46, from *Price WaterhouseCoopers Money Tree Survey*.

★ 1668 ★

Venture Capital (SIC 6211)

Venture Capital by State

Investments are shown in millions of dollars for the third quarter of the year.

California	$ 4,315.3
Massachusetts	1,212.8
Texas	508.3
Colorado	391.3
New York	348.4
Washington	302.3
Virginia	277.2
North Carolina	262.7
Pennsylvania	258.7
Georgia	249.1

Source: *Chicago Tribune*, November 17, 1998, p. 1, from PriceWaterhouseCoopers.

★ 1669 ★

Venture Capital (SIC 6211)

Venture Capital Industry - 1998

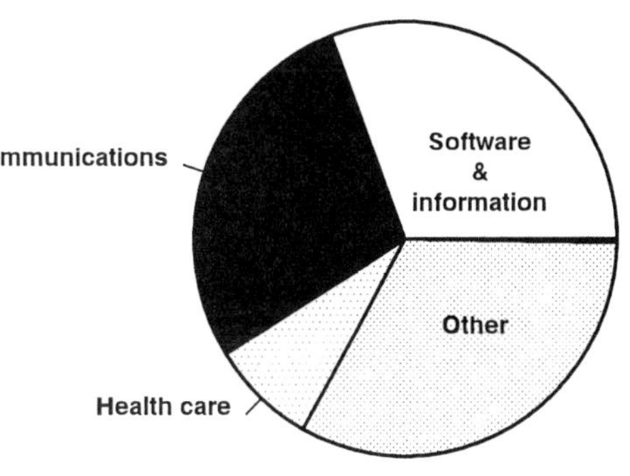

Data show share of total investments.

Software & information	31.3%
Communications	27.7
Health care	7.7
Other	33.3

Source: *Entrepeneur*, May 1999, p. 38, from PriceWaterhouseCoopers.

★ 1670 ★

Securities Exchanges (SIC 6231)

Largest Brokerage Firms in Buffalo, NY

Data show number of brokers.

Merrill Lynch	77
M&T Securities Inc.	55
Morgan Stanley Dean Witter	47
A.G. Edwards and Sons Inc.	42
Key Investments Inc.	42

Source: *Business First of Buffalo*, August 10, 1998, p. 14.

★ 1671 ★

Securities Exchanges (SIC 6231)

Securities Trading - 1998

Data share of Nasdaq trading for the fourth quarter of the year. Figures have been adjusted to eliminate double counted trades. ECN stands for electronic communication network.

Instinct	20.3%
Island ECN	6.2
Other ECNs	2.3
Traditional trading	71.2

Source: *New York Times*, May 12, 1999, p. C1, from Securities Industry Association, Credit Suisse First Boston, Putnam, Lovell de Guardia & Thornton, and Securities and Exchange Commission.

★ 1672 ★

Clearinghouses (SIC 6289)

Top Clearinghouse Firms

Market shares are shown in percent.

Bear Stearns	10.0%
Pershing	9.0
Fidelity	6.0
CSC	4.0
Southwest Securities	4.0
U.S. Clearing	4.0
Self clearers	12.0
Others	44.0

Source: *US Banker*, April 1999, p. 62, from Securities Industries Association, National Securities Clearing Corporation, Standard & Poor's, and Cerulli Associates.

SIC 63 - Insurance Carriers

★ 1673 ★

Insurance (SIC 6300)

Artisan Contracting Insurance Industry

Data show estimated premiums in millions of dollars. Artisan contractors offer $6.99 billion in premiums, or 5.5% of total commercial lines.

	($ mil.)	Share
West	$ 1,651.3	23.61%
Southeast	1,610.0	23.02
Northeast	1,566.2	22.39
Midwest	1,173.7	16.78
Southwest	993.8	14.21

Source: *Rough Notes*, March 1999, p. 95.

★ 1674 ★

Insurance (SIC 6300)

Largest Insurance Firms in Mexico - 1997

Market shares are shown in percent.

Comerical America	24.94%
Grupo Nacional Provincial	19.84
Monterrey Aetna	9.18
Inbursa	5.92
Tepeyac	3.50
Genesis	3.03
Bancomer	2.23
AIG Mexico	1.58
Aba/Seguros	1.53
Atlas	1.51
Other	26.74

Source: *Business Mexico*, September 1998, p. 38, from AMIS.

★ 1675 ★

Insurance (SIC 6300)

Largest Insurance Wholesalers

The premium volume of the largest U.S. based firms is shown in millions of dollars.

Swett & Crawford Group	$ 569.5
Crump Insurance Services Inc.	558.6
Tri-City Brokerages Inc.	435.0
Sherwood Insurance Services	335.0
Stewart Smith Group	302.8

Source: *Business Insurance*, September 7, 1998, p. 3.

★ 1676 ★

Insurance (SIC 6300)

Largest Professional Reinsurers in Canada - 1997

MunichRe

Swiss Re

EmployersRe

AXA Re

SCOR

Companies are ranked by net premiums written in millions of dollars.

MunichRe	$ 208.7
Swiss Re	161.6
EmployersRe	94.5
AXA Re	91.5
SCOR	89.2

Source: *Canadian Insurance*, July 1998, p. 11, from Stone & Cox Ltd.

★ 1677 ★

Insurance (SIC 6300)

Leading Claims Administrators

Firms are ranked by claims paid for self-insurers, in billions.

ESIS Inc.	$ 2.80
Sedgwick Claims Management	2.55
Harrington Benefit Services	2.25
RSKCo	1.96
Gallagher Bassett Services Inc.	1.91
The TPA Inc.	1.85
Crawford & Co.	1.80
CoreSource Inc.	1.62

Source: *Business Insurance*, February 15, 1999, p. 3.

★ 1678 ★

Insurance (SIC 6300)

Veterinary Insurance Industry

Data show estimated premiums in millions of dollars. Veterinary services offer $120.8 million in premiums, or 0.09% of total commercial lines.

	($ mil.)	Share
West	$ 29.66	24.55%
Northeast	26.47	21.91
Southeast	25.83	21.38
Midwest	21.23	17.57
Southwest	17.61	14.58

Source: *Rough Notes*, March 1999, p. 95.

★ 1679 ★

Life Insurance (SIC 6311)

Largest Life Insurers in North Carolina

Market shares are shown in percent.

Kemper Investors Life	16.5%
Hartford Life	12.5
Jefferson-Pilot	4.9
Metropolitan Life	4.0
Northwestern Mutual Life	3.8
Prudential	3.1
Massachusetts Mutual	1.9
New York Life	1.9
Other	51.4

Source: *Business North Carolina*, February 1999, p. 82, from North Carolina Department of Insurance.

★ 1680 ★

Life Insurance (SIC 6311)

Largest Life/Health Insurance Groups

Groups are ranked by assets in billions of dollars.

Prudential of America	$ 205.2
Metropolitan Life	183.2
Aegon/Transamerica	98.7
TIAA Group	93.8
Hartford Financial	91.1
New York Life	84.5
Aetna US Healthcare	77.1
Equitable	75.9
Cigna	74.2
Northwestern Mutual	71.1

Source: *Financial Times*, April 1, 1999, p. 20, from A.M. Best & Co.

★ 1681 ★

Life Insurance (SIC 6311)

Leading Life Insurers - 1997

Market shares are shown based on net premiums.

Metropolitan	7.0%
Northwestern Mutual	6.8
Prudential	6.6
New York Life	5.0
ITT Hartford	4.2
Mass Mutual	3.4
American General	2.8
The Guardian	2.7
State Farm	2.5
Equitable	2.4
Other	49.2

Source: *Investext*, Thomson Financial Networks, December 10, 1998, p. 70, from A.M. Best & Co.

★ 1682 ★

Life Insurance (SIC 6311)

Top Life Insurance Firms in Detroit, MI

Firms are ranked by total assets in millions of dollars.

Alexander Hamilton Life	$ 5,507.2
Royal Maccabees Life Insurance Co.	1,998.9
American Community Mutual Insurance Co.	182.9
Auto Club Life Insurance Co.	156.6
Vista Life Insurance Co.	56.9

Source: *Crain's Detroit Business*, September 28, 1998, p. 17.

★ 1683 ★

Life Insurance (SIC 6311)

Top Life Insurers in Canada - 1997

Market shares are shown in percent for the year ended December 31, 1997.

Sun Life Assurance	21.6%
Manufacturers Life Insurance	20.8
Great-West Life Assurance	19.9
Canada Life Assurance	10.6
London Life Assurance	7.1
Others	20.0

Source: "Report on Market Share." Retrieved June 1, 1999 from the World Wide Web: http://www.marketingmag.ca/index.cgi?, from Office of the Superintendent of Financial Institutions Canada.

★ 1684 ★

Auto Insurance (SIC 6321)

Auto Damage Insurance Industry - 1997

Market shares are shown in percent.

State Farm Group	19.5%
Allstate Ins. Group	11.7
Farmers Ins. Group	5.3
Nationwide Group	3.5
Progressive Group	3.4
USAA Group	2.9
Berkshire Hathaway	2.6
Amer. Family Ins. Group	1.7
Travelers PC Group	1.7
Liberty Mutual	1.6%
Other	46.1

Source: *Best's Review*, October 1998, p. 32, from A.M. Best & Co.

★ 1685 ★

Auto Insurance (SIC 6321)

Auto Insurance Market - 1997

Shares are shown based on commercial and private coverage. Total premiums reached $133.29 billion.

State Farm Group	18.1%
Allstate Ins Group	10.9
Farmers Ins. Group	5.3
Nationwide Group	3.7
Progressive Group	3.5
USAA Group	2.7
Berkshire Hathaway	2.6
Travelers PC Group	2.2
Liberty Mutual	1.9
Other	49.1

Source: *Best's Review*, July 1998, p. 43.

★ 1686 ★

Auto Insurance (SIC 6321)

Auto Liability Industry in Texas

Texas ranks third in the nation's auto liability market with total premiums reaching $6.5 billion. Market shares are shown in percent.

State Farm Group	23.1%
Farmers Ins. Group	12.5
Other	64.4

Source: *Best's Review*, October 1998, p. 38.

★ 1687 ★

Auto Insurance (SIC 6321)

Commercial Auto Insurance Industry - 1997

Market shares are shown in percent.

CNA Ins. Group	5.5%
Travelers PC Group	5.1
Zurich Ins. Group - U.S.	4.6
State Farm Group	3.6
Liberty Mutual	3.4

Continued on next page.

★ 1687 ★ *Continued*

Auto Insurance (SIC 6321)

Commercial Auto Insurance Industry - 1997

Market shares are shown in percent.

Amer. Inter. Group	3.2%
Old Republic Gen. Group	2.7
Nationwide Group	2.5
St. Paul Companies	2.5
Progressive Group	2.4
Other	64.5

Source: *Best's Review*, October 1998, p. 35, from A.M. Best & Co.

★ 1688 ★

Auto Insurance (SIC 6321)

Commercial Auto Insurance Market in Massachusetts

Massachusetts ranks 10th in the nation's commercial auto market with total premiums reaching $546.9 million. Market shares are shown in percent.

Arbella Ins. Group	15.8%
Travelers PC Group	13.1
Other	71.1

Source: *Best's Review*, October 1998, p. 45.

★ 1689 ★

Auto Insurance (SIC 6321)

Largest Auto Insurers - 1997

Market shares are shown in percent.

State Farm	21.3%
Allstate	12.3
Farmers Insurance	5.6
Nationwide Group	3.9
Progressive Corp.	3.7
USAA Group	3.2
Berkshire Hathaway	3.1
American Family	1.8
Liberty Mutual Group	1.7
Safeco	1.7
Other	41.7

Source: *Investext,* Thomson Financial Networks, January 4, 1999, p. 6.

★ 1690 ★

Auto Insurance (SIC 6321)

Largest Auto Insurers in Canada - 1998

Market shares are shown in percent for the year ended December 31, 1998.

CGU Group Canada Ltd.	9.1%
ING Canada	8.7
Co-Operators General Insurance	6.6
State Farm Insurance	6.1
Economical Insurance Group	4.9
AXA Canada	4.5
Wawanesa Mutual Insurance	3.9
Other	49.7

Source: "Report on Market Share." Retrieved June 1, 1999 from the World Wide Web: http://www.marketingmag.ca/index.cgi?, from *Canadian Insurance*.

★ 1691 ★

Auto Insurance (SIC 6321)

Private Auto Insurance Industry - 1997

Market shares are shown in percent.

State Farm Group	20.5%
Allstate Ins. Group	12.3
Farmers Ins. Group	6.0
Nationwide Group	3.9
Progressive Group	3.7
USAA Group	3.1
Berkshire Hathaway	3.0
Amer Family Ins Group	1.8
Liberty Mutual	1.7
Travelers PC Group	1.7
Other	42.3

Source: *Best's Review*, October 1998, p. 38, from A.M. Best & Co.

★ 1692 ★

Auto Insurance (SIC 6321)

Private Auto Insurance Market in West Virginia

Texas ranks 35th in the nation's private auto market with total premiums reaching $783.5 million. Market shares are shown in percent.

State Farm Group	34.1%
Nationwide Group	19.2
Other	46.7

Source: *Best's Review*, October 1998, p. 44.

★ 1693 ★

Health Insurance (SIC 6321)

Largest Accident/Health Insurers in North Carolina

Market shares are shown in percent.

Blue Cross and Blue Shield of NC	24.8%
Healthsource North Carolina	7.0
Partners National Health Plans of NC	5.6
United Healthcare of NC	4.7
Kaiser Foundation Health Plan of NC	3.9
Other	54.0

Source: *Business North Carolina*, February 1999, p. 82, from North Carolina Department of Insurance.

★ 1694 ★

Health Insurance (SIC 6321)

Largest Behavioral Health Care Vendors - 1997

Organizations are ranked by enrollment in millions.

Magellan Behavioral Health	58.7
VBH/Options	27.1
United Behavioral Health	13.8
Managed Health Network	8.2
MCC Behavioral Care	6.5

Source: *Business & Health*, August 1998, p. 51, from Open Minds.

★ 1695 ★

Health Insurance (SIC 6321)

Largest Physician Practice Management Firms - 1997

Companies are ranked by revenues in millions of dollars.

MedPartners	$ 6,300.0
FPA Medical Management	1,200.0
PhyCor	1,100.0
Physician Resource Group	411.6
PhyMatrix	346.5
American Oncology	321.8
Pediatrix Medical	128.9
ProMedCo Management	127.7
Orthodontic Centers of America	117.3
MedCath	110.9

Source: *Investor's Business Daily*, July 2, 1998, p. A4, from company reports and Piper Jaffray Inc.

★ 1696 ★

Health Insurance (SIC 6321)

U.S. Health Coverage

FEHBP stands for federal employees health benefits program.

Medicare	15.0%
Medicaid	13.0
FEHBP	4.0
CHAMPUS	3.0
Commercial private	24.0
Self-funded private	16.0
Uninsured	16.0
Other government	2.0

Source: *Continuing Care*, November 1998, p. 20, from American Association for Hospital Planning, Employee Benefit Research Institute, and Health Insurance Association of America.

★ 1697 ★

Health Plans (SIC 6324)

Health Plan Enrollments

Data show percent of employees enrolled. HMO stands for health manintenance organization. PPO stands for preferred provider organization.

	1997	1998
PPOs	35.0%	40.0%
HMOs	30.0	29.0
Point of service	20.0	18.0
Traditional indemnity	15.0	13.0

Source: *Business Insurance*, January 25, 1999, p. 6.

★ 1698 ★

Health Plans (SIC 6324)

Health Plan Market in Detroit, MI

Data show share of enrollees. PPO stands for preferred provider organization. HMO stands for health maintenance organization.

HMOs	31.0%
Traditional indemnity	30.0
PPO	28.0
Point of service	11.0

Source: *Detroit Free Press*, December 4, 1998, p. E1, from Hewitt Associates.

★ 1699 ★

Health Plans (SIC 6324)

HMOs by State

Data show number of licensed HMOs.

	No.	Share
Texas	69	8.47%
California	54	6.63
Indiana	51	6.26
Illinois	47	5.77
New York	47	5.77
Ohio	44	5.40
Florida	40	4.91
Missouri	33	4.05
Virginia	29	3.56
Wisconsin	25	3.07
Other	376	46.13

Source: *Business North Carolina*, January 1999, p. 60, from American Association of Health Plans.

★ 1700 ★

Health Plans (SIC 6324)

Largest HMO Doctor Networks

Plans are ranked by number of primary care physicians as of June 30, 1998

CIGNA HealthCare	81,385
Humana	73,500
Aetna U.S. Healthcare	55,000
Prudential Healthcare	40,746
PacifiCare Health Systems	20,359

Source: *Business Insurance*, December 28, 1998, p. 1.

★ 1701 ★

Health Plans (SIC 6324)

Largest HMO Plans

Plans are ranked by millions of enrollees as of June 30, 1998.

Kaiser Foundation	8.8
CIGNA HealthCare	6.3
Aetna U.S. Healthcare	6.2
UnitedHealth Group	6.0
Humana	3.8

Source: *Business Insurance*, December 28, 1998, p. 1.

★ 1702 ★

Health Plans (SIC 6324)

Largest HMOs - 1997

Data show enrollment.

Kaiser Permanente	8,054,722
United HealthCare/Humana	6,358,206
Aetna U.S. Healthcare	4,201,608
PacifiCare	4,027,065
Foundation Health Systems	3,507,096
Cigna	3,292,842
Prudential	2,435,410
Oxford Health Plan	1,736,300
NYLCare	1,265,992
Health Insurance Plan of Greater New York	1,110,696

Source: *Atlanta Journal-Constitution*, May 29, 1998, p. G1, from Interstudy.

★ 1703 ★

Health Plans (SIC 6324)

Largest HMOs in Colorado

Data show number of enrollees statewide.

PacifiCare of Colorado	378,265
Kaiser Foundation Health Plan of Colorado	363,850
HMO Colorado Inc.	203,141
CIGNA HealthCare of Colorado Inc.	162,644
United HealthCare of Colorado Inc.	159,373

Source: *Denver Business Journal*, February 12, 1999, p. 50.

★ 1704 ★

Health Plans (SIC 6324)

Largest Medicaid Health Plans in New York

Data show enrollment, in thousands.

Health-First	56.4
Metro-Plus	54.5
HIP	50.5
Oxford	38.8
Managed Healthcare Systems	30.5

Source: *Crain's New York Business*, October 5, 1998, p. 3, from United Hospital Fund.

★ 1705 ★

Health Plans (SIC 6324)

Largest Medicare HMO Plans

Plans are ranked by number of Medicare enrollees as of June 30, 1998

PacifiCare Health Systems	978,850
Kaiser Foundation	582,053
Aetna U.S. Healthcare Inc.	520,000
Humana	501,000
United Health Group	427,000

Source: *Business Insurance*, December 28, 1998, p. 1.

★ 1706 ★

Health Plans (SIC 6324)

Largest PPO Plans

Plans are ranked by millions of enrollees as of June 30, 1998. PPO stands for preferred provider organization.

CCN	31.8
MultiPlan Inc.	23.0
The First Health Network	14.8
CorVel Corp.	6.5
Private Healthcare Systems	5.6

Source: *Business Insurance*, December 28, 1998, p. 1.

★ 1707 ★

Health Plans (SIC 6324)

Largest PPOs in Colorado

Data show number of enrollees statewide. PPO stands for preferred-provider organization.

Sloans Lake Managed Care	487,897
Mountain Medical Affiliates Inc.	250,000
ADMAR Corp.	204,701
Private Healthcare Systems Inc.	170,000
Blue Cross & Blue Shield of Colorado	96,554

Source: *Denver Business Journal*, February 12, 1999, p. 10B.

★ 1708 ★

Health Plans (SIC 6324)

Largest Workers Comp PPOs

Plans are ranked by millions of enrollees as of June 30, 1998. PPO stands for preferred provider organization.

CCN	25.8
AnciCare	10.0
CorVel Corp.	6.5
Armada	2.5

Source: *Business Insurance*, December 28, 1998, p. 1.

★ 1709 ★

Property Insurance (SIC 6331)

Homeowners Insurance Leaders - 1997

Market shares are shown based on $28.9 billion in premiums.

State Farm Group	23.0%
Allstate Ins Group	11.3
Farmers Ins Group	6.7
Nationwide Group	3.6
Travelers PC Group	3.5
USAA Group	3.4
SAFECO Ins Companies	2.4
Chubb Grp of Ins Cos.	2.1
Amer Family Ins Group	1.8
Other	42.2

Source: *Best's Review*, July 1998, p. 43.

★ 1710 ★

Property Insurance (SIC 6331)

Homeowners Insurance Market in California

California leads the nation with $3.2 billion in premiums.

State Farm Group	23.3%
Farmers Ins Group	18.0
Other	58.7

Source: *Best's Review*, August 1998, p. 68.

★ 1711 ★

Property Insurance (SIC 6331)

Largest Home Insurance Providers in North Carolina - 1997

Market shares are shown based on premiums written.

State Farm Mutual Group	18.0%
Nationwide Group	17.9
North Carolina Farm Bureau Insurance	11.7
Allstate Insurance	10.6
Travelers Insurance Group	3.8
Lumbermens Mutual	3.1
Hartford Fire Group	2.4
United Services Auto Asso	2.4
Auto-Owners Insurance Group	2.0
Liberty Mutual Group	1.5%
Other	26.6

Source: *Investext,* Thomson Financial Networks, August 25, 1998, p. 2.

★ 1712 ★

Property Insurance (SIC 6331)

Largest Home Insurance Providers in South Carolina - 1997

Market shares are shown based on premiums written.

State Farm Mutual Group	28.4%
Allstate Insurance Co. Group	15.0
Nationwide Group	10.2
South Carolina Farm	9.1
Auto-Owners Insurance Group	4.1
United Services Auto Asso	3.9
Travelers Insurance Group	2.9
American Bankers Insurance	2.1
State Automobile Mutual	2.1
Continental Insurance Companies	1.9
Other	20.3

Source: *Investext,* Thomson Financial Networks, August 25, 1998, p. 2.

★ 1713 ★

Property Insurance (SIC 6331)

Largest Home Insurance Providers in Virginia - 1997

Market shares are shown based on premiums written.

State Farm Mutual Group	24.1%
Allstate Insurance Co. Group	14.6
Nationwide Group	10.8
Travelers Insurance Group	8.2
United Services Auto	7.1
Virginai Farm Bureau	3.7
Erie Ins. Exchange	3.6
USAA Casualty Insurance	2.5
Liberty Mutual	1.7
Federal Insurance	1.4
Other	22.3

Source: *Investext,* Thomson Financial Networks, August 25, 1998, p. 4.

★ 1714 ★

Property Insurance (SIC 6331)

Largest Property/Casualty Firms in Colorado

Firms are ranked by direct premiums written in millions of dollars.

State Farm Mutual	$ 518.7
Farmers Insurance Exchange	316.5
Colorado Compensation Insurance Authority	237.6
Allstate Insurance Co.	227.2
State Farm Fire & Casualty Co.	222.5

Source: *Denver Business Journal*, October 16, 1998, p. 6B.

★ 1715 ★

Property Insurance (SIC 6331)

Largest Property/Casualty Insurers

Companies are ranked by net premiums in millions of dollars.

Company	$ mil.
State Farm Group	$ 34,841.8
Allstate Insurance Group	18,237.1
CNA Insurance Group	9,860.9
American International Group	9,423.5
Farmers Insurance Group	9,113.8
Nationwide Group	8,375.3
Travelers PC Group	7,904.8
Liberty Mutual	5,920.9
Hartford Insurance Group	5,772.1
Zurich Insurance Group - U.S.	4,975.4

Source: *Industry Week*, January 18, 1999, p. 43, from *Best Week* and A.M. Best & Co.

★ 1716 ★

Property Insurance (SIC 6331)

Largest Property/Casualty Insurers in Canada

Market shares are shown in percent.

General Accident Group	7.61%
Royal & SunAlliance	6.33
Co-operators Group	6.20
ING Canada	5.81
AXA Canada Inc.	4.58
State Farm	4.15
Zurich Canada	3.78%
Other	61.54

Source: *Canadian Insurance Statistics*, 1998, p. 20.

★ 1717 ★

Property Insurance (SIC 6331)

Largest Property/Casualty Insurers in Canada - 1997

Market shares are shown based on net premiums.

General Accident Group	7.78%
ING Canada Inc.	6.86
Royal & SunAlliance Canada	5.75
Co-operators General Insurance	5.28
AXA Canada Inc.	5.01
Underwriters, members of Lloyd's	4.37
The Wawanesa Mutual Insurance Co.	4.13
Economical Insurance Group	3.90
State Farm Group	2.99
Dominion of Canada	2.87
Other	48.94

Source: *Investext,* Thomson Financial Networks, December 7, 1998, p. 3, from *Financial Post.*

★ 1718 ★

Property Insurance (SIC 6331)

Largest Property/Casualty Insurers in Florida - 1997

Firms are ranked by directly written premiums in millions of dollars.

State Farm Mutual Automobile	$ 1,767.1
State Farm Fire & Casualty Co.	948.6
Allstate Insurance Co.	900.6
Allstate Indemnity Co.	491.9
Nationwide Mutual	430.3

Source: *South Florida Business Journal*, June 26, 1998, p. 6B.

★ 1719 ★

Property Insurance (SIC 6331)

Largest Property/Casualty Insurers in North Carolina

Market shares are shown in percent.

Nationwide Mutual	7.2%
State Farm Mutual	7.2
N.C. Farm Bureau Mutual	6.5
Allstate	5.6
Nationwide Mutual Fire	3.8
State Farm Fire and Casualty	2.0
Integon Indemnity	1.9
Allstate Indemnity	1.8
Other	64.0

Source: *Business North Carolina*, February 1999, p. 82, from North Carolina Department of Insurance.

★ 1720 ★

Workers Compensation Insurance (SIC 6331)

Workers Compensation Insurance Market - 1997

Market shares are shown in percent.

Liberty Mutual Cos.	7.4%
Amer Intern Group	6.4
CNA Ins. Group	6.2
Travelers PC Group	5.4
Kemper Ins. Group	4.5
Hartford Ins. Group	4.3
Nationwide Group	3.2
Zurich Ins.Group - U.S.	3.2
Fremont General Group	2.8
Allianz of America	2.5
Other	54.1

Source: *Best's Review*, September 1998, p. 98, from A.M. Best & Co.

★ 1721 ★

Workers Compensation Insurance (SIC 6331)

Workers Compensation Market in Nevada - 1997

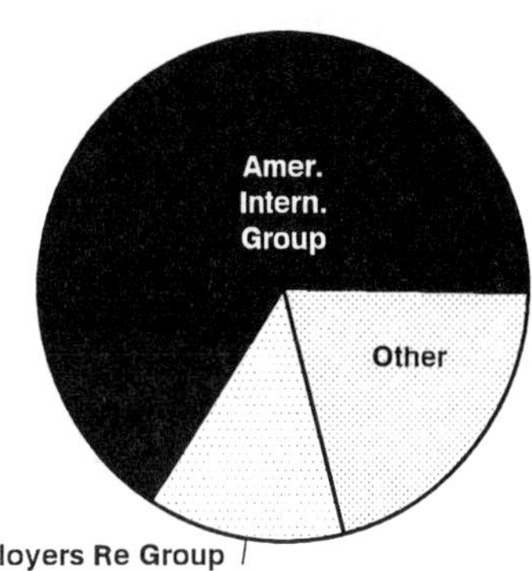

Market shares are shown in percent.

Amer. Intern. Group	65.6%
Employers Re Group	13.4
Other	21.0

Source: *Best's Review*, September 1998, p. 98, from A.M. Best & Co.

★ 1722 ★

Workers Compensation Insurance (SIC 6331)

Workers Compensation Market in North Dakota - 1997

Market shares are shown in percent.

Allianz of America	50.8%
Travelers PC Group	14.4
Other	34.8

Source: *Best's Review*, September 1998, p. 98, from A.M. Best & Co.

★ 1723 ★

Fidelity Insurance (SIC 6351)

Fidelity Insurance Industry in Hawaii - 1997

Market shares are shown in percent. New York lead the country with $107.1 million in written premiums.

CUNA Mutual Group	40.2%
Amer Intern Group	21.4
Other	38.4

Source: *Best's Review*, September 1998, p. 79.

★ 1724 ★

Fidelity Insurance (SIC 6351)

Leading Fidelity Insurance Writers - 1997

Market shares are shown in percent.

CUNA Mutual Group	15.7%
Chubb Group of Ins. Cos.	15.2
Amer. Inter. Group	12.1
Travelers PC Group	11.5
CNA Ins. Group	7.8
Zurich Ins. Group - U.S.	6.4
St. Paul Cos.	4.4
Hartford Ins. Group	4.0
Reliance Ins. Group	4.0
USF&G Group	1.9
Other	17.0

Source: *Best's Review*, September 1998, p. 74, from A.M. Best & Co.

★ 1725 ★

Liability Insurance (SIC 6351)

Product Liability Insurance Market in Michigan

According to the source, product liability is coverage for a company's liabity for losses or injuries to the buyer or user caused by a defect or a malfunction. Michigan ranks fourth in the nation with $132 million in premiums. Market shares are shown in percent.

Dorinco Reins Co.	55.9%
Zurich Ins Group - U.S.	5.9
Other	38.2

Source: *Best's Review*, August 1998, p. 70.

★ 1726 ★

Malpractice Insurance (SIC 6351)

Medical Malpractice Market - 1997

Market shares are shown based on direct premiums of $5.8 billion.

CNA Ins Group	7.0%
St Paul Companies	6.8
MLMIC Group	5.6
Health Care Indemn	4.5
Medical Protective	3.9
Amer Intern Group	3.6
Doctors' Co Ins Group	3.5%
Illinois St. Medical	3.3
Medical Int-In Ex Group	2.8
MMI Companies Group	2.8
Other	56.2

Source: *Best's Review*, July 1998, p. 45.

★ 1727 ★

Malpractice Insurance (SIC 6351)

Medical Malpractice Market in New Jersey

Market shares are shown in percent.

Medical Int-In Ex Gr	39.6%
Princeton Ins. Cos	35.4
Other	25.0

Source: *Best's Review*, August 1998, p. 71, from A.M. Best & Co.

★ 1728 ★

Malpractice Insurance (SIC 6351)

Medical Malpractice Market in Washington

Market shares are shown in percent.

Washington Phys Group	50.3%
Washington Cas Co.	16.1
Other	33.6

Source: *Best's Review*, August 1998, p. 71, from A.M. Best & Co.

★ 1729 ★

Surety Insurance (SIC 6351)

Leading Surety Insurance Writers - 1997

Market shares are shown in percent.

Amer. Intern. Group	7.8%
CNA Ins. Group	7.6
Reliance Inc. Group	6.7
Zurich Ins. Group - U.S.	6.3
United States F&G Group	6.1
Travelers PC Group	5.0
St. Paul Cos.	4.7
Safeco Ins Cos.	3.7
Allianz of America	3.5
Amwest Inc. Group	2.8
Other	45.8

Source: *Best's Review*, September 1998, p. 73, from A.M. Best & Co.

★ 1730 ★

Surety Insurance (SIC 6351)

Surety Insurance Industry in Delaware - 1997

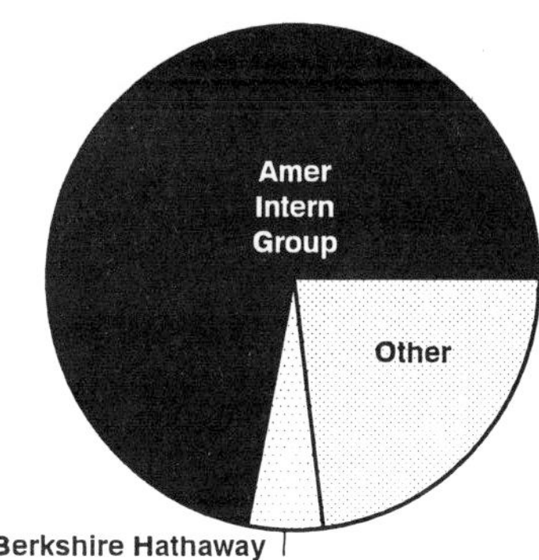

Market shares are shown in percent. California leads the industry with $339.6 million in premiums.

Amer Intern Group	72.2%
Berkshire Hathaway	4.6
Other	23.2

Source: *Best's Review*, September 1998, p. 79, from A.M. Best & Co.

★ 1731 ★

Surety Insurance (SIC 6351)

Surety Insurance Industry in South Dakota - 1997

Market shares are shown in percent. A total of $29.4 million in premiums were written.

HICA Holding Group	79.4%
CNA Ins Group	3.2
Other	17.4

Source: *Best's Review*, September 1998, p. 79.

★ 1732 ★

Pensions (SIC 6371)

Largest Corporate Pension Funds

Figures are in billions of dollars.

General Motors	$ 87.0
General Electric	58.7
IBM	52.6
Ford Motor	50.7
Lucent Technologies	49.8

Source: *Pensions & Investments*, January 25, 1999, p. 39.

★ 1733 ★

Pensions (SIC 6371)

Largest Pension Funds/Sponsors

Funds are ranked by assets in millions of dollars.

California Public Employees	$ 133,525
New York State Common	99,739
General Motors	87,000
California State Teachers	82,625
Florida State Board	77,525
New York State Teachers	71,077
Texas Teachers	69,464
Federal Retirement Thrift	64,452
New Jersey Division	63,324
General Electric	58,739

Source: *Pensions & Investments*, January 25, 1999, p. 30.

SIC 64 - Insurance Agents, Brokers, and Service

★ 1734 ★

Insurance Brokers (SIC 6411)

Largest Insurance Brokers - 1997

Companies are ranked by revenues in millions of dollars.

	Rev. ($ mil.)	Share
Marsh & McLennan	$ 2,620.2	12.1%
Aon Group Inc.	2,257.8	10.4
Sedgwick Group	643.1	3.0
Willis Corroon Group	600.8	2.8
Arthur J. Gallagher	417.3	1.9
Acordia Inc.	308.6	1.4
USI Insurance Services	236.2	1.1
Hilb, Rogal & Hamilton	161.8	0.7
Norwest Insurance Inc.	126.9	0.6
Poe & Brown Inc.	124.4	0.6

Source: *Investext,* Thomson Financial Networks, November 9, 1998, p. 9, from Business Insurance Rankings and Morgan Stanley Dean Witter Research.

SIC 65 - Real Estate

★ 1735 ★

Commercial Real Estate (SIC 6512)

Largest Commercial Space Developers in Florida - 1997

Data show new rentable square footage developed, in millions.

Codina Development Corporation	3.5
Michael Swerdlow Cos.	3.2
Stiles Corp.	1.9
Catalfumo Construction & Development Inc.	1.8
Tambone Real Estate Development Corp.	1.5

Source: *South Florida Business Journal*, October 30, 1998, p. 20B.

★ 1736 ★

Commercial Real Estate (SIC 6512)

Leasing in Downtown Manhattan

A total of 288 deals were conducted, covering 10,036,042 square feet. The table shows the leading industries.

Government	25.6%
Finance	23.1
Insurance	22.1
Legal services	10.5
Technology	4.5
Banking	3.8
Nonprofits	2.6
Communications	2.2
Other	5.6

Source: *Crain's New York Business*, February 1, 1999, p. 14.

★ 1737 ★

Shopping Centers (SIC 6512)

Largest Shopping Center Managers - 1998

Data show millions of square feet of gross leasable area managed.

Simon Property Group	164.9
General Growth Properties	98.8
CB Richard Ellis	64.2
Westfield Holdings Ltd.	60.8
Kimco Realty Corp.	60.6

Source: *Shopping Center World*, March 1999, p. 40.

★ 1738 ★

Shopping Centers (SIC 6512)

Largest Strip Center Managers - 1998

Data show millions of square feet of gross leasable area managed. Figures are as of April 30, 1998.

Kimco Realty Corp.	45.6
CB Richard Ellis	42.3
Developers Diversified Realty Corp.	34.3
Benderson Development Co. Inc.	33.8
Trammell Crow Co.	26.0

Source: *Shopping Center World*, August 1998, p. 61.

★ 1739 ★

Shopping Centers (SIC 6512)

Outlet Shopping Centers by Community - 1998

Data show number of outlet centers.

Orlando, FL	227
Central Valley, NY	220
Austin/San Antonio, TX	186
Kittery & Freeport, MA	183
Myrtle Beach, SC	177

Source: *Detroit Free Press*, June 27, 1999, p. 3C, from *Nation's Best Outlets, 1998*.

★ 1740 ★

Property Management (SIC 6531)

Largest Industrial Property Managers in Milwaukee, MN

Data show square footage managed.

Gerald Neil Inc.	$ 2,171,302
Prentiss Properties	2,064,804
CenterPoint Properties	1,400,000
MLG Management L.L.C.	965,000
James T. Barry Co./Colliers International	760,000

Source: *The Business Journal*, October 10, 1998, p. 26.

★ 1741 ★

Real Estate (SIC 6531)

Apartment Occupancy Rates

Data show regions with the highest occupancy rates. The average rate in the first quarter of 1998 was 94.9% with monthly rates of $780.

Newark, NJ	99.4%
Middlesex, NJ	99.1
Minneapolis	97.4
West Palm Beach, FL	97.4
San Diego	97.0
Washington D.C.	97.0

Source: *USA TODAY*, July 15, 1998, p. B1, from M/PF Research.

★ 1742 ★

Real Estate (SIC 6531)

Largest Master-Planned Communities

Data show acreage.

Irvine Ranch (CA)	110,000
Poinciana (FL)	47,000
Woodlands (TX)	25,000
Summerlin (NV)	22,500
Highlands Ranch (CO)	22,000

Source: *Wall Street Journal*, October 7, 1998, p. B1, from Woodlands Community Association.

★ 1743 ★

Real Estate (SIC 6531)

Largest Office Markets

Data show millions of square feet leased through June 1998.

Atlanta	6.9
Dallas	6.5
Houston	5.1
Boston	3.9
Chicago	3.8
Northern Virginia	3.8

Source: *USA TODAY*, September 30, 1998, p. B1, from Cushman & Wakefield.

★ 1744 ★

Real Estate (SIC 6531)

Largest Property Firms in South Florida

Firms ar ranked by current rentable square footage, in millions.

Codina Real Estate Management Inc.	10.7
Trammell Crow Co.	8.2
Cushman & Wakefield of Florida Inc.	5.5
Terranova Corp.	5.1
Continental Real Estate Cos.	4.7
Stiles Property Management	4.5
Adler Management Services Inc.	4.4
CB Richard Ellis	4.3
Easton-Babcock Management Inc.	3.6

Source: *South Florida Business Journal*, October 9, 1998, p. 8B.

★ 1745 ★

Real Estate (SIC 6531)

Who Owns Commercial Real Estate

REIT stands for real estate investment trust.

Corporations	43.1%
Partnerships	25.6
Not-for-profits	10.5
Government	6.0
REITs	3.6
Institutional investors	3.3
Financial institutions	2.9
Other	5.0

Source: *Building Operation Management*, May 1998, p. 12, from National Association of Real Estate Investment Trusts.

SIC 70 - Hotels and Other Lodging Places

★ 1746 ★

Hotels (SIC 7011)

Hotel Room Market in Mexico - 1996

5 stars	19.5%
4 stars	18.4
3 stars	17.0
2 stars	12.1
1 star	11.7
Other	21.3

Source: *National Trade Data Bank*, September 14, 1998, p. ISA980601, from SECTUR Estadistticas Basicas de la Actividad Turistica.

★ 1747 ★

Hotels (SIC 7011)

Largest Economy Lodging Chains

Chains are ranked by number of open guestrooms.

Days Inn of America	162,734
Super 8 Motels	107,225
Motel 6	88,432
Econo Lodge	45,850
Travelodge Hotels	42,264
Fairfield Inn by Marriott	37,568
Red Roof Inns	33,515
Knights Franchise Systems	18,009
Baymont Inns & Suites	16,562

Source: *Hotel & Motel Management*, February 1, 1999, p. 14, from Smith Travel Research.

★ 1748 ★

Hotels (SIC 7011)

Largest Hotel Companies - 1998

Data show number of guestrooms.

Cendant Corp.	516,262
Bass Hotels & Resorts	443,891
Marriott Hotels, Resorts & Suites	313,600
Best Western International	301,820
Choice Hotels International	287,444
Promus Hotel Corp.	186,920
Starwood Hotels & Resorts Worldwide	133,000
Patriot American Hospitality	105,000
Carlson Hospitality Worldwide	103,497
Hilton Hotels Corp.	103,151

Source: *Hotel & Motel Management*, September 21, 1998, p. 49.

★ 1749 ★

Hotels (SIC 7011)

Las Vegas Strip Market

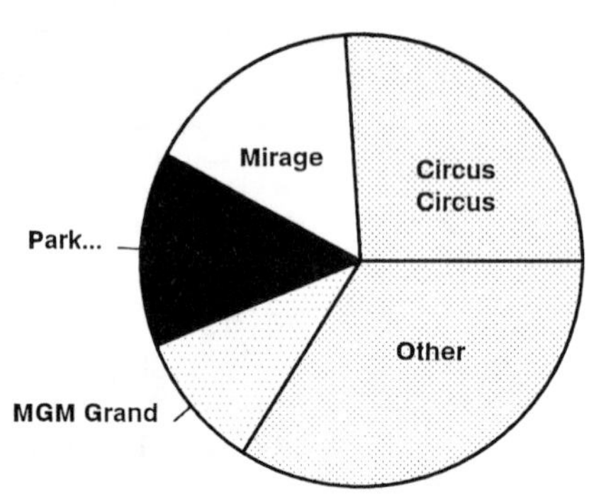

A total of 30.6 million people visited the Las Vegas Strip in 1998. Data show who controls the 68,216 hotel rooms in the region.

Circus Circus	25.6%
Mirage	16.3
Park Place Entertainment	13.6
MGM Grand	10.3
Other	34.2

Source: *Investor's Business Daily*, April 8, 1999, p. A9, from CIBC Oppenheimer.

★ 1750 ★

Hotels (SIC 7011)

U.S. Lodging Industry

Independents	30.6%
Economy	19.5
Midscale w/f&b	18.1
Upper upscale	12.3
Midscale w/o f&b	11.1
Upscale	8.4

Source: *Hotel & Motel Management*, February 1, 1999, p. 18.

★ 1751 ★

Trailer Parks (SIC 7033)

Trailer Park Occupancy in Phoenix, AZ

Data show occupancy rates.

Tuscon Area	95.0%
Yuma	95.0
Western region	87.0
Central region	83.0
Southeast region	82.0

Source: *Arizona Business*, July 1998, p. 2.

SIC 72 - Personal Services

★ 1752 ★

Funeral Services (SIC 7261)

Cremations by State

Data show the states with the highest rates of cremation.

Nevada	61.1%
Alaska	58.5
Hawaii	56.7
Washington	54.4
Arizona	53.0

Source: *USA TODAY*, January 12, 1999, p. A1, from Cremation Association of North America.

★ 1753 ★

Funeral Services (SIC 7261)

Leading Funeral Homes in Arkansas - 1997

Firms are ranked by number of services performed.

Roller Funeral Homes	3,000
Caruth-Hale Funeral Home Inc.	955
Edwards Funeral Home Inc.	850
Griffin-Leggett Healey & Roth Inc.	850
Ocker Funeral Home	450
Robinson & Son Inc.	450
Acklin and Son Funeral Home	405
North Little Rock Funeral Home Inc.	400
Huson Funeral Home	350
Sisco Funeral Chapel	347

Source: *Arkansas Business*, July 27, 1998, p. 39, from Arkansas Funeral Director and Embalmer Board.

★ 1754 ★

Tax Preparation (SIC 7291)

How We File Returns - 1998

1040	49.0%
Electronic filings	23.0
1040A	11.0
1040EZ	9.0
1040PC	7.0

Source: *Investor's Business Daily*, April 16, 1999, p. A4.

★ 1755 ★

Textile Rental (SIC 7299)

Textile Rental Industry

The market is shown by category.

	1996	1997
Dust control	10.5%	8.1%
Linen supply	10.8	6.0
Health care	2.3	4.7
Uniform rental	13.5	4.4
Other	62.9	76.8

Source: *Textile Rental*, October 1998, p. 36.

★ 1756 ★

Textile Rental (SIC 7299)

Uniform Rental Market

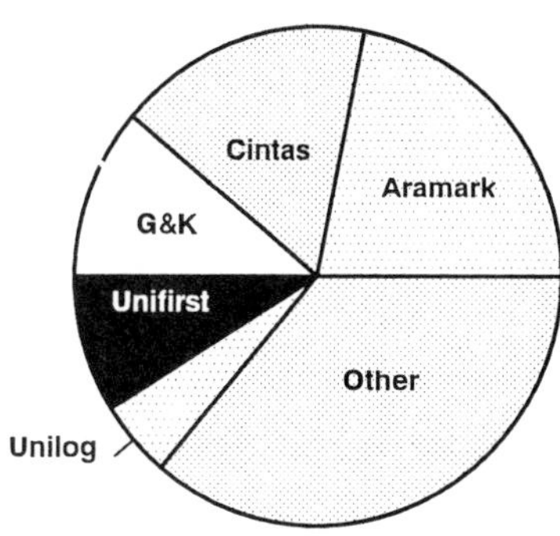

The uniform rental industry has been valued at $5.0 billion and comprises more than 700 companies. More than 25 million people wear some type of work garments, with approximately one-third wearing leased work wear. Other refers to small and medium sized private companies.

Aramark	22.0%
Cintas	17.0
G&K	11.0
Unifirst	9.0
Unilog	5.0
Other	36.0

Source: *Textile Rental*, October 1998, p. 50, from Cleary Gull Reiland & McDivitt.

★ 1757 ★

Weight Loss Services (SIC 7299)

Largest Weight Loss Firms - 1997

Firms are ranked by revenues in millions of dollars.

Weight Watchers	$ 1,000
Slim-Fast/Thompson Medical	721
Jenny Craig	365
Herbalife Intl.	193
Optifast	55
Shaklee	55

Source: *Advertising Age*, March 29, 1999, p. 53, from Marketdata.

SIC 73 - Business Services

★ 1758 ★

Advertising (SIC 7310)

Advertising Market - 1999

Total revenues reached $132.62 billion.

	($ mil.)	Share
Newspapers	$ 46,370	34.96%
Radio	16,598	12.51
Network TV	14,485	10.92
Local TV	12,910	9.73
Spot TV	11,045	8.33
Magazines	10,930	8.24
Cable TV	10,371	7.82
Outdoor	4,800	3.62
Syndication	2,820	2.13
Internet	2,300	1.73

Source: *Broadcasting & Cable*, January 4, 1999, p. 27.

★ 1759 ★

Advertising (SIC 7310)

Canada's Advertising Market

Television	24.7%
Daily newspapers	24.5
Catalogs	13.9
Yellow pages	11.1
Radio	9.9
Weekly newspapers	7.5
Magazines	5.5
Transit	2.5

Source: *Globe and Mail*, June 9, 1998, p. B4, from Radio Marketing Inc.

★ 1760 ★

Advertising (SIC 7310)

Largest Advertising Industries - 1997

Data show measured ad spending in millions of dollars.

Automotive	$ 6,507.4
Retail	3,404.3
Restaurants	1,917.9
Telephone	1,721.7
Food	1,659.4
Drugs & personal care	1,090.3
Financial services, brokers & insurance	980.0
Computers & electronics	841.6
Beer	569.2
Imaging/office machines	238.4

Source: *Automotive News*, July 20, 1998, p. 18, from Competitive Media Reporting.

★ 1761 ★

Advertising (SIC 7310)

Top Ad Markets - 1998

Billings are shown in billions of dollars.

New York City	$ 44.5
Chicago	13.8
Los Angeles	8.2
Detroit	8.1
Minneapolis	5.0
San Francisco	5.0
Boston	4.6
Dallas	2.9

Source: *Advertising Age*, April 19, 1999, p. S4.

★ 1762 ★

Advertising (SIC 7310)

Top Advertising Categories - 1998

Spending is shown in millions of dollars.

Automotive	$ 1,730.5
Direct response	1,616.2
Computers, office equipment	940.4
Drugs and remedies	807.9
Travel, hotels and resorts	644.8
Financial	607.1
Toiletries and cosmetics	594.1
Publishing & media	585.7

Source: *Mediaweek*, March 8, 1999, p. 42, from PIB/ Competitive Media Reporting.

★ 1763 ★

Advertising (SIC 7311)

Largest Ad Firms in Chicago, IL

Leo Burnett Co.
Foote Cone & Belding
DDB Needham Chicago
Frankel & Co.
J. Walter Thompson
Ogilvy & Mather Chicago
Euro RSCG tatham
Draftworldwide

Firms are ranked by local billings in millions of dollars.

Leo Burnett Co.	$ 2,649.3
Foote Cone & Belding	1,004.0
DDB Needham Chicago	972.0
Frankel & Co.	519.1
J. Walter Thompson	506.0
Ogilvy & Mather Chicago	452.0
Euro RSCG tatham	448.4
Draftworldwide	354.1

Source: *Crain's Chicago Business*, July 27, 1998, p. 17.

★ 1764 ★

Advertising (SIC 7311)

Largest Advertisers - 1998

Spending is shown in billions of dollars. Total media spending reached $79.3 billion.

General Motors Corp.	$ 2,121.5
Procter & Gamble Co.	1,725.0
DaimlerChrysler	1,411.1
Philip Morris Cos.	1,264.4
Ford Motor Co.	1,066.4
Time Warner	830.6
Walt Disney Co.	809.7
Sears, Roebuck & Co.	721.7
Unilever	691.2
Diageo	670.6

Source: *Advertising Age*, March 22, 1999, p. 6, from Competitive Media Reporting.

★ 1765 ★

Advertising (SIC 7311)

Top Ad Firms - 1998

Firms are ranked by gross income in millions of dollars.

Grey Advertising	$ 422.3
J. Walter Thompson Co.	414.6
Leo Burnett Co.	380.2
McCann-Erickson Worldwide	378.4
Young & Rubicam	344.0
BBDO Worldwide	336.6
DDB Needham Worldwide	316.6
Foote, Cone & Belding	298.0
Brann Worldwide	287.6
Ogilvy & Mather Worldwide	278.4

Source: *Advertising Age*, April 19, 1999, p. S4.

★ 1766 ★

Advertising (SIC 7311)

Top Ad Firms in Mexico - 1998

Figures show gross income in millions of dollars.

McCann-Erickson	$ 27,806
Young & Rubicam	16,301
Publicidad Ferrer y Asociados	14,394
Leo Burnett	13,813
BBDO Mexico	12,529
J. Walter Thompson	10,718
Panamer/Graficoncepto	9,517

Continued on next page.

★ 1766 ★ *Continued*
Advertising (SIC 7311)

Top Ad Firms in Mexico - 1998

Figures show gross income in millions of dollars.

Betancourt Barba Euro RSCG	$ 8,454
Bozell	8,039
Ammirati Puris Lintas	7,117

Source: *Advertising Age*, April 19, 1999, p. S34.

★ 1767 ★
Advertising (SIC 7311)

Top Advertisers in Canada - 1997

Spending is shown in millions of dollars. Total spending is expected to reach $5.4 billion in 1998.

General Motors Corp.	$ 93.0
BCE Inc.	65.4
Procter & Gamble Co.	62.4
Rogers Communications	54.2
Hudsons Bay Co.	53.2
Eaton's of Canada	50.4
Sears, Roebuck & Co.	49.0

Source: *Advertising Age International*, May 19, 1999, p. 37, from A.C. Nielsen.

★ 1768 ★
Advertising (SIC 7311)

Top Midwest Ad Firms - 1998

Firms are ranked by revenues in millions of dollars.

Leo Burnett	$ 396.2
J. Walter Thompson	151.0
Campbell-Ewald	131.6
DDB Needham	126.7
Bozell	109.0
Foote, Cone & Belding	97.5

Source: *Adweek*, April 19, 1999, p. 103.

★ 1769 ★
Advertising (SIC 7311)

Top New England Ad Firms - 1998

Firms are ranked by revenues in millions of dollars.

Hill, Holiday, Connors, Cosmopolus	$ 92.0
Arnold Communications	86.0
Mullen	38.1
Ingalls	17.1
Holland Mark Martin Edmund	17.0
Mintz & Hoke	11.1

Source: *Adweek*, April 19, 1999, p. 104.

★ 1770 ★
Advertising (SIC 7311)

Top Southeast Ad Firms - 1998

Firms are ranked by revenues in millions of dollars.

The Martin Agency	$ 54.3
Long Haymes Carr	32.7
WestWayne	25.7
Zimmerman & Partners Advertising	22.6
McKinney & Silver	20.8
BBDO South	20.8
Fitzgerald & Co.	20.7

Source: *Adweek*, April 19, 1999, p. 106.

★ 1771 ★
Advertising (SIC 7311)

Top Southwestern Ad Firms - 1998

Firms are ranked by revenues in millions of dollars.

Temerlin McClain	$ 61.0
GSD&M	56.1
The Richards Group	54.1
DDB Needham	24.7
Publicis	24.0
Ackerman McQueen	22.6
Fogarty Klein & Partners	21.7

Source: *Adweek*, April 19, 1999, p. 108.

★ 1772 ★

Advertising (SIC 7311)

Top Western Ad Firms - 1998

Firms are ranked by revenues in millions of dollars.

Firm	($ mil.)
TBWA/Chiat/Day	$ 150.0
Foote, Cone & Belding	88.5
Goldberg Moser O'Neill	67.5
Publicis & Hal Riney	63.2
Wieden & Kennedy	60.2
Rubin Postaer and Associates	56.4
McCann-Erickson	55.2

Source: *Adweek*, April 19, 1999, p. 109.

★ 1773 ★

Advertising (SIC 7312)

Largest Billboard Ad Categories - 1998

Sales reached $2.33 billion during the year. Data show the top categories.

	($ mil.)	Share
Local services/amusements	$ 190.9	14.15%
Public trans./hotels/resorts	176.8	13.10
Retail	162.7	12.06
Restaurants	158.1	11.72
Media/advertising	120.3	8.92
Auto dealers/services	120.3	8.92
Insurance/real estate	94.6	7.01
Auto accessories/equip	90.2	6.69
Financial	73.6	5.46
Misc.	161.7	11.98

Source: *Investor's Business Daily*, March 29, 1999, p. A2, from Outdoor Advertising Association of America.

★ 1774 ★

Advertising (SIC 7312)

Largest Outdoor Ad Firms

Infinity/Outdoor Systems

Clear Channel

Lamar Advertising

Chanceller

The largest firms are ranked by revenues in millions of dollars.

Firm	($ mil.)
Infinity/Outdoor Systems	$ 1,108
Clear Channel	813
Lamar Advertising	361
Chanceller	218

Source: *Wall Street Journal*, May 29, 1999, p. 4B, from Outdoor Advertising Association of America.

★ 1775 ★

Advertising (SIC 7312)

Top Outdoor Ad Firms - 1998

Companies are ranked by gross revenues in millions of dollars.

Firm	($ mil.)
Outdoor Systems Inc.	$ 746
Eller/Clear Channel Comm.	658
Transportation Display Inc.	390
Lamar Advertising Co.	308
AK Media	145
Whiteco	120
Martin Media/Chancellor Media	90
Adams Outdoor	80
Donrey Media Group	70
OCI Holdings	60

Source: *Advertising Age*, July 20, 1998, p. S21, from Morgan Stanley/Alex Brown.

★ 1776 ★

Advertising (SIC 7319)

Largest Cable TV Ad Firms

Companies are ranked by media billings in millions of dollars.

Euro RSCG Worldwide	$ 366.9
Grey Advertising	352.8
Leo Burnett Co.	328.5
D'Arcy Masius Benton & Bowles	310.0
BBDO Worldwide	308.6

Source: *Advertising Age*, April 19, 1999, p. S14.

★ 1777 ★

Advertising (SIC 7319)

Largest Drug Advertisers - 1997

Firms are ranked by spending in millions of dollars.

Glaxo Wellcome	$ 156.6
Merck	122.0
Bristol-Myers Squibb	107.3
Pfizer	90.0
Schering-Plough	70.0

Source: *Financial Times*, August 6, 1998, p. 4, from Competitive Media Reporting and Publishers Information Bureau.

★ 1778 ★

Advertising (SIC 7319)

Largest Insurance Advertisers

Spending is shown in millions of dollars for January - November 1998.

Allstate Corp.	$ 74.7
State Farm Mutual Auto	69.0
Berkshire Hathaway	68.4
Cendant Corp.	65.2
Blue Cross & Blue Shield	63.1

Source: *Best's Review*, May 1999, p. 26, from Competitive Media Reporting and Publishers Information Bureau.

★ 1779 ★

Advertising (SIC 7319)

Largest Magazine Ad Firms

Companies are ranked by media billings in millions of dollars.

Leo Burnett Co.	$ 935.9
Saatchi & Saatchi	488.8
McCann-Erickson Worldwide	454.2
J. Walter Thompson Co.	433.0
Young & Rubicam	418.1

Source: *Advertising Age*, April 19, 1999, p. S14.

★ 1780 ★

Advertising (SIC 7319)

Largest Magazine Advertisers - 1998

Spending is shown in millions of dollars.

General Motors	$ 459.3
Procter & Gamble Co.	407.3
Philip Morris Cos. Inc.	383.5
Chrysler Corp.	354.6
Ford Motor Corp.	291.3
Time Warner Inc.	180.0
Toyota Motor Co.	173.8
Unilever PLC	169.6
Sony Corp.	143.7
RJR Nabisco Corp.	135.2

Source: *Mediaweek*, March 8, 1999, p. 42, from PIB/ Competitive Media Reporting.

★ 1781 ★

Advertising (SIC 7319)

Largest Newspaper Ad Firms

Companies are ranked by media billings in millions of dollars.

Bernard Hodes Group	$ 595.2
TMP Worldwide	526.8
Nationwide Advertising Service	327.6
J. Walter Thompson Co.	286.0
McCann-Erickson Co.	185.6

Source: *Advertising Age*, April 19, 1999, p. S14.

★ 1782 ★

Advertising (SIC 7319)

Largest Newspaper Advertisers - 1998

Spending is shown in billions of dollars.

IBM Corp.	$ 44.35
Federated Department Stores	41.97
Time Warner	37.11
General Motors Corp.	36.00
Compaq	34.72
DaimlerChrysler	31.94
Ford Motor Co.	29.26
Citigroup	25.83
Walt Disney Co.	24.56

Source: *Advertising Age*, April 26, 1999, p. S4, from Competitive Media Reporting.

★ 1783 ★

Advertising (SIC 7319)

Largest Spot TV Ad Firms

Companies are ranked by media billings in millions of dollars.

BBDO Worldwide	$ 841.2
J. Walter Thompson Co.	705.0
Saatchi & Saatchi	653.5
McCann-Erickson Worldwide	643.7
Euro RSCG Worldwide	623.0

Source: *Advertising Age*, April 19, 1999, p. S14.

★ 1784 ★

Advertising (SIC 7319)

Largest Sunday Magazine Advertisers - 1998

Spending is shown in billions of dollars.

National Syndications	$ 126.68
Roll International Corp.	63.92
Bose Corp.	37.61
Bertelsmann	25.87
Bradford Exchange	22.00
Sony Corp.	20.49
DaimlerChrysler	20.43
Eli Lilly & Co.	19.56
Procter & Gamble Co.	16.75

Source: *Advertising Age*, April 26, 1999, p. S4, from Competitive Media Reporting.

★ 1785 ★

Advertising (SIC 7319)

Largest Syndicated TV Ad Firms

Companies are ranked by media billings in millions of dollars.

D'Arcy Masius Benton & Bowles	$ 292.0
Leo Burnett Co.	211.3
Euro RSCG Worldwide	170.2
Foote, Cone & Belding	122.0
McCann-Erickson Worldwide	121.3

Source: *Advertising Age*, April 19, 1999, p. S14.

★ 1786 ★

Advertising (SIC 7319)

Largest Web Advertisers - 1998

Spending is shown in millions of dollars. Total Web ad spending reached $1.0 billion.

	($ mil.)	Share
Microsoft Corp.	$ 34.8	3.48%
IBM Corp.	28.5	2.85
Compaq Computer Corp.	16.1	1.61
General Motors Corp.	12.7	1.27
Excite	12.3	1.23
Infoseek Corp.	9.3	0.93
AT&T Corp.	9.2	0.92
Hewlett-Packard Co.	8.0	0.80
Barnes & Noble	7.6	0.76
Datek Securities	7.6	0.76
Other	853.9	85.39

Source: *Advertising Age*, May 3, 1999, p. S18, from InterMedia Advertising Solutions.

★ 1787 ★

Advertising (SIC 7319)

Prescription Drug Ad Spending - 1998

Spending is shown in millions of dollars.

Antihistimines	$ 287.1
Cholesterol reducers	112.5
Hair loss	92.1
Inhaled nasal steroids	83.8
Smoking cessation	81.0
Anti-migraine	69.9

Continued on next page.

★ 1787 ★ *Continued*

Advertising (SIC 7319)

Prescription Drug Ad Spending - 1998

Spending is shown in millions of dollars.

Anti-ulcerants	$ 50.1
Bone density	45.0
Antidepressants	42.3
Antivirals	41.1

Source: *Investor's Business Daily*, May 24, 1999, p. A2, from Scott-Levin.

★ 1788 ★

Advertising (SIC 7319)

Top Business-to-Business Advertisers - 1998

Sales are shown in millions of dollars.

AT&T Corp.	$ 210.3
IBM Corp.	199.7
Microsoft Corp.	176.6
Compaq	172.4
MCI Communication Corp.	168.7
Hewlett-Packard	127.6
Sprint Corp.	115.2

Source: *Business Marketing*, September 1998, p. 20.

★ 1789 ★

Advertising (SIC 7319)

Top Computer/Software Advertisers - 1998

The top advertisers on cable television are ranked by spending in billions of dollars.

Microsoft Corp.	$ 25.62
Gateway Inc.	20.26
IBM Corp.	15.50
America Online Inc.	15.18
Dell Computer Corp.	14.34

Source: *Adweek*, April 12, 1999, p. 38, from Competitive Media Reporting.

★ 1790 ★

Advertising (SIC 7319)

Top Financial Advertisers - 1998

The top advertisers on cable television are ranked by spending in billions of dollars.

American Express Co.	$ 58.27
Visa USA Inc.	26.12
Countrywide Home Loans Inc.	19.17
Mastercard Intl Inc.	18.97
First USA Bank	18.55

Source: *Adweek*, April 12, 1999, p. 38, from Competitive Media Reporting.

★ 1791 ★

Advertising (SIC 7319)

Top Toy Advertisers - 1998

The top advertisers on cable television are ranked by spending in billions of dollars.

Mattel Inc.	$ 83.14
Hasbro Inc.	75.75
Nintendo Co.	24.74
Sony Corp.	16.53
Macandrews & Forbes Holdings	13.07

Source: *Adweek*, April 12, 1999, p. 38, from Competitive Media Reporting.

★ 1792 ★

Direct Marketing (SIC 7331)

Largest Direct Response Agencies - 1998

Agencies are ranked by billings in thousands of dollars.

Draft Worldwide	$ 1,337,452
Wunderman Cato Johnson	1,035,950
Bronner Slosberg Humphrey	848,414
Rapp Collins Worldwide	803,000
Blau Marketing Technologies	694,947
Ogilvy One	591,386
Grey Direct	368,100
Devon Direct	290,000

Source: *Adweek*, April 19, 1999, p. 99.

★ 1793 ★

Direct Marketing (SIC 7331)

Largest Mailing Service Firms in Phoenix, AZ - 1997

Companies are ranked by number of pieces of mail processed.

ADVO Inc.	1,070
PSI Group	245
Precision Direct Inc.	192
Al White's Mailing Inc.	175
Val-Pak of Arizona Inc.	150
International Mail Processing	121
Business Helpers Mail Center	113

Source: *The Business Journal Serving Phoenix and the Valley of the Sun*, August 7, 1998, p. 14.

★ 1794 ★

Direct Marketing (SIC 7331)

Top Direct Marketing Markets - 1997

The largest online markets are shown in millions of dollars.

Business services	$ 212.5
Computers	193.8
Communications	166.6
Office equipment	94.3
Printing/publishing	64.6

Source: *Target Marketing*, August 1998, p. 16, from Direct Marketing Association.

★ 1795 ★

Leasing (SIC 7350)

Largest Equipment Leasing Firms

Market shares are shown in percent.

GE Capital Corp.	19.3%
Newcourt	6.8
Associates Commercial Corp.	4.9
CIT	3.9
IBM Credit Corp.	3.6
Caterpillar Fin Services Corp.	2.9
Citicorp Global	2.8
NationsBanc Leasing	2.5%
First Union Leasing	2.1
John Deere Credit	2.0
Other	49.2

Source: *Investext,* Thomson Financial Networks, January 5, 1999, p. 57.

★ 1796 ★

Rental Services (SIC 7350)

Largest Rental Firms

Firms are ranked by revenues in millions of dollars.

United Rental Inc.	$ 1,400
HERC	600
Prime Service Inc.	500
Rental Service Corp.	500

Source: *Investor's Business Daily*, July 6, 1998, p. A6, from Rental Equipment Registar and company reports.

★ 1797 ★

Temp Agencies (SIC 7363)

Largest Staffing Firms - 1997

Market shares are shown in percent.

Manpower	5.1%
Adecco	4.3
Kelly Services	4.2
Accustaff	3.7
Olsten Staffing Services	3.1
CDI	2.8
Interim Services	2.5
Norrell	1.9
Robert Half International	1.8
Volt Staffing Services	1.6
Metamor Worldwide	1.4
Aerotak	1.1
TAC Worldwide Companies	1.1
Other	65.4

Source: *Investext,* Thomson Financial Networks, January 21, 1999, p. 5, from company reports and Interstate/ Johnson Lane estimates.

★ 1798 ★

Temp Agencies (SIC 7363)

Largest Temp Agencies

Adecco
Manpower
Olsten Corp.
Randstand Holding
Kelly Services
Vedior
Interim Services

Firms are ranked by revenues in billions of dollars.

Adecco	$ 9.12
Manpower	8.35
Olsten Corp.	4.43
Randstand Holding	4.22
Kelly Services	4.00
Vedior	3.47
Interim Services	1.78

Source: *Forbes*, January 11, 1999, p. 84, from BT Alex. Brown.

★ 1799 ★

Temp Agencies (SIC 7363)

Temp Agency Market - 1997

Data are based on 2.5 million workers.

Office/clerical	36.8%
Industrial	34.4
Technical	13.4
Professional/management	7.0
Health care	3.5
Other	4.9

Source: *New York Times*, June 24, 1998, p. C1, from National Association of Temporary and Staffing Services.

★ 1800 ★

Software (SIC 7372)

2D Plant Design/Drafting Market - 1997

Market shares are shown in percent.

Autodesk	33.0%
Jacobus	24.0
Intergraph	10.0
CadCentre	8.0
EA Systems	6.0
Other	17.0

Source: *Chemical Engineering*, July 1998, p. 156, from Daratech Inc.

★ 1801 ★

Software (SIC 7372)

3D Plant Design/Visualization Market - 1997

Market shares are shown in percent.

Intergraph	54.0%
CadCentre	18.0
Computervision	6.0
Rebis	6.0
EA Systems	5.0
IBM/Dassault	5.0
Other	16.0

Source: *Chemical Engineering*, July 1998, p. 156, from Daratech Inc.

★ 1802 ★

Software (SIC 7372)

Accounting Software Market - 1998

Shares are shown for the first seven months of the year.

Intuit	70.0%
Peachtree	14.3
Others	15.7

Source: *Investor's Business Daily*, August 19, 1998, p. A4, from PC Data Inc.

★ 1803 ★

Software (SIC 7372)

Adaptive Network Security Market - 1997

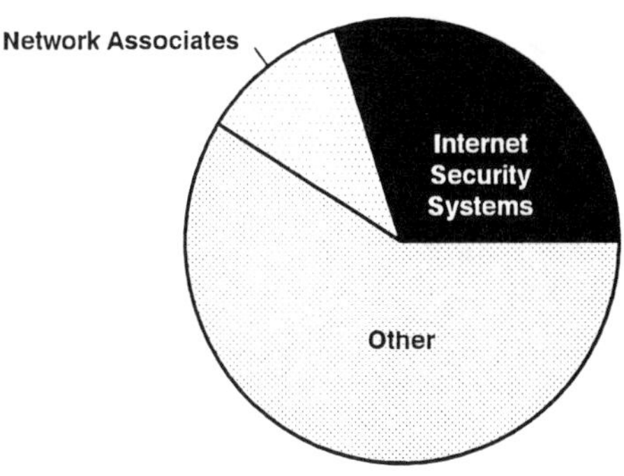

Market shares are shown in percent.

Internet Security Systems	30.0%
Network Associates	11.0
Other	59.0

Source: Retrieved May 18, 1999 from the World Wide Web: http:// www.sonic.net/cgi-bin/cif/cif/search-free.pl.

★ 1804 ★

Software (SIC 7372)

Antivirus Sales Vendors - 1998

Market shares are shown in percent as of August 1998.

Network Associates	40.6%
Symantec	39.6
Dr. Solomon	7.9
Computer Associates	7.1
Others	4.8

Source: Retrieved May 18, 1999 from the World Wide Web: http:// www.sonic.net/cgi-bin/cif/cif/search-free.pl.

★ 1805 ★

Software (SIC 7372)

Best-Selling Computer Games - 1998

Data show sales in thousands of units. Top producers include Havas Interactive, GT Interactive, Learning Co., Mattel, Activision and Microsoft.

Starcraft	746.5
Deer Hunter	620.9
Myst	539.6
Microsoft Flight Simulator	509.1
Deer Hunter II 3-D	470.8
Titanic: Adventures Out of Time	436.2
Lego Island	404.9
Age of Empires	367.2
Frogger	364.1
Riven: The Sequel to Myst	355.3
Diablo	354.1
Cabela's Big Game hunter	351.0
Unreal	291.3
Barbie Riding Club	288.3
Quake II	279.6

Source: *New York Times*, March 29, 1999, p. C2, from PC Data.

★ 1806 ★

Software (SIC 7372)

Business Desktop Market

Market shares are shown in percent.

Microsoft	35.0%
Symantec	10.0
Adobe	6.0
Corel	6.0
Other	43.0

Source: "Software Applications." Retrieved May 28, 1999 from the World Wide Web: http:// www.userwww.stsu.edu/~magpie5/mshare/ softapps.html, from PC Data Inc.

★ 1807 ★

Software (SIC 7372)

CAD Software Leaders

Unit shares are shown in percent. CAD stands for computer aided design.

Autodesk	34.3%
Expert Software	33.8
IMSI	18.0
Visio	11.1
Graphsoft	1.0
Other	1.8

Source: *Computer Reseller News*, March 29, 1999, p. 87, from PC Data.

★ 1808 ★

Software (SIC 7372)

Computer Language Market

Market shares are shown based on licenses sold.

	1998	2003
Visual Basic	33.5%	25.6%
Internet/HTML	12.4	23.1
C/C++	16.6	17.9
Java	4.1	15.1
Cobol	9.3	5.2
Other	24.1	13.1

Source: *Computerworld*, March 29, 1999, p. 6, from International Data Corp.

★ 1809 ★

Software (SIC 7372)

Customer Relationship Management Software

Market shares are shown in percent.

Siebel	22.0%
Aurum/Baan	10.0
Clarify	8.0
Vantive	8.0
Trilogy	6.0
Oracle/SAP	1.0
Others	45.0

Source: *Investor's Business Daily*, June 10, 1999, p. A10, from company reports, Southwest Securities, and First Call.

★ 1810 ★

Software (SIC 7372)

Database Application Software Market

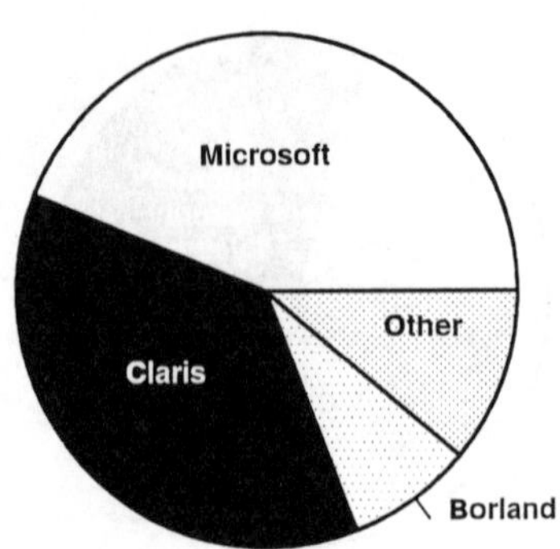

Market shares are shown in percent.

Microsoft	44.0%
Claris	37.0
Borland	8.0
Other	11.0

Source: "Business Desktop Applications." Retrieved May 28, 1999 from the World Wide Web: http://www.userwww.stsu.edu/~magpie5/mshare/busapps.html, from PC Data Inc.

★ 1811 ★

Software (SIC 7372)

Database Software Leaders - 1998

IBM	31.7%
Oracle	29.6
Microsoft	10.3
Others	28.4

Source: *New York Times*, May 24, 1999, p. C10, from Dataquest Inc.

★ 1812 ★

Software (SIC 7372)

E-Mail Software Leaders

Market shares are shown in percent.

Microsoft Outlook	17.0%
Microsoft Exchange Client	11.0
Microsoft Outlook Express	10.0
Eudora	9.0
CCMail	8.0

Continued on next page.

★ 1812 ★ *Continued*

Software (SIC 7372)

E-Mail Software Leaders

Market shares are shown in percent.

Lotus Notes	8.0%
Netscape Communicator	7.0
Netscape Navigator	7.0
Other	23.0

Source: *Investor's Business Daily*, August 13, 1998, p. A8, from Zona Research.

★ 1813 ★

Software (SIC 7372)

EDI Software Market - 1997

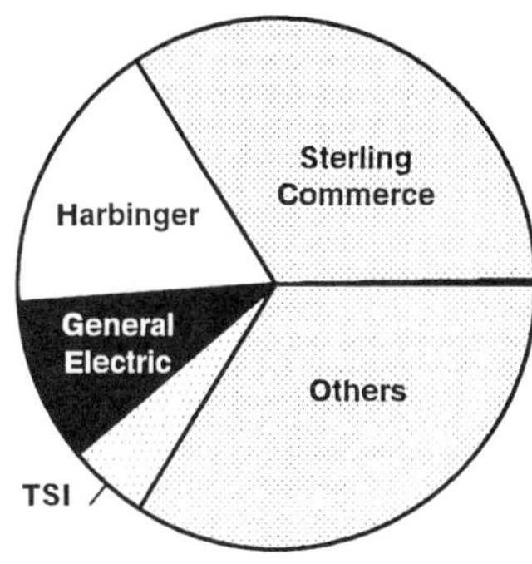

Shares are shown of the $413 million market in percent. EDI stands for electronic data interchange.

Sterling Commerce	34.0%
Harbinger	17.0
General Electric	10.0
TSI	5.0
Others	34.0

Source: *Investor's Business Daily*, August 20, 1998, p. A4, from company reports, Dataquest Inc., International Data Corp., and BT Alex Brown.

★ 1814 ★

Software (SIC 7372)

EDM Market Leaders - 1997

Market shares are shown in percent.

Documentum	11.3%
PC Docs	11.0
FileNet	5.7
Open Text	5.4
Info Dimensions	4.9
NOVASOFT	3.0
Cimage	2.8
Altris	2.7
Interleaf	1.7
Other	51.5

Source: *Investext*, Thomson Financial Networks, September 1, 1998, p. 12, from International Data Corp.

★ 1815 ★

Software (SIC 7372)

Educational Software Leaders - 1996

Market shares are shown in percent.

CUC Software	20.0%
The Learning Co.	19.0
Disney	12.0
Broderbund	8.0
Microsoft	4.0
Other	37.0

Source: "Software Applications." Retrieved May 28, 1999 from the World Wide Web: http://www.userwww.stsu.edu/~magpie5/mshare/softapps.html, from PC Data Inc.

★ 1816 ★

Software (SIC 7372)

Educational Software Market

Market shares are shown in percent.

Learning Company	35.9%
Cendant Software	28.3
Disney	6.2
Humongous	5.9
Broderbund	5.5

Source: "Software 101: Build Brand" Retrieved May 7, 1999 from the World Wide Web: http://more.abcnews.go.com/sections/business/DailyNews, from PC Data Inc.

★ 1817 ★

Software (SIC 7372)

Embedded Software Market - 2001

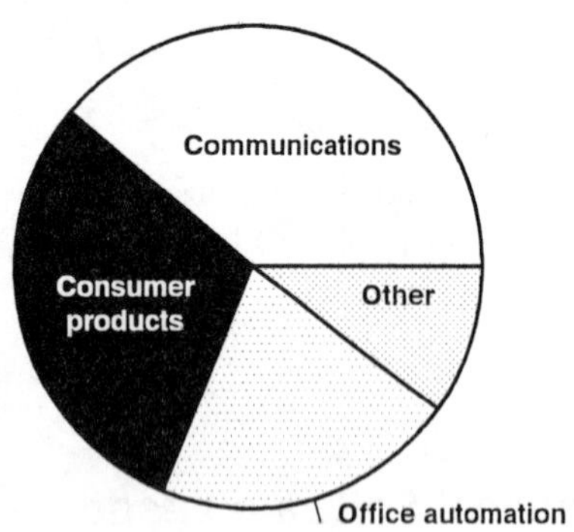

The market is estimated by segment.

Communications	39.0%
Consumer products	30.0
Office automation	21.0
Other	10.0

Source: *Investor's Business Daily*, August 6, 1998, p. A8, from Dain Rauscher Wessels and International Data Corp.

★ 1818 ★

Software (SIC 7372)

Enterprise Resource Planning Software Market

Market shares are shown in percent.

SAP	20.0%
SSA	19.0
Oracle	13.0
JBA Software Products	10.0
J.D. Edwards	10.0
Baan	7.0
Lawson Software	6.0
PeopleSoft	6.0
Intentia	5.0
QAD	4.0

Source: *Investor's Business Daily*, February 3, 1999, p. A7, from SMR Research Inc.

★ 1819 ★

Software (SIC 7372)

Enterprise Resource Planning Software Market - 1997

Market shares are shown in percent.

SAP	32.0%
Oracle	13.0
PeopleSoft	9.0
Baan Co.	7.0
J.D. Edwards	7.0
Others	32.0

Source: *New York Times*, November 8, 1998, p. 13, from AMR Research.

★ 1820 ★

Software (SIC 7372)

ERP Software Market

The market for enterprise resource planning software is shown in percent.

Manufacturing	35.0%
Services	16.0
Telecom/utilities	14.0
Financial	10.0
Government	5.0
Health care	5.0
Trade	4.0
Other	11.0

Source: *VAR Business*, May 10, 1999, p. 97, from Cahners In-Stat Group.

★ 1821 ★

Software (SIC 7372)

Financial Software Leaders

Market shares are shown in percent.

Intuit	84.0%
Peachtree	6.0
Black Financial	3.0
Microsoft	2.0
Other	5.0

Source: "Software Applications." Retrieved May 28, 1999 from the World Wide Web: http://www.userwww.stsu.edu/~magpie5/mshare/softapps.html, from PC Data Inc.

★ 1822 ★

Software (SIC 7372)

Firewall Market Vendors - 1997

Market shares are shown in percent.

Check Point Software	23.0%
Cisco Systems	19.0
Axent Technologies	7.0
Network Associates	6.0
Secure Computing	5.0
Others	40.0

Source: Retrieved May 18, 1999 from the World Wide Web: http:// www.sonic.net/cgi-bin/cif/cif/search-free.pl.

★ 1823 ★

Software (SIC 7372)

Game Software Leaders - 1996

Market shares are shown in percent.

CUC Software	15.0%
Electronic Arts	10.0
GT Interactive	9.0
Microsoft	6.0
Virgin	5.0
Other	55.0

Source: "Software Applications." Retrieved May 28, 1999 from the World Wide Web: http:// www.userwww.stsu.edu/~magpie5/mshare/ softapps.html, from PC Data Inc.

★ 1824 ★

Software (SIC 7372)

GameBoy Software Market

GameBoy controls 93% of the hand-held game device market. Figures are for the first six months of the year.

Nintendo	68.3%
THQ	12.8
Namco	4.3
Ubi Soft	2.6
Konami	2.2
Other	9.8

Source: *Investor's Business Daily*, October 22, 1998, p. A10, from NPD Group Inc. and Warburg Dillon Read.

★ 1825 ★

Software (SIC 7372)

Gene Sequencing Software Market - 1998

Market shares are shown in percent.

Oxford Molecular Group	26.0%
Gene Codes	10.0
Molecular Applications Group	9.0
Pangea Systems	9.0
DNAStar	8.0
Others	38.0

Source: *Chemical & Engineering News*, October 19, 1998, p. 29, from Frost & Sullivan.

★ 1826 ★

Software (SIC 7372)

Girl's Software Market

Mattel	64.5%
Learning Co.	21.6
Purple Moon	5.7
Other	8.2

Source: *Wall Street Journal*, March 19, 1999, p. A3.

★ 1827 ★

Software (SIC 7372)

Groupware Leaders - 1999

Data show millions of new users for the first quarter of the year.

Microsoft Exchange	1.9
Lotus Domino/Notes	1.4
Novell GroupWise	1.0

Source: "Market Reports." Retrieved June 1, 1999 from the World Wide Web: http:// www.itweb.co.za/office/ bmi/9906081105.htm, from International Data Corp.

★ 1828 ★

Software (SIC 7372)

Groupware Software Market

Market shares are shown in percent.

Lotus	33.3%
Microsoft	28.0
Novell	13.6
SoftArc	13.1
Netscape	3.7
TeamWare	1.7
Other	6.6

Source: *Forbes*, August 10, 1998, p. 107, from International Data Corp.

★ 1829 ★

Software (SIC 7372)

Hockey Game Market in Canada

The video game market is shown in percent.

EA	92.0%
Other	8.0

Source: *Marketing Magazine*, May 24, 1999, p. 10.

★ 1830 ★

Software (SIC 7372)

Intenet Browser Market - 1997

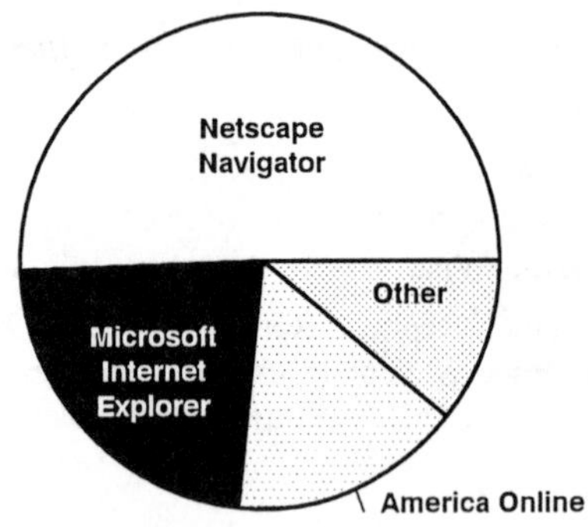

Netscape Navigator	50.5%
Microsoft Internet Explorer	22.8
America Online	16.1
Other	10.6

Source: *Wall Street Journal*, June 25, 1998, p. B8, from International Data Corp.

★ 1831 ★

Software (SIC 7372)

Internet Software Market - 1998

Market shares are shown for the first six months of the year. Microsoft includes AOL users.

Microsoft Internet Explorer	44.0%
Netscape Navigator	42.0
Other	14.0

Source: *PC Magazine*, November 17, 1998, p. 10, from International Data Corp.

★ 1832 ★

Software (SIC 7372)

Largest CAD/CAM Resellers/ Integrators - 1998

The top North American firms are ranked by sales in millions of dollars. CAD/CAM stands for computer aided design/computer aided manufacturing.

Rand Technology	$ 200
Advance Enterprise Solutions	85
Avcom Technologies	84
Integrated Systems Technology	65
Avatech Solutions	50

Source: *Computer Reseller News*, November 30, 1998, p. 69, from Daratech Inc.

★ 1833 ★

Software (SIC 7372)

Largest Educational Software Publishers - 1998

Market shares are shown in percent.

The Learning Company	42.0%
Havas Interactive	25.0
Other	33.0

Source: "PC Data Releases 1998 Software Sales Statistics." Retrieved June 1, 1999 from the World Wide Web: http:// www.pcdata.com/press/software, from PC Data.

★ 1834 ★
Software (SIC 7372)

Largest Entertainment Software Publishers - 1998

Market shares are shown in percent.

Havas Interactive	19.0%
Electronic Arts	13.0
Other	68.0

Source: "PC Data Releases 1998 Software Sales Statistics." Retrieved June 1, 1999 from the World Wide Web: http:// www.pcdata.com/press/software, from PC Data.

★ 1835 ★
Software (SIC 7372)

Largest Linux Vendors

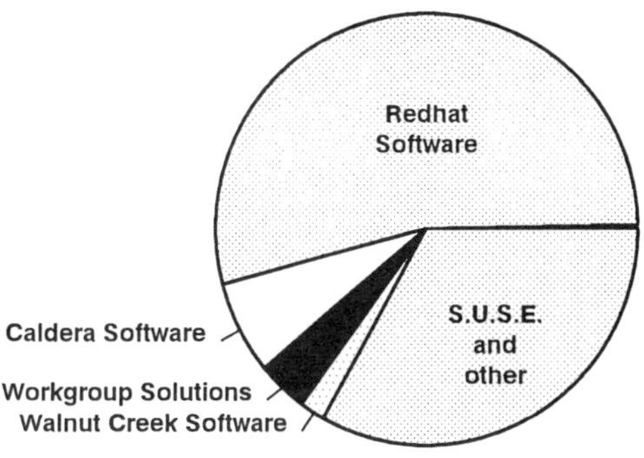

Linux software has been growing in popularity because of its price, reliability and power. As well, developers can easily modify the code for their own needs. Figures are in thousands of units.

	(000)	Share
Redhat Software	1,000	54.41%
Caldera Software	123	6.69
Workgroup Solutions	75	4.08
Walnut Creek Software	40	2.18
S.U.S.E. and other	600	32.64

Source: *Wall Street Journal*, October 22, 1998, p. B4, from International Data Corp.

★ 1836 ★
Software (SIC 7372)

Largest OR Software Sellers

Data show the leaders in the hospital market. Figures are based on a survey of 1,196 integrated health care delivery ssytems.

HBOC	38.0%
Medaphis/Per-Se	28.0
Meditech	6.0
Medical Systems Management	4.0
Self-developed	4.0
Other	20.0

Source: *OR Manager*, July 1998, p. 11, from Sheldon Dorenfest & Associates.

★ 1837 ★
Software (SIC 7372)

Largest PC Game Publishers - 1998

Firms are ranked by revenues in millions of dollars.

Havas Interactive	$ 236.3
Electronic Arts	170.1
Hasbro Interactive	118.5
GT Interactive	110.2
Microsoft	94.6
Learning Co.	84.9
Mattel	59.2
Activision	55.9
Interplay	44.6
Expert Software	14.6

Source: *Investor's Business Daily*, May 26, 1999, p. A6, from PC Data Inc.

★ 1838 ★

Software (SIC 7372)

Largest Reference Software Publishers - 1998

Market shares are shown in percent. Encyclopedias accounted for nearly 65% of reference software revenues.

The Learning Company	40.0%
Microsoft	30.0
IBM	12.0
Other	18.0

Source: "PC Data Releases 1998 Software Sales Statistics." Retrieved June 1, 1999 from the World Wide Web: http:// www.pcdata.com/press/software, from PC Data.

★ 1839 ★

Software (SIC 7372)

Largest Software Publishers - 1998

Market shares are shown in percent.

Microsoft	23.0%
The Learning Company	11.0
Other	66.0

Source: "PC Data Releases 1998 Software Sales Statistics." Retrieved June 1, 1999 from the World Wide Web: http:// www.pcdata.com/press/software, from PC Data.

★ 1840 ★

Software (SIC 7372)

Management Systems Software - 1997

EXE Technologies
McHugh
BDM International
Manhattan Associates
Catalyst
Optum

Market shares are shown in percent.

EXE Technologies	27.0%
McHugh	22.0
BDM International	16.0
Manhattan Associates	15.0
Catalyst	10.0
Optum	10.0

Source: *Investor's Business Daily*, February 3, 1999, p. A4, from Gartner Group Inc. and Hambrecht & Quist.

★ 1841 ★

Software (SIC 7372)

Messaging Software Leaders

Data show millions of seats as of June 1998.

Lotus Domino/Notes	21.9
Microsoft Exchange	15.0
Novell GroupWise	12.4
Netscape SuiteSpot	5.2
SoftArc	5.2

Source: *Wall Street Journal*, October 21, 1998, p. B6, from Dataquest Inc., International Data Corp., and Microsoft.

★ 1842 ★

Software (SIC 7372)

Messaging Software Market

Data show installed base, in millions of seats.

Notes	22.0
Exchange	13.1
GroupWise	8.8

Source: *Network World*, July 20, 1998, p. 8, from Electronic Mail & Messaging Systems.

★ 1843 ★
Software (SIC 7372)

Money Software Market

Market shares are shown in percent.

Quicken Deluxe	44.8%
Quicken	13.0
Quicken Suite	10.3
Money Financial Suite	7.5
Microsoft Money	4.5
Other	19.9

Source: *Investor's Business Daily*, October 2, 1998, p. 1, from PC Data.

★ 1844 ★
Software (SIC 7372)

Network Software Sales - 1997

Figures are estimated.

Unix	46.27%
Windows NT	34.54
Novell Netware	19.19

Source: *New York Times*, September 14, 1998, p. C2, from Novell, International Data Corp., and Bloomberg Financial Markets.

★ 1845 ★
Software (SIC 7372)

Numerical Control Software - 1999

Mold, tool & die	31.0%
Automotive	19.0
Aerospace	15.0
Machinery	12.0
Consumer products	9.0
Fabrication	6.0
Electric/electronic	3.0%
Government	3.0
Other	2.0

Source: *Tooling & Production*, June 1999, p. 46.

★ 1846 ★
Software (SIC 7372)

Office Suite Market

Market shares are shown in percent.

Microsoft	79.0%
Corel	16.0
Lotus	4.0

Source: "Business Desktop Applications." Retrieved May 28, 1999 from the World Wide Web: http://www.userwww.stsu.edu/~magpie5/mshare/busapps.html, from PC Data Inc.

★ 1847 ★
Software (SIC 7372)

Office Suite Sales - 1999

Shares are for April 1999.

Microsoft	93.0%
Corel	6.0
Lotus	1.0

Source: *New York Times*, June 7, 1999, p. C8, from PC Data.

★ 1848 ★
Software (SIC 7372)

Operating System Software

Market shares are shown in percent.

Windows NT	36.0%
Novell NetWare	27.0
Unix	23.0
Others	14.0

Source: *Investor's Business Daily*, August 20, 1998, p. A8, from International Data Corp.

★ 1849 ★

Software (SIC 7372)

Operating Systems Market - 1998

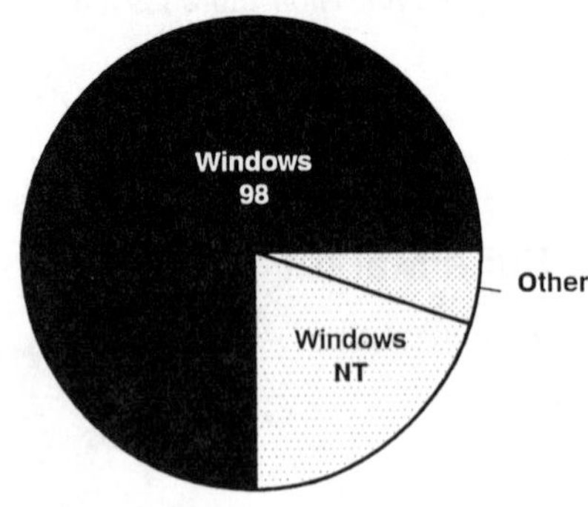

Market shares are shown based on shipments.

Windows 98	75.0%
Windows NT	20.0
Other	5.0

Source: *Investor's Business Daily*, July 7, 1998, p. A8, from Dataquest Inc. and Gartner Group Inc.

★ 1850 ★

Software (SIC 7372)

Operating Systems Market - 1998

The market is estimated.

Windows 98	51.3%
Windows 95	28.3
Windows NT	12.6
Windows 3.1	1.3
Non-Microsoft	6.5

Source: *Globe and Mail*, July 9, 1998, p. B1, from Dataquest Inc. and AdKnowledge.

★ 1851 ★

Software (SIC 7372)

Operating Systems Markets in Plants

Market shares are shown based on plant operations.

Windows NT single-user	26.0%
Multiuser/Windows NT	24.0
Unix	23.0
DEC's Open VMS	14.0
MS-DOS Windows 3.x	10.0
Other	4.0

Source: *Chemical Engineering*, November 1998, p. 53, from AMR Research.

★ 1852 ★

Software (SIC 7372)

Operating Systems Server Market - 1998

Windows NT	35.8%
NetWare 3.x, 4.x and 5.x	24.2
Unix	17.4
Linux	17.2
OS/2	3.0
Other	2.4

Source: *Wired*, May 1999, p. 141, from International Data Corp.

★ 1853 ★

Software (SIC 7372)

Packaged Software Sales in Mexico

Sales are shown in millions of dollars.

	1998	2000	Share
Application solutions	$ 268.72	$ 419.72	51.30%
Application tools	189.24	282.99	34.59
System software/ utilities	83.86	115.44	14.11

Source: *National Trade Data Bank*, October 23, 1998, p. ISA980901.

★ 1854 ★

Software (SIC 7372)

PC Game Vendors - 1998

Market shares are shown in percent. Figures are for the first six months of the year.

Cendant Software	17.2%
Electronic Arts	11.4
GT Interactive	9.9
Activision	5.1
Microsoft	5.1
Others	51.3

Source: Retrieved May 18, 1999 from the World Wide Web: http:// www.sonic.net/cgi-bin/cif/cif/search-free.pl.

★ 1855 ★

Software (SIC 7372)

Personal Productivity Software Leaders

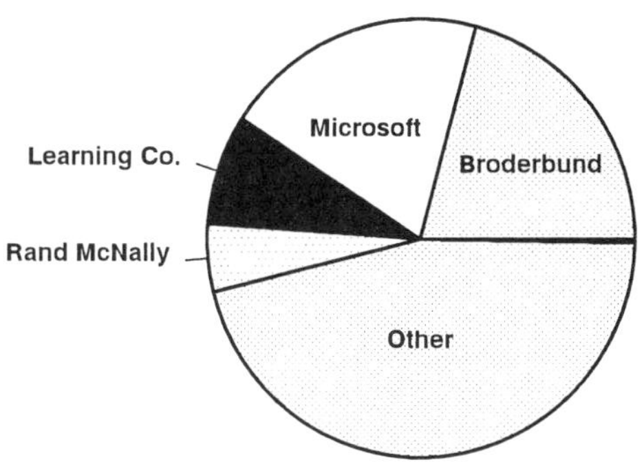

Market shares are shown in percent.

Broderbund	21.0%
Microsoft	20.0
Learning Co.	8.0
Rand McNally	5.0
Other	46.0

Source: "Software Applications." Retrieved May 28, 1999 from the World Wide Web: http:// www.userwww.stsu.edu/~magpie5/mshare/ softapps.html, from PC Data Inc.

★ 1856 ★

Software (SIC 7372)

Process Workflow Software - 1998

Market shares are shown in percent.

FileNet	16.3%
DST	9.5
Plexus	9.3
Eastman Software	9.2
Jetform	9.0
Staffware	7.8
Mosaix (Viewstar)	6.5
IBM	6.2
Other	26.2

Source: Retrieved May 18, 1999 from the World Wide Web: http:// www.sonic.net/cgi-bin/cif/cif/search-free.pl.

★ 1857 ★

Software (SIC 7372)

Reference Software Leaders

Market shares are shown in percent. Microsoft publishes Encarta multimedia encyclopedia, Bookshelf reference library, Cinemania movie guide and Automap Road Atlas.

Microsoft	39.0%
Learning Co.	12.0
American Business Information	11.0
Pro CD	11.0
Other	27.0

Source: "Software Applications." Retrieved May 28, 1999 from the World Wide Web: http:// www.userwww.stsu.edu/~magpie5/mshare/ softapps.html, from PC Data Inc.

★ 1858 ★

Software (SIC 7372)

Server Market - 1998

Market shares are shown for the second quarter of the year.

IBM	26.6%
Hewlett-Packard	14.4
Compaq/Digital	13.4
Sun	11.7
Siemens Nixdorf	4.6
Other	28.3

Source: *Investor's Business Daily*, October 19, 1998, p. A10, from Dataquest Inc.

★ 1859 ★

Software (SIC 7372)

Software Applications by Category

Client/server	85.0%
Host based	15.0

Source: Retrieved May 28, 1999 from the World Wide Web: http:// www.cif1.com/free/data/98Q3/ 98345146.htm.

★ 1860 ★

Software (SIC 7372)

Software Sales by Segment

Data show purchases by personal computer owners.

Entertainment	33.0%
Child education	7.0
Software suite	6.0
Reference/lifestyle	5.0
Drawing/graphics	4.0
Word processing	4.0
Adult education	3.0
Personal finance	3.0
Tax preparation	3.0
Utilties	3.0
Other	29.0

Source: *Detroit Free Press*, May 14, 1999, p. 2E, from Software & Information Industry Association.

★ 1861 ★

Software (SIC 7372)

Software Testing Tools Market - 1997

Market shares are shown in percent.

Mercury Interactive	34.5%
Rational Software	21.1
Segue Software	8.9
Compuware	7.3
Cyrano	5.7
AutoTester	3.9
Platinum Technology	3.5
Silicon Valley Networks	2.1
Softbridge	2.1
Other	10.9

Source: *Investor's Business Daily*, April 7, 1999, p. A10.

★ 1862 ★

Software (SIC 7372)

Speech-Recognition Market

Market shares are shown based on unit sales.

Dragon Systems	36.0%
IBM	31.0
Lernout & Hauspie	11.0
Others	22.0

Source: *New York Times*, March 1, 1999, p. C4, from PC Data and company reports.

★ 1863 ★

Software (SIC 7372)

Spreadsheet Software Market

Market shares are shown in percent.

Microsoft	60.0%
Lotus	35.0
Other	5.0

Source: "Business Desktop Applications." Retrieved May 28, 1999 from the World Wide Web: http:// www.userwww.stsu.edu/~magpie5/mshare/ busapps.html, from PC Data Inc.

★ 1864 ★

Software (SIC 7372)

Storage Software Market - 2002

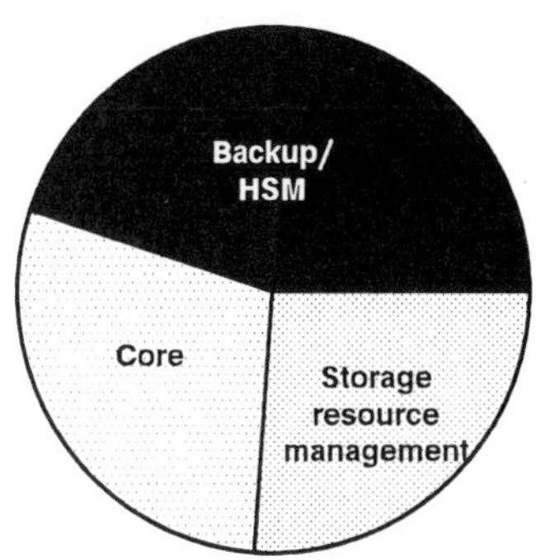

The market is estimated by category.

	($ mil.)	Share
Backup/HSM	$ 2,150	44.9%
Core	1,400	29.1
Storage resource management	1,240	26.0

Source: Retrieved May 18, 1999 from the World Wide Web: http:// www.sonic.net/cgi-bin/cif/cif/search-free.pl.

★ 1865 ★

Software (SIC 7372)

Streaming Media Software

The market is shown in percent.

RealNetworks	85.0%
Other	15.0

Source: *Investor's Business Daily*, April 6, 1999, p. a10.

★ 1866 ★

Software (SIC 7372)

Supply Chain Management

Shares are shown based on revenues.

	1998	2000
Software licenses	50.30%	52.07%
Implementation	29.58	28.56
Maintenance	13.52	14.50
Hardware	3.91	2.31
Other	2.69	2.56

Source: *Computerworld*, September 14, 1998, p. 46, from Advanced Manufacturing Research Inc.

★ 1867 ★

Software (SIC 7372)

Supply Chain Software Market

Market shares are shown in percent.

i2 Technologies	34.0%
Manugistics	24.0
PeopleSoft	7.0
Baan	5.0
Logility	5.0
Chesapeake	3.0
Numetrix	3.0
Paragon	3.0
SynQuest	3.0
Other	13.0

Source: *Traffic World*, October 12, 1998, p. 42, from Benchmarking Partners Inc.

★ 1868 ★

Software (SIC 7372)

Top Home PC Platform

Market shares are shown in percent.

Windows 95	60.0%
Windows 3.1	24.0
DOS	10.0
Macintosh	5.0

Source: Retrieved May 18, 1999 from the World Wide Web: http:// www.sonic.net/cgi-bin/cif/cif/search-free.pl.

★ 1869 ★

Software (SIC 7372)

Unix RDBMS Market - 1998

RDBMS stands for relational database management systems.

Oracle 7/8 and Oracle Lite	60.9%
Informix	13.2
IBM DB2	7.3
Sybase ASA	7.1
NCB	3.7
Others	7.8

Source: *Computer Reseller News*, April 5, 1999, p. 93, from Dataquest Inc.

★ 1870 ★
Software (SIC 7372)

Web Server Market

Market shares are shown in percent.

Apache	49.0%
Microsoft	22.0
Netscape	9.0
Other	20.0

Source: *Business Week*, June 29, 1998, p. 42, from Netcraft.

★ 1871 ★
Software (SIC 7372)

Web Server Software - 1998

Shares are shown as of January 1, 1999.

Apache	54.2%
Microsoft-IIS	23.3
Netscape-Enterprise	4.2
RapidSite	2.1
WebSite Pro	1.7
Other	14.4

Source: *Wired*, May 1999, p. 141, from International Data Corp.

★ 1872 ★
Software (SIC 7372)

Windows RDBMS Market - 1998

RDBMS stands for relational database management systems.

Oracle 7/8 and Oracle Life	46.1%
Microsoft SOL	29.7
IBM DB2	9.7
Sybase ASA	3.0
Others	11.5

Source: *Computer Reseller News*, April 5, 1999, p. 93, from Dataquest Inc. and Gartner Group.

★ 1873 ★
Software (SIC 7372)

Word Processing Market

Market shares are shown in percent.

Microsoft	62.0%
Corel	34.0
Lotus	3.0

Source: "Business Desktop Applications." Retrieved May 28, 1999 from the World Wide Web: http://www.userwww.stsu.edu/~magpie5/mshare/busapps.html, from PC Data Inc.

★ 1874 ★
Networks (SIC 7373)

ERP Database Server Market - 2000

Figures estimate the server market for enterprise resource planning software.

NT	50.0%
Unix	34.0
AS/400	15.0
Other	1.0

Source: *InfoWorld*, December 28, 1998, p. 47.

★ 1875 ★
Networks (SIC 7373)

Four-Way Server Market - 1998

Market shares are shown for the first three quarter of the year. Four-way servers contain four CPUs that share the same memory.

Compaq	45.0%
Dell	16.0
Hewlett-Packard	13.0
IBM	9.0
Others	17.0

Source: *Upside*, April 1999, p. 56, from International Data Corp.

★ 1876 ★
Networks (SIC 7373)

Top Server Makers in Mexico - 1998

Compaq	38.93%
Hewlett-Packard	24.48
IBM	14.52

Continued on next page.

★ 1876 ★ *Continued*

Networks (SIC 7373)

Top Server Makers in Mexico - 1998

Acer	11.96%
Dell	6.38
Digital	1.80
Lanix	0.93
Apple	0.18
Others	0.80

Source: *National Trade Data Bank*, April 1, 1999, p. ISA990201.

★ 1877 ★

Networks (SIC 7373)

UNIX Server Market - 1997

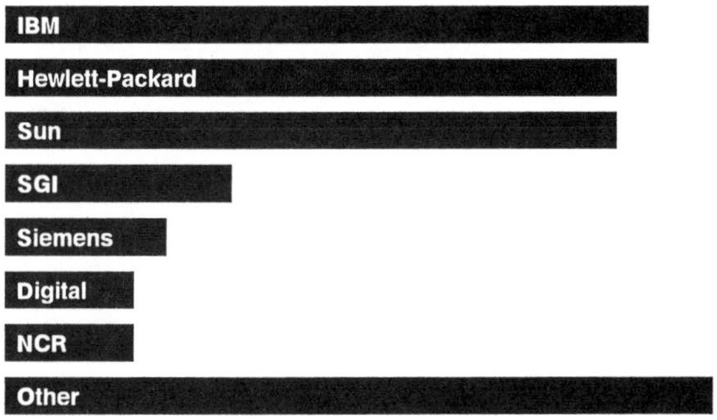

Market shares are shown in percent.

IBM	20.0%
Hewlett-Packard	19.0
Sun	19.0
SGI	7.0
Siemens	5.0
Digital	4.0
NCR	4.0
Other	22.0

Source: *Investor's Business Daily*, August 12, 1998, p. A8, from International Data Corp.

★ 1878 ★

Networks (SIC 7373)

Who Uses Servers in Mexico

Micro offices refers to 1-9 employees; small companies refers to 10-99 employees; medium companies refers to 100-499 employees; large companies refers to 500+ employees.

	2Q 1998	3Q 1998
Large companies	42.3%	51.3%
Medium companies	22.9	28.3
Small companies	16.0	14.4
Micro offices	6.6	3.7
Government	4.2	1.5
Education	1.6	0.8

Source: *National Trade Data Bank*, April 1, 1999, p. ISA990201.

★ 1879 ★

Networks (SIC 7373)

Wireless LAN Market - 1997

LAN stands for local area network.

Frequency hopping	65.0%
Direct-sequence	34.0
Other	1.0

Source: *Investor's Business Daily*, February 23, 1999, p. A6, from International Data Corp.

★ 1880 ★

Information Technology (SIC 7375)

Electronic Communication Networks

Market shares are estimated in percent.

Instinct	69.0%
Island	20.0
Tradebook	7.0
Archipelago (Tonto)	3.0
Other	1.0

Source: *Wall Street Journal*, December 23, 1998, p. C1, from Deutsche Bank Securities and BancBoston Robertson Stephens.

★ 1881 ★

Information Technology (SIC 7375)

High-Tech Industry in Georgia

Data show employment.

Communications services	59,500
Software services	26,000
Data processing/information services	16,000
Rental, maintenance/computer services	9,900
Communications equipment	7,100

Source: *Atlanta Journal-Constitution*, June 2, 1999, p. D4, from U.S. Bureau of Labor Statistics.

★ 1882 ★

Information Technology (SIC 7375)

Largest High-Tech Firms in Minnesota

Companies are ranked by annual revenues in millions of dollars. Products manufactured include data storage, imaging systems, software training and optical-mark readers.

Imation Corporation	$ 2,201.8
Ceridian Corporation	1,074.8
Analysts International Corporation	552.4
Hutchison Technology Inc.	453.2
National Computer Systems Inc.	406.0
DataCard Corporation	350.0
MTS Systems Corporation	303.5

Source: *Corporate Report*, September 1998, p. 57.

★ 1883 ★

Integrated Systems (SIC 7375)

Parts Data Management Systems Market

The market for PDM systems is expected to reach $2.5 billion in 2002. The system is a combination of a search engine and a database of parts. Market shares are shown in percent.

Documentum	8.0%
Metaphase	6.0
Parametric	6.0
Aspect	5.0
Sherpa	5.0
Computervision	4.0
IBM	4.0
Baan	3.0
EDS Unigraphics	3.0%
Intergraph	2.0
Other	54.0

Source: *Investor's Business Daily*, September 3, 1998, p. A4.

★ 1884 ★

Computer Services (SIC 7379)

Leading Outsourcing Companies for Banks

Vendors are ranked by outsourcing companies that provide services to commercial banks.

	Customers	Share
Fiserv Inc.	2,297	24.9%
Electronic Dats Systems Corp.	2,197	23.8
M&I Data Services	840	9.1
Alltel	565	6.1
Computer Services Inc.	291	3.2

Source: *ABA Banking Journal*, July 1998, p. 58, from Computer Based Solutions.

★ 1885 ★

Photofinishing (SIC 7384)

Photo Development Market - 1997

Distribution is shown by outlet.

Mass/discount	34.8%
Drug	24.3
Supermarkets	13.6
Stand-alone minilab	11.8
Mail order	6.6
Camera	5.8
Other	3.3

Source: *Photo Marketing*, January 1999, p. 45, from *1997-1998 PMA Industry Trends Report*.

★ 1886 ★

Interior Design (SIC 7389)

Largest Interior Design Firms

Firsm are ranked by fees in millions of dollars.

Callison Architecture	$ 24.6
Little & Associates Architects	10.5
The Amend Group	8.8
The Tricanco Group	7.3
Robert Young Associates	5.7
Marc-Michaels Interior Deisgn	5.5
Naomi Leff & Associates	4.7

Source: *Interior Design*, January 1999, p. 76.

★ 1887 ★

Mergers & Acquisitions (SIC 7389)

Largest Bank Deals

Deals are shown in billions of dollars. Acquirers are shown in parentheses. Data are from 1995 to the present.

CoreStates Financial (First Union)	$ 17.1
Barnett Banks (NationsBank)	15.5
First Interstate (Wells Fargo)	12.3
Mercantile Bancshares (Firstar)	10.7
CreStar Financial (SunTrust Banks)	9.6

Source: *Financial Times*, June 8, 1999, p. 18, from SNL Securities.

★ 1888 ★

Mergers & Acquisitions (SIC 7389)

Largest M&A Advisors to Depository Institutions - 1998

Data show announced deals in millions of dollars. Figures are for the first six months of the year.

Goldman, Sachs & Co.	$ 132,061.7
Merrill Lynch & Co.	95,301.5
NationsBanc Montgomery Securities Inc.	62,768.1
Credit Suisse First Boston Corp.	48,074.0
Morgan Stanley Dean Witter & Co.	30,338.4

Source: *US Banker*, September 1998, p. 84.

★ 1889 ★

Mergers & Acquisitions (SIC 7389)

Largest M&A Advisors to Thrift Institutions - 1998

Data show announced deals in millions of dollars. Figures are for the first six months of the year.

Lehman Brothers	$ 12,702.9
Credit Suisse First Boston Corp.	12,594.4
Goldman, Sachs & Co.	3,778.0
Salomon Smith Barney Inc.	3,394.1
Keefe, Bruyette & Woods Inc.	2,450.5

Source: *US Banker*, September 1998, p. 90.

★ 1890 ★

Mergers & Acquisitions (SIC 7389)

Largest M&A Law Firms - 1998

Data show value of completed deals in billions of dollars for the first nine months of the year.

Simpson Thacher & Bartlett	$ 254.7
Skadden Arps Slate Meagher & Flom	145.0
Shearman & Sterling	139.9
Cravath Swaine & Moore	122.6
Wachtell Lipton Rosen & Katz	118.1
Sullivan & Cromwell	111.1
Morris Nichols Arsht & Tunnell	102.7

Source: *Global Finance*, November 1998, p. 28.

★ 1891 ★

Mergers & Acquisitions (SIC 7389)

Largest Mergers in the Insurance Industry - 1998

Data show transaction value in billions of dollars. Figures are for the first six months of the year.

Travelers Corp. (Citicorp.)	$ 70,000
Berkshire Hathaway (General Re Corp.)	21,400
Commercial Union (General Accident)	11,500
Conseco (Green Tree Financial)	6,100
St. Paul Cos. (USF&G Corp.)	3,700

Source: *Business Insurance*, October 19, 1998, p. 3, from Conning & Co.

★ 1892 ★

Mergers & Acquisitions (SIC 7389)

Largest Physician Practice Mergers - 1998

Data show value of deals in millions of dollars. Acquirers are shown in parentheses.

Physician Reliance Network (American Oncology Resources)	$ 714.0
MedCath (Management-led buyout)	240.0
PrimeCare International (PhyCor)	118.3
Orange Coast Managed Care (FPA Medical Management)	42.4
Community Radiology Associates (American Physician Partners)	32.8

Source: *Modern Physician*, March 1999, p. 50, from Irving Levin Associates.

★ 1893 ★

Mergers & Acquisitions (SIC 7389)

Largest Telecom Dealers - 1998

The price of the deal is shown in billions of dollars. Acquirers are shown in parentheses.

Ameritech (SBC Communications)	$ 72.4
GTE (Bell Atlantic)	70.9
TCI (AT&T)	69.9
Teleport Communciations (AT&T)	11.0
Excel Communications (Teleglobe)	6.9

Source: *Industry Standard*, August 24, 1998, p. 32, from Securities Data Co.

SIC 75 - Auto Repair, Services, and Parking

★ 1894 ★

Truck Rental (SIC 7513)

Largest Truck Rental Services

Data show number of trucks in fleet.

U-Haul International Inc.	81,000
Ryder TRS	32,500
Rollins	30,000
Budget Rent-A-Truck	12,000

Source: Retrieved May 28, 1999 from the World Wide Web: http:// www.fleet-central.com/ARN/ TheStatistics/rentalmarket.htm.

★ 1895 ★

Auto Rental (SIC 7514)

Airport Car Rental Market

Shares of the market are shown in percent.

Hertz	29.7%
Avis	23.0
National	18.0
Budget	11.3
Alamo	9.8
Dollar/Thrifty	6.9
Other	1.3

Source: *Investor's Business Daily*, September 29, 1998, p. A4, from NationsBanc Montgomery Securities and Legg Mason Wood Walker.

★ 1896 ★

Auto Rental (SIC 7514)

Car Rental Market - 1998

Market shares are shown in percent for July 1998.

Hertz	29.0%
Avis	22.2
National	17.0
Alamo	12.1
Budget	10.8
Dollar/Thrifty	7.6
Other	1.4

Source: *Investext,* Thomson Financial Networks, December 9, 1998, p. 3.

★ 1897 ★

Auto Rental (SIC 7514)

Largest Car Rental Services

Data show number of cars.

Enterprise	355,000
Hertz	250,000
Avis	200,000
National	145,000
Alamo	130,000
Budget	125,000
Dollar	62,000
FRCS (Ford)	51,150
Thrifty	34,000
Republic Replacement	32,000

Source: Retrieved May 28, 1999 from the World Wide Web: http:// www.fleet-central.com/ARN/ TheStatistics/rentalmarekt.htm.

★ 1898 ★

Auto Rental (SIC 7514)

Local Car Rental Market

Shares of the local rental market are shown in percent.

Enterprise	20.0%
Avis	19.0
Hertz	16.0
Budget	11.0
Alamo	8.0
National	8.0
Thrifty	3.0
Dollar	2.0
Others	14.0

Source: *Consumer Reports Travel Letter*, September 1998, p. 208, from *Auto Rental News Fact Book, 1998.*

★ 1899 ★

Auto Repair Services (SIC 7539)

Brake Repair Services in Canada

Brake repairs were performed on approximately 7.3 million vehicles in 1996.

Ontario	39.0%
Quebec	26.0
British Columbia	12.0
Prairie	12.0
Maritime	11.0

Source: *National Trade Data Bank*, September 30, 1998, p. IMI980929, from *DesRosiers Automotive Consultants*.

★ 1900 ★

Auto Repair Services (SIC 7539)

Brake Repair Services Market in Canada

Shares are shown for the mechanically installed market.

Independent repair shop	38.0%
New car dealership	30.0
Specialty shop	13.0
Canadian Tire	7.0
Service Station	7.0%
Tire store	3.0
Department stores	1.0
Other	1.0

Source: *National Trade Data Bank*, September 30, 1998, p. IMI980929, from *DesRosiers Automotive Consultants*.

★ 1901 ★

Carwashes (SIC 7542)

Carwash Equipment Purchases

Data show the types of equipment added at carwashes.

In-bay automatics	21.3%
Vending machines	16.3
Vacuums	11.3
Fragrance dispensers	10.0
Bill changers	6.3
Foam brushes	5.0
Pre-soak	5.0
Fragrance/vacuum combos	3.8
Others	21.3

Source: *Auto Laundry News*, May 1999, p. 53.

★ 1902 ★

Auto Service (SIC 7549)

Oil Change Market in Canada

Ontario	32.0%
Quebec	25.0
Prairie provinces	17.0
British Columbia	12.0
Atlantic provinces	9.0
Other	5.0

Source: *National Trade Data Bank*, July 2, 1998, p. IMI980622.

SIC 78 - Motion Pictures

★ 1903 ★

Motion Pictures (SIC 7812)

Best-Selling DVDs

Data show the top selling digital video discs as sold through Videoscan as of May 1, 1999. VideoScan accounts for 75% of point of sale units sold through to consumers.

Lethal Weapon 4	192,000
Blade	167,000
Armageddon	160,000
Godzilla 1998	153,000
Tomorrow Never Dies	145,000

Source: Retrieved May 30, 1999 from the World Wide Web: http:// www.dvdfile.com/news/sales_statistics/ software.htm.

★ 1904 ★

Motion Pictures (SIC 7812)

DVD Leaders - 1999

Shares are shown for January 1, 1999 - May 1, 1999.

Warner	20.9%
Buena Vista	11.5
Columbia	10.1
Universal	9.4
New Line	9.2
Paramount	7.6
MGM	7.4
20th Century Fox	6.8
Other	17.1

Source: Retrieved May 30, 1999 from the World Wide Web: http:// www.dvdfile.com/news/sales_statistics/ software.htm.

★ 1905 ★

Motion Pictures (SIC 7812)

Largest Film/Video Production Firms in Florida - 1997

Data show gross billings in millions of dollars.

Five Star	$ 9.50
AFI/Filmworks	8.50
Multivision Video & Film	5.20
Bond Films & Associates	3.80
Paradise Productions	3.20

Source: *South Florida Business Journal*, September 18, 1998, p. 22A.

★ 1906 ★

Motion Pictures (SIC 7812)

Leading Adult Video Producers

Data show that 8,498 hard-core videos entered the retail market. Americans rented 686 million adult tapes generating $5 billion in sales and rentals. Figures show estimated sales in millions of dollars.

Vivid Video	$ 35
Metro Global Media	34
VCA	20

Source: *Forbes*, June 14, 1999, p. 216, from Showtime Event Television and company sources.

★ 1907 ★

Motion Pictures (SIC 7812)

Motion Pictures by Rating

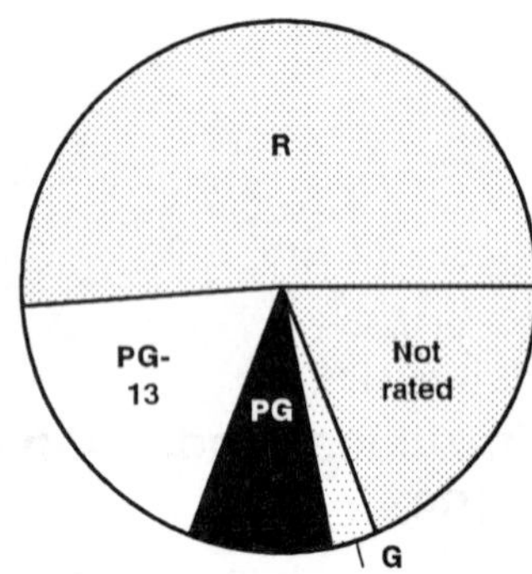

	No.	Share
R	177	50.72%
PG-13	63	18.05
PG	33	9.46
G	11	3.15
Not rated	65	18.62

Source: *Christian Science Monitor*, December 24, 1998, p. B10, from Exhibitor Relations.

★ 1908 ★

Motion Pictures (SIC 7812)

Top Films in Canada - 1998

Films are ranked by gross receipts in millions of dollars. Figures are for December 1997 - November 1998.

Titanic	$ 10.5
Les Boys	.3.7
Armageddon	3.0
Saving Private Ryan	2.1
Deep Impact	1.8
Good Will Hunting	1.7
Lethal Weapon 4	1.5
The Truman Show	1.5
Dr. Doolittle	1.4
Tomorrow Never Dies	1.4

Source: *Screen International*, December 11, 1998, p. 28, from Alex Films.

★ 1909 ★

Motion Pictures (SIC 7812)

Top Foreign Films in the United States - 1998

Films are ranked by gross receipts in millions of dollars.

Life is Beautiful	$ 5.2
Ma Vie En Rose	2.2
Live Flesh	1.7
The Thief	1.1
Men With Guns	0.9
The Celebration	0.8
Character	0.6

Source: *Screen International*, December 11, 1998, p. 30.

★ 1910 ★

Motion Pictures (SIC 7812)

Top Motion Picture Companies - 1998

Studios are ranked by box office grosses in millions of dollars.

Disney	$ 1,103.0
Paramount	1,085.0
Warner Bros.	749.7
Sony	749.4
Fox	729.3
New Line	537.0
Dreamworks	481.4
Miramax	402.7
Universal	376.8
MGM/UA	200.6

Source: *USA TODAY*, January 5, 1999, p. 8D.

★ 1911 ★

Motion Pictures (SIC 7812)

Top Movies - 1998

Films are ranked by gross revenues in millions of dollars.

Titanic	$ 488.19
Armageddon	201.57
Saving Private Ryan	190.80
There's Something About Mary	174.42
The Waterboy	147.89
Dr. Doolittle	144.15
Deep Impact	140.46

Continued on next page.

★ 1911 ★ *Continued*

Motion Pictures (SIC 7812)

Top Movies - 1998

Films are ranked by gross revenues in millions of dollars.

Godzilla	$ 136.31
Rush Hour	136.06
Good Will Hunting	134.06

Source: *Variety*, January 11, 1999, p. 33.

★ 1912 ★

Motion Pictures (SIC 7812)

Top Video Firms

Market shares are shown for the year ended December 27, 1998.

Warner Home Video	19.5%
Disney	19.2
Paramount Home Video	11.6
Fox	9.4
Columbia	8.7
Universal Home Video	8.0
Artisan Ent.	2.9
Anchor Bay	2.8
PolyGram Home Video	2.8
Other	15.1

Source: *Los Angeles Times*, January 6, 1999, p. C7, from VideoScan.

★ 1913 ★

Television Production (SIC 7812)

Spanish TV Market

Univision	85.0%
Telemundo	15.0

Source: *Fortune*, December 21, 1998, p. 56.

★ 1914 ★

Video Tapes (SIC 7812)

Exercise Video Market

Market shares of video sales are shown for the year ended February 7, 1999.

PPI Entertainment	15.9%
Living Arts	15.1
Sony	13.7
Anchor Bay	12.3%
Ventura Distribution	10.4
BMG Video	9.6
Warner Home Video	6.8
Goodtimes Hoem Video	6.3
Brentwood	3.4
Goldhill Home Media	2.1
Other	4.4

Source: *Los Angeles Times*, February 17, 1999, p. C8, from VideoScan.

★ 1915 ★

Video Tapes (SIC 7812)

Sports Video Leaders

Shares are shown of the sports video market for the year ended October 18, 1998.

Fox	29.7%
World Wrestling Federation	22.1
PolyGram Home Video	18.1
Warner Home Video	9.8
Simitar	3.5
Trimark	3.3
Madacy	2.2
Other	11.3

Source: *Los Angeles Times*, October 28, 1998, p. C8, from VideoScan.

★ 1916 ★

Video Tapes (SIC 7812)

TV Based Video Leaders

Shares are shown of the television-based video market for the year ended October 25, 1998.

Warner Home Video	23.7%
Fox	16.3
Artisan Entertainment	12.1
Disney	11.1
Paramount Home Video	9.0
Anchor Bay	7.6
PolyGram Home Video	4.4
Real Entertainment	4.3
Other	11.5

Source: *Los Angeles Times*, November 4, 1998, p. C10, from VideoScan.

★ 1917 ★

Video Tapes (SIC 7812)

Yoga Video Market

The market is shown in percent.

Living Arts	70.0%
Other	30.0

Source: *Forbes*, April 19, 1999, p. 114.

★ 1918 ★

Film Distribution (SIC 7822)

Top Film Distributors - 1998

Market shares are shown in percent.

Buena Vista	16.0%
Paramount	15.8
Sony	10.9
Warner Bros	10.9
20th Century Fox	10.6
New Line	7.8
Dreamworks SKG	6.9
Miramax	5.9
Universal	5.5
MGM/UA	2.9
Other	6.8

Source: *Entertainment Weekly*, February 5, 1999, p. 38, from *Variety*.

★ 1919 ★

Movie Theaters (SIC 7832)

Largest Movie Theater Chains

Market shares are shown based on 31,133 indoor screens as of June 30, 1998.

Regal/Act III	10.0%
Carmike Cinemas	9.0
Loews Cineplex	9.0
AMC Entertainment	8.0
United Artists	7.0
Cinemark	6.0
General Cinemas	4.0
National Amusements	4.0
Hoyts Cinemas	3.0
Edwards Cinemas	2.0
Other	38.0

Source: *Investext*, Thomson Financial Networks, August 17, 1998, p. 5, from EDI, company reports, and Schroder.

★ 1920 ★

Movie Theaters (SIC 7832)

Movie Theater Market in Canada

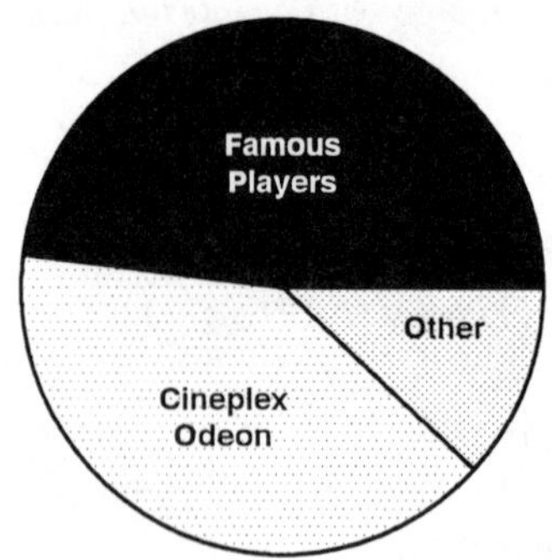

Market shares are estimated in percent.

Famous Players	48.0%
Cineplex Odeon	40.0
Other	12.0

Source: *Canadian Business*, December 11, 1998, p. 28.

★ 1921 ★

Video Tape Rental (SIC 7841)

Home Video Rental Market

Market shares are shown in percent.

Buena Vista	19.83%
Warner	16.98
Columbia TriStar	14.85
20th Century Fox	9.32
Paramount	8.77
Universal	7.45
New Line	7.15
PolyGram	3.33
MGM	3.17
DreamWorks	1.30
Other	7.85

Source: *Variety*, January 11, 1999, p. 20, from VidTrac.

★ 1922 ★

Video Tape Rental (SIC 7841)

Popular Movie Rentals

Data show the most rented videos of all time, ranked by grosses in millions of dollars.

Star Wars	$ 271
E.T. - The Extra Terrestrial	228
Jurassic Park	213
Return of the Jedi	192
Independence Day	177
The Empire Strikes Back	174
The Lion King	173
Forrest Gump	156

Source: *Christian Science Monitor*, August 14, 1998, p. 2, from *Variety*.

★ 1923 ★

Video Tape Rental (SIC 7841)

Top Movie Rental Chains - 1998

Data show millions of units rented.

Blockbuster Video	918.6
Hollywood Entertainment	203.0
Video Update	83.6
Movie Gallery	65.5

Source: *Chain Store Age*, June 1999, p. 46, from industry reports.

★ 1924 ★

Video Tape Rental (SIC 7841)

Video Store Leaders in Canada - 1998

Market shares are shown in percent for the year ended December 31, 1998.

Blockbuster Entertainment	19.2%
Rogers Video	11.4
Le Superclub Videotron	4.9
Jumbo Video	4.2
Video Update	3.9
Others	56.4

Source: "Report on Market Share." Retrieved June 1, 1999 from the World Wide Web: http://www.marketingmag.ca/index.cgi?, from *Video Store Magazine*.

★ 1925 ★

Concert Promotion (SIC 7929)

Top Concert Promoters - 1998

Promoters are ranked by gross revenues in millions of dollars. Figures are for December 1, 1997 - December 7, 1998.

TNA International Ltd./TNA USA	$ 238.43
Universal Concerts	168.79
Pace Concerts/Pace Entertainment/Pace Touring	122.55
Cellar Door	115.62
Delsener-Slater Enterprises	102.45
Bill Graham Presents	61.5
Jam Prods./Tinley Park	59.6
Metropolitan Entertainment	53.4

Source: *Amusement Business*, December 28, 1998, p. 12.

★ 1926 ★

Concert Promotion (SIC 7929)

Top Music Promoters in Michigan - 1998

Data show gross in millions of dollars.

Cellar Door	$ 22.7
Palace Sports & Entertainment	9.7
Belkin Prods.	8.7
PACE Touring	2.9
Brass Ring Prods.	2.4
Magicworks Entertainment	1.5
Metropolitan Entertainment Group	1.5

Source: *Amusement Business*, February 15, 1999, p. 20.

★ 1927 ★

Concert Promotion (SIC 7929)

Top Promoters - 1998

Promoters are ranked by gross revenues in millions of dollars. Figures are for December 1, 1997 - December 7, 1998.

Universal Concerts	$ 144.5
Delsener-Slater Enterprises	66.0
Pace Concerts/Pace Entertainment/Pace Touring	57.7
Cellar Door	52.0
Bill Graham Presents	34.4

Source: *Amusement Business*, December 28, 1998, p. 12.

★ 1928 ★

Entertainers (SIC 7929)

Leading Concert Tours - 1998

Earnings are shown in millions of dollars.

Elton John	$ 46.2
Dave Matthews Band	40.1
Celine Dion	38.1
Yanni	37.4
Garth Brooks	37.2
Eric Clapton	33.6
Shania Twain	33.5
Janet Jackson	33.1

Source: *Times-Picayune*, December 30, 1998, pp. A-12, from Pollstar.

★ 1929 ★

Entertainers (SIC 7929)

Top Touring Acts - 1998

Groups are ranked by gross revenues in millions of dollars. Figures are for December 1, 1997 - December 7, 1998.

The Rolling Stones	$ 193.3
U2	45.0
Elton John	40.0
Yanni	38.1
Garth Brooks	34.8
George Strait	32.9
Janet Jackson	32.2

Source: *Amusement Business*, December 28, 1998, p. 16, from Amusement Business Boxscore.

★ 1930 ★

Sports Promotion (SIC 7929)

Top Female Athletes

Data show annual endorsement income, in millions.

Monica Seles	$ 6.0
Steffi Graf	5.0
Kristi Yamaguchi	3.0
Anna Kournikova	2.0
Picabo Street	2.0
Tara Lipinski	2.0
Venus Williams	2.0

Source: *USA TODAY*, June 29, 1998, p. C1, from *Sports Business Journal*.

★ 1931 ★

Sports (SIC 7941)

Leading Major League Teams

Data show the leading major league teams by average home game attendance.

Colorado	47,311
Baltimore	45,333
Arizona	45,270
Cleveland	42,636
Atlanta	40,412

Source: *USA TODAY*, August 6, 1998, p. C1, from Major League Baseball.

★ 1932 ★

Sports (SIC 7941)

Popular Sports for Youth

Data show millions of participants.

Basketball	12,803
Soccer	6,971
Baseball	5,229
In-line skating	3,591
Football (touch)	3,590
Volleyball	3,022
Running/jogging	2,824
Softball	2,717
Football (tackle)	2,079
Fishing	2,021

Source: *Sporting Goods Dealer*, Fall 1998, p. 8, from Sporting Goods Manufacturers Association.

★ 1933 ★

Sports (SIC 7941)

Top Baseball Teams

Teams are ranked by current value in millions of dollars. Figures were calculated using revenues and operating income. See source for details.

New York Yankees	$ 362
Baltimore Orioles	323
Cleveland Indians	322
Colorado Rockies	303
Atlanta Braves	299
Texas Rangers	254
Seattle Mariners	251
Los Angeles Dodgers	236

Source: *Forbes*, December 14, 1998, p. 126, from *Amusement Business*, The Bonham Group, Marquee Global Sports Ventures, and *Inside the Ownership of Professional Sports Teams*.

★ 1934 ★

Sports (SIC 7941)

Top Basketball Teams

Teams are ranked by current value in millions of dollars. Figures were calculated using revenues and operating income. See source for details.

Chicago Bulls	$ 303
New York Knicks	296
Los Angeles Lakers	268

Continued on next page.

★ 1934 ★ *Continued*

Sports (SIC 7941)

Top Basketball Teams

Teams are ranked by current value in millions of dollars. Figures were calculated using revenues and operating income. See source for details.

Portland Trail Blazers	$ 245
Phoenix Suns	235
Washington Wizards	207
Detroit Pistons	206
Utah Jazz	200

Source: *Forbes*, December 14, 1998, p. 134, from *Amusement Business*, The Bonham Group, Marquee Global Sports Ventures, and *Inside the Ownership of Professional Sports Teams*.

★ 1935 ★

Sports (SIC 7941)

Top Football Teams

Teams are ranked by current value in millions of dollars. Figures were calculated using revenues and operating income. See source for details.

Dallas Cowboys	$ 413
Washington Redskins	403
Carolina Panthers	365
Tampa Bay Bucaneers	346
Miami Dolphins	340
Baltimore Ravens	329
Seattle Seahawks	324
St. Louis Rams	322
Tennessee Oilers	322

Source: *Forbes*, December 14, 1998, p. 134, from *Amusement Business*, The Bonham Group, Marquee Global Sports Ventures, and *Inside the Ownership of Professional Sports Teams*.

★ 1936 ★

Sports (SIC 7941)

Top Hockey Teams

Teams are ranked by current value in millions of dollars. Figures were calculated using revenues and operating income. See source for details.

New York Rangers	$ 195
Philadelphia Flyers	187
Boston Bruins	$ 185
Detroit Red Wings	184
Washington Capitals	178
Chicago Blackhawks	170
Montreal Canadiens	167
St. Louis Blues	154

Source: *Forbes*, December 14, 1998, p. 134, from *Amusement Business*, The Bonham Group, Marquee Global Sports Ventures, and *Inside the Ownership of Professional Sports Teams*.

★ 1937 ★

Sports (SIC 7941)

Top States for Soccer

Data show thousands of players for the average of 1995-97.

California	2,154
New York	1,354
Texas	1,277
Ohio	1,116
Pennyslvania	1,070
Michigan	781
New Jersey	643
Florida	613
Minnesota	561
North Carolina	467

Source: *USA TODAY*, June 16, 1999, p. 17A, from Soccer Industry Council of America.

★ 1938 ★

Health Clubs (SIC 7991)

Largest Health Clubs in San Francisco, CA

Data show memebership in the Bay Area.

24 Hour Fitness	400,000
Club One	38,000
Western Athletic Clubs	27,000
Bally Total Fitness Clubs	21,000
Leisure Sports Inc.	21,000
Club Sport of San Ramon	8,000
Prime Time Athletic Club	7,000
Jazzercise	5,500

Source: *San Francisco Business Journal*, January 8, 1999, p. 24.

★ 1939 ★

Amusement Parks (SIC 7996)

Largest Amusement Parks - 1998

Magic Kingdom
Epcot
Disney-MGM Studios
Universal Studios
Animal Kingdom
SeaWorld

Data show attendance, in millions.

Magic Kingdom	15.6
Epcot	10.6
Disney-MGM Studios	9.5
Universal Studios	8.9
Animal Kingdom	6.0
SeaWorld	4.9

Source: *Time*, May 31, 1999, p. 84, from *Amusement Business*.

★ 1940 ★

Amusement Parks (SIC 7996)

Top Waterparks - 1998

Data show attendance.

Wet 'N Wild	1,300,000
Blizzard Beach at Walt Disney World	1,280,000
Typhoon Lagoon at Walt Disney World	1,100,000
Schlitterbahn	877,000
Raging Waters	760,320
Water Country USA	650,000
Six Flags Hurricane Harbor at Six Flags Over Texas	600,000
Adventure Island	550,000
Noah's Ark	500,000

Source: *Amusement Business*, December 28, 1998, p. 78.

★ 1941 ★

Business Services (SIC 7999)

Most Contracted Services at Colleges

Foodservice	66.0%
Vending	57.7
Bookstores	39.2
Custodial, academic buildings	22.7
Laundry	22.7
Security, academic buildings	20.6

Source: *AS&U*, September 1998, p. 16, from *American School & University 5th Annual Privatization/Contract Services Survey.*

★ 1942 ★

Business Services (SIC 7999)

U.S. Outsouring Market

Sales are shown in billions of dollars.

	1998	2001
I.T.	$ 82.39	$ 183.79
Administration	24.65	39.94
Distribution	21.12	32.38
Facilities management	12.56	23.02
Customer service	6.81	15.19
Human resources	5.21	8.04
Marketing and sales	4.57	5.80

Source: *PC Week*, March 29, 1999, p. 72, from Outsouring Institute.

★ 1943 ★

National Parks (SIC 7999)

Most Visited National Parks - 1997

Data show millions of visitors.

Great Smoky Mountains	9.9
Grand Canyon	4.8
Olympic	3.8
Yosemite	3.7
Yellowstone	2.9

Source: *Christian Science Monitor*, July 10, 1998, p. 8.

★ 1944 ★

National Parks (SIC 7999)

Popular Recreation Sites - 1997

Data show number of visits.

Blue Ridge Pkwy.	18.3
Golden Gate NRA	13.8
Great Smoky Mountains NP	9.9
Lake Mead NRA	8.5
Gateway NRA	6.8
Natchez Trace Pkwy.	5.9
George Washington Mem. Pkwy.	5.8
Grand Canyon NP	4.7
Delaware Water Gap NRA	4.7

Source: *Congressional Digest*, January 1999, p. 8, from National Park Service.

★ 1945 ★

Sponsorship (SIC 7999)

Canadian Sponsorship Dollars - 1998

Data show estimated spending.

	($ mil.)	Share
Sports	$ 4,600	67.0%
Entertainment/tours/ attractions	675	10.0
Festivals, fairs	578	9.0
Causes	544	8.0
Arts	413	6.0

Source: *Globe and Mail*, July 17, 1998, p. B1, from IEG Inc.

★ 1946 ★

Sponsorship (SIC 7999)

Sponsorship in North America

Sports	67.0%
Entertainment tours, attractions	10.0
Festivals, fairs, annual events	9.0
Cause marketing	8.0
Arts	6.0

Source: *Investor's Business Daily*, May 20, 1999, p. A10, from *IEG Sponsorship Report*.

★ 1947 ★

Training (SIC 7999)

How Companies Conduct Training

	1997	2000
Classroom traning	78.0%	61.0%
Electronic technologies	9.0	23.0
Self paced methods	7.0	10.0
Other	6.0	6.0

Source: *Computerworld*, April 26, 1999, p. 61, from American Society for Training and Development.

SIC 80 - Health Services

★ 1948 ★

Surgery (SIC 8011)

Largest Outpatient Surgery Centers in Silicon Valley

Data show the number of times performed per year.

Stanford Hospital and Clinics	14,165
El Camino Surgery Center	8,000
Washington Outpatient Surgery Center	6,000
Valley Medical Center	4,500
Bonaventure Surgery Center	2,000

Source: *San Jose and Silicon Valley Business Jounral*, January 1, 1999, p. 14.

★ 1949 ★

Surgery (SIC 8011)

Where Knee Arthroscopy is Performed

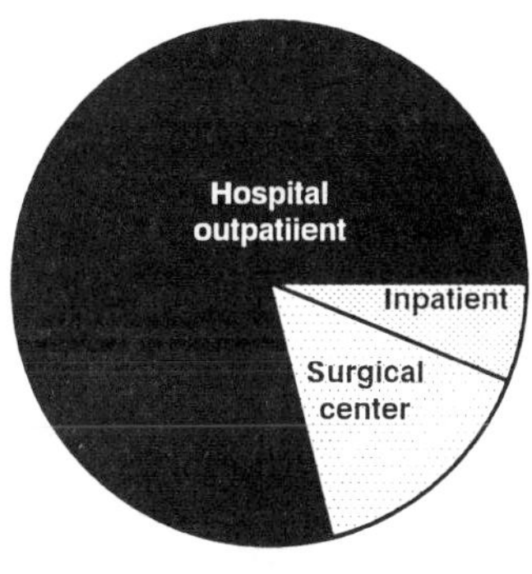

Figures are for 1995, the latest available.

Hospital outpatiient	79.0%
Surgical center	15.0
Inpatient	6.0

Source: *OR Manager*, August 1998, p. 26, from National Center for Health Statistics.

★ 1950 ★

Nursing Homes (SIC 8050)

Largest Assisted Living Chains

Chains are ranked by number of beds, managed or leased.

Alterra Healthcare Corp.	15,003
Emeritus Assisted Living	11,288
Marriott Senior Living Services	9,675
ARV Assisted Living	7,944
Atria Senior Quarters	7,600
Assisted Living Concepts	6,648
Sunrise Assisted Living	5,616
CareMatrix Corporation	5,096

Source: *Contemporary Long Term Care*, April 1999, p. 48.

★ 1951 ★

Nursing Homes (SIC 8050)

Largest Nursing Facilities - 1998

Chains are ranked by number of beds, managed or leased.

Beverly Enterprises	62,293
Mariner Post-Acute Network	49,656
Sun Healthcare Group	44,500
Integrated Health Services	42,859
HCR Manor Care	40,000
Vencor	38,362
Genesis Health Ventures	36,050

Source: *Contemporary Long Term Care*, April 1999, p. 44.

★ 1952 ★

Nursing Homes (SIC 8050)

Largest Nursing Home Chains

Data show number of beds.

Beverly Enterprises	63,376
Mariner Post-Acute Network	51,576
Sun Healthcare Group	47,103
Vencor	45,656
Genesis Health Ventures	42,317

Source: *Wall Street Journal*, July 24, 1998, p. B1, from CIBC Oppenheimer.

★ 1953 ★

Senior Citizen Housing (SIC 8052)

New Senior Housing - 1998

According to the source, there are 15,500 senior housing residences in the United States. Units under construction increased 11 percent from August 1997 to June 1998. CCRC stands for continuing care retirement communities.

Assisted living	75.0%
Congregate	15.0
Senior apts.	6.0
CCRCs	4.0

Source: *Provider*, September 1998, p. 13, from American Senior Housing Association.

★ 1954 ★

Hospitals (SIC 8060)

Largest Hospices in Arizona

Hospice of the Valley	456
Hospice Family Care Inc.	190
Dignita Hospice Care	130
Carondelet Hospice Services	87
Vista Care Hospice	80

Source: *The Business Journal Serving Phoenix and the Valley of the Sun*, January 15, 1999, p. 32.

★ 1955 ★

Hospitals (SIC 8060)

Largest Hospitals in Columbus, OH - 1997

Data show number of patient admissions.

Riverside Methodist Hospital	44,778
Ohio State University Hospital	27,133
Grant Medical Center	21,877
Mount Carmel Medical Center	19,482
Mount Carmel East Hospital	14,703

Source: *Business First*, July 17, 1998, p. 12.

★ 1956 ★

Hospitals (SIC 8060)

Largest Hospitals in New York

Hospitals are ranked by expenses in millions of dollars.

New York Presbyterian Hospital	$ 1,509
Montefiore Medical Center	910
Mount Sinai Hospital	882
Beth Israeli Medical Center	877
Memorial Sloan-Kettering Cancer Center	668

Source: *Crain's New York Business*, February 22, 1999, p. 14.

★ 1957 ★

Hospitals (SIC 8060)

Pediatric Hospital Affiliations in Miami, FL - 1997

The proposed market shares are shown.

Maiami Children's Hospital	32.0%
Jackson Memorial Hospital	31.3
Other	36.7

Source: *South Florida Business Journal*, March 5, 1999, p. 4, from Florida Hospital Association.

SIC 81 - Legal Services

★ 1958 ★

Legal Services (SIC 8111)

Largest Law Firms in San Francisco, CA

Data show number of lawyers in the Bay Area.

Wilson Sonelni Goodrich & Rosati	500
Morrison & Forester	324
Cooley Godward	295
Brobeck Phieger & Harrison	255
Littler Mendelson P.C.	239

Source: *San Francisco Business Journal*, September 18, 1998, p. 20.

SIC 82 - Educational Services

★ 1959 ★

Libraries (SIC 8231)

Largest U.S. Libraries

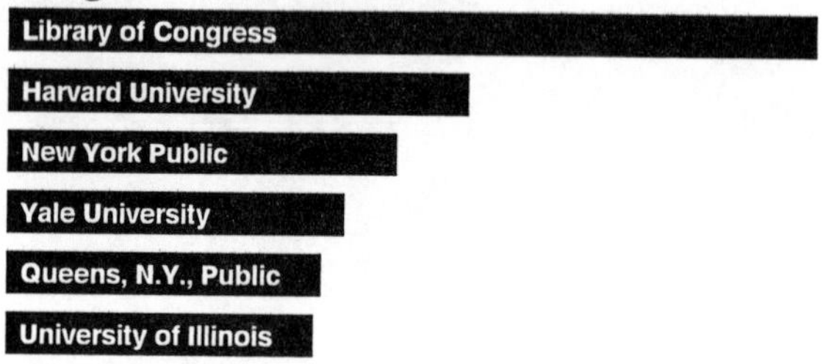

Library of Congress

Harvard University

New York Public

Yale University

Queens, N.Y., Public

University of Illinois

Data show the number of volumes.

Library of Congress	23,994,965
Harvard University	13,617,133
New York Public	11,445,971
Yale University	9,932,080
Queens, N.Y., Public	9,237,300
University of Illinois	9,024,296

Source: *USA TODAY*, October 14, 1998, p. D1, from American Library Association.

SIC 83 - Social Services

★ 1960 ★

Child Care (SIC 8351)

Largest Child Care Organizations

The largest organizations in North America are ranked by capacity.

KinderCare Learning Centers	144,000
La Petite Academy	98,477
Chilren's Learning Centers	65,545
Childtime Learning Centers	34,818
Bright Horizons Family Solutions	33,963
Children's Discovery Centers	27,183
Nobel Education Dynamics	27,000
New Horizons Child Care	11,363
Childcare Network	10,327
The Sunshine House	8,710

Source: *Child Care Information Exchange*, January 1999, p. 43.

★ 1961 ★

Charities (SIC 8399)

Charitable Donations - 1998

Category	Share
Religion	42.4%
Education	13.7
Gifts to foundations	9.4
Health	9.4
Human services	9.0
Public/society benefit organizations	6.1
Arts	5.9
Environment/wildlife	2.9
International affairs	1.2

Source: *The Economist*, May 29, 1999, p. 29, from American Association of Fund-Raising Counsel Trust for Philanthropy.

★ 1962 ★

Charities (SIC 8399)

Charitable Donations in the United States

Figures are based on a survey.

Category	Share
Church/synagogue	63.0%
United Way	40.0
School/college/university	38.0
Medical research	34.0
Environmental group	25.0
Arts group	14.0
Political group	12.0

Source: *USA TODAY*, April 9, 1999, p. A1, from Yankelovich Partners for Lutheran Brotherhood.

★ 1963 ★

Charities (SIC 8399)

Corporate Contributions - 1996

Category	Share
Education	30.0%
Health/human services	25.0
Civic/community	10.0
Cultural arts	9.0
Other	20.0

Source: *Industry Week*, September 7, 1998, p. 22, from Conference Board.

★ 1964 ★

Charities (SIC 8399)

Largest Charities in Minnesota

Companies are ranked by revenues in millions of dollars.

Billy Graham Evangelistic Association	$ 108.0
Ebenezer Social Ministries	88.0
United Way of Minneapolis Area	59.9
Amherst H. Wilder Foundation	59.5
Citizens Scholarship Foundation of America Inc.	47.1

Source: *Corporate Report*, November 1998, p. 58.

★ 1965 ★

Charities (SIC 8399)

Largest Foundations - 1998

Data show assets in billions of dollars.

Lilly Endowment	$ 15.38
Ford Foundation	10.70
David and Lucile Packard Foundation	9.60
Robert Wood Johnson Foundation	7.76
W.H. Kellogg Foundation	6.00
William H. Gates Foundation	5.20
Pew Charitable Trusts	4.73
John D. and Catherine T. MacArthur Foundation	4.10
Robert W. Woodruff Foundation	3.67
Andrew W. Mellon Foundation	3.30

Source: *The Chronicle of Philanthropy*, February 25, 1999, p. 9.

★ 1966 ★

Charities (SIC 8399)

Largest Foundations in Michigan

Foundations are ranked by assets in millions of dollars.

The Kresge Foundation	$ 2,200
Charles Stewart Mott Foundation	1,900
The Skillman Foundation	525
Herrick Foundation	248
Community Foundation for SE Michigan	191

Source: *Detroiter*, June 1999, p. 8, from Council of Michigan Foundations.

★ 1967 ★

Charities (SIC 8399)

Largest U.S. Charities - 1997

Organizations are ranked by total income in millions of dollars.

The National Council of YMCAs	$ 2,859.9
Salvation Army	2,500.0
Catholic Charities USA	2,218.9
American Red Cross	1,933.8
Shriners Hospitals for Children	1,393.7
Goodwill Industries International	1,360.0
Boy Scouts of America	648.6
YMCA of the USA	636.2
Girl Scouts of the USA	605.3
American Cancer Society Inc.	540.5

Source: *Christian Science Monitor*, December 14, 1998, p. 14, from *NonProfit Times*.

★ 1968 ★

Charities (SIC 8399)

Leading Philanthropists

Data show donations in millions of dollars.

George Soros	$ 2,000
Walter Annenberg	1,200
William/Flora Hewlett	835
Charles Feeney	700
Laurence S. Rockefeller	386
James/Virginia Stowers	331
Leslie/Abigail Wexner	303
Arnold Beckman	300
Jon/Karen Huntsman	275
Joan Kroc	250

Source: *Christian Science Monitor*, April 1, 1999, p. 20, from *Price's List of Lists*.

★ 1969 ★

Charities (SIC 8399)

Who Gives to Charity

Individuals	76.2%
Foundations	9.3
Bequests	8.8
Corporations	5.7

Source: *Investor's Business Daily*, October 13, 1998, p. A2, from *Christianity Today*.

SIC 84 - Museums, Botanical, Zoological Gardens

★ 1970 ★

Museums (SIC 8412)

Leading Museum Shows

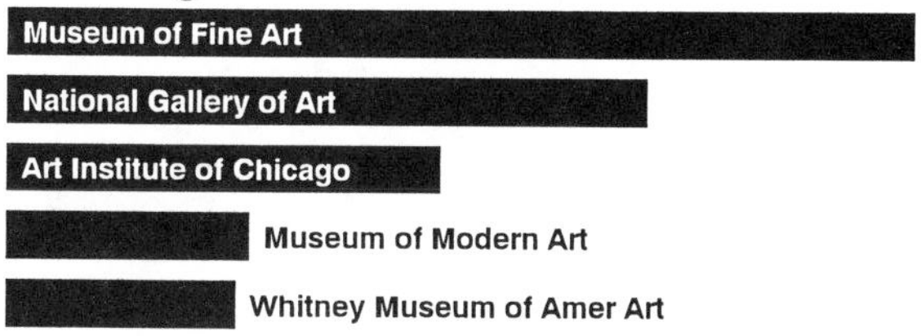

Museum of Fine Art

National Gallery of Art

Art Institute of Chicago

Museum of Modern Art

Whitney Museum of Amer Art

Data show attendance to date.

Museum of Fine Art (Monet)	490,000
National Gallery of Art (Van Gogh)	344,655
Art Institute of Chicago (Cassatt)	233,095
Museum of Modern Art (Pollock)	130,000
Whitney Museum of Amer Art (Rothko)	123,400

Source: *Newsweek*, December 21, 1998, p. 72.

SIC 86 - Membership Organizations

★ 1971 ★

Membership Organizations (SIC 8600)

Largest Membership Organizations

Organizations are ranked by millions of members.

American Automobile Association	35.29
American Association of Retired Persons	32.00
YMCA of the USA	14.80
National Congress of Parents and Teachers	6.50
National Right to Life Committee	6.00
Boy Scouts of America	5.83
National Comm. to Preserve Social Security and Medicare	5.50
Humane Society of the U.S.	5.30
American Farm Bureau Federation	4.70
Amateur Softball Association of America	4.50

Source: *Association Management*, May 1998, p. 32.

★ 1972 ★

Membership Organizations (SIC 8699)

Largest Frequent Flyer Programs

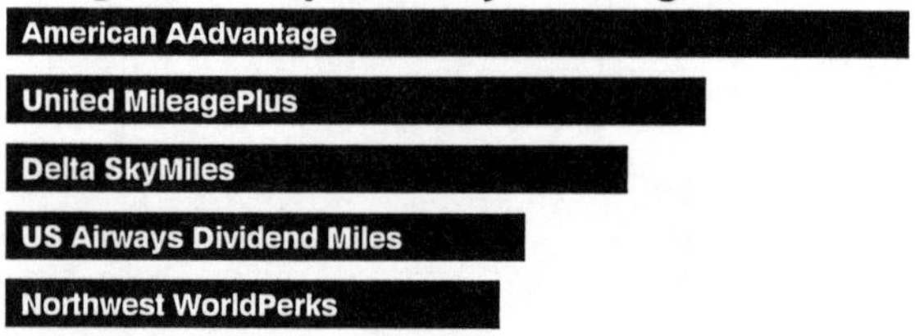

American AAdvantage
United MileagePlus
Delta SkyMiles
US Airways Dividend Miles
Northwest WorldPerks

Data show millions of members.

American AAdvantage	35.0
United MileagePlus	27.0
Delta SkyMiles	24.0
US Airways Dividend Miles	20.0
Northwest WorldPerks	18.5

Source: *USA TODAY*, June 1, 1999, p. 3B, from *Inside Flyer*.

SIC 87 - Engineering and Management Services

★ 1973 ★

Engineering Services (SIC 8711)

Largest Architect/Engineer Firms

Companies are ranked by revenues in millions of dollars.

Hellmuth, Obata + Kassabaum Inc.	$ 186.00
Ellerbe Becket	68.20
Leo A. Daly	63.70
SmithGroup	59.16
DLR Group	56.90

Source: *Building Design & Construction*, July 1998, p. 20.

★ 1974 ★

Engineering Services (SIC 8711)

Leading Engineering Firms

Companies are ranked by revenues in millions of dollars.

Fluor Daniel Inc.	$ 448.20
Jacobs Engineering Group Inc.	338.36
BE&K	264.00
Dames & Moore	229.20
Raytheon Engineers & Constructors	153.84

Source: *Building Design & Construction*, July 1998, p. 48.

★ 1975 ★

Architectural Services (SIC 8712)

Largest Architectural Firms in Cleveland, OH

Companies are ranked by number of locally registered architects.

GSI Architects	35
Van Dijk, Pace, Westlake Architects	31
Austin Co.	29
Dorsky Hodgson & Partners Inc.	26
KA Inc., Architecture	24

Source: *Crain's Cleveland Business*, May 17, 1999, p. 24.

★ 1976 ★

Architectural Services (SIC 8712)

Largest Architectural Firms in Dallas, TX - 1997

Companies are ranked by local billings in millions of dollars.

HKS Inc.	$ 79.9
Carter & Burgess Inc.	48.0
Corgan Associates Inc.	33.9
RTKL Associates Inc.	17.0
HDR Architecture Inc.	14.3

Source: *Dallas Business Journal*, December 4, 1998, p. B13.

★ 1977 ★
Architectural Services (SIC 8712)

Leading Architects

Companies are ranked by revenues in millions of dollars.

Gensler	$ 109.50
NBBJ	59.40
The Hillier Group	43.75
Thompson, Ventulett, Stainback & Associates	27.70
Zimmer Gunsul Frasca Partnership	26.00

Source: *Building Design & Construction*, July 1998, p. 12.

★ 1978 ★
Architectural Services (SIC 8712)

Retail Design Leaders - 1998

Firms are ranked by fees in millions of dollars.

Callison Architecture Inc.	$ 31.0
Pavlik Design Team	26.7
Retail Planning Associates Inc.	22.1
Frch Design Worldwide	16.0
MCG Architecture	14.0
Gensler	13.8
Design Forum	9.6
P.E.G. Park Architects P.C.	7.5
The Tricarico Group	7.3
Bergmeyer Associates Inc.	7.2

Source: *VM+SD*, February 1999, p. 50.

★ 1979 ★
Accounting Services (SIC 8721)

Largest Accounting Firms

Companies are ranked by fee income in millions of dollars.

Arthur Andersen	$ 6,828.0
Pricewaterhouse Coopers	5,853.0
Ernst & Young	5,545.0
Deloitte & Touche	4,700.0
KPMG	3,800.0
Grant Thornton	336.0
McGladrey & Pullen	$ 296.1
BDO Seidman	250.0
Crowe Chizek	118.2
Plante & Moran	104.7

Source: *Accountancy International*, February 1999, p. 8.

★ 1980 ★
Accounting Services (SIC 8721)

Largest Accounting Firms in Canada - 1998

Companies are ranked by revenues in millions of dollars.

KPMG	$ 607
Deloitte & Touche	570
Ernst & Young	449
Coopers & Lybrand	368
Price Waterhouse	352
Doane Raymond Grant Thornton	207
Arthur Andersen	146
BDO Dunwoody	136
Richter Usher & Wineberg	75
Meyers Norris Penny	40

Source: *Globe and Mail*, April 30, 1998, p. B13, from *The Bottom Line*.

★ 1981 ★
Accounting Services (SIC 8721)

Largest Accounting Firms in New England - 1998

Firms are ranked by revenues in millions of dollars.

Berry, Dunn, McNeil & Parker	$ 18.1
Tofias, Fleishman, Shapiro & Co.	16.8
Blum Shapiro & Co.	14.1
Baker, Newman & Noyes	12.3
Carlin, Charron & Rosen	11.2

Source: *Practical Accountant*, April 1999, p. S5.

★ 1982 ★

Accounting Services (SIC 8721)

Largest Accounting Firms in the Midwest States - 1998

Firms are ranked by revenues in millions of dollars.

Baird Kurtz & Dobson	$ 98.0
Larosn Allen Weishair & Co.	59.1
Eide Bailly	33.5
Rubin, Brown, Gornstein & Co.	18.7
Kennedy & Coe	18.2

Source: *Practical Accountant*, April 1999, p. S11.

★ 1983 ★

Accounting Services (SIC 8721)

Largest Accounting Firms in the Mountain States - 1998

Firms are ranked by revenues in millions of dollars.

Hein & Associates	$ 12.5
Galusha, Higgins and Galusha	11.0
Ehrhardt Keefer Steiner & Hottman	10.5
Anderson ZurMuehlen & Co.	7.9
Gelfond Hochstadt Pangburn & Co.	6.5

Source: *Practical Accountant*, April 1999, p. S12.

★ 1984 ★

Accounting Services (SIC 8721)

Largest Accounting Firms in the North Central States - 1998

Firms are ranked by revenues in millions of dollars.

Crowe, Chizek and Co.	$ 118.2
Plante & Moran	104.7
Clifton Gunderson	82.1
Olive LLP	58.0
Wipfli Ullrich Bertelson LLP	34.9

Source: *Practical Accountant*, April 1999, p. S10.

★ 1985 ★

Accounting Services (SIC 8721)

Largest Accounting Firms in the Northeast States - 1998

Firms are ranked by revenues in millions of dollars.

Constantin Associates	$ 85.1
Eisner	69.0
Resnick Fedder & Silverman	46.9
David Berdon & Co.	41.1
M.R. Weiser & Co.	33.0

Source: *Practical Accountant*, April 1999, p. S6.

★ 1986 ★

Accounting Services (SIC 8721)

Largest Accounting Firms in the Southeast States - 1998

Firms are ranked by revenues in millions of dollars.

Cherry, Bekaert & Holland	$ 31.0
Dixon Odom PLLC	23.8
Elliott, Davis & Co.	18.5
Crisp Hughes Evans	17.4
Kaufman Rossin & Co.	16.3

Source: *Practical Accountant*, April 1999, p. S7.

★ 1987 ★

Commercial Research (SIC 8732)

Largest Commercial Research Firms - 1998

Firms are ranked by research revenues in millions of dollars.

IMS Health	$ 412.3
Nielsen Media Research	401.9
Information Resources Inc.	397.0
A.C. Nielsen Corp.	390.4
VNU Marketing Information Services	343.0
Gartner Group	311.7
Westat	206.0
Arbitron Co.	194.5
NFO Worldwide	180.0
Maritz Marketing Research	126.8

Source: *Advertising Age*, May 24, 1999, p. S2.

★ 1988 ★

Commercial Research (SIC 8732)

Largest Research Firms

Firms are ranked by research revenues in millions of dollars.

A.C. Nielsen Corp.	$ 1,425.4
IMS Health Inc.	1,084.0
Information Resources Inc.	511.3
Nielsen Media Research	401.9
NFO Worldwide Inc.	275.4
Westat Inc.	205.4
The Arbitron Co.	194.5
Maritz Marketing Research Inc.	169.1
The Kantar Group Ltd.	150.6
The NPD Group Inc.	138.5

Source: *Marketing Magazine*, June 7, 1999, p. H4, from CASRO.

★ 1989 ★

Commercial Research (SIC 8732)

R&D Spending by State

Spending is shown in millions of dollars.

Texas	$ 319
California	274
Florida	256
New York	239
Pennsylvania	196

Source: *R&D Magazine*, January 1999, p. 20, from Battelle and State Science & Technology.

★ 1990 ★

Commercial Research (SIC 8732)

Research Spending by State

Investments are shown in millions of dollars. Total investments reached $177 billion.

	($ mil.)	Share
California	$ 36,133	20.41%
Michigan	13,276	7.50
New York	10,954	6.19
Masssachusetts	9,969	5.63
New Jersey	9,128	5.16
Other	97,540	55.11

Source: *R&D Magazine*, July 1998, p. 7, from National Patterns of R&D Resources, National Science Foundation.

★ 1991 ★

Commercial Research (SIC 8732)

Who Funds Research

Industry	66.5%
Federal gov't	28.9
Universities/nonprofit	4.6

Source: *USA TODAY*, April 1999, p. 11, from Batelle.

★ 1992 ★

Commercial Research (SIC 8732)

Who Performs R&D - 1999

Spending is shown in billions of dollars.

	($ bil.)	Share
Industry	$ 179.2	75.93%
University, nonprofit	39.5	16.74
Government	17.3	7.33

Source: *R&D Magazine*, January 1999, p. 15, from National Science Foundation.

★ 1993 ★

Construction Management (SIC 8741)

Largest Construction Management Firms

Companies are ranked by revenues in millions of dollars.

Bovis Inc.	$ 2,020.90
Gilbane Building Co.	1,790.42
Sverdrup Corp.	1,183.32
Heery International Inc.	1,120.00
3D/International	1,059.00

Source: *Building Design & Construction*, July 1998, p. 30.

★ 1994 ★

Construction Management (SIC 8741)

Largest Construction Management-At- Risk Firms

Firms are ranked by revenues in millions of dollars.

The Turner Corp.	$ 2,847.9
Fluor Daniel Inc.	2,073.0
Structure Tone Inc.	1,269.0
Brown & Root Inc.	1,213.0
Bovis Inc.	1,126.1

Continued on next page.

★ 1994 ★ *Continued*

Construction Management (SIC 8741)

Largest Construction Management-At- Risk Firms

Firms are ranked by revenues in millions of dollars.

Skanska (USA) Inc.	$ 1,118.0
Gilbane Building Co.	947.7
DPR Construction Inc.	894.1
Morse Diesel Intl. Inc.	815.0
Parsons Corp.	767.0

Source: *ENR*, June 15, 1998, p. 62.

★ 1995 ★

Construction Management (SIC 8741)

Largest Construction Management-For- Fee Firms

Firms are ranked by revenues in millions of dollars.

Foster Wheeler Corp.	$ 647.2
Fluor Daniel Inc.	345.0
CH2M Hill Cos.	310.2
Raytheon Engineers & Constructors Intl.	258.0
Bechtel Group Inc.	236.0
The Kvaerner Group	215.0
The M.W. Kellogg Co.	204.9
Parsons Corp.	191.0
Morrison Knudsen Corp.	181.0
ICF Kaiser International Inc.	153.7

Source: *ENR*, June 15, 1998, p. 62.

★ 1996 ★

Construction Management (SIC 8741)

Largest Design-Build Firms

Firms are ranked by revenues in millions of dollars.

Bechtel Group Inc.	$ 9,380.0
Fluor Daniel Inc.	7,358.0
McDermott International Inc.	1,620.7
Foster Wheeler Corp.	1,520.7
Raytheon Engineers & Constructors Intl.	1,379.0
The M.W. Kellogg Co.	1,308.5
Black & Veatch	1,157.0
ABB Lummus Global Inc.	1,131.1
Stone & Webster	689.0
Chicago Bridge & Iron Co.	633.0

Source: *ENR*, June 15, 1998, p. 62.

★ 1997 ★

Management Consulting (SIC 8742)

Largest Executive Search Firms - 1997

Firms are ranked by revenues in millions of dollars.

Korn/Ferry International	$ 157.2
Heidrick & Struggles	154.0
SpencerStuart	131.1
Russell Reynolds Associates	94.1
LAI	58.0

Source: *Best's Review*, December 1998, p. 37, from Kennedy Information.

★ 1998 ★

Management Consulting (SIC 8748)

Largest Executive Recruiters in New York

Data show number of recruiters.

Korn/Ferry International	95
Solomon Page Group	59
Johnson Smith & Knisely	41
A-L Associates Inc.	40
Russell Reynolds Associates	38

Source: *Crain's New York Business*, August 24, 1998, p. 12.

★ 1999 ★

Management Consulting (SIC 8748)

Largest Retail Consultants

Data are in millions of dollars.

Ernst & Young	$ 241
Deloitte Consulting	230
Andersen Consulting	229
PriceWaterhouseCoopers	188
KPMG Peat Marwick	161

Source: *Consultants News*, February 1999, p. 4, from Kennedy Information Research group estimates.

SIC 92 - Justice, Public Order, and Safety

★ 2000 ★

Crime (SIC 9220)

Piracy in Mexico

Data show the millions of dollars in losses that U.S. industries sustain from piracy in Mexico.

Software	$ 265
Cassettes and CDs	70
Videotapes	55
University textbooks	35

Source: *Wall Street Journal*, December 2, 1998, p. B1, from International Intellectual Property Alliance.

★ 2001 ★

Crime (SIC 9220)

Products Shoplifted

Cigarettes
HBC items
Analgesics
Liquor
Meat
Baby formula
Other

Retail theft reached $16 billion a year. HBC stands for health & beauty care.

Cigarettes	33.0%
HBC items	27.0
Analgesics	8.0
Liquor	8.0
Meat	8.0
Baby formula	7.0
Other	9.0

Source: *Supermarket Business*, May 1999, p. 83, from Food Marketing Institute.

★ 2002 ★

Prisons (SIC 9223)

Adult Private Corrections Market - 1997

Market shares are shown based on design capacity under contract.

Corrections Corporation of America	48.7%
Wackenhut Corrections Corporation	25.9
U.S. Corrections Corporation	4.9
Management and Training Corporation	4.0
Cornell Corrections	3.6
CiviGenics Inc.	3.3
The Bobby Ross Group	2.6
Correctional Services Corporation	2.5
Group 4 Prison Services ltd.	2.3
Other	2.2

Source: *Investext,* Thomson Financial Networks, October 20, 1998, p. 12, from Center for Studies in Criminology and Law, University of Florida.

★ 2003 ★

Prisons (SIC 9223)

Prisoners by State - 1997

California	157,547
Texas	140,729
New York	70,026
Georgia	36,450
Louisiana	29,265
New Jersey	28,361
Arizona	23,484

Source: *New York Times*, August 9, 1998, p. 14, from Bureau of Justice Statistics.

SIC 95 - Environmental Quality and Housing

★ 2004 ★

Environmental Services (SIC 9511)

Consulting/Remediation Market - 1997

The $11.7 billion market is shown in percent.

Remediation construction	40.0%
Remediation consulting	28.0
Water quality	20.0
Air	4.0
Multimedia	4.0
Solid waste	4.0

Source: *Civil Engineering*, September 1998, p. 19, from Farkas Berkowitz & Company.

★ 2005 ★

Environmental Services (SIC 9511)

Top Environmental Firms - 1997

Data show environmental revenues in millions of dollars.

U.S. Filter Corp.	$ 2,910.0
Bechtel Group Inc.	2,191.2
Philip Environ.Services Group	1,750.0
Foster Wheeler Corp.	1,131.0
CH2M Cos. Ltd.	927.1
ICF Kaiser International	885.0
International Technology Corp.	874.0
Fluor Daniel Inc.	793.0
Black & Veatch	706.0
Montgomery Watson Inc.	482.0

Source: *ENR*, July 6, 1998, p. 51.

★ 2006 ★

Social Spending (SIC 9512)

Bicycle Path/Pedestrian Facility Funding

Data show federal funding for bicycle and pedestrian paths. Figures are in millions of dollars for 1991-97.

Houston	$ 24.4
New York City	17.8
Dallas	4.1
Chicago	3.9
Philadelphia	3.8

Source: *Detroit Free Press*, May 14, 1999, p. 3B, from John F. Kennedy School of Government at Harvard University.

SOURCE INDEX

This index is divided into *primary sources* and *original sources*. Primary sources are the publications where the market shares were found. Original sources are sources cited in the primary sources. Numbers following the sources are entry numbers, arranged sequentially; the first number refers to the first appearance of the source in *Market Share Reporter*. All told, 979 organizations are listed.

Primary Sources

Original Sources

PLACE NAMES INDEX

This index shows countries, political entities, states and provinces, regions within countries, parks, airports, and cities. The numbers that follow listings are entry numbers; they are arranged sequentially so that the first mention of a place is listed first. The index shows references to more than 290 places.

PRODUCTS, SERVICES, NAMES, AND ISSUES INDEX

This index shows, in alphabetical order, references to products, services, personal names, and issues covered in *Market Share Reporter*, 10th Edition. More than 1,980 terms are included. Terms include subjects not readily categorized as products and services, including such subjects as *crime* and *welfare*. The numbers that follow each term refer to entry numbers and are arranged sequentially so that the first mention is listed first.

COMPANY INDEX

The more than 3,850 companies and institutions in this book are indexed here in alphabetical order. Numbers following the terms are entry numbers. They are arranged sequentially; the first entry number refers to the first mention of the company in *Market Share Reporter*. Although most organizations appear only once, some entities are referred to under abbreviations in the sources and these have not always been expanded.

BRANDS INDEX

This index shows more than 1,250 brands—including names of periodicals, television programs, popular movies, and other "brand-equivalent" names. Each brand name is followed by one or more numerals; these are entry numbers; they are arranged sequentially, with the first mention of the brand shown first.

Brands Index

APPENDIX I

SIC COVERAGE

This appendix lists the Standard Industrial Classification codes (SICs) included in *Market Share Reporter*. Page numbers are shown following each SIC category; the page shown indicates the first occurrence of an SIC. *NEC* stands for not elsewhere classified.

Food and Kindred Products

Tobacco Products

Textile Mill Products

Apparel and Other Textile Products

Lumber and Wood Products

Furniture and Fixtures

Paper and Allied Products

Transportation Equipment

Instruments and Related Products

Miscellaneous Manufacturing Industries

Railroad Transportation

Local and Interurban Passenger Transit

Trucking and Warehousing

Postal Service

Water Transportation

Transportation by Air

Pipelines, Except Natural Gas

Transportation Services

Communications

Electric, Gas, and Sanitary Services

Wholesale Trade - Durable Goods

SIC TO NAICS CONVERSION GUIDE

AGRICULTURE, FORESTRY, & FISHING

0111 Wheat
NAICS 11114 Wheat Farming
0112 Rice
NAICS 11116 Rice Farming
0115 Corn
NAICS 11115 Corn Farming
0116 Soybeans
NAICS 11111 Soybean Farming
0119 Cash Grains, nec
NAICS 11113 Dry Pea & Bean Farming
NAICS 11112 Oilseed Farming
NAICS 11115 Corn Farming
NAICS 111191 Oilseed & Grain Combination Farming
NAICS 111199 All Other Grain Farming
0131 Cotton
NAICS 11192 Cotton Farming
0132 Tobacco
NAICS 11191 Tobacco Farming
0133 Sugarcane & Sugar Beets
NAICS 111991 Sugar Beet Farming
NAICS 11193 Sugarcane Farming
0134 Irish Potatoes
NAICS 111211 Potato Farming
0139 Field Crops, Except Cash Grains, nec
NAICS 11194 Hay Farming
NAICS 111992 Peanut Farming
NAICS 111219 Other Vegetable & Melon Farming
NAICS 111998 All Other Miscellaneous Crop Farming
0161 Vegetables & Melons
NAICS 111219 Other Vegetable & Melon Farming
0171 Berry Crops
NAICS 111333 Strawberry Farming
NAICS 111334 Berry Farming
0172 Grapes
NAICS 111332 Grape Vineyards
0173 Tree Nuts
NAICS 111335 Tree Nut Farming
0174 Citrus Fruits
NAICS 11131 Orange Groves
NAICS 11132 Citrus Groves
0175 Deciduous Tree Fruits
NAICS 111331 Apple Orchards
NAICS 111339 Other Noncitrus Fruit Farming
0179 Fruits & Tree Nuts, nec
NAICS 111336 Fruit & Tree Nut Combination Farming
NAICS 111339 Other Noncitrus Fruit Farming
0181 Ornamental Floriculture & Nursery Products
NAICS 111422 Floriculture Production
NAICS 111421 Nursery & Tree Production
0182 Food Crops Grown under Cover
NAICS 111411 Mushroom Production
NAICS 111419 Other Food Crops Grown under Cover
0191 General Farms, Primarily Crop
NAICS 111998 All Other Miscellaneous Crop Farming
0211 Beef Cattle Feedlots
NAICS 112112 Cattle Feedlots
0212 Beef Cattle, Except Feedlots
NAICS 112111 Beef Cattle Ranching & Farming
0213 Hogs
NAICS 11221 Hog & Pig Farming
0214 Sheep & Goats
NAICS 11241 Sheep Farming
NAICS 11242 Goat Farming
0219 General Livestock, Except Dairy & Poultry
NAICS 11299 All Other Animal Production
0241 Dairy Farms
NAICS 112111 Beef Cattle Ranching & Farming
NAICS 11212 Dairy Cattle & Milk Production
0251 Broiler, Fryers, & Roaster Chickens
NAICS 11232 Broilers & Other Meat-type Chicken Production
0252 Chicken Eggs
NAICS 11231 Chicken Egg Production
0253 Turkey & Turkey Eggs
NAICS 11233 Turkey Production
0254 Poultry Hatcheries
NAICS 11234 Poultry Hatcheries
0259 Poultry & Eggs, nec
NAICS 11239 Other Poultry Production
0271 Fur-bearing Animals & Rabbits
NAICS 11293 Fur-bearing Animal & Rabbit Production
0272 Horses & Other Equines
NAICS 11292 Horse & Other Equine Production
0273 Animal Aquaculture
NAICS 112511 Finfish Farming & Fish Hatcheries
NAICS 112512 Shellfish Farming
NAICS 112519 Other Animal Aquaculture
0279 Animal Specialities, nec
NAICS 11291 Apiculture
NAICS 11299 All Other Animal Production
0291 General Farms, Primarily Livestock & Animal Specialties
NAICS 11299 All Other Animal Production
0711 Soil Preparation Services
NAICS 115112 Soil Preparation, Planting & Cultivating
0721 Crop Planting, Cultivating & Protecting
NAICS 48122 Nonscheduled Speciality Air Transportation
NAICS 115112 Soil Preparation, Planting & Cultivating
0722 Crop Harvesting, Primarily by Machine
NAICS 115113 Crop Harvesting, Primarily by Machine
0723 Crop Preparation Services for Market, Except Cotton Ginning
NAICS 115114 Postharvest Crop Activities
0724 Cotton Ginning
NAICS 115111 Cotton Ginning
0741 Veterinary Service for Livestock
NAICS 54194 Veterinary Services
0742 Veterinary Services for Animal Specialties
NAICS 54194 Veterinary Services
0751 Livestock Services, Except Veterinary
NAICS 311611 Animal Slaughtering
NAICS 11521 Support Activities for Animal Production
0752 Animal Specialty Services, Except Veterinary
NAICS 11521 Support Activities for Animal Production
NAICS 81291 Pet Care Services
0761 Farm Labor Contractors & Crew Leaders
NAICS 115115 Farm Labor Contractors & Crew Leaders
0762 Farm Management Services
NAICS 115116 Farm Management Services
0781 Landscape Counseling & Planning
NAICS 54169 Other Scientific & Technical Consulting Services
NAICS 54132 Landscape Architectural Services

0782 Lawn & Garden Services
NAICS 56173 Landscaping Services
0783 Ornamental Shrub & Tree Services
NAICS 56173 Landscaping Services
0811 Timber Tracts
NAICS 111421 Nursery & Tree Production
NAICS 11311 Timber Tract Operations
0831 Forest Nurseries & Gathering of Forest Products
NAICS 111998 All Other Miscellaneous Crop
NAICS 11321 Forest Nurseries & Gathering of Forest Products
0851 Forestry Services
NAICS 11531 Support Activities for Forestry
0912 Finfish
NAICS 114111 Finfish Fishing
0913 Shellfish
NAICS 114112 Shellfish Fishing
0919 Miscellaneous Marine Products
NAICS 114119 Other Marine Fishing
NAICS 111998 All Other Miscellaneous Crop Farming
0921 Fish Hatcheries & Preserves
NAICS 112511 Finfish Farming & Fish Hatcheries
NAICS 112512 Shellfish Farming
0971 Hunting, Trapping, & Game Propagation
NAICS 11421 Hunting & Trapping

MINING INDUSTRIES

1011 Iron Ores
NAICS 21221 Iron Ore Mining
1021 Copper Ores
NAICS 212234 Copper Ore & Nickel Ore Mining
1031 Lead & Zinc Ores
NAICS 212231 Lead Ore & Zinc Ore Mining
1041 Gold Ores
NAICS 212221 Gold Ore Mining
1044 Silver Ores
NAICS 212222 Silver Ore Mining
1061 Ferroalloy Ores, Except Vanadium
NAICS 212234 Copper Ore & Nickel Ore Mining
NAICS 212299 Other Metal Ore Mining
1081 Metal Mining Services
NAICS 213115 Support Activities for Metal Mining
NAICS 54136 Geophysical Surveying & Mapping Services
1094 Uranium-radium-vanadium Ores
NAICS 212291 Uranium-radium-vanadium Ore Mining
1099 Miscellaneous Metal Ores, nec
NAICS 212299 Other Metal Ore Mining
1221 Bituminous Coal & Lignite Surface Mining
NAICS 212111 Bituminous Coal & Lignite Surface Mining
1222 Bituminous Coal Underground Mining
NAICS 212112 Bituminous Coal Underground Mining
1231 Anthracite Mining
NAICS 212113 Anthracite Mining
1241 Coal Mining Services
NAICS 213114 Support Activities for Coal Mining
1311 Crude Petroleum & Natural Gas
NAICS 211111 Crude Petroleum & Natural Gas Extraction
1321 Natural Gas Liquids
NAICS 211112 Natural Gas Liquid Extraction
1381 Drilling Oil & Gas Wells
NAICS 213111 Drilling Oil & Gas Wells
1382 Oil & Gas Field Exploration Services
NAICS 48122 Nonscheduled Speciality Air Transportation
NAICS 54136 Geophysical Surveying & Mapping Services
NAICS 213112 Support Activities for Oil & Gas Field Operations
1389 Oil & Gas Field Services, nec
NAICS 213113 Other Oil & Gas Field Support Activities
1411 Dimension Stone
NAICS 212311 Dimension Stone Mining & Quarry
1422 Crushed & Broken Limestone
NAICS 212312 Crushed & Broken Limestone Mining & Quarrying
1423 Crushed & Broken Granite
NAICS 212313 Crushed & Broken Granite Mining & Quarrying
1429 Crushed & Broken Stone, nec
NAICS 212319 Other Crushed & Broken Stone Mining & Quarrying
1442 Construction Sand & Gravel
NAICS 212321 Construction Sand & Gravel Mining
1446 Industrial Sand
NAICS 212322 Industrial Sand Mining
1455 Kaolin & Ball Clay
NAICS 212324 Kaolin & Ball Clay Mining
1459 Clay, Ceramic, & Refractory Minerals, nec
NAICS 212325 Clay & Ceramic & Refractory Minerals Mining
1474 Potash, Soda, & Borate Minerals
NAICS 212391 Potash, Soda, & Borate Mineral Mining
1475 Phosphate Rock
NAICS 212392 Phosphate Rock Mining
1479 Chemical & Fertilizer Mineral Mining, nec
NAICS 212393 Other Chemical & Fertilizer Mineral Mining
1481 Nonmetallic Minerals Services Except Fuels
NAICS 213116 Support Activities for Non-metallic Minerals
NAICS 54136 Geophysical Surveying & Mapping Services
1499 Miscellaneous Nonmetallic Minerals, Except Fuels
NAICS 212319 Other Crushed & Broken Stone Mining or Quarrying
NAICS 212399 All Other Non-metallic Mineral Mining

CONSTRUCTION INDUSTRIES

1521 General Contractors-single-family Houses
NAICS 23321 Single Family Housing Construction
1522 General Contractors-residential Buildings, Other than Single-family
NAICS 23332 Commercial & Institutional Building Construction
NAICS 23322 Multifamily Housing Construction
1531 Operative Builders
NAICS 23321 Single Family Housing Construction
NAICS 23322 Multifamily Housing Construction
NAICS 23331 Manufacturing & Industrial Building Construction
NAICS 23332 Commercial & Institutional Building Construction
1541 General Contractors-industrial Buildings & Warehouses
NAICS 23332 Commercial & Institutional Building Construction
NAICS 23331 Manufacturing & Industrial Building Construction

1542 General Contractors-nonresidential Buildings, Other than Industrial Buildings & Warehouses
NAICS 23332 Commercial & Institutional Building Construction
1611 Highway & Street Construction, Except Elevated Highways
NAICS 23411 Highway & Street Construction
1622 Bridge, Tunnel, & Elevated Highway Construction
NAICS 23412 Bridge & Tunnel Construction
1623 Water, Sewer, Pipeline, & Communications & Power Line Construction
NAICS 23491 Water, Sewer & Pipeline Construction
NAICS 23492 Power & Communication Transmission Line Construction
1629 Heavy Construction, nec
NAICS 23493 Industrial Nonbuilding Structure Construction
NAICS 23499 All Other Heavy Construction
1711 Plumbing, Heating, & Air-conditioning
NAICS 23511 Plumbing, Heating & Air-conditioning Contractors
1721 Painting & Paper Hanging
NAICS 23521 Painting & Wall Covering Contractors
1731 Electrical Work
NAICS 561621 Security Systems Services
NAICS 23531 Electrical Contractors
1741 Masonry, Stone Setting & Other Stone Work
NAICS 23541 Masonry & Stone Contractors
1742 Plastering, Drywall, Acoustical & Insulation Work
NAICS 23542 Drywall, Plastering, Acoustical & Insulation Contractors
1743 Terrazzo, Tile, Marble, & Mosaic Work
NAICS 23542 Drywall, Plastering, Acoustical & Insulation Contractors
NAICS 23543 Tile, Marble, Terrazzo & Mosaic Contractors
1751 Carpentry Work
NAICS 23551 Carpentry Contractors
1752 Floor Laying & Other Floor Work, nec
NAICS 23552 Floor Laying & Other Floor Contractors
1761 Roofing, Siding, & Sheet Metal Work
NAICS 23561 Roofing, Siding, & Sheet Metal Contractors
1771 Concrete Work
NAICS 23542 Drywall, Plastering, Acoustical & Insulation Contractors
NAICS 23571 Concrete Contractors
1781 Water Well Drilling
NAICS 23581 Water Well Drilling Contractors
1791 Structural Steel Erection
NAICS 23591 Structural Steel Erection Contractors
1793 Glass & Glazing Work
NAICS 23592 Glass & Glazing Contractors
1794 Excavation Work
NAICS 23593 Excavation Contractors
1795 Wrecking & Demolition Work
NAICS 23594 Wrecking & Demolition Contractors
1796 Installation or Erection of Building Equipment, nec
NAICS 23595 Building Equipment & Other Machinery Installation Contractors
1799 Special Trade Contractors, nec
NAICS 23521 Painting & Wall Covering Contractors
NAICS 23592 Glass & Glazing Contractors
NAICS 56291 Remediation Services
NAICS 23599 All Other Special Trade Contractors

FOOD & KINDRED PRODUCTS

2011 Meat Packing Plants
NAICS 311611 Animal Slaughtering
2013 Sausages & Other Prepared Meats
NAICS 311612 Meat Processed from Carcasses
2015 Poultry Slaughtering & Processing
NAICS 311615 Poultry Processing
NAICS 311999 All Other Miscellaneous Food Manufacturing
2021 Creamery Butter
NAICS 311512 Creamery Butter Manufacturing
2022 Natural, Processed, & Imitation Cheese
NAICS 311513 Cheese Manufacturing
2023 Dry, Condensed, & Evaporated Dairy Products
NAICS 311514 Dry, Condensed, & Evaporated Milk Manufacturing
2024 Ice Cream & Frozen Desserts
NAICS 31152 Ice Cream & Frozen Dessert Manufacturing
2026 Fluid Milk
NAICS 311511 Fluid Milk Manufacturing
2032 Canned Specialties
NAICS 311422 Specialty Canning
NAICS 311999 All Other Miscellaneous Food Manufacturing
2033 Canned Fruits, Vegetables, Preserves, Jams, & Jellies
NAICS 311421 Fruit & Vegetable Canning
2034 Dried & Dehydrated Fruits, Vegetables, & Soup Mixes
NAICS 311423 Dried & Dehydrated Food Manufacturing
NAICS 311211 Flour Milling
2035 Pickled Fruits & Vegetables, Vegetables Sauces & Seasonings, & Salad Dressings
NAICS 311421 Fruit & Vegetable Canning
NAICS 311941 Mayonnaise, Dressing, & Other Prepared Sauce Manufacturing
2037 Frozen Fruits, Fruit Juices, & Vegetables
NAICS 311411 Frozen Fruit, Juice, & Vegetable Processing
2038 Frozen Specialties, nec
NAICS 311412 Frozen Specialty Food Manufacturing
2041 Flour & Other Grain Mill Products
NAICS 311211 Flour Milling
2043 Cereal Breakfast Foods
NAICS 31192 Coffee & Tea Manufacturing
NAICS 31123 Breakfast Cereal Manufacturing
2044 Rice Milling
NAICS 311212 Rice Milling
2045 Prepared Flour Mixes & Doughs
NAICS 311822 Flour Mixes & Dough Manufacturing from Purchased Flour
2046 Wet Corn Milling
NAICS 311221 Wet Corn Milling
2047 Dog & Cat Food
NAICS 311111 Dog & Cat Food Manufacturing
2048 Prepared Feed & Feed Ingredients for Animals & Fowls, Except Dogs & Cats
NAICS 311611 Animal Slaughtering
NAICS 311119 Other Animal Food Manufacturing
2051 Bread & Other Bakery Products, Except Cookies & Crackers
NAICS 311812 Commercial Bakeries
2052 Cookies & Crackers
NAICS 311821 Cookie & Cracker Manufacturing
NAICS 311919 Other Snack Food Manufacturing
NAICS 311812 Commercial Bakeries

2053 Frozen Bakery Products, Except Bread
NAICS 311813 Frozen Bakery Product Manufacturing
2061 Cane Sugar, Except Refining
NAICS 311311 Sugarcane Mills
2062 Cane Sugar Refining
NAICS 311312 Cane Sugar Refining
2063 Beet Sugar
NAICS 311313 Beet Sugar Manufacturing
2064 Candy & Other Confectionery Products
NAICS 31133 Confectionery Manufacturing from Purchased Chocolate
NAICS 31134 Non-chocolate Confectionery Manufacturing
2066 Chocolate & Cocoa Products
NAICS 31132 Chocolate & Confectionery Manufacturing from Cacao Beans
2067 Chewing Gum
NAICS 31134 Non-chocolate Confectionery Manufacturing
2068 Salted & Roasted Nuts & Seeds
NAICS 311911 Roasted Nuts & Peanut Butter Manufacturing
2074 Cottonseed Oil Mills
NAICS 311223 Other Oilseed Processing
NAICS 311225 Fats & Oils Refining & Blending
2075 Soybean Oil Mills
NAICS 311222 Soybean Processing
NAICS 311225 Fats & Oils Refining & Blending
2076 Vegetable Oil Mills, Except Corn, Cottonseed, & Soybeans
NAICS 311223 Other Oilseed Processing
NAICS 311225 Fats & Oils Refining & Blending
2077 Animal & Marine Fats & Oils
NAICS 311613 Rendering & Meat By-product Processing
NAICS 311711 Seafood Canning
NAICS 311712 Fresh & Frozen Seafood Processing
NAICS 311225 Edible Fats & Oils Manufacturing
2079 Shortening, Table Oils, Margarine, & Other Edible Fats & Oils, nec
NAICS 311225 Edible Fats & Oils Manufacturing
NAICS 311222 Soybean Processing
NAICS 311223 Other Oilseed Processing
2082 Malt Beverages
NAICS 31212 Breweries
2083 Malt
NAICS 311213 Malt Manufacturing
2084 Wines, Brandy, & Brandy Spirits
NAICS 31213 Wineries
2085 Distilled & Blended Liquors
NAICS 31214 Distilleries
2086 Bottled & Canned Soft Drinks & Carbonated Waters
NAICS 312111 Soft Drink Manufacturing
NAICS 312112 Bottled Water Manufacturing
2087 Flavoring Extracts & Flavoring Syrups nec
NAICS 31193 Flavoring Syrup & Concentrate Manufacturing
NAICS 311942 Spice & Extract Manufacturing
NAICS 311999 All Other Miscellaneous Food Manufacturing
2091 Canned & Cured Fish & Seafood
NAICS 311711 Seafood Canning
2092 Prepared Fresh or Frozen Fish & Seafoods
NAICS 311712 Fresh & Frozen Seafood Processing
2095 Roasted Coffee
NAICS 31192 Coffee & Tea Manufacturing
NAICS 311942 Spice & Extract Manufacturing
2096 Potato Chips, Corn Chips, & Similar Snacks
NAICS 311919 Other Snack Food Manufacturing
2097 Manufactured Ice
NAICS 312113 Ice Manufacturing
2098 Macaroni, Spaghetti, Vermicelli, & Noodles
NAICS 311823 Pasta Manufacturing
2099 Food Preparations, nec
NAICS 311423 Dried & Dehydrated Food Manufacturing
NAICS 111998 All Other Miscellaneous Crop Farming
NAICS 31134 Non-chocolate Confectionery Manufacturing
NAICS 311911 Roasted Nuts & Peanut Butter Manufacturing
NAICS 311991 Perishable Prepared Food Manufacturing
NAICS 31183 Tortilla Manufacturing
NAICS 31192 Coffee & Tea Manufacturing
NAICS 311941 Mayonnaise, Dressing, & Other Prepared Sauce Manufacturing
NAICS 311942 Spice & Extract Manufacturing
NAICS 311999 All Other Miscellaneous Food Manufacturing

TOBACCO PRODUCTS

2111 Cigarettes
NAICS 312221 Cigarette Manufacturing
2121 Cigars
NAICS 312229 Other Tobacco Product Manufacturing
2131 Chewing & Smoking Tobacco & Snuff
NAICS 312229 Other Tobacco Product Manufacturing
2141 Tobacco Stemming & Redrying
NAICS 312229 Other Tobacco Product Manufacturing
NAICS 31221 Tobacco Stemming & Redrying

TEXTILE MILL PRODUCTS

2211 Broadwoven Fabric Mills, Cotton
NAICS 31321 Broadwoven Fabric Mills
2221 Broadwoven Fabric Mills, Manmade Fiber & Silk
NAICS 31321 Broadwoven Fabric Mills
2231 Broadwoven Fabric Mills, Wool
NAICS 31321 Broadwoven Fabric Mills
NAICS 313311 Broadwoven Fabric Finishing Mills
NAICS 313312 Textile & Fabric Finishing Mills
2241 Narrow Fabric & Other Smallware Mills: Cotton, Wool, Silk, & Manmade Fiber
NAICS 313221 Narrow Fabric Mills
2251 Women's Full-length & Knee-length Hosiery, Except Socks
NAICS 315111 Sheer Hosiery Mills
2252 Hosiery, nec
NAICS 315111 Sheer Hosiery Mills
NAICS 315119 Other Hosiery & Sock Mills
2253 Knit Outerwear Mills
NAICS 315191 Outerwear Knitting Mills
2254 Knit Underwear & Nightwear Mills
NAICS 315192 Underwear & Nightwear Knitting Mills
2257 Weft Knit Fabric Mills
NAICS 313241 Weft Knit Fabric Mills
NAICS 313312 Textile & Fabric Finishing Mills
2258 Lace & Warp Knit Fabric Mills
NAICS 313249 Other Knit Fabric & Lace Mills
NAICS 313312 Textile & Fabric Finishing Mills
2259 Knitting Mills, nec
NAICS 315191 Outerwear Knitting Mills
NAICS 315192 Underwear & Nightwear Knitting Mills
NAICS 313241 Weft Knit Fabric Mills
NAICS 313249 Other Knit Fabric & Lace Mills

2261 Finishers of Broadwoven Fabrics of Cotton
NAICS 313311 Broadwoven Fabric Finishing Mills
2262 Finishers of Broadwoven Fabrics of Manmade Fiber & Silk
NAICS 313311 Broadwoven Fabric Finishing Mills
2269 Finishers of Textiles, nec
NAICS 313311 Broadwoven Fabric Finishing Mills
NAICS 313312 Textile & Fabric Finishing Mills
2273 Carpets & Rugs
NAICS 31411 Carpet & Rug Mills
2281 Yarn Spinning Mills
NAICS 313111 Yarn Spinning Mills
2282 Yarn Texturizing, Throwing, Twisting, & Winding Mills
NAICS 313112 Yarn Texturing, Throwing & Twisting Mills
NAICS 313312 Textile & Fabric Finishing Mills
2284 Thread Mills
NAICS 313113 Thread Mills
NAICS 313312 Textile & Fabric Finishing Mills
2295 Coated Fabrics, Not Rubberized
NAICS 31332 Fabric Coating Mills
2296 Tire Cord & Fabrics
NAICS 314992 Tire Cord & Tire Fabric Mills
2297 Nonwoven Fabrics
NAICS 31323 Nonwoven Fabric Mills
2298 Cordage & Twine
NAICS 314991 Rope, Cordage & Twine Mills
2299 Textile Goods, nec
NAICS 31321 Broadwoven Fabric Mills
NAICS 31323 Nonwoven Fabric Mills
NAICS 313312 Textile & Fabric Finishing Mills
NAICS 313221 Narrow Fabric Mills
NAICS 313113 Thread Mills
NAICS 313111 Yarn Spinning Mills
NAICS 314999 All Other Miscellaneous Textile Product Mills

APPAREL & OTHER FINISHED PRODUCTS MADE FROM FABRICS & SIMILAR MATERIALS

2311 Men's & Boys' Suits, Coats & Overcoats
NAICS 315211 Men's & Boys' Cut & Sew Apparel Contractors
NAICS 315222 Men's & Boys' Cut & Sew Suit, Coat, & Overcoat Manufacturing
2321 Men's & Boys' Shirts, Except Work Shirts
NAICS 315211 Men's & Boys' Cut & Sew Apparel Contractors
NAICS 315223 Men's & Boys' Cut & Sew Shirt, Manufacturing
2322 Men's & Boys' Underwear & Nightwear
NAICS 315211 Men's & Boys' Cut & Sew Apparel Contractors
NAICS 315221 Men's & Boys' Cut & Sew Underwear & Nightwear Manufacturing
2323 Men's & Boys' Neckwear
NAICS 315993 Men's & Boys' Neckwear Manufacturing
2325 Men's & Boys' Trousers & Slacks
NAICS 315211 Men's & Boys' Cut & Sew Apparel Contractors
NAICS 315224 Men's & Boys' Cut & Sew Trouser, Slack, & Jean Manufacturing
2326 Men's & Boys' Work Clothing
NAICS 315211 Men's & Boys' Cut & Sew Apparel Contractors
NAICS 315225 Men's & Boys' Cut & Sew Work Clothing Manufacturing
2329 Men's & Boys' Clothing, nec
NAICS 315211 Men's & Boys' Cut & Sew Apparel Contractors
NAICS 315228 Men's & Boys' Cut & Sew Other Outerwear Manufacturing
NAICS 315299 All Other Cut & Sew Apparel Manufacturing
2331 Women's, Misses', & Juniors' Blouses & Shirts
NAICS 315212 Women's & Girls' Cut & Sew Apparel Contractors
NAICS 315232 Women's & Girls' Cut & Sew Blouse & Shirt Manufacturing
2335 Women's, Misses' & Junior's Dresses
NAICS 315212 Women's & Girls' Cut & Sew Apparel Contractors
NAICS 315233 Women's & Girls' Cut & Sew Dress Manufacturing
2337 Women's, Misses' & Juniors' Suits, Skirts & Coats
NAICS 315212 Women's & Girls' Cut & Sew Apparel Contractors
NAICS 315234 Women's & Girls' Cut & Sew Suit, Coat, Tailored Jacket, & Skirt Manufacturing
2339 Women's, Misses' & Juniors' Outerwear, nec
NAICS 315999 Other Apparel Accessories & Other Apparel Manufacturing
NAICS 315212 Women's & Girls' Cut & Sew Apparel Contractors
NAICS 315299 All Other Cut & Sew Apparel Manufacturing
NAICS 315238 Women's & Girls' Cut & Sew Other Outerwear Manufacturing
2341 Women's, Misses, Children's, & Infants' Underwear & Nightwear
NAICS 315212 Women's & Girls' Cut & Sew Apparel Contractors
NAICS 315211 Men's & Boys' Cut & Sew Apparel Contractors
NAICS 315231 Women's & Girls' Cut & Sew Lingerie, Loungewear, & Nightwear Manufacturing
NAICS 315221 Men's & Boys' Cut & Sew Underwear & Nightwear Manufacturing
NAICS 315291 Infants' Cut & Sew Apparel Manufacturing
2342 Brassieres, Girdles, & Allied Garments
NAICS 315212 Women's & Girls' Cut & Sew Apparel Contractors
NAICS 315231 Women's & Girls' Cut & Sew Lingerie, Loungewear, & Nightwear Manufacturing
2353 Hats, Caps, & Millinery
NAICS 315991 Hat, Cap, & Millinery Manufacturing
2361 Girls', Children's & Infants' Dresses, Blouses & Shirts
NAICS 315291 Infants' Cut & Sew Apparel Manufacturing
NAICS 315223 Men's & Boys' Cut & Sew Shirt, Manufacturing
NAICS 315211 Men's & Boys' Cut & Sew Apparel Contractors
NAICS 315232 Women's & Girls' Cut & Sew Blouse & Shirt Manufacturing
NAICS 315233 Women's & Girls' Cut & Sew Dress Manufacturing
NAICS 315212 Women's & Girls' Cut & Sew Apparel Contractors
2369 Girls', Children's & Infants' Outerwear, nec
NAICS 315291 Infants' Cut & Sew Apparel Manufacturing
NAICS 315222 Men's & Boys' Cut & Sew Suit, Coat, & Overcoat Manufacturing
NAICS 315224 Men's & Boys' Cut & Sew Trouser, Slack, & Jean Manufacturing
NAICS 315228 Men's & Boys' Cut & Sew Other Outerwear Manufacturing
NAICS 315221 Men's & Boys' Cut & Sew Underwear & Nightwear Manufacturing
NAICS 315211 Men's & Boys' Cut & Sew Apparel Contractors

NAICS 315234 Women's & Girls' Cut & Sew Suit, Coat, Tailored Jacket, & Skirt Manufacturing
NAICS 315238 Women's & Girls' Cut & Sew Other Outerwear Manufacturing
NAICS 315231 Women's & Girls' Cut & Sew Lingerie, Loungewear, & Nightwear Manufacturing
NAICS 315212 Women's & Girls' Cut & Sew Apparel Contractors

2371 Fur Goods
NAICS 315292 Fur & Leather Apparel Manufacturing

2381 Dress & Work Gloves, Except Knit & All-leather
NAICS 315992 Glove & Mitten Manufacturing

2384 Robes & Dressing Gowns
NAICS 315231 Women's & Girls' Cut & Sew Lingerie, Loungewear, & Nightwear Manufacturing
NAICS 315221 Men's & Boys' Cut & Sew Underwear & Nightwear Manufacturing
NAICS 315211 Men's & Boys' Cut & Sew Apparel Contractors
NAICS 315212 Women's & Girls' Cut & Sew Apparel Contractors

2385 Waterproof Outerwear
NAICS 315222 Men's & Boys' Cut & Sew Suit, Coat, & Overcoat Manufacturing
NAICS 315234 Women's & Girls' Cut & Sew Suit, Coat, Tailored Jacket, & Skirt Manufacturing
NAICS 315228 Men's & Boys' Cut & Sew Other Outerwear Manufacturing
NAICS 315238 Women's & Girls' Cut & Sew Other Outerwear Manufacturing
NAICS 315291 Infants' Cut & Sew Apparel Manufacturing
NAICS 315999 Other Apparel Accessories & Other Apparel Manufacturing
NAICS 315211 Men's & Boys' Cut & Sew Apparel Contractors
NAICS 315212 Women's & Girls' Cut & Sew Apparel Contractors

2386 Leather & Sheep-lined Clothing
NAICS 315292 Fur & Leather Apparel Manufacturing

2387 Apparel Belts
NAICS 315999 Other Apparel Accessories & Other Apparel Manufacturing

2389 Apparel & Accessories, nec
NAICS 315999 Other Apparel Accessories & Other Apparel Manufacturing
NAICS 315299 All Other Cut & Sew Apparel Manufacturing
NAICS 315231 Women's & Girls' Cut & Sew Lingerie, Loungewear, & Nightwear Manufacturing
NAICS 315212 Women's & Girls' Cut & Sew Apparel Contractors
NAICS 315211 Mens' & Boys' Cut & Sew Apparel Contractors

2391 Curtains & Draperies
NAICS 314121 Curtain & Drapery Mills

2392 Housefurnishings, Except Curtains & Draperies
NAICS 314911 Textile Bag Mills
NAICS 339994 Broom, Brush & Mop Manufacturing
NAICS 314129 Other Household Textile Product Mills

2393 Textile Bags
NAICS 314911 Textile Bag Mills

2394 Canvas & Related Products
NAICS 314912 Canvas & Related Product Mills

2395 Pleating, Decorative & Novelty Stitching, & Tucking for the Trade
NAICS 314999 All Other Miscellaneous Textile Product Mills
NAICS 315211 Mens' & Boys' Cut & Sew Apparel Contractors
NAICS 315212 Women's & Girls' Cut & Sew Apparel Contractors

2396 Automotive Trimmings, Apparel Findings, & Related Products
NAICS 33636 Motor Vehicle Fabric Accessories & Seat Manufacturing
NAICS 315999 Other Apparel Accessories, & Other Apparel Manufacturing
NAICS 323113 Commercial Screen Printing
NAICS 314999 All Other Miscellaneous Textile Product Mills

2397 Schiffli Machine Embroideries
NAICS 313222 Schiffli Machine Embroidery

2399 Fabricated Textile Products, nec
NAICS 33636 Motor Vehicle Fabric Accessories & Seat Manufacturing
NAICS 315999 Other Apparel Accessories & Other Apparel Manufacturing
NAICS 314999 All Other Miscellaneous Textile Product Mills

LUMBER & WOOD PRODUCTS, EXCEPT FURNITURE

2411 Logging
NAICS 11331 Logging

2421 Sawmills & Planing Mills, General
NAICS 321913 Softwood Cut Stock, Resawing Lumber, & Planing
NAICS 321113 Sawmills
NAICS 321914 Other Millwork
NAICS 321999 All Other Miscellaneous Wood Product Manufacturing

2426 Hardwood Dimension & Flooring Mills
NAICS 321914 Other Millwork
NAICS 321999 All Other Miscellaneous Wood Product Manufacturing
NAICS 337139 Other Wood Furniture Manufacturing
NAICS 321912 Hardwood Dimension Mills

2429 Special Product Sawmills, nec
NAICS 321113 Sawmills
NAICS 321913 Softwood Cut Stock, Resawing Lumber, & Planing
NAICS 321999 All Other Miscellaneous Wood Product Manufacturing

2431 Millwork
NAICS 321911 Wood Window & Door Manufacturing
NAICS 321914 Other Millwork

2434 Wood Kitchen Cabinets
NAICS 337131 Wood Kitchen Cabinet & Counter Top Manufacturing

2435 Hardwood Veneer & Plywood
NAICS 321211 Hardwood Veneer & Plywood Manufacturing

2436 Softwood Veneer & Plywood
NAICS 321212 Softwood Veneer & Plywood Manufacturing

2439 Structural Wood Members, nec
NAICS 321913 Softwood Cut Stock, Resawing Lumber, & Planing
NAICS 321214 Truss Manufacturing
NAICS 321213 Engineered Wood Member Manufacturing

2441 Nailed & Lock Corner Wood Boxes & Shook
NAICS 32192 Wood Container & Pallet Manufacturing

2448 Wood Pallets & Skids
NAICS 32192 Wood Container & Pallet Manufacturing

2449 Wood Containers, nec
NAICS 32192 Wood Container & Pallet Manufacturing
2451 Mobile Homes
NAICS 321991 Manufactured Home Manufacturing
2452 Prefabricated Wood Buildings & Components
NAICS 321992 Prefabricated Wood Building Manufacturing
2491 Wood Preserving
NAICS 321114 Wood Preservation
2493 Reconstituted Wood Products
NAICS 321219 Reconstituted Wood Product Manufacturing
2499 Wood Products, nec
NAICS 339999 All Other Miscellaneous Manufacturing
NAICS 337139 Other Wood Furniture Manufacturing
NAICS 337148 Other Nonwood Furniture Manufacturing
NAICS 32192 Wood Container & Pallet Manufacturing
NAICS 321999 All Other Miscellaneous Wood Product Manufacturing

FURNITURE & FIXTURES

2511 Wood Household Furniture, Except Upholstered
NAICS 337122 Wood Household Furniture Manufacturing
2512 Wood Household Furniture, Upholstered
NAICS 337121 Upholstered Household Furniture Manufacturing
2514 Metal Household Furniture
NAICS 337124 Metal Household Furniture Manufacturing
2515 Mattresses, Foundations, & Convertible Beds
NAICS 33791 Mattress Manufacturing
NAICS 337132 Upholstered Wood Household Furniture Manufacturing
2517 Wood Television, Radio, Phonograph & Sewing Machine Cabinets
NAICS 337139 Other Wood Furniture Manufacturing
2519 Household Furniture, nec
NAICS 337143 Household Furniture (except Wood & Metal) Manufacturing
2521 Wood Office Furniture
NAICS 337134 Wood Office Furniture Manufacturing
2522 Office Furniture, Except Wood
NAICS 337141 Nonwood Office Furniture Manufacturing
2531 Public Building & Related Furniture
NAICS 33636 Motor Vehicle Fabric Accessories & Seat Manufacturing
NAICS 337139 Other Wood Furniture Manufacturing
NAICS 337148 Other Nonwood Furniture Manufacturing
NAICS 339942 Lead Pencil & Art Good Manufacturing
2541 Wood Office & Store Fixtures, Partitions, Shelving, & Lockers
NAICS 337131 Wood Kitchen Cabinet & Counter Top Manufacturing
NAICS 337135 Custom Architectural Woodwork, Millwork, & Fixtures
NAICS 337139 Other Wood Furniture Manufacturing
2542 Office & Store Fixtures, Partitions Shelving, & Lockers, Except Wood
NAICS 337145 Nonwood Showcase, Partition, Shelving, & Locker Manufacturing
2591 Drapery Hardware & Window Blinds & Shades
NAICS 33792 Blind & Shade Manufacturing
2599 Furniture & Fixtures, nec
NAICS 339113 Surgical Appliance & Supplies Manufacturing
NAICS 337139 Other Wood Furniture Manufacturing
NAICS 337148 Other Nonwood Furniture Manufacturing

PAPER & ALLIED PRODUCTS

2611 Pulp Mills
NAICS 32211 Pulp Mills
NAICS 322121 Paper Mills
NAICS 32213 Paperboard Mills
2621 Paper Mills
NAICS 322121 Paper Mills
NAICS 322122 Newsprint Mills
2631 Paperboard Mills
NAICS 32213 Paperboard Mills
2652 Setup Paperboard Boxes
NAICS 322213 Setup Paperboard Box Manufacturing
2653 Corrugated & Solid Fiber Boxes
NAICS 322211 Corrugated & Solid Fiber Box Manufacturing
2655 Fiber Cans, Tubes, Drums, & Similar Products
NAICS 322214 Fiber Can, Tube, Drum, & Similar Products Manufacturing
2656 Sanitary Food Containers, Except Folding
NAICS 322215 Non-folding Sanitary Food Container Manufacturing
2657 Folding Paperboard Boxes, Including Sanitary
NAICS 322212 Folding Paperboard Box Manufacturing
2671 Packaging Paper & Plastics Film, Coated & Laminated
NAICS 322221 Coated & Laminated Packaging Paper & Plastics Film Manufacturing
NAICS 326112 Unsupported Plastics Packaging Film & Sheet Manufacturing
2672 Coated & Laminated Paper, nec
NAICS 322222 Coated & Laminated Paper Manufacturing
2673 Plastics, Foil, & Coated Paper Bags
NAICS 322223 Plastics, Foil, & Coated Paper Bag Manufacturing
NAICS 326111 Unsupported Plastics Bag Manufacturing
2674 Uncoated Paper & Multiwall Bags
NAICS 322224 Uncoated Paper & Multiwall Bag Manufacturing
2675 Die-cut Paper & Paperboard & Cardboard
NAICS 322231 Die-cut Paper & Paperboard Office Supplies Manufacturing
NAICS 322292 Surface-coated Paperboard Manufacturing
NAICS 322298 All Other Converted Paper Product Manufacturing
2676 Sanitary Paper Products
NAICS 322291 Sanitary Paper Product Manufacturing
2677 Envelopes
NAICS 322232 Envelope Manufacturing
2678 Stationery, Tablets, & Related Products
NAICS 322233 Stationery, Tablet, & Related Product Manufacturing
2679 Converted Paper & Paperboard Products, nec
NAICS 322215 Non-folding Sanitary Food Container Manufacturing
NAICS 322222 Coated & Laminated Paper Manufacturing
NAICS 322231 Die-cut Paper & Paperboard Office Supplies Manufacturing
NAICS 322298 All Other Converted Paper Product Manufacturing

PRINTING, PUBLISHING, & ALLIED INDUSTRIES

2711 Newspapers: Publishing, or Publishing & Printing
NAICS 51111 Newspaper Publishers
2721 Periodicals: Publishing, or Publishing & Printing
NAICS 51112 Periodical Publishers
2731 Books: Publishing, or Publishing & Printing
NAICS 51223 Music Publishers
NAICS 51113 Book Publishers
2732 Book Printing
NAICS 323117 Book Printing
2741 Miscellaneous Publishing
NAICS 51114 Database & Directory Publishers
NAICS 51223 Music Publishers
NAICS 511199 All Other Publishers
2752 Commercial Printing, Lithographic
NAICS 323114 Quick Printing
NAICS 323110 Commercial Lithographic Printing
2754 Commercial Printing, Gravure
NAICS 323111 Commercial Gravure Printing
2759 Commercial Printing, nec
NAICS 323113 Commercial Screen Printing
NAICS 323112 Commercial Flexographic Printing
NAICS 323114 Quick Printing
NAICS 323115 Digital Printing
NAICS 323119 Other Commercial Printing
2761 Manifold Business Forms
NAICS 323116 Manifold Business Form Printing
2771 Greeting Cards
NAICS 323110 Commercial Lithographic Printing
NAICS 323111 Commercial Gravure Printing
NAICS 323112 Commercial Flexographic Printing
NAICS 323113 Commercial Screen Printing
NAICS 323119 Other Commercial Printing
NAICS 511191 Greeting Card Publishers
2782 Blankbooks, Loose-leaf Binders & Devices
NAICS 323110 Commercial Lithographic Printing
NAICS 323111 Commercial Gravure Printing
NAICS 323112 Commercial Flexographic Printing
NAICS 323113 Commercial Screen Printing
NAICS 323119 Other Commercial Printing
NAICS 323118 Blankbook, Loose-leaf Binder & Device Manufacturing
2789 Bookbinding & Related Work
NAICS 323121 Tradebinding & Related Work
2791 Typesetting
NAICS 323122 Prepress Services
2796 Platemaking & Related Services
NAICS 323122 Prepress Services

CHEMICALS & ALLIED PRODUCTS

2812 Alkalies & Chlorine
NAICS 325181 Alkalies & Chlorine Manufacturing
2813 Industrial Gases
NAICS 32512 Industrial Gas Manufacturing
2816 Inorganic Pigments
NAICS 325131 Inorganic Dye & Pigment Manufacturing
NAICS 325182 Carbon Black Manufacturing
2819 Industrial Inorganic Chemicals, nec
NAICS 325998 All Other Miscellaneous Chemical Product Manufacturing
NAICS 331311 Alumina Refining
NAICS 325131 Inorganic Dye & Pigment Manufacturing
NAICS 325188 All Other Basic Inorganic Chemical Manufacturing
2821 Plastics Material Synthetic Resins, & Nonvulcanizable Elastomers
NAICS 325211 Plastics Material & Resin Manufacturing
2822 Synthetic Rubber
NAICS 325212 Synthetic Rubber Manufacturing
2823 Cellulosic Manmade Fibers
NAICS 325221 Cellulosic Manmade Fiber Manufacturing
2824 Manmade Organic Fibers, Except Cellulosic
NAICS 325222 Noncellulosic Organic Fiber Manufacturing
2833 Medicinal Chemicals & Botanical Products
NAICS 325411 Medicinal & Botanical Manufacturing
2834 Pharmaceutical Preparations
NAICS 325412 Pharmaceutical Preparation Manufacturing
2835 In Vitro & in Vivo Diagnostic Substances
NAICS 325412 Pharmaceutical Preparation Manufacturing
NAICS 325413 In-vitro Diagnostic Substance Manufacturing
2836 Biological Products, Except Diagnostic Substances
NAICS 325414 Biological Product Manufacturing
2841 Soaps & Other Detergents, Except Speciality Cleaners
NAICS 325611 Soap & Other Detergent Manufacturing
2842 Speciality Cleaning, Polishing, & Sanitary Preparations
NAICS 325612 Polish & Other Sanitation Good Manufacturing
2843 Surface Active Agents, Finishing Agents, Sulfonated Oils, & Assistants
NAICS 325613 Surface Active Agent Manufacturing
2844 Perfumes, Cosmetics, & Other Toilet Preparations
NAICS 32562 Toilet Preparation Manufacturing
NAICS 325611 Soap & Other Detergent Manufacturing
2851 Paints, Varnishes, Lacquers, Enamels, & Allied Products
NAICS 32551 Paint & Coating Manufacturing
2861 Gum & Wood Chemicals
NAICS 325191 Gum & Wood Chemical Manufacturing
2865 Cyclic Organic Crudes & Intermediates, & Organic Dyes & Pigments
NAICS 32511 Petrochemical Manufacturing
NAICS 325132 Organic Dye & Pigment Manufacturing
NAICS 325192 Cyclic Crude & Intermediate Manufacturing
2869 Industrial Organic Chemicals, nec
NAICS 32511 Petrochemical Manufacturing
NAICS 325188 All Other Inorganic Chemical Manufacturing
NAICS 325193 Ethyl Alcohol Manufacturing
NAICS 32512 Industrial Gas Manufacturing
NAICS 325199 All Other Basic Organic Chemical Manufacturing
2873 Nitrogenous Fertilizers
NAICS 325311 Nitrogenous Fertilizer Manufacturing
2874 Phosphatic Fertilizers
NAICS 325312 Phosphatic Fertilizer Manufacturing
2875 Fertilizers, Mixing Only
NAICS 325314 Fertilizer Manufacturing
2879 Pesticides & Agricultural Chemicals, nec
NAICS 32532 Pesticide & Other Agricultural Chemical Manufacturing
2891 Adhesives & Sealants
NAICS 32552 Adhesive & Sealant Manufacturing
2892 Explosives
NAICS 32592 Explosives Manufacturing
2893 Printing Ink
NAICS 32591 Printing Ink Manufacturing

2895 Carbon Black
NAICS 325182 Carbon Black Manufacturing
2899 Chemicals & Chemical Preparations, nec
NAICS 32551 Paint & Coating Manufacturing
NAICS 311942 Spice & Extract Manufacturing
NAICS 325199 All Other Basic Organic Chemical Manufacturing
NAICS 325998 All Other Miscellaneous Chemical Product Manufacturing

PETROLEUM REFINING & RELATED INDUSTRIES

2911 Petroleum Refining
NAICS 32411 Petroleum Refineries
2951 Asphalt Paving Mixtures & Blocks
NAICS 324121 Asphalt Paving Mixture & Block Manufacturing
2952 Asphalt Felts & Coatings
NAICS 324122 Asphalt Shingle & Coating Materials Manufacturing
2992 Lubricating Oils & Greases
NAICS 324191 Petroleum Lubricating Oil & Grease Manufacturing 2999

RUBBER & MISCELLANEOUS PLASTICS PRODUCTS

3011 Tires & Inner Tubes
NAICS 326211 Tire Manufacturing
3021 Rubber & Plastics Footwear
NAICS 316211 Rubber & Plastics Footwear Manufacturing
3052 Rubber & Plastics Hose & Belting
NAICS 32622 Rubber & Plastics Hoses & Belting Manufacturing
3053 Gaskets, Packing, & Sealing Devices
NAICS 339991 Gasket, Packing, & Sealing Device Manufacturing
3061 Molded, Extruded, & Lathe-cut Mechanical Rubber Products
NAICS 326291 Rubber Product Manufacturing for Mechanical Use
3069 Fabricated Rubber Products, nec
NAICS 31332 Fabric Coating Mills
NAICS 326192 Resilient Floor Covering Manufacturing
NAICS 326299 All Other Rubber Product Manufacturing
3081 Unsupported Plastics Film & Sheet
NAICS 326113 Unsupported Plastics Film & Sheet Manufacturing
3082 Unsupported Plastics Profile Shapes
NAICS 326121 Unsupported Plastics Profile Shape Manufacturing
3083 Laminated Plastics Plate, Sheet, & Profile Shapes
NAICS 32613 Laminated Plastics Plate, Sheet, & Shape Manufacturing
3084 Plastic Pipe
NAICS 326122 Plastic Pipe & Pipe Fitting Manufacturing
3085 Plastics Bottles
NAICS 32616 Plastics Bottle Manufacturing
3086 Plastics Foam Products
NAICS 32615 Urethane & Other Foam Product Manufacturing
NAICS 32614 Polystyrene Foam Product Manufacturing
3087 Custom Compounding of Purchased Plastics Resins
NAICS 325991 Custom Compounding of Purchased Resin
3088 Plastics Plumbing Fixtures
NAICS 326191 Plastics Plumbing Fixtures Manufacturing
3089 Plastics Products, nec
NAICS 326122 Plastics Pipe & Pipe Fitting Manufacturing
NAICS 326121 Unsupported Plastics Profile Shape Manufacturing
NAICS 326199 All Other Plastics Product Manufacturing

LEATHER & LEATHER PRODUCTS

3111 Leather Tanning & Finishing
NAICS 31611 Leather & Hide Tanning & Finishing
3131 Boot & Shoe Cut Stock & Findings
NAICS 321999 All Other Miscellaneous Wood Product Manufacturing
NAICS 339993 Fastener, Button, Needle, & Pin Manufacturing
NAICS 316999 All Other Leather Good Manufacturing
3142 House Slippers
NAICS 316212 House Slipper Manufacturing
3143 Men's Footwear, Except Athletic
NAICS 316213 Men's Footwear Manufacturing
3144 Women's Footwear, Except Athletic
NAICS 316214 Women's Footwear Manufacturing
3149 Footwear, Except Rubber, nec
NAICS 316219 Other Footwear Manufacturing
3151 Leather Gloves & Mittens
NAICS 315992 Glove & Mitten Manufacturing
3161 Luggage
NAICS 316991 Luggage Manufacturing
3171 Women's Handbags & Purses
NAICS 316992 Women's Handbag & Purse Manufacturing
3172 Personal Leather Goods, Except Women's Handbags & Purses
NAICS 316993 Personal Leather Good Manufacturing
3199 Leather Goods, nec
NAICS 316999 All Other Leather Good Manufacturing

STONE, CLAY, GLASS, & CONCRETE PRODUCTS

3211 Flat Glass
NAICS 327211 Flat Glass Manufacturing
3221 Glass Containers
NAICS 327213 Glass Container Manufacturing
3229 Pressed & Blown Glass & Glassware, nec
NAICS 327212 Other Pressed & Blown Glass & Glassware Manufacturing
3231 Glass Products, Made of Purchased Glass
NAICS 327215 Glass Product Manufacturing Made of Purchased Glass
3241 Cement, Hydraulic
NAICS 32731 Hydraulic Cement Manufacturing
3251 Brick & Structural Clay Tile
NAICS 327121 Brick & Structural Clay Tile Manufacturing
3253 Ceramic Wall & Floor Tile
NAICS 327122 Ceramic Wall & Floor Tile Manufacturing
3255 Clay Refractories
NAICS 327124 Clay Refractory Manufacturing

3259 Structural Clay Products, nec
NAICS 327123 Other Structural Clay Product Manufacturing
3261 Vitreous China Plumbing Fixtures & China & Earthenware Fittings & Bathroom Accessories
NAICS 327111 Vitreous China Plumbing Fixture & China & Earthenware Fittings & Bathroom Accessories Manufacturing
3262 Vitreous China Table & Kitchen Articles
NAICS 327112 Vitreous China, Fine Earthenware & Other Pottery Product Manufacturing
3263 Fine Earthenware Table & Kitchen Articles
NAICS 327112 Vitreous China, Fine Earthenware & Other Pottery Product Manufacturing
3264 Porcelain Electrical Supplies
NAICS 327113 Porcelain Electrical Supply Manufacturing
3269 Pottery Products, nec
NAICS 327112 Vitreous China, Fine Earthenware, & Other Pottery Product Manufacturing
3271 Concrete Block & Brick
NAICS 327331 Concrete Block & Brick Manufacturing
3272 Concrete Products, Except Block & Brick
NAICS 327999 All Other Miscellaneous Nonmetallic Mineral Product Manufacturing
NAICS 327332 Concrete Pipe Manufacturing
NAICS 32739 Other Concrete Product Manufacturing
3273 Ready-mixed Concrete
NAICS 32732 Ready-mix Concrete Manufacturing
3274 Lime
NAICS 32741 Lime Manufacturing
3275 Gypsum Products
NAICS 32742 Gypsum & Gypsum Product Manufacturing
3281 Cut Stone & Stone Products
NAICS 327991 Cut Stone & Stone Product Manufacturing
3291 Abrasive Products
NAICS 332999 All Other Miscellaneous Fabricated Metal Product Manufacturing
NAICS 32791 Abrasive Product Manufacturing
3292 Asbestos Products
NAICS 33634 Motor Vehicle Brake System Manufacturing
NAICS 327999 All Other Miscellaneous Nonmetallic Mineral Product Manufacturing
3295 Minerals & Earths, Ground or Otherwise Treated
NAICS 327992 Ground or Treated Mineral & Earth Manufacturing
3296 Mineral Wool
NAICS 327993 Mineral Wool Manufacturing
3297 Nonclay Refractories
NAICS 327125 Nonclay Refractory Manufacturing
3299 Nonmetallic Mineral Products, nec
NAICS 32742 Gypsum & Gypsum Product Manufacturing
NAICS 327999 All Other Miscellaneous Nonmetallic Mineral Product Manufacturing

PRIMARY METALS INDUSTRIES

3312 Steel Works, Blast Furnaces , & Rolling Mills
NAICS 324199 All Other Petroleum & Coal Products Manufacturing
NAICS 331111 Iron & Steel Mills
3313 Electrometallurgical Products, Except Steel
NAICS 331112 Electrometallurgical Ferroalloy Product Manufacturing
NAICS 331492 Secondary Smelting, Refining, & Alloying of Nonferrous Metals
3315 Steel Wiredrawing & Steel Nails & Spikes
NAICS 331222 Steel Wire Drawing
NAICS 332618 Other Fabricated Wire Product Manufacturing
3316 Cold-rolled Steel Sheet, Strip, & Bars
NAICS 331221 Cold-rolled Steel Shape Manufacturing
3317 Steel Pipe & Tubes
NAICS 33121 Iron & Steel Pipes & Tubes Manufacturing from Purchased Steel
3321 Gray & Ductile Iron Foundries
NAICS 331511 Iron Foundries
3322 Malleable Iron Foundries
NAICS 331511 Iron Foundries
3324 Steel Investment Foundries
NAICS 331512 Steel Investment Foundries
3325 Steel Foundries, nec
NAICS 331513 Steel Foundries
3331 Primary Smelting & Refining of Copper
NAICS 331411 Primary Smelting & Refining of Copper
3334 Primary Production of Aluminum
NAICS 331312 Primary Aluminum Production
3339 Primary Smelting & Refining of Nonferrous Metals, Except Copper & Aluminum
NAICS 331419 Primary Smelting & Refining of Nonferrous Metals
3341 Secondary Smelting & Refining of Nonferrous Metals
NAICS 331314 Secondary Smelting & Alloying of Aluminum
NAICS 331423 Secondary Smelting, Refining, & Alloying of Copper
NAICS 331492 Secondary Smelting, Refining, & Alloying of Nonferrous Metals
3351 Rolling, Drawing, & Extruding of Copper
NAICS 331421 Copper Rolling, Drawing, & Extruding
3353 Aluminum Sheet, Plate, & Foil
NAICS 331315 Aluminum Sheet, Plate, & Foil Manufacturing
3354 Aluminum Extruded Products
NAICS 331316 Aluminum Extruded Product Manufacturing
3355 Aluminum Rolling & Drawing, nec
NAICS 331319 Other Aluminum Rolling & Drawing,
3356 Rolling, Drawing, & Extruding of Nonferrous Metals, Except Copper & Aluminum
NAICS 331491 Nonferrous Metal Rolling. Drawing, & Extruding
3357 Drawing & Insulating of Nonferrous Wire
NAICS 331319 Other Aluminum Rolling & Drawing
NAICS 331422 Copper Wire Drawing
NAICS 331491 Nonferrous Metal Rolling, Drawing, & Extruding
NAICS 335921 Fiber Optic Cable Manufacturing
NAICS 335929 Other Communication & Energy Wire Manufacturing
3363 Aluminum Die-castings
NAICS 331521 Aluminum Die-castings
3364 Nonferrous Die-castings, Except Aluminum
NAICS 331522 Nonferrous Die-castings
3365 Aluminum Foundries
NAICS 331524 Aluminum Foundries
3366 Copper Foundries
NAICS 331525 Copper Foundries
3369 Nonferrous Foundries, Except Aluminum & Copper
NAICS 331528 Other Nonferrous Foundries

3398 Metal Heat Treating
NAICS 332811 Metal Heat Treating
3399 Primary Metal Products, nec
NAICS 331111 Iron & Steel Mills
NAICS 331314 Secondary Smelting & Alloying of Aluminum
NAICS 331423 Secondary Smelting, Refining & Alloying of Copper
NAICS 331492 Secondary Smelting, Refining, & Alloying of Nonferrous Metals
NAICS 332618 Other Fabricated Wire Product Manufacturing
NAICS 332813 Electroplating, Plating, Polishing, Anodizing, & Coloring

FABRICATED METAL PRODUCTS, EXCEPT MACHINERY & TRANSPORTATION EQUIPMENT

3411 Metal Cans
NAICS 332431 Metal Can Manufacturing
3412 Metal Shipping Barrels, Drums, Kegs & Pails
NAICS 332439 Other Metal Container Manufacturing
3421 Cutlery
NAICS 332211 Cutlery & Flatware Manufacturing
3423 Hand & Edge Tools, Except Machine Tools & Handsaws
NAICS 332212 Hand & Edge Tool Manufacturing
3425 Saw Blades & Handsaws
NAICS 332213 Saw Blade & Handsaw Manufacturing
3429 Hardware, nec
NAICS 332439 Other Metal Container Manufacturing
NAICS 332919 Other Metal Valve & Pipe Fitting Manufacturing
NAICS 33251 Hardware Manufacturing
3431 Enameled Iron & Metal Sanitary Ware
NAICS 332998 Enameled Iron & Metal Sanitary Ware Manufacturing
3432 Plumbing Fixture Fittings & Trim
NAICS 332913 Plumbing Fixture Fitting & Trim Manufacturing
NAICS 332999 All Other Miscellaneous Fabricated Metal Product Manufacturing
3433 Heating Equipment, Except Electric & Warm Air Furnaces
NAICS 333414 Heating Equipment Manufacturing
3441 Fabricated Structural Metal
NAICS 332312 Fabricated Structural Metal Manufacturing
3442 Metal Doors, Sash, Frames, Molding, & Trim Manufacturing
NAICS 332321 Metal Window & Door Manufacturing
3443 Fabricated Plate Work
NAICS 332313 Plate Work Manufacturing
NAICS 33241 Power Boiler & Heat Exchanger Manufacturing
NAICS 33242 Metal Tank Manufacturing
NAICS 333415 Air-conditioning & Warm Air Heating Equipment & Commercial & Industrial Refrigeration Equipment Manufacturing
3444 Sheet Metal Work
NAICS 332322 Sheet Metal Work Manufacturing
NAICS 332439 Other Metal Container Manufacturing
3446 Architectural & Ornamental Metal Work
NAICS 332323 Ornamental & Architectural Metal Work Manufacturing
3448 Prefabricated Metal Buildings & Components
NAICS 332311 Prefabricated Metal Building & Component Manufacturing
3449 Miscellaneous Structural Metal Work
NAICS 332114 Custom Roll Forming
NAICS 332312 Fabricated Structural Metal Manufacturing
NAICS 332321 Metal Window & Door Manufacturing
NAICS 332323 Ornamental & Architectural Metal Work Manufacturing
3451 Screw Machine Products
NAICS 332721 Precision Turned Product Manufacturing
3452 Bolts, Nuts, Screws, Rivets, & Washers
NAICS 332722 Bolt, Nut, Screw, Rivet, & Washer Manufacturing
3462 Iron & Steel Forgings
NAICS 332111 Iron & Steel Forging
3463 Nonferrous Forgings
NAICS 332112 Nonferrous Forging
3465 Automotive Stamping
NAICS 33637 Motor Vehicle Metal Stamping
3466 Crowns & Closures
NAICS 332115 Crown & Closure Manufacturing
3469 Metal Stamping, nec
NAICS 339911 Jewelry Manufacturing
NAICS 332116 Metal Stamping
NAICS 332214 Kitchen Utensil, Pot & Pan Manufacturing
3471 Electroplating, Plating, Polishing, Anodizing, & Coloring
NAICS 332813 Electroplating, Plating, Polishing, Anodizing, & Coloring
3479 Coating, Engraving, & Allied Services, nec
NAICS 339914 Costume Jewelry & Novelty Manufacturing
NAICS 339911 Jewelry Manufacturing
NAICS 339912 Silverware & Plated Ware Manufacturing
NAICS 332812 Metal Coating, Engraving , & Allied Services to Manufacturers
3482 Small Arms Ammunition
NAICS 332992 Small Arms Ammunition Manufacturing
3483 Ammunition, Except for Small Arms
NAICS 332993 Ammunition Manufacturing
3484 Small Arms
NAICS 332994 Small Arms Manufacturing
3489 Ordnance & Accessories, nec
NAICS 332995 Other Ordnance & Accessories Manufacturing 3491
3492 Fluid Power Valves & Hose Fittings
NAICS 332912 Fluid Power Valve & Hose Fitting Manufacturing
3493 Steel Springs, Except Wire
NAICS 332611 Steel Spring Manufacturing
3494 Valves & Pipe Fittings, nec
NAICS 332919 Other Metal Valve & Pipe Fitting Manufacturing
NAICS 332999 All Other Miscellaneous Fabricated Metal Product Manufacturing
3495 Wire Springs
NAICS 332612 Wire Spring Manufacturing
NAICS 334518 Watch, Clock, & Part Manufacturing
3496 Miscellaneous Fabricated Wire Products
NAICS 332618 Other Fabricated Wire Product Manufacturing
3497 Metal Foil & Leaf
NAICS 322225 Laminated Aluminum Foil Manufacturing for Flexible Packaging Uses
NAICS 332999 All Other Miscellaneous Fabricated Metal Product Manufacturing
3498 Fabricated Pipe & Pipe Fittings
NAICS 332996 Fabricated Pipe & Pipe Fitting Manufacturing

3499 Fabricated Metal Products, nec
NAICS 337148 Other Nonwood Furniture Manufacturing
NAICS 332117 Powder Metallurgy Part Manufacturing
NAICS 332439 Other Metal Container Manufacturing
NAICS 33251 Hardware Manufacturing
NAICS 332919 Other Metal Valve & Pipe Fitting Manufacturing
NAICS 339914 Costume Jewelry & Novelty Manufacturing
NAICS 332999 All Other Miscellaneous Fabricated Metal Product Manufacturing

INDUSTRIAL & COMMERCIAL MACHINERY & COMPUTER EQUIPMENT

3511 Steam, Gas, & Hydraulic Turbines, & Turbine Generator Set Units
NAICS 333611 Turbine & Turbine Generator Set Unit Manufacturing
3519 Internal Combustion Engines, nec
NAICS 336399 All Other Motor Vehicle Parts Manufacturing
NAICS 333618 Other Engine Equipment Manufacturing
3523 Farm Machinery & Equipment
NAICS 333111 Farm Machinery & Equipment Manufacturing
NAICS 332323 Ornamental & Architectural Metal Work Manufacturing
NAICS 332212 Hand & Edge Tool Manufacturing
NAICS 333922 Conveyor & Conveying Equipment Manufacturing
3524 Lawn & Garden Tractors & Home Lawn & Garden Equipment
NAICS 333112 Lawn & Garden Tractor & Home Lawn & Garden Equipment Manufacturing
NAICS 332212 Hand & Edge Tool Manufacturing
3531 Construction Machinery & Equipment
NAICS 33651 Railroad Rolling Stock Manufacturing
NAICS 333923 Overhead Traveling Crane, Hoist, & Monorail System Manufacturing
NAICS 33312 Construction Machinery Manufacturing
3532 Mining Machinery & Equipment, Except Oil & Gas Field Machinery & Equipment
NAICS 333131 Mining Machinery & Equipment Manufacturing
3533 Oil & Gas Field Machinery & Equipment
NAICS 333132 Oil & Gas Field Machinery & Equipment Manufacturing
3534 Elevators & Moving Stairways
NAICS 333921 Elevator & Moving Stairway Manufacturing
3535 Conveyors & Conveying Equipment
NAICS 333922 Conveyor & Conveying Equipment Manufacturing
3536 Overhead Traveling Cranes, Hoists & Monorail Systems
NAICS 333923 Overhead Traveling Crane, Hoist & Monorail System Manufacturing
3537 Industrial Trucks, Tractors, Trailers, & Stackers
NAICS 333924 Industrial Truck, Tractor, Trailer, & Stacker Machinery Manufacturing
NAICS 332999 All Other Miscellaneous Fabricated Metal Product Manufacturing
NAICS 332439 Other Metal Container Manufacturing
3541 Machine Tools, Metal Cutting Type
NAICS 333512 Machine Tool Manufacturing
3542 Machine Tools, Metal Forming Type
NAICS 333513 Machine Tool Manufacturing
3543 Industrial Patterns
NAICS 332997 Industrial Pattern Manufacturing
3544 Special Dies & Tools, Die Sets, Jigs & Fixtures, & Industrial Molds
NAICS 333514 Special Die & Tool, Die Set, Jig, & Fixture Manufacturing
NAICS 333511 Industrial Mold Manufacturing
3545 Cutting Tools, Machine Tool Accessories, & Machinists' Precision Measuring Devices
NAICS 333515 Cutting Tool & Machine Tool Accessory Manufacturing
NAICS 332212 Hand & Edge Tool Manufacturing
3546 Power-driven Handtools
NAICS 333991 Power-driven Hand Tool Manufacturing
3547 Rolling Mill Machinery & Equipment
NAICS 333516 Rolling Mill Machinery & Equipment Manufacturing
3548 Electric & Gas Welding & Soldering Equipment
NAICS 333992 Welding & Soldering Equipment Manufacturing
NAICS 335311 Power, Distribution, & Specialty Transformer Manufacturing
3549 Metalworking Machinery, nec
NAICS 333518 Other Metalworking Machinery Manufacturing
3552
3553 Woodworking Machinery
NAICS 33321 Sawmill & Woodworking Machinery Manufacturing
3554 Paper Industries Machinery
NAICS 333291 Paper Industry Machinery Manufacturing
3555 Printing Trades Machinery & Equipment
NAICS 333293 Printing Machinery & Equipment Manufacturing
3556 Food Products Machinery
NAICS 333294 Food Product Machinery Manufacturing
3559 Special Industry Machinery, nec
NAICS 33322 Rubber & Plastics Industry Machinery Manufacturing
NAICS 333319 Other Commercial & Service Industry Machinery Manufacturing
NAICS 333295 Semiconductor Manufacturing Machinery
NAICS 333298 All Other Industrial Machinery Manufacturing
3561 Pumps & Pumping Equipment
NAICS 333911 Pump & Pumping Equipment Manufacturing
3562 Ball & Roller Bearings
NAICS 332991 Ball & Roller Bearing Manufacturing
3563 Air & Gas Compressors
NAICS 333912 Air & Gas Compressor Manufacturing
3564 Industrial & Commercial Fans & Blowers & Air Purification Equipment
NAICS 333411 Air Purification Equipment Manufacturing
NAICS 333412 Industrial & Commercial Fan & Blower Manufacturing
3565 Packaging Machinery
NAICS 333993 Packaging Machinery Manufacturing
3566 Speed Changers, Industrial High-speed Drives, & Gears
NAICS 333612 Speed Changer, Industrial High-speed Drive, & Gear Manufacturing
3567 Industrial Process Furnaces & Ovens
NAICS 333994 Industrial Process Furnace & Oven Manufacturing
3568 Mechanical Power Transmission Equipment, nec
NAICS 333613 Mechanical Power Transmission Equipment Manufacturing

3569 General Industrial Machinery & Equipment, nec
NAICS 333999 All Other General Purpose Machinery Manufacturing
3571 Electronic Computers
NAICS 334111 Electronic Computer Manufacturing
3572 Computer Storage Devices
NAICS 334112 Computer Storage Device Manufacturing
3575 Computer Terminals
NAICS 334113 Computer Terminal Manufacturing
3577 Computer Peripheral Equipment, nec
NAICS 334119 Other Computer Peripheral Equipment Manufacturing
3578 Calculating & Accounting Machines, Except Electronic Computers
NAICS 334119 Other Computer Peripheral Equipment Manufacturing
NAICS 333313 Office Machinery Manufacturing
3579 Office Machines, nec
NAICS 339942 Lead Pencil & Art Good Manufacturing
NAICS 334518 Watch, Clock, & Part Manufacturing
NAICS 333313 Office Machinery Manufacturing
3581 Automatic Vending Machines
NAICS 333311 Automatic Vending Machine Manufacturing
3582 Commercial Laundry, Drycleaning, & Pressing Machines
NAICS 333312 Commercial Laundry, Drycleaning, & Pressing Machine Manufacturing
3585 Air-conditioning & Warm Air Heating Equipment & Commercial & Industrial Refrigeration Equipment
NAICS 336391 Motor Vehicle Air Conditioning Manufacturing
NAICS 333415 Air Conditioning & Warm Air Heating Equipment & Commercial & Industrial Refrigeration Equipment Manufacturing
3586 Measuring & Dispensing Pumps
NAICS 333913 Measuring & Dispensing Pump Manufacturing
3589 Service Industry Machinery, nec
NAICS 333319 Other Commercial and Service Industry Machinery Manufacturing
3592 Carburetors, Pistons, Piston Rings & Valves
NAICS 336311 Carburetor, Piston, Piston Ring & Valve Manufacturing
3593 Fluid Power Cylinders & Actuators
NAICS 333995 Fluid Power Cylinder & Actuator Manufacturing
3594 Fluid Power Pumps & Motors
NAICS 333996 Fluid Power Pump & Motor Manufacturing
3596 Scales & Balances, Except Laboratory
NAICS 333997 Scale & Balance Manufacturing
3599 Industrial & Commercial Machinery & Equipment, nec
NAICS 336399 All Other Motor Vehicle Part Manufacturing
NAICS 332999 All Other Miscellaneous Fabricated Metal Product Manufacturing
NAICS 333319 Other Commercial & Service Industry Machinery Manufacturing
NAICS 33271 Machine Shops
NAICS 333999 All Other General Purpose Machinery Manufacturing

ELECTRONIC & OTHER ELECTRICAL EQUIPMENT & COMPONENTS, EXCEPT COMPUTER EQUIPMENT

3612 Power, Distribution, & Specialty Transformers
NAICS 335311 Power, Distribution, & Specialty Transformer Manufacturing
3613 Switchgear & Switchboard Apparatus
NAICS 335313 Switchgear & Switchboard Apparatus Manufacturing
3621 Motors & Generators
NAICS 335312 Motor & Generator Manufacturing
3624 Carbon & Graphite Products
NAICS 335991 Carbon & Graphite Product Manufacturing
3625 Relays & Industrial Controls
NAICS 335314 Relay & Industrial Control Manufacturing
3629 Electrical Industrial Apparatus, nec
NAICS 335999 All Other Miscellaneous Electrical Equipment & Component Manufacturing
3631 Household Cooking Equipment
NAICS 335221 Household Cooking Appliance Manufacturing
3632 Household Refrigerators & Home & Farm Freezers
NAICS 335222 Household Refrigerator & Home Freezer Manufacturing
3633 Household Laundry Equipment
NAICS 335224 Household Laundry Equipment Manufacturing
3634 Electric Housewares & Fans
NAICS 335211 Electric Housewares & Fan Manufacturing
3635 Household Vacuum Cleaners
NAICS 335212 Household Vacuum Cleaner Manufacturing
3639 Household Appliances, nec
NAICS 335212 Household Vacuum Cleaner Manufacturing
NAICS 333298 All Other Industrial Machinery Manufacturing
NAICS 335228 Other Household Appliance Manufacturing
3641 Electric Lamp Bulbs & Tubes
NAICS 33511 Electric Lamp Bulb & Part Manufacturing
3643 Current-carrying Wiring Devices
NAICS 335931 Current-carrying Wiring Device Manufacturing
3644 Noncurrent-carrying Wiring Devices
NAICS 335932 Noncurrent-carrying Wiring Device Manufacturing
3645 Residential Electric Lighting Fixtures
NAICS 335121 Residential Electric Lighting Fixture Manufacturing
3646 Commercial, Industrial, & Institutional Electric Lighting Fixtures
NAICS 335122 Commercial, Industrial, & Institutional Electric Lighting Fixture Manufacturing
3647 Vehicular Lighting Equipment
NAICS 336321 Vehicular Lighting Equipment Manufacturing
3648 Lighting Equipment, nec
NAICS 335129 Other Lighting Equipment Manufacturing
3651 Household Audio & Video Equipment
NAICS 33431 Audio & Video Equipment Manufacturing 3652
NAICS 51222 Integrated Record Production/distribution
3661 Telephone & Telegraph Apparatus
NAICS 33421 Telephone Apparatus Manufacturing
NAICS 334416 Electronic Coil, Transformer, & Other Inductor Manufacturing
NAICS 334418 Printed Circuit/electronics Assembly Manufacturing

3663 Radio & Television Broadcasting & Communication Equipment
NAICS 33422 Radio & Television Broadcasting & Wireless Communications Equipment Manufacturing
3669 Communications Equipment, nec
NAICS 33429 Other Communication Equipment Manufacturing
3671 Electron Tubes
NAICS 334411 Electron Tube Manufacturing
3672 Printed Circuit Boards
NAICS 334412 Printed Circuit Board Manufacturing
3674 Semiconductors & Related Devices
NAICS 334413 Semiconductor & Related Device Manufacturing
3675 Electronic Capacitors
NAICS 334414 Electronic Capacitor Manufacturing
3676 Electronic Resistors
NAICS 334415 Electronic Resistor Manufacturing
3677 Electronic Coils, Transformers, & Other Inductors
NAICS 334416 Electronic Coil, Transformer, & Other Inductor Manufacturing
3678 Electronic ConNECtors
NAICS 334417 Electronic ConNECtor Manufacturing
3679 Electronic Components, nec
NAICS 33422 Radio & Television Broadcasting & Wireless Communications Equipment Manufacturing
NAICS 334418 Printed Circuit/electronics Assembly Manufacturing
NAICS 336322 Other Motor Vehicle Electrical & Electronic Equipment Manufacturing
NAICS 334419 Other Electronic Component Manufacturing
3691 Storage Batteries
NAICS 335911 Storage Battery Manufacturing
3692 Primary Batteries, Dry & Wet
NAICS 335912 Dry & Wet Primary Battery Manufacturing
3694 Electrical Equipment for Internal Combustion Engines
NAICS 336322 Other Motor Vehicle Electrical & Electronic Equipment Manufacturing
3695 Magnetic & Optical Recording Media
NAICS 334613 Magnetic & Optical Recording Media Manufacturing
3699 Electrical Machinery, Equipment, & Supplies, nec
NAICS 333319 Other Commercial & Service Industry Machinery Manufacturing
NAICS 333618 Other Engine Equipment Manufacturing
NAICS 334119 Other Computer Peripheral Equipment Manufacturing Classify According to Function
NAICS 335129 Other Lighting Equipment Manufacturing
NAICS 335999 All Other Miscellaneous Electrical Equipment & Component Manufacturing

TRANSPORTATION EQUIPMENT

3711 Motor Vehicles & Passenger Car Bodies
NAICS 336111 Automobile Manufacturing
NAICS 336112 Light Truck & Utility Vehicle Manufacturing
NAICS 33612 Heavy Duty Truck Manufacturing
NAICS 336211 Motor Vehicle Body Manufacturing
NAICS 336992 Military Armored Vehicle, Tank, & Tank Component Manufacturing
3713 Truck & Bus Bodies
NAICS 336211 Motor Vehicle Body Manufacturing
3714 Motor Vehicle Parts & Accessories
NAICS 336211 Motor Vehicle Body Manufacturing
NAICS 336312 Gasoline Engine & Engine Parts Manufacturing
NAICS 336322 Other Motor Vehicle Electrical & Electronic Equipment Manufacturing
NAICS 33633 Motor Vehicle Steering & Suspension Components Manufacturing
NAICS 33634 Motor Vehicle Brake System Manufacturing
NAICS 33635 Motor Vehicle Transmission & Power Train Parts Manufacturing
NAICS 336399 All Other Motor Vehicle Parts Manufacturing
3715 Truck Trailers
NAICS 336212 Truck Trailer Manufacturing
3716 Motor Homes
NAICS 336213 Motor Home Manufacturing
3721 Aircraft
NAICS 336411 Aircraft Manufacturing
3724 Aircraft Engines & Engine Parts
NAICS 336412 Aircraft Engine & Engine Parts Manufacturing 3728
NAICS 336413 Other Aircraft Part & Auxiliary Equipment Manufacturing
3731 Ship Building & Repairing
NAICS 336611 Ship Building & Repairing
3732 Boat Building & Repairing
NAICS 81149 Other Personal & Household Goods Repair & Maintenance
NAICS 336612 Boat Building
3743 Railroad Equipment
NAICS 333911 Pump & Pumping Equipment Manufacturing
NAICS 33651 Railroad Rolling Stock Manufacturing
3751 Motorcycles, Bicycles, & Parts
NAICS 336991 Motorcycle, Bicycle, & Parts Manufacturing
3761 Guided Missiles & Space Vehicles
NAICS 336414 Guided Missile & Space Vehicle Manufacturing 3764
3769 Guided Missile Space Vehicle Parts & Auxiliary Equipment, nec
NAICS 336419 Other Guided Missile & Space Vehicle Parts & Auxiliary Equipment Manufacturing
3792 Travel Trailers & Campers
NAICS 336214 Travel Trailer & Camper Manufacturing
3795 Tanks & Tank Components
NAICS 336992 Military Armored Vehicle, Tank, & Tank Component Manufacturing
3799 Transportation Equipment, nec
NAICS 336214 Travel Trailer & Camper Manufacturing
NAICS 332212 Hand & Edge Tool Manufacturing
NAICS 336999 All Other Transportation Equipment Manufacturing

MEASURING, ANALYZING, & CONTROLLING INSTRUMENTS

3812 Search, Detection, Navigation, Guidance, Aeronautical, & Nautical Systems & Instruments
NAICS 334511 Search, Detection, Navigation, Guidance, Aeronautical, & Nautical System & Instrument Manufacturing
3821 Laboratory Apparatus & Furniture
NAICS 339111 Laboratory Apparatus & Furniture Manufacturing

3822 Automatic Controls for Regulating Residential & Commercial Environments & Appliances
NAICS 334512 Automatic Environmental Control Manufacturing for Regulating Residential, Commercial, & Appliance Use
3823 Industrial Instruments for Measurement, Display, & Control of Process Variables & Related Products
NAICS 334513 Instruments & Related Product Manufacturing for Measuring Displaying, & Controlling Industrial Process Variables
3824 Totalizing Fluid Meters & Counting Devices
NAICS 334514 Totalizing Fluid Meter & Counting Device Manufacturing
3825 Instruments for Measuring & Testing of Electricity & Electrical Signals
NAICS 334416 Electronic Coil, Transformer, & Other Inductor Manufacturing
NAICS 334515 Instrument Manufacturing for Measuring & Testing Electricity & Electrical Signals
3826 Laboratory Analytical Instruments
NAICS 334516 Analytical Laboratory Instrument Manufacturing
3827 Optical Instruments & Lenses
NAICS 333314 Optical Instrument & Lens Manufacturing
3829 Measuring & Controlling Devices, nec
NAICS 339112 Surgical & Medical Instrument Manufacturing
NAICS 334519 Other Measuring & Controlling Device Manufacturing
3841 Surgical & Medical Instruments & Apparatus
NAICS 339112 Surgical & Medical Instrument Manufacturing
3842 Orthopedic, Prosthetic, & Surgical Appliances & Supplies
NAICS 339113 Surgical Appliance & Supplies Manufacturing
NAICS 334510 Electromedical & Electrotherapeutic Apparatus Manufacturing
3843 Dental Equipment & Supplies
NAICS 339114 Dental Equipment & Supplies Manufacturing
3844 X-ray Apparatus & Tubes & Related Irradiation Apparatus
NAICS 334517 Irradiation Apparatus Manufacturing
3845 Electromedical & Electrotherapeutic Apparatus
NAICS 334517 Irradiation Apparatus Manufacturing
NAICS 334510 Electromedical & Electrotherapeutic Apparatus Manufacturing
3851 Ophthalmic Goods
NAICS 339115 Ophthalmic Goods Manufacturing
3861 Photographic Equipment & Supplies
NAICS 333315 Photographic & Photocopying Equipment Manufacturing
NAICS 325992 Photographic Film, Paper, Plate & Chemical Manufacturing
3873 Watches, Clocks, Clockwork Operated Devices & Parts
NAICS 334518 Watch, Clock, & Part Manufacturing

MISCELLANEOUS MANUFACTURING INDUSTRIES

3911 Jewelry, Precious Metal
NAICS 339911 Jewelry Manufacturing
3914 Silverware, Plated Ware, & Stainless Steel Ware
NAICS 332211 Cutlery & Flatware Manufacturing
NAICS 339912 Silverware & Plated Ware Manufacturing
3915 Jewelers' Findings & Materials, & Lapidary Work
NAICS 339913 Jewelers' Material & Lapidary Work Manufacturing
3931 Musical Instruments
NAICS 339992 Musical Instrument Manufacturing
3942 Dolls & Stuffed Toys
NAICS 339931 Doll & Stuffed Toy Manufacturing
3944 Games, Toys, & Children's Vehicles, Except Dolls & Bicycles
NAICS 336991 Motorcycle, Bicycle & Parts Manufacturing
NAICS 339932 Game, Toy, & Children's Vehicle Manufacturing
3949 Sporting & Athletic Goods, nec
NAICS 33992 Sporting & Athletic Good Manufacturing
3951 Pens, Mechanical Pencils & Parts
NAICS 339941 Pen & Mechanical Pencil Manufacturing
3952 Lead Pencils, Crayons, & Artist's Materials
NAICS 337139 Other Wood Furniture Manufacturing
NAICS 337139 Other Wood Furniture Manufacturing
NAICS 325998 All Other Miscellaneous Chemical Manufacturing
NAICS 339942 Lead Pencil & Art Good Manufacturing
3953 Marking Devices
NAICS 339943 Marking Device Manufacturing
3955 Carbon Paper & Inked Ribbons
NAICS 339944 Carbon Paper & Inked Ribbon Manufacturing
3961 Costume Jewelry & Costume Novelties, Except Precious Metals
NAICS 339914 Costume Jewelry & Novelty Manufacturing
3965 Fasteners, Buttons, Needles, & Pins
NAICS 339993 Fastener, Button, Needle & Pin Manufacturing
3991 Brooms & Brushes
NAICS 339994 Broom, Brush & Mop Manufacturing
3993 Signs & Advertising Specialties
NAICS 33995 Sign Manufacturing
3995 Burial Caskets
NAICS 339995 Burial Casket Manufacturing
3996 Linoleum, Asphalted-felt-base, & Other Hard Surface Floor Coverings, nec
NAICS 326192 Resilient Floor Covering Manufacturing
3999 Manufacturing Industries, nec
NAICS 337148 Other Nonwood Furniture Manufacturing
NAICS 321999 All Other Miscellaneous Wood Product Manufacturing
NAICS 31611 Leather & Hide Tanning & Finishing
NAICS 335121 Residential Electric Lighting Fixture Manufacturing
NAICS 325998 All Other Miscellaneous Chemical Product Manufacturing
NAICS 332999 All Other Miscellaneous Fabricated Metal Product Manufacturing
NAICS 326199 All Other Plastics Product Manufacturing
NAICS 323112 Commercial Flexographic Printing
NAICS 323111 Commercial Gravure Printing
NAICS 323110 Commercial Lithographic Printing
NAICS 323113 Commercial Screen Printing
NAICS 323119 Other Commercial Printing
NAICS 332212 Hand & Edge Tool Manufacturing
NAICS 339999 All Other Miscellaneous Manufacturing

TRANSPORTATION, COMMUNICATIONS, ELECTRIC, GAS, & SANITARY SERVICES

4011 Railroads, Line-haul Operating
NAICS 482111 Line-haul Railroads
4013 Railroad Switching & Terminal Establishments
NAICS 482112 Short Line Railroads
NAICS 48821 Support Activities for Rail Transportation
4111 Local & Suburban Transit
NAICS 485111 Mixed Mode Transit Systems
NAICS 485112 Commuter Rail Systems
NAICS 485113 Bus & Motor Vehicle Transit Systems
NAICS 485119 Other Urban Transit Systems
NAICS 485999 All Other Transit & Ground Passenger Transportation
4119 Local Passenger Transportation, nec
NAICS 62191 Ambulance Service
NAICS 48541 School & Employee Bus Transportation
NAICS 48711 Scenic & Sightseeing Transportation , Land
NAICS 485991 Special Needs Transportation
NAICS 485999 All Other Transit & Ground Passenger Transportation
NAICS 48532 Limousine Service
4121 Taxicabs
NAICS 48531 Taxi Service
4131 Intercity & Rural Bus Transportation
NAICS 48521 Interurban & Rural Bus Transportation
4141 Local Bus Charter Service
NAICS 48551 Charter Bus Industry
4142 Bus Charter Service, Except Local
NAICS 48551 Charter Bus Industry
4151 School Buses
NAICS 48541 School & Employee Bus Transportation
4173 Terminal & Service Facilities for Motor Vehicle Passenger Transportation
NAICS 48849 Other Support Activities for Road Transportation
4212 Local Trucking Without Storage
NAICS 562111 Solid Waste Collection
NAICS 562112 Hazardous Waste Collection
NAICS 562119 Other Waste Collection
NAICS 48411 General Freight Trucking, Local
NAICS 48421 Used Household & Office Goods Moving
NAICS 48422 Specialized Freight Trucking, Local
4213 Trucking, Except Local
NAICS 484121 General Freight Trucking, Long-distance, Truckload
NAICS 484122 General Freight Trucking, Long-distance, less than Truckload
NAICS 48421 Used Household & Office Goods Moving
NAICS 48423 Specialized Freight Trucking, Long-distance
4214 Local Trucking with Storage
NAICS 48411 General Freight Trucking, Local
NAICS 48421 Used Household & Office Goods Moving
NAICS 48422 Specialized Freight Trucking, Local
4215 Couriers Services Except by Air
NAICS 49211 Couriers
NAICS 49221 Local Messengers & Local Delivery
4221 Farm Product Warehousing & Storage
NAICS 49313 Farm Product Storage Facilities
4222 Refrigerated Warehousing & Storage
NAICS 49312 Refrigerated Storage Facilities
4225 General Warehousing & Storage
NAICS 49311 General Warehousing & Storage Facilities
NAICS 53113 Lessors of Miniwarehouses & Self Storage Units
4226 Special Warehousing & Storage, nec
NAICS 49312 Refrigerated Warehousing & Storage Facilities
NAICS 49311 General Warehousing & Storage Facilities
NAICS 49319 Other Warehousing & Storage Facilities
4231 Terminal & Joint Terminal Maintenance Facilities for Motor Freight Transportation
NAICS 48849 Other Support Activities for Road Transportation
4311 United States Postal Service
NAICS 49111 Postal Service
4412 Deep Sea Foreign Transportation of Freight
NAICS 483111 Deep Sea Freight Transportation
4424 Deep Sea Domestic Transportation of Freight
NAICS 483113 Coastal & Great Lakes Freight Transportation
4432 Freight Transportation on the Great Lakes - St. Lawrence Seaway
NAICS 483113 Coastal & Great Lakes Freight Transportation
4449 Water Transportation of Freight, nec
NAICS 483211 Inland Water Freight Transportation
4481 Deep Sea Transportation of Passengers, Except by Ferry
NAICS 483112 Deep Sea Passenger Transportation
NAICS 483114 Coastal & Great Lakes Passenger Transportation
4482 Ferries
NAICS 483114 Coastal & Great Lakes Passenger Transportation
NAICS 483212 Inland Water Passenger Transportation
4489 Water Transportation of Passengers, nec
NAICS 483212 Inland Water Passenger Transportation
NAICS 48721 Scenic & Sightseeing Transportation, Water
4491 Marine Cargo Handling
NAICS 48831 Port & Harbor Operations
NAICS 48832 Marine Cargo Handling
4492 Towing & Tugboat Services
NAICS 483113 Coastal & Great Lakes Freight Transportation
NAICS 483211 Inland Water Freight Transportation
NAICS 48833 Navigational Services to Shipping
4493 Marinas
NAICS 71393 Marinas
4499 Water Transportation Services, nec
NAICS 532411 Commercial Air, Rail, & Water Transportation Equipment Rental & Leasing
NAICS 48831 Port & Harbor Operations
NAICS 48833 Navigational Services to Shipping
NAICS 48839 Other Support Activities for Water Transportation
4512 Air Transportation, Scheduled
NAICS 481111 Scheduled Passenger Air Transportation
NAICS 481112 Scheduled Freight Air Transportation
4513 Air Courier Services
NAICS 49211 Couriers
4522 Air Transportation, Nonscheduled
NAICS 62191 Ambulance Services
NAICS 481212 Nonscheduled Chartered Freight Air Transportation
NAICS 481211 Nonscheduled Chartered Passenger Air Transportation
NAICS 48122 Nonscheduled Speciality Air Transportation
NAICS 48799 Scenic & Sightseeing Transportation , Other

4581 Airports, Flying Fields, & Airport Terminal Services
NAICS 488111 Air Traffic Control
NAICS 488112 Airport Operations, Except Air Traffic Control
NAICS 56172 Janitorial Services
NAICS 48819 Other Support Activities for Air Transportation
4612 Crude Petroleum Pipelines
NAICS 48611 Pipeline Transportation of Crude Oil
4613 Refined Petroleum Pipelines
NAICS 48691 Pipeline Transportation of Refined Petroleum Products
4619 Pipelines, nec
NAICS 48699 All Other Pipeline Transportation
4724 Travel Agencies
NAICS 56151 Travel Agencies
4725 Tour Operators
NAICS 56152 Tour Operators
4729 Arrangement of Passenger Transportation, nec
NAICS 488999 All Other Support Activities for Transportation
NAICS 561599 All Other Travel Arrangement & Reservation Services
4731 Arrangement of Transportation of Freight & Cargo
NAICS 541618 Other Management Consulting Services
NAICS 48851 Freight Transportation Arrangement
4741 Rental of Railroad Cars
NAICS 532411 Commercial Air, Rail, & Water Transportation Equipment Rental & Leasing
NAICS 48821 Support Activities for Rail Transportation
4783 Packing & Crating
NAICS 488991 Packing & Crating
4785 Fixed Facilities & Inspection & Weighing Services for Motor Vehicle Transportation
NAICS 48839 Other Support Activities for Water Transportation
NAICS 48849 Other Support Activities for Road Transportation
4789 Transportation Services, nec
NAICS 488999 All Other Support Activities for Transportation
NAICS 48711 Scenic & Sightseeing Transportation, Land
NAICS 48821 Support Activities for Rail Transportation
4812 Radiotelephone Communications
NAICS 513321 Paging
NAICS 513322 Cellular & Other Wireless Telecommunications
NAICS 51333 Telecommunications Resellers
4813 Telephone Communications, Except Radiotelephone
NAICS 51331 Wired Telecommunications Carriers
NAICS 51333 Telecommunications Resellers
4822 Telegraph & Other Message Communications
NAICS 51331 Wired Telecommunications Carriers
4832 Radio Broadcasting Stations
NAICS 513111 Radio Networks
NAICS 513112 Radio Stations
4833 Television Broadcasting Stations
NAICS 51312 Television Broadcasting
4841 Cable & Other Pay Television Services
NAICS 51321 Cable Networks
NAICS 51322 Cable & Other Program Distribution
4899 Communications Services, nec
NAICS 513322 Cellular & Other Wireless Telecommunications
NAICS 51334 Satellite Telecommunications
NAICS 51339 Other Telecommunications
4911 Electric Services
NAICS 221111 Hydroelectric Power Generation
NAICS 221112 Fossil Fuel Electric Power Generation
NAICS 221113 Nuclear Electric Power Generation
NAICS 221119 Other Electric Power Generation
NAICS 221121 Electric Bulk Power Transmission & Control
NAICS 221122 Electric Power Distribution
4922 Natural Gas Transmission
NAICS 48621 Pipeline Transportation of Natural Gas
4923 Natural Gas Transmission & Distribution
NAICS 22121 Natural Gas Distribution
NAICS 48621 Pipeline Transportation of Natural Gas
4924 Natural Gas Distribution
NAICS 22121 Natural Gas Distribution
4925 Mixed, Manufactured, or Liquefied Petroleum Gas Production And/or Distribution
NAICS 22121 Natural Gas Distribution
4931 Electric & Other Services Combined
NAICS 221111 Hydroelectric Power Generation
NAICS 221112 Fossil Fuel Electric Power Generation
NAICS 221113 Nuclear Electric Power Generation
NAICS 221119 Other Electric Power Generation
NAICS 221121 Electric Bulk Power Transmission & Control
NAICS 221122 Electric Power Distribution
NAICS 22121 Natural Gas Distribution
4932 Gas & Other Services Combined
NAICS 22121 Natural Gas Distribution
4939 Combination Utilities, nec
NAICS 221111 Hydroelectric Power Generation
NAICS 221112 Fossil Fuel Electric Power Generation
NAICS 221113 Nuclear Electric Power Generation
NAICS 221119 Other Electric Power Generation
NAICS 221121 Electric Bulk Power Transmission & Control
NAICS 221122 Electric Power Distribution
NAICS 22121 Natural Gas Distribution
4941 Water Supply
NAICS 22131 Water Supply & Irrigation Systems
4952 Sewerage Systems
NAICS 22132 Sewage Treatment Facilities
4953 Refuse Systems
NAICS 562111 Solid Waste Collection
NAICS 562112 Hazardous Waste Collection
NAICS 56292 Materials Recovery Facilities
NAICS 562119 Other Waste Collection
NAICS 562211 Hazardous Waste Treatment & Disposal
NAICS 562212 Solid Waste Landfills
NAICS 562213 Solid Waste Combustors & Incinerators
NAICS 562219 Other Nonhazardous Waste Treatment & Disposal
4959 Sanitary Services, nec
NAICS 488112 Airport Operations, Except Air Traffic Control
NAICS 56291 Remediation Services
NAICS 56171 Exterminating & Pest Control Services
NAICS 562998 All Other Miscellaneous Waste Management Services
4961 Steam & Air-conditioning Supply
NAICS 22133 Steam & Air-conditioning Supply
4971 Irrigation Systems
NAICS 22131 Water Supply & Irrigation Systems

WHOLESALE TRADE

5012 Automobiles & Other Motor Vehicles
NAICS 42111 Automobile & Other Motor Vehicle Wholesalers

5013 Motor Vehicle Supplies & New Parts
NAICS 44131 Automotive Parts & Accessories Stores - Retail
NAICS 42112 Motor Vehicle Supplies & New Part Wholesalers
5014 Tires & Tubes
NAICS 44132 Tire Dealers - Retail
NAICS 42113 Tire & Tube Wholesalers
5015 Motor Vehicle Parts, Used
NAICS 42114 Motor Vehicle Part Wholesalers
5021 Furniture
NAICS 44211 Furniture Stores
NAICS 42121 Furniture Wholesalers
5023 Home Furnishings
NAICS 44221 Floor Covering Stores
NAICS 42122 Home Furnishing Wholesalers
5031 Lumber, Plywood, Millwork, & Wood Panels
NAICS 44419 Other Building Material Dealers
NAICS 42131 Lumber, Plywood, Millwork, & Wood Panel Wholesalers
5032 Brick, Stone & Related Construction Materials
NAICS 44419 Other Building Material Dealers
NAICS 42132 Brick, Stone & Related Construction Material Wholesalers
5033 Roofing, Siding, & Insulation Materials
NAICS 42133 Roofing, Siding, & Insulation Material Wholesalers
5039 Construction Materials, nec
NAICS 44419 Other Building Material Dealers
NAICS 42139 Other Construction Material Wholesalers
5043 Photographic Equipment & Supplies
NAICS 42141 Photographic Equipment & Supplies Wholesalers
5044 Office Equipment
NAICS 42142 Office Equipment Wholesalers
5045 Computers & Computer Peripheral Equipment & Software
NAICS 42143 Computer & Computer Peripheral Equipment & Software Wholesalers
NAICS 44312 Computer & Software Stores - Retail
5046 Commercial Equipment, nec
NAICS 42144 Other Commercial Equipment Wholesalers
5047 Medical, Dental, & Hospital Equipment & Supplies
NAICS 42145 Medical, Dental & Hospital Equipment & Supplies Wholesalers
NAICS 446199 All Other Health & Personal Care Stores - Retail
5048 Ophthalmic Goods
NAICS 42146 Ophthalmic Goods Wholesalers
5049 Professional Equipment & Supplies, nec
NAICS 42149 Other Professional Equipment & Supplies Wholesalers
NAICS 45321 Office Supplies & Stationery Stores - Retail
5051 Metals Service Centers & Offices
NAICS 42151 Metals Service Centers & Offices
5052 Coal & Other Minerals & Ores
NAICS 42152 Coal & Other Mineral & Ore Wholesalers
5063 Electrical Apparatus & Equipment Wiring Supplies, & Construction Materials
NAICS 44419 Other Building Material Dealers
NAICS 42161 Electrical Apparatus & Equipment, Wiring Supplies & Construction Material Wholesalers
5064 Electrical Appliances, Television & Radio Sets
NAICS 42162 Electrical Appliance, Television & Radio Set Wholesalers
5065 Electronic Parts & Equipment, Not Elsewhere Classified
NAICS 42169 Other Electronic Parts & Equipment Wholesalers
5072 Hardware
NAICS 42171 Hardware Wholesalers
5074 Plumbing & Heating Equipment & Supplies
NAICS 44419 Other Building Material Dealers
NAICS 42172 Plumbing & Heating Equipment & Supplies Wholesalers
5075 Warm Air Heating & Air-conditioning Equipment & Supplies
NAICS 42173 Warm Air Heating & Air-conditioning Equipment & Supplies Wholesalers
5078 Refrigeration Equipment & Supplies
NAICS 42174 Refrigeration Equipment & Supplies Wholesalers
5082 Construction & Mining Machinery & Equipment
NAICS 42181 Construction & Mining Machinery & Equipment Wholesalers
5083 Farm & Garden Machinery & Equipment
NAICS 42182 Farm & Garden Machinery & Equipment Wholesalers
NAICS 44421 Outdoor Power Equipment Stores - Retail
5084 Industrial Machinery & Equipment
NAICS 42183 Industrial Machinery & Equipment Wholesalers
5085 Industrial Supplies
NAICS 42183 Industrial Machinery & Equipment Wholesalers
NAICS 42184 Industrial Supplies Wholesalers
NAICS 81131 Commercial & Industrial Machinery & Equipment Repair & Maintenence
5087 Service Establishment Equipment & Supplies
NAICS 42185 Service Establishment Equipment & Supplies Wholesalers
NAICS 44612 Cosmetics, Beauty Supplies, & Perfume Stores
5088 Transportation Equipment & Supplies, Except Motor Vehicles
NAICS 42186 Transportation Equipment & Supplies Wholesalers
5091 Sporting & Recreational Goods & Supplies
NAICS 42191 Sporting & Recreational Goods & Supplies Wholesalers
5092 Toys & Hobby Goods & Supplies
NAICS 42192 Toy & Hobby Goods & Supplies Wholesalers
5093 Scrap & Waste Materials
NAICS 42193 Recyclable Material Wholesalers
5094 Jewelry, Watches, Precious Stones, & Precious Metals
NAICS 42194 Jewelry, Watch , Precious Stone, & Precious Metal Wholesalers
5099 Durable Goods, nec
NAICS 42199 Other Miscellaneous Durable Goods Wholesalers
5111 Printing & Writing Paper
NAICS 42211 Printing & Writing Paper Wholesalers
5112 Stationery & Office Supplies
NAICS 45321 Office Supplies & Stationery Stores
NAICS 42212 Stationery & Office Supplies Wholesalers
5113 Industrial & Personal Service Paper
NAICS 42213 Industrial & Personal Service Paper Wholesalers
5122 Drugs, Drug Proprietaries, & Druggists' Sundries
NAICS 42221 Drugs, Drug Proprietaries, & Druggists' Sundries Wholesalers

5131 Piece Goods, Notions, & Other Dry Goods
NAICS 313311 Broadwoven Fabric Finishing Mills
NAICS 313312 Textile & Fabric Finishing Mills
NAICS 42231 Piece Goods, Notions, & Other Dry Goods Wholesalers
5136 Men's & Boys' Clothing & Furnishings
NAICS 42232 Men's & Boys' Clothing & Furnishings Wholesalers
5137 Women's Children's & Infants' Clothing & Accessories
NAICS 42233 Women's, Children's, & Infants' Clothing & Accessories Wholesalers
5139 Footwear
NAICS 42234 Footwear Wholesalers
5141 Groceries, General Line
NAICS 42241 General Line Grocery Wholesalers
5142 Packaged Frozen Foods
NAICS 42242 Packaged Frozen Food Wholesalers
5143 Dairy Products, Except Dried or Canned
NAICS 42243 Dairy Products Wholesalers
5144 Poultry & Poultry Products
NAICS 42244 Poultry & Poultry Product Wholesalers
5145 Confectionery
NAICS 42245 Confectionery Wholesalers
5146 Fish & Seafoods
NAICS 42246 Fish & Seafood Wholesalers
5147 Meats & Meat Products
NAICS 311612 Meat Processed from Carcasses
NAICS 42247 Meat & Meat Product Wholesalers
5148 Fresh Fruits & Vegetables
NAICS 42248 Fresh Fruit & Vegetable Wholesalers
5149 Groceries & Related Products, nec
NAICS 42249 Other Grocery & Related Product Wholesalers
5153 Grain & Field Beans
NAICS 42251 Grain & Field Bean Wholesalers
5154 Livestock
NAICS 42252 Livestock Wholesalers
5159 Farm-product Raw Materials, nec
NAICS 42259 Other Farm Product Raw Material Wholesalers
5162 Plastics Materials & Basic Forms & Shapes
NAICS 42261 Plastics Materials & Basic Forms & Shapes Wholesalers
5169 Chemicals & Allied Products, nec
NAICS 42269 Other Chemical & Allied Products Wholesalers
5171 Petroleum Bulk Stations & Terminals
NAICS 454311 Heating Oil Dealers
NAICS 454312 Liquefied Petroleum Gas Dealers
NAICS 42271 Petroleum Bulk Stations & Terminals
5172 Petroleum & Petroleum Products Wholesalers, Except Bulk Stations & Terminals
NAICS 42272 Petroleum & Petroleum Products Wholesalers
5181 Beer & Ale
NAICS 42281 Beer & Ale Wholesalers
5182 Wine & Distilled Alcoholic Beverages
NAICS 42282 Wine & Distilled Alcoholic Beverage Wholesalers
5191 Farm Supplies
NAICS 44422 Nursery & Garden Centers - Retail
NAICS 42291 Farm Supplies Wholesalers
5192 Books, Periodicals, & Newspapers
NAICS 42292 Book, Periodical & Newspaper Wholesalers
5193 Flowers, Nursery Stock, & Florists' Supplies
NAICS 42293 Flower, Nursery Stock & Florists' Supplies Wholesalers
NAICS 44422 Nursery & Garden Centers - Retail
5194 Tobacco & Tobacco Products
NAICS 42294 Tobacco & Tobacco Product Wholesalers
5198 Paint, Varnishes, & Supplies
NAICS 42295 Paint, Varnish & Supplies Wholesalers
NAICS 44412 Paint & Wallpaper Stores
5199 Nondurable Goods, nec
NAICS 54189 Other Services Related to Advertising
NAICS 42299 Other Miscellaneous Nondurable Goods Wholesalers

RETAIL TRADE

5211 Lumber & Other Building Materials Dealers
NAICS 44411 Home Centers
NAICS 42131 Lumber, Plywood, Millwork & Wood Panel Wholesalers
NAICS 44419 Other Building Material Dealers
5231 Paint, Glass, & Wallpaper Stores
NAICS 42295 Paint, Varnish & Supplies Wholesalers
NAICS 44419 Other Building Material Dealers
NAICS 44412 Paint & Wallpaper Stores
5251 Hardware Stores
NAICS 44413 Hardware Stores
5261 Retail Nurseries, Lawn & Garden Supply Stores
NAICS 44422 Nursery & Garden Centers
NAICS 453998 All Other Miscellaneous Store Retailers
NAICS 44421 Outdoor Power Equipment Stores
5271 Mobile Home Dealers
NAICS 45393 Manufactured Home Dealers
5311 Department Stores
NAICS 45211 Department Stores
5331 Variety Stores
NAICS 45299 All Other General Merchandise Stores
5399 Miscellaneous General Merchandise Stores
NAICS 45291 Warehouse Clubs & Superstores
NAICS 45299 All Other General Merchandise Stores
5411 Grocery Stores
NAICS 44711 Gasoline Stations with Convenience Stores
NAICS 44511 Supermarkets & Other Grocery Stores
NAICS 45291 Warehouse Clubs & Superstores
NAICS 44512 Convenience Stores
5421 Meat & Fish Markets, Including Freezer Provisioners
NAICS 45439 Other Direct Selling Establishments
NAICS 44521 Meat Markets
NAICS 44522 Fish & Seafood Markets
5431 Fruit & Vegetable Markets
NAICS 44523 Fruit & Vegetable Markets
5441 Candy, Nut, & Confectionery Stores
NAICS 445292 Confectionary & Nut Stores
5451 Dairy Products Stores
NAICS 445299 All Other Specialty Food Stores
5461 Retail Bakeries
NAICS 722213 Snack & Nonalcoholic Beverage Bars
NAICS 311811 Retail Bakeries
NAICS 445291 Baked Goods Stores
5499 Miscellaneous Food Stores
NAICS 44521 Meat Markets
NAICS 722211 Limited-service Restaurants
NAICS 446191 Food Supplement Stores
NAICS 445299 All Other Specialty Food Stores
5511 Motor Vehicle Dealers
NAICS 44111 New Car Dealers

5521 Motor Vehicle Dealers
NAICS 44112 Used Car Dealers
5531 Auto & Home Supply Stores
NAICS 44132 Tire Dealers
NAICS 44131 Automotive Parts & Accessories Stores
5541 Gasoline Service Stations
NAICS 44711 Gasoline Stations with Convenience Store
NAICS 44719 Other Gasoline Stations
5551 Boat Dealers
NAICS 441222 Boat Dealers
5561 Recreational Vehicle Dealers
NAICS 44121 Recreational Vehicle Dealers
5571 Motorcycle Dealers
NAICS 441221 Motorcycle Dealers
5599 Automotive Dealers, nec
NAICS 441229 All Other Motor Vehicle Dealers
5611 Men's & Boys' Clothing & Accessory Stores
NAICS 44811 Men's Clothing Stores
NAICS 44815 Clothing Accessories Stores
5621 Women's Clothing Stores
NAICS 44812 Women's Clothing Stores
5632 Women's Accessory & Specialty Stores
NAICS 44819 Other Clothing Stores
NAICS 44815 Clothing Accessories Stores
5641 Children's & Infants' Wear Stores
NAICS 44813 Children's & Infants' Clothing Stores
5651 Family Clothing Stores
NAICS 44814 Family Clothing Stores
5661 Shoe Stores
NAICS 44821 Shoe Stores
5699 Miscellaneous Apparel & Accessory Stores
NAICS 315 Included in Apparel Manufacturing Subsector Based on Type of Garment Produced
NAICS 44819 Other Clothing Stores
NAICS 44815 Clothing Accessories Stores
5712 Furniture Stores
NAICS 337133 Wood Household Furniture, Except Upholstered, Manufacturing
NAICS 337131 Wood Kitchen Cabinet & Counter Top Manufacturing
NAICS 337132 Upholstered Household Furniture Manufacturing
NAICS 44211 Furniture Stores
5713 Floor Covering Stores
NAICS 44221 Floor Covering Stores
5714 Drapery, Curtain, & Upholstery Stores
NAICS 442291 Window Treatment Stores
NAICS 45113 Sewing, Needlework & Piece Goods Stores
NAICS 314121 Curtain & Drapery Mills
5719 Miscellaneous Homefurnishings Stores
NAICS 442291 Window Treatment Stores
NAICS 442299 All Other Home Furnishings Stores
5722 Household Appliance Stores
NAICS 443111 Household Appliance Stores
5731 Radio, Television, & Consumer Electronics Stores
NAICS 443112 Radio, Television, & Other Electronics Stores
NAICS 44131 Automotive Parts & Accessories Stores
5734 Computer & Computer Software Stores
NAICS 44312 Computer & Software Stores
5735 Record & Prerecorded Tape Stores
NAICS 45122 Prerecorded Tape, Compact Disc & Record Stores
5736 Musical Instrument Stores
NAICS 45114 Musical Instrument & Supplies Stores
5812 Eating & Drinking Places
NAICS 72211 Full-service Restaurants
NAICS 722211 Limited-service Restaurants
NAICS 722212 Cafeterias
NAICS 722213 Snack & Nonalcoholic Beverage Bars
NAICS 72231 Foodservice Contractors
NAICS 72232 Caterers
NAICS 71111 Theater Companies & Dinner Theaters
5813 Drinking Places
NAICS 72241 Drinking Places
5912 Drug Stores & Proprietary Stores
NAICS 44611 Pharmacies & Drug Stores
5921 Liquor Stores
NAICS 44531 Beer, Wine & Liquor Stores
5932 Used Merchandise Stores
NAICS 522298 All Other Non-depository Credit Intermediation
NAICS 45331 Used Merchandise Stores
5941 Sporting Goods Stores & Bicycle Shops
NAICS 45111 Sporting Goods Stores
5942 Book Stores
NAICS 451211 Book Stores
5943 Stationery Stores
NAICS 45321 Office Supplies & Stationery Stores
5944 Jewelry Stores
NAICS 44831 Jewelry Stores
5945 Hobby, Toy, & Game Shops
NAICS 45112 Hobby, Toy & Game Stores
5946 Camera & Photographic Supply Stores
NAICS 44313 Camera & Photographic Supplies Stores
5947 Gift, Novelty, & Souvenir Shops
NAICS 45322 Gift, Novelty & Souvenir Stores
5948 Luggage & Leather Goods Stores
NAICS 44832 Luggage & Leather Goods Stores
5949 Sewing, Needlework, & Piece Goods Stores
NAICS 45113 Sewing, Needlework & Piece Goods Stores
5961 Catalog & Mail-order Houses
NAICS 45411 Electronic Shopping & Mail-order Houses
5962 Automatic Merchandising Machine Operator
NAICS 45421 Vending Machine Operators
5963 Direct Selling Establishments
NAICS 72233 Mobile Caterers
NAICS 45439 Other Direct Selling Establishments
5983 Fuel Oil Dealers
NAICS 454311 Heating Oil Dealers
5984 Liquefied Petroleum Gas Dealers
NAICS 454312 Liquefied Petroleum Gas Dealers
5989 Fuel Dealers, nec
NAICS 454319 Other Fuel Dealers
5992 Florists
NAICS 45311 Florists
5993 Tobacco Stores & Stands
NAICS 453991 Tobacco Stores
5994 News Dealers & Newsstands
NAICS 451212 News Dealers & Newsstands
5995 Optical Goods Stores
NAICS 339117 Eyeglass & Contact Lens Manufacturing
NAICS 44613 Optical Goods Stores
5999 Miscellaneous Retail Stores, nec
NAICS 44612 Cosmetics, Beauty Supplies & Perfume Stores
NAICS 446199 All Other Health & Personal Care Stores
NAICS 45391 Pet & Pet Supplies Stores

NAICS 45392 Art Dealers
NAICS 443111 Household Appliance Stores
NAICS 443112 Radio, Television & Other Electronics Stores
NAICS 44831 Jewelry Stores
NAICS 453999 All Other Miscellaneous Store Retailers

FINANCE, INSURANCE, & REAL ESTATE

6011 Federal Reserve Banks
NAICS 52111 Monetary Authorities-central Banks
6019 Central Reserve Depository Institutions, nec
NAICS 52232 Financial Transactions Processing, Reserve, & Clearing House Activities
6021 National Commercial Banks
NAICS 52211 Commercial Banking
NAICS 52221 Credit Card Issuing
NAICS 523991 Trust, Fiduciary & Custody Activities
6022 State Commercial Banks
NAICS 52211 Commercial Banking
NAICS 52221 Credit Card Issuing
NAICS 52219 Other Depository Intermediation
NAICS 523991 Trust, Fiduciary & Custody Activities
6029 Commercial Banks, nec
NAICS 52211 Commercial Banking
6035 Savings Institutions, Federally Chartered
NAICS 52212 Savings Institutions
6036 Savings Institutions, Not Federally Chartered
NAICS 52212 Savings Institutions
6061 Credit Unions, Federally Chartered
NAICS 52213 Credit Unions
6062 Credit Unions, Not Federally Chartered
NAICS 52213 Credit Unions
6081 Branches & Agencies of Foreign Banks
NAICS 522293 International Trade Financing
NAICS 52211 Commercial Banking
NAICS 522298 All Other Non-depository Credit Intermediation
6082 Foreign Trade & International Banking Institutions
NAICS 522293 International Trade Financing
6091 Nondeposit Trust Facilities
NAICS 523991 Trust, Fiduciary, & Custody Activities
6099 Functions Related to Deposit Banking, nec
NAICS 52232 Financial Transactions Processing, Reserve, & Clearing House Activities
NAICS 52313 Commodity Contracts Dealing
NAICS 523991 Trust, Fiduciary, & Custody Activities
NAICS 523999 Miscellaneous Financial Investment Activities
NAICS 52239 Other Activities Related to Credit Intermediation
6111 Federal & Federally Sponsored Credit Agencies
NAICS 522293 International Trade Financing
NAICS 522294 Secondary Market Financing
NAICS 522298 All Other Non-depository Credit Intermediation
6141 Personal Credit Institutions
NAICS 52221 Credit Card Issuing
NAICS 52222 Sales Financing
NAICS 522291 Consumer Lending
6153 Short-term Business Credit Institutions, Except Agricultural
NAICS 52222 Sales Financing
NAICS 52232 Financial Transactions Processing, Reserve, & Clearing House Activities
NAICS 522298 All Other Non-depository Credit Intermediation
6159 Miscellaneous Business Credit Institutions
NAICS 52222 Sales Financing
NAICS 532 Included in Rental & Leasing Services Subsector by Type of Equipment & Method of Operation
NAICS 522293 International Trade Financing
NAICS 522298 All Other Non-depository Credit Intermediation
6162 Mortgage Bankers & Loan Correspondents
NAICS 522292 Real Estate Credit
NAICS 52239 Other Activities Related to Credit Intermediation
6163 Loan Brokers
NAICS 52231 Mortgage & Other Loan Brokers
6211 Security Brokers, Dealers, & Flotation Companies
NAICS 52311 Investment Banking & Securities Dealing
NAICS 52312 Securities Brokerage
NAICS 52391 Miscellaneous Intermediation
NAICS 523999 Miscellaneous Financial Investment Activities
6221 Commodity Contracts Brokers & Dealers
NAICS 52313 Commodity Contracts Dealing
NAICS 52314 Commodity Brokerage
6231 Security & Commodity Exchanges
NAICS 52321 Securities & Commodity Exchanges
6282 Investment Advice
NAICS 52392 Portfolio Management
NAICS 52393 Investment Advice
6289 Services Allied with the Exchange of Securities or Commodities, nec
NAICS 523991 Trust, Fiduciary, & Custody Activities
NAICS 523999 Miscellaneous Financial Investment Activities
6311 Life Insurance
NAICS 524113 Direct Life Insurance Carriers
NAICS 52413 Reinsurance Carriers
6321 Accident & Health Insurance
NAICS 524114 Direct Health & Medical Insurance Carriers
NAICS 52519 Other Insurance Funds
NAICS 52413 Reinsurance Carriers
6324 Hospital & Medical Service Plans
NAICS 524114 Direct Health & Medical Insurance Carriers
NAICS 52519 Other Insurance Funds
NAICS 52413 Reinsurance Carriers
6331 Fire, Marine, & Casualty Insurance
NAICS 524126 Direct Property & Casualty Insurance Carriers
NAICS 52519 Other Insurance Funds
NAICS 52413 Reinsurance Carriers
6351 Surety Insurance
NAICS 524126 Direct Property & Casualty Insurance Carriers
NAICS 52413 Reinsurance Carriers
6361 Title Insurance
NAICS 524127 Direct Title Insurance Carriers
NAICS 52413 Reinsurance Carriers
6371 Pension, Health, & Welfare Funds
NAICS 52392 Portfolio Management
NAICS 524292 Third Party Administration for Insurance & Pension Funds
NAICS 52511 Pension Funds
NAICS 52512 Health & Welfare Funds
6399 Insurance Carriers, nec
NAICS 524128 Other Direct Insurance Carriers

6411 Insurance Agents, Brokers, & Service
NAICS 52421 Insurance Agencies & Brokerages
NAICS 524291 Claims Adjusters
NAICS 524292 Third Party Administrators for Insurance & Pension Funds
NAICS 524298 All Other Insurance Related Activities
6512 Operators of Nonresidential Buildings
NAICS 71131 Promoters of Performing Arts, Sports & Similar Events with Facilities
NAICS 53112 Lessors of Nonresidential Buildings
6513 Operators of Apartment Buildings
NAICS 53111 Lessors of Residential Buildings & Dwellings
6514 Operators of Dwellings Other than Apartment Buildings
NAICS 53111 Lessors of Residential Buildings & Dwellings
6515 Operators of Residential Mobile Home Sites
NAICS 53119 Lessors of Other Real Estate Property
6517 Lessors of Railroad Property
NAICS 53119 Lessors of Other Real Estate Property
6519 Lessors of Real Property, nec
NAICS 53119 Lessors of Other Real Estate Property
6531 Real Estate Agents & Managers
NAICS 53121 Offices of Real Estate Agents & Brokers
NAICS 81399 Other Similar Organizations
NAICS 531311 Residential Property Managers
NAICS 531312 Nonresidential Property Managers
NAICS 53132 Offices of Real Estate Appraisers
NAICS 81222 Cemeteries & Crematories
NAICS 531399 All Other Activities Related to Real Estate
6541 Title Abstract Offices
NAICS 541191 Title Abstract & Settlement Offices
6552 Land Subdividers & Developers, Except Cemeteries
NAICS 23311 Land Subdivision & Land Development
6553 Cemetery Subdividers & Developers
NAICS 81222 Cemeteries & Crematories
6712 Offices of Bank Holding Companies
NAICS 551111 Offices of Bank Holding Companies
6719 Offices of Holding Companies, nec
NAICS 551112 Offices of Other Holding Companies
6722 Management Investment Offices, Open-end
NAICS 52591 Open-end Investment Funds
6726 Unit Investment Trusts, Face-amount Certificate Offices, & Closed-end Management Investment Offices
NAICS 52599 Other Financial Vehicles
6732 Education, Religious, & Charitable Trusts
NAICS 813211 Grantmaking Foundations
6733 Trusts, Except Educational, Religious, & Charitable
NAICS 52392 Portfolio Management
NAICS 523991 Trust, Fiduciary, & Custody Services
NAICS 52519 Other Insurance Funds
NAICS 52592 Trusts, Estates, & Agency Accounts
6792 Oil Royalty Traders
NAICS 523999 Miscellaneous Financial Investment Activities
NAICS 53311 Owners & Lessors of Other Non-financial Assets
6794 Patent Owners & Lessors
NAICS 53311 Owners & Lessors of Other Non-financial Assets
6798 Real Estate Investment Trusts
NAICS 52593 Real Estate Investment Trusts
6799 Investors, nec
NAICS 52391 Miscellaneous Intermediation
NAICS 52392 Portfolio Management
NAICS 52313 Commodity Contracts Dealing
NAICS 523999 Miscellaneous Financial Investment Activities

SERVICE INDUSTRIES

7011 Hotels & Motels
NAICS 72111 Hotels & Motels
NAICS 72112 Casino Hotels
NAICS 721191 Bed & Breakfast Inns
NAICS 721199 All Other Traveler Accommodation
7021 Rooming & Boarding Houses
NAICS 72131 Rooming & Boarding Houses
7032 Sporting & Recreational Camps
NAICS 721214 Recreational & Vacation Camps
7033 Recreational Vehicle Parks & Campsites
NAICS 721211 Rv & Campgrounds
7041 Organization Hotels & Lodging Houses, on Membership Basis
NAICS 72111 Hotels & Motels
NAICS 72131 Rooming & Boarding Houses
7211 Power Laundries, Family & Commercial
NAICS 812321 Laundries, Family & Commercial
7212 Garment Pressing, & Agents for Laundries
NAICS 812391 Garment Pressing & Agents for Laundries
7213 Linen Supply
NAICS 812331 Linen Supply
7215 Coin-operated Laundry & Drycleaning
NAICS 81231 Coin-operated Laundries & Drycleaners
7216 Drycleaning Plants, Except Rug Cleaning
NAICS 812322 Drycleaning Plants
7217 Carpet & Upholstery Cleaning
NAICS 56174 Carpet & Upholstery Cleaning Services
7218 Industrial Launderers
NAICS 812332 Industrial Launderers
7219 Laundry & Garment Services, nec
NAICS 812331 Linen Supply
NAICS 81149 Other Personal & Household Goods Repair & Maintenance
NAICS 812399 All Other Laundry Services
7221 Photographic Studios, Portrait
NAICS 541921 Photographic Studios, Portrait
7231 Beauty Shops
NAICS 812112 Beauty Salons
NAICS 812113 Nail Salons
NAICS 611511 Cosmetology & Barber Schools
7241 Barber Shops
NAICS 812111 Barber Shops
NAICS 611511 Cosmetology & Barber Schools
7251 Shoe Repair Shops & Shoeshine Parlors
NAICS 81143 Footwear & Leather Goods Repair
7261 Funeral Services & Crematories
NAICS 81221 Funeral Homes
NAICS 81222 Cemeteries & Crematories
7291 Tax Return Preparation Services
NAICS 541213 Tax Preparation Services
7299 Miscellaneous Personal Services, nec
NAICS 62441 Child Day Care Services
NAICS 812191 Diet & Weight Reducing Centers
NAICS 53222 Formal Wear & Costume Rental
NAICS 812199 Other Personal Care Services
NAICS 81299 All Other Personal Services
7311 Advertising Agencies
NAICS 54181 Advertising Agencies
7312 Outdoor Advertising Services
NAICS 54185 Display Advertising

7313 Radio, Television, & Publishers' Advertising Representatives
NAICS 54184 Media Representatives
7319 Advertising, nec
NAICS 481219 Other Nonscheduled Air Transportation
NAICS 54183 Media Buying Agencies
NAICS 54185 Display Advertising
NAICS 54187 Advertising Material Distribution Services
NAICS 54189 Other Services Related to Advertising
7322 Adjustment & Collection Services
NAICS 56144 Collection Agencies
NAICS 561491 Repossession Services
7323 Credit Reporting Services
NAICS 56145 Credit Bureaus
7331 Direct Mail Advertising Services
NAICS 54186 Direct Mail Advertising
7334 Photocopying & Duplicating Services
NAICS 561431 Photocopying & Duplicating Services
7335 Commercial Photography
NAICS 48122 Nonscheduled Speciality Air Transportation
NAICS 541922 Commercial Photography
7336 Commercial Art & Graphic Design
NAICS 54143 Commercial Art & Graphic Design Services
7338 Secretarial & Court Reporting Services
NAICS 56141 Document Preparation Services
NAICS 561492 Court Reporting & Stenotype Services
7342 Disinfecting & Pest Control Services
NAICS 56172 Janitorial Services
NAICS 56171 Exterminating & Pest Control Services
7349 Building Cleaning & Maintenance Services, nec
NAICS 56172 Janitorial Services
7352 Medical Equipment Rental & Leasing
NAICS 532291 Home Health Equipment Rental
NAICS 53249 Other Commercial & Industrial Machinery & Equipment Rental & Leasing
7353 Heavy Construction Equipment Rental & Leasing
NAICS 23499 All Other Heavy Construction
NAICS 532412 Construction, Mining & Forestry Machinery & Equipment Rental & Leasing
7359 Equipment Rental & Leasing, nec
NAICS 53221 Consumer Electronics & Appliances Rental
NAICS 53231 General Rental Centers
NAICS 532299 All Other Consumer Goods Rental
NAICS 532412 Construction, Mining & Forestry Machinery & Equipment Rental & Leasing
NAICS 532411 Commercial Air, Rail, & Water Transportation Equipment Rental & Leasing
NAICS 562991 Septic Tank & Related Services
NAICS 53242 Office Machinery & Equipment Rental & Leasing
NAICS 53249 Other Commercial & Industrial Machinery & Equipment Rental & Leasing
7361 Employment Agencies
NAICS 541612 Human Resources & Executive Search Consulting Services
NAICS 56131 Employment Placement Agencies
7363 Help Supply Services
NAICS 56132 Temporary Help Services
NAICS 56133 Employee Leasing Services
7371 Computer Programming Services
NAICS 541511 Custom Computer Programming Services
7372 Prepackaged Software
NAICS 51121 Software Publishers
NAICS 334611 Software Reproducing
7373 Computer Integrated Systems Design
NAICS 541512 Computer Systems Design Services
7374 Computer Processing & Data Preparation & Processing Services
NAICS 51421 Data Processing Services
7375 Information Retrieval Services
NAICS 514191 On-line Information Services
7376 Computer Facilities Management Services
NAICS 541513 Computer Facilities Management Services
7377 Computer Rental & Leasing
NAICS 53242 Office Machinery & Equipment Rental & Leasing
7378 Computer Maintenance & Repair
NAICS 44312 Computer & Software Stores
NAICS 811212 Computer & Office Machine Repair & Maintenance
7379 Computer Related Services, nec
NAICS 541512 Computer Systems Design Services
NAICS 541519 Other Computer Related Services
7381 Detective, Guard, & Armored Car Services
NAICS 561611 Investigation Services
NAICS 561612 Security Guards & Patrol Services
NAICS 561613 Armored Car Services
7382 Security Systems Services
NAICS 561621 Security Systems Services
7383 News Syndicates
NAICS 51411 New Syndicates
7384 Photofinishing Laboratories
NAICS 812921 Photo Finishing Laboratories
NAICS 812922 One-hour Photo Finishing
7389 Business Services, nec
NAICS 51224 Sound Recording Studios
NAICS 51229 Other Sound Recording Industries
NAICS 541199 All Other Legal Services
NAICS 81299 All Other Personal Services
NAICS 54137 Surveying & Mapping Services
NAICS 54141 Interior Design Services
NAICS 54142 Industrial Design Services
NAICS 54134 Drafting Services
NAICS 54149 Other Specialized Design Services
NAICS 54189 Other Services Related to Advertising
NAICS 54193 Translation & Interpretation Services
NAICS 54135 Building Inspection Services
NAICS 54199 All Other Professional, Scientific & Technical Services
NAICS 71141 Agents & Managers for Artists, Athletes, Entertainers & Other Public Figures
NAICS 561422 Telemarketing Bureaus
NAICS 561432 Private Mail Centers
NAICS 561439 Other Business Service Centers
NAICS 561491 Repossession Services
NAICS 56191 Packaging & Labeling Services
NAICS 56179 Other Services to Buildings & Dwellings
NAICS 561599 All Other Travel Arrangement & Reservation Services
NAICS 56192 Convention & Trade Show Organizers
NAICS 561591 Convention & Visitors Bureaus
NAICS 52232 Financial Transactions, Processing, Reserve & Clearing House Activities
NAICS 561499 All Other Business Support Services
NAICS 56199 All Other Support Services
7513 Truck Rental & Leasing, Without Drivers
NAICS 53212 Truck, Utility Trailer & Rv Rental & Leasing

7514 Passenger Car Rental
NAICS 532111 Passenger Cars Rental
7515 Passenger Car Leasing
NAICS 532112 Passenger Cars Leasing
7519 Utility Trailer & Recreational Vehicle Rental
NAICS 53212 Truck, Utility Trailer & Rv Rental & Leasing
7521 Automobile Parking
NAICS 81293 Parking Lots & Garages
7532 Top, Body, & Upholstery Repair Shops & Paint Shops
NAICS 811121 Automotive Body, Paint, & Upholstery Repair & Maintenance
7533 Automotive Exhaust System Repair Shops
NAICS 811112 Automotive Exhaust System Repair
7534 Tire Retreading & Repair Shops
NAICS 326212 Tire Retreading
NAICS 811198 All Other Automotive Repair & Maintenance
7536 Automotive Glass Replacement Shops
NAICS 811122 Automotive Glass Replacement Shops
7537 Automotive Transmission Repair Shops
NAICS 811113 Automotive Transmission Repair
7538 General Automotive Repair Shops
NAICS 811111 General Automotive Repair
7539 Automotive Repair Shops, nec
NAICS 811118 Other Automotive Mechanical & Electrical Repair & Maintenance
7542 Carwashes
NAICS 811192 Car Washes
7549 Automotive Services, Except Repair & Carwashes
NAICS 811191 Automotive Oil Change & Lubrication Shops
NAICS 48841 Motor Vehicle Towing
NAICS 811198 All Other Automotive Repair & Maintenance
7622 Radio & Television Repair Shops
NAICS 811211 Consumer Electronics Repair & Maintenance
NAICS 443112 Radio, Television & Other Electronics Stores
7623 Refrigeration & Air-conditioning Services & Repair Shops
NAICS 443111 Household Appliance Stores
NAICS 81131 Commercial & Industrial Machinery & Equipment Repair & Maintenance
NAICS 811412 Appliance Repair & Maintenance
7629 Electrical & Electronic Repair Shops, nec
NAICS 443111 Household Appliance Stores
NAICS 811212 Computer & Office Machine Repair & Maintenance
NAICS 811213 Communication Equipment Repair & Maintenance
NAICS 811219 Other Electronic & Precision Equipment Repair & Maintenance
NAICS 811412 Appliance Repair & Maintenance
NAICS 811211 Consumer Electronics Repair & Maintenance
7631 Watch, Clock, & Jewelry Repair
NAICS 81149 Other Personal & Household Goods Repair & Maintenance
7641 Reupholster & Furniture Repair
NAICS 81142 Reupholstery & Furniture Repair
7692 Welding Repair
NAICS 81149 Other Personal & Household Goods Repair & Maintenance
7694 Armature Rewinding Shops
NAICS 81131 Commercial & Industrial Machinery & Equipment Repair & Maintenance
NAICS 335312 Motor & Generator Manufacturing
7699 Repair Shops & Related Services, nec
NAICS 561622 Locksmiths
NAICS 562991 Septic Tank & Related Services
NAICS 56179 Other Services to Buildings & Dwellings
NAICS 48839 Other Supporting Activities for Water Transportation
NAICS 45111 Sporting Goods Stores
NAICS 81131 Commercial & Industrial Machinery & Equipment Repair & Maintenance
NAICS 11521 Support Activities for Animal Production
NAICS 811212 Computer & Office Machine Repair & Maintenance
NAICS 811219 Other Electronic & Precision Equipment Repair & Maintenance
NAICS 811411 Home & Garden Equipment Repair & Maintenance
NAICS 811412 Appliance Repair & Maintenance
NAICS 81143 Footwear & Leather Goods Repair
NAICS 81149 Other Personal & Household Goods Repair & Maintenance
7812 Motion Picture & Video Tape Production
NAICS 51211 Motion Picture & Video Production
7819 Services Allied to Motion Picture Production
NAICS 512191 Teleproduction & Other Post-production Services
NAICS 56131 Employment Placement Agencies
NAICS 53222 Formal Wear & Costumes Rental
NAICS 53249 Other Commercial & Industrial Machinery & Equipment Rental & Leasing
NAICS 541214 Payroll Services
NAICS 71151 Independent Artists, Writers, & Performers
NAICS 334612 Prerecorded Compact Disc , Tape, & Record Manufacturing
NAICS 512199 Other Motion Picture & Video Industries
7822 Motion Picture & Video Tape Distribution
NAICS 42199 Other Miscellaneous Durable Goods Wholesalers
NAICS 51212 Motion Picture & Video Distribution
7829 Services Allied to Motion Picture Distribution
NAICS 512199 Other Motion Picture & Video Industries
NAICS 51212 Motion Picture & Video Distribution
7832 Motion Picture Theaters, Except Drive-ins.
NAICS 512131 Motion Picture Theaters, Except Drive-in
7833 Drive-in Motion Picture Theaters
NAICS 512132 Drive-in Motion Picture Theaters
7841 Video Tape Rental
NAICS 53223 Video Tapes & Disc Rental
7911 Dance Studios, Schools, & Halls
NAICS 71399 All Other Amusement & Recreation Industries
NAICS 61161 Fine Arts Schools
7922 Theatrical Producers & Miscellaneous Theatrical Services
NAICS 56131 Employment Placement Agencies
NAICS 71111 Theater Companies & Dinner Theaters
NAICS 71141 Agents & Managers for Artists, Athletes, Entertainers & Other Public Figures
NAICS 71112 Dance Companies
NAICS 71131 Promoters of Performing Arts, Sports, & Similar Events with Facilities
NAICS 71132 Promoters of Performing Arts, Sports, & Similar Events Without Facilities
NAICS 51229 Other Sound Recording Industries
NAICS 53249 Other Commercial & Industrial Machinery & Equipment Rental & Leasing
7929 Bands, Orchestras, Actors, & Other Entertainers & Entertainment Groups
NAICS 71113 Musical Groups & Artists
NAICS 71151 Independent Artists, Writers, & Performers

NAICS 71119 Other Performing Arts Companies
7933 Bowling Centers
NAICS 71395 Bowling Centers
7941 Professional Sports Clubs & Promoters
NAICS 711211 Sports Teams & Clubs
NAICS 71141 Agents & Managers for Artists, Athletes, Entertainers , & Other Public Figures
NAICS 71132 Promoters of Arts, Sports & Similar Events Without Facilities
NAICS 71131 Promoters of Arts, Sports, & Similar Events with Facilities
NAICS 711219 Other Spectator Sports
7948 Racing, Including Track Operations
NAICS 711212 Race Tracks
NAICS 711219 Other Spectator Sports
7991 Physical Fitness Facilities
NAICS 71394 Fitness & Recreational Sports Centers
7992 Public Golf Courses
NAICS 71391 Golf Courses & Country Clubs
7993 Coin Operated Amusement Devices
NAICS 71312 Amusement Arcades
NAICS 71329 Other Gambling Industries
NAICS 71399 All Other Amusement & Recreation Industries
7996 Amusement Parks
NAICS 71311 Amusement & Theme Parks
7997 Membership Sports & Recreation Clubs
NAICS 48122 Nonscheduled Speciality Air Transportation
NAICS 71391 Golf Courses & Country Clubs
NAICS 71394 Fitness & Recreational Sports Centers
NAICS 71399 All Other Amusement & Recreation Industries
7999 Amusement & Recreation Services, nec
NAICS 561599 All Other Travel Arrangement & Reservation Services
NAICS 48799 Scenic & Sightseeing Transportation, Other
NAICS 71119 Other Performing Arts Companies
NAICS 711219 Other Spectator Sports
NAICS 71392 Skiing Facilities
NAICS 71394 Fitness & Recreational Sports Centers
NAICS 71321 Casinos
NAICS 71329 Other Gambling Industries
NAICS 71219 Nature Parks & Other Similar Institutions
NAICS 61162 Sports & Recreation Instruction
NAICS 532292 Recreational Goods Rental
NAICS 48711 Scenic & Sightseeing Transportation, Land
NAICS 48721 Scenic & Sightseeing Transportation, Water
NAICS 71399 All Other Amusement & Recreation Industries
8011 Offices & Clinics of Doctors of Medicine
NAICS 621493 Freestanding Ambulatory Surgical & Emergency Centers
NAICS 621491 Hmo Medical Centers
NAICS 621112 Offices of Physicians, Mental Health Specialists
NAICS 621111 Offices of Physicians
8021 Offices & Clinics of Dentists
NAICS 62121 Offices of Dentists
8031 Offices & Clinics of Doctors of Osteopathy
NAICS 621111 Offices of Physicians
NAICS 621112 Offices of Physicians, Mental Health Specialists
8041 Offices & Clinics of Chiropractors
NAICS 62131 Offices of Chiropractors
8042 Offices & Clinics of Optometrists
NAICS 62132 Offices of Optometrists
8043 Offices & Clinics of Podiatrists
NAICS 621391 Offices of Podiatrists
8049 Offices & Clinics of Health Practitioners, nec
NAICS 62133 Offices of Mental Health Practitioners
NAICS 62134 Offices of Physical, Occupational, & Speech Therapists & Audiologists
NAICS 621399 Offices of All Other Miscellaneous Health Practitioners
8051 Skilled Nursing Care Facilities
NAICS 623311 Continuing Care Retirement Communities
NAICS 62311 Nursing Care Facilities
8052 Intermediate Care Facilities
NAICS 623311 Continuing Care Retirement Communities
NAICS 62321 Residential Mental Retardation Facilities
NAICS 62311 Nursing Care Facilities
8059 Nursing & Personal Care Facilities, nec
NAICS 623311 Continuing Care Retirement Communities
NAICS 62311 Nursing Care Facilities
8062 General Medical & Surgical Hospitals
NAICS 62211 General Medical & Surgical Hospitals
8063 Psychiatric Hospitals
NAICS 62221 Psychiatric & Substance Abuse Hospitals
8069 Specialty Hospitals, Except Psychiatric
NAICS 62211 General Medical & Surgical Hospitals
NAICS 62221 Psychiatric & Substance Abuse Hospitals
NAICS 62231 Specialty Hospitals
8071 Medical Laboratories
NAICS 621512 Diagnostic Imaging Centers
NAICS 621511 Medical Laboratories
8072 Dental Laboratories
NAICS 339116 Dental Laboratories
8082 Home Health Care Services
NAICS 62161 Home Health Care Services
8092 Kidney Dialysis Centers
NAICS 621492 Kidney Dialysis Centers
8093 Specialty Outpatient Facilities, nec
NAICS 62141 Family Planning Centers
NAICS 62142 Outpatient Mental Health & Substance Abuse Centers
NAICS 621498 All Other Outpatient Care Facilities
8099 Health & Allied Services, nec
NAICS 621991 Blood & Organ Banks
NAICS 54143 Graphic Design Services
NAICS 541922 Commercial Photography
NAICS 62141 Family Planning Centers
NAICS 621999 All Other Miscellaneous Ambulatory Health Care Services
8111 Legal Services
NAICS 54111 Offices of Lawyers
8211 Elementary & Secondary Schools
NAICS 61111 Elementary & Secondary Schools
8221 Colleges, Universities, & Professional Schools
NAICS 61131 Colleges, Universities & Professional Schools
8222 Junior Colleges & Technical Institutes
NAICS 61121 Junior Colleges
8231 Libraries
NAICS 51412 Libraries & Archives
8243 Data Processing Schools
NAICS 611519 Other Technical & Trade Schools
NAICS 61142 Computer Training
8244 Business & Secretarial Schools
NAICS 61141 Business & Secretarial Schools
8249 Vocational Schools, nec
NAICS 611513 Apprenticeship Training
NAICS 611512 Flight Training
NAICS 611519 Other Technical & Trade Schools

8299 Schools & Educational Services, nec
NAICS 48122 Nonscheduled speciality Air Transportation
NAICS 611512 Flight Training
NAICS 611692 Automobile Driving Schools
NAICS 61171 Educational Support Services
NAICS 611691 Exam Preparation & Tutoring
NAICS 61161 Fine Arts Schools
NAICS 61163 Language Schools
NAICS 61143 Professional & Management Development Training Schools
NAICS 611699 All Other Miscellaneous Schools & Instruction
8322 Individual & Family Social Services
NAICS 62411 Child & Youth Services
NAICS 62421 Community Food Services
NAICS 624229 Other Community Housing Services
NAICS 62423 Emergency & Other Relief Services
NAICS 62412 Services for the Elderly & Persons with Disabilities
NAICS 624221 Temporary Shelters
NAICS 92215 Parole Offices & Probation Offices
NAICS 62419 Other Individual & Family Services
8331 Job Training & Vocational Rehabilitation Services
NAICS 62431 Vocational Rehabilitation Services
8351 Child Day Care Services
NAICS 62441 Child Day Care Services
8361 Residential Care
NAICS 623312 Homes for the Elderly
NAICS 62322 Residential Mental Health & Substance Abuse Facilities
NAICS 62399 Other Residential Care Facilities
8399 Social Services, nec
NAICS 813212 Voluntary Health Organizations
NAICS 813219 Other Grantmaking & Giving Services
NAICS 813311 Human Rights Organizations
NAICS 813312 Environment, Conservation & Wildlife Organizations
NAICS 813319 Other Social Advocacy Organizations
8412 Museums & Art Galleries
NAICS 71211 Museums
NAICS 71212 Historical Sites
8422 Arboreta & Botanical or Zoological Gardens
NAICS 71213 Zoos & Botanical Gardens
NAICS 71219 Nature Parks & Other Similar Institutions
8611 Business Associations
NAICS 81391 Business Associations
8621 Professional Membership Organizations
NAICS 81392 Professional Organizations
8631 Labor Unions & Similar Labor Organizations
NAICS 81393 Labor Unions & Similar Labor Organizations
8641 Civic, Social, & Fraternal Associations
NAICS 81341 Civic & Social Organizations
NAICS 81399 Other Similar Organizations
NAICS 92115 American Indian & Alaska Native Tribal Governments
NAICS 62411 Child & Youth Services
8651 Political Organizations
NAICS 81394 Political Organizations
8661 Religious Organizations
NAICS 81311 Religious Organizations
8699 Membership Organizations, nec
NAICS 81341 Civic & Social Organizations
NAICS 81391 Business Associations
NAICS 813312 Environment, Conservation, & Wildlife Organizations
NAICS 561599 All Other Travel Arrangement & Reservation Services
NAICS 81399 Other Similar Organizations
8711 Engineering Services
NAICS 54133 Engineering Services
8712 Architectural Services
NAICS 54131 Architectural Services
8713 Surveying Services
NAICS 48122 Nonscheduled Air Speciality Transportation
NAICS 54136 Geophysical Surveying & Mapping Services
NAICS 54137 Surveying & Mapping Services
8721 Accounting, Auditing, & Bookkeeping Services
NAICS 541211 Offices of Certified Public Accountants
NAICS 541214 Payroll Services
NAICS 541219 Other Accounting Services
8731 Commercial Physical & Biological Research
NAICS 54171 Research & Development in the Physical Sciences & Engineering Sciences
NAICS 54172 Research & Development in the Life Sciences
8732 Commercial Economic, Sociological, & Educational Research
NAICS 54173 Research & Development in the Social Sciences & Humanities
NAICS 54191 Marketing Research & Public Opinion Polling
8733 Noncommercial Research Organizations
NAICS 54171 Research & Development in the Physical Sciences & Engineering Sciences
NAICS 54172 Research & Development in the Life Sciences
NAICS 54173 Research & Development in the Social Sciences & Humanities
8734 Testing Laboratories
NAICS 54194 Veterinary Services
NAICS 54138 Testing Laboratories
8741 Management Services
NAICS 56111 Office Administrative Services
NAICS 23 Included in Construction Sector by Type of Construction
8742 Management Consulting Services
NAICS 541611 Administrative Management & General Management Consulting Services
NAICS 541612 Human Resources & Executive Search Services
NAICS 541613 Marketing Consulting Services
NAICS 541614 Process, Physical, Distribution & Logistics Consulting Services
8743 Public Relations Services
NAICS 54182 Public Relations Agencies
8744 Facilities Support Management Services
NAICS 56121 Facilities Support Services
8748 Business Consulting Services, nec
NAICS 61171 Educational Support Services
NAICS 541618 Other Management Consulting Services
NAICS 54169 Other Scientific & Technical Consulting Services
8811 Private Households
NAICS 81411 Private Households
8999 Services, nec
NAICS 71151 Independent Artists, Writers, & Performers
NAICS 51221 Record Production
NAICS 54169 Other Scientific & Technical Consulting Services
NAICS 51223 Music Publishers
NAICS 541612 Human Resources & Executive Search Consulting Services
NAICS 514199 All Other Information Services

NAICS 54162 Environmental Consulting Services

PUBLIC ADMINISTRATION

9111 Executive Offices
NAICS 92111 Executive Offices
9121 Legislative Bodies
NAICS 92112 Legislative Bodies
9131 Executive & Legislative Offices, Combined
NAICS 92114 Executive & Legislative Offices, Combined
9199 General Government, nec
NAICS 92119 All Other General Government
9211 Courts
NAICS 92211 Courts
9221 Police Protection
NAICS 92212 Police Protection
9222 Legal Counsel & Prosecution
NAICS 92213 Legal Counsel & Prosecution
9223 Correctional Institutions
NAICS 92214 Correctional Institutions
9224 Fire Protection
NAICS 92216 Fire Protection
9229 Public Order & Safety, nec
NAICS 92219 All Other Justice, Public Order, & Safety
9311 Public Finance, Taxation, & Monetary Policy
NAICS 92113 Public Finance
9411 Administration of Educational Programs
NAICS 92311 Administration of Education Programs
9431 Administration of Public Health Programs
NAICS 92312 Administration of Public Health Programs
9441 Administration of Social, Human Resource & Income Maintenance Programs
NAICS 92313 Administration of Social, Human Resource & Income Maintenance Programs
9451 Administration of Veteran's Affairs, Except Health Insurance
NAICS 92314 Administration of Veteran's Affairs
9511 Air & Water Resource & Solid Waste Management
NAICS 92411 Air & Water Resource & Solid Waste Management
9512 Land, Mineral, Wildlife, & Forest Conservation
NAICS 92412 Land, Mineral, Wildlife, & Forest Conservation
9531 Administration of Housing Programs
NAICS 92511 Administration of Housing Programs
9532 Administration of Urban Planning & Community & Rural Development
NAICS 92512 Administration of Urban Planning & Community & Rural Development
9611 Administration of General Economic Programs
NAICS 92611 Administration of General Economic Programs
9621 Regulations & Administration of Transportation Programs
NAICS 488111 Air Traffic Control
NAICS 92612 Regulation & Administration of Transportation Programs
9631 Regulation & Administration of Communications, Electric, Gas, & Other Utilities
NAICS 92613 Regulation & Administration of Communications, Electric, Gas, & Other Utilities
9641 Regulation of Agricultural Marketing & Commodity
NAICS 92614 Regulation of Agricultural Marketing & Commodity
9651 Regulation, Licensing, & Inspection of Miscellaneous Commercial Sectors
NAICS 92615 Regulation, Licensing, & Inspection of Miscellaneous Commercial Sectors
9661 Space Research & Technology
NAICS 92711 Space Research & Technology
9711 National Security
NAICS 92811 National Security
9721 International Affairs
NAICS 92812 International Affairs
9999 Nonclassifiable Establishments
NAICS 99999 Unclassified Establishments

NAICS TO SIC CONVERSION GUIDE

AGRICULTURE, FORESTRY, FISHING, & HUNTING

11111 Soybean Farming
SIC 0116 Soybeans
11112 Oilseed Farming
SIC 0119 Cash Grains, nec
11113 Dry Pea & Bean Farming
SIC 0119 Cash Grains, nec
11114 Wheat Farming
SIC 0111 Wheat
11115 Corn Farming
SIC 0115 Corn
SIC 0119 Cash Grains, nec
11116 Rice Farming
SIC 0112 Rice
111191 Oilseed & Grain Combination Farming
SIC 0119 Cash Grains, nec
111199 All Other Grain Farming
SIC 0119 Cash Grains, nec
111211 Potato Farming
SIC 0134 Irish Potatoes
111219 Other Vegetable & Melon Farming
SIC 0161 Vegetables & Melons
SIC 0139 Field Crops Except Cash Grains
11131 Orange Groves
SIC 0174 Citrus Fruits
11132 Citrus Groves
SIC 0174 Citrus Fruits
111331 Apple Orchards
SIC 0175 Deciduous Tree Fruits
111332 Grape Vineyards
SIC 0172 Grapes
111333 Strawberry Farming
SIC 0171 Berry Crops
111334 Berry Farming
SIC 0171 Berry Crops
111335 Tree Nut Farming
SIC 0173 Tree Nuts
111336 Fruit & Tree Nut Combination Farming
SIC 0179 Fruits & Tree Nuts, nec
111339 Other Noncitrus Fruit Farming
SIC 0175 Deciduous Tree Fruits
SIC 0179 Fruit & Tree Nuts, nec
111411 Mushroom Production
SIC 0182 Food Crops Grown Under Cover
111419 Other Food Crops Grown Under Cover
SIC 0182 Food Crops Grown Under Cover
111421 Nursery & Tree Production
SIC 0181 Ornamental Floriculture & Nursery Products
SIC 0811 Timber Tracts
111422 Floriculture Production
SIC 0181 Ornamental Floriculture & Nursery Products
11191 Tobacco Farming
SIC 0132 Tobacco
11192 Cotton Farming
SIC 0131 Cotton
11193 Sugarcane Farming
SIC 0133 Sugarcane & Sugar Beets
11194 Hay Farming
SIC 0139 Field Crops, Except Cash Grains, nec
111991 Sugar Beet Farming
SIC 0133 Sugarcane & Sugar Beets
111992 Peanut Farming
SIC 0139 Field Crops, Except Cash Grains, nec
111998 All Other Miscellaneous Crop Farming
SIC 0139 Field Crops, Except Cash Grains, nec
SIC 0191 General Farms, Primarily Crop
SIC 0831 Forest Products
SIC 0919 Miscellaneous Marine Products
SIC 2099 Food Preparations, nec
112111 Beef Cattle Ranching & Farming
SIC 0212 Beef Cattle, Except Feedlots
SIC 0241 Dairy Farms
112112 Cattle Feedlots
SIC 0211 Beef Cattle Feedlots
11212 Dairy Cattle & Milk Production
SIC 0241 Dairy Farms
11213 Dual Purpose Cattle Ranching & Farming
No SIC equivalent
11221 Hog & Pig Farming
SIC 0213 Hogs
11231 Chicken Egg Production
SIC 0252 Chicken Eggs
11232 Broilers & Other Meat Type Chicken Production
SIC 0251 Broiler, Fryers, & Roaster Chickens
11233 Turkey Production
SIC 0253 Turkey & Turkey Eggs
11234 Poultry Hatcheries
SIC 0254 Poultry Hatcheries
11239 Other Poultry Production
SIC 0259 Poultry & Eggs, nec
11241 Sheep Farming
SIC 0214 Sheep & Goats
11242 Goat Farming
SIC 0214 Sheep & Goats
112511 Finfish Farming & Fish Hatcheries
SIC 0273 Animal Aquaculture
SIC 0921 Fish Hatcheries & Preserves
112512 Shellfish Farming
SIC 0273 Animal Aquaculture
SIC 0921 Fish Hatcheries & Preserves
112519 Other Animal Aquaculture
SIC 0273 Animal Aquaculture
11291 Apiculture
SIC 0279 Animal Specialties, nec
11292 Horse & Other Equine Production
SIC 0272 Horses & Other Equines
11293 Fur-Bearing Animal & Rabbit Production
SIC 0271 Fur-Bearing Animals & Rabbits
11299 All Other Animal Production
SIC 0219 General Livestock, Except Dairy & Poultry
SIC 0279 Animal Specialties, nec
SIC 0291 General Farms, Primarily Livestock & Animal Specialties;
11311 Timber Tract Operations
SIC 0811 Timber Tracts
11321 Forest Nurseries & Gathering of Forest Products
SIC 0831 Forest Nurseries & Gathering of Forest Products
11331 Logging
SIC 2411 Logging

114111 Finfish Fishing
SIC 0912 Finfish
114112 Shellfish Fishing
SIC 0913 Shellfish
114119 Other Marine Fishing
SIC 0919 Miscellaneous Marine Products
11421 Hunting & Trapping
SIC 0971 Hunting & Trapping, & Game Propagation;
115111 Cotton Ginning
SIC 0724 Cotton Ginning
115112 Soil Preparation, Planting, & Cultivating
SIC 0711 Soil Preparation Services
SIC 0721 Crop Planting, Cultivating, & Protecting
115113 Crop Harvesting, Primarily by Machine
SIC 0722 Crop Harvesting, Primarily by Machine
115114 Other Postharvest Crop Activities
SIC 0723 Crop Preparation Services For Market, Except Cotton Ginning
115115 Farm Labor Contractors & Crew Leaders
SIC 0761 Farm Labor Contractors & Crew Leaders
115116 Farm Management Services
SIC 0762 Farm Management Services
11521 Support Activities for Animal Production
SIC 0751 Livestock Services, Except Veterinary
SIC 0752 Animal Specialty Services, Except Veterinary
SIC 7699 Repair Services, nec
11531 Support Activities for Forestry
SIC 0851 Forestry Services

MINING

211111 Crude Petroleum & Natural Gas Extraction
SIC 1311 Crude Petroleum & Natural Gas
211112 Natural Gas Liquid Extraction
SIC 1321 Natural Gas Liquids
212111 Bituminous Coal & Lignite Surface Mining
SIC 1221 Bituminous Coal & Lignite Surface Mining
212112 Bituminous Coal Underground Mining
SIC 1222 Bituminous Coal Underground Mining
212113 Anthracite Mining
SIC 1231 Anthracite Mining
21221 Iron Ore Mining
SIC 1011 Iron Ores
212221 Gold Ore Mining
SIC 1041 Gold Ores
212222 Silver Ore Mining
SIC 1044 Silver Ores
212231 Lead Ore & Zinc Ore Mining
SIC 1031 Lead & Zinc Ores
212234 Copper Ore & Nickel Ore Mining
SIC 1021 Copper Ores
212291 Uranium-Radium-Vanadium Ore Mining
SIC 1094 Uranium-Radium-Vanadium Ores
212299 All Other Metal Ore Mining
SIC 1061 Ferroalloy Ores, Except Vanadium
SIC 1099 Miscellaneous Metal Ores, nec
212311 Dimension Stone Mining & Quarrying
SIC 1411 Dimension Stone
212312 Crushed & Broken Limestone Mining & Quarrying
SIC 1422 Crushed & Broken Limestone
212313 Crushed & Broken Granite Mining & Quarrying
SIC 1423 Crushed & Broken Granite
212319 Other Crushed & Broken Stone Mining & Quarrying
SIC 1429 Crushed & Broken Stone, nec
SIC 1499 Miscellaneous Nonmetallic Minerals, Except Fuels
212321 Construction Sand & Gravel Mining
SIC 1442 Construction Sand & Gravel
212322 Industrial Sand Mining
SIC 1446 Industrial Sand
212324 Kaolin & Ball Clay Mining
SIC 1455 Kaolin & Ball Clay
212325 Clay & Ceramic & Refractory Minerals Mining
SIC 1459 Clay, Ceramic, & Refractory Minerals, nec
212391 Potash, Soda, & Borate Mineral Mining
SIC 1474 Potash, Soda, & Borate Minerals
212392 Phosphate Rock Mining
SIC 1475 Phosphate Rock
212393 Other Chemical & Fertilizer Mineral Mining
SIC 1479 Chemical & Fertilizer Mineral Mining, nec
212399 All Other Nonmetallic Mineral Mining
SIC 1499 Miscellaneous Nonmetallic Minerals, Except Fuels
213111 Drilling Oil & Gas Wells
SIC 1381 Drilling Oil & Gas Wells
213112 Support Activities for Oil & Gas Operations
SIC 1382 Oil & Gas Field Exploration Services
SIC 1389 Oil & Gas Field Services, nec
213113 Other Gas & Field Support Activities
SIC 1389 Oil & Gas Field Services, nec
213114 Support Activities for Coal Mining
SIC 1241 Coal Mining Services
213115 Support Activities for Metal Mining
SIC 1081 Metal Mining Services
213116 Support Activities for Nonmetallic Minerals, Except Fuels
SIC 1481 Nonmetallic Minerals Services, Except Fuels

UTILITIES

221111 Hydroelectric Power Generation
SIC 4911 Electric Services
SIC 4931 Electric & Other Services Combined
SIC 4939 Combination Utilities, nec
221112 Fossil Fuel Electric Power Generation
SIC 4911 Electric Services
SIC 4931 Electric & Other Services Combined
SIC 4939 Combination Utilities, nec
221113 Nuclear Electric Power Generation
SIC 4911 Electric Services
SIC 4931 Electric & Other Services Combined
SIC 4939 Combination Utilities, nec
221119 Other Electric Power Generation
SIC 4911 Electric Services
SIC 4931 Electric & Other Services Combined
SIC 4939 Combination Utilities, nec
221121 Electric Bulk Power Transmission & Control
SIC 4911 Electric Services
SIC 4931 Electric & Other Services Combined
SIC 4939 Combination Utilities, NEC
221122 Electric Power Distribution
SIC 4911 Electric Services
SIC 4931 Electric & Other Services Combined
SIC 4939 Combination Utilities, nec
22121 Natural Gas Distribution
SIC 4923 Natural Gas Transmission & Distribution
SIC 4924 Natural Gas Distribution

SIC 4925 Mixed, Manufactured, or Liquefied Petroleum Gas Production and/or Distribution
SIC 4931 Electronic & Other Services Combined
SIC 4932 Gas & Other Services Combined
SIC 4939 Combination Utilities, nec
22131 Water Supply & Irrigation Systems
SIC 4941 Water Supply
SIC 4971 Irrigation Systems
22132 Sewage Treatment Facilities
SIC 4952 Sewerage Systems
22133 Steam & Air-Conditioning Supply
SIC 4961 Steam & Air-Conditioning Supply

CONSTRUCTION

23311 Land Subdivision & Land Development
SIC 6552 Land Subdividers & Developers, Except Cemeteries
23321 Single Family Housing Construction
SIC 1521 General contractors-Single-Family Houses
SIC 1531 Operative Builders
23322 Multifamily Housing Construction
SIC 1522 General Contractors-Residential Building, Other Than Single-Family
SIC 1531 Operative Builders
23331 Manufacturing & Industrial Building Construction
SIC 1531 Operative Builders
SIC 1541 General Contractors-Industrial Buildings & Warehouses
23332 Commercial & Institutional Building Construction
SIC 1522 General Contractors-Residential Building Other than Single-Family
SIC 1531 Operative Builders
SIC 1541 General Contractors-Industrial Buildings & Warehouses
SIC 1542 General Contractor-Nonresidential Buildings, Other than Industrial Buildings & Warehouses
23411 Highway & Street Construction
SIC 1611 Highway & Street Construction, Except Elevated Highways
23412 Bridge & Tunnel Construction
SIC 1622 Bridge, Tunnel, & Elevated Highway Construction
2349 Other Heavy Construction
23491 Water, Sewer, & Pipeline Construction
SIC 1623 Water, Sewer, Pipeline, & Communications & Power Line Construction
23492 Power & Communication Transmission Line Construction
SIC 1623 Water, Sewer, Pipelines, & Communications & Power Line Construction
23493 Industrial Nonbuilding Structure Construction
SIC 1629 Heavy Construction, nec
23499 All Other Heavy Construction
SIC 1629 Heavy Construction, nec
SIC 7353 Construction Equipment Rental & Leasing
23511 Plumbing, Heating & Air-Conditioning Contractors
SIC 1711 Plumbing, Heating & Air-Conditioning
23521 Painting & Wall Covering Contractors
SIC 1721 Painting & Paper Hanging
SIC 1799 Special Trade Contractors, nec
23531 Electrical Contractors
SIC 1731 Electrical Work
23541 Masonry & Stone Contractors
SIC 1741 Masonry, Stone Setting & Other Stone Work
23542 Drywall, Plastering, Acoustical & Insulation Contractors
SIC 1742 Plastering, Drywall, Acoustical, & Insulation Work
SIC 1743 Terrazzo, Tile, Marble & Mosaic work
SIC 1771 Concrete Work
23543 Tile, Marble, Terrazzo & Mosaic Contractors
SIC 1743 Terrazzo, Tile, Marble, & Mosaic Work
23551 Carpentry Contractors
SIC 1751 Carpentry Work
23552 Floor Laying & Other Floor Contractors
SIC 1752 Floor Laying & Other Floor Work, nec
23561 Roofing, Siding &,Sheet Metal Contractors
SIC 1761 Roofing, Siding, & Sheet Metal Work
23571 Concrete Contractors
SIC 1771 Concrete Work
23581 Water Well Drilling Contractors
SIC 1781 Water Well Drilling
23591 Structural Steel Erection Contractors
SIC 1791 Structural Steel Erection
23592 Glass & Glazing Contractors
SIC 1793 Glass & Glazing Work
SIC 1799 Specialty Trade Contractors, nec
23593 Excavation Contractors
SIC 1794 Excavation Work
23594 Wrecking & Demolition Contractors
SIC 1795 Wrecking & Demolition Work
23595 Building Equipment & Other Machinery Installation Contractors
SIC 1796 Installation of Erection of Building Equipment, nec
23599 All Other Special Trade Contractors
SIC 1799 Special Trade Contractors, nec

FOOD MANUFACTURING

311111 Dog & Cat Food Manufacturing
SIC 2047 Dog & Cat Food
311119 Other Animal Food Manufacturing
SIC 2048 Prepared Feeds & Feed Ingredients for Animals & Fowls, Except Dogs & Cats
311211 Flour Milling
SIC 2034 Dehydrated Fruits, Vegetables & Soup Mixes
SIC 2041 Flour & Other Grain Mill Products
311212 Rice Milling
SIC 2044 Rice Milling
311213 Malt Manufacturing
SIC 2083 Malt
311221 Wet Corn Milling
SIC 2046 Wet Corn Milling
311222 Soybean Processing
SIC 2075 Soybean Oil Mills
SIC 2079 Shortening, Table Oils, Margarine, & Other Edible Fats & Oils, nec
311223 Other Oilseed Processing
SIC 2074 Cottonseed Oil Mills
SIC 2079 Shortening, Table Oils, Margarine & Other Edible Fats & Oils, nec
SIC 2076 Vegetable Oil Mills, Except Corn, Cottonseed, & Soybean
311225 Edible Fats & Oils Manufacturing
SIC 2077 Animal & Marine Fats & Oil, nec
SIC 2074 Cottonseed Oil Mills
SIC 2075 Soybean Oil Mills

SIC 2076 Vegetable Oil Mills, Except Corn, Cottonseed, & Soybean
SIC 2079 Shortening, Table Oils, Margarine, & Other Edible Fats & Oils, nec
31123 Breakfast Cereal Manufacturing
SIC 2043 Cereal Breakfast Foods
311311 Sugarcane Mills
SIC 2061 Cane Sugar, Except Refining
311312 Cane Sugar Refining
SIC 2062 Cane Sugar Refining
311313 Beet Sugar Manufacturing
SIC 2063 Beet Sugar
31132 Chocolate & Confectionery Manufacturing from Cacao Beans
SIC 2066 Chocolate & Cocoa Products
31133 Confectionery Manufacturing from Purchased Chocolate
SIC 2064 Candy & Other Confectionery Products
31134 Non-Chocolate Confectionery Manufacturing
SIC 2064 Candy & Other Confectionery Products
SIC 2067 Chewing Gum
SIC 2099 Food Preparations, nec
311411 Frozen Fruit, Juice & Vegetable Processing
SIC 2037 Frozen Fruits, Fruit Juices, & Vegetables
311412 Frozen Specialty Food Manufacturing
SIC 2038 Frozen Specialties, NEC
311421 Fruit & Vegetable Canning
SIC 2033 Canned Fruits, Vegetables, Preserves, Jams, & Jellies
SIC 2035 Pickled Fruits & Vegetables, Vegetable Sauces, & Seasonings & Salad Dressings
311422 Specialty Canning
SIC 2032 Canned Specialties
311423 Dried & Dehydrated Food Manufacturing
SIC 2034 Dried & Dehydrated Fruits, Vegetables & Soup Mixes
SIC 2099 Food Preparation, nec
311511 Fluid Milk Manufacturing
SIC 2026 Fluid Milk
311512 Creamery Butter Manufacturing
SIC 2021 Creamery Butter
311513 Cheese Manufacturing
SIC 2022 Natural, Processed, & Imitation Cheese
311514 Dry, Condensed, & Evaporated Milk Manufacturing
SIC 2023 Dry, Condensed & Evaporated Dairy Products
31152 Ice Cream & Frozen Dessert Manufacturing
SIC 2024 Ice Cream & Frozen Desserts
311611 Animal Slaughtering
SIC 0751 Livestock Services, Except Veterinary
SIC 2011 Meat Packing Plants
SIC 2048 Prepared Feeds & Feed Ingredients for Animals & Fowls, Except Dogs & Cats
311612 Meat Processed from Carcasses
SIC 2013 Sausages & Other Prepared Meats
SIC 5147 Meat & Meat Products
311613 Rendering & Meat By-product Processing
SIC 2077 Animal & Marine Fats & Oils
311615 Poultry Processing
SIC 2015 Poultry Slaughtering & Processing
311711 Seafood Canning
SIC 2077 Animal & Marine Fats & Oils
SIC 2091 Canned & Cured Fish & Seafood
311712 Fresh & Frozen Seafood Processing
SIC 2077 Animal & Marine Fats & Oils
SIC 2092 Prepared Fresh or Frozen Fish & Seafood
311811 Retail Bakeries
SIC 5461 Retail Bakeries
311812 Commercial Bakeries
SIC 2051 Bread & Other Bakery Products, Except Cookies & Crackers
SIC 2052 Cookies & Crackers
311813 Frozen Bakery Product Manufacturing
SIC 2053 Frozen Bakery Products, Except Bread
311821 Cookie & Cracker Manufacturing
SIC 2052 Cookies & Crackers
311822 Flour Mixes & Dough Manufacturing from Purchased Flour
SIC 2045 Prepared Flour Mixes & Doughs
311823 Pasta Manufacturing
SIC 2098 Macaroni, Spaghetti, Vermicelli & Noodles
31183 Tortilla Manufacturing
SIC 2099 Food Preparations, nec
311911 Roasted Nuts & Peanut Butter Manufacturing
SIC 2068 Salted & Roasted Nuts & Seeds
SIC 2099 Food Preparations, nec
311919 Other Snack Food Manufacturing
SIC 2052 Cookies & Crackers
SIC 2096 Potato Chips, Corn Chips, & Similar Snacks
31192 Coffee & Tea Manufacturing
SIC 2043 Cereal Breakfast Foods
SIC 2095 Roasted Coffee
SIC 2099 Food Preparations, nec
31193 Flavoring Syrup & Concentrate Manufacturing
SIC 2087 Flavoring Extracts & Flavoring Syrups
311941 Mayonnaise, Dressing & Other Prepared Sauce Manufacturing
SIC 2035 Pickled Fruits & Vegetables, Vegetable Seasonings, & Sauces & Salad Dressings
SIC 2099 Food Preparations, nec
311942 Spice & Extract Manufacturing
SIC 2087 Flavoring Extracts & Flavoring Syrups
SIC 2095 Roasted Coffee
SIC 2099 Food Preparations, nec
SIC 2899 Chemical Preparations, nec
311991 Perishable Prepared Food Manufacturing
SIC 2099 Food Preparations, nec
311999 All Other Miscellaneous Food Manufacturing
SIC 2015 Poultry Slaughtering & Processing
SIC 2032 Canned Specialties
SIC 2087 Flavoring Extracts & Flavoring Syrups
SIC 2099 Food Preparations, nec

BEVERAGE & TOBACCO PRODUCT MANUFACTURING

312111 Soft Drink Manufacturing
SIC 2086 Bottled & Canned Soft Drinks & Carbonated Water
312112 Bottled Water Manufacturing
SIC 2086 Bottled & Canned Soft Drinks & Carbonated Water
312113 Ice Manufacturing
SIC 2097 Manufactured Ice
31212 Breweries
SIC 2082 Malt Beverages
31213 Wineries
SIC 2084 Wines, Brandy, & Brandy Spirits
31214 Distilleries
SIC 2085 Distilled & Blended Liquors

31221 Tobacco Stemming & Redrying
SIC 2141 Tobacco Stemming & Redrying
312221 Cigarette Manufacturing
SIC 2111 Cigarettes
312229 Other Tobacco Product Manufacturing
SIC 2121 Cigars
SIC 2131 Chewing & Smoking Tobacco & Snuff
SIC 2141 Tobacco Stemming & Redrying

TEXTILE MILLS

313111 Yarn Spinning Mills
SIC 2281 Yarn Spinning Mills
SIC 2299 Textile Goods, nec
313112 Yarn Texturing, Throwing & Twisting Mills
SIC 2282 Yarn Texturing, Throwing, Winding Mills
313113 Thread Mills
SIC 2284 Thread Mills
SIC 2299 Textile Goods, NEC
31321 Broadwoven Fabric Mills
SIC 2211 Broadwoven Fabric Mills, Cotton
SIC 2221 Broadwoven Fabric Mills, Manmade Fiber & Silk
SIC 2231 Broadwoven Fabric Mills, Wool
SIC 2299 Textile Goods, nec
313221 Narrow Fabric Mills
SIC 2241 Narrow Fabric & Other Smallware Mills: Cotton, Wool, Silk & Manmade Fiber
SIC 2299 Textile Goods, nec
313222 Schiffli Machine Embroidery
SIC 2397 Schiffli Machine Embroideries
31323 Nonwoven Fabric Mills
SIC 2297 Nonwoven Fabrics
SIC 2299 Textile Goods, nec
313241 Weft Knit Fabric Mills
SIC 2257 Weft Knit Fabric Mills
SIC 2259 Knitting Mills nec
313249 Other Knit Fabric & Lace Mills
SIC 2258 Lace & Warp Knit Fabric Mills
SIC 2259 Knitting Mills nec
313311 Broadwoven Fabric Finishing Mills
SIC 2231 Broadwoven Fabric Mills, Wool
SIC 2261 Finishers of Broadwoven Fabrics of Cotton
SIC 2262 Finishers of Broadwoven Fabrics of Manmade Fiber & Silk
SIC 2269 Finishers of Textiles, nec
SIC 5131 Piece Goods & Notions
313312 Textile & Fabric Finishing Mills
SIC 2231 Broadwoven Fabric Mills, Wool
SIC 2257 Weft Knit Fabric Mills
SIC 2258 Lace & Warp Knit Fabric Mills
SIC 2269 Finishers of Textiles, nec
SIC 2282 Yarn Texturizing, Throwing, Twisting, & Winding Mills
SIC 2284 Thread Mills
SIC 2299 Textile Goods, nec
SIC 5131 Piece Goods & Notions
31332 Fabric Coating Mills
SIC 2295 Coated Fabrics, Not Rubberized
SIC 3069 Fabricated Rubber Products, nec

TEXTILE PRODUCT MILLS

31411 Carpet & Rug Mills
SIC 2273 Carpets & Rugs
314121 Curtain & Drapery Mills
SIC 2391 Curtains & Draperies
SIC 5714 Drapery, Curtain, & Upholstery Stores
314129 Other Household Textile Product Mills
SIC 2392 Housefurnishings, Except Curtains & Draperies
314911 Textile Bag Mills
SIC 2392 Housefurnishings, Except Curtains & Draperies
SIC 2393 Textile Bags
314912 Canvas & Related Product Mills
SIC 2394 Canvas & Related Products
314991 Rope, Cordage & Twine Mills
SIC 2298 Cordage & Twine
314992 Tire Cord & Tire Fabric Mills
SIC 2296 Tire Cord & Fabrics
314999 All Other Miscellaneous Textile Product Mills
SIC 2299 Textile Goods, nec
SIC 2395 Pleating, Decorative & Novelty Stitching, & Tucking for the Trade
SIC 2396 Automotive Trimmings, Apparel Findings, & Related Products
SIC 2399 Fabricated Textile Products, nec

APPAREL MANUFACTURING

315111 Sheer Hosiery Mills
SIC 2251 Women's Full-Length & Knee-Length Hosiery, Except socks
SIC 2252 Hosiery, nec
315119 Other Hosiery & Sock Mills
SIC 2252 Hosiery, nec
315191 Outerwear Knitting Mills
SIC 2253 Knit Outerwear Mills
SIC 2259 Knitting Mills, nec
315192 Underwear & Nightwear Knitting Mills
SIC 2254 Knit Underwear & Nightwear Mills
SIC 2259 Knitting Mills, nec
315211 Men's & Boys' Cut & Sew Apparel Contractors
SIC 2311 Men's & Boys' Suits, Coats, & Overcoats
SIC 2321 Men's & Boys' Shirts, Except Work Shirts
SIC 2322 Men's & Boys' Underwear & Nightwear
SIC 2325 Men's & Boys' Trousers & Slacks
SIC 2326 Men's & Boys' Work Clothing
SIC 2329 Men's & Boys' Clothing, nec
SIC 2341 Women's, Misses', Children's, & Infants' Underwear & Nightwear
SIC 2361 Girls', Children's, & Infants' Dresses, Blouses & Shirts
SIC 2369 Girls', Children's, & Infants' Outerwear, nec
SIC 2384 Robes & Dressing Gowns
SIC 2385 Waterproof Outerwear
SIC 2389 Apparel & Accessories, nec
SIC 2395 Pleating, Decorative & Novelty Stitching, & Tucking for the Trade
315212 Women's & Girls' Cut & Sew Apparel Contractors
SIC 2331 Women's, Misses', & Juniors' Blouses & Shirts
SIC 2335 Women's, Misses' & Juniors' Dresses
SIC 2337 Women's, Misses', & Juniors' Suits, Skirts, & Coats
SIC 2339 Women's, Misses', & Juniors' Outerwear, nec

SIC 2341 Women's, Misses', Children's, & Infants' Underwear & Nightwear
SIC 2342 Brassieres, Girdles, & Allied Garments
SIC 2361 Girls', Children's, & Infants' Dresses, Blouses, & Shirts
SIC 2369 Girls', Children's, & Infants' Outerwear, nec
SIC 2384 Robes & Dressing Gowns
SIC 2385 Waterproof Outerwear
SIC 2389 Apparel & Accessories, nec
SIC 2395 Pleating, Decorative & Novelty Stitching, & Tucking for the Trade

315221 Men's & Boys' Cut & Sew Underwear & Nightwear Manufacturing
SIC 2322 Men's & Boys' Underwear & Nightwear
SIC 2341 Women's, Misses', Children's, & Infants' Underwear & Nightwear
SIC 2369 Girls', Children's, & Infants' Outerwear, nec
SIC 2384 Robes & Dressing Gowns

315222 Men's & Boys' Cut & Sew Suit, Coat & Overcoat Manufacturing
SIC 2311 Men's & Boys' Suits, Coats, & Overcoats
SIC 2369 Girls', Children's, & Infants' Outerwear, nec
SIC 2385 Waterproof Outerwear

315223 Men's & Boys' Cut & Sew Shirt Manufacturing
SIC 2321 Men's & Boys' Shirts, Except Work Shirts
SIC 2361 Girls', Children's, & Infants' Dresses, Blouses, & Shirts

315224 Men's & Boys' Cut & Sew Trouser, Slack & Jean Manufacturing
SIC 2325 Men's & Boys' Trousers & Slacks
SIC 2369 Girls', Children's, & Infants' Outerwear, NEC

315225 Men's & Boys' Cut & Sew Work Clothing Manufacturing
SIC 2326 Men's & Boys' Work Clothing

315228 Men's & Boys' Cut & Sew Other Outerwear Manufacturing
SIC 2329 Men's & Boys' Clothing, nec
SIC 2369 Girls', Children's, & Infants' Outerwear, nec
SIC 2385 Waterproof Outerwear

315231 Women's & Girls' Cut & Sew Lingerie, Loungewear & Nightwear Manufacturing
SIC 2341 Women's, Misses', Children's, & Infants' Underwear & Nightwear
SIC 2342 Brassieres, Girdles, & Allied Garments
SIC 2369 Girls', Children's, & Infants' Outerwear, nec
SIC 2384 Robes & Dressing Gowns
SIC 2389 Apparel & Accessories, NEC

315232 Women's & Girls' Cut & Sew Blouse & Shirt Manufacturing
SIC 2331 Women's, Misses', & Juniors' Blouses & Shirts
SIC 2361 Girls', Children's, & Infants' Dresses, Blouses & Shirts

315233 Women's & Girls' Cut & Sew Dress Manufacturing
SIC 2335 Women's, Misses', & Juniors' Dresses
SIC 2361 Girls', Children's, & Infants' Dresses, Blouses & Shirts

315234 Women's & Girls' Cut & Sew Suit, Coat, Tailored Jacket & Skirt Manufacturing
SIC 2337 Women's, Misses', & Juniors' Suits, Skirts, & Coats
SIC 2369 Girls', Children's, & Infants' Outerwear, nec
SIC 2385 Waterproof Outerwear

315238 Women's & Girls' Cut & Sew Other Outerwear Manufacturing
SIC 2339 Women's, Misses', & Juniors' Outerwear, nec
SIC 2369 Girls', Children's, & Infants' Outerwear, nec
SIC 2385 Waterproof Outerwear

315291 Infants' Cut & Sew Apparel Manufacturing
SIC 2341 Women's, Misses', Children's, & Infants' Underwear & Nightwear
SIC 2361 Girls', Children's, & Infants' Dresses, Blouses, & Shirts
SIC 2369 Girls', Children's, & Infants' Outerwear, nec
SIC 2385 Waterproof Outerwear

315292 Fur & Leather Apparel Manufacturing
SIC 2371 Fur Goods
SIC 2386 Leather & Sheep-lined Clothing

315299 All Other Cut & Sew Apparel Manufacturing
SIC 2329 Men's & Boys' Outerwear, nec
SIC 2339 Women's, Misses', & Juniors' Outerwear, nec
SIC 2389 Apparel & Accessories, nec

315991 Hat, Cap & Millinery Manufacturing
SIC 2353 Hats, Caps, & Millinery

315992 Glove & Mitten Manufacturing
SIC 2381 Dress & Work Gloves, Except Knit & All-Leather
SIC 3151 Leather Gloves & Mittens

315993 Men's & Boys' Neckwear Manufacturing
SIC 2323 Men's & Boys' Neckwear

315999 Other Apparel Accessories & Other Apparel Manufacturing
SIC 2339 Women's, Misses', & Juniors' Outerwear, nec
SIC 2385 Waterproof Outerwear
SIC 2387 Apparel Belts
SIC 2389 Apparel & Accessories, nec
SIC 2396 Automotive Trimmings, Apparel Findings, & Related Products
SIC 2399 Fabricated Textile Products, nec

LEATHER & ALLIED PRODUCT MANUFACTURING

31611 Leather & Hide Tanning & Finishing
SIC 3111 Leather Tanning & Finishing
SIC 3999 Manufacturing Industries, nec

316211 Rubber & Plastics Footwear Manufacturing
SIC 3021 Rubber & Plastics Footwear

316212 House Slipper Manufacturing
SIC 3142 House Slippers

316213 Men's Footwear Manufacturing
SIC 3143 Men's Footwear, Except Athletic

316214 Women's Footwear Manufacturing
SIC 3144 Women's Footwear, Except Athletic

316219 Other Footwear Manufacturing
SIC 3149 Footwear Except Rubber, NEC

316991 Luggage Manufacturing
SIC 3161 Luggage

316992 Women's Handbag & Purse Manufacturing
SIC 3171 Women's Handbags & Purses

316993 Personal Leather Good Manufacturing
SIC 3172 Personal Leather Goods, Except Women's Handbags & Purses

316999 All Other Leather Good Manufacturing
SIC 3131 Boot & Shoe Cut Stock & Findings
SIC 3199 Leather Goods, nec

WOOD PRODUCT MANUFACTURING

321113 Sawmills
SIC 2421 Sawmills & Planing Mills, General
SIC 2429 Special Product Sawmills, nec
321114 Wood Preservation
SIC 2491 Wood Preserving
321211 Hardwood Veneer & Plywood Manufacturing
SIC 2435 Hardwood Veneer & Plywood
321212 Softwood Veneer & Plywood Manufacturing
SIC 2436 Softwood Veneer & Plywood
321213 Engineered Wood Member Manufacturing
SIC 2439 Structural Wood Members, nec
321214 Truss Manufacturing
SIC 2439 Structural Wood Members, nec
321219 Reconstituted Wood Product Manufacturing
SIC 2493 Reconstituted Wood Products
321911 Wood Window & Door Manufacturing
SIC 2431 Millwork
321912 Hardwood Dimension Mills
SIC 2426 Hardwood Dimension & Flooring Mills
321913 Softwood Cut Stock, Resawing Lumber, & Planing
SIC 2421 Sawmills & Planing Mills, General
SIC 2429 Special Product Sawmills, nec
SIC 2439 Structural Wood Members, nec
321914 Other Millwork
SIC 2421 Sawmills & Planing Mills, General
SIC 2426 Hardwood Dimension & Flooring Mills
SIC 2431 Millwork
32192 Wood Container & Pallet Manufacturing
SIC 2441 Nailed & Lock Corner Wood Boxes & Shook
SIC 2448 Wood Pallets & Skids
SIC 2449 Wood Containers, NEC
SIC 2499 Wood Products, nec
321991 Manufactured Home Manufacturing
SIC 2451 Mobile Homes
321992 Prefabricated Wood Building Manufacturing
SIC 2452 Prefabricated Wood Buildings & Components
321999 All Other Miscellaneous Wood Product Manufacturing
SIC 2426 Hardwood Dimension & Flooring Mills
SIC 2499 Wood Products, nec
SIC 3131 Boot & Shoe Cut Stock & Findings
SIC 3999 Manufacturing Industries, nec
SIC 2421 Sawmills & Planing Mills, General
SIC 2429 Special Product Sawmills, nec

PAPER MANUFACTURING

32211 Pulp Mills
SIC 2611 Pulp Mills
322121 Paper Mills
SIC 2611 Pulp Mills
SIC 2621 Paper Mills
322122 Newsprint Mills
SIC 2621 Paper Mills
32213 Paperboard Mills
SIC 2611 Pulp Mills
SIC 2631 Paperboard Mills
322211 Corrugated & Solid Fiber Box Manufacturing
SIC 2653 Corrugated & Solid Fiber Boxes
322212 Folding Paperboard Box Manufacturing
SIC 2657 Folding Paperboard Boxes, Including Sanitary
322213 Setup Paperboard Box Manufacturing
SIC 2652 Setup Paperboard Boxes
322214 Fiber Can, Tube, Drum, & Similar Products Manufacturing
SIC 2655 Fiber Cans, Tubes, Drums, & Similar Products
322215 Non-Folding Sanitary Food Container Manufacturing
SIC 2656 Sanitary Food Containers, Except Folding
SIC 2679 Converted Paper & Paperboard Products, NEC
322221 Coated & Laminated Packaging Paper & Plastics Film Manufacturing
SIC 2671 Packaging Paper & Plastics Film, Coated & Laminated
322222 Coated & Laminated Paper Manufacturing
SIC 2672 Coated & Laminated Paper, nec
SIC 2679 Converted Paper & Paperboard Products, nec
322223 Plastics, Foil, & Coated Paper Bag Manufacturing
SIC 2673 Plastics, Foil, & Coated Paper Bags
322224 Uncoated Paper & Multiwall Bag Manufacturing
SIC 2674 Uncoated Paper & Multiwall Bags
322225 Laminated Aluminum Foil Manufacturing for Flexible Packaging Uses
SIC 3497 Metal Foil & Leaf
322231 Die-Cut Paper & Paperboard Office Supplies Manufacturing
SIC 2675 Die-Cut Paper & Paperboard & Cardboard
SIC 2679 Converted Paper & Paperboard Products, nec
322232 Envelope Manufacturing
SIC 2677 Envelopes
322233 Stationery, Tablet, & Related Product Manufacturing
SIC 2678 Stationery, Tablets, & Related Products
322291 Sanitary Paper Product Manufacturing
SIC 2676 Sanitary Paper Products
322292 Surface-Coated Paperboard Manufacturing
SIC 2675 Die-Cut Paper & Paperboard & Cardboard
322298 All Other Converted Paper Product Manufacturing
SIC 2675 Die-Cut Paper & Paperboard & Cardboard
SIC 2679 Converted Paper & Paperboard Products, NEC

PRINTING & RELATED SUPPORT ACTIVITIES

323110 Commercial Lithographic Printing
SIC 2752 Commercial Printing, Lithographic
SIC 2771 Greeting Cards
SIC 2782 Blankbooks, Loose-leaf Binders & Devices
SIC 3999 Manufacturing Industries, nec
323111 Commercial Gravure Printing
SIC 2754 Commercial Printing, Gravure
SIC 2771 Greeting Cards
SIC 2782 Blankbooks, Loose-leaf Binders & Devices
SIC 3999 Manufacturing Industries, nec
323112 Commercial Flexographic Printing
SIC 2759 Commercial Printing, NEC
SIC 2771 Greeting Cards
SIC 2782 Blankbooks, Loose-leaf Binders & Devices
SIC 3999 Manufacturing Industries, nec
323113 Commercial Screen Printing
SIC 2396 Automotive Trimmings, Apparel Findings, & Related Products
SIC 2759 Commercial Printing, nec
SIC 2771 Greeting Cards
SIC 2782 Blankbooks, Loose-leaf Binders & Devices
SIC 3999 Manufacturing Industries, nec

323114 Quick Printing
SIC 2752 Commercial Printing, Lithographic
SIC 2759 Commercial Printing, nec
323115 Digital Printing
SIC 2759 Commercial Printing, nec
323116 Manifold Business Form Printing
SIC 2761 Manifold Business Forms
323117 Book Printing
SIC 2732 Book Printing
323118 Blankbook, Loose-leaf Binder & Device Manufacturing
SIC 2782 Blankbooks, Loose-leaf Binders & Devices
323119 Other Commercial Printing
SIC 2759 Commercial Printing, nec
SIC 2771 Greeting Cards
SIC 2782 Blankbooks, Loose-leaf Binders & Devices
SIC 3999 Manufacturing Industries, nec
323121 Tradebinding & Related Work
SIC 2789 Bookbinding & Related Work
323122 Prepress Services
SIC 2791 Typesetting
SIC 2796 Platemaking & Related Services

PETROLEUM & COAL PRODUCTS MANUFACTURING

32411 Petroleum Refineries
SIC 2911 Petroleum Refining
324121 Asphalt Paving Mixture & Block Manufacturing
SIC 2951 Asphalt Paving Mixtures & Blocks
324122 Asphalt Shingle & Coating Materials Manufacturing
SIC 2952 Asphalt Felts & Coatings
324191 Petroleum Lubricating Oil & Grease Manufacturing
SIC 2992 Lubricating Oils & Greases
324199 All Other Petroleum & Coal Products Manufacturing
SIC 2999 Products of Petroleum & Coal, nec
SIC 3312 Blast Furnaces & Steel Mills

CHEMICAL MANUFACTURING

32511 Petrochemical Manufacturing
SIC 2865 Cyclic Organic Crudes & Intermediates, & Organic Dyes & Pigments
SIC 2869 Industrial Organic Chemicals, nec
32512 Industrial Gas Manufacturing
SIC 2813 Industrial Gases
SIC 2869 Industrial Organic Chemicals, nec
325131 Inorganic Dye & Pigment Manufacturing
SIC 2816 Inorganic Pigments
SIC 2819 Industrial Inorganic Chemicals, nec
325132 Organic Dye & Pigment Manufacturing
SIC 2865 Cyclic Organic Crudes & Intermediates, & Organic Dyes & Pigments
325181 Alkalies & Chlorine Manufacturing
SIC 2812 Alkalies & Chlorine
325182 Carbon Black Manufacturing
SIC 2816 Inorganic pigments
SIC 2895 Carbon Black
325188 All Other Basic Inorganic Chemical Manufacturing
SIC 2819 Industrial Inorganic Chemicals, nec
SIC 2869 Industrial Organic Chemicals, nec
325191 Gum & Wood Chemical Manufacturing
SIC 2861 Gum & Wood Chemicals
325192 Cyclic Crude & Intermediate Manufacturing
SIC 2865 Cyclic Organic Crudes & Intermediates & Organic Dyes & Pigments
325193 Ethyl Alcohol Manufacturing
SIC 2869 Industrial Organic Chemicals
325199 All Other Basic Organic Chemical Manufacturing
SIC 2869 Industrial Organic Chemicals, nec
SIC 2899 Chemical & Chemical Preparations, nec
325211 Plastics Material & Resin Manufacturing
SIC 2821 Plastics Materials, Synthetic & Resins, & Nonvulcanizable Elastomers
325212 Synthetic Rubber Manufacturing
SIC 2822 Synthetic Rubber
325221 Cellulosic Manmade Fiber Manufacturing
SIC 2823 Cellulosic Manmade Fibers
325222 Noncellulosic Organic Fiber Manufacturing
SIC 2824 Manmade Organic Fibers, Except Cellulosic
325311 Nitrogenous Fertilizer Manufacturing
SIC 2873 Nitrogenous Fertilizers
325312 Phosphatic Fertilizer Manufacturing
SIC 2874 Phosphatic Fertilizers
325314 Fertilizer Manufacturing
SIC 2875 Fertilizers, Mixing Only
32532 Pesticide & Other Agricultural Chemical Manufacturing
SIC 2879 Pesticides & Agricultural Chemicals, nec
325411 Medicinal & Botanical Manufacturing
SIC 2833 Medicinal Chemicals & Botanical Products
325412 Pharmaceutical Preparation Manufacturing
SIC 2834 Pharmaceutical Preparations
SIC 2835 In-Vitro & In-Vivo Diagnostic Substances
325413 In-Vitro Diagnostic Substance Manufacturing
SIC 2835 In-Vitro & In-Vivo Diagnostic Substances
325414 Biological Product Manufacturing
SIC 2836 Biological Products, Except Diagnostic Substance
32551 Paint & Coating Manufacturing
SIC 2851 Paints, Varnishes, Lacquers, Enamels & Allied Products
SIC 2899 Chemicals & Chemical Preparations, nec
32552 Adhesive & Sealant Manufacturing
SIC 2891 Adhesives & Sealants
325611 Soap & Other Detergent Manufacturing
SIC 2841 Soaps & Other Detergents, Except Specialty Cleaners
SIC 2844 Toilet Preparations
325612 Polish & Other Sanitation Good Manufacturing
SIC 2842 Specialty Cleaning, Polishing, & Sanitary Preparations
325613 Surface Active Agent Manufacturing
SIC 2843 Surface Active Agents, Finishing Agents, Sulfonated Oils, & Assistants
32562 Toilet Preparation Manufacturing
SIC 2844 Perfumes, Cosmetics, & Other Toilet Preparations
32591 Printing Ink Manufacturing
SIC 2893 Printing Ink
32592 Explosives Manufacturing
SIC 2892 Explosives
325991 Custom Compounding of Purchased Resin
SIC 3087 Custom Compounding of Purchased Plastics Resin
325992 Photographic Film, Paper, Plate & Chemical Manufacturing
SIC 3861 Photographic Equipment & Supplies

325998 All Other Miscellaneous Chemical Product Manufacturing
SIC 2819 Industrial Inorganic Chemicals, nec
SIC 2899 Chemicals & Chemical Preparations, nec
SIC 3952 Lead Pencils & Art Goods
SIC 3999 Manufacturing Industries, nec

PLASTICS & RUBBER PRODUCTS MANUFACTURING

326111 Unsupported Plastics Bag Manufacturing
SIC 2673 Plastics, Foil, & Coated Paper Bags
326112 Unsupported Plastics Packaging Film & Sheet Manufacturing
SIC 2671 Packaging Paper & Plastics Film, Coated, & Laminated
326113 Unsupported Plastics Film & Sheet Manufacturing
SIC 3081 Unsupported Plastics Film & Sheets
326121 Unsupported Plastics Profile Shape Manufacturing
SIC 3082 Unsupported Plastics Profile Shapes
SIC 3089 Plastics Product, nec
326122 Plastics Pipe & Pipe Fitting Manufacturing
SIC 3084 Plastics Pipe
SIC 3089 Plastics Products, nec
32613 Laminated Plastics Plate, Sheet & Shape Manufacturing
SIC 3083 Laminated Plastics Plate, Sheet & Profile Shapes
32614 Polystyrene Foam Product Manufacturing
SIC 3086 Plastics Foam Products
32615 Urethane & Other Foam Product Manufacturing
SIC 3086 Plastics Foam Products
32616 Plastics Bottle Manufacturing
SIC 3085 Plastics Bottles
326191 Plastics Plumbing Fixture Manufacturing
SIC 3088 Plastics Plumbing Fixtures
326192 Resilient Floor Covering Manufacturing
SIC 3069 Fabricated Rubber Products, nec
SIC 3996 Linoleum, Asphalted-Felt-Base, & Other Hard Surface Floor Coverings, nec
326199 All Other Plastics Product Manufacturing
SIC 3089 Plastics Products, nec
SIC 3999 Manufacturing Industries, nec
326211 Tire Manufacturing
SIC 3011 Tires & Inner Tubes
326212 Tire Retreading
SIC 7534 Tire Retreading & Repair Shops
32622 Rubber & Plastics Hoses & Belting Manufacturing
SIC 3052 Rubber & Plastics Hose & Belting
326291 Rubber Product Manufacturing for Mechanical Use
SIC 3061 Molded, Extruded, & Lathe-Cut Mechanical Rubber Goods
326299 All Other Rubber Product Manufacturing
SIC 3069 Fabricated Rubber Products, nec

NONMETALLIC MINERAL PRODUCT MANUFACTURING

327111 Vitreous China Plumbing Fixture & China & Earthenware Fittings & Bathroom Accessories Manufacturing
SIC 3261 Vitreous China Plumbing Fixtures & China & Earthenware Fittings & Bathroom Accessories
327112 Vitreous China, Fine Earthenware & Other Pottery Product Manufacturing
SIC 3262 Vitreous China Table & Kitchen Articles
SIC 3263 Fine Earthenware Table & Kitchen Articles
SIC 3269 Pottery Products, nec
327113 Porcelain Electrical Supply Manufacturing
SIC 3264 Porcelain Electrical Supplies
327121 Brick & Structural Clay Tile Manufacturing
SIC 3251 Brick & Structural Clay Tile
327122 Ceramic Wall & Floor Tile Manufacturing
SIC 3253 Ceramic Wall & Floor Tile
327123 Other Structural Clay Product Manufacturing
SIC 3259 Structural Clay Products, nec
327124 Clay Refractory Manufacturing
SIC 3255 Clay Refractories
327125 Nonclay Refractory Manufacturing
SIC 3297 Nonclay Refractories
327211 Flat Glass Manufacturing
SIC 3211 Flat Glass
327212 Other Pressed & Blown Glass & Glassware Manufacturing
SIC 3229 Pressed & Blown Glass & Glassware, nec
327213 Glass Container Manufacturing
SIC 3221 Glass Containers
327215 Glass Product Manufacturing Made of Purchased Glass
SIC 3231 Glass Products Made of Purchased Glass
32731 Hydraulic Cement Manufacturing
SIC 3241 Cement, Hydraulic
32732 Ready-Mix Concrete Manufacturing
SIC 3273 Ready-Mixed Concrete
327331 Concrete Block & Brick Manufacturing
SIC 3271 Concrete Block & Brick
327332 Concrete Pipe Manufacturing
SIC 3272 Concrete Products, Except Block & Brick
32739 Other Concrete Product Manufacturing
SIC 3272 Concrete Products, Except Block & Brick
32741 Lime Manufacturing
SIC 3274 Lime
32742 Gypsum & Gypsum Product Manufacturing
SIC 3275 Gypsum Products
SIC 3299 Nonmetallic Mineral Products, nec
32791 Abrasive Product Manufacturing
SIC 3291 Abrasive Products
327991 Cut Stone & Stone Product Manufacturing
SIC 3281 Cut Stone & Stone Products
327992 Ground or Treated Mineral & Earth Manufacturing
SIC 3295 Minerals & Earths, Ground or Otherwise Treated
327993 Mineral Wool Manufacturing
SIC 3296 Mineral Wool
327999 All Other Miscellaneous Nonmetallic Mineral Product Manufacturing
SIC 3272 Concrete Products, Except Block & Brick
SIC 3292 Asbestos Products
SIC 3299 Nonmetallic Mineral Products, nec

PRIMARY METAL MANUFACTURING

331111 Iron & Steel Mills
SIC 3312 Steel Works, Blast Furnaces , & Rolling Mills
SIC 3399 Primary Metal Products, nec
331112 Electrometallurgical Ferroalloy Product Manufacturing
SIC 3313 Electrometallurgical Products, Except Steel

33121 Iron & Steel Pipes & Tubes Manufacturing from Purchased Steel
SIC 3317 Steel Pipe & Tubes
331221 Cold-Rolled Steel Shape Manufacturing
SIC 3316 Cold-Rolled Steel Sheet, Strip & Bars
331222 Steel Wire Drawing
SIC 3315 Steel Wiredrawing & Steel Nails & Spikes
331311 Alumina Refining
SIC 2819 Industrial Inorganic Chemicals, nec
331312 Primary Aluminum Production
SIC 3334 Primary Production of Aluminum
331314 Secondary Smelting & Alloying of Aluminum
SIC 3341 Secondary Smelting & Refining of Nonferrous Metals
SIC 3399 Primary Metal Products, nec
331315 Aluminum Sheet, Plate & Foil Manufacturing
SIC 3353 Aluminum Sheet, Plate, & Foil
331316 Aluminum Extruded Product Manufacturing
SIC 3354 Aluminum Extruded Products
331319 Other Aluminum Rolling & Drawing
SIC 3355 Aluminum Rolling & Drawing, nec
SIC 3357 Drawing & Insulating of Nonferrous Wire
331411 Primary Smelting & Refining of Copper
SIC 3331 Primary Smelting & Refining of Copper
331419 Primary Smelting & Refining of Nonferrous Metal
SIC 3339 Primary Smelting & Refining of Nonferrous Metals, Except Copper & Aluminum
331421 Copper Rolling, Drawing & Extruding
SIC 3351 Rolling, Drawing, & Extruding of Copper
331422 Copper Wire Drawing
SIC 3357 Drawing & Insulating of Nonferrous Wire
331423 Secondary Smelting, Refining, & Alloying of Copper
SIC 3341 Secondary Smelting & Refining of Nonferrous Metals
SIC 3399 Primary Metal Products, nec
331491 Nonferrous Metal Rolling, Drawing & Extruding
SIC 3356 Rolling, Drawing & Extruding of Nonferrous Metals, Except Copper & Aluminum
SIC 3357 Drawing & Insulating of Nonferrous Wire
331492 Secondary Smelting, Refining, & Alloying of Nonferrous Metal
SIC 3313 Electrometallurgical Products, Except Steel
SIC 3341 Secondary Smelting & Reining of Nonferrous Metals
SIC 3399 Primary Metal Products, nec
331511 Iron Foundries
SIC 3321 Gray & Ductile Iron Foundries
SIC 3322 Malleable Iron Foundries
331512 Steel Investment Foundries
SIC 3324 Steel Investment Foundries
331513 Steel Foundries,
SIC 3325 Steel Foundries, nec
331521 Aluminum Die-Castings
SIC 3363 Aluminum Die-Castings
331522 Nonferrous Die-Castings
SIC 3364 Nonferrous Die-Castings, Except Aluminum
331524 Aluminum Foundries
SIC 3365 Aluminum Foundries
331525 Copper Foundries
SIC 3366 Copper Foundries
331528 Other Nonferrous Foundries
SIC 3369 Nonferrous Foundries, Except Aluminum & Copper

FABRICATED METAL PRODUCT MANUFACTURING

332111 Iron & Steel Forging
SIC 3462 Iron & Steel Forgings
332112 Nonferrous Forging
SIC 3463 Nonferrous Forgings
332114 Custom Roll Forming
SIC 3449 Miscellaneous Structural Metal Work
332115 Crown & Closure Manufacturing
SIC 3466 Crowns & Closures
332116 Metal Stamping
SIC 3469 Metal Stampings, nec
332117 Powder Metallurgy Part Manufacturing
SIC 3499 Fabricated Metal Products, nec
332211 Cutlery & Flatware Manufacturing
SIC 3421 Cutlery
SIC 3914 Silverware, Plated Ware, & Stainless Steel Ware
332212 Hand & Edge Tool Manufacturing
SIC 3423 Hand & Edge Tools, Except Machine Tools & Handsaws
SIC 3523 Farm Machinery & Equipment
SIC 3524 Lawn & Garden Tractors & Home Lawn & Garden Equipment
SIC 3545 Cutting Tools, Machine Tools Accessories, & Machinist Precision Measuring Devices
SIC 3799 Transportation Equipment, nec
SIC 3999 Manufacturing Industries, nec
332213 Saw Blade & Handsaw Manufacturing
SIC 3425 Saw Blades & Handsaws
332214 Kitchen Utensil, Pot & Pan Manufacturing
SIC 3469 Metal Stampings, nec
332311 Prefabricated Metal Building & Component Manufacturing
SIC 3448 Prefabricated Metal Buildings & Components
332312 Fabricated Structural Metal Manufacturing
SIC 3441 Fabricated Structural Metal
SIC 3449 Miscellaneous Structural Metal Work
332313 Plate Work Manufacturing
SIC 3443 Fabricated Plate Work
332321 Metal Window & Door Manufacturing
SIC 3442 Metal Doors, Sash, Frames, Molding & Trim
SIC 3449 Miscellaneous Structural Metal Work
332322 Sheet Metal Work Manufacturing
SIC 3444 Sheet Metal Work
332323 Ornamental & Architectural Metal Work Manufacturing
SIC 3446 Architectural & Ornamental Metal Work
SIC 3449 Miscellaneous Structural Metal Work
SIC 3523 Farm Machinery & Equipment
33241 Power Boiler & Heat Exchanger Manufacturing
SIC 3443 Fabricated Plate Work
33242 Metal Tank Manufacturing
SIC 3443 Fabricated Plate Work
332431 Metal Can Manufacturing
SIC 3411 Metal Cans
332439 Other Metal Container Manufacturing
SIC 3412 Metal Shipping Barrels, Drums, Kegs, & Pails
SIC 3429 Hardware, nec
SIC 3444 Sheet Metal Work
SIC 3499 Fabricated Metal Products, nec
SIC 3537 Industrial Trucks, Tractors, Trailers, & Stackers
33251 Hardware Manufacturing
SIC 3429 Hardware, nec
SIC 3499 Fabricated Metal Products, nec

332611 Steel Spring Manufacturing
SIC 3493 Steel Springs, Except Wire
332612 Wire Spring Manufacturing
SIC 3495 Wire Springs
332618 Other Fabricated Wire Product Manufacturing
SIC 3315 Steel Wiredrawing & Steel Nails & Spikes
SIC 3399 Primary Metal Products, nec
SIC 3496 Miscellaneous Fabricated Wire Products
33271 Machine Shops
SIC 3599 Industrial & Commercial Machinery & Equipment, nec
332721 Precision Turned Product Manufacturing
SIC 3451 Screw Machine Products
332722 Bolt, Nut, Screw, Rivet & Washer Manufacturing
SIC 3452 Bolts, Nuts, Screws, Rivets, & Washers
332811 Metal Heat Treating
SIC 3398 Metal Heat Treating
332812 Metal Coating, Engraving , & Allied Services to Manufacturers
SIC 3479 Coating, Engraving, & Allied Services, nec
332813 Electroplating, Plating, Polishing, Anodizing & Coloring
SIC 3399 Primary Metal Products, nec
SIC 3471 Electroplating, Plating, Polishing, Anodizing, & Coloring
332911 Industrial Valve Manufacturing
SIC 3491 Industrial Valves
332912 Fluid Power Valve & Hose Fitting Manufacturing
SIC 3492 Fluid Power Valves & Hose Fittings
SIC 3728 Aircraft Parts & Auxiliary Equipment, nec
332913 Plumbing Fixture Fitting & Trim Manufacturing
SIC 3432 Plumbing Fixture Fittings & Trim
332919 Other Metal Valve & Pipe Fitting Manufacturing
SIC 3429 Hardware, nec
SIC 3494 Valves & Pipe Fittings, nec
SIC 3499 Fabricated Metal Products, nec
332991 Ball & Roller Bearing Manufacturing
SIC 3562 Ball & Roller Bearings
332992 Small Arms Ammunition Manufacturing
SIC 3482 Small Arms Ammunition
332993 Ammunition Manufacturing
SIC 3483 Ammunition, Except for Small Arms
332994 Small Arms Manufacturing
SIC 3484 Small Arms
332995 Other Ordnance & Accessories Manufacturing
SIC 3489 Ordnance & Accessories, nec
332996 Fabricated Pipe & Pipe Fitting Manufacturing
SIC 3498 Fabricated Pipe & Pipe Fittings
332997 Industrial Pattern Manufacturing
SIC 3543 Industrial Patterns
332998 Enameled Iron & Metal Sanitary Ware Manufacturing
SIC 3431 Enameled Iron & Metal Sanitary Ware
332999 All Other Miscellaneous Fabricated Metal Product Manufacturing
SIC 3291 Abrasive Products
SIC 3432 Plumbing Fixture Fittings & Trim
SIC 3494 Valves & Pipe Fittings, nec
SIC 3497 Metal Foil & Leaf
SIC 3499 Fabricated Metal Products, NEC
SIC 3537 Industrial Trucks, Tractors, Trailers, & Stackers
SIC 3599 Industrial & Commercial Machinery & Equipment, nec
SIC 3999 Manufacturing Industries, nec

MACHINERY MANUFACTURING

333111 Farm Machinery & Equipment Manufacturing
SIC 3523 Farm Machinery & Equipment
333112 Lawn & Garden Tractor & Home Lawn & Garden Equipment Manufacturing
SIC 3524 Lawn & Garden Tractors & Home Lawn & Garden Equipment
33312 Construction Machinery Manufacturing
SIC 3531 Construction Machinery & Equipment
333131 Mining Machinery & Equipment Manufacturing
SIC 3532 Mining Machinery & Equipment, Except Oil & Gas Field Machinery & Equipment
333132 Oil & Gas Field Machinery & Equipment Manufacturing
SIC 3533 Oil & Gas Field Machinery & Equipment
33321 Sawmill & Woodworking Machinery Manufacturing
SIC 3553 Woodworking Machinery
33322 Rubber & Plastics Industry Machinery Manufacturing
SIC 3559 Special Industry Machinery, nec
333291 Paper Industry Machinery Manufacturing
SIC 3554 Paper Industries Machinery
333292 Textile Machinery Manufacturing
SIC 3552 Textile Machinery
333293 Printing Machinery & Equipment Manufacturing
SIC 3555 Printing Trades Machinery & Equipment
333294 Food Product Machinery Manufacturing
SIC 3556 Food Products Machinery
333295 Semiconductor Machinery Manufacturing
SIC 3559 Special Industry Machinery, nec
333298 All Other Industrial Machinery Manufacturing
SIC 3559 Special Industry Machinery, nec
SIC 3639 Household Appliances, nec
333311 Automatic Vending Machine Manufacturing
SIC 3581 Automatic Vending Machines
333312 Commercial Laundry, Drycleaning & Pressing Machine Manufacturing
SIC 3582 Commercial Laundry, Drycleaning & Pressing Machines
333313 Office Machinery Manufacturing
SIC 3578 Calculating & Accounting Machinery, Except Electronic Computers
SIC 3579 Office Machines, nec
333314 Optical Instrument & Lens Manufacturing
SIC 3827 Optical Instruments & Lenses
333315 Photographic & Photocopying Equipment Manufacturing
SIC 3861 Photographic Equipment & Supplies
333319 Other Commercial & Service Industry Machinery Manufacturing
SIC 3559 Special Industry Machinery, nec
SIC 3589 Service Industry Machinery, nec
SIC 3599 Industrial & Commercial Machinery & Equipment, nec
SIC 3699 Electrical Machinery, Equipment & Supplies, nec
333411 Air Purification Equipment Manufacturing
SIC 3564 Industrial & Commercial Fans & Blowers & Air Purification Equipment
333412 Industrial & Commercial Fan & Blower Manufacturing
SIC 3564 Industrial & Commercial Fans & Blowers & Air Purification Equipment
333414 Heating Equipment Manufacturing
SIC 3433 Heating Equipment, Except Electric & Warm Air Furnaces

SIC 3634 Electric Housewares & Fans

333415 Air-Conditioning & Warm Air Heating Equipment & Commercial & Industrial Refrigeration Equipment Manufacturing

SIC 3443 Fabricated Plate Work

SIC 3585 Air-Conditioning & Warm Air Heating Equipment & Commercial & Industrial Refrigeration Equipment

333511 Industrial Mold Manufacturing

SIC 3544 Special Dies & Tools, Die Sets, Jigs & Fixtures, & Industrial Molds

333512 Machine Tool Manufacturing

SIC 3541 Machine Tools, Metal Cutting Type

333513 Machine Tool Manufacturing

SIC 3542 Machine Tools, Metal Forming Type

333514 Special Die & Tool, Die Set, Jig & Fixture Manufacturing

SIC 3544 Special Dies & Tools, Die Sets, Jigs & Fixtures, & Industrial Molds

333515 Cutting Tool & Machine Tool Accessory Manufacturing

SIC 3545 Cutting Tools, Machine Tool Accessories, & Machinists' Precision Measuring Devices

333516 Rolling Mill Machinery & Equipment Manufacturing

SIC 3547 Rolling Mill Machinery & Equipment

333518 Other Metalworking Machinery Manufacturing

SIC 3549 Metalworking Machinery, nec

333611 Turbine & Turbine Generator Set Unit Manufacturing

SIC 3511 Steam, Gas, & Hydraulic Turbines, & Turbine Generator Set Units

333612 Speed Changer, Industrial High-Speed Drive & Gear Manufacturing

SIC 3566 Speed Changers, Industrial High-Speed Drives, & Gears

333613 Mechanical Power Transmission Equipment Manufacturing

SIC 3568 Mechanical Power Transmission Equipment, nec

333618 Other Engine Equipment Manufacturing

SIC 3519 Internal Combustion Engines, nec

SIC 3699 Electrical Machinery, Equipment & Supplies, nec

333911 Pump & Pumping Equipment Manufacturing

SIC 3561 Pumps & Pumping Equipment

SIC 3743 Railroad Equipment

333912 Air & Gas Compressor Manufacturing

SIC 3563 Air & Gas Compressors

333913 Measuring & Dispensing Pump Manufacturing

SIC 3586 Measuring & Dispensing Pumps

333921 Elevator & Moving Stairway Manufacturing

SIC 3534 Elevators & Moving Stairways

333922 Conveyor & Conveying Equipment Manufacturing

SIC 3523 Farm Machinery & Equipment

SIC 3535 Conveyors & Conveying Equipment

333923 Overhead Traveling Crane, Hoist & Monorail System Manufacturing

SIC 3536 Overhead Traveling Cranes, Hoists, & Monorail Systems

SIC 3531 Construction Machinery & Equipment

333924 Industrial Truck, Tractor, Trailer & Stacker Machinery Manufacturing

SIC 3537 Industrial Trucks, Tractors, Trailers, & Stackers

333991 Power-Driven Hand Tool Manufacturing

SIC 3546 Power-Driven Handtools

333992 Welding & Soldering Equipment Manufacturing

SIC 3548 Electric & Gas Welding & Soldering Equipment

333993 Packaging Machinery Manufacturing

SIC 3565 Packaging Machinery

333994 Industrial Process Furnace & Oven Manufacturing

SIC 3567 Industrial Process Furnaces & Ovens

333995 Fluid Power Cylinder & Actuator Manufacturing

SIC 3593 Fluid Power Cylinders & Actuators

333996 Fluid Power Pump & Motor Manufacturing

SIC 3594 Fluid Power Pumps & Motors

333997 Scale & Balance Manufacturing

SIC 3596 Scales & Balances, Except Laboratory

333999 All Other General Purpose Machinery Manufacturing

SIC 3599 Industrial & Commercial Machinery & Equipment, nec

SIC 3569 General Industrial Machinery & Equipment, nec

COMPUTER & ELECTRONIC PRODUCT MANUFACTURING

334111 Electronic Computer Manufacturing

SIC 3571 Electronic Computers

334112 Computer Storage Device Manufacturing

SIC 3572 Computer Storage Devices

334113 Computer Terminal Manufacturing

SIC 3575 Computer Terminals

334119 Other Computer Peripheral Equipment Manufacturing

SIC 3577 Computer Peripheral Equipment, nec

SIC 3578 Calculating & Accounting Machines, Except Electronic Computers

SIC 3699 Electrical Machinery, Equipment & Supplies, nec

33421 Telephone Apparatus Manufacturing

SIC 3661 Telephone & Telegraph Apparatus

33422 Radio & Television Broadcasting & Wireless Communications Equipment Manufacturing

SIC 3663 Radio & Television Broadcasting & Communication Equipment

SIC 3679 Electronic Components, nec

33429 Other Communications Equipment Manufacturing

SIC 3669 Communications Equipment, nec

33431 Audio & Video Equipment Manufacturing

SIC 3651 Household Audio & Video Equipment

334411 Electron Tube Manufacturing

SIC 3671 Electron Tubes

334412 Printed Circuit Board Manufacturing

SIC 3672 Printed Circuit Boards

334413 Semiconductor & Related Device Manufacturing

SIC 3674 Semiconductors & Related Devices

334414 Electronic Capacitor Manufacturing

SIC 3675 Electronic Capacitors

334415 Electronic Resistor Manufacturing

SIC 3676 Electronic Resistors

334416 Electronic Coil, Transformer, & Other Inductor Manufacturing

SIC 3661 Telephone & Telegraph Apparatus

SIC 3677 Electronic Coils, Transformers, & Other Inductors

SIC 3825 Instruments for Measuring & Testing of Electricity & Electrical Signals

334417 Electronic Connector Manufacturing

SIC 3678 Electronic Connectors

334418 Printed Circuit/Electronics Assembly Manufacturing

SIC 3679 Electronic Components, nec

SIC 3661 Telephone & Telegraph Apparatus

334419 Other Electronic Component Manufacturing
SIC 3679 Electronic Components, nec
334510 Electromedical & Electrotherapeutic Apparatus Manufacturing
SIC 3842 Orthopedic, Prosthetic & Surgical Appliances & Supplies
SIC 3845 Electromedical & Electrotherapeutic Apparatus
334511 Search, Detection, Navigation, Guidance, Aeronautical, & Nautical System & Instrument Manufacturing
SIC 3812 Search, Detection, Navigation, Guidance, Aeronautical, & Nautical Systems & Instruments
334512 Automatic Environmental Control Manufacturing for Residential, Commercial & Appliance Use
SIC 3822 Automatic Controls for Regulating Residential & Commercial Environments & Appliances
334513 Instruments & Related Products Manufacturing for Measuring, Displaying, & Controlling Industrial Process Variables
SIC 3823 Industrial Instruments for Measurement, Display, & Control of Process Variables; & Related Products
334514 Totalizing Fluid Meter & Counting Device Manufacturing
SIC 3824 Totalizing Fluid Meters & Counting Devices
334515 Instrument Manufacturing for Measuring & Testing Electricity & Electrical Signals
SIC 3825 Instruments for Measuring & Testing of Electricity & Electrical Signals
334516 Analytical Laboratory Instrument Manufacturing
SIC 3826 Laboratory Analytical Instruments
334517 Irradiation Apparatus Manufacturing
SIC 3844 X-Ray Apparatus & Tubes & Related Irradiation Apparatus
SIC 3845 Electromedical & Electrotherapeutic Apparatus
334518 Watch, Clock, & Part Manufacturing
SIC 3495 Wire Springs
SIC 3579 Office Machines, nec
SIC 3873 Watches, Clocks, Clockwork Operated Devices, & Parts
334519 Other Measuring & Controlling Device Manufacturing
SIC 3829 Measuring & Controlling Devices, nec
334611 Software Reproducing
SIC 7372 Prepackaged Software
334612 Prerecorded Compact Disc , Tape, & Record Reproducing
SIC 3652 Phonograph Records & Prerecorded Audio Tapes & Disks
SIC 7819 Services Allied to Motion Picture Production
334613 Magnetic & Optical Recording Media Manufacturing
SIC 3695 Magnetic & Optical Recording Media

ELECTRICAL EQUIPMENT, APPLIANCE, & COMPONENT MANUFACTURING

33511 Electric Lamp Bulb & Part Manufacturing
SIC 3641 Electric Lamp Bulbs & Tubes
335121 Residential Electric Lighting Fixture Manufacturing
SIC 3645 Residential Electric Lighting Fixtures
SIC 3999 Manufacturing Industries, nec
335122 Commercial, Industrial & Institutional Electric Lighting Fixture Manufacturing
SIC 3646 Commercial, Industrial, & Institutional Electric Lighting Fixtures
335129 Other Lighting Equipment Manufacturing
SIC 3648 Lighting Equipment, nec
SIC 3699 Electrical Machinery, Equipment, & Supplies, nec
335211 Electric Housewares & Fan Manufacturing
SIC 3634 Electric Housewares & Fans
335212 Household Vacuum Cleaner Manufacturing
SIC 3635 Household Vacuum Cleaners
SIC 3639 Household Appliances, nec
335221 Household Cooking Appliance Manufacturing
SIC 3631 Household Cooking Equipment
335222 Household Refrigerator & Home Freezer Manufacturing
SIC 3632 Household Refrigerators & Home & Farm Freezers
335224 Household Laundry Equipment Manufacturing
SIC 3633 Household Laundry Equipment
335228 Other Household Appliance Manufacturing
SIC 3639 Household Appliances, nec
335311 Power, Distribution & Specialty Transformer Manufacturing
SIC 3548 Electric & Gas Welding & Soldering Equipment
SIC 3612 Power, Distribution, & Speciality Transformers
335312 Motor & Generator Manufacturing
SIC 3621 Motors & Generators
SIC 7694 Armature Rewinding Shops
335313 Switchgear & Switchboard Apparatus Manufacturing
SIC 3613 Switchgear & Switchboard Apparatus
335314 Relay & Industrial Control Manufacturing
SIC 3625 Relays & Industrial Controls
335911 Storage Battery Manufacturing
SIC 3691 Storage Batteries
335912 Dry & Wet Primary Battery Manufacturing
SIC 3692 Primary Batteries, Dry & Wet
335921 Fiber-Optic Cable Manufacturing
SIC 3357 Drawing & Insulating of Nonferrous Wire
335929 Other Communication & Energy Wire Manufacturing
SIC 3357 Drawing & Insulating of Nonferrous Wire
335931 Current-Carrying Wiring Device Manufacturing
SIC 3643 Current-Carrying Wiring Devices
335932 Noncurrent-Carrying Wiring Device Manufacturing
SIC 3644 Noncurrent-Carrying Wiring Devices
335991 Carbon & Graphite Product Manufacturing
SIC 3624 Carbon & Graphite Products
335999 All Other Miscellaneous Electrical Equipment & Component Manufacturing
SIC 3629 Electrical Industrial Apparatus, nec
SIC 3699 Electrical Machinery, Equipment, & Supplies, nec

TRANSPORTATION EQUIPMENT MANUFACTURING

336111 Automobile Manufacturing
SIC 3711 Motor Vehicles & Passenger Car Bodies
336112 Light Truck & Utility Vehicle Manufacturing
SIC 3711 Motor Vehicles & Passenger Car Bodies
33612 Heavy Duty Truck Manufacturing
SIC 3711 Motor Vehicles & Passenger Car Bodies
336211 Motor Vehicle Body Manufacturing
SIC 3711 Motor Vehicles & Passenger Car Bodies
SIC 3713 Truck & Bus Bodies
SIC 3714 Motor Vehicle Parts & Accessories
336212 Truck Trailer Manufacturing
SIC 3715 Truck Trailers

336213 Motor Home Manufacturing
SIC 3716 Motor Homes
336214 Travel Trailer & Camper Manufacturing
SIC 3792 Travel Trailers & Campers
SIC 3799 Transportation Equipment, nec
336311 Carburetor, Piston, Piston Ring & Valve Manufacturing
SIC 3592 Carburetors, Pistons, Piston Rings, & Valves
336312 Gasoline Engine & Engine Parts Manufacturing
SIC 3714 Motor Vehicle Parts & Accessories
336321 Vehicular Lighting Equipment Manufacturing
SIC 3647 Vehicular Lighting Equipment
336322 Other Motor Vehicle Electrical & Electronic Equipment Manufacturing
SIC 3679 Electronic Components, nec
SIC 3694 Electrical Equipment for Internal Combustion Engines
SIC 3714 Motor Vehicle Parts & Accessories
33633 Motor Vehicle Steering & Suspension Components Manufacturing
SIC 3714 Motor Vehicle Parts & Accessories
33634 Motor Vehicle Brake System Manufacturing
SIC 3292 Asbestos Products
SIC 3714 Motor Vehicle Parts & Accessories
33635 Motor Vehicle Transmission & Power Train Parts Manufacturing
SIC 3714 Motor Vehicle Parts & Accessories
33636 Motor Vehicle Fabric Accessories & Seat Manufacturing
SIC 2396 Automotive Trimmings, Apparel Findings, & Related Products
SIC 2399 Fabricated Textile Products, nec
SIC 2531 Public Building & Related Furniture
33637 Motor Vehicle Metal Stamping
SIC 3465 Automotive Stampings
336391 Motor Vehicle Air-Conditioning Manufacturing
SIC 3585 Air-Conditioning & Warm Air Heating Equipment & Commercial & Industrial Refrigeration Equipment
336399 All Other Motor Vehicle Parts Manufacturing
SIC 3519 Internal Combustion Engines, nec
SIC 3599 Industrial & Commercial Machinery & Equipment, NEC
SIC 3714 Motor Vehicle Parts & Accessories
336411 Aircraft Manufacturing
SIC 3721 Aircraft
336412 Aircraft Engine & Engine Parts Manufacturing
SIC 3724 Aircraft Engines & Engine Parts
336413 Other Aircraft Part & Auxiliary Equipment Manufacturing
SIC 3728 Aircraft Parts & Auxiliary Equipment, nec
336414 Guided Missile & Space Vehicle Manufacturing
SIC 3761 Guided Missiles & Space Vehicles
336415 Guided Missile & Space Vehicle Propulsion Unit & Propulsion Unit Parts Manufacturing
SIC 3764 Guided Missile & Space Vehicle Propulsion Units & Propulsion Unit Parts
336419 Other Guided Missile & Space Vehicle Parts & Auxiliary Equipment Manufacturing
SIC 3769 Guided Missile & Space Vehicle Parts & Auxiliary Equipment
33651 Railroad Rolling Stock Manufacturing
SIC 3531 Construction Machinery & Equipment
SIC 3743 Railroad Equipment
336611 Ship Building & Repairing
SIC 3731 Ship Building & Repairing
336612 Boat Building
SIC 3732 Boat Building & Repairing
336991 Motorcycle, Bicycle, & Parts Manufacturing
SIC 3944 Games, Toys, & Children's Vehicles, Except Dolls & Bicycles
SIC 3751 Motorcycles, Bicycles & Parts
336992 Military Armored Vehicle, Tank & Tank Component Manufacturing
SIC 3711 Motor Vehicles & Passenger Car Bodies
SIC 3795 Tanks & Tank Components
336999 All Other Transportation Equipment Manufacturing
SIC 3799 Transportation Equipment, nec

FURNITURE & RELATED PRODUCT MANUFACTURING

337121 Upholstered Household Furniture Manufacturing
SIC 2512 Wood Household Furniture, Upholstered
SIC 2515 Mattress, Foundations, & Convertible Beds
SIC 5712 Furniture
337122 Nonupholstered Wood Household Furniture Manufacturing
SIC 2511 Wood Household Furniture, Except Upholstered
SIC 5712 Furniture Stores
337124 Metal Household Furniture Manufacturing
SIC 2514 Metal Household Furniture
337125 Household Furniture Manufacturing
SIC 2519 Household Furniture, NEC
337127 Institutional Furniture Manufacturing
SIC 2531 Public Building & Related Furniture
SIC 2599 Furniture & Fixtures, nec
SIC 3952 Lead Pencils, Crayons, & Artist's Materials
SIC 3999 Manufacturing Industries, nec
337129 Wood Television, Radio, & Sewing Machine Cabinet Manufacturing
SIC 2517 Wood Television, Radio, Phonograph, & Sewing Machine Cabinets
337131 Wood Kitchen & Counter Top Manufacturing
SIC 2434 Wood Kitchen Cabinets
SIC 2541 Wood Office & Store Fixtures, Partitions, Shelving, & Lockers
SIC 5712 Furniture Stores
337132 Upholstered Wood Household Furniture Manufacturing
SIC 2515 Mattresses, Foundations, & Convertible Beds
SIC 5712 Furniture Stores
337133 Wood Household Furniture
SIC 5712 Furniture Stores
337134 Wood Office Furniture Manufacturing
SIC 2521 Wood Office Furniture
337135 Custom Architectural Woodwork, Millwork, & Fixtures
SIC 2541 Wood Office & Store Fixtures, Partitions, Shelving, and Lockers
337139 Other Wood Furniture Manufacturing
SIC 2426 Hardwood Dimension & Flooring Mills
SIC 2499 Wood Products, nec
SIC 2517 Wood Television, Radio, Phonograph, & Sewing Machine Cabinets
SIC 2531 Public Building & Related Furniture
SIC 2541 Wood Office & Store Fixtures, Partitions., Shelving, & Lockers
SIC 2599 Furniture & Fixtures, nec
SIC 3952 Lead Pencils, Crayons, & Artist's Materials

337141 Nonwood Office Furniture Manufacturing
SIC 2522 Office Furniture, Except Wood
337143 Household Furniture Manufacturing
SIC 2519 Household Furniture, NEC
337145 Nonwood Showcase, Partition, Shelving, & Locker Manufacturing
SIC 2542 Office & Store Fixtures, Partitions, Shelving, & Lockers, Except Wood
337148 Other Nonwood Furniture Manufacturing
SIC 2499 Wood Products, NEC
SIC 2531 Public Building & Related Furniture
SIC 2599 Furniture & Fixtures, nec
SIC 3499 Fabricated Metal Products, nec
SIC 3952 Lead Pencils, Crayons, & Artist's Materials
SIC 3999 Manufacturing Industries, nec
337212 Custom Architectural Woodwork & Millwork Manufacturing
SIC 2541 Wood Office & Store Fixtures, Partitions, Shelving, & Lockers
337214 Nonwood Office Furniture Manufacturing
SIC 2522 Office Furniture, Except Wood
337215 Showcase, Partition, Shelving, & Locker Manufacturing
SIC 2542 Office & Store Fixtures, Partitions, Shelving & Lockers, Except Wood
SIC 2541 Wood Office & Store Fixtures, Partitions, Shelving, & Lockers
SIC 2426 Hardwood Dimension & Flooring Mills
SIC 3499 Fabricated Metal Products, nec
33791 Mattress Manufacturing
SIC 2515 Mattresses, Foundations & Convertible Beds
33792 Blind & Shade Manufacturing
SIC 2591 Drapery Hardware & Window Blinds & Shades

MISCELLANEOUS MANUFACTURING

339111 Laboratory Apparatus & Furniture Manufacturing
SIC 3829 Measuring & Controlling Devices, nec
339112 Surgical & Medical Instrument Manufacturing
SIC 3841 Surgical & Medical Instruments & Apparatus
SIC 3829 Measuring & Controlling Devices, nec
339113 Surgical Appliance & Supplies Manufacturing
SIC 2599 Furniture & Fixtures, nec
SIC 3842 Orthopedic, Prosthetic, & Surgical Appliances & Supplies
339114 Dental Equipment & Supplies Manufacturing
SIC 3843 Dental Equipment & Supplies
339115 Ophthalmic Goods Manufacturing
SIC 3851 Opthalmic Goods
SIC 5995 Optical Goods Stores
339116 Dental Laboratories
SIC 8072 Dental Laboratories 339117 Eyeglass & Contact Lens Manufacturing
SIC 5995 Optical Goods Stores
339911 Jewelry Manufacturing
SIC 3469 Metal Stamping, nec
SIC 3479 Coating, Engraving, & Allied Services, nec
SIC 3911 Jewelry, Precious Metal
339912 Silverware & Plated Ware Manufacturing
SIC 3479 Coating, Engraving, & Allied Services, nec
SIC 3914 Silverware, Plated Ware, & Stainless Steel Ware
339913 Jewelers' Material & Lapidary Work Manufacturing
SIC 3915 Jewelers' Findings & Materials, & Lapidary Work
339914 Costume Jewelry & Novelty Manufacturing
SIC 3479 Coating, Engraving, & Allied Services, nec
SIC 3499 Fabricated Metal Products, nec
SIC 3961 Costume Jewelry & Costume Novelties, Except Precious Metal
33992 Sporting & Athletic Goods Manufacturing
SIC 3949 Sporting & Athletic Goods, nec
339931 Doll & Stuffed Toy Manufacturing
SIC 3942 Dolls & Stuffed Toys
339932 Game, Toy, & Children's Vehicle Manufacturing
SIC 3944 Games, Toys, & Children's Vehicles, Except Dolls & Bicycles
339941 Pen & Mechanical Pencil Manufacturing
SIC 3951 Pens, Mechanical Pencils, & Parts
339942 Lead Pencil & Art Good Manufacturing
SIC 2531 Public Buildings & Related Furniture
SIC 3579 Office Machines, nec
SIC 3952 Lead Pencils, Crayons, & Artists' Materials
339943 Marking Device Manufacturing
SIC 3953 Marking Devices
339944 Carbon Paper & Inked Ribbon Manufacturing
SIC 3955 Carbon Paper & Inked Ribbons
33995 Sign Manufacturing
SIC 3993 Signs & Advertising Specialties
339991 Gasket, Packing, & Sealing Device Manufacturing
SIC 3053 Gaskets, Packing, & Sealing Devices
339992 Musical Instrument Manufacturing
SIC 3931 Musical Instruments
339993 Fastener, Button, Needle & Pin Manufacturing
SIC 3965 Fasteners, Buttons, Needles, & Pins
SIC 3131 Boat & Shoe Cut Stock & Findings
339994 Broom, Brush & Mop Manufacturing
SIC 3991 Brooms & Brushes
SIC 2392 Housefurnishings, Except Curtains & Draperies
339995 Burial Casket Manufacturing
SIC 3995 Burial Caskets
339999 All Other Miscellaneous Manufacturing
SIC 2499 Wood Products, NEC
SIC 3999 Manufacturing Industries, nec

WHOLESALE TRADE

42111 Automobile & Other Motor Vehicle Wholesalers
SIC 5012 Automobiles & Other Motor Vehicles
42112 Motor Vehicle Supplies & New Part Wholesalers
SIC 5013 Motor Vehicle Supplies & New Parts
42113 Tire & Tube Wholesalers
SIC 5014 Tires & Tubes
42114 Motor Vehicle Part Wholesalers
SIC 5015 Motor Vehicle Parts, Used
42121 Furniture Wholesalers
SIC 5021 Furniture
42122 Home Furnishing Wholesalers
SIC 5023 Homefurnishings
42131 Lumber, Plywood, Millwork & Wood Panel Wholesalers
SIC 5031 Lumber, Plywood, Millwork, & Wood Panels
SIC 5211 Lumber & Other Building Materials Dealers - Retail
42132 Brick, Stone & Related Construction Material Wholesalers
SIC 5032 Brick, Stone, & Related Construction Materials
42133 Roofing, Siding & Insulation Material Wholesalers
SIC 5033 Roofing, Siding, & Insulation Materials

42139 Other Construction Material Wholesalers
SIC 5039 Construction Materials, nec
42141 Photographic Equipment & Supplies Wholesalers
SIC 5043 Photographic Equipment & Supplies
42142 Office Equipment Wholesalers
SIC 5044 Office Equipment
42143 Computer & Computer Peripheral Equipment & Software Wholesalers
SIC 5045 Computers & Computer Peripherals Equipment & Software
42144 Other Commercial Equipment Wholesalers
SIC 5046 Commercial Equipment, nec
42145 Medical, Dental & Hospital Equipment & Supplies Wholesalers
SIC 5047 Medical, Dental & Hospital Equipment & Supplies
42146 Ophthalmic Goods Wholesalers
SIC 5048 Ophthalmic Goods
42149 Other Professional Equipment & Supplies Wholesalers
SIC 5049 Professional Equipment & Supplies, nec
42151 Metal Service Centers & Offices
SIC 5051 Metals Service Centers & Offices
42152 Coal & Other Mineral & Ore Wholesalers
SIC 5052 Coal & Other Mineral & Ores
42161 Electrical Apparatus & Equipment, Wiring Supplies & Construction Material Wholesalers
SIC 5063 Electrical Apparatus & Equipment, Wiring Supplies & Construction Materials
42162 Electrical Appliance, Television & Radio Set Wholesalers
SIC 5064 Electrical Appliances, Television & Radio Sets
42169 Other Electronic Parts & Equipment Wholesalers
SIC 5065 Electronic Parts & Equipment, nec
42171 Hardware Wholesalers
SIC 5072 Hardware
42172 Plumbing & Heating Equipment & Supplies Wholesalers
SIC 5074 Plumbing & Heating Equipment & Supplies
42173 Warm Air Heating & Air-Conditioning Equipment & Supplies Wholesalers
SIC 5075 Warm Air Heating & Air-Conditioning Equipment & Supplies
42174 Refrigeration Equipment & Supplies Wholesalers
SIC 5078 Refrigeration Equipment & Supplies
42181 Construction & Mining Machinery & Equipment Wholesalers
SIC 5082 Construction & Mining Machinery & Equipment
42182 Farm & Garden Machinery & Equipment Wholesalers
SIC 5083 Farm & Garden Machinery & Equipment
42183 Industrial Machinery & Equipment Wholesalers
SIC 5084 Industrial Machinery & Equipment
SIC 5085 Industrial Supplies
42184 Industrial Supplies Wholesalers
SIC 5085 Industrial Supplies
42185 Service Establishment Equipment & Supplies Wholesalers
SIC 5087 Service Establishment Equipment & Supplies Wholesalers
42186 Transportation Equipment & Supplies Wholesalers
SIC 5088 Transportation Equipment and Supplies, Except Motor Vehicles
42191 Sporting & Recreational Goods & Supplies Wholesalers
SIC 5091 Sporting & Recreational Goods & Supplies
42192 Toy & Hobby Goods & Supplies Wholesalers
SIC 5092 Toys & Hobby Goods & Supplies
42193 Recyclable Material Wholesalers
SIC 5093 Scrap & Waste Materials
42194 Jewelry, Watch, Precious Stone & Precious Metal Wholesalers
SIC 5094 Jewelry, Watches, Precious Stones, & Precious Metals
42199 Other Miscellaneous Durable Goods Wholesalers
SIC 5099 Durable Goods, nec
SIC 7822 Motion Picture & Video Tape Distribution
42211 Printing & Writing Paper Wholesalers
SIC 5111 Printing & Writing Paper
42212 Stationary & Office Supplies Wholesalers
SIC 5112 Stationery & Office Supplies
42213 Industrial & Personal Service Paper Wholesalers
SIC 5113 Industrial & Personal Service Paper
42221 Drug, Drug Proprietaries & Druggists' Sundries Wholesalers
SIC 5122 Drugs, Drug Proprietaries, & Druggists' Sundries
42231 Piece Goods, Notions & Other Dry Goods Wholesalers
SIC 5131 Piece Goods, Notions, & Other Dry Goods
42232 Men's & Boys' Clothing & Furnishings Wholesalers
SIC 5136 Men's & Boys' Clothing & Furnishings
42233 Women's, Children's, & Infants' & Accessories Wholesalers
SIC 5137 Women's, Children's, & Infants' Clothing & Accessories
42234 Footwear Wholesalers
SIC 5139 Footwear
42241 General Line Grocery Wholesalers
SIC 5141 Groceries, General Line
42242 Packaged Frozen Food Wholesalers
SIC 5142 Packaged Frozen Foods
42243 Dairy Product Wholesalers
SIC 5143 Dairy Products, Except Dried or Canned
42244 Poultry & Poultry Product Wholesalers
SIC 5144 Poultry & Poultry Products
42245 Confectionery Wholesalers
SIC 5145 Confectionery
42246 Fish & Seafood Wholesalers
SIC 5146 Fish & Seafoods
42247 Meat & Meat Product Wholesalers
SIC 5147 Meats & Meat Products
42248 Fresh Fruit & Vegetable Wholesalers
SIC 5148 Fresh Fruits & Vegetables
42249 Other Grocery & Related Products Wholesalers
SIC 5149 Groceries & Related Products, nec
42251 Grain & Field Bean Wholesalers
SIC 5153 Grain & Field Beans
42252 Livestock Wholesalers
SIC 5154 Livestock
42259 Other Farm Product Raw Material Wholesalers
SIC 5159 Farm-Product Raw Materials, nec
42261 Plastics Materials & Basic Forms & Shapes Wholesalers
SIC 5162 Plastics Materials & Basic Forms & Shapes
42269 Other Chemical & Allied Products Wholesalers
SIC 5169 Chemicals & Allied Products, nec
42271 Petroleum Bulk Stations & Terminals
SIC 5171 Petroleum Bulk Stations & Terminals
42272 Petroleum & Petroleum Products Wholesalers
SIC 5172 Petroleum & Petroleum Products Wholesalers, Except Bulk Stations & Terminals
42281 Beer & Ale Wholesalers
SIC 5181 Beer & Ale

42282 Wine & Distilled Alcoholic Beverage Wholesalers
SIC 5182 Wine & Distilled Alcoholic Beverages
42291 Farm Supplies Wholesalers
SIC 5191 Farm Supplies
42292 Book, Periodical & Newspaper Wholesalers
SIC 5192 Books, Periodicals, & Newspapers
42293 Flower, Nursery Stock & Florists' Supplies Wholesalers
SIC 5193 Flowers, Nursery Stock, & Florists' Supplies
42294 Tobacco & Tobacco Product Wholesalers
SIC 5194 Tobacco & Tobacco Products
42295 Paint, Varnish & Supplies Wholesalers
SIC 5198 Paints, Varnishes, & Supplies
SIC 5231 Paint, Glass & Wallpaper Stores
42299 Other Miscellaneous Nondurable Goods Wholesalers
SIC 5199 Nondurable Goods, nec

RETAIL TRADE

44111 New Car Dealers
SIC 5511 Motor Vehicle Dealers, New and Used
44112 Used Car Dealers
SIC 5521 Motor Vehicle Dealers, Used Only
44121 Recreational Vehicle Dealers
SIC 5561 Recreational Vehicle Dealers
441221 Motorcycle Dealers
SIC 5571 Motorcycle Dealers
441222 Boat Dealers
SIC 5551 Boat Dealers
441229 All Other Motor Vehicle Dealers
SIC 5599 Automotive Dealers, NEC
44131 Automotive Parts & Accessories Stores
SIC 5013 Motor Vehicle Supplies & New Parts
SIC 5731 Radio, Television, & Consumer Electronics Stores
SIC 5531 Auto & Home Supply Stores
44132 Tire Dealers
SIC 5014 Tires & Tubes
SIC 5531 Auto & Home Supply Stores
44211 Furniture Stores
SIC 5021 Furniture
SIC 5712 Furniture Stores
44221 Floor Covering Stores
SIC 5023 Homefurnishings
SIC 5713 Floor Coverings Stores
442291 Window Treatment Stores
SIC 5714 Drapery, Curtain, & Upholstery Stores
SIC 5719 Miscellaneous Homefurnishings Stores
442299 All Other Home Furnishings Stores
SIC 5719 Miscellaneous Homefurnishings Stores
443111 Household Appliance Stores
SIC 5722 Household Appliance Stores
SIC 5999 Miscellaneous Retail Stores, nec
SIC 7623 Refrigeration & Air-Conditioning Service & Repair Shops
SIC 7629 Electrical & Electronic Repair Shops, nec
443112 Radio, Television & Other Electronics Stores
SIC 5731 Radio, Television, & Consumer Electronics Stores
SIC 5999 Miscellaneous Retail Stores, nec
SIC 7622 Radio & Television Repair Shops
44312 Computer & Software Stores
SIC 5045 Computers & Computer Peripheral Equipment & Software
SIC 7378 Computer Maintenance & Repair
SIC 5734 Computer & Computer Software Stores
44313 Camera & Photographic Supplies Stores
SIC 5946 Camera & Photographic Supply Stores
44411 Home Centers
SIC 5211 Lumber & Other Building Materials Dealers
44412 Paint & Wallpaper Stores
SIC 5198 Paints, Varnishes, & Supplies
SIC 5231 Paint, Glass, & Wallpaper Stores
44413 Hardware Stores
SIC 5251 Hardware Stores
44419 Other Building Material Dealers
SIC 5031 Lumber, Plywood, Millwork, & Wood Panels
SIC 5032 Brick, Stone, & Related Construction Materials
SIC 5039 Construction Materials, nec
SIC 5063 Electrical Apparatus & Equipment, Wiring Supplies, & Construction Materials
SIC 5074 Plumbing & Heating Equipment & Supplies
SIC 5211 Lumber & Other Building Materials Dealers
SIC 5231 Paint, Glass, & Wallpaper Stores
44421 Outdoor Power Equipment Stores
SIC 5083 Farm & Garden Machinery & Equipment
SIC 5261 Retail Nurseries, Lawn & Garden Supply Stores
44422 Nursery & Garden Centers
SIC 5191 Farm Supplies
SIC 5193 Flowers, Nursery Stock, & Florists' Supplies
SIC 5261 Retail Nurseries, Lawn & Garden Supply Stores
44511 Supermarkets & Other Grocery Stores
SIC 5411 Grocery Stores
44512 Convenience Stores
SIC 5411 Grocery Stores
44521 Meat Markets
SIC 5421 Meat & Fish Markets, Including Freezer Provisioners
SIC 5499 Miscellaneous Food Stores
44522 Fish & Seafood Markets
SIC 5421 Meat & Fish Markets, Including Freezer Provisioners
44523 Fruit & Vegetable Markets
SIC 5431 Fruit & Vegetable Markets
445291 Baked Goods Stores
SIC 5461 Retail Bakeries
445292 Confectionery & Nut Stores
SIC 5441 Candy, Nut & Confectionery Stores
445299 All Other Specialty Food Stores
SIC 5499 Miscellaneous Food Stores
SIC 5451 Dairy Products Stores
44531 Beer, Wine & Liquor Stores
SIC 5921 Liquor Stores
44611 Pharmacies & Drug Stores
SIC 5912 Drug Stores & Proprietary Stores
44612 Cosmetics, Beauty Supplies & Perfume Stores
SIC 5087 Service Establishment Equipment & Supplies
SIC 5999 Miscellaneous Retail Stores, nec
44613 Optical Goods Stores
SIC 5995 Optical Goods Stores
446191 Food Supplement Stores
SIC 5499 Miscellaneous Food Stores
446199 All Other Health & Personal Care Stores
SIC 5047 Medical, Dental, & Hospital Equipment & Supplies
SIC 5999 Miscellaneous Retail Stores, nec
44711 Gasoline Stations with Convenience Stores
SIC 5541 Gasoline Service Station
SIC 5411 Grocery Stores
44719 Other Gasoline Stations
SIC 5541 Gasoline Service Station

44811 Men's Clothing Stores
SIC 5611 Men's & Boys' Clothing & Accessory Stores
44812 Women's Clothing Stores
SIC 5621 Women's Clothing Stores
44813 Children's & Infants' Clothing Stores
SIC 5641 Children's & Infants' Wear Stores
44814 Family Clothing Stores
SIC 5651 Family Clothing Stores
44815 Clothing Accessories Stores
SIC 5611 Men's & Boys' Clothing & Accessory Stores
SIC 5632 Women's Accessory & Specialty Stores
SIC 5699 Miscellaneous Apparel & Accessory Stores
44819 Other Clothing Stores
SIC 5699 Miscellaneous Apparel & Accessory Stores
SIC 5632 Women's Accessory & Specialty Stores
44821 Shoe Stores
SIC 5661 Shoe Stores
44831 Jewelry Stores
SIC 5999 Miscellaneous Retailer, nec
SIC 5944 Jewelry Stores
44832 Luggage & Leather Goods Stores
SIC 5948 Luggage & Leather Goods Stores
45111 Sporting Goods Stores
SIC 7699 Repair Shops & Related Services, NEC
SIC 5941 Sporting Goods Stores & Bicycle Shops
45112 Hobby, Toy & Game Stores
SIC 5945 Hobby, Toy, & Game Stores
45113 Sewing, Needlework & Piece Goods Stores
SIC 5714 Drapery, Curtain, & Upholstery Stores
SIC 5949 Sewing, Needlework, & Piece Goods Stores
45114 Musical Instrument & Supplies Stores
SIC 5736 Musical Instruments Stores
451211 Book Stores
SIC 5942 Book Stores
451212 News Dealers & Newsstands
SIC 5994 News Dealers & Newsstands
45122 Prerecorded Tape, Compact Disc & Record Stores
SIC 5735 Record & Prerecorded Tape Stores
45211 Department Stores
SIC 5311 Department Stores
45291 Warehouse Clubs & Superstores
SIC 5399 Miscellaneous General Merchandise Stores
SIC 5411 Grocery Stores
45299 All Other General Merchandise Stores
SIC 5399 Miscellaneous General Merchandise Stores
SIC 5331 Variety Stores
45311 Florists
SIC 5992 Florists
45321 Office Supplies & Stationery Stores
SIC 5049 Professional Equipment & Supplies, nec
SIC 5112 Stationery & Office Supplies
SIC 5943 Stationery Stores
45322 Gift, Novelty & Souvenir Stores
SIC 5947 Gift, Novelty, & Souvenir Shops
45331 Used Merchandise Stores
SIC 5932 Used Merchandise Stores
45391 Pet & Pet Supplies Stores
SIC 5999 Miscellaneous Retail Stores, NEC
45392 Art Dealers
SIC 5999 Miscellaneous Retail Stores, nec
45393 Manufactured Home Dealers
SIC 5271 Mobile Home Dealers
453991 Tobacco Stores
SIC 5993 Tobacco Stores & Stands
453999 All Other Miscellaneous Store Retailers
SIC 5999 Miscellaneous Retail Stores, nec
SIC 5261 Retail Nurseries, Lawn & Garden Supply Stores
45411 Electronic Shopping & Mail-Order Houses
SIC 5961 Catalog & Mail-Order Houses
45421 Vending Machine Operators
SIC 5962 Automatic Merchandise Machine Operators
454311 Heating Oil Dealers
SIC 5171 Petroleum Bulk Stations & Terminals
SIC 5983 Fuel Oil Dealers
454312 Liquefied Petroleum Gas Dealers
SIC 5171 Petroleum Bulk Stations & Terminals
SIC 5984 Liquefied Petroleum Gas Dealers
454319 Other Fuel Dealers
SIC 5989 Fuel Dealers, nec
45439 Other Direct Selling Establishments
SIC 5421 Meat & Fish Markets, Including Freezer Provisioners
SIC 5963 Direct Selling Establishments

TRANSPORTATION & WAREHOUSING

481111 Scheduled Passenger Air Transportation
SIC 4512 Air Transportation, Scheduled
481112 Scheduled Freight Air Transportation
SIC 4512 Air Transportation, Scheduled
481211 Nonscheduled Chartered Passenger Air Transportation
SIC 4522 Air Transportation, Nonscheduled
481212 Nonscheduled Chartered Freight Air Transportation
SIC 4522 Air Transportation, Nonscheduled
481219 Other Nonscheduled Air Transportation
SIC 7319 Advertising, nec
48122 Nonscheduled Speciality Air Transportation
SIC 0721 Crop Planting, Cultivating, & Protecting
SIC 1382 Oil & Gas Field Exploration Services
SIC 4522 Air Transportation, Nonscheduled
SIC 7335 Commercial Photography
SIC 7997 Membership Sports & Recreation Clubs
SIC 8299 Schools & Educational Services, nec
SIC 8713 Surveying Services
482111 Line-Haul Railroads
SIC 4011 Railroads, Line-Haul Operating
482112 Short Line Railroads
SIC 4013 Railroad Switching & Terminal Establishments
483111 Deep Sea Freight Transportation
SIC 4412 Deep Sea Foreign Transportation of Freight
483112 Deep Sea Passenger Transportation
SIC 4481 Deep Sea Transportation of Passengers, Except by Ferry
483113 Coastal & Great Lakes Freight Transportation
SIC 4424 Deep Sea Domestic Transportation of Freight
SIC 4432 Freight Transportation on the Great Lakes - St. Lawrence Seaway
SIC 4492 Towing & Tugboat Services
483114 Coastal & Great Lakes Passenger Transportation
SIC 4481 Deep Sea Transportation of Passengers, Except by Ferry
SIC 4482 Ferries
483211 Inland Water Freight Transportation
SIC 4449 Water Transportation of Freight, nec
SIC 4492 Towing & Tugboat Services

483212 Inland Water Passenger Transportation
SIC 4482 Ferries
SIC 4489 Water Transportation of Passengers, nec
48411 General Freight Trucking, Local
SIC 4212 Local Trucking without Storage
SIC 4214 Local Trucking with Storage
484121 General Freight Trucking, Long-Distance, Truckload
SIC 4213 Trucking, Except Local
484122 General Freight Trucking, Long-Distance, Less Than Truckload
SIC 4213 Trucking, Except Local
48421 Used Household & Office Goods Moving
SIC 4212 Local Trucking Without Storage
SIC 4213 Trucking, Except Local
SIC 4214 Local Trucking With Storage
48422 Specialized Freight Trucking, Local
SIC 4212 Local Trucking without Storage
SIC 4214 Local Trucking with Storage
48423 Specialized Freight Trucking, Long-Distance
SIC 4213 Trucking, Except Local
485111 Mixed Mode Transit Systems
SIC 4111 Local & Suburban Transit
485112 Commuter Rail Systems
SIC 4111 Local & Suburban Transit
485113 Bus & Motor Vehicle Transit Systems
SIC 4111 Local & Suburban Transit
485119 Other Urban Transit Systems
SIC 4111 Local & Suburban Transit
48521 Interurban & Rural Bus Transportation
SIC 4131 Intercity & Rural Bus Transportation
48531 Taxi Service
SIC 4121 Taxicabs
48532 Limousine Service
SIC 4119 Local Passenger Transportation, nec
48541 School & Employee Bus Transportation
SIC 4151 School Buses
SIC 4119 Local Passenger Transportation, nec
48551 Charter Bus Industry
SIC 4141 Local Charter Bus Service
SIC 4142 Bus Charter Services, Except Local
485991 Special Needs Transportation
SIC 4119 Local Passenger Transportation, nec
485999 All Other Transit & Ground Passenger Transportation
SIC 4111 Local & Suburban Transit
SIC 4119 Local Passenger Transportation, nec
48611 Pipeline Transportation of Crude Oil
SIC 4612 Crude Petroleum Pipelines
48621 Pipeline Transportation of Natural Gas
SIC 4922 Natural Gas Transmission
SIC 4923 Natural Gas Transmission & Distribution
48691 Pipeline Transportation of Refined Petroleum Products
SIC 4613 Refined Petroleum Pipelines
48699 All Other Pipeline Transportation
SIC 4619 Pipelines, nec
48711 Scenic & Sightseeing Transportation, Land
SIC 4119 Local Passenger Transportation, nec
SIC 4789 Transportation Services, nec
SIC 7999 Amusement & Recreation Services, nec
48721 Scenic & Sightseeing Transportation, Water
SIC 4489 Water Transportation of Passengers, nec
SIC 7999 Amusement & Recreation Services, nec
48799 Scenic & Sightseeing Transportation, Other
SIC 4522 Air Transportation, Nonscheduled
SIC 7999 Amusement & Recreation Services, nec
488111 Air Traffic Control
SIC 4581 Airports, Flying Fields, & Airport Terminal Services
SIC 9621 Regulation & Administration of Transportation Programs
488112 Airport Operations, except Air Traffic Control
SIC 4581 Airports, Flying Fields, & Airport Terminal Services
SIC 4959 Sanitary Services, nec
488119 Other Airport Operations
SIC 4581 Airports, Flying Fields, & Airport Terminal Services
SIC 4959 Sanitary Services, nec
48819 Other Support Activities for Air Transportation
SIC 4581 Airports, Flying Fields, & Airport Terminal Services
48821 Support Activities for Rail Transportation
SIC 4013 Railroad Switching & Terminal Establishments
SIC 4741 Rental of Railroad Cars
SIC 4789 Transportation Services, nec
48831 Port & Harbor Operations
SIC 4491 Marine Cargo Handling
SIC 4499 Water Transportation Services, nec
48832 Marine Cargo Handling
SIC 4491 Marine Cargo Handling
48833 Navigational Services to Shipping
SIC 4492 Towing & Tugboat Services
SIC 4499 Water Transportation Services, nec
48839 Other Support Activities for Water Transportation
SIC 4499 Water Transportation Services, nec
SIC 4785 Fixed Facilities & Inspection & Weighing Services for Motor Vehicle Transportation
SIC 7699 Repair Shops & Related Services, nec
48841 Motor Vehicle Towing
SIC 7549 Automotive Services, Except Repair & Carwashes
48849 Other Support Activities for Road Transportation
SIC 4173 Terminal & Service Facilities for Motor Vehicle Passenger Transportation
SIC 4231 Terminal & Joint Terminal Maintenance Facilities for Motor Freight Transportation
SIC 4785 Fixed Facilities & Inspection & Weighing Services for Motor Vehicle Transportation
48851 Freight Transportation Arrangement
SIC 4731 Arrangement of Transportation of Freight & Cargo
488991 Packing & Crating
SIC 4783 Packing & Crating
488999 All Other Support Activities for Transportation
SIC 4729 Arrangement of Passenger Transportation, nec
SIC 4789 Transportation Services, nec
49111 Postal Service
SIC 4311 United States Postal Service
49211 Couriers
SIC 4215 Courier Services, Except by Air
SIC 4513 Air Courier Services
49221 Local Messengers & Local Delivery
SIC 4215 Courier Services, Except by Air
49311 General Warehousing & Storage Facilities
SIC 4225 General Warehousing & Storage
SIC 4226 Special Warehousing & Storage, nec
49312 Refrigerated Storage Facilities
SIC 4222 Refrigerated Warehousing & Storage
SIC 4226 Special Warehousing & Storage, nec
49313 Farm Product Storage Facilities
SIC 4221 Farm Product Warehousing & Storage
49319 Other Warehousing & Storage Facilities
SIC 4226 Special Warehousing & Storage, nec

INFORMATION

51111 Newspaper Publishers
SIC 2711 Newspapers: Publishing or Publishing & Printing
51112 Periodical Publishers
SIC 2721 Periodicals: Publishing or Publishing & Printing
51113 Book Publishers
SIC 2731 Books: Publishing or Publishing & Printing
51114 Database & Directory Publishers
SIC 2741 Miscellaneous Publishing
511191 Greeting Card Publishers
SIC 2771 Greeting Cards
511199 All Other Publishers
SIC 2741 Miscellaneous Publishing
51121 Software Publishers
SIC 7372 Prepackaged Software
51211 Motion Picture & Video Production
SIC 7812 Motion Picture & Video Tape Production
51212 Motion Picture & Video Distribution
SIC 7822 Motion Picture & Video Tape Distribution
SIC 7829 Services Allied to Motion Picture Distribution
512131 Motion Picture Theaters, Except Drive-Ins.
SIC 7832 Motion Picture Theaters, Except Drive-In
512132 Drive-In Motion Picture Theaters
SIC 7833 Drive-In Motion Picture Theaters
512191 Teleproduction & Other Post-Production Services
SIC 7819 Services Allied to Motion Picture Production
512199 Other Motion Picture & Video Industries
SIC 7819 Services Allied to Motion Picture Production
SIC 7829 Services Allied to Motion Picture Distribution
51221 Record Production
SIC 8999 Services, nec
51222 Integrated Record Production/Distribution
SIC 3652 Phonograph Records & Prerecorded Audio Tapes & Disks
51223 Music Publishers
SIC 2731 Books: Publishing or Publishing & Printing
SIC 2741 Miscellaneous Publishing
SIC 8999 Services, nec
51224 Sound Recording Studios
SIC 7389 Business Services, nec
51229 Other Sound Recording Industries
SIC 7389 Business Services, nec
SIC 7922 Theatrical Producers & Miscellaneous Theatrical Services
513111 Radio Networks
SIC 4832 Radio Broadcasting Stations
513112 Radio Stations
SIC 4832 Radio Broadcasting Stations
51312 Television Broadcasting
SIC 4833 Television Broadcasting Stations
51321 Cable Networks
SIC 4841 Cable & Other Pay Television Services
51322 Cable & Other Program Distribution
SIC 4841 Cable & Other Pay Television Services
51331 Wired Telecommunications Carriers
SIC 4813 Telephone Communications, Except Radiotelephone
SIC 4822 Telegraph & Other Message Communications
513321 Paging
SIC 4812 Radiotelephone Communications
513322 Cellular & Other Wireless Telecommunications
SIC 4812 Radiotelephone Communications
SIC 4899 Communications Services, nec
51333 Telecommunications Resellers
SIC 4812 Radio Communications
SIC 4813 Telephone Communications, Except Radiotelephone
51334 Satellite Telecommunications
SIC 4899 Communications Services, NEC
51339 Other Telecommunications
SIC 4899 Communications Services, NEC
51411 News Syndicates
SIC 7383 News Syndicates
51412 Libraries & Archives
SIC 8231 Libraries
514191 On-Line Information Services
SIC 7375 Information Retrieval Services
514199 All Other Information Services
SIC 8999 Services, nec
51421 Data Processing Services
SIC 7374 Computer Processing & Data Preparation & Processing Services

FINANCE & INSURANCE

52111 Monetary Authorities - Central Bank
SIC 6011 Federal Reserve Banks
52211 Commercial Banking
SIC 6021 National Commercial Banks
SIC 6022 State Commercial Banks
SIC 6029 Commercial Banks, nec
SIC 6081 Branches & Agencies of Foreign Banks
52212 Savings Institutions
SIC 6035 Savings Institutions, Federally Chartered
SIC 6036 Savings Institutions, Not Federally Chartered
52213 Credit Unions
SIC 6061 Credit Unions, Federally Chartered
SIC 6062 Credit Unions, Not Federally Chartered
52219 Other Depository Credit Intermediation
SIC 6022 State Commercial Banks
52221 Credit Card Issuing
SIC 6021 National Commercial Banks
SIC 6022 State Commercial Banks
SIC 6141 Personal Credit Institutions
52222 Sales Financing
SIC 6141 Personal Credit Institutions
SIC 6153 Short-Term Business Credit Institutions, Except Agricultural .
SIC 6159 Miscellaneous Business Credit Institutions
522291 Consumer Lending
SIC 6141 Personal Credit Institutions
522292 Real Estate Credit
SIC 6162 Mortgage Bankers & Loan Correspondents
522293 International Trade Financing
SIC 6081 Branches & Agencies of Foreign Banks
SIC 6082 Foreign Trade & International Banking Institutions
SIC 6111 Federal & Federally-Sponsored Credit Agencies
SIC 6159 Miscellaneous Business Credit Institutions
522294 Secondary Market Financing
SIC 6111 Federal & Federally Sponsored Credit Agencies
522298 All Other Nondepository Credit Intermediation
SIC 5932 Used Merchandise Stores
SIC 6081 Branches & Agencies of Foreign Banks
SIC 6111 Federal & Federally-Sponsored Credit Agencies
SIC 6153 Short-Term Business Credit Institutions, Except Agricultural
SIC 6159 Miscellaneous Business Credit Institutions

52231 Mortgage & Other Loan Brokers
SIC 6163 Loan Brokers
52232 Financial Transactions Processing, Reserve, & Clearing House Activities
SIC 6019 Central Reserve Depository Institutions, nec
SIC 6099 Functions Related to Depository Banking, nec
SIC 6153 Short-Term Business Credit Institutions, Except Agricultural
SIC 7389 Business Services, nec
52239 Other Activities Related to Credit Intermediation
SIC 6099 Functions Related to Depository Banking, nec
SIC 6162 Mortgage Bankers & Loan Correspondents
52311 Investment Banking & Securities Dealing
SIC 6211 Security Brokers, Dealers, & Flotation Companies
52312 Securities Brokerage
SIC 6211 Security Brokers, Dealers, & Flotation Companies
52313 Commodity Contracts Dealing
SIC 6099 Functions Related to depository Banking, nec
SIC 6799 Investors, nec
SIC 6221 Commodity Contracts Brokers & Dealers
52314 Commodity Brokerage
SIC 6221 Commodity Contracts Brokers & Dealers
52321 Securities & Commodity Exchanges
SIC 6231 Security & Commodity Exchanges
52391 Miscellaneous Intermediation
SIC 6211 Securities Brokers, Dealers & Flotation Companies
SIC 6799 Investors, nec
52392 Portfolio Management
SIC 6282 Investment Advice
SIC 6371 Pension, Health, & Welfare Funds
SIC 6733 Trust, Except Educational, Religious, & Charitable
SIC 6799 Investors, nec
52393 Investment Advice
SIC 6282 Investment Advice
523991 Trust, Fiduciary & Custody Activities
SIC 6021 National Commercial Banks
SIC 6022 State Commercial Banks
SIC 6091 Nondepository Trust Facilities
SIC 6099 Functions Related to Depository Banking, nec
SIC 6289 Services Allied With the Exchange of Securities or Commodities, nec
SIC 6733 Trusts, Except Educational, Religious, & Charitable
523999 Miscellaneous Financial Investment Activities
SIC 6099 Functions Related to Depository Banking, nec
SIC 6211 Security Brokers, Dealers, & Flotation Companies
SIC 6289 Services Allied With the Exchange of Securities or Commodities, nec
SIC 6799 Investors, nec
SIC 6792 Oil Royalty Traders
524113 Direct Life Insurance Carriers
SIC 6311 Life Insurance
524114 Direct Health & Medical Insurance Carriers
SIC 6324 Hospital & Medical Service Plans
SIC 6321 Accident & Health Insurance
524126 Direct Property & Casualty Insurance Carriers
SIC 6331 Fire, Marine, & Casualty Insurance
SIC 6351 Surety Insurance
524127 Direct Title Insurance Carriers
SIC 6361 Title Insurance
524128 Other Direct Insurance Carriers
SIC 6399 Insurance Carriers, nec
52413 Reinsurance Carriers
SIC 6311 Life Insurance
SIC 6321 Accident & Health Insurance
SIC 6324 Hospital & Medical Service Plans
SIC 6331 Fire, Marine, & Casualty Insurance
SIC 6351 Surety Insurance
SIC 6361 Title Insurance
52421 Insurance Agencies & Brokerages
SIC 6411 Insurance Agents, Brokers & Service
524291 Claims Adjusters
SIC 6411 Insurance Agents, Brokers & Service
524292 Third Party Administration for Insurance & Pension Funds
SIC 6371 Pension, Health, & Welfare Funds
SIC 6411 Insurance Agents, Brokers & Service
524298 All Other Insurance Related Activities
SIC 6411 Insurance Agents, Brokers & Service
52511 Pension Funds
SIC 6371 Pension, Health, & Welfare Funds
52512 Health & Welfare Funds
SIC 6371 Pension, Health, & Welfare Funds
52519 Other Insurance Funds
SIC 6321 Accident & Health Insurance
SIC 6324 Hospital & Medical Service Plans
SIC 6331 Fire, Marine, & Casualty Insurance
SIC 6733 Trusts, Except Educational, Religious, & Charitable
52591 Open-End Investment Funds
SIC 6722 Management Investment Offices, Open-End
52592 Trusts, Estates, & Agency Accounts
SIC 6733 Trusts, Except Educational, Religious, & Charitable
52593 Real Estate Investment Trusts
SIC 6798 Real Estate Investment Trusts
52599 Other Financial Vehicles
SIC 6726 Unit Investment Trusts, Face-Amount Certificate Offices, & Closed-End Management Investment Offices

REAL ESTATE & RENTAL & LEASING

53111 Lessors of Residential Buildings & Dwellings
SIC 6513 Operators of Apartment Buildings
SIC 6514 Operators of Dwellings Other Than Apartment Buildings
53112 Lessors of Nonresidential Buildings
SIC 6512 Operators of Nonresidential Buildings
53113 Lessors of Miniwarehouses & Self Storage Units
SIC 4225 General Warehousing & Storage
53119 Lessors of Other Real Estate Property
SIC 6515 Operators of Residential Mobile Home Sites
SIC 6517 Lessors of Railroad Property
SIC 6519 Lessors of Real Property, nec
53121 Offices of Real Estate Agents & Brokers
SIC 6531 Real Estate Agents Managers
531311 Residential Property Managers
SIC 6531 Real Estate Agents & Managers
531312 Nonresidential Property Managers
SIC 6531 Real Estate Agents & Managers
53132 Offices of Real Estate Appraisers
SIC 6531 Real Estate Agents & Managers
531399 All Other Activities Related to Real Estate
SIC 6531 Real Estate Agents & Managers
532111 Passenger Car Rental
SIC 7514 Passenger Car Rental
532112 Passenger Car Leasing
SIC 7515 Passenger Car Leasing

53212 Truck, Utility Trailer, & RV Rental & Leasing
SIC 7513 Truck Rental & Leasing Without Drivers
SIC 7519 Utility Trailers & Recreational Vehicle Rental
53221 Consumer Electronics & Appliances Rental
SIC 7359 Equipment Rental & Leasing, nec
53222 Formal Wear & Costume Rental
SIC 7299 Miscellaneous Personal Services, nec
SIC 7819 Services Allied to Motion Picture Production
53223 Video Tape & Disc Rental
SIC 7841 Video Tape Rental
532291 Home Health Equipment Rental
SIC 7352 Medical Equipment Rental & Leasing
532292 Recreational Goods Rental
SIC 7999 Amusement & Recreation Services, nec
532299 All Other Consumer Goods Rental
SIC 7359 Equipment Rental & Leasing, nec
53231 General Rental Centers
SIC 7359 Equipment Rental & Leasing, nec
532411 Commercial Air, Rail, & Water Transportation Equipment Rental & Leasing
SIC 4499 Water Transportation Services, nec
SIC 4741 Rental of Railroad Cars
SIC 7359 Equipment Rental & Leasing, nec
532412 Construction, Mining & Forestry Machinery & Equipment Rental & Leasing
SIC 7353 Heavy Construction Equipment Rental & Leasing
SIC 7359 Equipment Rental & Leasing, nec
53242 Office Machinery & Equipment Rental & Leasing
SIC 7359 Equipment Rental & Leasing
SIC 7377 Computer Rental & Leasing
53249 Other Commercial & Industrial Machinery & Equipment Rental & Leasing
SIC 7352 Medical Equipment Rental & Leasing
SIC 7359 Equipment Rental & Leasing, nec
SIC 7819 Services Allied to Motion Picture Production
SIC 7922 Theatrical Producers & Miscellaneous Theatrical Services
53311 Owners & Lessors of Other Nonfinancial Assets
SIC 6792 Oil Royalty Traders
SIC 6794 Patent Owners & Lessors

PROFESSIONAL, SCIENTIFIC, & TECHNICAL SERVICES

54111 Offices of Lawyers
SIC 8111 Legal Services
541191 Title Abstract & Settlement Offices
SIC 6541 Title Abstract Offices
541199 All Other Legal Services
SIC 7389 Business Services, nec
541211 Offices of Certified Public Accountants
SIC 8721 Accounting, Auditing, & Bookkeeping Services
541213 Tax Preparation Services
SIC 7291 Tax Return Preparation Services
541214 Payroll Services
SIC 7819 Services Allied to Motion Picture Production
SIC 8721 Accounting, Auditing, & Bookkeeping Services
541219 Other Accounting Services
SIC 8721 Accounting, Auditing, & Bookkeeping Services
54131 Architectural Services
SIC 8712 Architectural Services
54132 Landscape Architectural Services
SIC 0781 Landscape Counseling & Planning
54133 Engineering Services
SIC 8711 Engineering Services
54134 Drafting Services
SIC 7389 Business Services, nec
54135 Building Inspection Services
SIC 7389 Business Services, nec
54136 Geophysical Surveying & Mapping Services
SIC 8713 Surveying Services
SIC 1081 Metal Mining Services
SIC 1382 Oil & Gas Field Exploration Services
SIC 1481 Nonmetallic Minerals Services, Except Fuels
54137 Surveying & Mapping Services
SIC 7389 Business Services, nec
SIC 8713 Surveying Services
54138 Testing Laboratories
SIC 8734 Testing Laboratories
54141 Interior Design Services
SIC 7389 Business Services, nec
54142 Industrial Design Services
SIC 7389 Business Services, nec
54143 Commercial Art & Graphic Design Services
SIC 7336 Commercial Art & Graphic Design
SIC 8099 Health & Allied Services, nec
54149 Other Specialized Design Services
SIC 7389 Business Services, nec
541511 Custom Computer Programming Services
SIC 7371 Computer Programming Services
541512 Computer Systems Design Services
SIC 7373 Computer Integrated Systems Design
SIC 7379 Computer Related Services, nec
541513 Computer Facilities Management Services
SIC 7376 Computer Facilities Management Services
541519 Other Computer Related Services
SIC 7379 Computer Related Services, nec
541611 Administrative Management & General Management Consulting Services
SIC 8742 Management Consulting Services
541612 Human Resources & Executive Search Consulting Services
SIC 8742 Management Consulting Services
SIC 7361 Employment Agencies
SIC 8999 Services, nec
541613 Marketing Consulting Services
SIC 8742 Management Consulting Services
541614 Process, Physical, Distribution & Logistics Consulting Services
SIC 8742 Management Consulting Services
541618 Other Management Consulting Services
SIC 4731 Arrangement of Transportation of Freight & Cargo
SIC 8748 Business Consulting Services, nec
54162 Environmental Consulting Services
SIC 8999 Services, nec
54169 Other Scientific & Technical Consulting Services
SIC 0781 Landscape Counseling & Planning
SIC 8748 Business Consulting Services, nec
SIC 8999 Services, nec
54171 Research & Development in the Physical Sciences & Engineering Sciences
SIC 8731 Commercial Physical & Biological Research
SIC 8733 Noncommercial Research Organizations

54172 Research & Development in the Life Sciences
SIC 8731 Commercial Physical & Biological Research
SIC 8733 Noncommercial Research Organizations
54173 Research & Development in the Social Sciences & Humanities
SIC 8732 Commercial Economic, Sociological, & Educational Research
SIC 8733 Noncommercial Research Organizations
54181 Advertising Agencies
SIC 7311 Advertising Agencies
54182 Public Relations Agencies
SIC 8743 Public Relations Services
54183 Media Buying Agencies
SIC 7319 Advertising, nec
54184 Media Representatives
SIC 7313 Radio, Television, & Publishers' Advertising Representatives
54185 Display Advertising
SIC 7312 Outdoor Advertising Services
SIC 7319 Advertising, nec
54186 Direct Mail Advertising
SIC 7331 Direct Mail Advertising Services
54187 Advertising Material Distribution Services
SIC 7319 Advertising, NEC
54189 Other Services Related to Advertising
SIC 7319 Advertising, nec
SIC 5199 Nondurable Goods, nec
SIC 7389 Business Services, nec
54191 Marketing Research & Public Opinion Polling
SIC 8732 Commercial Economic, Sociological, & Educational Research
541921 Photography Studios, Portrait
SIC 7221 Photographic Studios, Portrait
541922 Commercial Photography
SIC 7335 Commercial Photography
SIC 8099 Health & Allied Services, nec
54193 Translation & Interpretation Services
SIC 7389 Business Services, NEC
54194 Veterinary Services
SIC 0741 Veterinary Services for Livestock
SIC 0742 Veterinary Services for Animal Specialties
SIC 8734 Testing Laboratories
54199 All Other Professional, Scientific & Technical Services
SIC 7389 Business Services

MANAGEMENT OF COMPANIES & ENTERPRISES

551111 Offices of Bank Holding Companies
SIC 6712 Offices of Bank Holding Companies
551112 Offices of Other Holding Companies
SIC 6719 Offices of Holding Companies, nec
551114 Corporate, Subsidiary, & Regional Managing Offices
No SIC equivalent

ADMINISTRATIVE & SUPPORT, WASTE MANAGEMENT & REMEDIATION SERVICES

56111 Office Administrative Services
SIC 8741 Management Services
56121 Facilities Support Services
SIC 8744 Facilities Support Management Services
56131 Employment Placement Agencies
SIC 7361 Employment Agencies
SIC 7819 Services Allied to Motion Pictures Production
SIC 7922 Theatrical Producers & Miscellaneous Theatrical Services
56132 Temporary Help Services
SIC 7363 Help Supply Services
56133 Employee Leasing Services
SIC 7363 Help Supply Services
56141 Document Preparation Services
SIC 7338 Secretarial & Court Reporting
561421 Telephone Answering Services
SIC 7389 Business Services, nec
561422 Telemarketing Bureaus
SIC 7389 Business Services, nec
561431 Photocopying & Duplicating Services
SIC 7334 Photocopying & Duplicating Services
561432 Private Mail Centers
SIC 7389 Business Services, nec
561439 Other Business Service Centers
SIC 7334 Photocopying & Duplicating Services
SIC 7389 Business Services, nec
56144 Collection Agencies
SIC 7322 Adjustment & Collection Services
56145 Credit Bureaus
SIC 7323 Credit Reporting Services
561491 Repossession Services
SIC 7322 Adjustment & Collection
SIC 7389 Business Services, nec
561492 Court Reporting & Stenotype Services
SIC 7338 Secretarial & Court Reporting
561499 All Other Business Support Services
SIC 7389 Business Services, NEC
56151 Travel Agencies
SIC 4724 Travel Agencies
56152 Tour Operators
SIC 4725 Tour Operators
561591 Convention & Visitors Bureaus
SIC 7389 Business Services, nec
561599 All Other Travel Arrangement & Reservation Services
SIC 4729 Arrangement of Passenger Transportation, nec
SIC 7389 Business Services, nec
SIC 7999 Amusement & Recreation Services, nec
SIC 8699 Membership Organizations, nec
561611 Investigation Services
SIC 7381 Detective, Guard, & Armored Car Services
561612 Security Guards & Patrol Services
SIC 7381 Detective, Guard, & Armored Car Services
561613 Armored Car Services
SIC 7381 Detective, Guard, & Armored Car Services
561621 Security Systems Services
SIC 7382 Security Systems Services
SIC 1731 Electrical Work
561622 Locksmiths
SIC 7699 Repair Shops & Related Services, nec
56171 Exterminating & Pest Control Services
SIC 4959 Sanitary Services, NEC
SIC 7342 Disinfecting & Pest Control Services
56172 Janitorial Services
SIC 7342 Disinfecting & Pest Control Services
SIC 7349 Building Cleaning & Maintenance Services, nec
SIC 4581 Airports, Flying Fields, & Airport Terminal Services

56173 Landscaping Services
SIC 0782 Lawn & Garden Services
SIC 0783 Ornamental Shrub & Tree Services
56174 Carpet & Upholstery Cleaning Services
SIC 7217 Carpet & Upholstery Cleaning
56179 Other Services to Buildings & Dwellings
SIC 7389 Business Services, nec
SIC 7699 Repair Shops & Related Services, nec
56191 Packaging & Labeling Services
SIC 7389 Business Services, nec
56192 Convention & Trade Show Organizers
SIC 7389 Business Services, NEC
56199 All Other Support Services
SIC 7389 Business Services, nec
562111 Solid Waste Collection
SIC 4212 Local Trucking Without Storage
SIC 4953 Refuse Systems
562112 Hazardous Waste Collection
SIC 4212 Local Trucking Without Storage
SIC 4953 Refuse Systems
562119 Other Waste Collection
SIC 4212 Local Trucking Without Storage
SIC 4953 Refuse Systems
562211 Hazardous Waste Treatment & Disposal
SIC 4953 Refuse Systems
562212 Solid Waste Landfill
SIC 4953 Refuse Systems
562213 Solid Waste Combustors & Incinerators
SIC 4953 Refuse Systems
562219 Other Nonhazardous Waste Treatment & Disposal
SIC 4953 Refuse Systems
56291 Remediation Services
SIC 1799 Special Trade Contractors, nec
SIC 4959 Sanitary Services, nec
56292 Materials Recovery Facilities
SIC 4953 Refuse Systems
562991 Septic Tank & Related Services
SIC 7359 Equipment Rental & Leasing, nec
SIC 7699 Repair Shops & Related Services, nec
562998 All Other Miscellaneous Waste Management Services
SIC 4959 Sanitary Services, nec

EDUCATIONAL SERVICES

61111 Elementary & Secondary Schools
SIC 8211 Elementary & Secondary Schools
61121 Junior Colleges
SIC 8222 Junior Colleges & Technical Institutes
61131 Colleges, Universities & Professional Schools
SIC 8221 Colleges, Universities, & Professional Schools
61141 Business & Secretarial Schools
SIC 8244 Business & Secretarial Schools
61142 Computer Training
SIC 8243 Data Processing Schools
61143 Professional & Management Development Training Schools
SIC 8299 Schools & Educational Services, nec
611511 Cosmetology & Barber Schools
SIC 7231 Beauty Shops
SIC 7241 Barber Shops
611512 Flight Training
SIC 8249 Vocational Schools, nec
SIC 8299 Schools & Educational Services, nec
611513 Apprenticeship Training
SIC 8249 Vocational Schools, nec
611519 Other Technical & Trade Schools
SIC 8249 Vocational Schools, NEC
SIC 8243 Data Processing Schools
61161 Fine Arts Schools
SIC 8299 Schools & Educational Services, nec
SIC 7911 Dance Studios, Schools, & Halls
61162 Sports & Recreation Instruction
SIC 7999 Amusement & Recreation Services, nec
61163 Language Schools
SIC 8299 Schools & Educational Services, nec
611691 Exam Preparation & Tutoring
SIC 8299 Schools & Educational Services, nec
611692 Automobile Driving Schools
SIC 8299 Schools & Educational Services, nec
611699 All Other Miscellaneous Schools & Instruction
SIC 8299 Schools & Educational Services, nec
61171 Educational Support Services
SIC 8299 Schools & Educational Services nec
SIC 8748 Business Consulting Services, nec

HEALTH CARE & SOCIAL ASSISTANCE

621111 Offices of Physicians
SIC 8011 Offices & Clinics of Doctors of Medicine
SIC 8031 Offices & Clinics of Doctors of Osteopathy
621112 Offices of Physicians, Mental Health Specialists
SIC 8011 Offices & Clinics of Doctors of Medicine
SIC 8031 Offices & Clinics of Doctors of Osteopathy
62121 Offices of Dentists
SIC 8021 Offices & Clinics of Dentists
62131 Offices of Chiropractors
SIC 8041 Offices & Clinics of Chiropractors
62132 Offices of Optometrists
SIC 8042 Offices & Clinics of Optometrists
62133 Offices of Mental Health Practitioners
SIC 8049 Offices & Clinics of Health Practitioners, nec
62134 Offices of Physical, Occupational & Speech Therapists & Audiologists
SIC 8049 Offices & Clinics of Health Practitioners, nec
621391 Offices of Podiatrists
SIC 8043 Offices & Clinics of Podiatrists
621399 Offices of All Other Miscellaneous Health Practitioners
SIC 8049 Offices & Clinics of Health Practitioners, nec
62141 Family Planning Centers
SIC 8093 Speciality Outpatient Facilities, NEC
SIC 8099 Health & Allied Services, nec
62142 Outpatient Mental Health & Substance Abuse Centers
SIC 8093 Specialty Outpatient Facilities, nec
621491 HMO Medical Centers
SIC 8011 Offices & Clinics of Doctors of Medicine
621492 Kidney Dialysis Centers
SIC 8092 Kidney Dialysis Centers
621493 Freestanding Ambulatory Surgical & Emergency Centers
SIC 8011 Offices & Clinics of Doctors of Medicine
621498 All Other Outpatient Care Centers
SIC 8093 Specialty Outpatient Facilities, nec
621511 Medical Laboratories
SIC 8071 Medical Laboratories
621512 Diagnostic Imaging Centers
SIC 8071 Medical Laboratories

62161 Home Health Care Services
SIC 8082 Home Health Care Services
62191 Ambulance Services
SIC 4119 Local Passenger Transportation, nec
SIC 4522 Air Transportation, Nonscheduled
621991 Blood & Organ Banks
SIC 8099 Health & Allied Services, nec
621999 All Other Miscellaneous Ambulatory Health Care Services
SIC 8099 Health & Allied Services, nec
62211 General Medical & Surgical Hospitals
SIC 8062 General Medical & Surgical Hospitals
SIC 8069 Specialty Hospitals, Except Psychiatric
62221 Psychiatric & Substance Abuse Hospitals
SIC 8063 Psychiatric Hospitals
SIC 8069 Specialty Hospitals, Except Psychiatric
62231 Specialty Hospitals
SIC 8069 Specialty Hospitals, Except Psychiatric
62311 Nursing Care Facilities
SIC 8051 Skilled Nursing Care Facilities
SIC 8052 Intermediate Care Facilities
SIC 8059 Nursing & Personal Care Facilities, nec
62321 Residential Mental Retardation Facilities
SIC 8052 Intermediate Care Facilities
62322 Residential Mental Health & Substance Abuse Facilities
SIC 8361 Residential Care
623311 Continuing Care Retirement Communities
SIC 8051 Skilled Nursing Care Facilities
SIC 8052 Intermediate Care Facilities
SIC 8059 Nursing & Personal Care Facilities, nec
623312 Homes for the Elderly
SIC 8361 Residential Care
62399 Other Residential Care Facilities
SIC 8361 Residential Care
62411 Child & Youth Services
SIC 8322 Individual & Family Social Services
SIC 8641 Civic, Social, & Fraternal Organizations
62412 Services for the Elderly & Persons with Disabilities
SIC 8322 Individual & Family Social Services
62419 Other Individual & Family Services
SIC 8322 Individual & Family Social Services
62421 Community Food Services
SIC 8322 Individual & Family Social Services
624221 Temporary Shelters
SIC 8322 Individual & Family Social Services
624229 Other Community Housing Services
SIC 8322 Individual & Family Social Services
62423 Emergency & Other Relief Services
SIC 8322 Individual & Family Social Services
62431 Vocational Rehabilitation Services
SIC 8331 Job Training & Vocational Rehabilitation Services
62441 Child Day Care Services
SIC 8351 Child Day Care Services
SIC 7299 Miscellaneous Personal Services, nec

ARTS, ENTERTAINMENT, & RECREATION

71111 Theater Companies & Dinner Theaters
SIC 5812 Eating Places
SIC 7922 Theatrical Producers & Miscellaneous Theatrical Services
71112 Dance Companies
SIC 7922 Theatrical Producers & Miscellaneous Theatrical Services
71113 Musical Groups & Artists
SIC 7929 Bands, Orchestras, Actors, & Entertainment Groups
71119 Other Performing Arts Companies
SIC 7929 Bands, Orchestras, Actors, & Entertainment Groups
SIC 7999 Amusement & Recreation Services, nec
711211 Sports Teams & Clubs
SIC 7941 Professional Sports Clubs & Promoters
711212 Race Tracks
SIC 7948 Racing, Including Track Operations
711219 Other Spectator Sports
SIC 7941 Professional Sports Clubs & Promoters
SIC 7948 Racing, Including Track Operations
SIC 7999 Amusement & Recreation Services, nec
71131 Promoters of Performing Arts, Sports & Similar Events with Facilities
SIC 6512 Operators of Nonresidential Buildings
SIC 7922 Theatrical Procedures & Miscellaneous Theatrical Services
SIC 7941 Professional Sports Clubs & Promoters
71132 Promoters of Performing Arts, Sports & Similar Events without Facilities
SIC 7922 Theatrical Producers & Miscellaneous Theatrical Services
SIC 7941 Professional Sports Clubs & Promoters
71141 Agents & Managers for Artists, Athletes, Entertainers & Other Public Figures
SIC 7389 Business Services, nec
SIC 7922 Theatrical Producers & Miscellaneous Theatrical Services
SIC 7941 Professional Sports Clubs & Promoters
71151 Independent Artists, Writers, & Performers
SIC 7819 Services Allied to Motion Picture Production
SIC 7929 Bands, Orchestras, Actors, & Other Entertainers & Entertainment Services
SIC 8999 Services, nec
71211 Museums
SIC 8412 Museums & Art Galleries
71212 Historical Sites
SIC 8412 Museums & Art Galleries
71213 Zoos & Botanical Gardens
SIC 8422 Arboreta & Botanical & Zoological Gardens
71219 Nature Parks & Other Similar Institutions
SIC 7999 Amusement & Recreation Services, nec
SIC 8422 Arboreta & Botanical & Zoological Gardens
71311 Amusement & Theme Parks
SIC 7996 Amusement Parks
71312 Amusement Arcades
SIC 7993 Coin-Operated Amusement Devices
71321 Casinos
SIC 7999 Amusement & Recreation Services, nec
71329 Other Gambling Industries
SIC 7993 Coin-Operated Amusement Devices
SIC 7999 Amusement & Recreation Services, nec
71391 Golf Courses & Country Clubs
SIC 7992 Public Golf Courses
SIC 7997 Membership Sports & Recreation Clubs
71392 Skiing Facilities
SIC 7999 Amusement & Recreation Services, nec
71393 Marinas
SIC 4493 Marinas

71394 Fitness & Recreational Sports Centers
SIC 7991 Physical Fitness Facilities
SIC 7997 Membership Sports & Recreation Clubs
SIC 7999 Amusement & Recreation Services, nec
71395 Bowling Centers
SIC 7933 Bowling Centers
71399 All Other Amusement & Recreation Industries
SIC 7911 Dance Studios, Schools, & Halls
SIC 7993 Amusement & Recreation Services, nec
SIC 7997 Membership Sports & Recreation Clubs
SIC 7999 Amusement & Recreation Services, nec

ACCOMMODATION & FOODSERVICES

72111 Hotels & Motels
SIC 7011 Hotels & Motels
SIC 7041 Organization Hotels & Lodging Houses, on Membership Basis
72112 Casino Hotels
SIC 7011 Hotels & Motels
721191 Bed & Breakfast Inns
SIC 7011 Hotels & Motels
721199 All Other Traveler Accommodation
SIC 7011 Hotels & Motels
721211 RV Parks & Campgrounds
SIC 7033 Recreational Vehicle Parks & Campgrounds
721214 Recreational & Vacation Camps
SIC 7032 Sporting & Recreational Camps
72131 Rooming & Boarding Houses
SIC 7021 Rooming & Boarding Houses
SIC 7041 Organization Hotels & Lodging Houses, on Membership Basis
72211 Full-Service Restaurants
SIC 5812 Eating Places
722211 Limited-Service Restaurants
SIC 5812 Eating Places
SIC 5499 Miscellaneous Food Stores
722212 Cafeterias
SIC 5812 Eating Places
722213 Snack & Nonalcoholic Beverage Bars
SIC 5812 Eating Places
SIC 5461 Retail Bakeries
72231 Foodservice Contractors
SIC 5812 Eating Places
72232 Caterers
SIC 5812 Eating Places
72233 Mobile Caterers
SIC 5963 Direct Selling Establishments
72241 Drinking Places
SIC 5813 Drinking Places

OTHER SERVICES

811111 General Automotive Repair
SIC 7538 General Automotive Repair Shops
811112 Automotive Exhaust System Repair
SIC 7533 Automotive Exhaust System Repair Shops
811113 Automotive Transmission Repair
SIC 7537 Automotive Transmission Repair Shops
811118 Other Automotive Mechanical & Electrical Repair & Maintenance
SIC 7539 Automotive Repair Shops, nec
811121 Automotive Body, Paint & Upholstery Repair & Maintenance
SIC 7532 Top, Body, & Upholstery Repair Shops & Paint Shops
811122 Automotive Glass Replacement Shops
SIC 7536 Automotive Glass Replacement Shops
811191 Automotive Oil Change & Lubrication Shops
SIC 7549 Automotive Services, Except Repair & Carwashes
811192 Car Washes
SIC 7542 Carwashes
811198 All Other Automotive Repair & Maintenance
SIC 7534 Tire Retreading & Repair Shops
SIC 7549 Automotive Services, Except Repair & Carwashes
811211 Consumer Electronics Repair & Maintenance
SIC 7622 Radio & Television Repair Shops
SIC 7629 Electrical & Electronic Repair Shops, nec
811212 Computer & Office Machine Repair & Maintenance
SIC 7378 Computer Maintenance & Repair
SIC 7629 Electrical & Electronic Repair Shops, nec
SIC 7699 Repair Shops & Related Services, nec
811213 Communication Equipment Repair & Maintenance
SIC 7622 Radio & Television Repair Shops
SIC 7629 Electrical & Electronic Repair Shops, nec
811219 Other Electronic & Precision Equipment Repair & Maintenance
SIC 7629 Electrical & Electronic Repair Shops, nec
SIC 7699 Repair Shops & Related Services, NEC
81131 Commercial & Industrial Machinery & Equipment Repair & Maintenance
SIC 7699 Repair Shops & Related Services, nec
SIC 7623 Refrigerator & Air-Conditioning Service & Repair Shops
SIC 7694 Armature Rewinding Shops
811411 Home & Garden Equipment Repair & Maintenance
SIC 7699 Repair Shops & Related Services, nec
811412 Appliance Repair & Maintenance
SIC 7623 Refrigeration & Air-Conditioning Service & Repair Shops
SIC 7629 Electrical & Electronic Repair Shops, NEC
SIC 7699 Repairs Shops & Related Services, nec
81142 Reupholstery & Furniture Repair
SIC 7641 Reupholstery & Furniture Repair
81143 Footwear & Leather Goods Repair
SIC 7251 Shoe Repair & Shoeshine Parlors
SIC 7699 Repair Shops & Related Services
81149 Other Personal & Household Goods Repair & Maintenance
SIC 3732 Boat Building & Repairing
SIC 7219 Laundry & Garment Services, nec
SIC 7631 Watch, Clock, & Jewelry Repair
SIC 7692 Welding Repair
SIC 7699 Repair Shops & Related Services, nec
812111 Barber Shops
SIC 7241 Barber Shops
812112 Beauty Salons
SIC 7231 Beauty Shops
812113 Nail Salons
SIC 7231 Beauty Shops
812191 Diet & Weight Reducing Centers
SIC 7299 Miscellaneous Personal Services, nec

812199 Other Personal Care Services
SIC 7299 Miscellaneous Personal Services, nec,
81221 Funeral Homes
SIC 7261 Funeral Services & Crematories
81222 Cemeteries & Crematories
SIC 6531 Real Estate Agents & Managers
SIC 6553 Cemetery Subdividers & Developers
SIC 7261 Funeral Services & Crematories
81231 Coin-Operated Laundries & Drycleaners
SIC 7215 Coin-Operated Laundry & Drycleaning
812321 Laundries, Family & Commercial
SIC 7211 Power Laundries, Family & Commercial
812322 Drycleaning Plants
SIC 7216 Drycleaning Plants, Except Rug Cleaning
812331 Linen Supply
SIC 7213 Linen Supply
SIC 7219 Laundry & Garment Services, nec,
812332 Industrial Launderers
SIC 7218 Industrial Launderers
812391 Garment Pressing, & Agents for Laundries
SIC 7212 Garment Pressing & Agents for Laundries
812399 All Other Laundry Services
SIC 7219 Laundry & Garment Services, NEC
81291 Pet Care Services
SIC 0752 Animal Speciality Services, Except Veterinary
812921 Photo Finishing Laboratories
SIC 7384 Photofinishing Laboratories
812922 One-Hour Photo Finishing
SIC 7384 Photofinishing Laboratories
81293 Parking Lots & Garages
SIC 7521 Automobile Parking
81299 All Other Personal Services
SIC 7299 Miscellaneous Personal Services, nec
SIC 7389 Miscellaneous Business Services
81311 Religious Organizations
SIC 8661 Religious Organizations
813211 Grantmaking Foundations
SIC 6732 Educational, Religious, & Charitable Trust
813212 Voluntary Health Organizations
SIC 8399 Social Services, nec
813219 Other Grantmaking & Giving Services
SIC 8399 Social Services, NEC
813311 Human Rights Organizations
SIC 8399 Social Services, nec
813312 Environment, Conservation & Wildlife Organizations
SIC 8399 Social Services, nec
SIC 8699 Membership Organizations, nec
813319 Other Social Advocacy Organizations
SIC 8399 Social Services, NEC
81341 Civic & Social Organizations
SIC 8641 Civic, Social, & Fraternal Organizations
SIC 8699 Membership Organizations, nec
81391 Business Associations
SIC 8611 Business Associations
SIC 8699 Membership Organizations, nec
81392 Professional Organizations
SIC 8621 Professional Membership Organizations
81393 Labor Unions & Similar Labor Organizations
SIC 8631 Labor Unions & Similar Labor Organizations
81394 Political Organizations
SIC 8651 Political Organizations
81399 Other Similar Organizations
SIC 6531 Real Estate Agents & Managers
SIC 8641 Civic, Social, & Fraternal Organizations
SIC 8699 Membership Organizations, nec
81411 Private Households
SIC 8811 Private Households

PUBLIC ADMINISTRATION

92111 Executive Offices
SIC 9111 Executive Offices
92112 Legislative Bodies
SIC 9121 Legislative Bodies
92113 Public Finance
SIC 9311 Public Finance, Taxation, & Monetary Policy
92114 Executive & Legislative Offices, Combined
SIC 9131 Executive & Legislative Offices, Combined
92115 American Indian & Alaska Native Tribal Governments
SIC 8641 Civic, Social, & Fraternal Organizations
92119 All Other General Government
SIC 9199 General Government, nec
92211 Courts
SIC 9211 Courts
92212 Police Protection
SIC 9221 Police Protection
92213 Legal Counsel & Prosecution
SIC 9222 Legal Counsel & Prosecution
92214 Correctional Institutions
SIC 9223 Correctional Institutions
92215 Parole Offices & Probation Offices
SIC 8322 Individual & Family Social Services
92216 Fire Protection
SIC 9224 Fire Protection
92219 All Other Justice, Public Order, & Safety
SIC 9229 Public Order & Safety, nec
92311 Administration of Education Programs
SIC 9411 Administration of Educational Programs
92312 Administration of Public Health Programs
SIC 9431 Administration of Public Health Programs
92313 Administration of Social, Human Resource & Income Maintenance Programs
SIC 9441 Administration of Social, Human Resource & Income Maintenance Programs
92314 Administration of Veteran's Affairs
SIC 9451 Administration of Veteran's Affairs, Except Health Insurance
92411 Air & Water Resource & Solid Waste Management
SIC 9511 Air & Water Resource & Solid Waste Management
92412 Land, Mineral, Wildlife, & Forest Conservation
SIC 9512 Land, Mineral, Wildlife, & Forest Conservation
92511 Administration of Housing Programs
SIC 9531 Administration of Housing Programs
92512 Administration of Urban Planning & Community & Rural Development
SIC 9532 Administration of Urban Planning & Community & Rural Development
92611 Administration of General Economic Programs
SIC 9611 Administration of General Economic Programs
92612 Regulation & Administration of Transportation Programs
SIC 9621 Regulations & Administration of Transportation Programs
92613 Regulation & Administration of Communications, Electric, Gas, & Other Utilities
SIC 9631 Regulation & Administration of Communications, Electric, Gas, & Other Utilities

92614 Regulation of Agricultural Marketing & Commodities
SIC 9641 Regulation of Agricultural Marketing & Commodities
92615 Regulation, Licensing, & Inspection of Miscellaneous Commercial Sectors
SIC 9651 Regulation, Licensing, & Inspection of Miscellaneous Commercial Sectors
92711 Space Research & Technology
SIC 9661 Space Research & Technology
92811 National Security
SIC 9711 National Security
92812 International Affairs
SIC 9721 International Affairs
99999 Unclassified Establishments
SIC 9999 Nonclassifiable Establishments

APPENDIX III

ANNOTATED SOURCE LIST

The following listing provides the names, publishers, addresses, telephone and fax numbers (if available), and frequency of publications for the primary sources used in *Market Share Reporter*.

ABA Banking Journal, Simmons-Boardman Publishing Corp., 345 Hudson St., New York, NY 10014-4502, *Telephone:* (212) 620-7200.

Accountancy International, The American Institute of Certified Public Accountants, 1211 Avenue of the Americas, New York, NY 10036, *Telephone:* (212) 596-6200, *Fax:* (212) 596-6213. *Published:* monthly.

Adhesives Age, Communication Channels Inc., 6255 Barfield Rd., Atlanta, GA 30328, *Telephone:* (404) 256-9800, *Fax:* (404) 256-3116, *Published::* monthly.

Advertising Age, Crain Communications, Inc., 220 E. 42nd St., New York, NY 10017, *Telephone:* (212) 210-0725, *Fax:* (212) 210-0111, *Published:* weekly.

Advertising Age International, Crain Communications, Inc., 220 E. 42nd St., New York, NY 10017, *Telephone:* (212) 210-0725, *Fax:* (212) 210-0111.

Adweek, BPI Communications, Merchandise Mart, Suite 936, Chicago, IL 60654, *Telephone:* (800) 722-6658, *Fax:* (312) 464-8540, *Published:* weekly.

Aftermarket Business, Advanstar Communications, Inc., 7500 Old Oak Blvd., Cleveland, OH 44130-3343, *Published*: monthly.

Agri Finance, Century Publishing Co., 990 Grove St., Evanston, IL 60201-4370, *Telephone:* (708) 491-6440, *Fax:* (708) 647-7055, *Published:* 9x/yr.

Agricultural Outlook, USGPO, Superintendent of Documents, Washington D.C. 20402, *Telephone:* (202) 783-3238, *Fax:* (202) 275-0019.

Air Cargo World, Journal of Commerce Inc., 1230 National Press Building, Washington D.C. 20045, *Telphone*: (202) 783-1148, *Published*: monthly.

Air Conditioning, Heating and Refrigeration News, Business News Publishing Co., P.O. Box 2600, Troy MI 48007, *Telephone:* (313) 362-3700, *Fax:* (313) 362-0317.

American Clinical Laboratory, International Scientific Communications Inc., 30 Controls Drive, P.O. Box 870, Shelton, CT 06484-0870, *Telephone*: (203) 926-9300, *Fax:* (203) 926-9310.

American Ink Maker, MacNair-Dorland Co., 445 Broadhollow Rd., Melville, NY 11747, *Telephone:* (212) 279-4456. *Published:* monthly.

American Machinist, Penton Publishing, 1100 Superior Ave., Cleveland, OH 44114, *Telephone:* (216) 696-7000, *Fax:* (216) 696-0836, *Published:* monthly.

American Metal Market, Capital Cities Media Inc., 825 7th Avenue, New York, NY 10019, *Telephone:* (800) 360-7600, *Published:* daily, except Saturdays, Sundays, and holidays, *Price:* $560 per year (U.S., Canada, and Mexico).

American Nurseryman, American Nurseryman Publishing Co., 77 W. Washington St., Ste 2100, Chicago,

IL 60602-2801, *Telephone:* (312) 782-5505, *Fax*: (312) 782-3232, *Published:* 2x/mo.

American Printer, Maclean Hunter Publishing Co., 29 N. Wacker Dr., Chicago, IL 60606. *Published:* monthly.

American Vegetable Grower, Meister Publishing Co., 37733 Euclid Ave., Willoughby, OH 44094-5992, *Telephone:* (216) 942-2000, *Fax:* (216) 942-0662. *Published:* monthly.

Amusement Business, BPI Communications Inc., Box 24970, Nashville, TN 37202, *Telephone:* (615) 321-4250, *Fax:* (615) 327-1575. *Published:* weekly.

Angus Journal, 3201 Frederick Blvd, Saint Joseph, MO 64506, *Telephone:* (816) 233-0563, *Fax:* (816) 233-0508.

Appliance, Dana Chase Publications Inc., 1110 Jorie Blvd., CS 9019, Ste. 203, Hinsdale, IL 60521, *Telephone:* (708) 990 - 3484, *Fax:* (708) 990 - 0078, *Published:* monthly, *Price:* $60.

Appliance Manufacturer, Business News Publishing Co., 755 W. Big Beaver Rd., Ste. 1000, Troy, MI 48084-4900, *Telephone:* (313) 362-3700, *Fax:* (313) 244-6439, *Published:* monthly.

Arizona Business, 3111 N. Central, Phoenix, AZ 85012, *Telephone:* (602) 277-6045, *Published:* weekly.

Arkansas Business, 201 E. Markham, P.O. Box 3686, Little Rock, AR 72203, *Telephone:* (501)372-1443 Fax: (501) 375-3623, *Published:* weekly, *Price:* $38 per year.

AS&U (American School and University), North American Publishing Co., 401 N. Broad St., Philadelphia, PA 19106, *Telephone:* (215) 238-4200, *Fax:* (215) 238-4227, *Published:* monthly.

The Asian Wall Street Journal, Dow Jones & Co. Inc., 200 Liberty Street, New York, NY 10281, *Telephone:* (212) 416-2242, *Fax*: (212) 416-4438.

Assembly, Hitchcock Publishing Co., 191 S. Gary Ave., Carol Stream, IL 60188, *Telephone:* (708) 665 - 1000, *Fax:* (708) 462 - 2225.

Association Management, American Society of Association Executives, 1575 Eye St., Washington DC 20005, *Published:* monthly, *Price:* $24 per year to members, $30 per year for nonmembers.

ATI, Billian Publishing, 2100 Powers Ferry NW, Ste. 300, Atlanta, GA 30339, *Telephone:* (404) 955-5656, *Fax:* (404) 952-0669, *Published:* monthly.

Atlanta Journal-Constitution, 72 Marietta St., NW Atlanta, GA 30303, *Telephone:* (404) 526 - 5151, *Published:* daily.

Auto Laundry News, E.W. Williams Publications Co., 370 Lexington Ave., New York, NY 10017-6658, *Published:* monthly, *Price:* $25 per year.

Automotive Engineering International, Society of Automotive Enginners Inc., 400 Commonwealth Drive, Warrendale, PA 15096, *Telephone:* (412) 776-4841, *Fax:* (412) 776-9765.

Automotive Industries, Capital Cities/ABC/Chilton Co., Chilton Way, Radnor PA 19089, *Telephone*: (215) 961-4255, *Fax:* (215) 964 -4251.

Automotive News, Crain Communications Inc., 380 Woodbridge, Detroit, MI 48207 *Telephone:* (313) 446-6000, *Fax:* (313) 446-0347.

Bakery Production and Marketing, Cahners Publishing Co., 455 N. Cityfront Plaza Dr., Chicago, IL 60611, *Telephone:* (312) 222-2000.

Baltimore Business Journal, American City Business Journals, 117 Water St., Baltimore, MD 21202, *Telephone:* (410) 576-1161, *Fax:* (301) 383-321, *Published:* weekly.

The Baltimore Sun, The Baltimore Sun Co., P.O. Box 17166, Baltimore, MD 21203-7166, *Telephone:* (800) 829-8000, *Published:* daily.

Bank Systems & Technology, Miller Freeman Inc., 1515 Broadway, New York, NY 10036, *Telephone:* (212) 869-1300, *Fax:* (212) 302-6273.

The Banker, Greystoke Place, Feteer Lane, London. England EC4A IND, *Telephone*: (071) 405-6969, *Published:* monthly.

Banking Strategies, Bank Administration Institute, One North Franklin, Chicago, IL 60606, *Telephone:* (312) 553-4600, *Price:* $59.

Best's Review, A.M. Best Co. Inc., Ambest Rd., Oldwick, NJ 08858, *Telephone:* (908) 439-2200, *Fax:* (908) 439-3363, *Published:* monthly.

Better Crops, 655 Engineering Dr., Ste. 1110, Norcross, GA 30092-2821, *Telephone*: (404) 447-0335.

Beverage Industry, Advanstar Communications, Inc., 7500 Oald Oak Blvd., Cleveland OH 44130, *Telephone:* (216) 243-8100, *Fax:* (216) 891-2651, *Published:* monthly, *Price:* $40 per year.

Beverage World, Keller International Publishing Corp., 150 Great Neck Rd., Great Neck, NY 11021, *Telephone:* (516) 829-9210, *Fax:* (516) 829-5414, *Published:* monthly.

Billboard, BPI Communications, 1515 Broadway, 14th FL, New York, NY 10036, *Telephone*: (212) 764-7300, *Fax:* (212) 536-5358.

Boating Industry, Communication Channels, Inc., 6151 Powers Ferry Road, Atlanta, GA 30339, *Telephone:* (404) 955-2500, *Published:* monthly.

Bobbin, Bobbin Blenheim Media Corp., 1110 Shop Rd., PO Box 1986, Columbia, SC 29202, *Telephone:* (803) 771-7500, *Fax*: (803) 799-1461.

The Boston Globe, Globe Newspaper Co., P.O. Box 2378, Boston, MA 02107, *Telephone:* (617) 929-2000, *Published:* daily.

Brandweek, Adweek L.P., 1515 Broadway, New York, NY 10036, *Telephone:* (212) 536-5336. *Published:* weekly, except no issue in the last week of Dec.

Broadcasting & Cable, Cahners Publishing Co., 1705 DeSales Street, N.W., Washington, DC 20036, *Telephone:* (800) 554-5729 or (202) 659-2340, *Fax:* (202) 331-1732.

Broiler Industry, Watt Publishing Co., 122 S. Wesley Ave., Mount Morris, IL 61054-1497, *Telephone:* (815) 734-4171, *Fax:* (815) 734-4201, *Published:* monthly.

Builder, Hanley-Wood Inc., 655 15th St. N.W., Ste. 475, Washington, D.C. 20005, *Telephone:* (202) 737-0717, *Fax:* (202) 737-2439, *Published:* monthly.

Building Design & Construction, Cahners Publishing, 1350 E. Touhy Ave., Des Plaines, IL 60017-5080, *Telephone:* (708) 635-8800, *Published:* monthly.

Building Material Dealer, National Lumbermens Publishing Corp., 1405 Lilac Drive N, No. 131, Minneapolis, MN 55422, Telephone: (612) 544-1597, Fax: (612) 544-820, *Published:* monthly.

Building Operation & Management, Trade Press Publishing Corp., 2100 W. Florist Ave., Milwaukee, WI 53209, *Telephone:* (414) 228-7701, *Fax:* (414) 228-1134, *Published:* monthly.

Business & Commercial Aviation, 4 International Drive, Ste. 260, Rye Brook, NY 10573 - 1065, *Telephone:* (914) 939-0300, *Fax:* (914) 939-1100, *Published*: monthly, *Price:* $42.

Business & Health, Medical Economics Publishing Co., 5 Paragon Dr., Montvale, NJ 07645-1184, *Telephone:* (201) 358-7208, *Published:* 14x/yr.

Business Communications Review, BCR Enterprises, Inc., 950 York Rd., Hinsdale, IL 60521, *Telephone:* (800) 227-1324, *Published:* monthly.

Business First, 200 E. Rich St., Columbus, OH 43215, *Telephone:* (614) 461-4040.

Business First of Buffalo, 472 Delaware St., Buffalo, NY 14202.

Business Insurance, Crain Communications, Inc., 740 N. Rush St., Chicago IL 60611, *Published:* monthly.

The Business Journal, American City Business Journals, 2025 N. Summit Ave., Milwaukee, WI 53202. *Telephone:* (414) 278- 7788, *Fax:* (414) 278-7028.

The Business Journal - Serving Phoenix and the Valley of the Sun, 3737 N. 7th St., Ste. 200, Phoenix, AZ 85014, *Telephone:* (602) 230-8400, *Fax:* (602) 230-0955, *Published:* weekly, *Cost:* $46.

Business Marketing, Crain Communications, 740 N. Rush St., Chicago, IL 60611, *Telephone*: (312) 649-5200, *Published:* monthly.

Business Mexico, American Chamber of Commerce, A.C., Lucerna 78, Col. Juarez, DEl. Cuauhtemoc, Mexico City, Mexico, *Telephone:* 705-0995. *Published:* monthly.

Business North Carolina, 5435 77 Center Dr., No. 50, Charlotte, NC 28217-0711 *Telephone:* (704) 523-6987 *Published:* monthly.

Business Week, McGraw-Hill Inc., 1221 Avenue of the Americas, New York, NY 10020. *Published:* weekly, *Price:* U.S.: $46.95 per year; Canada: $69 CDN per year.

Cablevision, Chilton Publications, P.O. Box 7698, Riverton, NJ 08077-7698, *Telephone:* (609) 786-0501. *Published:* twice monthly, *Price:* U.S.: $55 per year, $99 for 2 years; Elsewhere via surface mail: $85 per year, $159 for 2 years.

Canadian Business, CB Media Limited, 70 Esplanade, Second Floor, Toronto MSE IR2 Canada, *Telephone:* (416) 364-4266, *Fax:* (416) 364-2783. *Published:* monthly, *Price:* Canada: $24 per year, $60 for 3 years; Elsewhere: $40 per year, $100 for 3 years.

Canadian Insurance, Stone & Cox Ltd., 111 Peter St., Ste. 202, Toronto, ON Canada M5V 2H1, *Telephone,* (416) 599-0772, *Fax*: (416) 599-0867.

Canadian Insurance Statistics, Stone & Cox Ltd., 111 Peter St., Ste. 202, Toronto, ON Canada M5V 2H1, *Telephone,* (416) 599-0772, *Fax*: (416) 599-0867.

Canadian Mining Journal, Southam Magazine Group, PO Box 1144, Lewiston, NY 14092, *Published:* 4x/yr.

Catalog Age, Cowles Business Media Inc., 911 Hope St., Six River Bend Center, Box 4949, Stanford CT 06907-0949, *Telephone:* (203) 358-9900, *Published:* monthly.

Ceramic Bulletin, American Ceramic Society, 735 Ceramic Place, Westerville, OH 43081-8720, *Published:* monthly, *Price*: $50 for nonmembers and libraries, inccluded in membership dues.

Ceramic Industry, Business News Publishing Co., 5900 Harper Road, Suite 109, Solon, OH 44139, *Telephone:* (216) 498-9214, *Fax:* (216) 498-9121. *Published:* monthly, *Price:* U.S.: $53 per year; Mexico: $63; Canada: $66.71 (includes postage & GST).

Chain Store Age, Lebhar-Friedman Inc., 425 Park Ave., New York, NY 10022, *Telephone:* (212) 371-9400, *Fax:* (212) 319-4129. *Published:* monthly.

Chemical & Engineering News, American Chemical Society, Dept. L-0011, Columbus, OH 43210, *Telephone:* (800) 333-9511 or (614) 447-3776. *Published:* weekly, except last week in December, *Price:* U.S.: $100 per year, $198 for 2 years; elsewhere: $148 per year, $274 for 2 years.

Chemical Engineering, McGraw-Hill Inc., 1221 Avenue of the Americas, New York, NY 10020, *Telephone:* (212) 512-2000. *Published:* monthly.

Chemical Market Reporter, Schnell Publishing Co., Inc., 80 Broad St., New York, NY 1004-2203, *Telephone:* (212) 248-4177, *Fax:* (212) 248-4903, *Published:* weekly.

Chemical Week, Chemical Week Associates, P.O. Box 7721, Riverton, NJ 08077-7721, *Telephone:* (609) 786-0401, *Published:* weekly, except four combination issues (total of 49 issues), *Price:* U.S.: $99 per year; Canada: $129 per year. Single copies $8 in U.S. and $10 elsewhere.

The Chicago Tribune, 435 N. Michigan Ave., Chicago, IL 60611, *Telephone:* (312) 222-3232. *Published:* daily.

Child Care Information Exchange, Exchange Press Inc., P.O. 2890, Redmond, WA 98073, *Telephone:* (800) 221-2864, *Published:* bimonthly, *Price:* $35 per year.

The Christian Science Monitor, Christian Science Publishing Society, One Norway St., Boston, MA 02115, *Telephone:* (800) 456-2220, *Published:* daily, except weekends and holidays.

The Chronicle of Philanthropy, 1255 23rd Street, NW, Ste 775, Washington D.C. 20037, *Telephone:* (202) 466-1200, *Fax:* (202) 296-2691.

Civil Engineering, American Society of Civil Engineers, 345 E. 47th St., New York, NY 10017-2398, *Telephone:* (212) 705-7463., *Price:* $72.

Commercial Carrier Journal, Capital Cities/ABC/Chilton Co., Chilton Way, Radnor, PA 19089, *Telephone:* (215) 964-4000, *Fax:* (215) 964-4981.

Computer Design, PennWell Publishing Co., 1 Technology Park Drive, Westford, MA 01886, *Telephone:* (508) 692-0700, *Published:* 24x/yr.

Computer Reseller News, CMP Media Inc., One Jericho Plaza, Jericho, New York 11753, *Published:* weekly, *Pricet*: $199; Canada $224

Computerworld, P.O. Box 2043, Marion, OH 43305-2403, *Telephone:* (800) 669-1002, *Published*: weekly.

Computing Canada, Plesman Publications Ltd., 2005 Sheppard Ave. E., 4th Fl., Willowsdale, ON, Canada M2J 5B1, *Telephone:* (416) 497-9562, *Fax:* (416) 497-9427. *Published:* biweekly.

Congressional Digest, U.S. Dept. of Commerce, Superintendent of Documents, USGPO, Washington DC 20402, *Telephone:* (202) 783-3238.

The Construction Specifier, Construction Specifications Institute, 601 Madison St., Alexandria, VA 22314, Telephone: (703) 684-0300, Published: monthly.

Consultants News, Kennedy Publications, Templeton Road, Fitzwilliam, NH 03447, *Telephone:* (603) 585-6544, *Fax:* (603) 585-6401, Published: monthly, *Price:* $158 per year.

Consumer Reports Travel Letter, Consumers Union of U.S., Inc., 101 Truman Ave., Yonkers, NY 10703-1057, *Telephone:* (914) 378-2000, *Fax:* (914) 378-2900, *Published:* monthly, *Price:* $18.

Contemporary Long Term Care, Bill Communications Inc., P.O. Box 3599, Akron, OH 44309-3599, *Telephone:* (216) 867-4402, *Fax:* (216) 867-0019.

Continuing Care, Stevens Publishing Corporation, 225 N. New Rd., Waco, TX 76710, *Telephone:* (817) 776-9000, *Fax:* (817) 776-9018.

Contractor, Cahners Publishing Co., 44 Cook St., Denver, CO. 80206-5800, *Telephone:* (708) 390-2676, *Fax:* (708) 390-2690, *Published:* monthly.

Control Engineering, Cahners Publishing Co., 1350 E. Touhy Ave., Des Plaines, IL 60018, *Telephone*: (708) 635-8800, *Fax:* (708) 390-2618.

Cornell Hotel and Restaurant Administration Quarterly, Cornell University of School of Hotel Administration, Statlet Hall, Ithaca, NY 14853, *Telephone:* (607) 255-5093, *Fax:* (607) 257-1204, *Published:* 6x/yr., *Price:* $62; $102 institutions; $90 foreign.

Corporate Report Minnesota, Corporate Report Inc., 5500 Wayzata Blvd., Suite 800, Minneapolis, MN 55416, *Telephone:* (612) 591-2531. *Published:*

monthly, *Price:* $29 per year, $47 for 2 years, $63 for three years. Back issues $3.95 each.

Crain's Chicago Business, Crain Communications Inc., 740 N. Rush St., Chicago, IL 60611, *Telephone:* (312) 649-5411.

Crain's Cleveland Business, Crain Communications, Inc., 1725 Merriman Rd., Ste. 300, Akron, OH 44313-5251, *Telephone:* (216) 836-9180, *Fax:* (216) 836-1005, *Published:* weekly.

Crain's Detroit Business, Crain Communications Inc., 1400 Woodbridge, Detroit, MI 48207-3187, *Telephone:* (313) 446-6000. *Published:* weekly, except semiweekly the fourth week in May.

Crain's New York Business, Crain Communications, Inc., 220 E. 42nd St., New York, NY 10017, *Telephone:* (212) 210-0100, *Fax:* (212) 210-0799. *Published:* weekly.

Dairy Foods, Gorman Publishing Co., 8750 W. Bryn Mawr Ave., Chicago, IL 60062, *Telephone:* (312) 693-3200. *Published:* monthly, except semimonthly in Aug.

Dallas Business Journal, American City Business Journals, American City Business Journals, 4131 N Central Expy, Ste. 310, Dallas, TX 75204, *Telephone:* (214) 520-1010, *Fax:* (214) 528-4686.

Dallas Morning News, 508 Young St., P.O. Box 655237, Dallas, TX 75265, *Telephone:* (214) 977-8222, *Fax:* (214) 977-8776, *Published:* daily.

DCI, Advanstar Communications Inc., 7500 Old Oak Blvd., Cleveland, OH 44310, *Published*: monthly.

Denver Business Journal, 1700 Broadway, Ste. 515, Denver, CO 80290, Telephone: (303) 837-3500, Fax: (303) 837-3535, *Published:* weekly.

The Des Moines Register, P.O. Box 957, Des Moines, IA 50304, *Telephone*: (515) 284-8000, *Fax:* (515) 284-8103, *Published*: daily.

Design Build, McGraw-Hill, Two Penn Plaza, New York, NY 10121-2298, *Telephone:* (212) 904-2000, *Published:* quarterly.

Detroit Free Press, Knight-Ridder, Inc., 1 Herald Plaza, Miami, FL 33132, *Telephone:* (305) 376-3800, *Published:* daily.

The Detroiter, Detroit Regional Chamber, One Woodward Avenue, Suite 1700, P.O. Box 33840, Detroit, MI 48322-0840, *Telephone:* (313) 593-0373, *Published*: monthly, *Price*: $14 chamber members; $18 nonmembers.

Direct Marketing, Hoke Communications Inc., 224 7th St., Garden City, NY 11530, *Telephone:* (516) 746-6700, *Fax:* (516) 294-8141, *Published:* monthly, *Cost:* $56.

Discount Merchandiser, Schwartz Publications, 233 Park Ave. S., New York, NY 10003, *Telephone:* (212) 979-4860, *Fax:* (212) 979-7431, *Published:* monthly.

Discount Store News, Lebhar-Friedman Inc., 425 Park Ave, New York, NY 10022, *Telephone:* (212) 756-5100, *Fax:* (212) 756-5125, *Published:* weekly.

DNR, Cahners Publishing Co., 275 Washington St., Newton, MA 02158, *Telephone:* (617) 558-4243, *Fax:* (617) 558-4759, *Published:* 2x/mo.

Do-It-Yourself-Retailing, National Retail Hardware Assn., 5822 W. 74th St., Indianapolis, IN 46278-1756, *Telephone:* (317) 297-1190, *Fax:* (317) 328-4354, *Published:* monthly, *Price: $8; $2 single issue.*

E-Media Professional, Online Inc., 462 Danbury Road, Wilton, CT 06897-2126, *Published:* monthly, *Cost:* $55; $98 corporate.

The Economist, The Economist Bldg, 111 W. 57th St., New York, NY 10019, *Telephone:* (212) 541-5730, *Fax:* (212) 541-9378, *Published:* weekly, *Cost:* $110; $3.50 per single issue.

Egg Industry, Watt Publishing Co., 122 S. Wesley Ave., Mount Morris, IL 61054-1497, *Telephone:* (815) 734-4171, *Fax:* (815) 734-4201, *Published:* bimonthly.

Electronic Business, CMP Publications Inc., 8773 South Ridgeline Blvd., Highlands Ranch, CO, 80126-2329, *Telephone:* (516) 562-5000, *Fax:* (516) 562-5409, *Published:* monthly.

Electronic Design, 222 Rosewood Drive, Danvers, MA 01923.

Electronic News, Electronic News Publishing Corp., 488 Madison Ave., New York, NY 10022, *Telephone:* (212) 909-5924, *Published:* weekly, except last week of Dec.

Electronic Packaging & Production, Cahners Publishing Co., 1350 E. Touhy Ave., P.O. Box 5080, Des Plaines, IL 60017-5080, *Telephone*: (708) 635-8800, *Fax*: (708) 635-9950, *Published:* monthly.

Electronic Servicing & Technology, CQ Communications, 76 N. Broadway, Hicksville, NY 11801, *Telephone:* (516) 681-2922.

Engineering & Mining Journal, Maclean Hunter Publishing Co., 29 Wacker Dr., Chicago, IL 60606, *Fax:* (312) 726-2574, *Published:* monthly.

ENR **,** McGraw-Hill Inc., Fulfillment Manager, ENR, P.O. Box 518, Highstown, NJ 08520, *Telephone:* (609) 426-7070 or (212) 512-3549, *Fax:* (212) 512-3150, *Published:* weekly, *Price:* U.S.: $89 per year; Canada: $75 per year. Single copies $5 in U.S.

Entertainment Weekly, Time-Warner Inc., 1675 Broadway, New York, NY 10019, Published: weekly.

Entrepreneur Magazine, Entrepreneur Inc., 2392 Morse Ave., Irvine, CA 92714, *Telephone:* (714) 261-2325, *Fax:* (714) 755-4211.

European Chemical News, Reed Business Publishing Co., Quadrant House, Sutton, Surrey SM2 5AS, U.K., *Telephone:* 081-6613500, *Published:* weekly.

European Rubber Journal, Crain Communications Ltd., 20-22 Bedford Row, London WC1R 4EW, UK *Telephone:* (071) 831-9511, *Fax:* (071) 430-2176, *Published:* monthly, except August.

Farm Journal, 230 W. Washington Sq., Philadelphia, PA 19106, *Telephone:* (215) 829-4700, *Published:* 13x/yr, *Price:* $14 per year.

Feedstuffs, Miller Publishing Co., 12400 Whitewater Dr., Ste. 1600, Minnetonka, MN 55343, *Telephone:* (612) 931-0211.

The Financial Gleaner, 7 North Street, P.O. Box 40, Kingston Jamaica, WI, *Telephone*: (876) 922-3400, *Published:* daily.

The Financial Post, The Financial Post Company, 333 King St., East, Toronto M5A 4N2, Canada, *Telephone:* (800) 387-9011. *Published:* monthly with 5-day per week newspaper, *Price:* $182 per year; weekend mail subscription $49.95 includes magazine and annual issues.

Financial Services Online, 1 Penn Plaza, 17th Fl, New York, NY 10001-2006, *Published:* monthly.

Financial Times, FT Publications Inc., 14 East 60th Street, New York, NY 21002, *Telephone:* (212) 752-4500, *Fax:* (212) 319-0704, *Published:* daily, except for Sundays and holidays, *Price:* $425.

Food Management, Chilton Co., One Chilton Way, Radnor, PA 19089, *Telephone:* (215) 964-4000. *Published:* monthly, *Price:* solicited only from professionals in field: $55 per year, $100 for 2 years; educational rate: $28 per year.

Food Technology, Institute of Food Technologists, 221 N. LaSalle St., Ste 300, Chicago, IL 60601, *Telephone:* (312) 782-8424.

Forbes, Forbes, Inc., P.O. Box 10048, Des Moines, IA 50340-0048, *Telephone:* (800) 888-9896, *Published:* 27 issues per year, *Price:* U.S.: $54 per year; Canada: $95 per year (includes GST).

Forest Products Journal, Forest Products Society, 2801 Marshall Court, Madison, WI 53705-2295, *Published:* monthly, except combined issues in July/August and November/December, *Price:* U.S.: $115 per year; Canada/Mexico: $125; single copies $12 each plus shipping and handling.

Fortune, Time Inc., Time & Life Building, Rockefeller Center, New York, NY 10020-1393, *Published:* twice monthly, except two issues combined into a single issue at year-end, *Price:* U.S.: $57 per year; Canada: $65 per year.

Fruit Grower, Meister Publishing Co., 37733 Euclid Ave., Willoughsby, OH 44094-5992.

Furniture Today, Cahners Publishing Co., 200 S. Main St., P.O. Box 2754, High Point, NC 27261, *Telephone:* (919) 889-0113, *Published:* weekly.

Gas Engineering & Management, The Journal of the Institution of Gas Engineers, 21 Portland Place, London W1N 3AF.

Gifts & Decorative Accessories, Cahners Busienss Information, 345 Hudson Street, New York, NY 10014, *Telephone:* (212) 519-7200, *Fax:* (212) 519-7431, *Published:* monthly.

Global Finance, Global Finance Joint Venture, 11 W. 19th St. 2nd Fl., New York, NY 1011, *Telephone:* (212)337-5900, *Fax:* (212) 697-8331, *Published:* monthly.

Globe and Mail, 444 Front St. W., Toronto, ON, Canada M5V 2S9, *Telephone:* (416) 585-5000, *Fax:* (416) 585-5085, *Published:* Mon.-Sat. (morn.).

Grocery Headquarters, Delta Communications Inc., 455 N. Cityfront Plaza Drive, Chicago, IL 60611, *Telephone:* (312) 222-2000, *Fax:* (312) 222-2026, *Published:* monthly.

Grounds Maintenance, Intertec Publishing Co., 9800 Metcalf Ave., Overland Park, KS 66212-2215, *Published:* monthly.

Health Industry Today, Business Word, 5350 S. Roslyn St., Ste. 400, Englewood, CO 80111-2125, *Published:* monthly.

Heavy Construction News, Maclean Hunter Ltd., 777 Bay St., Tortonto, ON, Canada M5w 1A7, *Telephone:* (416) 596-5000.

Hereford World, 11020 NW Ambassador Drive, Kansas City, MO 64153-2034, *Telephone:* (816) 891-8400.

HFN, 7 E. 12th St., New York, NY 10003. *Published:* weekly.

Hoard's Dairyman, W.D. Hoard & Sons Co., P.O. Box 801, Fort Atkainson, WI 53538-0801, *Telephone:* (414) 563-5551, *Fax:* (414) 563-7298.

Hotel & Motel Management, Advanstar Communications, Inc., 7500 Old Oak Blvd., Cleveland, OH 44130, *Telephone:* (216) 826-2839.

Household and Personal Products Industry, Rodman Publishing, 17 S. Franklin Turnpike, Box 555, Ramsey, NJ 07446, *Telephone:* (201) 825-2552, *Fax:* (201) 825-0553, *Published:* monthly.

Implement & Tractor, Farm Press Publications, Inc., PO Box 1420, Clarksdale, MS 38614, *Telephone:* (601) 624-8503, *Fax:* (601) 627-1977. *Published:* monthly, *Price:* $15 per year.

In-Plant Graphics, Innes Publishing Co., P.O. Box 368, Northbrook, IL 60065, *Fax:* (708) 564-8361.

Inc., Goldhirsh Group Inc., 38 Commercial Wharf, Boston, MA 02110, *Published:* monthly.

Industrial Distribution, Cahners Publishing Company, 275 Washington Street, Newton, MA 02158, *Telephone:* (617) 964-3030, *Published:* monthly.

The Industry Standard, Internet Industy Publishing, 315 Pacific Ave., San Francisco, CA 94111-1701, *Telephone:* (415) 733-5400, *Fax:* (415) 733-5401, *Published:* weekly.

Industry Week, Penton Publishing, 1100 Superior Ave., Cleveland, OH 44114-2542, *Telephone*: (216) 696-7000, *Fax:* (216) 696-7670.

Infoworld, Infoworld Publishing Co., 155 Bovet Rd., Ste. 800, San Mateo, CA 94402, *Telephone:* (415) 572-7341, *Published:* weekly.

Injection Molding, Abby Communications Inc., 10 Fairmont Ave., Chatham, NJ 07928, *Telephone:* (973) 635-5646, *Published*: monthly.

Interavia, Swissair Centre, 31 Route de l'Aeroport, P.O. Box 437, 1215 Geneva 15, Switzerland, Switzerland, *Telephone*: (902) 788-2788, *Published:* monthly, Price: $128 per year.

Interior Design, Cahners Publishing Co., 249 W. 17th St., New York, NY 10011, *Telephone:* (212) 463-6694.

Investext, The Investext Group, 22 Pittsburgh Street, Boston, MA 02210. Investext is an online database of full-text company and industry research reports produced by more than 385 investment banks and brokerage firms around the globe. Approximately 400 new reports are added daily. The Investext database is available on the Investext Group's online and CD-ROM products and via most major online business providers. Reports and research services may also be ordered by phone. Telephone: 800-662-7878 (U.S.), +44-171-815-3860 (U.K./Europe), 852-2522-4159 (Hong Kong), 03-5213-7300.

Investor's Business Daily, P.O. Box 661750, Los Angeles, CA 90066-8950, *Published:* daily, except weekends and holidays, *Cost:* $128 per year.

Jewelers Circular Keystone, Chilton Co., Chilton Way, Radnor PA 19089, *Telephone:* (212) 887-8452, *Published*: monthly.

Journal of Commerce, Journal of Commerce, Inc., Two World Trade Center, 27th Floor, New York, NY 10048, *Telephone:* (212) 837-7000, *Fax:* (212) 837-7035.

Latin Trade, Freedom Communications Inc., 200 South Bicauyne Blvd., Suite 1150, Miami, FL 33131, *Published:* monthly.

Logistics Management, 1924 W. Mall, Vancouver, BC, Canada, V6t 1Zs.

Los Angeles Times, The Times Mirror Company, Times Mirror Square, Los Angeles, CA 90053, *Telephone:* (800) LA TIMES.

LP/GAS, Advanstar Communications Inc., 131 West First Street, Duluth, MN 55802-2065, *Published:* monthly, *Cost*: $40 one year.

The Manufacturing Confectioner, The Manufacturing Confectioner Publishing Company, 175 Rock Rd., Glen Rock, NJ 07452, *Telephone:* (201) 652-2655, *Fax:* (201) 652-3419, *Published:* 12 times per year, *Price:* $25 per year, single copies $10 each, except $25 for April and July issues.

Marketing Magazine, Maclean Hunter Canadian Publishing, P.O. Box 4541, Buffalo, NY 14240-4541, *Telephone:* (800) 567-0444, *Fax:* (416) 946-1679, *Price:* Canada: $59.50 per year, $98.50 for 2 years, $125 for 3 years; U.S.: $90 per year.

Mediaweek, ADWEEK, L.P., P.O. Box 1976, Danbury, CT 06813-1976, *Telephone:* (800) 722-6658, *Published:* weekly, except first week of July, last week of August, and Last two weeks of December, *Price:* U.S.: $95 per year, $170 for 2 years; Canada: $230 per year.

Medical Tribune, PressCorps Inc., 444 Park Avenue South, Suite 102, *Telephone*: (212) 686-8584, *Fax:* (212) 686-5310, *Published:* semimonthly.

Metro Magazine Fact Book, Bobbit Publishing Co., 2512 Artesia Boulevard, Redondo Beach, CA 90278.

Mexico Business, 3033 Chimey Rd., Suite 300, Houston, TX 77056, *Published:* monthly, combined issues in Jan./Feb. and July/Aug.

Michigan Retailer, Michigan Retailers Association, 221 North Pine Street, Lansing, MI 48933, *Published:* 10x/yr. *Cost:* $20.

Minerals Yearbook: Metals and Minerals, Superintendent of Documents, U.S. Govt. Printing Office, Washington, DC 20402, *Telephone:* (202) 783-3238.

Mining Engineering, Society for Mining, Metallurgy and Exploration Inc., 8307 Shaffer Parkway, Littleton CO 80127-5002, *Telephone:* (303) 973-9550, *Fax:* (303) 973-3845, *Published*: monthly.

Modern Casting, American Foundrymen's Society, 505 State St., Des Plaines, IL 60016-8399, *Telephone:* (708) 824-0181.

Modern Healthcare, Crain Communications, Inc., 740 N. Rush St., Chicago, IL 60611-2590, *Telephone:* (312) 649-5350, *Fax:* (312) 280-3189, *Published:* weekly.

Modern Physician, Crain Communications Inc., 740 N. Rush St., Chicago, IL 60611-2590.

Modern Plastics, McGraw-Hill, Inc., Attn. Fulfillment Manager, P.O. Box 481, Highstown, NJ 08520, *Telephone:* (800) 525-5003, *Published:* monthly, *Price:* U.S.: $41.75 per year, $62.70 for 2 years, $83.50 for 3 years; Canada:$CDN 53 per year, $CDN 80 for 2 years, $CDN 106 for 3 years.

Music Trades, P.O. Box 432, 80 West St., Englewood, NJ 07631, *Telephone:* (201) 871-1965, *Fax:* (201) 871-0455, *Published:* monthly.

National Petroleum News, Hunter Publishing Limited Partnership, Circulation Dept., National Petroleum News, 25 Northwest Point Blvd., Suite 800, Elk Grove Village, IL 60007, *Telephone:* (708) 427-9512, *Published:* monthly, except semimonthly in June, *Price:* U.S.: $60 per year for those in petroleum marketing industry, $75 per year for others; Canada: $69 per year for those in petroleum marketing industry, $84 per year for others.

National Trade Data Bank, STAT-USA, U.S. Department of Commerce, Washington D.C., 20230, *Telephone:* (202) 482-1986, *Fax:* (202) 482-2164.

National Underwriter, The National Underwriter Co., 505 Gest St., Cincinnati, OH 45203, *Telephone:* (800) 543-0874, *Fax:* (800) 874-1916, *Published:* weekly, except last week in December, *Price:* U.S.: $77 per year, $130 for 2 years; Canada: $112 per year, $130 for 2 years.

Nation's Restaurant News, Lebhar-Friedman, Inc., Subscription Dept., P.O. Box 31179, Tampa, FL 33631-3179, *Telephone:* (800) 447-7133. *Published:* weekly on Mondays, except the first Monday in July and the last Monday in December, *Price:* $34.50 per year and $55 for 2 years for professionals in the field; $89 per year for those allied to field.

Network World, Network World, Inc., 161 Worcester Rd., Framingham, MA 01701-9172, *Telephone:* (508) 875-6400, *Published:* weekly.

New Steel, Chilton Publishing Company, One Chilton Way, Radnor, PA 19089, *Telephone:* (212) 887-8560, *Published:* monthly.

The New York Times, New York Times Co., 229 W. 43rd St., New York, NY 10036, *Telephone:* (212) 556-1234. *Published:* daily.

Newsweek, The Newsweek Building, Livingston, NJ 07039-1666, *Telephone:* (800) 631-1040, *Published:* weekly, *Price:* U.S.: $41.08 per year; Canada: $61.88 per year (send to P.O. Box 4012, Postal Station A, Toronto, ON M5W 2K1).

Nursery Retailer, Brantwood Publications, Inc., 3023 Eastland Blvd., Ste. 103, Clearwater, FL 34621-4106, *Telephone:* (813) 796-3877, *Fax:* (813) 791-4126, *Published:* 6x/yr.

Oil & Gas Journal, PennWell Publishing Co., 3050 Post Oak Blvd., Ste. 200, Houston, TX 77056, *Telephone:* (713) 621-9720, *Fax:* (713) 963-6285.

OR Manager, 2170 S. Parker Rd., Ste. 300, Denver, CO 80231-5711, *Telephone:* (303) 755-6300.

Packaging Technology & Engineering, North American Publishing Co., 401 N Broad St, Philadelphia, PA

19108, *Published*: monthly, *Price:* U.S. $83; Canada $113.

Paperboard Packaging, Advanstar Communications Inc., 131 West First Street, Duluth, MN 55802, *Telephone:* (218) 723-9477, *Fax:* (218) 723-9437, *Published:* monthly, *Price:* U.S.: $39 per year, $58 for 2 years; Canada: $59 per year, $88 for 2 years.

PC Magazine, 28 E 28th St., New York, NY 10016-7930, *Telephone:* (212) 503-5255, *Published:* weekly.

PC Week, Ziff-Davis Publishing Company L.P., Customer Service Dept., PC WEEK, P.O. Box 1770, Riverton, NJ 08077-7370, *Telephone:* (609) 461-210, *Published:* weekly, except combined issue at year-end, *Price:* U.S.: $160 per year; Canada/Mexico: $200 per year.

Pensions & Investments, Crain Communications Inc., 220 E. 42nd St., New York, NY 10017, *Telephone:* (212) 210-0227, *Fax:* (212) 210-0117, *Published:* biweekly

Philadelphia Inquirer, Philadelphia Newspapers Inc., 400 N. Broad St., Box 8263, Philadelphia, PA 19101, *Telephone:* (215) 854-2000, *Published:* daily.

Photo Marketing, Photo Marketing Association International, 3000 Picture Place, Jackson, MI 49201, *Telephone:* (517) 788-8100, *Fax:* (517) 788-8371. *Published:* monthly, *Price:* U.S.: $35 per year/with Newsline $50, $55 for 2 years/$65 with Newsline; Canada: $35 per year/$50 with Newsline, $55 for 2 years/$70 with Newsline (payable in Canadian funds plus GST).

Photonics Spectra, Laurin Publishing Co., Inc., Berkshire Common, PO Box 4949, Pittsfield, MA 01202, *Telephone:* (413) 499-0514, *Fax:* (413) 442-3180, *Published:* monthly.

PIMA's Papermaker, Paper Industry Management Assn., 2400 E Oakton St., Arlington heights, IL 60005, *Published:* monthly.

Pipeline & Gas Journal, Oildom Publishing Co. of Texas, Inc., 3314 Mercer St., Houston, TX 77027, *Telephone:* (713) 622-0676, *Fax:* (713) 623-4768, *Published:* monthly, *Price:* free to qualitifed subscribers; all others $15 per year.

Pit & Quarry, Edgell Communications, Inc., 7500 Old Oak Blvd., Cleveland, OH 44130, *Telephone:* (216) 243-8100, *Fax:* (216) 891-2726, *Published:* monthly.

Plants, Sites & Parks, Pocral Inc., 10100 W Sample Road, No. 201, Coral Springs, FL 33065, *Telephone:* (305) 755-7048, *Published:* monthly.

Plastics News, Crain Communications, 965 E. Jefferson, Detroit, MI 48207-3185, *Published:* weekly.

Playthings, Geyer-McAllister Publications, Inc., 51 Madison Ave., New York, NY 10010, *Telephone:* (212) 689-4411, *Fax:* (212) 683-7929, *Published:* monthly, except semimonthly in May.

PR Week, PR Publications Ltd., 220 Fifth Ave., New York, NY 10001, *Telephone*: (212) 532-9200, *Fax:* (212) 532-9200, *Published*: 49x/yr.

Practical Accountant, Faulkner & Gray, Inc., 11 Penn Plaza, 17th Floor, New York, NY 10001, *Telephone:* (800) 535-8403 or (212) 967-7060, *Published:* monthly, *Price:* U.S.: $60 per year; Elsewhere: $79 per year.

Professional Builder, Cahners Publishing Co., 1350 E. Touhy Ave., Des Plaines, IL 60018, *Published:* monthly.

Progressive Grocer, 263 Tresser Blvd., Stamford, CT 06901, *Telephone:* (203) 325-3500, *Published:* monthly, *Price:* U.S.: $75 per year; Canada: $86 per year; single copies $9 each.

Provider, American Health Care Association, 5615 W. Cermak Rd., Cicero, IL 60650, *Published:* monthly.

Publishers Weekly, Cahners Publishing Company, ESP Computer Services, 19110 Van Ness Ave., Torrance, CA 90501-1170, *Telephone:* (800) 278-2991, *Published:* weekly, *Price:* U.S.: $129 per year; Canada: $177 per year (includes GST).

Pulp & Paper, Miller Freeman Inc., P.O. Box 1065, Skokie, IL 60076-8065, *Telephone:* (800) 682-8297, *Published:* monthly, *Price:* free to those in pulp, paper, and board manufacturing and paper converting firms; Others in U.S.: $100 per year.

Purchasing, Cahners Publishing Company, 44 Cook St., Denver, CO 80217-3377, *Telephone:* (303) 388-4511. *Published:* semimonthly, except monthly in January, February, July, August, December, and one extra issue in March and September, *Price:* U.S.: $84.95 per year; Canada: $133.95 per year; Mexico: $124.95 per year.

Quick Frozen Foods International, E.W. Williams Publications Co., 2125 Center Ave., Ste. 305, Fort Lee, NJ 07024, *Telephone:* (201) 592-7007, *Fax:* (201) 592-7171, *Published:* quarterly.

R&D Magazine, Cahners Publishing Company, 275 Washington St., Newton, MA 02158, *Telephone:* (708) 635-8800, *Fax:* (708) 390-2618, *Published*: monthly.

Railway Age, Simmons-Boardman Publishing, 345 Hudson St., New York, NY 10014, *Telephone:* (212) 620-7200, *Fax:* (212) 633-1165, *Published:* monthly.

Restaurants & Institutions, Cahners Publishing Co., 1350 Touhy Ave., Cahners Plaza, Des Plaines, IL 60017-5080, *Telephone:* (312) 635-8800.

Rough Notes, Rough Notes Co. Inc., 11690 Technologies Dr., Carmel, IN 46032-5600, *Published:* monthly, *Cost:* $25.

Rubber & Plastics News, Crain Communications, 1725 Merriman Road, Ste. 300, Akron, OH 44313, *Telephone:* (330) 836-9180, *Fax*:(330)836-1005, *Published:* weekly.

RV Business, TL Enterprises Inc., 29901 Agoura Rd., Agoura Hills, CA 91309, *Telephone:* (818) 991-4980, *Fax:* (818) 597-2403, *Published:* monthly.

Sacramento Business Journal, 1401 21st St., Sacramento, CA 95814-5221, *Telephone:* (916) 447-7661, *Fax:* (916) 444-7779, *Published:* weekly.

Sales & Marketing Management, Times Mirror Magazines, Inc., 2 Park Ave., New York, NY 10016, *Telephone:* (212) 592-6300, *Fax:* (212) 592-6300, Published: 15x/yr.

San Francisco Business Journal, American City Business Journals, 21st St., Sacramento, CA 96814-5221, *Telephone*: (916) 444-7779.

San Jose and Silicon Valley Business Journal, 56 N 3rd St., San Jose, CA 95112, *Telephone:* (408) 295-3800, *Fax:* (408) 295-5028, *Published:* weekly.

Screen International, EMAP Media, 33-39 Bowling Green Lane, London EC1R ODA, *Telephone:* 44 (0)171 396-8000, *Published:* weekly.

Security Distribution & Marketing, Cahners Publishing Co., 1350 E. Touhy Ave., Des Plaines, IL 60018, *Telephone:* (708) 635--8800, *Fax:* (708) 299-8622.

Security Managmeent, America Society for Industrial Security, 1655 N Fort Myer Dr., Ste. 1200, Arlington, VA 22209, Telephone: (703) 522-5800.

Semiconductor International, Cahners Publishing, 1350 Touhy Ave., Des Plaines, IL 60018, *Telephone*: (708) 635-8800, Published: monthly.

Shopping Center World, Communications Channels, Inc., 6255 Barfield Rd., Altanta, GA 30328, *Telephone:* (404) 256-9800.

Site Selection, Conway Data, Inc., 40 Technology Park/Atlanta, Norcross, GA 30092-9990, *Telephone:* (404) 446-6996.

Small Farm Today Supplement, Missouri Farm Publishing Inc., 3903 W. Ridge Trail Rd., Clark, MO 65243.

Smart Computing, Sandhills Publishing, 120 W Harvest Drive, Lincoln, NE 68521, *Published:* monthly.

Snack Food & Wholesale Bakery, Stagnito Publishing Co., 1935 Shermer Rd., Ste. 100, Northbrook, IL 60062-5354, *Telephone:* (708) 205-5660, *Fax:* (708)

205-5680, *Published:* monthly, *Price:* free to qualified subscribers; $45 per year to all others.

Soap/Cosmetic/Chemical Specialties, 455 Broad Hollow Road, Melville, NY 11747-4722, *Published:* monthly.

South Florida Business Journal, American City Business Journals, 7950 NW 53 St., Ste. 210, Miami, FL 33166, *Telephone:* (305) 594-2100, *Fax:* (305) 594-1892.

Sporting Goods Business, Gralla Publications, Inc., 1515 Broadway, New York, NY 10036, *Telephone:* (212) 869-1300.

Sporting Goods Dealer, Times Mirror Magazines, Inc., 2 Park Ave., New York, NY 10016, *Telephone:* (212) 779-5000, *Fax:* (212) 213-3540, *Published:* monthly.

Sportstyle, Fairchild Publications, 7 W. 34th St., New York, NY 10001, *Telephone:* (212) 630-4000, *Fax:* (212) 630-3726.

Spray Technology & Marketing, Indsutry Publications, Inc., 389 Passaic Ave., Fairfield, NJ 07004, *Telephone:* (201) 227-5151, *Fax:* (201) 227-921, *Published:* monthly.

Stores, NRF Enterprises Inc., 100 West 31st St., New York, NY 10001, *Published:* monthly, *Price:* U.S./Canada: $49 per year, $80 for 2 years, $120 for 3 years.

Successful Farming, Meredith Corp., 1716 Locust St., Des Moines, IA 50309, *Telephone:* (515) 284-3000, *Fax:* (515) 284-2700.

Supermarket Business, Howfrey Communications, Inc., 1086 Teaneck Rd., Teaneck, NJ 07666, *Telephone:* (201) 833-1900, *Published:* monthly.

Supermarket News, Fairchild Publications, 7 W. 34th St., New York, NY 10001, *Telephone:* (212) 630-4750, *Fax:* (212) 630-4760.

Swimming Pool/Spa Age, Intersec Publishing Co., 6151 Powers Ferry Road, NW, Atlanta, GA 30339, *Telephone:* (770) 955-2500, *Published:* monthly.

Target Marketing, North American Publishing Co., 401 N Broad Street, Philadelphia, PA 19108, *Telephone:* (215) 238-5300, *Fax:* (215) 238-5457.

Telecommunications, Horizon House Publications, Inc., 685 Canton St., Norwood, CA 02062, *Telephone:* (617) 769-9750, *Fax:* (617) 762-9071.

Telephony, Intersec Publishing Corp., 9800 Metcalf, Overland Park, KS 66282-2960, *Published:* monthly.

Textile Asia, Tak Yan Commercial Bldg., 11th Fl., 30-32 D'Aguilar St., Hong Kong, *Telephone:* (5) 247467, *Published:* monthly.

Textile Rental, Textile Rental Services Assn. of America, 1130 E. Hallandale Beach Blvd, Hallandale, FL 33009, *Published:* monthly, *Price:* $90 per year.

Textile World, Maclean Hunter Publishing Co., Circulation Dept., 29 N. Wacker Dr., Chicago, IL 60606, *Price:* U.S./Canada: $45 per year, $75 for 2 years, $105 for 3 years.

Time, Time, Inc., Time & Life Bldg., Rockefeller Center, New York, NY 10020-1393, *Telephone:* (800) 843-8463, *Published:* weekly.

Times-Picauyne, Times-Picauyne Publishing Co., 800 Howard Ave., New Orleans, LA 70140, *Telephone:* (504) 826-3300, *Published:* daily.

Tire Business, Crain Commincations, Inc., 1725 Merriman Rd., Ste. 300, Akron, OH 44313-5251, *Telephone:* (216) 836-9180, *Fax:* (216) 836-1005.

Tooling & Production, Huebcore Communications Inc., 29100 Aurora Rd., Ste. 200, Solon, OH 44139, *Published:* monthly, *Price:* $90 per year.

Toronto Star, One Yong Street, Toronto, Ontario M5E 1E6, Telephone: (416) 367-2000, *Published:* daily.

Traffic World, Journal of Commerce Inc., Two World Trade Center, New York, NY 10048, *Published:* weekly, except last week of December, *Price:* $159 per year.

Transport Topics, American Trucking Assn., 2200 Mill Road, Alexandria, VA 22314, *Telephone*: (703) 838-1770.

Upside, Upside Media Inc., 2015 Pioneer Court, San Mateo, CA 94403, *Telephone:* (650) 377-0950, *Fax:* (650) 377-1962, *Published*: monthly.

U.S. Distribution Journal, BMT Publications Inc., 7 Penn Plaza, New York, NY 10001, *Telephone:* (212) 594-4120. *Published:* monthly, plus one additional issue in Dec.

U.S. Mexico Business, 3033 Chimney Road, Suite 300, Houston, TX 77056, *Published:* monthly.

U.S. News & World Report, 2400 N. St. NW, Washington, D.C. 20037, *Telephone:* (202) 955-200,. *Published:* weekly.

US Banker, Kalo Communications, 60 E. 42nd St., Ste. 3810, New York, NY 10165, Telephone: (212) 599-3310.

USA TODAY, Gannett Co., Inc., 1000 Wilson Blvd., Arlington, VA 22229, *Telephone:* (703) 276-3400. *Published:* Mon.-Fri.

VAR Business, CMP Media Inc., 1 Jericho Plaza A, Jericho NY 11753, *Telephone:* (516) 733-6700, *Published:* weekly.

Variety, 475 Park Ave., South, New York, NY 10016, *Telephone:* (212) 779-1100, *Fax:* (212) 779-0026. *Published:* weekly.

Vending Times, Vending Times Inc., 545 8th Ave., New York, NY 10018, *Telephone:* (212) 714-0101, *Fax:* (212) 564-0196, *Published:* monthly.

VM + SD, ST Publications Inc., 407 Gilbert Ave., Cincinnati, OH 45202, *Telephone:* (513) 421-2050, *Published:* monthly, *Price:* $39 per year.

Wall Street Journal, Dow Jones & Co. Inc., 200 Liberty St., New York, NY 10281, *Telephone:* (212) 416-2000. *Published:* Mon.-Fri.

WARD's Auto World, Ward's Communications, 28 W. Adams, Detroit, MI 48226, *Telephone:* (313) 962-4456. *Published:* monthly.

WARD's Dealer Business, Ward's Communications, 28 W. Adams, Detroit, MI 48226, *Telephone:* (313) 962-4456. *Published:* monthly.

The Washington Post, The Washington Post, 1150 15th St., N.W., Washington, DC 20071, *Published:* weekly.

Windows, Ziff-Davis, One Park Ave., New York, NY 10016, *Published:* monthly.

Wines & Vines, Hiaring Co., 1800 Lincoln Ave., San Rafael, CA 94901-1298, *Telephone:* (415) 453-9700, *Fax:* (415) 453-2517, *Published:* monthly, *Price:* $32 per year without directory; $77.50 per year including directory.

Wired, 520 3rd St., 4th Fl., San Francisco, CA 94107-1815, Telephone: (415) 276-5000, *Published*: monthly, *Price:* $39.95; Corporate: $80.

Wood & Wood Products, Vance Publishing Corp., 400 Knightsbridge Pkway., Lincolnshire, IL 60069, *Telephone:* (708) 634-4347, *Fax:* (708) 634-4379, Published: monthly, except semimonthly in March.

Wood Digest, Johnson Hill Press, 1233 Janesville Ave., Fort Atkinson, WI 53538, *Telephone:* (414) 563-6388, *Fax*: (414) 563-1702.

World Trade, Freedom Magazines, 17702 Cowan, Ste. 100, Irvine, CA 92714-6035.

WWD, Fairchild Publications, 7 E. 12th St., New York, NY 10003, *Telephone:* (212) 741-4000, *Fax:* (212) 337-3225. *Published:* weekly.

Yahoo!Internet Life, Ziff Davis Inc., Ona Park Ave., New York, NY 10016, Published: monthly.